D0923070

3 1232 00118 3302

NARRATIVE AND DRAMATIC SOURCES OF SHAKESPEARE

Volume V

THE ROMAN PLAYS:

JULIUS CÆSAR

ANTONY AND CLEOPATRA

CORIOLANUS

Volumes published

I. EARLY COMEDIES, POEMS, ROMEO AND JULIET

II. THE COMEDIES (1597-1603)

III. EARLIER ENGLISH HISTORY PLAYS:
HENRY VI, RICHARD III, RICHARD II

IV. LATER ENGLISH HISTORY PLAYS:
KING JOHN, HENRY IV, HENRY V,
HENRY VIII

V. THE ROMAN PLAYS:
JULIUS CÆSAR
ANTONY AND CLEOPATRA
CORIOLANUS

NARRATIVE AND DRAMATIC SOURCES OF SHAKESPEARE

Edited by
GEOFFREY BULLOUGH
Professor of English Language and Literature,
King's College, London

Volume V

THE ROMAN PLAYS:
JULIUS CÆSAR
ANTONY AND CLEOPATRA
CORIOLANUS

LONDON: Routledge and Kegan Paul

NEW YORK: Columbia University Press

1964

First published 1964
by Routledge and Kegan Paul Ltd
Broadway House, 68-74 Carter Lane
London, E.C.4
and Columbia University Press
Columbia University, New York
Made and printed in Great Britain
by William Clowes and Sons, Limited
London and Beccles

Library of Congress Catalog Card Number: 57–9969

To
Stephen and Patricia

PREFACE

THIS volume was originally intended to include consideration both of the Roman plays and of the other plays on ostensibly 'classical' themes. While gathering the material, however, I came to see the advisability of lengthening the Introductions so as to trace the growth of the Caesar and Cleopatra legends, and of omitting as little as possible of the three major Lives in Plutarch. Moreover, realizing that no modern editions of the Countess of Pembroke's *Antonie* and Samuel Daniel's *Cleopatra* are accessible to students, I determined to include complete texts of these plays, since they are valuable not only as sources or analogues but also for themselves as dramatic experiments in the classical mode. (In these as in other texts I have occasionally amended punctuation and spelling, but as seldom and slightly as possible.) In consequence what was meant to be one volume must become two, and *Titus Andronicus*, *Troilus and Cressida*, *Timon* and *Pericles* will be discussed in Volume VI, leaving the four greatest tragedies and the Romances for Vol. VII.

My thanks are extended to the Librarians of the British Museum, King's College, London, and the University Libraries of London and Edinburgh, and to my colleagues Professor H. H. Scullard, Mr A. W. Lintott and Mr F. M. Guercio for help in interpretation and translation. I am grateful to the Council of the Malone Society for permission to quote passages from its edition of *Caesar's Revenge*. I owe much, as before, to Miss Rosemary Jackson for her secretarial assistance and care for detail, and to her and my wife for aid with the proofs.

CONTENTS OF VOLUME V

LIST OF ABBREVIATIONS

1. *Shakespeare's Works and Apocrypha*

Ado	*Much Ado about Nothing*
AFev	*Arden of Feversham*
AShrew	*The Taming of A Shrew*
AYL	*As You Like It*
CE	*Comedy of Errors*
Cor	*Coriolanus*
Cym	*Cymbeline*
Ham	*Hamlet*
1H4	*Henry the Fourth, Part I*
2H4	*Henry the Fourth, Part II*
H5	*Henry the Fifth*
1H6	*Henry the Sixth, Part I*
2H6	*Henry the Sixth, Part II*
3H6	*Henry the Sixth, Part III*
H8	*Henry the Eighth*
KJ	*King John*
LComp	*Lover's Complaint*
Lear	*King Lear*
LLL	*Love's Labour's Lost*
Luc	*The Rape of Lucrece*
Mac	*Macbeth*
MM	*Measure for Measure*
MND	*A Midsummer Night's Dream*
More	*Sir Thomas More*
MV	*The Merchant of Venice*
MWW	*The Merry Wives of Windsor*
NobKin	*Two Noble Kinsmen*
Oth	*Othello*
Per	*Pericles*
PhT	*The Phoenix and the Turtle*
PPil	*The Passionate Pilgrim*
R2	*King Richard the Second*
R3	*King Richard the Third*
RJ	*Romeo and Juliet*
Son	*Sonnets*
TA	*Titus Andronicus*
Tem	*The Tempest*
TGV	*Two Gentlemen of Verona*
Tim	*Timon of Athens*
TN	*Twelfth Night*
TrC	*Troilus and Cressida*
TSh	*The Taming of The Shrew*
VA	*Venus and Adonis*
WT	*The Winter's Tale*

2. *Modern Editions and Other Works*

Arden	The Arden Shakespeare
Camb	The New Cambridge edition, edited by J. Dover Wilson, A. Quiller-Couch, &c.
Coll	*Shakespeare's Library*, edited J. Payne Collier, 2 vols.
ELH	*English Literary History* (Johns Hopkins University, Washington D.C.)
ElSt	E. K. Chambers, *The Elizabethan Stage*, 4 vols.
EngHist Soc	English Historical Society
EngStud	*Englische Studien*

Hol.	Holinshed's *Chronicles*
JEGP	*The Journal of English and Germanic Philology*
Jest Books	*Shakespeare Jest Books*, edited W. C. Hazlitt
Lee	Sir Sidney Lee, *Life of Shakespeare*
MalSoc	Malone Society Reprints
MedSt	E. K. Chambers, *The Medieval Stage*, 2 vols.
MLN	*Modern Language Notes*
MLR	*The Modern Language Review*
MPhil	*Modern Philology*
New Arden	The Arden Edition of Shakespeare (revised and reset)
N&Q	*Notes & Queries*
Oxf.	The Oxford Edition of Shakespeare, text by W. J. Craig; Introductory Studies by E. Dowden
PhilQ	*Philological Quarterly*
PMLA	Publications of the Modern Language Association of America
RES	*The Review of English Studies*
ShJb	Jahrbuch der deutschen Shakespeare—Gesellschaft
ShLib	*Shakespeare's Library*, 6 vols. 2nd Edn. 1875, edited J. P. Collier and W. C. Hazlitt
ShQ	*Shakespeare Quarterly*
Sh.Soc Trans.	*Transactions of the New Shakespeare Society*
SPhil	*Studies in Philology*
Sh Survey	*Shakespeare Survey*
Texas	*University of Texas Studies in English*
TLS	*The Times Literary Supplement* (London)
TR	*The Troublesome Raigne of King John*
Var.	*The New Variorum edition*, ed. H. H. Furness, &c.
WSh	E. K. Chambers, *William Shakespeare*, 2 vols.

3. *Other Abbreviations*

Arg	Argument
Chor	Chorus
Prol	Prologue
Rev.	Review
F	Folio edition
n.d.	No date
S.R.	The Stationer's Register
STC	*A Short-Title Catalogue of Books printed . . 1475–1640* (1950)

JULIUS CÆSAR

INTRODUCTION

JULIUS CÆSAR was not published till the First Folio (1623) in which it appears with few errors or misprints. It seems to have been printed from a clean prompt-copy or a transcript made from it. T. S. Dorsch (*New Arden*, xxiv) suggests that the printers used 'a careful scribal copy of Shakespeare's "fine papers" which had been used as the prompt-book'. There are few textual cruces, and no clear signs of revision except in the two differing accounts of Portia's death (IV.3.146–56 and 180–94) where Messala's relation was probably written first and Brutus' account written second to replace it but the earlier one printed by mistake as well.

The date of composition has been placed variously, but there is a reference to III.2 in John Weever's *The Mirror of Martyrs, or the Life and Death of Sir John Oldcastle* (1601):

> The many-headed multitude were drawne
> By *Brutus* speach, that Cæsar was ambitious,
> When eloquent *Mark Antonie* had showne
> His vertues, who but *Brutus* then was vicious?

Weever plagiarized from Edmund Fairfax's *Godfrey of Bulloigne* (1600),[1] so the reference proves that Shakespeare's play was well known in 1600. In all probability it was the play seen in the new Globe Theatre in the autumn of 1599 by the Swiss traveller Thomas Platter.[2]

The date 1599 agrees with other references, such as Ben Jonson's humorous use of 'Et tu, Brute' in *Every Man out of his Humour* (V.6.79) and Samuel Nicholson's use of the same phrase in *Acolastus his Afterwitte* (1600).[3] The play was popular, as Leonard Digges declared in lines (published in the 1640

[1] T. S. Dorsch, *New Arden*, viii.
[2] *WSh* ii, 322; from G. Binz, *Anglia* xxii, 456.
[3] Cf. *New Arden* viii–xi and *WSh* i, 397 for these and other allusions.

edition of Shakespeare's poems) comparing Shakespeare and Jonson to the latter's disadvantage:

> So have I seen, when Cesar would appeare,
> And on the Stage at halfe-sword parley were,
> *Brutus* and *Cassius*; oh how the Audience
> Were ravished, with what wonder they went thence . . .

The popularity of *Julius Cæsar* was caused not only by its dramatic effectiveness but also by its individual approach to the traditions and feelings which had grown up round the name of Caius Julius Cæsar. To explore the long history of the 'Cæsar-Mythos' is outside our present terms of reference, but although Shakespeare's main source was North's *Plutarch*, he seems to have dipped into other authorities, and it may well be that his handling of the material was affected by a complex tradition which, arising from the divergent attitudes of classical historians, had been modified in the Middle Ages and Renaissance in legend, scholarship and creative writing.

The life and personality of Julius Cæsar have always been of intense interest to biographers and historians. The range of his activities, his far-flung conquests, his political achievements, the manner of his death and what came after it, were so dramatic and well documented as to attract students of military history and of the Roman state (especially of the decline and fall of the Republic) and many explorers of the 'Great Man's' rôle in human affairs. His personality remained an enigma, interpreted differently by men of different political persuasions. In classical times he was praised or blamed as the pivot of Rome's transformation from Republic to Empire. In the Middle Ages he was a figure of bizarre legend. In the Renaissance he was regarded in the light of new political theories and of a new study of ancient documents; and the opposed views of him then formed endured until the nineteenth century, when opinions as diverse as those of Mommsen and Oman were still possible.[1] To trace the course and nature of his fame helps to explain the conflict of attitudes which affected dramatic representations of Cæsar and those associated with him, and

[1] Th. Mommsen, *History of Rome* (1854–6); C. Oman, *Seven Roman Statesmen*, 1902.

may throw light on the curiously ambivalent attitude apparent in Shakespeare's plays on Cæsar and Antony. In the following summary attention will mainly be centred on works current in the sixteenth century and contributing to the Renaissance tradition.[1]

Gaius Julius Cæsar (100–44 B.C.) wrote some of his own life-story in his two military memoirs. The *Commentarii de Bello Gallico* (*Gallic Wars*) comprise seven books about his relations with the Gauls, the Germans and the Britons between 59 B.C. and 52 B.C. Cæsar's aim in this was to justify to people at home his activities beyond the Alps. The *De Bello Civili* in three books was intended to describe and justify his war against Pompey. Both works are soldierly, cool and ostensibly objective accounts in which great exploits and endurances are narrated in a flat simple style which conceals the artfulness of the apologia and the egocentricity of the narrator while making clear his military genius, determination and command over the legions entrusted to him. Three books on the wars in Egypt, Africa and Spain (48–45 B.C.) may have been written by someone else, but in the Renaissance were usually regarded as his own.

Much light is thrown on the tangled affairs of Rome during the Civil Wars by the correspondence and speeches of the great orator and statesman Marcus Tullius Cicero (106–43 B.C.) who though not of the highest rank by birth had risen quickly to the Consulship and had suppressed the conspiracy of Catiline.

Afterwards he was exiled, but Pompey had him recalled. During the ensuing struggle between Cæsar and Pompey he lived mainly in retirement, practising law and writing his works on public affairs (*De Republica*, *De Legibus*), ethics (*Old Age*, *Friendship*) and rhetoric (*Brutus*, *De Oratore*).

Cicero's attitude to Julius Cæsar varied from time to time. On the whole he admired the younger man's active genius but mistrusted his political ambition. Cæsar, who was not above using gangster methods to increase his influence, had played a somewhat ambiguous part during the Catiline affair. Cicero sided with Pompey in the Civil War but was reconciled after Pharsalia to Cæsar, who treated him with courtesy, tolerating

[1] I am indebted to Gundolf, *The Mantle of Cæsar*, 1929, and also to Dr E. Schanzer, whose essay on 'Julius Cæsar' I read in draft after I had written most of this section. See his *Shakespeare's Problem Plays*, 1963.

the man of words as an unreliable friend and an irresolute foe. Cicero was not invited to join Brutus' conspiracy, but his Republican sentiments made him greet the assassination of Cæsar as a virtuous act, and he corresponded with Brutus and Cassius as their fortunes declined. 'It would seem' (he wrote to the latter[1]) 'that we have been delivered, not from a tyranny, but only from a tyrant. For though we have slain the tyrant, we still watch that tyrant's every word.' Cicero hated Antony, and in letters and speeches (the *Philippics*) he painted a lurid portrait of 'that crazy and desperate fellow' who spent his time either plotting 'to avenge the death of Cæsar' or 'exhausted with debauchery and wine . . . practising in [his] licentious house all forms of impurity'. He regretted that Antony had been spared: 'I wish you had invited me to your banquet on the Ides of March; there would have been no leavings' (to Cassius, February, 43 B.C.). 'The only refuge for honest folk is with you and Brutus', he declared a month or so later; 'if we have Cassius and Brutus back in Rome we shall think we have our Republic again.' When Antony claimed that the two friends were exiled, Cicero cried, 'What men so boorish, when they see these men, as not to think that they themselves have reaped the fullest harvest life can give? What future generation indeed shall be found so unmindful, what literature so ungrateful, as not to enshrine their glory in an immortal record?'[2]

Brutus and Cassius never returned; so Cicero looked to Octavian to save Rome from Antony's drunkenness and corruption; but after a while Octavian turned from him, and Antony had his revenge when Cicero was proscribed in 43 B.C. and murdered.

Although the *Familiar Epistles* of Cicero were not Englished until 1620 (by J. Webbe), they were widely known in the Renaissance. In England a Latin edition printed by H. Bynneman in 1571 was followed by others in 1574 (T. March), 1575 and 1579 (T. Vautrollier), 1585 (J. Jackson and E. Bollifant), 1591 (R. Robinson). They were used in schools and universities to teach the art of prose writing. The *Philippics* were printed by R. Pynson in 1521, and the ethical writings were among the most widely studied of Latin works. Insofar as Tudor England

[1] May, 44 B.C. *Letters to Friends,* Loeb ii, Bk. xii, 1, p. 516.
[2] *Philippics* II, trans. W. C. A. Ker, Loeb, p. 97.

had any sense of Roman values it was owing largely to Cicero. Shakespeare may have read something of him in Latin. Cicero's account of major oratorical styles (in his dialogue *Brutus* or *De Claris Oratoribus*) may have coloured the funeral speeches. Cicero distinguishes the dry, reserved Stoic manner from the richer, more highly coloured way of speaking, praising on the one hand the plain oratory of Cato and Brutus himself, and on the other the more lavish art of an earlier Marcus Antonius, a victim of the Marian persecution in 87 B.C.

> 'Stoic oratory (says Cicero in the dialogue) is too closely knit and too compact for a popular audience;' and Brutus himself declares, 'practically all adherents of the Stoic school are very able in precise argument; they work by rule and system and are fairly architects in the use of words; but transfer them from discussion to oratorical presentation, and they are found poor and unresourceful.'[1]

How true this is of Brutus' speech at the funeral! Yet Cicero praised Brutus for combining the virtues of several schools in his eloquence. So Shakespeare has given us a Stoic speech rather than that which Cicero's Brutus would probably have made.

> 'As for Antonius (wrote Cicero) nothing relevant escaped his attention, and it was all set in proper place for the greatest force and effectiveness . . . In the matter of choosing words (and choosing them more for weight than for charm), in placing them and tying them into compact sentences, Antonius controlled everything by purpose and by something like deliberate art. This same quality was still more noticeable in the embellishment which he gave to his thought by figurative expression. [His voice] . . . in passages of pathos it had a touching quality well-suited to winning confidence and to stirring compassion.'[2]

This was a different Antony, but it holds good of the Antony of the play, whose oration is so consciously contrived to move the emotions of the audience.

[1] *Brutus*, trans. G. L. Henderson and H. M. Hubbell, Loeb edn. 1942, xxxi, 120 and 118, pp. 107–9.

[2] *Ibid.*, pp. 123–5.

Among other contemporaries hostile to Cæsar the poet Catullus (c. 84–54 B.C.) could be held to represent the younger nobility during Cæsar's rise to power, afraid of losing their class-privileges through his bribery of the mob, and inimical towards the apostle of central government and authoritarian efficiency. Personal factors also made Catullus write satiric epigrams against the successful man of the world, and insist, 'Nil nimium studeo, Cæsar, tibi velle placere.' Ere he died, some years before Cæsar, Catullus had come to think better of him.

On the other side Sallust (Gaius Sallustius Crispus, 86–34 B.C.) owed much to Julius Cæsar, because, after he had been degraded from the Senate in 50 B.C. for licentious conduct, Cæsar had him reinstated and made governor of Numidia. After his patron's murder Sallust retired from public life and wrote a history of the years 78–67 B.C. of which little remains, and short accounts of the Jugurthine war and the Catiline conspiracy. In this last he defended Cæsar and showed the incompetence and corruption of the aristocrats in the Senate who opposed him. Sallust preferred the magnificence of Cæsar to the acknowledged virtue of the stoic Cato. Most previous historians had been annalists, but Sallust unified his work by his strong partisanship, and began the glorification of Cæsar which flourished under Augustus and the later emperors of the Julian line. His works were well known in the Renaissance but not published in England until 1615, and although his *Jugurthine War* was translated by Sir A. Barclay in about 1520 and twice reprinted, the *Catiline Conspiracy* was not translated until Thomas Heywood did both works in 1608/9.[1] Shakespeare may possibly have read Sallust, and a brief excerpt from Heywood is given below [Text IV].

The Emperor Augustus's own memoirs down to 24 B.C. are lost, but were used by the imperialists Velleius Paterculus and Suetonius. Another influential work now lost was the relevant portion of Titus Livius's great *History of Rome from the Foundation of the City* to 9 B.C. which contained 142 books of which the 35 extant in full do not go beyond 167 B.C. The remainder are represented by various resumés, including one made in the first

[1] *The two most worthy and notable histories, the Conspiracy of Catiline and the Warre which Jugurtha maintained* . . . 2 pts. For J. Haggard, 1608–9.

century A.D. and the epitomes of Florus, Eutropius and Orosius. Livy (59 B.C.–A.D. 17) was a supporter of the Republic and Senate, with a liking for Pompey and considerable respect for Brutus and Cassius. A saga-writer rather than a historian (in any modern sense), he organized with superb style his carefully selected material so as to portray the civic and private virtues of early Rome as a moral standard by which to judge the later decay of the Republic.

At the imperial court there was a natural tendency to praise Julius Cæsar as the saviour of Rome from degenerate democracy and the founder of the new order. Under Tiberius, Gaius Velleius Paterculus, an army officer devoted to the Emperor, under whom he had served in the Danube and Rhine campaigns, spent his retirement in writing a *Compendium of Roman History* in two books, of which the second covers 146 B.C. to A.D. 30. The first forty chapters of this extend to Julius Cæsar's consulship, the next sixteen to his death, the next twenty-eight to Actium (31 B.C.). So Velleius gave good measure to Cæsar, whom he admired as 'scion of the noble Julian house, descendant (as all antiquarians agree) of Anchises and Venus . . . one whose soul rose above the limit of man's nature, and indeed his powers of belief.' The bias is plainly anti-republican.

Little known in the Middle Ages, Velleius was printed in 1520 from a copy found by the Tacitus scholar Beatus Rhenanus in the Abbey of Murbach. Ascham cited his opinion of Cicero, Chapman his reference to Homer, but he was not translated into English until 1632, when Sir R. Le Grys made a version [1] which has been used for some excerpts below [Text V].

The appearance of Cæsar and his group in collections of anecdotes about great men began with the *Noteworthy Deeds and Sayings* (*Facta et Dicta Memorabilia*) of Valerius Maximus, also in the reign of Tiberius. This contained nine books in which the stories were arranged under subjects. Thus Book i (concerning religious matters, portents, dreams, apparitions) contains the story of an apparition seen by Cassius before Philippi; Book ii (on old institutions) has a description of Cato's power over the people; Book v contains the story of Cæsar's grief over Pompey's head, Portia's death by swallowing fire, and Antony's honour-

[1] *Velleius Paterculus, his Romane historie*, trans. Sr. R. Le Grys. M. F[lesher] for R. Simme, 1632.

able treatment of Brutus's corpse; Book vi includes Brutus' cool words when advised not to fight at Philippi, but calls him 'the Murtherer of his own Virtues, before he was the Parricide of the Parent of his countrey (for by one foul deed he overthrew them all, and defil'd his memory with an unexpiable detestation.'[1] Because of his heavy moralizing and his value as a source-book for illustrations, Valerius was much read in the Middle Ages and Renaissance. Chaucer named and used him; Sir Thomas Elyot translated several anecdotes in his *Governour*. There is however no particular reason to think that Shakespeare used for his Roman plays this book of wise saws and ancient instances.

With the epic *Pharsalia* by Seneca's grandson Marcus Annæus Lucanus (A.D. 39–65), the imperial cult of Cæsar received a setback. A native of Cordoba, he became a favourite of Nero, who however became jealous of his poetic powers and began to treat him badly. After joining a plot against the Emperor, Lucan was forced to commit suicide, aged only twenty-six. Lucan belonged to the new school of rhetorical poets and sought to improve on Virgil by an unconventional approach and by adding sensational and realistic ingredients to the epic. Maybe because the Emperor was jealous of Julius Cæsar's versatile genius, more certainly because the young poet idealized the aristocratic rule of the ancient Senate, Lucan's poem on the Civil Wars favoured Pompey and Cato rather than their conqueror:

> Pompey could bide no equal,
> Nor Cæsar no superior: which of both
> Had justest cause, unlawful 'tis to judge:
> Each side had great partakers; Cæsar's cause
> The gods abetted, Cato lik'd the other . . .
> Cæsar's renown for war was less, he restless,
> Shaming to strive but where he did subdue;
> When ire or hope provok'd heady and bold;
> At all times charging home, and making havoc;
> Urging his fortune, trusting in the gods,

[1] *Romæ antiquæ Descriptio* . . . Written in Latine by that famous Historian Quintus Valerius Maximus: And now carefully rendred into English. Together with the Life of the Author, 1678. J. C. for Samuel Speed.

Destroying what withstood his proud desires,
And glad when blood and ruin made him way.
(Marlowe's trans. Bk i, 125–51)

Cæsar's invasion of Italy was one of many criminal acts:

Here, here, saith he,
An end of peace; here end polluted laws;
Hence leagues and covenants; Fortune thee I follow,
War and the Destinies shall try my cause. (*ibid.* 226-29)

At Pharsalia Pompey was 'intent on escaping tyranny, Cæsar on imposing it.' Cæsar ordered his men to kill, not the ordinary men, but the senators. Lucan shows Brutus, on Pompey's side, carving a way through the opposing ranks in an effort to reach and kill Cæsar (Bk. vii). In Bk. ix the spirit of the dead Pompey seats itself first in Cato's breast and then in Brutus'. Cæsar's motives were invariably bad. When he wept over Pompey's head (Bk. ix) he was 'pretending sorrow that a relative's corpse had been mutilated, so as to make an excuse for withholding gratitude from the King who sent him this disgusting present.'[1] Not content with this Lucan gives a long speech by Cæsar supporting the fiction of grief.

In contrast with this harsh portrait the poet gives others equally brilliant if not always consistent: the ageing Pompey resting on his laurels as a warrior, lapped in false security, but doomed (Bk. i); Cato the austere puritan who never did any act of self-indulgence; Brutus going by night to Cato's door to ask whether he should take part in the Pompeian war and on whose side (Bk. ii); Cleopatra and her spell over Cæsar (Bk. x) —of which more later.

With his violent depiction of battles and sufferings, the liberal use of portents and omens, the substitution of magic for the Virgilian gods, the rhetorical language and 'strong lines', Lucan influenced other Roman poets of the eclectic Silver Age. Quintilian called him an orator rather than a poet, but he was admired in the Middle Ages and Renaissance. Dante thought him the fourth greatest poet; Petrarch and Tasso quoted him; the French classical dramatists from Garnier onwards drew freely on him, and many editions of the *Pharsalia* appeared in

[1] Lucan, *Pharsalia,* trans. R. Graves, 1956, p. 223.

France and Italy. In England there was one in 1589. Christopher Marlowe translated the first Book and although this was not printed until 1600 it may possibly have been known to Shakespeare. A version by Sir A. Gorges appeared in 1614, a better one by Thomas May in 1627.

If Lucan's epic was the product of mingled adulation and hatred of a particular emperor, the works of Publius Cornelius Tacitus (c. A.D. 55–120) had a more stable moral foundation. In his *Annals* Tacitus traced the sombre story of the Cæsars and their crimes till the fall of Domitian. Beginning with the deaths of Brutus and Cassius he summarized the gradual assumption of single rule by Augustus, who 'little by little taking upon him, . . . drew to himselfe the affaires of Senate, the dutie of magistrates and lawes, without contradiction of any',[1] until no trace was left of the old Roman independence of spirit. The peace of Augustus seemed preferable to the freedom which had brought civil war.

In his account of Augustus' funeral Tacitus summed up the two sides of the Emperor's record; on the one hand, his just revenge for Julius' murder, his moderation; on the other hand, his ambition, his proscriptions, his self-interest; and Tacitus does not forget the significance of Brutus and Cassius when, describing the funeral of Brutus' sister Julia, he writes, 'The images of twentie noble houses, were carried before her . . . But *Cassius* and *Brutus* did shine above the rest, because their images were not seene' (*Annals*, iii, lxxvi).

The works of Tacitus were frequently reprinted during the Renaissance on the Continent, and the *Annals* were translated by R. Grenewey in 1598. Shakespeare may have read this version before writing *Henry V* (cf. Vol. IV, p. 361). From Tacitus the dramatist may have learned to depict Augustus as a cold and calculating man governed by self-interest, and to regard his punishment of the conspirators and even of Antony as no unmixed blessings.

Plutarch's parallel *Lives of the Greeks and Romans* makes a fascinating contrast with such political partiality. Plutarch (c. A.D. 46–120) was a Greek who lived mainly in Chæronea, his native town, though he went on several embassies to Rome and gave lectures there. His other major work, the *Moral Essays*

[1] R. Grenewey's translation [Text VI].

(*Moralia*) reveals the ethical nature of his approach to history, the beauty of character and style which made them so popular in the Renaissance, his great breadth of human interests and curiosity about the world. History for him was the biographies of great men, and since he knew both the Greek civilization and the Roman which had supplanted it he conceived the plan of a series of Lives from various periods, each pair being explored as individuals then briefly compared. There was no attempt at a general survey or comparison of the two national cultures, though he was aware of 'the tragedy of Athens, the drama of Rome' (Wyndham). Plutarch was interested primarily in the characters and careers of individual men, which he traced chronologically and surrounded with anecdotes to illustrate their traits: 'The noblest deedes doe not alwayes shew men's vertues and vices, but often times a light occasion, a word, or some sporte, makes men's natural dispositions and manners appear more plaine, then the famous battells wonne . . .' (*Life of Alexander*). He paired off men of similar character or men in like situations or at similar periods of national history. Thus Theseus goes with Romulus (both founders of states and civilizers), Alcibiades with Coriolanus (traitors), Alexander and Cæsar (conquerors cut off in their prime), Dion and Brutus (liberators), Demetrius and Antony (extreme in vice and virtue). But he does not show them merely as creatures of one master passion; they are men among men.

In the Renaissance the *Lives* were edited many times, but the important translation for us was that made in French by Jacques Amyot of Melun (1513–93), professor at Bourges and later Bishop of Auxerre, who also translated Heliodorus' *Aethiopica* (1546), *Daphnis and Chloe* (1559), and several hitherto unknown books of Diodorus Siculus which he discovered in Italy (1554). His version of the *Parallel Lives* first appeared in 1559, that of the *Moralia* in 1572. Sir Thomas North's translation of Amyot's *Lives* came in 1579, and this was certainly Shakespeare's main source for *Julius Cæsar*, *Antony and Cleopatra* and *Coriolanus*. The relationship of Amyot to Plutarch and to North has been examined by Wyndham[1] and others. Plutarch was less favourable to Cicero and Octavian than might have been expected; his view of Antony showed some sympathy.

[1] Introduction to *Plutarch's Lives* (Tudor Translations), 1895, i, lxviii–lxxxvii.

After Plutarch the *Lives of the Twelve Cæsars* (*Vitae Duodecim Cæsarum*) of Caius Suetonius Tranquillus (fl. A.D. 93–138) seem somewhat trivial. A friend of the younger Pliny and patronized by Trajan and Hadrian, Suetonius was a compiler of some merit. He lacked Plutarch's idealism, insight and power of sustained narrative, but his titbits of gossip are often illuminating. The *Lives* were first printed at Rome in 1470. The first English translation, by Philemon Holland, was published in 1606. There is nothing in Shakespeare's plays to prove that he had read Suetonius, but the latter's attempt to weigh Cæsar's virtues against his faults of womanizing and arrogance contributed to the balanced view of the dictator [Text VII].

Appian of Alexandria (c. A.D. 95–165), a Greek in the Roman civil service under Trajan and Hadrian, wrote a history on roughly geographical lines, discussing the major wars of Rome in various parts of the world—Spain (Bk. VI), Carthage (Bk. VIII), Syria (Bk. XI) and so on. Books XIII–XVII, on the Civil Wars, are extant. A Latin version was made by Peter Candidus for Pope Nicolas V in 1452.

The Greek work was first printed by C. Estienne at Paris in 1551. Another Latin translation, by Sigismund Geslen, was published at Basle in 1554; a French version by Claude de Seyssel in 1544; an Italian one taken from Candidus by Braccio appeared in 1544 and was often reprinted. The English translation by W. B. was published by Henry Bynneman in 1578.[1] Shakespeare may well have read this for *Julius Cæsar* and *Antony and Cleopatra*.

Appian tried to keep a balance in describing Cæsar's enigmatic behaviour after destroying Pompey: his disregard of his personal safety, his acceptance of honours, his refusal to be called King. His determination to move against the Parthians is ascribed to several motives.

Similarly Appian is cautious about the motives of the conspirators, who 'killed him . . . eyther for envie . . . or as they said, for the love of their country's libertie'. Brutus acted 'either as an ingrate man, or ignorant of his mothers faulte, or dis-

[1] For a fuller discussion of, and longer extracts from, this translation see *Shakespeare's Appian*, ed. Ernest Schanzer, Liverpool University Press, 1956. Mr Schanzer thinks W. B. may have been William Barker (fl. 1570) who also translated Xenophon's *Cyropædia* (1567).

trustfull, or ashamed, or very desirous of his countrys libertie, preferring it before all other things, or that he was descended of the auntient Brutus, that drove out the Kings: or that he was incensed and rebuked of the people.'

Appian's most striking contribution to the Cæsar legend consisted in his portrait of Antony, not as Plutarch's 'plain blunt man' but as one who combined 'boldnesse vehement' with 'dissimulation extreame', who wrought 'deceytefully', 'artificially' and with 'sutteltie'. Appian also developed the speeches of several characters considerably, and especially those of Brutus (to the people at the Capital) and Antony (in the Senate and in Cæsar's 'funeral sermon') [Text VIII]. As Dr Schanzer has shown, the histrionic behaviour of Appian's Antony may have suggested to Shakespeare important aspects of his treatment in *Julius Cæsar*.

Also well known in the Renaissance was the *Epitome* of Livy by Lucius Florus, in two books extending to the reign of Augustus. First published in 1470–2 these were often reprinted. An English translation (by E. M. B. (Bolton)) did not appear until 1619, but Florus was well known to English schoolboys. Florus, who lived in Hadrian's time, meant his work to be a panegyric of Rome. In it he divided Roman history into four ages and considered the decline of the state from triumph over foreign enemies to civil war as due to 'the too much rankness of prosperitie.'

Florus praised Cæsar for his great deeds and his clemency. He used his power for good and when he was offered the kingship 'it was unknowne whether it were with his good liking', but he was partly to blame for the Civil War and his death was poetic justice. Florus looked back wistfully to 'the state of the ancient libertie', yet since civil war followed Cæsar's death, 'we are to be glad notwithstanding, that the whole power of Rome came to be setled upon *Octavius*, first *Cæsar Augustus*', who brought unity by his single rule. Florus was antagonistic to Brutus and Cassius, and also to Antony, whom he regarded as 'of his owne nature troublesome to peace, and troublesome to commonweale' [Text IX].

Cassius Dio Cocceianus (c. A.D. 155–230), son of a senator, was a Greek from Bithynia who rose to be consul, and then devoted twenty-two years of his retirement to a vast *History of*

Rome in Greek in eighty books of which little remain except those covering 69 B.C. to A.D. 46. Epitomes made in Byzantium in the eleventh and twelfth centuries give some idea of the rest. A supporter of the Emperors, Dio Cassius expatiated on the wavering nature of the Roman people. Cæsar's difficulties with his soldiers, who expected large rewards, are shown, and the mixture of cunning and kindliness with which he treated them. His triumphs are described at length, his arrogant showmanship, his projected reforms, and the undemocratic privileges offered him by the Senate—the title of Imperator and decrees 'by which they declared him a monarch out and out'. Brutus was roused to plot against him when an image of Cæsar was set up on the Capitol along with those of the kings and of the Brutus who overthrew the Tarquins.

Coming to Cæsar's death Dio Cassius was downright in his condemnation of the assassins who 'added a new name to the annals of infamy . . . and brought upon the Romans seditions and civil wars once more after a state of harmony'. The historian compared democracy and monarchy, to the latter's advantage, as 'a most practical form of government to live under'. By not reflecting on these things Brutus and Cassius 'made themselves the cause of countless ills both to themselves and to all the rest of mankind then living' (XLIV).

On the other hand, Cæsar is shown as smitten with conceit and false security, being 'encouraged to believe that he should never be plotted against by the men who had voted him such honours'. 'Either by some heaven-sent fatuity or even through excess of joy' he received the senators sitting, which 'afforded his slayers one of their chief excuses for their plot against him.'

Brutus was the leader of the plot, being excited by pamphlets and secret writings, by his relationship to Cato, and strengthened by the fortitude of his wife. 'After this he obtained as an associate Gaius Cassius', and together they gathered others round them.

Dio Cassius loved to invent speeches for his characters, as when Cæsar tried to persuade the Senate that he had not 'become so elated or puffed up by my great good fortune as to desire also to play the tyrant over you', when Cicero attacked Antony, and when Antony roused the mob by a speech 'which was very ornate and brilliant to be sure, but out of place on that occasion' (XLIV). Before the fight at Philippi portents and omens are used to show that Heaven wished men to know that it was a supreme struggle in which they were engaged (XLVII). The deaths of the conspirators made it clear that 'justice and the Divine Will seem to have led to suffer death themselves men who had killed their benefactor, one who had attained such eminence in both virtue and good fortune' (XLVIII).

Hostile on the whole to Antony, Dio Cassius reserved the full force of his criticism for his account of Cæsar's war against him and Cleopatra (L–LI). The events after Julius Cæsar's death led inevitably to the unification of the Empire under Augustus. There is no proof that Shakespeare knew the *History*, but it helped to form the climate of opinion in which Cicero, Plutarch, Appian and others were read in Tudor days.

Compared with this, the *Breviarium ab Urbe Condita* of Eutropius in the fourth century had little new to offer. An English translation, by Nicolas Haward 'studiente of Thavies Inn', appeared in 1564. In Eutropius we once more see an impartial view attempted. Cæsar's conquests are celebrated and his grief at Pompey's murder approved, but his conduct thereafter at Rome is reprehended: 'he began to demean himself very disorderly and againste the usage of the Romaine libertye', and this excited 'the commons and Senate' against him. The two Bruti were the chief conspirators. Antony performed 'divers heinous actes' for which he was overthrown in battle by Octavian before they were reconciled and formed the triumvirate with Lepidus. Octavian's rule, when he became Augustus, was admirable.

By the end of the classical epoch the main features of the chief characters in the fall of the Republic were well established. Usually two aspects of each of them were contrasted. Julius Cæsar appeared as a man of paradox. On the one hand there was general agreement on his martial skill, energy, eloquence, power over his legions and the plebeians; on his kindness to his friends and soldiers, his moderation in diet, his frequent clemency. On the other hand he was widely regarded as capable of great ruthlessness, a despiser of religion, lustful, guileful, above all ambitious. Opinions were divided on whether he sought the Civil War and Pompey's death, but most ancient writers agreed that inordinate ambition was his lifelong driving-force; he could not bear to be second, and he wished to rule the state, possibly as hereditary monarch, certainly as a 'tyrant' in the Greek sense of the word. Though some writers thought his murder might be justified, the majority regarded it as a wicked act. The ambivalence found in Cicero and developed by Plutarch affected the whole Cæsar-tradition, and we can see later historians striving towards a balanced view which would take account of both sides of his personality and career.

Few ancient historians considered the assassination as anything but a gross mistake fraught with evil consequences. The conspirators on the whole were condemned. Brutus shared the double reputation of Cæsar. He was noble in his Republican and Stoic principles, yet he killed his benefactor, and though he did it for the best political motives the result proved him wrong. Either political circumstances or the gods themselves avenged Cæsar within a short time. Antony also had two sides. He was a man of lax principles and loose life, yet he was Cæsar's faithful friend and avenger. Afterwards he declined rapidly through his enmity towards Octavian and his luxurious life in Egypt, and he deserved his miserable fate at the hands of Cæsar's heir, who himself combined the virtues of the avenger and peacebringer with a coldly calculating strain.

Thus already in the ancient world we can see a realization that the chief figures in the events between Pharsalia and Actium were men of mixed motives, with good and bad points in their public and private lives.

As Gundolf has shown, the Middle Ages found magic in the name of Cæsar and attached it to many legends. In one he became the father of the fairy king Oberon by the fairy Morgana; in a poem on Huon of Bordeaux he was the son of the fairy Brünhilde and grandson of Judas Maccabaeus. Perceforest made his murder an act of private revenge by Brutus; elsewhere it was done by friends of Virgil because Cæsar's daughter had laughed at the poet. Especially in France and Italy Cæsar became a paladin like Hector, Aeneas, Alexander, King Arthur. He became one of the Nine Worthies[1] (though sometimes Pompey replaces him, as in *Love's Labour's Lost*, V.2).

[1] They were Hector, Alexander, Julius Cæsar from the classical world; Joshua, David and Judas Maccabæus from Hebrew story; Arthur, Charlemagne and Godfrey of Boulogne from the romances.

Having conquered many lands he was said to have founded many cities, Worms, Mainz, Ghent and Worcester. He built a Louvre in Paris, and the Tower of London (as Shakespeare's Prince Edward recalled in *Richard III*, III.1.68–77):

PRINCE I do not like the Tower, of any place:
Did Julius Cæsar build that place, my lord?
BUCKINGHAM He did, my gracious lord, begin that place,
Which, since, succeeding ages have re-edified.
PRINCE Is it upon record, or else reported
Successively from age to age, he built it?
BUCKINGHAM Upon record, my gracious lord.
PRINCE But say, my lord, it were not register'd,
Methinks the truth should live from age to age,
As 'twas retail'd to all posterity,
Even to the general all-ending day.

Alexander the Great was more easily regarded as a hero of romance, yet Cæsar took to himself the qualities of the enchanter, the epic and chivalric hero. Emperors and popes traced their descent from him and boasted of their likeness to him; thus Boniface VIII wrote, 'I am Cæsar, I am Emperor.' But although there were many who admired the column in Rome alleged to mark the tomb of his ashes, others remembered the fate of mortality:

Cæsar, tantus eras quantus et orbis,
Sed nunc in modico clauderis antro.

For many churchmen Cæsar was an enemy of virtue. Anselm indeed called him an anti-Christ, like Nero and Julian the Apostate. St Thomas Aquinas in his *De Regimine Principum* (c. 1270) treated him as an abuser of power and as a moral example, now of mildness, now of cruelty, with no attempt at a historical view. Unlike these two Dante presented a favourable view of Cæsar. In the *Inferno*, Canto 4, 'Cesare armato con gli occhi grifagni' ('Cæsar, armed, with falcon's eyes') is seen in the green fields of the castle in Limbo, with Electra, Hector and Aeneas. In *Paradiso*, Canto 6, 74–8, the spirit in Mercury, sketching the history of the Roman Empire, tells of Cæsar's glory in war 'of such a flight as neither tongue nor pen could follow', and of Augustus' prowess.

Dante's aim being to advocate a unified rule against division and dissension, he naturally thought little of Brutus and Cassius and placed them in the lowest reach of the *Inferno* (Canto 34, 61–9) with Judas Iscariot, as traitors to their benefactors, each in one of the three mouths of Satan, 'Lo imperador del doloroso regno.' Cato however appears in *Purgatorio* as a hero of liberty. This extreme view of Brutus, with no palliation for his noble soul, was not common. Petrarch was in two minds about Brutus. In his *Trionfi* he praises Cicero the versatile orator, leader, writer, even more than Julius Cæsar, whom he saw as a slave of Cupid and a friend of Fame. Cato and Brutus were to be admired as champions of liberty. Petrarch also wrote a work on famous men, of which the biography of Cæsar formed half. Here in contrast with his awestruck admiration for Cæsar, he takes a different view of Brutus—as ungrateful, treacherous and foolish. In the Renaissance this biography was often ascribed to one Julius Celsus and as such widely read, translated and copied. Petrarch did much to give the Cæsar legend scholarly details and new admirers. Compared with him Boccaccio showed little historical sense, telling of Cæsar's death in the *Amorosa Visione* and also in the *De Casibus Illustrium Virorum* which Chaucer used for the *Monk's Tale*.

> By wisedom, manhede, and by greet labour
> From humble bed to roial magestie
> Up roos he, Julius the conquerour,
> That wan al thoccident, by land and see
> By strength of hand, or elles by tretee,

and vanquished Pompey. Brutus and Cassius are evil men

> That ever hadde of his hye estaat envye.

Cæsar's manliness and 'honesty' were shown when before he died he cast his mantle over his hips

> For no man sholde seen his privetee.

Chaucer's (or Boccaccio's) authorities were Lucan, Suetonius and Valerius Maximus for a history which showed that to Cæsar and Pompey

> Fortune was first freend and sithe foo.

So Cæsar's is a tragedy of changing Fortune, not of desert.

Against this view the Ciceronian tradition in the Renaissance restored the good name of Brutus as the lover of freedom. Poggio Bracciolini thought Cæsar inferior to Cicero because he was a bad citizen and an evildoer.

The image of Cæsar entered the minds of aspiring rulers in the sixteenth century. Henry VIII was praised by Erasmus for having Cæsar's strength of will, Ptolemy Philadelphus' love of learning, Augustus' reason, Trajan's clemency, Theodosius' piety. In an age of great monarchs Cæsar became a pattern, and Pedro Mexia's *Lives of the Emperors from Cæsar to Charles V* praised him lavishly. So did the *Life of Cæsar* by Schiapollaria (1578). On the other hand Colet warned the King to imitate Christ rather than Cæsar or Alexander. Martin Luther saw Cæsar as a tyrant who destroyed the Roman commonwealth, and Montaigne, while admiring Cæsar's writings and his humane qualities, also thought him an enemy of liberty. Jean Bodin viewed Cæsar from a Machiavellian standpoint as exemplifying the art of rule, and saw his weaknesses as political rather than moral failings. A famous German historian Johan Carion, in his *Chronica* (1532; and often translated), having like some medieval writers ascribed Pompey's downfall to retribution for sacrilege in the Temple at Jerusalem, where he was said to have entered the Holy of Holies, describes the conspiracy against Cæsar:

> 'Cassius, having been rebuffed in purchasing to be prætor in Rome, which he aspired to be, and moreover hating Cæsar, was the first to put forward that Cæsar must be killed, and by subtlety drew Brutus into that plot. Thereupon the authority of Brutus caused the others to join.'

The death of Cæsar 'this great personage, must not only be placed among examples of the inconstancy of human things, but also of the ingratitude and disloyalty of men. For several of the murderers had been saved from death by Cæsar, and (what is more) honoured with great riches and estates. Also his death did not put the Republic into better order, although Cicero and other Senators tried to make peace.' Carion proved by dates that Cæsar could not possibly have behaved as a tyrant during the short interval between his arriving in Rome and his death. So he defended Cæsar, but he thought little of his avengers—their triumvirate was filled with cruelty.

The other side was taken by G. Botero in the *Observations upon the Lives of Alexander, Cæsar and Scipio* (trans. 1602). Cæsar, wrote Botero,

> 'had placed the principalitie and signorie of Rome (or at least an extraordinarie and singular potencie) for the end of his thoughts and the reward of his labours'

He had been involved in many conspiracies against the Republic; he governed 'not as Consull, but as a Dictator'. His aim in collecting disgraced and bankrupt followers was because such men 'did wish with al their hearts, That the waters might bee troubled, and the state perturbed'. A cynical opportunist, he reconciled himself to his enemies for sheer expediency, using Crassus and Pompey to suppress the Senate's authority and to advance his own interests until he could do without them. Botero praises Cæsar's energy in the war, and his principal military virtues, but writes more about the reasons for condemning him—'his ambitious projects' and 'those meanes which hee used to attain thereunto', 'his annihilating of the authority of the Senat: and in oppressing of the Optimates, and the better sort of Cittizens; finally, in not making any difference twixt right and wrong.' In addition he succumbed to ambition, let himself be 'honoured above reason by flatterers and sycophants', and sought 'the Title and Crowne of a King'.

These two works sum up the opposite verdicts on Cæsar. For the most part a balanced judgement was attempted by both schools of Renaissance historians, and it is not surprising therefore to find in the literary treatment of Julius Cæsar before Shakespeare a weighing of pros and cons, a representation of good and bad characteristics.

Renaissance educationists and writers of 'courtesy-books' frequently illustrated their ethical teaching from ancient history. In *The Governour*, a book which Shakespeare seems to have known well, Sir Thomas Elyot claimed that Lucan was 'very expedient to be lerned' for his account of the Civil Wars (I.x). A noble heart should be 'trayned to delite in histories', and to 'begynne with Titus Livius'. Livy was valuable for the study of war. 'Julius Cesar and Salust for their compendious writynge, to the understandynge wherof is required an exact and perfect jugement', should be reserved till a later stage of study (I.xi). 'Also there be dyvers orations, as well in all the bokes of the said autors as in the historie of Cornelius Tacitus, which be very delectable, and for counsayles very expedient to be had in memorie.'

Discussing the several qualities of a good prince Elyot uses Cæsar's swimming at Alexandria to illustrate physical prowess (I.xvii), praises his industry (I.xxiii), his learning (I.xxv), his placability (II.vi), his diligence 'as well in commune causes as private, concernynge the defence and assistance of innocents' (III.x). Under Affability he ascribes the discontent with Cæsar and the plot against him to Cæsar's own fault in withdrawing from Affability—a view which Shakespeare may possibly have recalled in his portrayal of Cæsar as pontifical, critical of Cassius etc., and lacking in the geniality found in Pescetti's *Il Cesare* [Text X a]. Elsewhere Pompey and Cæsar are made illustrations of Ambition, a 'vice following Magnanimitie' [Text X b]. Brutus and Cassius are treated as examples of disloyalty [Text X c].

As Professor T. J. B. Spencer has shown[1] in a perceptive essay, 'The really important and interesting and relevant political lessons were those connected with *princes*' and 'in spite of literary admiration for Cicero, the Romans in the imagination of the sixteenth century were Suetonian and Tacitan rather than Plutarchan'. Various factors contributed to this. Under the Tudor régime civil war was regarded as the worst of public evils and an ever-recurring possibility, so the history of Rome under Cæsar and the Triumvirate was a terrible illustration of the results of internecine strife, personal ambition and intrigue, a perfect Mirror for Magistrates. Moreover an age which regarded a benevolent monarchy as the most desirable form of government and distinguished this from selfish tyranny and democracy—as witness many other treatises besides Fulke Greville's on that subject—found it easy to agree that both the gods and human needs brought about the replacement of the Roman Republic by the Roman Empire. Cæsar's arrogation of more than kingly privileges to himself might be reprehended, but the bringing of the world under Augustus' wise

[1] 'Shakespeare and the Elizabethan Romans', in *Sh. Survey*, 10, 1957.

and peaceful rule could be seen as a lesson for Tudor and Jacobean England.[1] So the translator of Appian saw the fate of Julius Cæsar's murderers as an *exemplum* of 'How God plagueth them that conspire againste theyr Prince' and declared his wish 'to affray all men from disloyaltie toward their Soveraigne', while his title page advertised his book as providing 'finally, an evident demonstration, that peoples rule must give place, and Princes power prevayle.'

In an age of princes the works of Suetonius and Tacitus were topical, and full of salutary lessons. The conflicts at imperial courts were not only more easily understood than the earlier history of Rome, but more sensational, appealing to the Elizabethans' love of luxury, cruelty, revenge and exemplary justice. Hence works like Richard Reynolds' *Chronicle of all the noble Emperours of the Romaines, from Julius Cæsar orderly*, ... (1571). Yet the number of histories of Rome written in the sixteenth century was few compared with the number of editions of the Roman historians themselves, and no later Emperor outshone the glory of Pompey and Cæsar.

The English attitude to Julius Cæsar preserved its medieval ambivalence, and his popularity owed perhaps as much to the fact that the British withstood his invasions as to his versatile genius and terrible fate. In his *Preface* to his *Mirror for Magistrates* (1559) Baldwin declared that 'it were . . . a goodlye and a notable matter to searche and dyscorse one whole storye from the fyrst beginning of the inhabitynge of the yle', but the first edition, starting where Lydgate left off, had nothing about the early history of Britain. In the additions made by John Higgins in 1574 however this gap was partially filled by sixteen tragedies from early British history which included the tragedy of *Cordila*, Lear's daughter, and *Perrex* (told in *Gorboduc*) and concluded with the tale of Nennius, 'a worthy Britayne, [who] the very paterne of a valiaunt, noble, and faithful subjecte encountring with Julius Cæsar at his firste comming into this Islande, was by him death wounded, yet nathelesse he gate Cæsar's swoorde: put him to flighte: slewe therewith Labienus a Tribune of the Romaynes, endured fight till hys countreymen wan the battayle, died fiftene dayes after.'

[1] Cf. J. E. Phillips, *The State in Shakespeare's Greek and Roman Plays*, Columbia U.P. 1940, Ch. ix.

The story of Irenglas in the 1575 edition likewise told of the time

> When *Cæsar* so with shamefull flight recoylde,
> And left our *Britayne* land unconquerde first
> (Which only thought, our realme & us, t'ave spoild).

For the definitive edition of the Baldwin-Higgins *Mirror* in 1587, the tragedy of *Caius Julius Cesar* was added along with those of Nero, Caligula and other Romans. In this poem Cæsar's ghost explained his inclusion in a work of British history by his invasions and conquest of Britain, and went on to describe not only these but also his triumphs over the Pompeians and his death at the hands of 'the traitor Brutus' and other envious traducers of his fame. His fall was also due to Fortune and to Jove's justice, because of the thousands whose deaths he had caused. I give part of this dreary piece as an example of pre-Shakespearian moralizing [Text XI]. There is no evidence that Shakespeare used it, but he may have glanced through *The Mirror* while writing *Julius Cæsar*, since Cassius' 'The fault dear Brutus lies not in our stars . . .' may be a recollection of that other rebel Glendower who in his Complaint declares, 'For they be faultes that foyle men, not their fates' (cf. Vol. IV, p. 203).

There is no evidence that Roman themes found any popularity on the public stage before Shakespeare, although the Revels Accounts mention several pieces performed at court by child-actors between 1574 and 1581. Roman plays came next from members of the court circle revolving round Sidney's sister, Mary Countess of Pembroke, and their attempts to naturalize French Senecanism in closet drama. In writing *Julius Cæsar* Shakespeare may well have been the initiator of a fashion in the popular theatre.

For the early Renaissance there was no great gulf between classical legend and history, and the pseudo-Senecan Latin *Octavia* was as valid an influence as Seneca's plays of Greek mythology. This play, the first Roman history-drama to survive, dealt with the sorrows of Nero's wife whom he divorced to marry Poppaea, banished, and sent away by ship with a band of murderers. This play, translated by Thomas Nuce in 1561 was a 'series of disquisitions and discussions . . . suggested by a single impressive historical situation' (MacCallum). Along with other Senecan dramas, it directly influenced the rise of Senecanism in France and England through the côteries linking Buchanan, Muret and Garnier in France, and the Pembroke circle in England.[1] In France the Cæsar story inspired the Latin *Julius Cæsar* of M. A. Muret (1544), Montaigne's tutor, a short piece of 600 lines which laid down a pattern of construction to be followed by many successors.

Act 1 is a soliloquy by Cæsar in which he looks forward to death because life holds no more conquests for him.

> Let others count their triumph when they will
> And name themselves from conquered provinces.
> To be called Cæsar's more. Whoever seeks
> Elsewhere new titles, takes something there away . . .
> I must seek heaven, since earth is base to me.

In Act 2 Brutus chides himself for not destroying the tyrant.

> Art thou unmoved by thy ancestors' virtues
> And by thy name, O Brutus; by the hard lot
> Of the groaning land, oppressèd by the tyrant
> And calling for thy aid; by the appeals
> In which the citizens lament that Brutus comes not
> To avenge the state? If these things move thee little
> Thy wife now charges thee to be a man
> Who in her blood hath proved her faith to thee,
> Thus witnessing herself thy Cato's offspring . . .
> Though he indeed be no king but dictator
> If yet the fact is so, what recks the name? . . .
> What though he gave me honours, even my life,
> My country matters more than all of these.
> Who gratitude will show to his country's tyrant,
> Inept in gratitude, is proved ungrateful.

The entry of Cassius shows that the plot has been made, the day has come and Cæsar will be slain. Cassius wishes Antony to be killed also, but Brutus refuses, for he wishes only to destroy tyranny.

[1] Cf. H. B. Charlton, *The Senecan Tradition in Renaissance Tragedy*, Manchester Univ. Press, 1946.

CASS. Then let it be destroyed from its deepest roots,
Lest when cut down it sprout again hereafter.
BRU. Under one trunk the whole root lies dependent.
CASS. Seems it thus so to thee? I'll say no more.
Thy will be done. We follow thee our leader.

After this the Chorus celebrates those who remove tyrants.

In Act III Calpurnia, entering from her room in great distress, tells her nurse that she has dreamed that Cæsar was dead in her arms, bloody from many wounds. The nurse declares that dreams are meaningless, that Cæsar's clemency and wisdom have removed any danger. Calpurnia however says that she will ask her husband to stay at home. The Chorus prays that all may be well.

In Act IV Calpurnia appeals to Cæsar, who reluctantly agrees to stay. Decimus Brutus however says that it would be shameful if Cæsar, ruler of the world, were ruled by a woman. He advises him at least to go and dismiss the Senate lest they think that he neglects and despises them. Cæsar goes, declaring that it is better to die once than to live in perpetual fear, and with regrettable *hubris* declares that he would not stay even though three hundred prophets, no not even if a god were to appear and warn him. The Chorus recalls Cassandra's prophecies as proof that sometimes women's advice should be followed.

When Act V opens, the assassination is over. Brutus and Cassius enter triumphant:

BRUT. Breathe again, Citizens. Cæsar is slain . . .
In Senate which he overthrew he lies o'erthrown.

Cassius flourishes his sword yet warm with blood, crying that the impious one who vexed Rome with criminal fury and blind madness is dead. They go out and Calpurnia enters to lament that her dream has proved true.

The Chorus joins her lament and demands revenge. Cæsar's ghostly voice bids them not mourn, for he is now one of the immortals:

Those who attacked me (a god I foretell truth)
With furious mind, shall not escape unpunished.
My virtue's heir, and heir too of my sceptre,

My sister's grandson, punishment shall claim
As best he chooses.

The Chorus rejoices in the happiness of the soul freed from the body.

Already in Muret we find many details repeated in later Cæsar plays. Cæsar is somewhat boastful, yet he is swayed first by his wife and then by Decimus Brutus. On the other hand he is not superstitious and once his mind is made up he is resolute with an arrogance drawn from the chroniclers who called him the enemy of the augurs. No evidence of Cæsar's tyranny is produced, but Brutus and Cassius both assert it, and after the murder Brutus calls Cæsar

the terror of his country,
The Senate's foe, the slaughterer of innocents,
The Law's ruin, plague of public right.

The speeches compress into the last day impressions of Brutus' personality which extend over a longer period. Thus in Act 2 he explains his own delay in coming to the help of the state, and refers to the citizens' petitions as though he had not yet decided what to do, although Cassius' entry makes it clear that the murder is already decided on and will take place that day. Brutus is the man of principle setting public duty above private gratitude; his connection with Cato and the earlier Brutus is recalled. He refuses to kill Antony. Cassius is a lesser man, swayed by Brutus' personality; he is more violent in his fury both before and after the murder. As MacCallum points out, 'more noticeable than any of these details, are the divided admiration and divided sympathy the author bestows both on Brutus and Cæsar—which are obvious even in the wavering utterances of the Chorus' (p. 26).

Fourteen years after Muret his play was adapted into French by a Huguenot, Jacques Grévin, who doubled its length, and while keeping the construction, introduced new characters and made the whole more theatrical. Grévin enriches the first Act by bringing in Mark Antony to flatter Cæsar and show his devotion. To enlarge Act II, Decimus Brutus is introduced. Act III combines the material of Muret's Acts 3 and 4 bringing together Calpurnia's dream and her attempts to keep Cæsar at home. Grévin's Act IV is new. To make more of the assassination and describe the scene at the Senate house, a Messenger is introduced to tell the news to Calpurnia and her Nurse.

In Act V a speech by Decimus Brutus is added, and instead of hearing Cæsar's voice we see Mark Antony first addressing the soldiers and then going off to stir the citizens to avenge Cæsar. In general attitude Grévin follows his master closely, recognizing the greatness of the antagonists, as appears in Brutus' speech claiming eternal fame:

And when they speak of Cæsar and of Rome,
May they remember that there was a man
Brutus, avenger of all cruelty
Who with one blow regained our liberty.
When they shall call Cæsar the Empire's master,
May they say just as oft that Brutus killed him.
When they say Cæsar was the first Emperor,
Let them say equally Brutus was the avenger.
Thus may his glory be for ever paled
By his who'll be his mortal enemy.

This indeed occurred, and most Renaissance playwrights praised both men while not concealing their weaknesses. Note that in most of these dramas, as in the *Octavia*, the antagonists are kept apart. Brutus does not meet Cæsar on the stage. Decimus Brutus is the link between the parties; and there is no exchange of opposed views, no quarrel, only statements not fortified by debate. Monologue is more important than dialogue, and action is almost entirely lacking.

Less directly bearing on Shakespeare's theme was the *Cornélie* of Garnier (1573, publd. 1574), who had already written a play on Portia in 1568. This play celebrated the sorrows of Cornelia the wife of Pompey the Great, and daughter of Metellus Scipio, who after Pompey's death fought on against Cæsar in Africa. Cicero is an important character. In Act I he utters a long soliloquy on the decline of Rome through desire of conquest. In Act II he tries to comfort Cornelia who blames herself for marrying Pompey after the death of her first husband Cassius. In Act III after she has told an illboding dream in which she saw Pompey's ghost, Cicero announces Cæsar's victory over Scipio and the latter's death. Cornelia receives the urn containing her husband's ashes and utters curses on Julius Cæsar. In Act IV Cassius and Decimus Brutus show their hostility to Cæsar before Cæsar and Antony enter. Antony wants severe measures to be used against Cæsar's vanquished foes, but Cæsar is for clemency. A chorus of Cæsar's friends sing of his great services to Rome. Act V is something of an anti-climax; in it a Messenger tells of Scipio's defeat and death and Cornelia declares that after the obsequies of Pompey and Scipio she will kill herself.

This piece is entirely undramatic, a series of rhetorical disquisitions often derived from Lucan. Cicero is treated as the wisest of the Romans. The republican sentiments of Cassius and Decimus Brutus owe much to Muret and Grévin. Antony is Cæsar's admirer and chief supporter. Cæsar is self-consciously grandiose, but asserts that he was forced against his wishes to wage civil war, and that he gets no pleasure from a victory involving the death of one Roman citizen. He is self-confident, asserting that his former enemies owe their lives and wealth to his bounty. Antony agrees but declares that their debt is greater to their fatherland and that they regard Cæsar as the ravisher of its rights.

Cornélie was translated into English by Thomas Kyd (1594) and Shakespeare may well have known his *Cornelia*, which had a second edition in 1595.

More interesting in some respects than Grévin's *César* is the Italian *Il Cesare* of Orlando Pescetti (1594). A possible connexion between this play and Shakespeare's was argued by Gregor Sarrazin [1] and by Alexander Boecker who thought that Shakespeare was probably indebted to Pescetti in his first three Acts.

Il Cesare elaborates the simple outlines of Muret and Grévin, using material from Appian, Plutarch, Suetonius and Lucan. The play starts with a long Prologue in heaven in which Venus and Mars bitterly resent the imminent death of Cæsar but are placated by Jove who declares that his apparent injustice is for the good of mankind.

In Act I Brutus and Cassius, meeting at the temple in the early morning before the assassination, speak of Cæsar's tyranny, discuss whether Antony should be killed, and are

[1] 'Shakespeare und Orlando Pescetti', in *EngSt.*, Bd. 46, 1913, pp. 347–54; A. Boecker, *A Probable Italian Source of Shakespeare's Julius Cæsar*, New York, 1913.

interrupted by Portia, who wishes she were a man so that she could join the plotters. She reproaches them for keeping their intentions secret from her and is with difficulty persuaded to go indoors and wait.

Act II begins with Calpurnia telling her Nurse about her evil dream before entering the temple. Brutus and Portia return and Brutus learns that his wife has wounded herself to prove her constancy. In a tender love-scene she asserts her resolve not to live on should he die. They overhear Calpurnia announce that she will keep her husband at home. Brutus prays Jove to make Cæsar go to the Senate.

In Act III Cæsar with Antony praises Lepidus' hospitality and shows some fear lest fortune turn against him. Advised by Antony to take precautions against his enemies he proposes to create a special guard for his person. He intends to make war on the Parthians. Antony soliloquizes on Cæsar's glory and hopes to obtain power for himself should Cæsar die. A priest describes the bad omens and auguries. Importuned by Calpurnia, Cæsar nevertheless refuses to stay at home.

At the start of Act IV Brutus and Cassius fear the discovery of their plot should the assassination be impossible that day. They discuss the evil effects of tyranny on the individual soul. Meanwhile Cæsar has decided not to go to the Senate but he is finally persuaded by Decimus Brutus to do so. On their way they are accosted by Lenate, whose private talk with Cæsar makes Cassius fear that he is betraying the plot. Brutus says that he will kill himself if need be, but it is soon obvious that Lenate has not revealed anything.

Before Act V opens the murder has been accomplished. Brutus briefly addresses the citizens and calls on Cicero to bid them rejoice. Calpurnia grieves, and a Messenger describes the murder. Three Choruses sing—the Citizens of liberty, the Ladies of war, the Soldiers of Cæsar's worth. The Soldiers demand vengeance. A second Messenger describes the confusion caused by the murder, the flight of Antony, and his probable alliance with Lepidus against the republicans. The play ends lamenting the decay of Rome, which a Chorus has already ascribed to neglect of religion.

Pescetti's characters are more fully developed than those in preceding Senecan dramas. His Cæsar is gracious and genial, arrogant and superstitious; his Brutus patriotic, scholarly and altruistic. Pescetti emphasizes the friendship between Brutus and Cassius and that between Cæsar and Antony, makes much of the discussion whether to kill Antony, of Calpurnia's endeavours to keep her husband at home. As Boecker declares, he seems to have introduced into drama the scenes between Brutus and Portia in which she demands his full confidence and tells how she wounded herself. Pescetti also introduces the suspense caused by Popilius Lena's approach to Cæsar. He makes much of the portents and of Cæsar's indecision.

The parallels between *Il Cesare* and *Julius Cæsar* are close, but Shakespeare could have got from Appian and Plutarch most of what Boecker thought he took from Pescetti. The Portia parallel is striking, but, being obliged to develop her part in the play, which otherwise would contain only one woman, Shakespeare would easily hit on such a scene as that between Portia and Brutus in II.1.233ff. The timing of this conversation, in the early morning, and her insistence on her masculine reliability (II.1.291–8) are both close to Pescetti. But Shakespeare makes short work of her 'voluntary wound'.

There are few verbal parallels, but one at least is interesting. Pescetti's Brutus, refusing to have Antony slain, declares

> Col troncar della testa all' altre membre
> Troncasi ogni vigore, ogni possanza.

Compare II.1.162–6:

> Our course will seem too bloody, Caius Cassius,
> To cut the head off and then hack the limbs,
> Like wrath in death and envy afterwards;
> For Antony is but a limb of Cæsar.
> Let us be sacrificers, but not butchers, Caius.

Shakespeare does not develop the idea of sacrificial ritual, but earlier in Pescetti (Act I) Brutus tells Cassius that Cæsar will be killed in the Senate as 'an offering and a sacrifice to liberty.'

Despite this and the other approximations it seems unlikely that Shakespeare would read *Il Cesare*. The parallels then are all the more remarkable, as showing some kinship between two very different minds working on the same materials in different literary traditions. I give below [Text XII] a translation of the most relevant parts of Pescetti's play, including some of the Prologue with its interesting defence by Jove of his seeming hostility to men (compare *Samson Agonistes*).

Apart from these plays on the last phase of Cæsar's life there were others on *Antony and Cleopatra* of which more will be said later. Thus eight years after Muret, Jodelle wrote *Cléopâtre Captive* (played 1552). In 1578 Garnier's *Marc Antoine* was successfully acted; and the translation of this play by Mary Sidney, Countess of Pembroke (pubd. 1592, 1595) was an attempt to apply the views on tragedy which she and her circle shared with her dead brother Sir Philip Sidney (see *Apologie for Poetry*). Others in her group followed suit. Kyd's *Cornelia* was dedicated to the Countess of Suffolk, Mary Sidney's aunt. Samuel Daniel's *Cleopatra* (1594) was addressed to Lady Mary. Samuel Brandon's *Vertuous Octavia* (written 1598) was a tragedy of Antony's wife. Sidney's friend, Fulke Greville, wrote a play on *Antony and Cleopatra* which he destroyed when Essex fell because its comments on the heroic general destroyed by his love for a false queen might have compromised him. Sir William Alexander's *Julius Cæsar* (1607) was the last fruit of the aristocratic Senecanism in England which derived mainly from Grévin and Garnier.

In the Universities too the period of Julius Cæsar inspired dramas. A *Cæsar Interfectus* by R. Eedes was played at Christ Church, Oxford, in 1581/2. The epilogue alone is extant, but shows an interesting parallel to the short, clipped Senecan style of Brutus' speech [Text XIII]. At the same college in 1588 an *Octavia* was put on; and probably some time in the nineties Trinity College, Oxford, performed a long play in English, *The Tragedie of Cæsar and Pompey, or Cæsar's Revenge* (not pubd. till 1607), based largely on Appian's *Bella Civilia*. The date of this play has been disputed, but its reminiscences of Marlowe's *Tamburlaine*, Daniel's *Rosamund* (1592), and Books I–III of Spenser's *Færie Queene* seem to place it before Shakespeare's *Julius Cæsar*.

Although this play is very unlike Shakespeare's in general conduct and characterization, it has certain likenesses to *Julius Cæsar* which have made Mr E. Schanzer consider that Shakespeare probably 'was acquainted with *Cæsar's Revenge* and that its importance as a source is only second to Plutarch'.[1] The summary and extracts from the play given below [Text XIV] show that it combines loosely several themes within the framework of a Senecan tragedy. The political dissension working through the whole from Pharsalia to Philippi is forced on our notice by the figure of Discord herself who acts as Chorus before each Act and at the end of the piece. There is the story of Pompey's end, when defeated at Pharsalia he flees to Egypt and is there murdered. There is the spell cast by Cleopatra over Cæsar and Antony; a spell which Cæsar at least throws off when he returns to Rome. Antony's love is left hanging in the air to foreshadow his later fate. Halfway through Act II we approach the matter of Shakespeare's play in the opposition to Cæsar in Rome (II.4; III.1) where Cassius takes the lead and draws Brutus in (III.3; III.5). Cæsar's pride and prudence are revealed in his triumph, in his refusal of the kingly title. His indecision after his wife's dream is emphasized. After the murder (III.6) there are formal speeches by Antony and Octavian over Cæsar's body (IV.1). Cæsar's Ghost appears (IV.3) to regret that the quarrels between Antony and Octavian hinder his revenge. The Ghost appears to Brutus both before (V.1) and during the Battle, and so ends the play.

Cæsar's Revenge resembles *Julius Cæsar* in covering a greater extent of time than the French Senecan dramas or their academic English imitators. Its course from Act II, Sc. 4 onwards is not unlike that of Shakespeare's play, with scenes alternating between the conspirators and Cæsar's party. The seduction of Brutus, the indecision of Cæsar, the journey to Pompey's Theatre, the murder, are shown in both, and both include speeches over the body. These might be expected in a play following the course of history without overmuch care for the Unities of place and time. *Cæsar's Revenge* also transforms the 'evil spirit' or 'evil genius' of the Roman chroniclers into Cæsar's Ghost. The fact that it appears three times, on the second pursuing the unfortunate Brutus during the battle, may perhaps have made Shakespeare resolve to keep its appearance on the stage to a minimum; hence in *Julius Cæsar* its second appearance is merely referred to (V.5.16–19). I am particularly struck by the parallels educed by Mr Schanzer, between

[1] 'A Neglected Source of *Julius Cæsar*', *N&Q*, Vol. 199, May, 1954, pp. 196–7.

Antony's violent prophecy in *Julius Cæsar* (III.1.258–75) and the sanguinary speeches of *Cæsar's Revenge*, and especially by his reference to 'Cæsar's spirit ranging for revenge, With Ate by his side come hot from hell'. This may possibly be a reminiscence of *Cæsar's Revenge* (2526ff) where Discord and the Ghost gloat over the dead, and Discord announces that she will return to Hell, while Cæsar's Ghost will go to Elysium. Brutus in this play is a cruder character than in Shakespeare, but he is depicted as melancholy when Cassius addresses him in III.3 (1390): 'But see where melancholy Brutus walks' (Cf. *JC* I.2.37–46). Brutus also, after declaring in IV.2, 1943–4

> I that before fear'd not to do the deede,
> Shall never now repent it being done

realizes his 'sad ingratitude' when the Ghost appears before the battle (2270–80) and he begs the spirit to slay him. Shakespeare's Brutus is nearer to that of the French Senecans, for he gives little sign of remorse, and he never calls death 'the guerdon that my deeds deserve'. In *Julius Cæsar*, Brutus' doubts of their plot's justice come early: once committed he never looks back or reproaches himself morally. Nevertheless *Cæsar's Revenge* portrays a more thoughtful Brutus than most plays on the theme. Thus it is by no means certain that Shakespeare knew *Cæsar's Revenge*, but the parallels are interesting as showing two dissimilar writers working over the same ground within a few years of one another.

Of Shakespeare's classical knowledge Dr Johnson declared, accepting Ben Jonson's 'small Latin, less Greek', 'It is most likely that he learned *Latin* sufficiently to make him acquainted with construction, but that he never advanced to an easy perusal of the *Roman* authors' (*Preface to Shakespeare*). Recent enquiries[1] show that Shakespeare could certainly read Latin and both remembered much of what he had read at school and kept up some study of it. This does not mean that he used Latin authorities closely like a modern classical scholar or like Ben

[1] Notably by T. W. Baldwin, *Shakspere's Small Latine and Lesse Greeke*, 2 vols. Urbana, 1944; V. K. Whitaker, *Shakespeare's Use of Learning*, Huntington Library, 1953; J. A. K. Thomson, *Shakespeare and the Classics*, 1952; P. Simpson, 'Shakespeare's Use of Latin Authors', in *Studies in Elizabethan Drama*, Oxford, 1955; J. D. Wilson, 'Shakespeare's "small Latin"—how much?', in *Sh. Survey*, 10, 1957.

Jonson for *Sejanus* and *Catiline*, but he read more easily in Latin than Dr Johnson supposed.

At the better grammar schools of the time the relevant authors studied were Ovid, Cicero, Cæsar, Sallust and Livy. At Eton the boys in the fifth form read Valerius Maximus and Lucius Florus. There is no reason to suppose that Shakespeare knew all these, but if he went to Stratford Grammar School he would be able not only to read but to imitate the style of several of them, and his memory, though fallible,[1] was so extraordinarily good that we can confidently assert that if he wished to consult any of the major Roman historians in Latin he could do so profitably and without great difficulty. There is however no proof that he did so for *Julius Cæsar*.

He used English translations whenever possible. It is likely that he wrote with North's Plutarch by his side; that he consulted the translation of Appian; and for the portents before the assassination remembered, or consulted again, the end of Golding's version of the *Metamorphoses*, Virgil's *Georgics*, Bk. I, and Lucan's account of the portents of civil war after Cæsar had crossed the Rubicon.[2]

Other works probably used included the *Mirror for Magistrates*, Sir Thomas Elyot's *The Governour*, Kyd's *Cornelia* and maybe *Cæsar's Revenge*, but the main source for *Julius Cæsar*, *Antony and Cleopatra* and *Coriolanus* was Plutarch's *Lives* in which can be found almost everything historical in these plays. For *Julius Cæsar* he used at least the *Lives* of *Cæsar*, *Brutus* and *Mark Antony*, and he may also have read the biographies of Cato and Cicero. All three major *Lives* contain the main incidents of his plot, and treat Cæsar, the conspirators and Antony in much the same way, although the emphasis naturally changes in each biography [Texts I, II, III and *AC* Text I].

From the start Shakespeare shows his skill in compressing the events of months into a few days or hours, and in combining elements from his three *Lives* to make a consistent pattern of urgency, without going into political and historical details which would involve long explanations. For his purpose a succession of telling strokes is more important than strict

[1] Examples of confusion or error are given by Simpson, *op. cit.*, pp. 6–8.

[2] Cf. K. Muir, *Shakespeare's Sources*, I, Ch. vii, for a lucid summary of Shakespeare's indebtedness in the Roman plays.

authenticity. He begins his play with Cæsar's triumph on returning to Rome after defeating Pompey's sons. This triumph offended many Romans—and especially former followers of Pompey—because it celebrated the overthrow of 'the sons of the noblest man in Rome, whom fortune had overthrown' (*Cæsar*, *inf.* 77). The tribune Marullus expresses this sentiment (I.1.35–55) when with his colleague Flavius he orders the disrobing of Cæsar's images on which (*Brutus*, *inf.* 95) 'Cæsar's flatterers . . put diadems.' (Shakespeare calls them 'ceremonies', 'trophies', and 'scarfs'.) The tribunes become Pompeian sympathizers, whereas in Plutarch they were anti-monarchists, imprisoning 'them that first saluted Cæsar as king' (*inf.* 81). The working folk in I.1 are thoughtless admirers of Cæsar but not necessarily monarchical in sentiment. Maybe the cobbler among them came from the statement in the *Life of Brutus* that the appeals to Brutus to liberate them were *not* written by 'cobblers, tapsters, or suchlike base mechanical people' (*inf.* 96).

The triumph was held in October, 45 B.C. and the feast of the Lupercal was not until February 15, 44 B.C.; but Shakespeare combines the two in order to show Cæsar soaring towards kingship but receiving a setback in the next scene. The triumphal procession perhaps suggested Cæsar's entry in I.2, going to take his seat 'in a chair of gold, apparelled in triumphing manner' to watch Antony and others run the sacred course (*inf.* 81). To prepare for Calpurnia's important part later he introduces her here and refers to her sterility (as Plutarch never did). The first warning of Cæsar's danger is given by the Soothsayer, who in Plutarch had done so 'long time before'. The Soothsayer is to be seen again later.

For the conversation between Brutus and Cassius which follows (I.2.25–177) Shakespeare drew on the *Life of Brutus*, but ascribed the recent coolness between him and Cassius, not to their rivalry for the prætorship (*inf.* 93–6), but to Brutus' disturbed mind. In Plutarch not only is Cassius more direct in mentioning the danger that 'Cæsar should be called King by the Senate' (*inf.* 96), but Brutus is more forceful in his reaction: 'I mean not to hold my peace, but to withstand it, and rather die than lose my liberty.' Shakespeare's Cassius finds it necessary to bring to Brutus' consciousness thoughts which he has been suppressing (I.2.51–70). Brutus, confessing that he would not have Cæsar king, adds 'yet I love him well', a reference maybe to the fact that Cæsar had forgiven him his part with Pompey in the Civil War, but his virtue makes him set justice ('the general good' (l. 85)) above his personal wishes. 'That Brutus could evil away with the tyranny, and that Cassius hated the tyrant' (*inf.* 94) is shown in lines 81ff, when Cassius belittles Cæsar by distorting qualities described more favourably by Plutarch. Thus Plutarch and other authorities told how Cæsar's prowess in swimming enabled him to escape from the Egyptians in Alexandria. Any reader of the Roman chroniclers would doubt Cassius' veracity at 99–115, or at least recall the other story. Similarly Cassius builds on Plutarch's statement that Cæsar was 'often subject to headache, and otherwhile to the falling sickness: (the which took him the first time, as it is reported in Corduba, a city of Spain)' (*inf.* 66) as a proof of weakness (119–28), whereas Plutarch insisted that Cæsar did *not* give way to his ailments. In the light of the sources this dialogue shows Cassius as a mean and partial enemy; and I cannot believe that Shakespeare meant us to think much worse of Cæsar for it. What moves Brutus is not this envious malice but his own fears which agree with Cassius' closing reference (157–60) to Lucius Junius Brutus who drove out the Tarquins. Brutus' reply ends the discussion, 'What you would work me to, I have some aim', and, referring to his own previous reflections, suggests, not that he will take part in a murder-plot, but that he may withdraw from Rome: 'Brutus had rather be a villager . . .' With this for the moment Cassius must be content. The winning of Brutus to the conspiracy is not so easy in the play as in Plutarch.

We are not shown Antony offering the crown to Cæsar. Shakespeare may have thought that this would show Cæsar in too bad a light. More probably he wished to keep our attention mainly on the conspirators and their enmity. But we see Cæsar departing from the festival angry that the mob applauded him when he refused to be king, Calpurnia disturbed, and Cicero furious that the offer was made (I.2.177–87). Having heard Cassius' opinion of Cæsar we now hear Cæsar's of Cassius, contrasting his 'pale looks' and 'carrion-lean' figure with Antony's sleek plumpness and love of music. Plutarch's Cæsar included Brutus in this stricture (*inf.* 82, 94) for he did not trust him. In Shakespeare he shows no fear of Brutus, but the dramatist never brings the two together before the murder, in this resembling the French Senecan playwrights. The denigration of Cæsar by Cassius is now followed by Casca's account of his behaviour when offered the crown—a narrative which throws as much light on the jeering narrator as on the dictator. Here Shakespeare follows Plutarch's *Life of Antonius* rather than that of Cæsar; in the former Cæsar in a rage offered his neck to the crowd (*inf.* 264), whereas in the *Cæsar* he had done this to allay their anger after he had neglected to rise to greet the Senate (*inf.* 80). Brutus' disgust at Casca's manner is shown in his two interruptions (252, 260) and at the end he comments on the decline of Casca from 'quick mettle' to 'blunt fellow'. The ignorance of Greek which Casca claims in describing Cicero's reaction is belied by Plutarch who asserts that during the assassination Casca spoke Greek to his brother. He alludes to the mockery of Cicero as 'the Grecian scholar' (*Life of Cicero*). Shakespeare's Casca is of the sneering 'malcontent' type to which Thersites in *Troilus and Cressida* belongs.

Cassius' soliloquy after the departure of Brutus accords with the view of him as a scheming politician already given. Plutarch insists that Brutus by going along with Cæsar 'might have been one of Cæsar's chiefest friends' and possibly his successor, adding that Cassius' friends 'prayed him to beware of Cæsar's sweet enticements' which were intended 'not to honour his virtue, but to weaken his constant mind, framing it to the bent of his bow' (*inf. Brutus* 94). Shakespeare's Cassius in referring to favourable signs in Brutus ('I will come home to you . . .'), recalls (in 305–8) the pliability hinted at in Plutarch, and boasts of his own firmness (312–13). Cassius himself is going to throw in at Brutus' windows the propagandist appeals which in Plutarch came from those 'that desired change' (*Cæsar*), 'his friends and countrymen' (*Brutus*).

Between I.2 and the events of I.3 and II.1 a month actually passed, but Shakespeare obscures this by Brutus' reference in I.2 to a meeting with Cassius 'tomorrow', and by making Cassius at I.3.144 ask Casca to throw writings through Brutus' windows. II.1 follows closely on the stormy night-scene I.3. On the other hand Brutus indicates in II.1.61 that some days have gone by 'Since Cassius first did whet me against Cæsar' and he has had time to give Ligarius reasons for joining the plot (II.1.215–19). Shakespeare is using 'double time', but not systematically; he is aware of the lapse of time in Plutarch, but also wishes to give speed and continuity to the play while omitting some historical incidents.

In I.3 the movements of the conspirators are set against the unnatural portents which Plutarch (*inf.* 83, cf. 153) described as preceding the death of Cæsar. Shakespeare adds to them, from Marlowe's *Lucan* and maybe other accounts of prodigies. He shows their effect on some important personages: Casca terrified, Cicero calm and unconcerned as befits one affected by stoicism, Cassius seeing them as omens of 'some monstrous state', but quick to turn even the supernatural to political advantage by comparing these 'strange eruptions' with Cæsar's prodigious growth. When the gossip Casca (I.3.85–8) announces that Cæsar is to be made 'king of all the provinces of the Empire of Rome out of Italy' (*inf.* 84), Cassius threatens to commit suicide (89–102), blames Cæsar's tyranny upon the sheepish Romans and makes Casca commit himself before Cinna enters, on his way to a meeting of the plotters 'in Pompey's porch' (where Plutarch set the assassination).

In Plutarch after Cassius has won Brutus over, Brutus' anxiety about the conspiracy's success will not let him sleep (*inf.* 98); the two of them approached 'all their acquaintance whom they trusted, and laid their heads together, consulting upon it'. Shakespeare in II.1 has used the historian's materials for a different purpose, to show Brutus, sleepless through doubts about the justice of killing Cæsar, resolving his conflict in soliloquy, reading the appeals thrown through his window, whispering his decision to Cassius (l. 100), taking the plotters' hands and discussing with them whom to include in their number.

The inadequate reasons for Brutus' decision will be considered later; they are fortified by the citizens' appeals to his republican ancestry, but he hates the necessity for conspiratorial meetings by night (77–81) and the hypocritical affability (81–2) which Plutarch said he put on by day (*inf.* 98). Whereas Plutarch in the *Life of Brutus* praised the loyalty of the plotters in their secrecy, 'having never taken oaths together nor taken or given any caution or assurance, etc.' (*inf.* 97), Shakespeare gives the credit for this to Brutus, making him reject at length Cassius' suggestion of an oath (II.1.113–40). Brutus also is made responsible for not acquainting Cicero with their scheme, not because as Plutarch wrote, he was timid and old, but because he would never follow other men's lead (141–53). Here, as in the decision not to kill Antony with Cæsar, the mental ascendancy of Brutus over his fellows is shown.

After his friends have gone, a brief indication of Brutus' gentleness towards his servant is followed by that favourite feature of previous Cæsar plays, a colloquy between Brutus and his wife Portia, in which she reveals more of his recent mental disturbance, shows her love, and demands, as Cato's daughter, to share his counsels. Shakespeare makes less of her self-inflicted wound than did some of his predecessors, and to avoid wearisome iteration keeps Brutus' explanation offstage. The coming of the sick Ligarius (whom Shakespeare following Plutarch calls Caius instead of Quintus) ends the scene with another touch of noble resolution.

In II.2 we are back among the portents of the night in I.3 though in fact Calpurnia's dream occurred on the night before the Ides of March. Cæsar, like Brutus in II.1, finds sleep difficult, but Shakespeare omits the noises in his chamber except the 'fumbling lamentable speeches' of his wife (*inf.* 83). She has already told him her dream, which is not revealed to the audience until 76–9, but after Cæsar has sent to have auguries taken (5–6) she supports her demand that he stay at home with a list of prodigies which, expanding Plutarch's account, may owe something to Marlowe's *Lucan* (I.557–79), *Cæsar's Revenge* and perhaps Savile's *Histories of Tacitus*, which described portents before the destruction of Jerusalem by Titus in A.D. 70 (V.xiii).

In Shakespeare as in Plutarch she has not previously been superstitious (II.2.13–14); nor was Cæsar himself. Indeed he was accused of impiety for his refusal to accept auguries which did not suit him (*inf.* 149, 154). In Plutarch however he 'did fear and suspect somewhat', moved by his wife's fears and by the unfavourable report of the 'soothsayers' (*inf.* 84). Shakespeare makes him less easily swayed, until Calpurnia beseeches him on her knees to let Antony tell the Senators that he is not well, when he agrees to fall in with his wife's 'humour' (25–56).

Insisting on Cæsar's natural fearlessness Shakespeare introduces (32–7) a reference to his saying that 'it was better to die once than always to be afraid of death' (*inf.* 78). Those who suppose that he 'did fear . . . somewhat' and was glad to blame it on his wife must ignore his first words to Decius Brutus when he prefers to risk offending the Senators rather than 'send a lie' or 'be afeard to tell grey beards the truth' (57–68). Behind this and Decius' desire for a reason lies Shakespeare's knowledge that Cæsar was already suspected of despising the Senate. Calpurnia's dream, now related, includes details not in Plutarch—but based on him—that Cæsar's statue ran blood (as Pompey's did at the assassination—*inf.* 86) and that Romans 'did bathe their hands in it' (as did the conspirators in III.1.105–13). Decius' favourable interpretation is Shakespeare's invention and recalls the opposite interpretations of Gloucester's dream in *2 Henry VI* I.2. He appeals to Cæsar's fear of misrepresentation as in Plutarch, but Shakespeare brings Brutus, Antony and others to take him to the Senate, and includes an aged Senator, Publius, who is not in the plot and who will be introduced again after the murder to prove the conspirators' goodwill toward the Senate (III.1.85–93). In an aside Brutus grieves over the treacherous part he has to play (II.2.126–9). The introduction (II.3) of the rhetorician Artemidorus with his paper giving the names of the plotters (as in the *Mirror for Magistrates* [Text XI]), excites suspense which is increased by Portia's fears in II.4.

Shakespeare might have made an occasion for Brutus to show his Stoic constancy here, for Plutarch says (*inf. Brutus* 100) that he was informed that 'his wife was dying' but 'he left not off the care of his country and commonwealth, neither went home to his house for any news he heard'. In some of Shakespeare's plays such an anticipation of his behaviour when she really died might have been used. But in *Julius Cæsar* there is less repetition than usual.

The reappearance of the Soothsayer, his reply to Cæsar's merry greeting, and the importunate attempt of Artemidorus to get his 'schedule' read, link the two scenes and make the action continuous. Suspense grows when Popilius Lena goes to speak to Cæsar (III.1.13–24) but Brutus is unperturbed (Cf. *inf.* 101).

The murder of Cæsar follows Plutarch in its general outline. In Plutarch's *Cæsar* Trebonius drew off Antony; in *Brutus* it was Decius Brutus. Shakespeare follows the former account. Shakespeare's Cæsar is overfull of dignity and brags of his immoveable resolution in his response to the appeals on behalf of Metellus' exiled brother (named by Shakespeare Publius, without warrant). Plutarch's version of the stabbing may have influenced the stage-business at lines 73–7. Cæsar's cry 'Et tu, Brute?' may have been ultimately inspired by the cry in Suetonius' *Julius Cæsar:* 'And thou, my son?' but they occur in *The True Tragedie of Richard Duke of Yorke* (printed 1595) and are approached in *Cæsar's Revenge* [Text XIV]. Maybe Shakespeare wished to avoid any allusion to the tradition that Brutus was the illegitimate son of Julius Cæsar by Servilia.

The next lines embroider Plutarch's narrative (*inf.* 86, 102); the senators fleeing afraid (though needlessly as Brutus and Cassius tell the aged Publius); the flight of Antony (not however to another man's house, as in Plutarch); the blooding of the murderers (not in the act of assassination as in Plutarch's *Brutus* but in solemn ritual (105–7)); their march, sword in hand, to the market place, led by Brutus.

The coming of Antony's messenger asking for safe-conduct, followed closely by his master, is Shakespeare's invention in order to bring the avenger into contact with the assassins as soon as possible. Shakespeare therefore speeds things up, omitting the Senate-meeting (next day) at which the wily Antony joined with Cicero to get pardon and honours for the liberators and 'sent them his son for a pledge'. His Antony is more forthright and courageous, ready to face death along with Cæsar, but also to shake hands one by one with the chief murderers. His ambiguous attitude (III.1.204–22) is on the surface that of many senators and others in Rome who mourned the death of Cæsar but were willing to be persuaded that it was necessary and to take advantage of its consequences (*inf.* 104). Shakespeare cunningly makes it obvious, by Cassius' misgiving (144–6) and Antony's own speeches, that the latter is unsatisfied and dangerous, and when he persuades Brutus to let him speak at Cæsar's funeral, despite Cassius' warnings (227–53) we expect some striking outcome. In Plutarch Brutus first made a speech in the Capitol 'to win the favour of the people and to justify that they had done.' He afterwards spoke in the market-place on the day after the murder. The *Life of Cæsar* asserts that the people gave them 'such audience that it seemed they neither greatly reproved nor allowed the fact: for by their silence they shewed that they were sorry for Cæsar's death, and also that they did reverence Brutus.' According to the *Life of Brutus*, Brutus was heard quietly, 'howbeit, immediately after, they shewed that they were not all contented with the murther . . . Insomuch that the conspirators returned again into the Capitol.' (*Brutus*, *inf.* 103). Cæsar's funeral was discussed in the Senate two days after the murder, and there Antony proposed, and Brutus supported, public obsequies and the reading of Cæsar's will. By omitting the Senate's part in the business Shakespeare has focused attention on the main antagonists and by shifting Brutus' speech to the funeral has made the contrast between them and the weakness of Brutus' judgement the more apparent. Plutarch observed that his major errors were two, to oppose the killing of Antony, and then to let him have his way over the funeral arrangements. Shakespeare adds two other proofs of Brutus' lack of realism—his belief that Antony would be their friend (III.I.143) and his confidence that by speaking first he could prevent Antony from moving the people against them (*ibid.*, 231–52). 'The infatuation is almost incredible', wrote MacCallum, commenting on Brutus' 'Quixotic exaltation'. Indeed, his is the *hubris* of the moral fanatic, and the audience foresees the end when Antony makes his exultant soliloquy (254–75), which is framed however in terms more suited to the Civil Wars of Pompey and Cæsar than to what actually happened after Cæsar's death. Shakespeare probably had *Cæsar's Revenge* or Marlowe's Lucan in mind when he wrote

> Domestic fury and fierce civil strife
> Shall cumber all the parts of Italy . . .

Antony's attempt to keep the young Octavius Cæsar away from Rome until after the funeral (276–97) is presented by Shakespeare as prompted by fears for the boy's safety. But behind lies the knowledge that Antony was hostile to Cæsar's heir and treated him contemptuously when he arrived in Rome from

Apollonia (where he had been studying and waiting to accompany Cæsar against the Parthians) in May 44 B.C. Only in 43 B.C. did Antony and Octavius become temporary and uneasy allies.

Omitting Brutus' first oration in the Capitol and the lapse of a night or two during which Antony had supper with Cassius, and Lepidus with Brutus, Shakespeare goes straight to the second climax of his play, the scene at Cæsar's funeral when Brutus, foolishly leaving Antony to come as chief mourner with Cæsar's body, makes his speech to satisfy the plebeians about his actions. Cassius goes off to make a speech elsewhere, so he is absent when Antony turns the tables on Brutus. Plutarch tells us nothing about the latter's oration, but elsewhere he gives a specimen of Brutus' epistolary style which 'counterfeited that brief compendious manner of speech of the Lacedæmonians' (*inf.* 91). M. Macmillan in the old Arden edition of the play pointed out that in his speech Brutus makes repeated use of conditional clauses ('If any, speak . . .) and of the word 'offended' found in the letter. Shakespeare may have imitated this letter. But he may possibly also have known Cicero's dialogue on the great orators of Rome (*Brutus or De Claris Oratoribus*) drafted shortly before Cæsar's murder and including Brutus among the interlocutors (*sup.* 7).

Brutus' speech in the play is a careful piece of craftsmanship, formally correct but inflexible in its marshalling of antithetical qualities and rhetorical questions. The tone is reasonable but begs the question: Was Cæsar's ambition deleterious to Rome? *Would* his rule have made them all slaves? Of these implications there is no evidence. When Brutus declares 'The question of his death is enroll'd in the Capitol' (III.2.38–41), he refers to something outside the play, namely the Senate resolutions which tried to offend nobody, pardoning Cæsar's murderers but confirming the legality of Cæsar's edicts. When Brutus declares that Antony 'shall receive the benefit of his dying, a place in the commonwealth', he probably refers to a letter in Cicero's correspondence in which Brutus and Cassius desired Antony 'to be great and honest in a free republic' (MacCallum). The effect of his speech is disconcerting, for some ardent plebeians want him crowned as Cæsar. This agrees with Plutarch's *Cæsar* in which they 'wished Brutus only their prince and governor above all other.' Antony barely keeps the terms of his agreement with the conspirators, admitting ambiguously that for Brutus' sake he finds himself beholden to them all. For the circumstances, material and effects of Antony's speech, Shakespeare drew mainly on the *Life of Antony*, but he took some details from the other two *Lives*. None of them however gave many details of what Antony said or how he said it. In Appian there is a long and finely wrought oration which was probably invented by that late historian. It contains nothing to indicate that Shakespeare used it, but he may well have read it in the Elizabethan translation, and the excerpt given below [Text VIII] may be interesting to compare with the dramatist's brilliant creation which, without entirely breaking faith with Brutus, nevertheless by its mingling of grief, frankness, irony, innuendo and appeal to the mob's self-interest swings the latter away from Brutus to a furious lust for revenge. Analysis of the speech shows him using some of Brutus' rhetorical devices—conditional clauses and the repetition of phrases, but more subtly. As in Plutarch, 'he mingled his oration with lamentable words; and by amplifying of matters did greatly move their hearts and affections unto pity and compassion' (*Antonius*, *inf.* 265). Pathos and amplification are indeed major devices of Shakespeare's *Antony*. Plutarch's *Cæsar* attributed the people's riot to the reading of Cæsar's testament and the exposure of his body 'al bemangled with gashes of swords' (*inf.* 87). By combining this with the other two accounts and making Antony the adroit manipulator of these two crucial incidents Shakespeare gets suspense and action into the oration, with a superb climax or 'climbing figure' in his changing description of the murderers: 'honourable men', 'envious Casca'—'well beloved Brutus', 'bloody treason', 'traitors'. The scene ends with the announcement of Octavius' arrival in Rome and Antony's expression of pleasure at the news. Brutus and Cassius have fled. In Plutarch's *Brutus* they do this only after the murder of Cinna the poet has proved the extreme hatred of the mob against them.

The Cinna episode (III.3, *Brutus*, *inf.* 105) gives Shakespeare an opportunity for a scene of macabre humour such as he had made of a popular riot in the Jack Cade scenes of 2 *Henry VI*. It illustrates once more the irrationality of the mob, as easily swayed to murder as to hero-worship and warm sympathy. At the beginning of Act IV we see the double nature of another group of men when the new triumvirate, Antony, Octavius and Lepidus having met, as they did in autumn 43 B.C., to divide the empire between them, draw up a list of proscriptions, but 'could hardly agree whom they would put to death: for every one of them would kill their enemies, and save their kinsmen and friends' (*Antonius*, *inf.* 268). The scene starts when 'in their greedy desire to be revenged of their enemies, they spurned all reverence of blood and holiness of friendship at their feet.' Since Octavius has arrived in Rome the meeting takes place there, not on an island off the coast. J. Dover Wilson (*Camb*, 169) has suggested that the scene may have been added later 'to form a link with *Antony and Cleopatra*.' More probably Shakespeare already had the possibility of a sequel in mind when he made Antony the dominant figure in the second half of the play, ignoring both the quarrels between him and Octavius and his defeat by the latter before they joined to destroy Brutus and Cassius. He wished to keep Antony to the fore, yet in pursuance of his general plan for this play of showing all parties in an unfavourable as well as a favourable light, he took the opportunity of revealing the ruthlessness and grasping ambition in both Antony and Octavius. Hence their sacrifice of kinsmen and friends, and Antony's contempt for Lepidus, his desire to 'cut off some charge' in the legacies he has just proclaimed so effectively to the Roman people. The scene, with its portrayal of Cæsar's avengers on the brink of dissension, also goes well with the next two scenes in which their opponents are also seen quarrelling. In the *Life of Brutus* Brutus and Cassius fell out at Sardis over 'tales and complaints' from their 'captains', until they were interrupted by the cynic poet Marcus Phaonius. Next day they quarrelled again about the condemnation by Brutus of Lucius Pella for 'robbery and pilfering in his office.' (*inf. Brutus*, 115). Shakespeare changes the order of events somewhat. Cassius greets Brutus (much as he did in I.2) by accusing him of unfriendliness, this time for condemning Lucius Pella for taking bribes. Brutus retorts by accusing Cassius of having 'an itching palm', an allusion to 'the extreme covetousness and cruelty of Cassius to the Rhodians' (*inf.* 113). Brutus' reminder that they had slain Julius Cæsar 'But for supporting robbers', gives us the only concrete reference in the play to any evil act done by the dead dictator. Brutus did not mention it earlier (II.1.10–34) because Shakespeare wished him to base his decision entirely on principle, and the decision was to be seen as without a sufficient cause. Shakespeare would find it not only in the *Life of Brutus* (*inf.* 115) but also in the *Antonius* (*inf.* 261), but he is following the former biography closely here. The argument about which of the two is the better soldier is invented by Shakespeare but based on his knowledge that Cassius 'was the elder man' and a more experienced general, and also exceedingly choleric (*inf.* 110). The quarrel deepens when Brutus, self-righteously asserting his inability to extort money 'from the hard hands of peasants', says that Cassius had refused him 'certain sums of gold'. Actually Cassius' friends had urged him to refuse it but he had sent Brutus a third of all he had (*Brutus*, *inf.* 111). So Cassius is right when he says 'I denied you not.' In Plutarch the poet's intrusion stops their quarrel only temporarily. In Shakespeare the better nature and mutual loyalty of the two friends have already brought about a reconciliation when he forces his way into the tent and serves as a comic epilogue which also makes it appear that the hot-tempered Cassius has a richer sense of humour than Brutus, who chides the fatuous intruder impatiently, thus making a link with what follows. The idea of making him a bad poet comes from North's doggerel translation of a perfectly good line quoted in Plutarch from Homer.

Shakespeare has shown the two chief groups at their worst, but that he wishes us now to see Brutus and Cassius in a better light than their antagonists appears in the next part of the scene, into which he transfers from the end of Plutarch's *Life of Brutus* the account of Portia's death. The two announcements of it have naturally excited debate. In the Folio text Brutus first tells Cassius of it to excuse his loss of temper, describing how she swallowed fire in grief at her husband's absence and at the growing power of his enemies (142–57). A few lines further on, after the approach of Octavius and Mark Antony towards Philippi, and news of the proscription by which Cicero has been slain (cf. *inf.* 108), Messala asks Brutus if he has had any news of his wife. Brutus says 'Nothing, Messala', and the latter tries to break it to him.

> Then like a Roman hear the truth I tell;
> For certain she is dead, and by strange manner. (86–7)

Brutus asks for no details but closes the subject with inhuman stoicism, which excites the wonder and admiration of Messala and Cassius (188–94).

There is some inconsistency here, for in the first account tidings of her death came with tidings of the enemy's strength (150–4); and he must have news of it somehow. Some critics have argued that both passages are meant to be acted, that Brutus wanted to give Messala a lesson in Roman fortitude. Even at the expense of lying, and of pretending not to know what he had already spoken about to Cassius? I agree with the critics who see an uncancelled duplication in the Folio text, and regard the second piece of dialogue (180–94) as the original, the first piece (142–57) as Shakespeare's revised, and greatly improved, version; improved because it helps to explain to Cassius and the audience the uncharacteristic anger of the first part of the scene, brings out Cassius' sympathy, portrays the conflict in Brutus' mind between grief and self-restraint, and gives us another glimpse of Portia's noble love and desperation, already seen in II.4. Plutarch gave two different theories about the cause of her suicide, one ascribing it to loneliness and political despair (*inf.* 131–2), the other to illness. Shakespeare's first version avoided choosing between them but made Brutus cold and unnatural in his reaction. In the revised version the dramatist chose the more fitting motive and also revealed Brutus' humanity.

The discussion about the advisability of awaiting the enemy's attack or marching to meet them at Philippi follows Plutarch, who attributed Brutus' insistence on the latter plan to his customary desire for immediate and decisive action whatever the consequences (*inf.* 118). He overrides Cassius' more cautious opinion and Cassius gives way against his better judgement, full of remorse for the 'ill beginning of the night', i.e. their quarrel. His warm loyalty is paralleled by Brutus' consideration for Lucius and his officers (239–70). Behind Brutus' wakefulness here is Plutarch's statement that Brutus 'slept very little' and often spent most of the night 'in despatching of his weightiest causes', but would then 'read some book till the third watch of the night, at what time the captains . . . did use to come to him'. This is not the sleepless Brutus of II.1, worn with mental conflict. Having acted on the decision then made he has never regretted it openly, yet he is anxious and 'much forgetful', his longing for music is a longing for a lost harmony; there is perhaps a reminiscence of Gethsemane in the inability of his boy to watch with him one hour; and in the words 'If I do live, I will be good to thee' there lurks a doubt which is justified when the apparition enters.

In Plutarch the visitant is not identified as Cæsar's ghost (cf. IV.3.273 *s.d.* and V.5.17) but as Brutus' 'evil spirit', or 'genius', and the comments of classical scholars in the Renaissance showed that this was akin to the Bad Angel which haunted Marlowe's Faustus (*inf.* 116). The 'evil spirit' came to warn a man of approaching doom whether deserved or not. Dramatic tradition however had already turned it into Cæsar's ghost. In *Cæsar's Revenge* it urges Antony and Octavius to seek 'a just revenge' (l. 2051) rather than fight one another, appears to Brutus twice (2281 and 2502), and ends the play exulting with Discord. Shakespeare's ghost, following Plutarch closely, is laconic, and Brutus, quickly recovering from his fear, courageously accepts what it forebodes. He would like to think it a figment of his imagination, but knows it is not and is unafraid ('Ill spirit, I would hold more talk with thee'); yet he wakes his boy and officers and questions them. He shows no sign of conscience. The ghost is an evil portent, no more.

Coming at the beginning of the fifth Act to Philippi, Shakespeare omits the sickness of Octavius which endangered his cause, and the delay of ten days before the two armies were ranged on the plains. Octavius' reference to the enemy's coming down from the hills links V.1 with the discussion in IV.3.195–211. Antony misjudges the courage of the enemy. His reference to their 'bravery' comes from North's remark that 'For bravery and rich furniture, Brutus' army far excelled Cæsar's' (*inf.* 117). There is a moment of disagreement between Octavius and Antony when the former insists on leading the right wing of the army (V.1.16–20), refusing to be overborne by the more experienced Antony. This really happened in the opposite camp (*inf.* 120), but Shakespeare transfers it, presumably to show that both partnerships were marred by discord. But whereas Brutus and Cassius came together harmoniously the tart exchange between Antony and Octavius symbolizes an uneasy relationship which in Plutarch had already been marked by mutual mistrust and open combat.

The wordy warfare between the leaders before the battle (21–66) has no parallel in Plutarch but was a common feature of Elizabethan plays. After it Cassius protests to Messala that, like Pompey at Pharsalia, he is compelled against his will to stake all on one battle. This comes from Plutarch (*inf.* 119) and is used to introduce a passage in which Cassius declares that the unlucky omens have turned him 'from Epicurus' opinion' (Plutarch) that the gods ignore human affairs, and make him half inclined to believe that they will be defeated, though he is 'fresh of spirit' and ready for the worst (71–92). The portents include some which in Plutarch came before Brutus' second battle (*inf.* 127). Brutus declares that as a Stoic he considers suicide 'cowardly and vile' and has blamed Cato for taking that way out (*inf.* 120), but when Cassius asks if he could endure being taken a prisoner to Rome he vigorously rejects the idea, now thinking as a soldier rather than as a philosophic advocate of patience. Their parting is affectionate and dignified.

The next scene (V.2), where Brutus sends written orders ordering Cassius to attack Octavius' men is so short that it might seem unnecessary, but V.3 shows that Brutus, misjudging the situation, has attacked too early. He has pressed his superiority over Octavius, leaving Cassius exposed to the full brunt of Antony's onset (*inf.* 121). Cassius is urged to flee, but first sends Titinius to see whether the troops coming towards them are friends or foes. Pindarus mistakenly thinks Titinius has been captured, whereupon the impetuous Cassius, despairing of victory, enlists Pindarus' aid to kill himself 'with the same sword, with the which he strake Cæsar' (*inf.* 88), just before Titinius returns with Messala to announce Brutus' victory and give Cassius a garland of victory. Titinius places the garland on the dead man's brow and kills himself with Cassius' sword. Plutarch writes that Cassius' death and its aftermath were the result of misunderstanding: 'For nothing undid them but that Brutus went not to help Cassius, thinking he had overcome them as himself had done; and Cassius on the other side tarried not for Brutus, thinking he had been overthrown as himself was' (*inf. Brutus* 122). Shakespeare lays no blame on Brutus but has Titinius address Cassius' body, 'Alas, thou hast misconstrued everything' (V.3.84). What a world of truth there is in this!

Shakespeare now omits the considerable time which elapsed before the second battle, the evil plight of both armies, the misconduct of Cassius' forces and the sea-victory which might have changed Brutus' fortunes had he heard of it in time (*inf.* 126). The second battle is telescoped into the first, and as soon as Brutus has ordered Cassius to be buried at Thassos he continues the fight. The young Cato is killed (V.4), Lucilius, disguised as Brutus, is captured and treated honourably by Antony as in Plutarch (*inf.* 129), Brutus is defeated, without any of Plutarch's details (*inf.* 130), and, asking first one then another of his officers to kill him, declares that the ghost of Cæsar has appeared to him again 'last night, here in Philippi fields, I know my hour is come' (V.5.1–29). Taking leave of life he boasts nobly that in all his life 'I found no man but he was true to me', gets Strato to hold his sword, and runs upon it, thus following Plutarch's account (*inf.* 131). Messala and Strato are taken into the service of Octavius, and the play ends with Antony and Octavius speaking magnanimously of their great enemy. Antony's epitaph takes over from Plutarch the contrast between Brutus' disinterestedness and the envy which motivated the other conspirators (V.5.68–75).

In action *Julius Cæsar* is a tragic chronicle with three main foci: the seduction of Brutus; the assassination and its concomitants; and the vengeance of Antony in which his rise and Octavius' are contrasted with the decline and fall of Brutus and Cassius. The foregoing analysis shows that Shakespeare drew freely throughout on Plutarch's three *Lives*. Probably the fact that he had three biographies before him suggested a threefold division in which first Brutus was the main (though not the only) centre of interest, then Cæsar, and lastly Antony with Octavius. Having to piece together the deeds and motives of the participants out of three accounts Shakespeare was encouraged not to make any of them—the noble conspirator, the world-famous victim, the dexterous avenger—into the sole hero of his play. His own interest seems to have been divided between them, and since in Plutarch and other histories none of the three was above reproach, and all were portrayed with a mixture of approval and disapproval, the paradoxes of motivation and morality seem to have seized Shakespeare's imagination and inspired or fortified his disinclination to make any one of them the central figure. Rather he prefers to give a balanced view, pointing out the mingled good and evil in their behaviour, without explicit moralizing or Senecan rant. Not for him in 1599 the diatribes of Discord and the Ghost which girdle *Cæsar's Revenge*. His studies in English history had shown him how mixed was human nature both in politics and private life; and the comedies he was perhaps already writing or planning (*All's Well*, etc.) were to be darker in tone than his previous ones because in them romance was to be treated realistically in the light of deep ethical conflict.

So Julius Cæsar is not the 'hero', although he is the pivot of the tragedy. He is the world-victor, as even Cassius bitterly admits:

> Why man, he doth bestride the narrow world
> Like a Colossus (I.2.133–4)

He has got 'the start of the majestic world', to 'bear the palm alone'. He has conquered the Pompeys, and Shakespeare could depend on his audience to have the right initial awe of Cæsar's greatness. In order not to make his personality dominate the play Shakespeare must play him down, and without destroying his legend reveal him not as godlike but as a man subject to other men's weaknesses.

Here we touch on one of Shakespeare's major difficulties. In discussing English history he could rely on his audience's knowing a good deal about the events of the past 250 years, for the reigns of the kings since Edward III were associated with heroic or terrible events still often recalled in religious, political and imaginative writings. Most of the barons in the plays from *Henry VI* to *Henry IV* were ancestors, direct or collateral, of Elizabethan nobles, and their family legends were widely known. The great battles of the past, the exiles, usurpations, murders and intrigues which Hall, Grafton, Holinshed and others had described were common knowledge. No such acquaintance with the details of Roman history could be assumed among the citizens who came to see Julius Cæsar killed in the Capitol. Shakespeare himself could not have extracted from Plutarch or Appian or other authorities so clear an idea of the complex issues involved as was given to modern students by Mommsen, Oman and G. Walter. He seems to have wished to compose an objective and impartial picture of the interrelationship of Brutus and Cassius, Cæsar, Antony and Octavius, while entering as little as possible into the complexities of the political situation. He was forced to simplify, to depart from Plutarch, not only to avoid bewildering the spectators with recondite allusions but also in order to treat the main characters with even-handed justice and divided sympathy.

To expatiate on Cæsar's past exploits and the reforms which as Dictator he was planning for Rome, his acts of generosity (including his honouring of his late enemy Brutus) would be to make Brutus into the criminal Dante thought him. On the other hand, the assassination of Cæsar, the strong ruler who had brought order out of chaos, must not seem a virtuous act. Shakespeare was no republican but a defender of the Tudor monarchy which had brought peace out of civil war and was always afraid of a relapse. Yet in following Plutarch's portrait of Brutus and making him a noble sinner, an altruistic murderer, the dramatist must not give tangible proof that Brutus' suspicions of Cæsar's intentions were wrong.

Hence Shakespeare walks a tightrope in depicting the two chief antagonists, and succeeds by ignoring particular political issues. We do not see Cæsar insulting the Senate and we are not reminded of his egoistic actions, sins against tradition, or love affairs (even Cleopatra is not mentioned); but he is viewed well on this side idolatry, and portrayed as a lover of pomp and circumstance whose tragedy is less ambition than a self-conscious arrogance not justified by the physical or mental qualities shown in the play. We see him patronizing his followers and now displaying bland indifference to warnings which we know have fatal significance, now vacillating (like any mediocre husband) between uxoriousness and public duty. Unlike Pescetti's Cæsar, who is thoroughly scared and about to surround himself with an impenetrable guard, Shakespeare's Cæsar perishes through a false sense of security, an assurance which misjudges the situation and the men around him. We should not believe all that the envious Cassius and Casca say against him, but some of it strikes home during the first two Acts. The balance is adjusted however by the assassination and Antony's use of it. With his death Cæsar becomes a martyr, once more the Cæsar of popular legend.

Similarly Brutus might easily in his crucial soliloquy (II.1) have mentioned several illboding signs of anti-republican ambition in Cæsar's behaviour since crossing the Rubicon. Instead Shakespeare makes him admit:

> The abuse of greatness is when it disjoins
> Remorse from power; and, to speak truth of Cæsar,
> I have not known when his affections sway'd
> More than his reason (II.1.18–21)

His decision to join the conspiracy is founded on the supposition that if crowned Cæsar would change his nature ('Then lest he may, prevent'). In depriving Brutus of any substantial reason for the assassination Shakespeare distorts the historic situation, and illustrates the lack of judgement which marks Brutus' character throughout the play. His tragedy therefore is that of a man of the noblest moral principles whose idealism blinds him to the realities of politics, and to the nature of his fellow-conspirators and of the Roman populace. The good man is led to perform an act of murderous injustice. Cæsar is killed undeservedly on a presupposition of what he might become; but his story is not ended with his death. 'We all stand up against the spirit of Cæsar', says Brutus (II.1.167) meaning the autocratic ambition of Cæsar. But the spirit of Cæsar lives on in Antony and Octavius, and finally conquers. Moreover by transforming Brutus' 'evil spirit' or 'genius' into Cæsar's ghost Shakespeare makes the Battle of Philippi a personal triumph for the dead man as well as for his avengers.

The ambivalent treatment of Cæsar and Brutus is also extended to Antony. If the glory of Cæsar's past made it unnecessary for Shakespeare to prove the Dictator's heroic worth in any striking fashion, so the shadow of Antony's future makes it unnecessary to expatiate on his sensual weaknesses beyond letting Cæsar mention his love of plays, music and laughter (I.2.200–3), and showing him running the course at the Lupercal when Brutus refers to his quick, gamesome spirit (I.2.28–9). In this play favourable aspects of Antony are to the fore since he is to be Cæsar's avenger, 'a shrewd contriver' turning the tables on Brutus in the funeral scene and taking the lead in the war against the assassins. The weakness of Brutus' judgement of men is shown both in his insistence on sparing Antony's life against the advice of the more worldly-wise Cassius, and in his self-confident assurance that he could hold the people despite anything Antony, by permission, could say. Antony gains his oratorical victory in the market-place by a dexterity which we can admire, since the conspirators have put themselves in the wrong. But the other side of his character is not forgotten. Immediately after he has stirred up the mob and given his blessing to 'mischief', we see the innocent poet Cinna murdered; and in the next scene (IV.1) Antony not only takes a lead in the proscription but treats Lepidus in a contemptuous and deceitful manner which surprises Octavius. The devoted friend of Cæsar proves to be moved by greed and ambition. Acts IV and V indeed press home the ambivalent treatment of the two sides, for if the mask of piety slips from the face of the avenger, the high-principled solidarity of the Republicans is seen endangered in the quarrel about bribery, money and military skill between Brutus and Cassius.

That Shakespeare wished to avoid writing just another tragedy of revenge like *The Tragedy of Pompey and Cæsar* is made clear, for sympathy with Brutus and Cassius, if shaken, is not lost. Their reconciliation, manly enough in itself, is made touching by news of Portia's death, Brutus' noble grief and Cassius' warm-hearted feeling for his friend. They are gallant and loyal as they go down in defeat, and their deaths are truly Roman. On the other hand the behaviour of Antony and Octavius in their hour of victory reflects credit on them too. So the play ends in a manner which dignifies all parties in the conflict. Nobody is portrayed with total praise or total blame, but the greatest praise is given to Brutus who, despite his misguided act, is recognized to have exemplified a perfect balance of virtues: 'This was a man!'

Julius Cæsar is a play about a triple group-relationship—with Cæsar at the centre of one group, Brutus of another, Antony of the third—and of their interaction in a great conflict which involves the fate of Rome. Unlike the French Senecans Shakespeare does not explore the political principles involved; he refers little to the horrors of the Pompeian wars (so luridly described by Lucan) and he neither prophesies the strife that followed Philippi nor treats what happens as part of a divinely-ordained movement from republic to monarchy. The play lacks the overt didacticism of the English Histories. Its emphasis is not on political theory but on the traits of individual men as shown in their public connections.

The play is not a 'problem play' in the sense that we are left undecided how to regard the characters. The ambivalence of presentation is not intended to confuse or offer alternative interpretations. We are meant to accept both sides as true to life and to modulate from approval to disapproval as Plutarch himself did in his *Lives*. For what Shakespeare learned from Plutarch was to represent more clearly than before the paradoxes of human motive, the mixture of good and evil in the same person. The heroic Cæsar may be pompous, deaf and epileptic; the sensual Antony may achieve nobility; the stoic Brutus be tetchy with his friend. In *Julius Cæsar* the dramatist achieves a somewhat detached tolerance in his attitude towards historical figures, and at the same time a critical attitude towards politics and those who take part in it. The romantic hero-worship of *Henry V* has given place to a shrewd look at the inner weaknesses of public men. But the mood is still benevolent and the ancient world has a certain grandeur.

I. Source

PLUTARCH'S LIVES OF THE NOBLE GRECIANS AND ROMANES translated by Sir Thomas North (1579)

The Lives of the Noble Grecians and Romanes compared together by that Grave Learned Philosopher and Historiographer Plutarke of Chæronea. Translated out of Greeke into French by James Amyot . . . and out of French into Englishe by Thomas North. T. Vautrollier. 1579.

THE LIFE OF JULIUS CÆSAR

At what time Sylla was made Lord of all, he would have had Cæsar put away his wife Cornelia, the daughter of Cinna Dictator: but when he saw, he could neither with any promise nor threate bring him to it, he tooke her joynter away from him. The cause of Cæsars ill will unto Sylla, was by meanes of mariage: for Marius thelder, maried his fathers own sister, by whom he had Marius the younger, whereby Cæsar and he were cosin germaines.[1] Sylla being troubled in waightie matters, putting to death so many of his enemies, when he came to be conqueror, he made no reckoning of Cæsar: but he was not contented to be hidden in safety, but came and made sute unto the people for the Priesthoodshippe that was voyde, when he had scant any heare on his face. Howbeit he was repulsed by Syllaes meanes, that secretly was against him. Who, when he was determined to have killed him, some of his frendes told him, that it was to no purpose to put so young a boy as he to death. But Sylla told them agaìne, that they did not consider that there were many Marians in that young boy. Cæsar understanding that, stale out of Rome, and hidde him selfe a long time in the contrie of the Sabines, wandring still from place to place. But one day being

[1] *In margin:* 'Cæsar joyned with Cinna and Marius.'

caried from house to house, he fell into the handes of Syllaes souldiers, who searched all those places, and tooke them whom they found hidden. Cæsar bribed the Captaine, whose name was Cornelius, with two talentes which he gave him. After he had escaped them thus, he went unto the sea side, and tooke shippe,[1] and sailed into Bithynia to goe unto king Nicomedes. When he had bene with him a while, he tooke sea againe, and was taken by pyrates about the Ile of Pharmacusa[2]: for those pyrates kept all uppon that sea coast, with a great fleete of shippes and botes. They asking him at the first twentie talentes for his ransome, Cæsar laughed them to scorne, as though they knew not what a man they had taken, and of him selfe promised them fiftie talents. Then he sent his men up and downe to get him this money, so that he was left in maner alone among these theeves of the Cilicians, (which are the cruellest butchers in the world) with one of his frends, and two of his slaves only: and yet he made so litle reckoning of them, that when he was desirous to sleepe, he sent unto them to commaunde them to make no noyse. Thus was he eight and thirtie dayes among them, not kept as prisoner, but rather waited uppon by them as a Prince. All this time he woulde boldly exercise him selfe in any sporte or pastime they would goe to. And other while also he woulde wryte verses, and make orations, and call them together to say them before them: and if any of them seemed as though they had not understoode him, or passed not for them, he called them blockeheades, and brute beastes, and laughing, threatned them that he would hang them up. But they were as merie with the matter as could be, and tooke all in good parte, thinking that this his bold speach came, through the simplicity of his youth. So when his raunsome was come from the citie of Miletum, they being payed their money, and he againe set at libertie: he then presently armed, and manned out certaine ships out of the haven of Miletum, to follow those theeves, whom he found yet riding at ancker in the same Iland. So he tooke the most of them, and had the spoile of their goods, but for their bodies, he brought them into the city of Pergamum, and there committed them to prison, whilest he him selfe went to speake with Junius, who had the government of Asia, as unto whom the execution of these pirats did belong, for that he was Prætor of that contrie.[3] But this Prætor having a great fancie to be fingering of the money, bicause there was good store of it: answered, that he would consider of these prisoners at better leasure. Cæsar leaving Junius there,

[1] *In margin:* 'Cæsar tooke sea, and went unto Nicomedes, king of Bithynia.'
[2] *In margin:* 'Cæsar taken of pirats.'
[3] *In margin:* 'Junius Prætor of Asia.'

returned againe unto Pergamum, and there hung up all these theeves openly upon a crosse, as he had oftentimes promised them in the Ile he would doe, when they thought he did but jeast. Afterwardes when Syllaes power beganne to decay, Cæsars frendes wrote unto him, to pray him to come home againe. But he sailed first unto Rhodes, to studie there a time under Apollonius the sonne of Molon, whose scholler also Cicero was, for he was a very honest man, and an excellent good Rethoritian. It is reported that Cæsar had an excellent naturall gift to speake well before the people, and besides that rare gift, he was excellently well studied, so that doutlesse he was counted the second man for eloquence in his time,[1] and gave place to the first, bicause he would be the first and chiefest man of warre and authoritie, being not yet comen to the degree of perfection to speake well, which his nature coulde have performed in him, bicause he was geven rather to followe warres and to mannage great matters, which in thende brought him to be Lord of all Rome. And therefore in a booke he wrote against that which Cicero made in the praise of Cato, he prayeth the readers not to compare the stile of a souldier, with the eloquence of an excellent Orator, that had followed it the most part of his life. . . Now Cæsar immediatly wan many mens good willes at Rome, through his eloquence, in pleading of their causes: and the people loved him marvelously also, bicause of the curteous manner he had to speake to every man, and to use them gently, being more ceremonious therein, then was looked for in one of his yeres. Furthermore, he ever kept a good bourde, and fared well at his table, and was very liberall besides[2]: the which in deede did advaunce him forward, and brought him in estimacion with the people.[3] His enemies judging that this favor of the common people would soone quaile, when he could no longer hold out that charge and expence: suffered him to runne on, till by litle and litle he was growen to be of great strength and power. But in fine, when they had thus geven him the bridell to grow to this greatnes, and that they could not then pull him backe, though in dede in sight it would turne one day to the destruction of the whole state and common wealth of Rome: too late they found, that there is not so litle a beginning of any thing, but continuaunce of time will soone make it strong, when through contempt there is no impediment to hinder the greatnes. Thereuppon, Cicero like a wise ship-master that feareth the calmnes of the sea, was the first man that mistrusting his manner of dealing in the common wealth, found out his craft and malice, which he cunningly cloked

[1] *In margin:* 'Cæsars eloquence.'
[2] *In margin:* 'Cæsar loved hospitalitie.'
[3] *In margin:* 'Cæsar a follower of the people.'

under the habit of outward curtesie and familliaritie.[1] And yet, sayd he, when I consider howe finely he combeth his faire bush of heare, and how smooth it lyeth, and that I see him scrat his head with one finger only: my minde gives me then, that such a kinde of man should not have so wicked a thought in his head, as to overthrow the state of the common wealth. But this was long time after that . . .

Now for that he was very liberal in expences, buying (as some thought) but a vaine and short glorie of the favor of the people: (where in deede he bought good cheape the greatest thinges that coulde be.) Some say, that before he bare any office in the common wealth, he was growen in debt, to the summe of thirteene hundred talentes.[2] Furthermore, bicause he was made overseer of the worke, for the high way going unto Appius, he disbursed a great summe of his owne money towardes the charges of the same. And on the other side, when he was made Ædilis, for that he did show the people the pastime of three hundred and twentie cople of sword players, and did besides exceede all other in sumptuousnes in the sportes and common feastes which he made to delight them withall: (and did as it were drowne all the stately shewes of others in the like, that had gone before him) he so pleased the people, and wan their love therwith, that they devised daily to give him new offices for to requite him. At that time there were two factions in Rome, to wit, the faction of Sylla, which was very strong and of great power, and the other of Marius, which then was under foote and durst not shew it selfe. But Cæsar, bicause he would renue it again, even at that time when he being Ædilis, all the feasts and common sports were in their greatest ruffe: he secretly caused images of Marius to be made, and of victories that caried triumphes, and those he set up one night within the Capitol. The next morning when every man saw the glistering of these golden images excellently well wrought, shewing by the inscriptions, that they were the victories which Marius had wonne apon the Cimbres: every one marveled much at the boldnes of him that durst set them up there, knowing well enough who it was. Hereuppon, it ranne straight through all the citie, and everie man came thither to see them. Then some cried out apon Cæsar, and sayd it was a tyranny which he ment to set up, by renuing of such honors as before had bene troden under foote, and forgotten, by common decree and open proclamation[3]: and that it was no more but a baite to gage the peoples good wils, which he had set out in the stately shewes of his common playes, to see if he

[1] *In margin:* 'Ciceroes judgement of Cæsar.'
[2] *In margin:* 'Cæsars prodigality.'
[3] *In margin:* 'Cæsar accused to make a rebellion in the state.'

had brought them to his lure, that they would abide such partes to be played, and a new alteracion of things to be made . . . [Cæsar was elected Pontifex Maximus, to the alarm of the Senate.] Then Catulus and Piso fell flatly out with Cicero, and condemned him, for that he did not bewray Cæsar, when he knew that he was of conspiracie with Catiline, and had oportunitie to have done it.[1] For when Catiline was bent and determined, not onely to overthrow the state of the common wealth, but utterly to destroy the Empire of Rome, he scaped out of the handes of justice for lacke of sufficient proofe, before his full treason and determination was knowen. Notwithstanding he left Lentulus and Cethegus in the citie, companions of his conspiracie: unto whom, whether Cæsar did geve any secret helpe or comfort, it is not well knowen. [But Cæsar pleaded in the Senate for leniency to them.] This opinion was thought more gentle, and withall was uttered with such a passing good grace and eloquence, that not only they which were to speake after him did approve it: but such also as had spoken to the contrarie before, revoked their opinion and stucke to his, until it came to Cato and Catulus to speake. They both did sharpely invey against him, but Cato chiefly: who in his oration made Cæsar suspected to be of the conspiracie, and stowtly spake against him, insomuch that the offenders were put into the hands of the officers to be put to death.[2] Cæsar comming out of the Senate, a company of young men which garded Cicero for the safetie of his person, did sette apon him with their swordes drawen. But some say, that Curio covered Cæsar with his gowne, and tooke him out of their handes. And Cicero selfe, when the young men looked apon him, beckened with his head that they should not kil him, either fearing the fury of the people, or els that he thought it too shamefull and wicked a parte. But if that were true, I marvell why Cicero did not put it into his booke he wrote of his Consulshippe. But certainly they blamed him afterwards, for that he tooke not the oportunitie offered him against Cæsar, onely for overmuch feare of the people, that loved him verie dearely . . . [Cato, fearing a revolt, got the Senate to give free corn to the poor.] This counsell quenched a present great feare, and did in happie time scatter and disperse abroade the best parte of Cæsars force and power, at such time as he was made Prætor, and that for respect of his office he was most to be feared. Yet all the time he was officer, he never sought any alteracion in the common wealth . . .

The government of the province of Spayne being fallen unto

[1] *In margin:* 'Cæsar suspected to be confederate with Catiline in his conspiracy.'
[2] *In margin:* 'Catoes oration against Cæsar.'

Cæsar for that he was Prætor: his creditors came and cried out apon him, and were importunate of him to be payed.[1] Cæsar being unable to satisfie them, was compelled to goe unto Crassus, who was the richest man of all Rome, and that stoode in neede of Cæsars boldnes and corage to withstand Pompeys greatnes in the common wealth. Crassus became his suretie unto his greediest creditors for the summe of eight hundred and thirtie talentes[2]: whereuppon they suffered Cæsar to departe to the government of his province. In his jorney it is reported, that passinge over the mountaines of the Alpes, they came through a litle poore village that had not many householdes, and yet poore cotages. There, his frendes that did accompanie him, asked him merily, if there were any contending for offices in that towne, and whether there were any strife there amongest the noble men for honor. Cæsar speaking in good earnest, aunswered: I can not tell that said he, but for my parte, I had rather be the chiefest man here, then the second person in Rome. An other time also when he was in Spayne, reading the history of Alexanders actes, when he had red it, he was sorowfull a good while after, and then burst out in weeping. His frends seeing that, marveled what should be the cause of his sorow. He aunswered them, Doe ye not thinke sayd he, that I have good cause to be heavie, when king Alexander being no older than my selfe is now, had in old time wonne so many nations and contries: and that I hitherunto have done nothing worthy of my selfe? Therefore when he was come into Spayne, he was very carefull of his busines, and had in few dayes joyned ten new ensignes more of footemen, unto the other twenty which he had before.[3] Then marching forward against the Callæcians and Lusitanians, he conquered all, and went as farre as the great sea Oceanum, subduing all the people which before knew not the Romanes for their Lordes. There he tooke order for pacifying of the warre, and did as wisely take order for the establishing of peace . . . He having wonne great estimacion by this good order taken, returned from his government very riche, and his souldiers also full of rich spoyles, who called him Imperator, to say soveraine Captaine.[4] . . .

Pompey and Crassus, two of the greatest personages of the city of Rome, being at jarre together, Cæsar made them frends, and by that meanes got unto him selfe the power of them both[5]: for, by colour of that gentle acte and frendshippe of his, he subtilly (unwares

[1] *In margin:* 'Cæsar Prætor of Spaine.'
[2] *In margin:* 'Crassus surety for Cæsar to his creditors.'
[3] *In margin:* 'Cæsars actes in Spayne.'
[4] *In margin:* 'Cæsars souldiers called him Imperator.'
[5] *In margin:* 'Cæsar reconcileth Pompey and Crassus together.'

to them all) did greatly alter and chaunge the state of the common wealth. For it was not the private discord betwene Pompey and Cæsar, as many men thought, that caused the civill warre: but rather it was their agreement together, who joyned all their powers first to overthrowe the state of the Senate and nobilitie, and afterwardes they fell at jarre one with an other. But Cato, that then foresaw and prophecied many times what woulde followe, was taken but for a vaine man[1]: but afterwardes they found him a wiser man, then happie in his counsell. Thus Cæsar being brought unto the assemblie of the election, in the middest of these two noble persons, whom he had before reconciled together: he was there chosen Consull, with Calphurnius Bibulus, without gaine saying or contradiction of any man.[2] Now when he was entred into his office, he beganne to put foorth lawes meeter for a seditious Tribune of the people, than for a Consull: bicause by them he preferred the division of landes,[3] and distributing of corne to everie citizen, Gratis, to please them withall. But when the noble men of the Senate were against his devise, he desiring no better occasion, beganne to crie out, and to protest, that by the overhardnesse and austeritie of the Senate, they drave him against his will to leane unto the people: and thereupon having Crassus on thone side of him, and Pompey on thother, he asked them openly in thassemblie, if they did geve their consent unto the lawes which he had put forth. They both aunswered, they did. Then he prayed them to stande by him against those that threatned him with force of sworde to let him. Crassus gave him his worde, he would. Pompey also did the like, and added thereunto, that he would come with his sword and target both, against them that would withstand him with their swords. These wordes offended much the Senate, being farre unmeete for his gravetie, and undecent for the majestie and honor he caried, and most of all uncomely for the presence of the Senate whome he should have reverenced: and were speaches fitter for a rash light headed youth, than for his person. Howbeit the common people on thother side, they rejoyced. Then Cæsar bicause he would be more assured of Pompeis power and frendshippe, he gave him his daughter Julia in mariage,[4] which was made sure before unto Servilius Cæpio, and promised him in exchaunge Pompeis wife, the which was sure also unto Faustus the sonne of Sylla. And shortly after also, Cæsar selfe did marie Calphurnia the daughter of Piso, whom he caused to be

[1] *In margin:* 'Catoes foresight and prophecy.'

[2] *In margin:* 'Cæsars first Consulship with Calphurnius Bibulus.'

[3] *In margin:* 'Cæsars lawes. *Lex agraria.*'

[4] *In margin:* 'Cæsar maried his daughter Julia unto Pompey.'

made Consul, to succeede him the next yeare following.[1] Cato then cried out with open mouth, and called the gods to witnes, that it was a shamefull matter, and not to be suffered, that they should in that sorte make havoke of the Empire of Rome, by such horrible bawdie matches, distributing among them selves through those wicked mariages, the governments of the provinces, and of great armies. [Cæsar lost much esteem by trying to send Cato to prison.] But after he had played this parte, there were few Senators that would be President of the Senate under him, but left the citie, bicause they could not away with his doinges . . . The shamefullest parte that Cæsar played while he was Consul, seemeth to be this: when he chose P. Clodius Tribune of the people, that had offred his wife such dishonor, and profaned the holy auncient misteries of the women, which were celebrated in his owne house. Clodius sued to be Tribune to no other end, but to destroy Cicero: and Cæsar selfe also departed not from Rome to his army, before he had set them together by the eares, and driven Cicero out of Italy.[2] All these things they say he did, before the warres with the Gaules. But the time of the great armies and conquests he made afterwards, and of the warre in the which he subdued al the Gaules: (entring into an other course of life farre contrarie unto the first) made him to be knowen for as valliant a souldier and as excellent a Captaine to lead men, as those that afore him had bene counted the wisest and most valliantest Generalles that ever were, and that by their valliant deedes had atchieved great honor.[3] For whosoever would compare the house of the Fabians, of the Scipioes, of the Metellians, yea those also of his owne time, or long before him, as Sylla, Marius, the two Lucullians, and Pompey selfe,

Whose fame ascendeth up unto the heavens:

it will appeare that Cæsars prowes and deedes of armes, did excell them all together. The one, in the hard contries where he made warres: an other, in enlarging the realmes and contries which he joyned unto the Empire of Rome: an other, in the multitude and power of his enemies whome he overcame: an other, in the rudenesse and austere nature of men with whom he had to doe, whose maners afterwardes he softned and made civill: an other, in curtesie and clemencie which he used unto them whome he had conquered: an other in great bountie and liberality bestowed upon them that served under him in those warres: and in fine, he excelled them all

[1] *In margin:* 'Cæsar maried Calphurnia the daughter of Piso.'
[2] *In margin:* 'Cæsar by Clodius, drave Cicero out of Italy.'
[3] *In margin:* 'Cæsar, a valliant souldier, and a skilfull Captaine.'

in the number of battells he had fought, and in the multitude of his enemies he had slaine in battell. For in lesse then tenne yeares warre in Gaule he tooke by force and assault above eight hundred townes[1]: he conquered three hundred severall nations: and having before him in battell thirty hundred thowsand souldiers, at sundrie times he slue tenne hundred thowsand of them, and tooke as many more prisoners. Furthermore, he was so entirely beloved of his souldiers, that to doe him service (where otherwise they were no more then other men in any private quarrell) if Cæsars honor were touched, they were invincible, and would so desperatly venter them selves, and with such furie, that no man was able to abide them[2]. . . . Nowe Cæsars selfe did breede this noble corage and life in them. First, for that he gave them bountifully, and did honor them also, shewing thereby, that he did not heape up riches in the warres to maintaine his life afterwards in wantonnesse and pleasure, but that he did keepe it in store, honorably to reward their valliant service: and that by so much he thought him selfe riche, by howe much he was liberall in rewarding of them that had deserved it. Furthermore, they did not wonder so much at his valliantnesse in putting him selfe at every instant in such manifest daunger, and in taking so extreame paines as he did, knowing that it was his greedie desire of honor that set him a fire, and pricked him forward to doe it: but that he alwayes continued all labour and hardnesse, more then his bodie could beare, that filled them all with admiration. For, concerning the constitucion of his bodie, he was leane, white, and soft skinned, and often subject to headache, and otherwhile to the falling sickenes[3]: (the which tooke him the first time, as it is reported, in Corduba, a citie of Spayne)[4] but yet therefore yeelded not to the disease of his bodie,[5] to make it a cloke to cherishe him withall, but contrarilie, tooke the paines of warre, as a medicine to cure his sicke bodie fighting alwayes with his disease, travelling continually, living soberly, and commonly lying abroade in the field. For the most nights he slept in his coch or litter, and thereby bestowed his rest, to make him alwayes able to do some thing: and in the day time, he would travell up and downe the contrie to see townes, castels, and strong places. He had alwayes a secretarie with him in his coche, who did still wryte as he went by the way, and a souldier behinde him that caried his sword. He made such speede the first

[1] *In margin:* 'Cæsars conquestes in Gaule.'
[2] *In margin:* 'The love and respect of Cæsars souldiers unto him.'
[3] *In margin:* 'Cæsar had the falling sickenes.' Cf. I.2.252.
[4] I.2.119: 'He had a fever when he was in Spain.'
[5] Contrast Cassius' slander, I.2.118–30.

time he came from Rome, when he had his office: that in eight dayes, he came to the river of Rhone. He was so excellent a rider of horse from his youth, that holding his handes behinde him, he would galloppe his horse upon the spurre. In his warres in Gaule, he did further exercise him selfe to indite letters as he rode by the way, and did occupie two secretaries at once with as much as they could wryte: and as Oppius wryteth, more then two at a time. And it is reported, that Cæsar was the first that devised frendes might talke together by wryting ciphers in letters, when he had no leasure to speake with them for his urgent busines, and for the great distaunce besides from Rome. How litle accompt Cæsar made of his dyet, this example doth prove it.[1] Cæsar supping one night in Milane with his frende Valerius Leo, there was served sparrage to his bourde, and oyle of perfume put into it in stead of sallet oyle. He simplie eate it, and found no fault, blaming his frendes that were offended: and told them, that it had bene enough for them to have absteyned to eate of that they misliked, and not to shame their frend, and how that he lacked good manner that found fault with his frend.[2] An other time as he travelled through the contrie, he was driven by fowle weather on the sodaine to take a poore mans cottage, that had but one litle cabin in it, and that was so narrowe, that one man could but scarce lye in it. Then he sayd to his frendes that were about him: Greatest roomes are meetest for greatest men, and the most necessarie roomes, for the sickest persons. And thereuppon he caused Oppius that was sicke to lye there all night: and he him selfe, with the rest of his frendes, lay with out dores, under the easing of the house. . . . [Plutarch describes Cæsar's victories in Gaul and over the Nervii, etc.]

The jorney he made also into England, was a noble enterprise, and very commendable.[3] For he was the first that sailed the west Ocean with an army by sea, and that passed through the sea Atlanticum with his army, to make warre in that so great and famous Ilande: (which many auncient wryters would not beleve that it was so in deede, and did make them vary about it, saying that it was but a fable and a lye) and was the first that enlarged the Romane Empire, beyonde the earth inhabitable. For twise he passed over the narrowe sea against the firme lande of Gaule, and fighting many battells there, did hurt his enemies more, then enriche his owne men: bicause, of men hardlie brought up, and poore, there was nothing to be gotten. Whereuppon his warre had not

[1] *In margin:* 'The temperance of Cæsar in his dyet.'
[2] *In margin:* 'Cæsars civilitie not to blame his frend.'
[3] *In margin:* 'Cæsars jorney into England.'

such successe as he looked for, and therefore takinge pledges onely of the kinge, and imposing a yearely tribute apon him, to be payed unto the people of Rome: he returned againe into Gaule. There he was no sooner landed, but he founde letters ready to be sent over the sea unto him: in the which he was advertised from Rome, of the death of his Daughter, that she was dead with child by Pompey.[1] For the which, Pompey and Cæsar both, were marvelous sorowfull: and their friends mourned also, thinking that this alliance which mainteined the common wealth (that otherwise was very tickle) in good peace and concord, was now severed, and broken a sonder, and the rather likely, bicause the childe lived not long after the mother. So the common people at Rome tooke the corps of Julia, in dispite of the Tribunes, and buried it in the fielde of Mars. . . .

Nowe Cæsar had of long time determined to destroy Pompey, and Pompey him also. For Crassus being killed amongest the Parthians, who onely did see, that one of them two must needes fall: nothing kept Cæsar from being the greatest person, but bicause he destroied not Pompey, that was the greater: neither did any thing let Pompey to withstand that it should not come to passe, but bicause he did not first overcome Cæsar, whom onely he feared. For till then, Pompey had not long feared him, but alwayes before set light by him, thinking it an easie matter for him to put him downe when he would, sithe he had brought him to that greatnes he was come unto.[2] But Cæsar contrarily, having had that drift in his head from the beginning, like a wrestler that studieth for trickes to overthrowe his adversary: he went farre from Rome, to exercise him selfe in the warres of Gaule, where he did trayne his armie, and presently by his valiant deedes did increase his fame and honor. By these meanes became Cæsar as famous as Pompey in his doings, and lacked no more to put his enterprise in execution, but some occasions of culler,[3] which Pompey partly gave him, and partly also the tyme delivered him, but chiefly, the hard fortune and ill government of that tyme of the common wealth at Rome. For they that made sute for honor and offices, bought the voyces of the people with ready money, which they gave out openly to usury, without shame or feare.[4] Thereupon, the common people that had sold their voyces for money, came to the market place at the day of election, to fight for him that had hyered them: not with their voices, but with their bowes, slings, and swordes. So that the assembly seldom

[1] *In margin:* 'The death of Julia, Cæsars Daughter.'

[2] *In margin:* 'The discord betwixt Cæsar and Pompey, and the cause of the civill warres.'

[3] *In margin:* 'Cæsars craftines.'

[4] *In margin:* 'The peoples voices bought at Rome for money.'

tyme brake up, but that the pulpit for orations was defiled and sprinckled with the bloode of them that were slayne in the market place, the citie remayning all that tyme without government of Magistrate, like a shippe left without a Pilote. Insomuch, as men of deepe judgement and discression seing such furie and madnes of the people, thought them selves happy if the common wealth were no worse troubled, then with the absolut state of a Monarchy and soveraine Lord to governe them. Furthermore, there were many that were not affraid to speake it openly, that there was no other help to remedy the troubles of the common wealth, but by the authority of one man only, that should commaund them all: and that this medicine must be ministred by the hands of him, that was the gentlest Phisition, meaning covertly Pompey. Now Pompey used many fine speeches, making semblance as though he would none of it, and yet cunningly under hand did lay all the yrons in the fire he could, to bring it to passe, that he might be chosen Dictator. . . . [The rivalry between Pompey and Cæsar came to a head when Cæsar was asked to dismiss his army.] When he was come unto the litle ryver of Rubicon, which devideth Gaule on this side the Alpes from Italy: he stayed uppon a sodaine.[1] For, the nearer he came to execute his purpose, the more remorse he had in his conscience, to thinke what an enterprise he tooke in hand: and his thoughts also fell out more doubtfull, when he entred into consideration of the desperatnes of his attempt. So he fell into many thoughts with him selfe, and spake never a word, waving sometime one way, sometime an other way, and often times chaunged his determination, contrary to him selfe. So did he talke much also with his friends he had with him, amongest whom was Asinius Pollio, telling them what mischieves the beginning of this passage over that river would breede in the world, and how much their posteritie and them that lived after them, would speake of it in time to come. But at length, casting from him with a noble courage, all those perillous thoughts to come, and speaking these words which valiant men commonly say, that attempt daungerous and desperat enterprises, 'A desperat man feareth no daunger, come on'[2]: he passed over the river, and when he was come over, he ranne with his coche and never staied, so that before day light he was within the citie of Ariminum, and tooke it.[3] It is said, that the night before he passed over this river, he dreamed a damnable dreame, that he carnally knew his mother.[4] The citie of Ariminum being taken, and the rumor thereof dispersed through

[1] *In margin:* 'Cæsars doubtfull thoughts at the river of Rubicon.'

[2] *In margin:* 'The Greeke useth this phrase of speech, cast the dye.'

[3] *In margin:* 'Cæsar tooke the citie of Ariminum.'

[4] *In margin:* 'Cæsars damnable dreame.'

all Italy, even as if it had bene open warre both by sea and land, and as if all the lawes of Rome, together with thextreme bounds and confines of the same had bene broken up: a man would have sayd, that not onely the men and women for feare, as experience proved at other times, but whole cities them selves leaving their habitations, fled from one place to another through all Italy. And Rome it selfe also was immediatly filled with the flowing repaire of all the people their neighbours thereabouts, which came thither from all partes like droves of cattell, that there was neither officer nor Magistrate that could any more commaund them by authoritie, neither by any perswasion of reason bridle such a confused and disorderly multitude: so that Rome had in maner destroyed it selfe for lacke of rule and order.[1] For in all places, men were of contrary opinions, and there were daungerous sturres and tumults every where: bicause they that were glad of this trouble, could keepe in no certaine place, but running up and downe the citie, when they met with others in divers places, that seemed either to be affraid or angry with this tumult (as otherwise it is impossible in so great a citie) they flatly fell out with them, and boldly threatned them with that that was to come. Pompey him selfe, who at that time was not a litle amazed, was yet much more troubled with the ill wordes some gave him on the one side, and some on the other. . . . For they brought him so many lyes, and put so many examples of feare before him, as if Cæsar had bene already at their heeles, and had wonne all: so that in the ende he yelded unto them, and gave place to their furie and madnes, determining (seeing all thinges in such tumult and garboyle) that there was no way but to forsake the citie, and thereuppon commaunded the Senate to follow him, and not a man to tary there, unles he loved tyrannie, more then his owne libertie and the common wealth.[2] Thus the Consuls them selves, before they had done their common sacrifices accustomed at their going out of the citie, fled every man of them. So did likewise the moste parte of the Senators, taking their owne thinges in haste, such as came first to hande, as if by stealth they had taken them from another. And there were some of them also that alwayes loved Cæsar, whose witts were then so troubled and besides them selves, with the feare they had conceyved: that they also fled, and followed the streame of this tumult, without manifest cause or necessitie. But above all thinges, it was a lamentable sight to see the citie it selfe, that in this feare and trouble was left at all adventure, as a shippe tossed in storme of sea, forsaken of her Pilots, and dispairing of her

[1] *In margin:* 'Rome in uprore with Cæsars comming.'
[2] *In margin:* 'Pompey flyeth from Rome.'

safetie. This their departure being thus miserable, yet men esteemed their banishment (for the love they bare unto Pompey) to bee their naturall contry, and reckoned Rome no better then Cæsars campe. . . . Now Cæsar having assembled a great and dreadfull power together, went straight where he thought to finde Pompey him selfe. But Pompey taried not his comming,[1] but fled into the citie of Brundusium, from whence he had sent the two Consuls before with that armie he had, unto Dyrrachium: and he him selfe also went thither afterwards, when he understoode that Cæsar was come, as you shall heare more amply hereafter in his life. Cæsar lacked no good will to follow him, but wanting shippes to take the seas, he returned forthwith to Rome: So that in lesse then three skore dayes, he was Lord of all Italy, without any blood shed. Who when he was come to Rome, and found it much quietter then he looked for, and many Senatours there also: he curteously intreated them, and prayed them to send unto Pompey, to pacifie all matters betweene them, apon reasonable conditions. But no man did attempt it, eyther bicause they feared Pompey for that they had forsaken him, or els for that they thought Cæsar ment not as he spake, but that they were wordes of course, to culler his purpose withall. And when Metellus also, one of the Tribunes, would not suffer him to take any of the common treasure out of the temple of Saturne, but tolde him that it was against the lawe: Tushe, sayd he, tyme of warre and lawe are two thinges.[2] If this that I doe, quoth he, doe offende thee, then get thee hence for this tyme: for warre can not abyde this francke and bolde speeche. But when warres are done, and that we are all quiet agayne, then thou shalt speake in the pulpit what thou wilt: and yet I doe tell thee this of favor, impayring so much my right, for thou art myne, both thou, and all them that have risen against me, and whom I have in my hands. When he had spoken thus unto Metellus, he went to the temple dore where the treasure laye: and finding no keyes there, he caused Smythes to be sent for, and made them breake open the lockes.[3] Metellus thereuppon beganne agayne to withstande him, and certen men that stoode by praysed him in his doing: but Cæsar at length speaking biggely to him, threatned him he would kill him presently, if he troubled him any more: and told him furthermore, Younge man, quoth he, thow knowest it is harder for me to tell it thee, than to doe it. That word made Metellus quake for feare, that he gotte him away rowndly: and ever after that, Cæsar had all at his commaundement

[1] *In margin:* 'Pompey flyeth into Epirus.'
[2] *In margin:* '*Silent leges inter arma.*'
[3] *In margin:* 'Cæsar taketh money out of the temple of Saturne.'

for the warres. From thence he went into Spayne, to make warre with Petreius and Varro, Pompeys Lieuetenants[1]: first to gette their armies and provinces into his hands which they governed, that afterwardes he might follow Pompey the better, leaving never an enemie behinde him. In this jorney he was oftentymes him selfe in daunger, through the ambushes that were layde for him in divers straunge sortes and places, and likely also to have lost all his armie for lacke of vittells. All this notwithstanding, he never left following of Pompeys Lieuetenants, provoking them to battell, and intrenching them in: untill he had gotten their campe and armies into his handes, albeit that the Lieuetenants them selves fled unto Pompey. When Cæsar returned agayne to Rome, Piso his father in lawe gave him counsell to sende Ambassadors unto Pompey, to treate of peace. But Isauricus, to flatter Cæsar, was against it. Cæsar beeing then created Dictator by the Senate,[2] called home againe all the banished men, and restored their children to honor, whose fathers before had beene slayne in Syllaes tyme: and did somewhat cutte of the usuries that did oppresse them, and besides, did make some such other ordinances as those, but very fewe. For he was Dictator but eleven dayes onely, and then did yeld it uppe of him selfe, and made him selfe Consul, with Servilius Isauricus,[3] and after that determined to followe the warres. . . . [The war against Pompey is traced until Cæsar's victory at Pharsalia.] Then Pompey seeing his horsemen from the other winge of his battell, so scattered and dispersed, flying away: forgate that he was any more Pompey the great which he had bene before, but rather was like a man whose wittes the goddes had taken from him, being affrayde and amazed with the slaughter sent from above, and so retyred into his tent speaking never a worde, and sate there to see the ende of this battell. Untill at length all his army beeing overthrowen, and put to flight,[4] the enemies came, and gotte up upon the rampers and defence of his campe, and fought hande to hande with them that stoode to defende the same. Then as a man come to him selfe agayne, he spake but this onely worde: What, even into our campe? So in haste, casting of his coate armor and apparell of a generall, he shifted him, and put on such, as became his miserable fortune, and so stale out of his campe. Furthermore, what he did after this overthrowe, and howe he had put him selfe into the handes of the Ægyptians, by whome he was miserably slayne: we have sette it forthe at large in

[1] *In margin:* 'Cæsars jorney into Spayne, against Pompeys Lieuetenants.'
[2] *In margin:* 'Cæsar Dictator.'
[3] *In margin:* 'Cæsar and Isauricus Consulls.'
[4] *In margin:* 'Pompeys flight.'

his life. Then Cæsar entring into Pompeys campe, and seeing the bodies layed on the grounde that were slayne, and others also that were a killing, sayde, fetching a great sighe: It was their owne doing, and against my will. For Caius Cæsar, after he had wonne so many famous conquests, and overcome so many great battells, had beene utterly condemned notwithstanding, if he had departed from his armie. Asinius Pollio writeth, that he spake these wordes then in Latyn, which he afterwards wrote in Greeke, and sayeth furthermore, that the moste parte of them which were put to the sworde in the campe, were slaves and bondmen, and that there were not slayne in all at this battell, above six thowsand souldiers. As for them that were taken prisoners, Cæsar did put many of them amongest his legions, and did pardon also many men of estimation, amonge whome Brutus was one, that afterwardes slue Cæsar him selfe[1]: and it is reported, that Cæsar was very sory for him, when he could not immediatly be founde after the battell, and that he rejoyced againe, when he knewe he was alyve, and that he came to yeelde him selfe unto him. . . .

Then he came into Alexandria, after Pompey was slaine: and detested Theodotus, that presented him Pompeys heade, and turned his head at toe side bicause he would not see it. Notwithstanding, he tooke his seale, and beholding it, wept. Furthermore, he curteously used all Pompeys friendes and familiers, who wandring up and downe the contry, were taken of the king of Ægypt, and wanne them all to be at his commaundement. Continuing these curtesies, he wrote unto his friendes at Rome,[2] that the greatest pleasure he tooke of his victorie, was, that he dayly saved the lives of some of his contry men that bare armes against him. And for the warre he made in Alexandria, some say, he needed not have done it, but that he willingly did it for the love of Cleopatra[3]: wherein he wanne litle honor, and besides did put his person in great daunger. Others doe lay the fault upon the king of Ægypts Ministers, but specially on Pothinus the Euenuke, who bearing thc greatest swaye of all the kinges servaunts, after he had caused Pompey to be slaine,[4] and driven Cleopatra from the Court, secretly layd waite all the wayes he could, how he might likewise kill Cæsar. Wherefore Cæsar hearing an inckling of it, beganne thenceforth to spend all the night long in feasting and bancketing, that his person might be in the

[1] *In margin:* 'Brutus that slue Cæsar, taken prisoner at the battell of Pharsalia.' Not mentioned by Shakespeare.

[2] *In margin:* 'Cæsars clemency in victory.'

[3] *In margin:* 'The cause of Cæsars warre in Alexandria.'

[4] *In margin:* 'Pothinus the Euenuke caused Pompey to be slayne.'

better safetie . . . and thereupon secretly sent for Cleopatra which was in the contry to come unto him.[1] She onely taking Apollodorus Sicilian of all her friendes, tooke a litle bote, and went away with him in it in the night, and came and landed hard by the foote of the castell. Then having no other meane to come in to the court, without being knowen, she laid her selfe downe upon a mattresse or flock-bed,[2] which Apollodorus her frend tied and bound up together like a bundel with a great leather thong, and so tooke her up on his backe, and brought her thus hamperd in this fardell unto Cæsar, in at the castell gate. This was the first occasion, (as it is reported) that made Cæsar to love her: but afterwards, when he sawe her sweete conversation and pleasaunt entertainment, he fell then in further liking with her, and did reconcile her again unto her brother the king, with condition, that they two joyntly should raigne together. Upon this newe reconciliation, a great feast being prepared, a slave of Cæsars that was his barber, the fearefullest wretch that lived, stil busily prying and listening abroad in every corner, being mistrust-full by nature: found that Pothinus and Achillas did lie in waite to kill his Maister Cæsar. This beeing proved unto Cæsar, he did sette such sure watch about the hall, where the feaste was made, that in fine, he slue the Euenuke Pothinus him selfe.[3] Achillas on thother side, saved him selfe, and fled unto the kinges campe, where he raysed a marvelous daungerous and difficult warre for Cæsar: bicause he having then but a few men about him as he had, he was to fight against a great and strong city. The first daunger he fell into, was for the lacke of water he had: for that his enemies had stopped the mouth of the pipes, the which conveyed the water unto the castell. The seconde daunger he had, was, that seeing his enemies came to take his shippes from him, he was driven to repulse that daunger with fire, the which burnt the arsenall where the shippes lay, and that notable librarie of Alexandria withall.[4] The third daunger was in the battell by sea, that was fought by the tower of Phar: where meaning to helpe his men that fought by sea, he lept from the peere, into a boate. Then the Ægyptians made towardes him with their owers, on everie side: but he leaping into the sea, with great hazard saved him selfe by swimming. It is sayd, that then holding divers bookes in his hand, he did never let them go, but kept them alwayes upon his head above water, and swamme with the

[1] *In margin:* 'Cleopatra came to Cæsar.'

[2] *In margin:* 'Cleopatra trussed up in a mattresse, and so brought to Cæsar, upon Apollodorus backe.' Shaw used this incident in *Cæsar and Cleopatra,* Act III.

[3] Pothinus is still alive in *AC* III.6.14.

[4] *In margin:* 'The great library of Alexandria burnt.'

other hand,[1] notwithstanding that they shot marvelously at him, and was driven somtime to ducke into the water: howbeit the boate was drowned presently. In fine, the king comming to his men that made warre with Cæsar, he went against him, and gave him battell, and wanne it with great slaughter, and effusion of blood. But for the king, no man could ever tell what became of him after. Thereuppon Cæsar made Cleopatra his sister, Queene of Ægypt,[2] who being great with childe by him, was shortly brought to bedde of a sonne, whom the Alexandrians named Cæsarion.[3] From thence he went into Syria, and so going into Asia . . . fought a great battell with king Pharnaces, by the citie of Zela, where he slue his armie, and drave him out of all the realme of Ponte. And bicause he would advertise one of his frendes of the sodainnes of this victorie, he onely wrote three words unto Anitius at Rome: *Veni, Vidi, Vici*: to wit, I came, I saw, I overcame.[4] These three wordes ending all with like sound and letters in the Latin, have a certaine short grace, more pleasaunt to the eare, then can be well expressed in any other tongue. After this, he returned againe into Italie, and came to Rome, ending his yeare for the which he was made Dictator the seconde time, which office before was never graunted for one whole yeare, but unto him. Then he was chosen Consul for the yeare following. . . . He was much misliked also for the desperate parts and madnes of Dolabella, for the covetousnes of Anitius, for the dronkennes of Antonius and Cornificius, which made Pompeys house be pulled downe and builded up againe, as a thing not bigge enough for him, wherewith the Romanes were marvelously offended. Cæsar knew all this well enough, and would have bene contented to have redressed them: but to bring his matters to passe he pretended, he was driven to serve his turne by such instrumentes. After the battell of Pharsalia, Cato and Scipio being fled into Africke, king Iuba joyned with them, and leavied a great puisant army. Wherefore Cæsar determined to make warre with them, and in the middest of winter, he tooke his jorney into Sicile. . . . [In Africa he had setbacks before defeating Scipio.]

Then following this first good happe he had, he went forthwith to set apon the campe of Afranius, the which he tooke at the first onset, and the campe of the Numidians also, king Juba being fled. Thus in a litle peece of the day only, he tooke three campes, and

[1] *In margin:* 'Cæsars swimming with bookes in his hand.' Suetonius develops this. Contrast Cassius, I.2.99–115.

[2] *In margin:* 'Cæsar made Cleopatra Queene of Ægypt.'

[3] *In margin:* 'Cæsarion. Cæsars sonne, begotten of Cleopatra.'

[4] *In margin:* 'Cæsar wryteth three wordes to certifie his victory.'

slue fifty thowsand of his enemies, and lost but fifty of his souldiers.[1] In this sorte is set downe theffect of this battell by some wryters. Yet others doe wryte also, that Cæsar selfe was not there in person at thexecution of this battell. For as he did set his men in battell ray, the falling sickenesse tooke him,[2] whereunto he was geven, and therefore feeling it comming, before he was overcome withall, he was caried into a castell not farre from thence, where the battell was fought, and there tooke his rest till thextremity of his disease had left him. Now, for the Prætors and Consulls that scaped from this battell, many of them being taken prisoners, did kill them selves, and others also Cæsar did put to death: but he being specially desirous of all men else to have Cato alive in his hands, he went with all possible speede unto the citie of Utica, whereof Cato was Governor, by meanes whereof he was not at the battell. Notwithstanding being certified by the way that Cato had slaine him selfe with his owne handes, he then made open shew that he was very sory for it, but why or wherfore, no man could tell.[3] But this is true, that Cæsar sayd at that present time: O Cato, I envy thy death, bicause thou diddest envy my glory, to save thy life. This notwithstanding, the booke that he wrote afterwardes against Cato being dead, did shew no very great affection nor pitiefull hart towardes him. For how could he have pardoned him, if living he had had him in his handes: that being dead did speake so vehemently against him?[4] Notwithstanding, men suppose he would have pardoned him, if he had taken him alive, by the clemencie he shewed unto Cicero, Brutus, and divers others that had borne armes against him. . . .

Cæsar being now returned out of Africke, first of all made an oration to the people, wherein he greatly praised and commended this his last victorie, declaring unto them, that he had conquered so many contries unto the Empire of Rome, that he coulde furnishe the common wealth yearely, with two hundred thowsande busshells of wheate, and twenty hundred thowsand pound weight of oyle. Then he made three triumphes, the one for Ægypt, the other for the kingdom of Ponte, and the third for Africke: not bicause he had overcome Scipio there, but king Juba. Whose sonne being likewise called Juba, being then a young boy, was led captive in the showe of this triumphe.[5] But this his imprisonment fel out happily for him: for where he was but a barbarous Numidian, by the study he fell

[1] *In margin:* 'Cæsars great victorie and small losse.'
[2] *In margin:* 'Cæsar trobled with the falling sickenes.'
[3] *In margin:* 'Cæsar was sory for the death of Cato.'
[4] *In margin:* 'Cæsar wrote against Cato being dead.'
[5] *In margin:* 'Juba, the sonne of king Juba, a famous historiographer.'

unto when he was prisoner, he came afterwards to be reckoned one of the wisest historiographers of the Græcians. After these three triumphes ended, he very liberally rewarded his souldiers, and to curry favor with the people, he made great feasts and common sportes. For he feasted all the Romanes at one time, at two and twenty thowsand tables,[1] and gave them the pleasure to see divers sword players to fight at the sharpe, and battells also by sea, for the remembraunce of his daughter Julia, which was dead long afore. Then after all these sportes, he made the people (as the manner was) to be mustered[2]: and where there were at the last musters before, three hundred and twenty thowsande citizens, at this muster only there were but a hundred and fifty thowsand. Such misery and destruction had this civill warre brought unto the common wealth of Rome, and had consumed such a number of Romanes, not speaking at all of the mischieves and calamities it had brought unto all the rest of Italie, and to the other provinces pertaining to Rome. After all these thinges were ended, he was chosen Consul the fourth time,[3] and went into Spayne to make warre with the sonnes of Pompey: who were yet but very young, but had notwithstanding raised a marvelous great army together, and shewed to have had manhoode and corage worthie to commaunde such an armie, insomuch as they put Cæsar him selfe in great daunger of his life. The greatest battell that was fought betwene them in all this warre, was by the citie of Munda.[4] . . . This was the last warre that Cæsar made. But the triumphe he made into Rome for the same, did as much offend the Romanes, and more, then any thing that ever he had done before: bicause he had not overcome Captaines that were straungers, nor barbarous kinges, but had destroyed the sonnes of the noblest man in Rome, whom fortune had overthrowen.[5] And bicause he had plucked up his race by the rootes, men did not thinke it meete for him to triumphe so, for the calamities of his contrie, rejoycing at a thing for the which he had but one excuse to alleage in his defence, unto the gods and men: that he was compelled to doe that he did. And the rather they thought it not meete, bicause he had never before sent letters nor messengers unto the common wealth at Rome, for any victorie that he had ever wonne in all the civill warres: but did alwayes for shame refuse the glorie of it. This notwithstanding, the Romanes inclining to Cæsars prosperity, and taking the bit in the

[1] *In margin:* 'Cæsars feasting of the Romanes.'

[2] *In margin:* 'The muster taken of the Romanes.'

[3] *In margin:* 'Cæsar Consull the fourth time.'

[4] *In margin:* 'Battell fought betwixt Cæsar and the young Pompeyes, by the city of Munda.'

[5] *In margin:* 'Cæsars triumphe of Pompeis sonnes.' Cf. I.1.35–58.

mouth, supposing that to be ruled by one man alone, it would be a good meane for them to take breth a litle, after so many troubles and miseries as they had abidden in these civill warres: they chose him perpetuall Dictator.[1] This was a plaine tyranny: for to this absolute power of Dictator, they added this, never to be affraied to be deposed. Cicero propounded before the Senate, that they should geve him such honors, as were meete for a man: howbeit others afterwardes added to, honors beyonde all reason. For, men striving who shoulde most honor him, they made him hatefull and troublesome to them selves that most favored him, by reason of the unmeasurable greatnes and honors which they gave him. Thereuppon, it is reported, that even they that most hated him, were no lesse favorers and furtherers of his honors, then they that most flattered him: bicause they might have greater occasions to rise, and that it might appeare they had just cause and colour to attempt that they did against him. And now for him selfe, after he had ended his civill warres, he did so honorably behave him selfe, that there was no fault to be founde in him: and therefore me thinkes, amongest other honors they gave him, he rightly deserved this, that they should builde him a temple of clemency, to thanke him for his curtesie he had used unto them in his victorie.[2] For he pardoned many of them that had borne armes against him, and furthermore, did preferre some of them to honor and office in the common wealth: as amongest others, Cassius and Brutus, both the which were made Prætors.[3] And where Pompeys images had bene throwen downe, he caused them to be set up againe[4]: whereupon Cicero sayd then, that Cæsar setting up Pompeys images againe, he made his owne to stand the surer. And when some of his frends did counsell him to have a gard for the safety of his person, and some also did offer them selves to serve him: he would never consent to it, but sayd, it was better to dye once, then alwayes to be affrayed of death[5]. But to win him selfe the love and good will of the people, as the honorablest gard and best safety he could have: he made common feasts againe, and generall distributions of corne. Furthermore,[6] to gratifie the souldiers also, he replenished many cities againe with inhabitantes, which before had bene destroyed, and placed them there that had no place to repaire unto: of the which the noblest and chiefest cities were these two, Carthage, and Corinthe, and it chaunced so, that

[1] *In margin:* 'Cæsar Dictator perpetuall.' Not mentioned by Shakespeare.

[2] *In margin:* 'The temple of clemency, dedicated unto Cæsar, for his curtesie.'

[3] *In margin:* 'Cassius and Brutus Prætors.' Not in Shakespeare.

[4] Cf. Cæsar's in I.1.67–8.

[5] *In margin:* 'Cæsars saying of death.' Cf. II.2.32–3.

[6] *In margin:* 'Good will of subjectes, the best gard and safety for Princes.'

like as aforetime they had bene both taken and destroyed together, even so were they both set a foote againe, and replenished with people, at one selfe time. And as for great personages, he wanne them also, promising some of them, to make them Prætors and Consulls in time to come, and unto others, honors and preferrements, but to all men generally good hope, seeking all the wayes he coulde to make everie man contented with his raigne. . . . Furthermore, Cæsar being borne to attempt all great enterprises, and having an ambitious desire besides to covet great honors: the prosperous good successe he had of his former conquestes bred no desire in him quietly to enjoy the frutes of his labours, but rather gave him hope of thinges to come, still kindling more and more in him, thoughts of greater enterprises, and desire of new glory, as if that which he had present, were stale and nothing worth.[1] This humor of his was no other but an emulation with him selfe as with an other man, and a certaine contencion to overcome the thinges he prepared to attempt. For he was determined, and made preparacion also, to make warre with the Persians. Then when he had overcome them, to passe through Hyrcania (compassing in the sea Caspium, and mount Caucasus) into the realme of Pontus, and so to invade Scythia: and overrunning all the contries, and people adjoyning unto high Germany, and Germany it selfe, at length to returne by Gaule into Italie, and so to enlarge the Romane Empire round, that it might be every way compassed in with the great sea Oceanum. But whilest he was preparing for this voiage, he attempted to cut the barre of the straight of Peloponnesus, in the place where the city of Corinthe standeth. Then he was minded to bring the rivers of Anienes and Tiber, straight from Rome, unto the citie of Circees, with a deepe channell and high banckes cast up on either side, and so to fall into the sea at Terracina, for the better safety and commodity of the marchants that came to Rome to trafficke there. Furthermore, he determined to draine and seawe all the water of the marisses betwext the cities of Nomentum and Setium, to make it firme land, for the benefit of many thowsandes of people: and on the sea coast next unto Rome, to cast great high bankes, and to clense all the haven about Ostia, of rockes and stones hidden under the water, and to take away all other impedimentes that made the harborough daungerous for shippes, and to make new havens and arsenalls meete to harbor such shippes, as did continually trafficke thither. All these thinges were purposed to be done, but tooke no effecte. But, the ordinaunce of the kalender, and reformation of the yeare, to take away all confusion of time, being exactly calculated

[1] Cf. Flavius on his ambition, I.1.75–8.

by the Mathematicians, and brought to perfection, was a great commoditie unto all men.[1] . . . But the chiefest cause that made him mortally hated, was the covetous desire he had to be called king[2]: which first gave the people just cause, and next his secret enemies, honest colour to beare him ill will. This notwithstanding, they that procured him this honor and dignity, gave it out among the people, that it was written in the Sybilline prophecies, how the Romanes might overcome the Parthians, if they made warre with them, and were led by a king, but otherwise that they were unconquerable. And furthermore they were so bold besides, that Cæsar returning to Rome from the citie of Alba, when they came to salute him, they called him king. But the people being offended, and Cæsar also angry, he said he was not called king, but Cæsar. Then every man keeping silence, he went his way heavy and sorowfull. When they had decreed divers honors for him in the Senate, the Consulls and Prætors accompanied with the whole assembly of the Senate, went unto him in the market place, where he was set by the pulpit for orations, to tell him what honors they had decreed for him in his absence. But he sitting still in his majesty, disdaining to rise up unto them when they came in, as if they had bene private men, aunswered them: that his honors had more neede to be cut of, then enlarged. This did not onely offend the Senate, but the common people also, to see that he should so lightly esteeme of the Magistrates of the common wealth: insomuch as every man that might lawfully goe his way, departed thence very sorrowfully. Thereupon also Cæsar rising, departed home to his house, and tearing open his doblet coller,[3] making his necke bare, he cried out alowde to his frendes, that his throte was readie to offer to any man that would come and cut it. Notwithstanding, it is reported, that afterwardes to excuse this folly, he imputed it to his disease,[4] saying, that their wittes are not perfit which have his disease of the falling evil, when standing of their feete they speake to the common people, but are soone troubled with a trembling of their body, and a sodaine dimnes and guidines. But that was not true. For he would have risen up to the Senate, but Cornelius Balbus one of his frendes (but rather a flatterer) would not let him, saying: What, doe you not remember that you are Cæsar, and will you not let them reverence you, and doe their dueties? Besides these occasions and offences, there followed also his shame and reproache, abusing the Tribunes

[1] *In margin:* 'Cæsar reformed the inequality of the yeare.' Shakespeare ignores all these projects.

[2] *In margin:* 'Why Cæsar was hated.' Cf. Cassius, I.2.155–60.

[3] Cf. I.2.263 when offered the crown.

[4] I.2.265–9.

of the people in this sorte. At that time, the feast Lupercalia[1] was celebrated, the which in olde time men say was the feast of sheapheards or heard men, and is much like unto the feast of the Lycæians in Arcadia. But howesoever it is, that day there are divers noble mens sonnes, young men, (and some of them Magistrats them selves that governe then) which run naked through the city, striking in sport them they meete in their way, with leather thonges, heare and all on, to make them geve place. And many noble women, and gentle women also, goe of purpose to stand in their way,[2] and doe put forth their handes to be striken, as schollers hold them out to their schoolemaster, to be striken with the ferula: perswading them selves that being with childe, they shall have good deliverie, and also being barren, that it will make them to conceive with child.[3] Cæsar sate to beholde that sport upon the pulpit for orations, in a chayer of gold, apparelled in triumphing manner. Antonius, who was Consull at that time, was one of them that ranne this holy course.[4] So when he came into the market place, the people made a lane for him to runne at libertie, and he came to Cæsar, and presented him a Diadeame wreathed about with laurell.[5] Whereuppon there rose a certaine crie of rejoycing, not very great, done onely by a few, appointed for the purpose. But when Cæsar refused the Diadeame, then all the people together made an outcrie of joy. Then Antonius offering it him againe, there was a second shoute of joy, but yet of a few. But when Cæsar refused it againe the second time, then all the whole people showted.[6] Cæsar having made this proofe, found that the people did not like of it, and thereuppon rose out of his chayer,[7] and commaunded the crowne to be caried unto Jupiter in the Capitoll. After that, there were set up images of Cæsar in the city with Diadeames upon their heades, like kinges. Those, the two Tribunes, Flavius and Marullus, went and pulled downe[8]: and furthermore, meeting with them that first saluted Cæsar as king, they committed them to prison. The people followed them rejoycing at it, and called them Brutes: bicause of Brutus, who had in old time driven the kings out of Rome, and that brought the kingdom of one person, unto the government of the Senate and people. Cæsar was so offended withall, that he deprived Marullus and Flavius of their Tribuneshippes,[9] and accusing them, he spake also against the people, and called them Bruti, and Cumani, to witte, beastes, and fooles. Hereuppon the people went straight unto Marcus Brutus,

[1] *In margin:* 'The feast Lupercalia.' [2] I.2.3–4. [3] Cf. I.2.7–9.
[4] *In margin:* 'Antonius being Consull, was one of the Lupercalians.'
[5] *In margin:* 'Antonius presented the Diademe to Cæsar.' I.2.232–48.
[6] Three times in I.2.240–5. [7] He swoons, I.2.245–50. [8] I.1.67–72.
[9] I.2.283–4.

who from his father came of the first Brutus, and by his mother, of the house of the Servilians, a noble house as any was in Rome, and was also nephew and sonne in law of Marcus Cato. Notwithstanding, the great honors and favor Cæsar shewed unto him, kept him backe that of him selfe alone, he did not conspire nor consent to depose him of his kingdom.[1] For Cæsar did not onely save his life, after the battell of Pharsalia when Pompey fled, and did at his request also save many more of his frendes besides: but furthermore, he put a marvelous confidence in him.[2] For he had already preferred him to the Prætorshippe for that yeare, and furthermore was appointed to be Consul, the fourth yeare after that, having through Cæsars frendshippe, obtained it before Cassius, who likewise made sute for the same[3]: and Cæsar also, as it is reported, sayd in this contention, In deede Cassius hath alleaged best reason, but yet shall not be chosen before Brutus. Some one day accusing Brutus while he practised this conspiracy,[4] Cæsar would not heare of it, but clapping his hande on his bodie, told them, Brutus will looke for this skinne: meaning thereby, that Brutus for his vertue, deserved to rule after him, but yet, that for ambitions sake, he woulde not shewe him selfe unthankefull nor dishonorable. Nowe they that desired chaunge, and wished Brutus only their Prince and Governour above all other: they durst not come to him them selves to tell him what they woulde have him to doe, but in the night did cast sundrie papers into the Prætors seate where he gave audience,[5] and the most of them to this effect: Thou sleepest Brutus, and art not Brutus in deede.[6] Cassius finding Brutus ambition sturred up the more by these seditious billes, did pricke him forwarde, and egge him on the more, for a private quarrell he had conceived against Cæsar[7]: the circumstance whereof, we have sette downe more at large in Brutus life. Cæsar also had Cassius in great gelouzie, and suspected him much: whereuppon he sayd on a time to his frendes, What will Cassius doe, thinke ye? I like not his pale lookes. An other time when Cæsars frendes complained unto him of Antonius, and Dolabella, that they pretended some mischiefe towardes him: he aunswered them againe, As for those fatte men and smooth comed heades, quoth he, I never reckon of them: but these pale visaged and carian leane people, I feare them most, meaning Brutus and Cassius.[8] Certainly, destenie may easier be foreseene, then avoyded: considering the straunge and

[1] Hence I.2.46–7.
[2] *In margin:* 'Cæsar saved Marcus Brutus life, after the battell of Pharsalia.'
[3] Hence perhaps I.2.32–6.
[4] *In margin:* 'Brutus conspireth against Cæsar.'
[5] I.3.140–4. [6] II.1.46. [7] *In margin:* 'Cassius stirreth up Brutus against Cæsar.'
[8] I.2.191–4. Brutus not included.

wonderfull signes that were sayd to be seene before Cæsars death.[1] For, touching the fires in the element, and spirites running up and downe in the night, and also these solitarie birdes to be seene at noone dayes sittinge in the great market place: are not all these signes perhappes worth the noting, in such a wonderfull chaunce as happened? But Strabo the Philosopher wryteth, that divers men were seene going up and downe in fire: and furthermore, that there was a slave of the souldiers, that did cast a marvelous burning flame out of his hande, insomuch as they that saw it, thought he had bene burnt, but when the fire was out, it was found he had no hurt.[2] Cæsar selfe also doing sacrifice unto the goddes, found that one of the beastes which was sacrificed had no hart: and that was a straunge thing in nature, how a beast could live without a hart.[3] Furthermore, there was a certaine Soothsayer that had geven Cæsar warning long time affore, to take heede of the day of the Ides of Marche, (which is the fifteenth of the moneth) for on that day he shoulde be in great daunger.[4] That day being come, Cæsar going unto the Senate house, and speaking merily to the Soothsayer, tolde him, The Ides of Marche be come: So be they, softly aunswered the Soothsayer, but yet are they not past.[5] And the very day before, Cæsar supping with Marcus Lepidus, sealed certaine letters as he was wont to do at the bord: so talke falling out amongest them, reasoning what death was best: he preventing their opinions, cried out alowde, Death unlooked for.[6] Then going to bedde the same night as his manner was, and lying with his wife Calpurnia, all the windowes and dores of his chamber flying open, the noyse awooke him, and made him affrayed when he saw such light[7]: but more, when he heard his wife Calpurnia, being fast a sleepe, weepe and sigh, and put forth many fumbling lamentable speaches. For she dreamed that Cæsar was slaine, and that she had him in her armes.[8] Others also doe denie that she had any suche dreame, as amongest other, Titus Livius wryteth, that it was in this sorte. The Senate having set upon the toppe of Cæsars house, for an ornament and setting foorth of the same, a certaine pinnacle: Calpurnia dreamed that she sawe it broken downe, and that she thought she lamented and wept for it. Insomuch that Cæsar rising in the morning, she prayed him if it were possible, not to goe out of the dores that day, but to adjorne the session of the Senate, untill an other day. And if that he made no reckoning of her dreame, yet that he woulde searche

[1] *In margin:* 'Predictions, and foreshewes of Cæsars death.'
[2] I.3.15–18. [3] II.2.39–40.
[4] *In margin:* 'Cæsars day of his death prognosticated by a Soothsayer.' I.2.15–24.
[5] III.1.1–2. [6] Cf. II.2.32–7. [7] Hinted at in II.2.10–12.
[8] *In margin:* 'The dreame of Calpurnia, Cæsars wife.' Cf. II.2.1–3; 76–81.

further of the Soothsayers by their sacrifices, to knowe what should happen him that day.[1] Thereby it seemed that Cæsar likewise did feare and suspect somewhat, bicause his wife Calpurnia untill that time, was never geven to any feare or supersticion[2]: and then, for that he saw her so troubled in minde with this dreame she had. But much more afterwardes, when the Soothsayers having sacrificed many beastes one after an other, tolde him that none did like them[3]: then he determined to sende Antonius to adjorne the session of the Senate.[4] But in the meane time came Decius Brutus, surnamed Albinus, in whom Cæsar put such confidence, that in his last will and testament he had appointed him to be his next heire, and yet was of the conspiracie with Cassius and Brutus: he fearing that if Cæsar did adjorne the session that day, the conspiracie woulde out, laughed the Soothsayers to scorne,[5] and reproved Cæsar, saying: that he gave the Senate occasion to mislike with him, and that they might thinke he mocked them, considering that by his commaundement they were assembled, and that they were readie willingly to graunt him all thinges, and to proclaime him king of all the provinces of the Empire of Rome out of Italie, and that he should weare his Diademe in all other places, both by sea and land.[6] And furthermore, that if any man should tell them from him, they should departe for that present time, and returne againe when Calpurnia shoulde have better dreames: what would his enemies and ill willers say, and how could they like of his frendes wordes? And who could perswade them otherwise, but that they would thinke his dominion a slaverie unto them, and tirannicall in him selfe?[7] And yet if it be so, sayd he, that you utterly mislike of this day, it is better that you goe your selfe in person, and saluting the Senate, to dismisse them till an other time. Therewithall he tooke Cæsar by the hand, and brought him out of his house.[8] Cæsar was not gone farre from his house, but a bondman, a straunger, did what he could to speake with him[9]: and when he sawe he was put backe by the great prease and multitude of people that followed him, he went straight unto his house, and put him selfe into Calpurniaes handes to be kept, till Cæsar came backe againe, telling her that he had great matters to imparte unto him. And one Artemidorus also borne in the Ile of Gnidos, a Doctor of Rethoricke in the Greeke tongue, who by meanes of his profession was verie familliar with certaine of Brutus confederates, and therefore knew the most parte

[1] II.2.5–9. [2] II.2.13–14. [3] II.2.37–40 etc. [4] II.2.52–6.
[5] *In margin:* 'Decius Brutus Albinus perswasion to Cæsar.' II.2.57–104.
[6] II.2.93–6. [7] II.2.96–101; 119.
[8] *In margin:* 'Decius Brutus brought Cæsar into the Senate house.'
[9] *In margin:* 'The tokens of the conspiracy against Cæsar.'

of all their practises against Cæsar: came and brought him a litle bill wrytten with his owne hand, of all that he ment to tell him.[1] He marking howe Cæsar received all the supplications that were offered him, and that he gave them straight to his men that were about him, pressed neerer to him, and sayed: Cæsar, reade this memoriall to your selfe, and that quickely, for they be matters of great waight and touche you neerely.[2] Cæsar tooke it of him, but coulde never reade it, though he many times attempted it, for the number of people that did salute him: but holding it still in his hande, keeping it to him selfe, went on withall into the Senate house.[3] Howbeit other are of opinion, that it was some man else that gave him that memoriall, and not Artemidorus, who did what he could all the way as he went to geve it Cæsar, but he was alwayes repulsed by the people. For these things, they may seeme to come by chaunce: but the place where the murther was prepared, and where the Senate were assembled, and where also there stoode up an image of Pompey dedicated by him selfe amongest other ornamentes which he gave unto the Theater[4]: all these were manifest proofes that it was the ordinaunce of some god, that made this treason to be executed, specially in that verie place. It is also reported, that Cassius (though otherwise he did favour the doctrine of Epicurus) beholding the image of Pompey, before they entred into the action of their traiterous enterprise: he did softely call upon it, to aide him. But the instant daunger of the present time, taking away his former reason, did sodainly put him into a furious passion, and made him like a man halfe besides him selfe. Now Antonius, that was a faithfull frende to Cæsar, and a valliant man besides of his handes,[5] him, Decius Brutus Albinus entertained out of the Senate house, having begon a long tale of set purpose.[6] So Cæsar comming into the house, all the Senate stoode up on their feete to doe him honor. Then parte of Brutus companie and confederates stoode rounde about Cæsars chayer, and parte of them also came towardes him, as though they made sute with Metellus Cimber, to call home his brother againe from banishment: and thus prosecuting still their sute, they followed Cæsar, till he was set in his chayer. Who, denying their petitions, and being offended with them one after an other, bicause the more they were denied, the more they pressed upon him, and were the earnester with him[7]: Metellus at length, taking his gowne with both his handes, pulled it over his necke, which was the

[1] II.3. [2] III.1.3–7. [3] Cf. III.1.8–12.
[4] *In margin:* 'The place where Cæsar was slaine.'
[5] *In margin:* 'Antonius, Cæsars faithfull frend.'
[6] Trebonius in III.1.25–6. [7] III.1.27–75.

signe geven the confederates to sette apon him. Then Casca[1] behinde him strake him in the necke with his sword, howbeit the wounde was not great nor mortall, bicause it seemed, the feare of such a develishe attempt did amaze him, and take his strength from him, that he killed him not at the first blowe. But Cæsar turning straight unto him, caught hold of his sword, and held it hard: and they both cried out, Cæsar in Latin: O vile traitor Casca, what doest thou? and Casca in Greeke to his brother, Brother, helpe me.[2] At the beginning of this sturre, they that were present, not knowing of the conspiracie were so amazed with the horrible sight they sawe: that they had no power to flie, neither to helpe him, not so much, as once to make any outcrie. They on thother side that had conspired his death, compassed him in on everie side with their swordes drawen in their handes, that Cæsar turned him no where, but he was striken at by some, and still had naked swords in his face, and was hacked and mangeled amonge them, as a wilde beaste taken of hunters.[3] For it was agreed among them, that every man should geve him a wound, bicause all their partes should be in this murther: and then Brutus him selfe gave him one wounde about his privities. Men reporte also, that Cæsar did still defende him selfe against the rest, running everie waye with his bodie: but when he sawe Brutus with his sworde drawen in his hande, then he pulled his gowne over his heade, and made no more resistaunce,[4] and was driven either casually, or purposedly, by the counsell of the conspirators, against the base[5] whereupon Pompeys image stoode, which ranne all of a goare bloude, till he was slaine. Thus it seemed, that the image tooke just revenge of Pompeys enemie, being throwen downe on the ground at his feete, and yelding up his ghost there, for the number of wounds he had upon him. For it is reported, that he had three and twenty wounds apon his body[6]: and divers of the conspirators did hurt them selves, striking one body with so many blowes. When Cæsar was slaine, the Senate (though Brutus stood in the middest amongest them as though he would have sayd somewhat touching this fact) presently ran out of the house, and flying, filled all the city with marvelous feare and tumult. Insomuch as some did shut to their dores, others forsooke their shops and warehouses, and others ranne to the place to see what the matter was: and others also that had seene it, ran home to their houses againe.[7] But Antonius and

[1] *In margin:* 'Casca, the first that strake at Cæsar.' III.1.76.
[2] Contrast I.2.281. [3] Contrast Brutus's wish, II.1.173–4.
[4] III.1.77; III.2.184–9. [5] III.1.115–6.
[6] *In margin:* 'Cæsar slaine and had 23 wounds apon him.'
[7] III.1.97–8.

Lepidus, which were two of Cæsars chiefest frends, secretly conveying them selves away, fled into other mens houses, and forsooke their owne.[1] Brutus and his confederats on thother side, being yet hotte with this murther they had committed, having their swordes drawen in their hands, came all in a troupe together out of the Senate, and went into the market place,[2] not as men that made countenaunce to flie, but otherwise boldly holding up their heades like men of corage, and called to the people to defende their libertie, and stayed to speake with every great personage whome they met in their way. Of them, some followed this troupe, and went amongest them, as if they had bene of the conspiracie, and falsely chalenged parte of the honor with them: among them was Caius Octavius, and Lentulus Spinther. But both of them were afterwards put to death, for their vaine covetousnes of honor, by Antonius, and Octavius Cæsar the younger: and yet had no parte of that honor for the which they were put to death, neither did any man beleve that they were any of the confederates, or of counsell with them. For they that did put them to death, tooke revenge rather of the will they had to offend, then of any fact they had committed. The next morning, Brutus and his confederates came into the market place to speake unto the people, who gave them such audience, that it seemed they neither greatly reproved, nor allowed the fact: for by their great silence they showed, that they were sory for Cæsars death, and also that they did reverence Brutus.[3] Nowe the Senate graunted generall pardonne for all that was paste, and to pacifie every man, ordained besides, that Cæsars funeralls[4] shoulde bee honored as a god, and established all thinges that he had done: and gave certaine provinces also, and convenient honors unto Brutus and his confederates, whereby every man thought all things were brought to good peace and quietnes againe. But when they had opened Cæsars testament,[5] and found a liberall legacie of money, bequeathed unto every citizen of Rome,[6] and that they saw his body (which was brought into the market place) al bemangled with gashes of swordes[7]: then there was no order to keepe the multitude and common people quiet, but they plucked up formes, tables, and stooles, and layed them all about the body, and setting them a fire, burnt the corse. Then when the fire was well kindled, they tooke the firebrandes, and went unto their houses that had slaine Cæsar, to

[1] Cf. III.1.96.

[2] *In margin:* 'The murtherers of Cæsar doe goe to the Capitoll (*sic.*).' III.1.108–10; 119–21.

[3] III.2.1–10. Cassius speaks elsewhere.

[4] *In margin:* 'Cæsars funeralls.'

[5] Cf. Antony, III.2.130–240.

[6] III.2.240–2.

[7] III.2.174–97; 223–9.

set them a fire.[1] Other also ranne up and downe the citie to see if they could meete with any of them, to cut them in peeces: howbeit they could meete with never a man of them, bicause they had locked them selves up safely in their houses. There was one of Cæsars frends called Cinna,[2] that had a marvelous straunge and terrible dreame the night before. He dreamed that Cæsar bad him to supper, and that he refused, and would not goe: then that Cæsar tooke him by the hand, and led him against his will. Now Cinna hearing at that time, that they burnt Cæsars body in the market place, notwithstanding that he feared his dreame, and had an agew on him besides: he went into the market place to honor his funeralls. When he came thither, one of meane sorte asked what his name was? He was straight called by his name. The first man told it to an other, and that other unto an other, so that it ranne straight through them all, that he was one of them that murdered Cæsar: (for in deede one of the traitors to Cæsar, was also called Cinna as him selfe) wherefore taking him for Cinna the murderer, they fell upon him with such furie, that they presently dispatched him in the market place.[3] This sturre and furie made Brutus and Cassius more affrayed, then of all that was past, and therefore within fewe dayes after, they departed out of Rome[4]: and touching their doings afterwards, and what calamity they suffered till their deathes, we have wrytten it at large, in the life of Brutus. Cæsar dyed at six and fifty yeres of age: and Pompey also lived not passing foure yeares more then he. So he reaped no other frute of all his raigne and dominion, which he had so vehemently desired all his life, and pursued with such extreame daunger: but a vaine name only, and a superficiall glory, that procured him the envy and hatred of his contrie. But his great prosperitie and good fortune that favored him all his life time, did continue afterwards in the revenge of his death, pursuing the murtherers both by sea and land, till they had not left a man more to be executed, of al them that were actors or counsellers in the conspiracy of his death.[5] Furthermore, of all the chaunces that happen unto men upon the earth, that which came to Cassius above all other, is most to be wondered at. For he being overcome in battell at the jorney of Philippes, slue him selfe with the same sworde, with the which he strake Cæsar.[6] Againe, of signes in the element, the great comet which seven nightes together was seene very bright after

[1] Cf. III.2.204–31; 255.

[2] *In margin:* 'Cinnaes dreame of Cæsar.' III.3.1–2. Cf. *inf.* 105.

[3] *In margin:* 'The murther of Cinna.' III.3.5–39.

[4] III.2.268–9.

[5] *In margin:* 'The revenge of Cæsars death.'

[6] *In margin:* 'Cassius being overthrowen at the battell of Philippes, slue himselfe with the selfe same sword wherewith he strake Cæsar.' V.3.41–6.

Cæsars death, the eight night after was never seene more.[1] Also the brightnes of the sunne was darkened, the which all that yeare through rose very pale, and shined not out, whereby it gave but small heate: therefore the ayer being very clowdy and darke, by the weakenes of the heate that could not come foorth, did cause the earth to bring foorth but raw and unrype frute, which rotted before it could rype. But above all, the ghost that appeared unto Brutus shewed plainly, that the goddes were offended with the murther of Cæsar.[2] The vision was thus: Brutus being ready to passe over his army from the citie of Abydos, to the other coast lying directly against it, slept every night (as his manner was) in his tent, and being yet awake, thinking of his affaires: (for by reporte he was as carefull a Captaine, and lived with as litle sleepe, as ever man did) he thought he heard a noyse at his tent dore, and looking towards the light of the lampe that waxed very dimme, he saw a horrible vision of a man, of a wonderfull greatnes, and dreadfull looke, which at the first made him marvelously afraid.[3] But when he sawe that it did him no hurt, but stoode by his bedde side, and sayd nothing: at length he asked him what he was. The image aunswered him: I am thy ill angell, Brutus, and thou shalt see me by the citie of Philippes. Then Brutus replied againe, and sayd: Well, I shall see thee then.[4] Therewithall, the spirit presently vanished from him. After that time Brutus being in battell neere unto the citie of Philippes, against Antonius and Octavius Cæsar, at the first battell he wan the victorie, and overthrowing all them that withstoode him, he drave them into young Cæsars campe, which he tooke. The second battell being at hand, this spirit appeared again unto him, but spake never a word.[5] Thereuppon Brutus knowing he should dye,[6] did put him selfe to all hazard in battell, but yet fighting could not be slaine. So seeing his men put to flight and overthrowen, he ranne unto a litle rocke not farre of, and there setting his swordes point to his brest, fell upon it, and slue him selfe, but yet as it is reported, with the helpe of his frend, that dispatched him.[7]

THE END OF CÆSARS LIFE

[1] *In margin:* 'Wonders seene in the element after Cæsar's death. A great Comet.'
[2] *In margin:* 'Brutus vision.'
[3] *In margin:* 'A spirit appeared unto Brutus.' IV.3.273–85.
[4] IV.3.280–85.
[5] *In margin:* 'The second appearing of the spirit, unto Brutus.' V.5.17–19.
[6] V.5.20. [7] V.5.43–51; 65.

II. Source

PLUTARCH'S LIVES OF THE NOBLE GRECIANS AND ROMANES

translated by Sir Thomas North (1579)

THE LIFE OF MARCUS BRUTUS

Marcus Brutus came of that Junius Brutus, for whome the auncient Romanes made his statue of brasse to be set up in the Capitoll, with the images of the kings, holding a naked sword in his hand: bicause he had valliantly put downe the Tarquines from their kingdom of Rome.[1] But that Junius Brutus being of a sower stearne nature, not softned by reason, being like unto sword blades of too hard a temper: was so subject to his choller and malice he bare unto the tyrannes, that for their sakes he caused his owne sonnes to be executed. But this Marcus Brutus in contrarie maner, whose life we presently wryte, having framed his manners of life by the rules of vertue and studie of Philosophie, and having imployed his wit, which was gentle and constant, in attempting of great things: me thinkes he was rightly made and framed unto vertue.[2] So that his verie enemies which wish him most hurt, bicause of his conspiracy against Julius Cæsar: if there were any noble attempt done in all this conspiracie, they referre it whollie unto Brutus, and all the cruell and violent actes unto Cassius, who was Brutus familiar frend, but not so well geven, and condicioned as he. . . . Marcus Cato the Philosopher was brother unto Servilia M. Brutus mother[3]: whom Brutus studied most to follow of all the other Romanes, bicause he was his Uncle, and afterwards he maried his daughter. Now touching the Græcian Philosophers, there was no sect nor Philosopher of them, but he heard and liked it: but above all the rest, he loved Platoes sect best, and did not much geve him selfe to the new nor meane Academy as they call it, but altogether to the old Academy.[4] Therefore he did ever greatly esteeme the Philosopher Antiochus, of the citie of Ascalon: but he was more familiar with his brother

[1] *In margin:* 'The parentage of Brutus.'
[2] *In margin:* 'Brutus maners.'
[3] *In margin:* 'Servilia Catoes sister.'
[4] *In margin:* 'Brutus studies.' 'Brutus followed the olde Academyks.'

Ariston, who for learning and knowledge was inferior to many other Philosophers, but for wisedom and curtesie, equall with the best and chiefest. . . . He was properly learned in the Latine tongue, and was able to make long discourse in it, beside that he could also plead verie well in Latine. But for the Græke tongue, they do note in some of his Epistells, that he counterfeated that briefe compendious maner of speach of the Lacedæmonians.[1] As when the warre was begonne, he wrote unto the Pargamenians in this sorte: I understand you have geven Dolobella money: if you have done it willingly, you confesse you have offended me: if against your wills, shewe it then by geving me willinglie. An other time againe unto the Samians[2]: Your counsels be long, your doinges be slowe, consider the ende. And in an other Epistell he wrote unto the Patareians: The Xanthians despising my good wil, have made their contrie a grave of dispaire: and the Patareians that put them selves into my protection, have lost no jot of their libertie. And therefore whilest you have libertie, either choose the judgement of the Patareians, or the fortune of the Xanthians. These were Brutus manner of letters which were honored for their briefenes.

So Brutus being but a young stripling went into Cyprus with his Uncle Cato, who was sent against Ptolomy king of Ægypt.[3] . . . Afterwards when the Empire of Rome was devided into factions, and that Cæsar and Pompey both were in armes one against the other, and that all the Empire of Rome was in garboyle and uprore: it was thought then that Brutus woulde take parte with Cæsar, bicause Pompey not long before had put his father unto death. But Brutus preferring the respect of his contrie and common wealth, before private affection, and perswading himselfe that Pompey had juster cause to enter into armes then Cæsar: he then tooke parte with Pompey,[4] though oftentimes meting him before, he thought scorne to speake to him, thinking it a great sinne and offence in him, to speake to the murtherer of his father. But then submitting him selfe unto Pompey, as unto the head of the common wealth: he sailed into Sicilia, Lieutenant under Sestius that was Governor of that province. But when he saw that there was no way to rise, nor to do any noble exployts, and that Cæsar and Pompey were both camped together, and fought for victory: he went of him selfe unsent for into Macedon, to be partaker of the daunger. It is reported that Pompey being glad, and wondering at his comming when he sawe

[1] *In margin:* 'Brutus maner of wryting his Epistells in Græke.'

[2] *In margin:* 'A briefe letter to the Samians.' Cf. his funeral oration, III.2.12ff.

[3] *In margin:* 'Brutus followed Cato into Cyprus.'

[4] *In margin:* 'Brutus taketh parte with Pompey.'

him come to him: he rose out of his chaire, and went and imbraced him before them all, and used him as honorablie, as he could have done the noblest man that tooke his parte. Brutus being in Pompeys campe, did nothing but studie all day long, except he were with Pompey, and not only the dayes before, but the selfe same day also before the great battell was fought in the fieldes of Pharsalia, where Pompey was overthrowen.[1] It was in the middest of sommer, and the sunne was verie hotte, besides that the campe was lodged neere unto marishes, and they that caried his tent, taried long before they came: whereuppon, being verie wearie with travell, scant any meate came into his mouth at dinner time. Furthermore, when others slept, or thought what woulde happen the morrowe after: he fell to his booke, and wrote all day long till night, wryting a breviarie of Polybius.[2] It is reported that Cæsar did not forgette him, and that he gave his Captaines charge before the battell, that they shoulde beware they killed not Brutus in fight, and if he yeelded willinglie unto them, that then they shoulde bring him unto him: but if he resisted, and woulde not be taken, then that they shoulde lette him goe, and doe him no hurte.[3] Some saye he did this for Serviliaes sake, Brutus mother. For when he was a young man, he had bene acquainted with Servilia, who was extreamelie in love with him.[4] And bicause Brutus was borne in that time when their love was hottest, he perswaded him selfe that he begat him. . . . So, after Pompeys overthrowe at the battell of Pharsalia, and that he fledde to the sea: when Cæsar came to beseege his campe, Brutus went out of the campe gates unseene of any man, and lept into a marishe full of water and reedes. Then when night was come, he crept out, and went unto the citie of Larissa: from whence he wrote unto Cæsar, who was verie glad that he had scaped, and sent for him to come unto him. When Brutus was come, he did not onelie pardon him, but also kept him alwayes about him, and did as muche honor and esteeme him, as any man he had in his companie.[5] Nowe no man coulde tell whither Pompey was fledde, and all were marvelous desirous to knowe it: wherefore Cæsar walking a good waye alone with Brutus, he did aske him which way he thought Pompey tooke. Cæsar perceiving by his talke that Brutus gessed certainlie whither Pompey shoulde be fledde: he left all other wayes, and tooke his jorney directlie towardes Ægypt. Pompey, as Brutus had conjectured, was in deede fledde into Ægypt, but there he was villanouslie

[1] *In margin:* 'Brutus exercise in Pompeys campe.'
[2] *In margin:* 'Brutus studied in Pompeis campe.'
[3] *In margin:* 'Julius Cæsar carefull of Brutus safety.'
[4] *In margin:* 'Julius Cæsar loved Servilia, Brutus mother.'
[5] *In margin:* 'Brutus saved by Julius Cæsar, after the battell of Pharsalia.'

slayne. Furthermore, Brutus obteyned pardon of Cæsar for Cassius; and defending also the king[1] of Lybiaes cause, he was overlayed with a worlde of accusacions against him, howebeit intreating for him, he saved him the best parte of his realme and kingdome. They say also that Cæsar sayd, when he hearde Brutus pleade: I knowe not, sayd he, what this young man woulde, but what he woulde, he willeth it vehementlie. For as Brutus gravetie and constant minde woulde not graunt all men their requests that sued unto him, but being moved with reason and discretion, did alwayes encline to that which was good and honest: even so when it was moved to followe any matter, he used a kinde of forcible and vehement perswasion that calmed not, till he had obteyned his desire. For by flattering of him, a man coulde never obteyne any thing at his handes, nor make him to doe that which was unjust. Further, he thought it not meete for a man of calling and estimacion, to yeelde unto the requestes and intreaties of a shamelesse and importunate suter, requesting thinges unmeete: the which notwithstanding, some men doe for shame, bicause they dare deny nothing. . . .

Now there were divers sortes of Prætorshippes at Rome, and it was looked for, that Brutus or Cassius would make sute for the chiefest Prætorshippe, which they called the Prætorshippe of the citie: bicause he that had that office, was as a Judge to minister justice unto the citizens. Therfore they strove one against the other,[2] though some say that there was some litle grudge betwext them for other matters before, and that this contencion did sette them further out, though they were allyed together. For Cassius had maried Junia, Brutus sister.[3] Others say, that this contencion betwext them came by Cæsar himselfe, who secretly gave either of them both hope of his favour. So their sute for the Prætorshippe was so followed and laboured of either partie, that one of them put an other in sute of lawe. Brutus with his vertue and good name contended against many noble exploytes in armes, which Cassius had done against the Parthians. So Cæsar after he had heard both their objections, he told his frendes with whom he consulted about this matter: Cassius cause is the juster, sayd he, but Brutus must be first preferred. Thus Brutus had the first Prætorshippe, and Cassius the second: who thanked not Cæsar so much for the Prætorshippe he had, as he was angrie with him for that he had lost.[4] But Brutus in many other thinges tasted of the benefite of Cæsars favour in any thing he requested. For if he had listed, he might have bene one of Cæsars

[1] *In margin:* 'This king was Juba . . .'

[2] *In margin:* 'Brutus and Cassius contend for the Prætorship of the citie.'

[3] *In margin:* 'Cassius maried Junia, Brutus sister.' Cf. IV.3.95.

[4] *In margin:* 'The first cause of Cassius malice against Cæsar.'

chiefest frendes, and of greatest authoritie and credit about him. Howebeit Cassius frendes did disswade him from it (for Cassius and he were not yet reconciled together sithence their first contencion and strife for the Prætorship) and prayed him to beware of Cæsars sweete intisements, and to flie his tyrannicall favors: the which they sayd Cæsar gave him, not to honor his vertue, but to weaken his constant minde, framing it to the bent of his bowe. Now Cæsar on the other side did not trust him overmuch, nor was not without tales brought unto him against him[1]: howbeit he feared his great minde, authority, and frends. Yet on the other side also, he trusted his good nature, and fayer condicions. For, intelligence being brought him one day, that Antonius and Dolabella did conspire against him: he aunswered, that these fat long heared men made him not affrayed, but the leane and whitely faced fellowes, meaning that, by Brutus and Cassius.[2] At an other time also when one accused Brutus unto him, and bad him beware of him: What, sayd he againe, clapping his hand on his brest: thinke ye that Brutus will not tarie till this bodie dye?[3] Meaning that none but Brutus after him was meete to have suche power as he had. And surelie, in my opinion, I am perswaded that Brutus might in dede have come to have bene the chiefest man of Rome, if he could have contented him selfe for a time and have bene next unto Cæsar, and to have suffred his glorie and authoritie, which he had gotten by his great victories, to consume with time. But Cassius being a chollericke man, and hating Cæsar privatlie, more then he did the tyrannie openlie: he incensed Brutus against him.[4] It is also reported, that Brutus coulde evill away with the tyrannie, and that Cassius hated the tyranne: making many complayntes for the injuries he had done him, and amongest others, for that he had taken away his Lyons from him. Cassius had provided them for his sportes, when he should be Ædilis, and they were found in the citie of Megara, when it was wonne by Calenus, and Cæsar kept them. The rumor went, that these Lyons did marvelous great hurt to the Magarians. For when the citie was taken, they brake their cages where they were tied up, and turned them loose, thinking they would have done great mischiefe to the enemies, and have kept them from setting uppon them: but the Lyons contrarie to expectacion, turned upon them selves that fled unarmed, and did so cruelly tare some in peces, that it pitied their enemies to see them. And this was the cause, as some do report, that made Cassius conspire against Cæsar. But this holdeth

[1] *In margin:* 'Cæsar suspected Brutus.' [2] I.2.188–942.

[3] *In margin:* 'Cæsars saying of Brutus.'

[4] *In margin:* 'Cassius incenseth Brutus against Cæsar.'

no water. For Cassius even from his cradell could not abide any maner of tyrans,[1] as it appeared when he was but a boy, and went unto the same schoole that Faustus, the sonne of Sylla did. And Faustus bragging among other boyes, highly boasted of his fathers kingdom: Cassius rose up on his feete, and gave him two good whirts on the eare. Faustus governors would have put this matter in sute against Cassius: but Pompey woulde not suffer them, but caused the two boyes to be brought before him, and asked them howe the matter came to passe. Then Cassius, as it is wrytten of him, said unto the other: Goe to, Faustus, speake againe and thou darest, before this noble man here, the same wordes that made me angrie with thee, that my fistes may walke once againe about thine eares. Suche was Cassius hotte stirring nature. But for Brutus, his frendes and contrie men, both by divers procurementes, and sundrie rumors of the citie, and by many bills also, did openlie call and procure him to doe that he did.[2] For, under the image of his auncester Junius Brutus, that drave the kinges out of Rome,[3] they wrote: O, that it pleased the goddes thou wert now alive, Brutus: and againe, that thou wert here amonge us nowe. His tribunall (or chaire) where he gave audience during the time he was Prætor, was full of suche billes: Brutus, thou art a sleepe, and art not Brutus in deede.[4] And of all this, Cæsars flatterers were the cause: who beside many other exceeding and unspeakeable honors they dayly devised for him, in the night time they did put Diadeames uppon the heades of his images, supposinge thereby to allure the common people to call him kinge, in steade of Dictator. Howebeit it turned to the contrarie, as we have wrytten more at large in Julius Cæsars life. Nowe when Cassius felt his frendes, and did stirre them up against Cæsar: they all agreed and promised to take parte with him, so Brutus were the chiefe of their conspiracie. For they told him, that so high an enterprise and attempt as that, did not so muche require men of manhoode, and courage to drawe their swordes: as it stoode them uppon to have a man of suche estimacion as Brutus, to make everie man boldlie thinke, that by his onelie presence the fact were holie, and just. If he tooke not this course, then that they shoulde goe to it with fainter hartes, and when they had done it, they shoulde be more fearefull: bicause everie man woulde thinke that Brutus woulde not have refused to have made one with them, if the cause had bene good and honest. Therefore Cassius considering this matter with him selfe, did first of all speake to Brutus, since they grewe straunge

[1] *In margin:* 'Cassius an enemie of tyrans.'

[2] *In margin:* 'How Brutus was incensed against Cæsar.'

[3] I.3.145–7.

[4] I.3.142–4; II.1.46.

together for the sute they had for the Prætorshippe.[1] So when he was reconciled to him againe, and that they had imbraced one an other: Cassius asked him if he were determined to be in the Senate house, the first day of the moneth of Marche, bicause he heard say that Cæsars frendes shoulde move the counsell that day, that Cæsar shoulde be called king by the Senate. Brutus aunswered him he would not be there. But if we be sent for sayd Cassius: howe then? For my selfe then sayd Brutus, I meane not to holde my peace, but to withstande it, and rather dye then lose my libertie. Cassius being bolde, and taking holde of this worde: Why, quoth he, what Romane is he alive that will suffer thee to dye for the libertie? What, knowest thou not that thou art Brutus?[2] Thinkest thou that they be cobblers, tapsters, or suche like base mechanicall people, that wryte these billes and scrowles which are founde dayly in thy Prætor's chaire, and not the noblest men and best citizens that doe it? No, be thou well assured, that of other Prætors they looke for giftes, common distribucions amongest the people, and for common playes, and to see fensers fight at the sharpe, to shew the people pastime: but at thy handes, they specially require (as a due det unto them) the taking away of the tyranny, being fully bent to suffer any extremity for thy sake, so that thou wilt shew thy selfe to be the man thou art taken for, and that they hope thou art. Thereuppon he kissed Brutus, and imbraced him: and so each taking leave of other, they went both to speake with their frendes about it. Nowe amongest Pompeys frendes, there was one called Caius Ligarius,[3] who had bene accused unto Cæsar for taking parte with Pompey, and Cæsar discharged him. But Ligarius thanked not Cæsar so muche for his discharge, as he was offended with him for that he was brought in daunger by his tyrannicall power.[4] And therefore in his hearte he was alway his mortall enemie, and was besides verie familiar with Brutus, who went to see him beinge sicke in his bedde, and sayed unto him: O Ligarius, in what a time art thou sicke! Ligarius risinge uppe in his bedde, and taking him by the right hande, sayed unto him: Brutus, sayed he, if thou hast any great enterprise in hande worthie of thy selfe, I am whole. After that time they beganne to feele all their acquaintaunce whome they trusted, and layed their heades together consultinge uppon it, and did not onelie picke out

[1] *In margin:* 'Cassius praieth Brutus first, to helpe him to put downe the tyran.' I.2.25–62.

[2] I.2.141–6.

[3] *In margin:* 'In an other place they cal him Quintus.' [i.e. in *Life of Cæsar*]. Cf. II.1.215–17.

[4] *In margin:* 'Brutus maketh Ligarius one of the conspiracie.' II.1.218–20; 310–34. Cf. Cæsar, II.2.111–13.

their frendes, but all those also whome they thought stowt enough to attempt any desperate matter, and that were not affrayed to loase their lives. For this cause they durst not acquaint Cicero with their conspiracie, although he was a man whome they loved dearelie, and trusted best[1]: for they were affrayed that he being a coward by nature, and age also having increased his feare, he woulde quite turne and alter all their purpose, and quenche the heate of their enterprise, the which speciallie required hotte and earnest execucion, seeking by perswasion to bring all thinges to suche safetie, as there should be no perill.[2] Brutus also did let other of his frendes alone, as Statilius Epicurian, and Faonius, that made profession to followe Marcus Cato. Bicause that having cast out wordes a farre of, disputing together in Philosophie to feele their mindes: Faonius aunswered, that civill warre was worse then tyrannicall government usurped against the lawe.[3] And Statilius tolde him also, that it were an unwise parte of him, to put his life in daunger, for a sight of ignoraunt fooles and asses. Labeo was present at this talke, and maintayned the contrarie against them both. But Brutus helde his peace, as though it had bene a doubtfull matter, and a harde thing to have decided. But afterwardes, being out of their companie, he made Labeo privie to his intent: who verie readilie offered him selfe to make one. And they thought good also to bring in an other Brutus to joyne with him, surnamed Albinus: who was no man of his handes him selfe, but bicause he was able to bring good force of a great number of slaves, and fensers at the sharpe, whome he kept to shewe the people pastime with their fighting, besides also that Cæsar had some trust in him. Cassius and Labeo tolde Brutus Albinus of it at the first, but he made them no aunswere. But when he had spoken with Brutus him selfe alone, and that Brutus had tolde him he was the chiefe ringleader of all this conspiracie: then he willinglie promised him the best aide he coulde. Furthermore, the onlie name and great calling of Brutus, did bring on the most of them to geve consent to this conspiracie. Who having never taken othes together, nor taken or geven any caution or assuraunce, nor binding them selves one to an other by any religious othes[4]: they all kept the matter so secret to them selves, and coulde so cunninglie handle it, that notwithstanding the goddes did reveale it by manifest signes and tokens from above, and by predictions of sacrifices: yet all this woulde not be beleved. Nowe Brutus, who knewe verie well

[1] *In margin:* 'They do hide the conspiracy against Cæsar, from Cicero.'
[2] Cf. their reasons in II.1.141–51.
[3] *In margin:* 'Civill warre worse then tyrannicall government.'
[4] *In margin:* 'The wonderfull faith and secresie of the Conspirators of Cæsars death.' Cf. II.1.112–40.

that for his sake all the noblest, valliantest, and most couragious men of Rome did venter their lives, waying with him selfe the greatnesse of the daunger: when he was out of his house, he did so frame and facion his countenaunce and lookes, that no man coulde discerne he had any thing to trouble his minde. But when night came that he was in his owne house, then he was cleane chaunged. For, either care did wake him against his will when he woulde have slept, or else oftentimes of him selfe he fell into suche deepe thoughtes of this enterprise, casting in his minde all the daungers that might happen: that his wife lying by him, founde that there was some marvelous great matter that troubled his minde, not beinge wont to be in that taking, and that he coulde not well determine with him selfe.[1] His wife Porcia (as we have tolde you before) was the daughter of Cato,[2] whome Brutus maried being his cosin, not a maiden, but a younge widowe after the death of her first husbande Bibulus, by whome she had also a younge sonne called Bibulus, who afterwardes wrote a booke of the actes and jeastes[3] of Brutus, extant at this present day. This young Ladie being excellentlie well seene in Philosophie,[4] loving her husbande well, and being of a noble courage, as she was also wise: bicause she woulde not aske her husbande what he ayled before she had made some proofe by her selfe, she tooke a litle rasor suche as barbers occupie to pare mens nayles, and causinge all her maydes and women to goe out of her chamber, gave her selfe a greate gashe withall in her thigh, that she was straight all of a gore bloode, and incontinentlie after, a vehement fever tooke her, by reason of the payne of her wounde.[5] Then perceiving her husbande was marvelouslie out of quiet, and that he coulde take no rest[6]: even in her greatest payne of all, she spake in this sorte unto him[7]: 'I being, O Brutus, (sayed she) the daughter 'of Cato, was maried unto thee, not to be thy beddefellowe and 'companion in bedde and at borde onelie, like a harlot[8]: but to 'be partaker also with thee, of thy good and evill fortune. Nowe for 'thy selfe, I can finde no cause of faulte in thee touchinge our 'matche: but for my parte, howe may I showe my duetie towardes 'thee, and howe muche I woulde doe for thy sake, if I can not 'constantlie beare a secret mischaunce or griefe with thee, which 'requireth secrecy and fidelity? I confesse, that a womans wit com-'monly is too weake to keepe a secret safely: but yet, Brutus, good

[1] II.1.61–9. [2] *In margin:* 'Porcia, Catoes daughter, wife unto Brutus.'
[3] gestes, deeds. [4] *In margin:* 'Porcia studied in Philosophie.'
[5] *In margin:* 'The corage of Porcia.' [6] Cf. II.1.237–68.
[7] *In margin:* 'Porciaes words unto her husband Brutus.'
[8] *In margin:* 'Great difference betwext a wife and a harlot.' II.1.279–87.

'educacion, and the companie of vertuous men, have some power to 'reforme the defect of nature. And for my selfe, I have this benefit 'moreover: that I am the daughter of Cato, and wife of Brutus.[1] 'This notwithstanding, I did not trust to any of these things before: 'untill that now I have found by experience, that no paine nor 'griefe whatsoever can overcome me.' With those wordes she shewed him her wounde on her thigh, and tolde him what she had done to prove her selfe.[2] Brutus was amazed to heare what she sayd unto him, and lifting up his handes to heaven, he besought the goddes to geve him the grace he might bring his enterprise to so good passe, that he might be founde a husband, worthie of so noble a wife as Porcia: so he then did comfort her the best he coulde.[3] Now a day being appointed for the meeting of the Senate, at what time they hoped Cæsar woulde not faile to come: the conspirators determined then to put their enterprise in execucion, bicause they might meete safelie at that time without suspicion, and the rather, for that all the noblest and chiefest men of the citie woulde be there. Who when they should see suche a great matter executed, would everie man then set to their handes, for the defence of their libertie. Furthermore, they thought also that the appointment of the place where the counsell shoulde be kept, was chosen of purpose by divine providence, and made all for them. For it was one of the porches about the Theater, in the which there was a certaine place full of seates for men to sit in, where also was set up the image of Pompey, which the citie had made and consecrated in honor of him: when he did beawtifie that parte of the citie with the Theater he built, with divers porches about it. In this place was the assembly of the Senate appointed to be, just on the fifteenth day of the moneth of March, which the Romanes call, Idus Martias: so that it seemed some god of purpose had brought Cæsar thither to be slaine, for revenge of Pompeys death. So when the day was come, Brutus went out of his house with a dagger by his side under his long gowne, that no bodie sawe nor knewe, but his wife onelie.[4] The other conspirators were all assembled at Cassius house, to bring his sonne into the market place, who on that day did put on the mans gowne, called Toga Virilis: and from thence they came all in a troupe together unto Pompeys porche, looking that Cæsar woulde straight come thither. But here is to be noted, the wonderfull assured constancie of these conspirators, in so daungerous and waightie an enterprise as they had undertaken.[5] For many of them being Prætors, by reason of their office, whose duetie is to minister justice to everie bodie: they

[1] II.1.292–95. [2] II.1.299–302. [3] II.1.302–8. [4] Cf. II.4.39–41.
[5] *In margin:* 'The wonderfull constancy of the conspirators, in killing of Cæsar.'

did not onelie with great quietnesse and curtesie heare them that spake unto them, or that pleaded matters before them, and gave them attentive eare, as if they had had no other matter in their heades: but moreover, they gave just sentence, and carefullie dispatched the causes before them. So there was one among them, who being condemned in a certaine summe of money, refused to pay it, and cried out that he did appeale unto Cæsar. Then Brutus casting his eyes uppon the conspirators, sayd, Cæsar shall not lette me to see the lawe executed. Notwithstanding this, by chaunce there fell out many misfortunes unto them, which was enough to have marred the enterprise.[1] The first and chiefest was, Cæsars long tarying, who came verie late to the Senate: for bicause the signes of the sacrifices appeared unluckie, his wife Calpurnia kept him at home, and the Soothsayers bad him beware he went not abroade.[2] The seconde cause was, when one came unto Casca being a conspirator, and taking him by the hande, sayd unto him: O Casca, thou keptest it close from me, but Brutus hath tolde me all. Casca being amazed at it, the other went on with his tale, and sayd: Why, howe nowe, howe commeth it to passe thou art thus riche, that thou doest sue to be Ædilis? Thus Casca being deceived by the others doubtfull wordes, he tolde them it was a thowsand to one, he blabbed not out all the conspiracie. An other Senator called Popilius Læna, after he had saluted Brutus and Cassius more frendlie then he was wont to doe: he rounded softlie in their eares, and told them, I pray the goddes you may goe through with that you have taken in hande, but withall, dispatche I reade you, for your enterprise is bewrayed. When he had sayd, he presentlie departed from them, and left them both affrayed that their conspiracie woulde out.[3] Nowe in the meane time, there came one of Brutus men post hast unto him, and tolde him his wife was a dying. For Porcia being verie carefull and pensive for that which was to come, and being too weake to away with so great and inward griefe of minde: she coulde hardlie keepe within, but was frighted with everie litle noyse and crie she hearde, as those that are taken and possest with the furie of the Bacchantes, asking every man that came from the market place, what Brutus did, and still sent messenger after messenger, to knowe what newes.[4] At length, Cæsars comming being prolonged as you have heard, Porciaes weakenesse was not able to holde out any lenger, and thereuppon she sodainlie swounded, that she had no leasure to goe

[1] *In margin:* 'Sundrie misfortunes to have broken of the enterprise.'

[2] II.1. 193–201. [3] III.1.13–17.

[4] *In margin:* 'The weakenes of Porcia, notwithstanding her former corage.' II.4.1–20.

to her chamber, but was taken in the middest of her house, where her speache and sences failed her. Howbeit she soone came to her selfe againe, and so was layed in her bedde, and tended by her women. When Brutus heard these newes, it grieved him, as it is to be presupposed:[1] yet he left not of the care of his contrie and common wealth, neither went home to his house for any newes he heard. Nowe, it was reported that Cæsar was comming in his litter: for he determined not to stay in the Senate all that day (bicause he was affrayed of the unluckie signes of the sacrifices) but to adjorne matters of importaunce unto the next session, and counsell holden, faining him selfe not to be well at ease. When Cæsar came out of his litter: Popilius Læna, that had talked before with Brutus and Cassius, and had prayed the goddes they might bring this enterprise to passe: went unto Cæsar, and kept him a long time with a talke. Cæsar gave good eare unto him. Wherefore the conspirators (if so they shoulde be called) not hearing what he sayd to Cæsar, but conjecturing by that he had tolde them a litle before, that his talke was none other but the verie discoverie of their conspiracie: they were affrayed everie man of them, and one looking in an others face, it was easie to see that they were all of a minde, that it was no tarying for them till they were apprehended, but rather that they should kill them selves with their owne handes. And when Cassius and certeine other clapped their handes on their swordes under their gownes to draw them: Brutus marking the countenaunce and gesture of Læna, and considering that he did use him selfe rather like an humble and earnest suter, then like an accuser: he sayd nothing to his companion (bicause there were many amongest them that were not of the conspiracie) but with a pleasaunt countenaunce encouraged Cassius.[2] And immediatlie after, Læna went from Cæsar, and kissed his hande: which shewed plainlie that it was for some matter concerning him selfe, that he had held him so long in talke. Nowe all the Senators being entred first into this place or chapter house where the counsell should be kept: all the other conspirators straight stoode about Cæsars chaire, as if they had had some thing to have sayd unto him. And some say, that Cassius casting his eyes upon Pompeys image, made his prayer unto it, as if it had bene alive. Trebonius[3] on thother side, drewe Antonius atoside, as he came into the house where the Senate sate, and helde him with a long talke without. When Cæsar was come into the house,

[1] Not in the play.

[2] *In margin:* 'Brutus with his countenaunce encoraged his fearefull consortes.' III.1.18–24.

[3] *In margin:* 'In Cæsars life it is sayd, it was Decius Brutus Albinus, that kept Antonius with a talke without.' Trebonius in III.1.25–6.

all the Senate rose to honor him at his comming in. So when he was set, the conspirators flocked about him, and amongst them they presented one Tullius Cimber,[1] who made humble sute for the calling home againe of his brother that was banished. They all made as though they were intercessors for him, and tooke him by the handes, and kissed his head and brest. Cæsar at the first, simplie refused their kindnesse and intreaties: but afterwardes, perceiving they still pressed on him, he violently thrust them from him.[2] Then Cimber with both his hands plucked Cæsars gowne over his shoulders, and Casca that stoode behinde him, drew his dagger first, and strake Cæsar upon the shoulder, but gave him no great wound.[3] Cæsar feeling him selfe hurt, tooke him straight by the hande he held his dagger in, and cried out in Latin: O traitor, Casca, what doest thou? Casca on thother side cried in Græke,[4] and called his brother to helpe him. So divers running on a heape together to flie uppon Cæsar, he looking about him to have fledde, sawe Brutus with a sworde drawen in his hande readie to strike at him: then he let Cascaes hande goe, and casting his gowne over his face, suffered everie man to strike at him that woulde.[5] Then the conspirators thronging one upon an other bicause everie man was desirous to have a cut at him, so many swords and daggers lighting upon one bodie, one of them hurte an other, and among them Brutus caught a blowe on his hande, bicause he would make one in murdering of him, and all the rest also were every man of them bloudied.[6] Cæsar being slaine in this maner, Brutus standing in the middest of the house, would have spoken, and stayed the other Senators that were not of the conspiracie, to have tolde them the reason why they had done this facte.[7] But they as men both affrayd and amazed, fled one upon anothers necke in haste to get out at the dore, and no man followed them. For it was set downe, and agreed betwene them, that they should kill no man but Cæsar onely,[8] and should intreate all the rest to looke to defend their libertie. All the conspirators, but Brutus, determining upon this matter, thought it good also to kill Antonius, bicause he was a wicked man, and that in nature favored tyranny: besides also, for that he was in great estimation with souldiers, having bene conversant of long time amongest them: and specially, having a mind bent to great enterprises, he was also of great authoritie at that time, being Consul with

[1] *In margin:* 'In Cæsars life he is called Metellus Cimber.' So in III.1.27.
[2] *In margin:* 'The murther of Cæsar.' III.1.29ff.
[3] *In margin:* 'Casca, the first that wounded him.' III.1.76.
[4] Casca pretended not to know Greek, I.2.277–82.
[5] Cf. III.1.77. [6] Contrast III.1.105–7. [7] III.1.82–3. [8] III.1.91.

Cæsar. But Brutus would not agree to it.[1] First, for that he sayd it was not honest: secondly, bicause he told them there was hope of chaunge in him. For he did not mistrust, but that Antonius being a noble minded and coragious man (when he should knowe that Cæsar was dead) would willingly helpe his contry to recover her libertie, having them an example unto him, to follow their corage and vertue. So Brutus by this meanes saved Antonius life, who at that present time disguised him selfe, and stale away.[2] But Brutus and his consorts, having their swords bloudy in their handes, went straight to the Capitoll,[3] perswading the Romanes as they went, to take their libertie againe. Now, at the first time when the murther was newly done, there were sodaine outcryes of people that ranne up and downe the citie, the which in deede did the more increase the feare and tumult. But when they saw they slue no man, neither did spoyle or make havock of any thing: then certaine of the Senators, and many of the people imboldening them selves, went to the Capitoll unto them. There a great number of men being assembled one after another: Brutus made an oration unto them to winne the favor of the people, and to justifie that they had done. All those that were by, sayd they had done well, and cryed unto them that they should boldly come downe from the Capitoll. Whereuppon, Brutus and his companions came boldly downe into the market place. The rest followed in trowpe, but Brutus went formost, very honorably compassed in round about with the noblest men of the citie, which brought him from the Capitoll, thorough the market place, to the pulpit for orations. When the people saw him in the pulpit, although they were a multitude of rakehells of all sortes, and had a good will to make some sturre: yet being ashamed to doe it for the reverence they bare unto Brutus, they kept silence, to heare what he would say.[4] When Brutus began to speake, they gave him quiet audience: howbeit immediatly after, they shewed that they were not all contented with the murther.[5] For when another called Cinna would have spoken, and began to accuse Cæsar: they fell into a great uprore among them, and marvelously reviled him. Insomuch that the conspirators returned againe into the Capitol. There Brutus being affrayd to be beseeged, sent back againe the noble men that came thither with him, thinking it no reason, that they which were no partakers of the murther, should be partakers of the daunger. Then the next morning the Senate

[1] *In margin:* 'Why Antonius was not slayne with Cæasr.' II.1.154–91.

[2] III.1.96.

[3] *In margin:* 'Brutus with his consorts went unto the Capitoll.' Cf. III.1.108: 'to the market-place.'

[4] Transferred to the funeral, III.2.1–8.

[5] Contrast III.2.48–54.

being assembled, and holden within the temple of the goddesse Tellus, to wete the earth: and Antonius, Plancus, and Cicero, having made a motion to the Senate in that assembly, that they should take an order to pardon and forget all that was past, and to stablishe friendship and peace againe: it was decreed, that they should not onely be pardoned, but also that the Consuls should referre it to the Senate what honors should be appoynted unto them.[1] This being agreed upon, the Senate brake up, and Antonius the Consul, to put them in hart that were in the Capitoll, sent them his sonne for a pledge. Upon this assurance, Brutus and his companions came downe from the Capitoll, where every man saluted and imbraced eche other, among the which, Antonius him selfe did bid Cassius to supper to him: and Lepidus also bad Brutus, and so one bad another, as they had friendship and acquaintance together.[2] The next day following, the Senate being called againe to counsell, did first of all commend Antonius, for that he had wisely stayed and quenched the beginning of a civill warre: then they also gave Brutus and his consorts great prayses, and lastly they appoynted them severall governments of provinces. For unto Brutus, they appoynted Creta: Africk, unto Cassius: Asia, unto Trebonius: Bithynia, unto Cimber: and unto the other Decius Brutus Albinus, Gaule on this side the Alpes. When this was done, they came to talke of Cæsars will and testament, and of his funeralls and tombe.[3] Then Antonius thinking good his testament should be red openly, and also that his body should be honorably buried, and not in hugger mugger, least the people might thereby take occasion to be worse offended if they did otherwise: Cassius stowtly spake against it.[4] But Brutus went with the motion, and agreed unto it: wherein it seemeth he committed a second fault. For the first fault he did was, when he would not consent to his fellow conspirators, that Antonius should be slayne: and therefore he was justly accused, that thereby he had saved and strengthened a stronge and grievous enemy of their conspiracy. The second fault was, when he agreed that Cæsars funeralls should be as Antonius would have them: the which in deede marred all.[5] For first of all, when Cæsars testament was openly red amonge them, whereby it appeared that he bequeathed unto every Citizen of Rome, 75 Drachmas a man, and that he left his gardens and arbors unto the people, which he had on this side

[1] *In margin:* 'Honors decreed for the murtherers of Cæsar.' Shakespeare omits the Senate meeting.

[2] Shakespeare substitutes the 'reconciliation scene'. III.i.124–253.

[3] *In margin:* 'Cæsars will, and funeralls.' III.i.240–1.

[4] Compare III.i.226 ff.

[5] *In margin:* 'Brutus committed two great faults after Cæsars death.'

of the river of Tyber, in the place where now the temple of Fortune is built: the people then loved him, and were marvelous sory for him.[1] Afterwards when Cæsars body was brought into the market place, Antonius making his funerall oration in praise of the dead,[2] according to the auncient custom of Rome, and perceiving that his wordes moved the common people to compassion: he framed his eloquence to make their harts yerne the more, and taking Cæsars gowne all bloudy in his hand, he layed it open to the sight of them all, shewing what a number of cuts and holes it had upon it. Therewithall the people fell presently into such a rage and mutinie,[3] that there was no more order kept amongest the common people. For some of them cryed out, Kill the murtherers: others plucked up, formes, tables, and stalles about the market place, as they had done before at the funeralls of Clodius, and having layed them all on a heape together, they set them on fire, and thereuppon did put the bodye of Cæsar, and burnt it in the middest of the most holy places.[4] And furthermore, when the fire was thoroughly kindled, some here, some there, tooke burning fire brands, and ranne with them to the murtherers houses that had killed him, to set them a fire.[5] Howbeit the conspirators foreseeing the daunger before, had wisely provided for them selves, and fled. But there was a Poet called Cinna, who had bene no partaker of the conspiracy, but was alway one of Cæsars chiefest friends: he dreamed the night before, that Cæsar bad him to supper with him, and that he refusing to goe, Cæsar was very importunate with him, and compelled him, so that at length he led him by the hand into a great darke place, where being marvelously affrayd, he was driven to follow him in spite of his hart.[6] This dreame put him all night into a fever, and yet notwithstanding, the next morning when he heard that they caried Cæsars body to buriall, being ashamed not to accompany his funerals: he went out of his house, and thrust him self into the prease of the common people that were in a great uprore. And bicause some one called him by his name, Cinna: the people thinking he had bene that Cinna, who in an oration he made had spoken very evill of Cæsar, they falling upon him in their rage, slue him outright in the market place.[7] This made Brutus and his companions more affrayd, then any other thing, next unto the chaunge of Antonius. Wherefore they got them out of Rome,[8] and kept at the first in the citie of Antium,

[1] III.2.238–52. [2] *In margin:* 'Antonius funerall oration for Cæsar.'
[3] III.2.170–230. [4] III.2.253–6. [5] III.2.257–60.
[6] *In margin:* 'The straunge dreame of Cinna the Poet.' III.3.1–4.
[7] *In margin:* 'The murder of Cinna the Poet, being mistaken for an other of that name.' III.3.27–38.
[8] *In margin:* 'Brutus and his consorts doe flye from Rome.' III.2.268–9.

hoping to returne againe to Rome, when the furie of the people were a litle asswaged. The which they hoped would be quickly, considering that they had to deale with a fickle and unconstant multitude, easye to be caried, and that the Senate stoode for them: who notwithstanding made no enquiery of them that had torne poore Cinna the Poet in peeces, but caused them to be sought for and apprehended, that went with fire brands to set fire of the conspirators houses. The people growing weary now of Antonius pride and insolency, who ruled all things in manner with absolute power: they desired that Brutus might returne againe, and it was also looked for, that Brutus would come him selfe in person to playe the playes which were due to the people, by reason of his office of Prætorship. But Brutus understanding that many of Cæsars souldiers which served under him in the warres, and that also had lands and houses given them in the cities where they lay, did lye in wayte for him to kill him, and that they dayly by small companies came by one and by one into Rome: he durst no more returne thither, but yet the people had the pleasure and pastyme in his absence, to see the games and sportes he made them, which were sumptuouslie set foorth and furnished with all thinges necessarie, sparing for no cost.[1]

. . . Now the state of Rome standing in these termes, there fell out an other chaunge and alteracion, when the younge man Octavius Cæsar came to Rome.[2] He was the sonne of Julius Cæsars Nece, whome he had adopted for his sonne, and made his heire, by his last will and testament. But when Julius Cæsar his adopted father was slayne, he was in the citie of Apollonia, where he studied tarying for him, bicause he was determined to make warre with the Parthians[3]: but when he heard the newes of his death, he returned againe to Rome, where to begin to curry favor with the common people, he first of all tooke upon him his adopted fathers name, and made distribution amonge them of the money which his father had bequeathed unto them.[4] By this meanes he troubled Antonius sorely, and by force of money, got a great number of his fathers souldiers together, that had served in the warres with him. And Cicero him selfe, for the great malice he bare Antonius, did favor his proceedings. But Brutus marvelously reproved him for it.[5] . . . Now, the citie of Rome being devided in two factions, some taking part with Antonius, other also leaning unto Octavius Cæsar, and

[1] *In margin:* 'Brutus playes and sportes at Rome in his absence.'

[2] *In margin:* 'Octavius Cæsars comming to Rome.' Antony tries to delay him, III.1.287–90, but he arrives, III.2.262–7.

[3] Cf. III.1.278.

[4] Cf. Antony, IV.1.8–9.

[5] *In margin:* 'Brutus reproved Cicero, for taking part with Octavius Cæsar.'

the souldiers making port-sale[1] of their service to him that would give most: Brutus seeing the state of Rome would be utterly overthrowen, he determined to goe out of Italy, and went a foote through the contry of Luke, unto the citie of Elea, standing by the sea. There Porcia being ready to depart from her husband Brutus,[2] and to returne to Rome, did what she could to dissemble the griefe and sorow she felt at her hart: but a certaine paynted table bewrayed her in the ende, although untill that time she alwayes shewed a constant and pacient mind. The devise of the table was taken out of the Greeke stories, howe Andromachè accompanied her husband Hector, when he went out of the citie of Troy, to goe to the warres, and how Hector delivered her his litle sonne, and how her eyes were never of him.[3] Porcia seeing this picture, and likening her selfe to be in the same case, she fell a weeping: and comming thither oftentymes in a day to see it, she wept still. Acilius one of Brutus friendes perceiving that, rehearsed the verses Andromachè speaketh to this purpose in Homer:

Thou Hector art my father, and my mother, and my brother,
And husband eke, and [all] in all: I mind not any other.

Then Brutus smyling aunswered againe: But yet (sayd he) I can not for my part say unto Porcia, as Hector aunswered Andromachè in the same place of the Poet:

Tush, meddle thou with weying dewly out
Thy mayds their task, and pricking on a clowt. [*Iliad*, vi]

For in deede, the weake constitution of her body, doth not suffer her to performe in shew, the valliant acts that we are able to doe: but for corage and constant minde, she shewed her selfe as stowt in the defence of her contry, as any of us. Bibulus, the sonne of Porcia, reporteth this story thus. Now Brutus imbarking at Elea in Luke, he sayled directly towards Athens. When he arrived there, the people of Athens received him with common joyes of rejoycing, and honorable decrees made for him.[4] He lay with a friend of his, with whome he went daily to heare the lectures of Theomnestus Academick Philosopher, and of Cratippus the Peripatetick, and so would talke with them in Philosophie, that it seemed he left all other matters, and gave him selfe onely unto studye: howbeit secretly

[1] Sale to the highest bidder.
[2] *In margin:* 'Porciaes sorowfull returne to Rome for the absence of her husband Brutus.'
[3] *In margin:* 'The story of Hector and Andromachè set forth in painted tables.'
[4] *In margin:* 'How Brutus bestowed his time at Athens.'

notwithstanding, he made preparation for warre. . . . [Examples of Brutus' clemency are given. Octavius and Antony quarrel.] So Brutus preparing to goe into Asia, newes came unto him of the great chaunge at Rome. For Octavius Cæsar was in armes, by commaundement, and authoritie from the Senate, against Marcus Antonius. But after that he had driven Antonius out of Italy, the Senate then began to be affrayd of him: bicause he sued to be Consul, which was contrary to the law, and kept a great army about him, when the Empire of Rome had no neede of them. On the other side, Octavius Cæsar perceiving the Senate stayed not there, but turned unto Brutus that was out of Italy, and that they appoynted him the government of certaine provinces: then he began to be affrayd for his part, and sent unto Antonius to offer him his friendship.[1] Then comming on with his armye neare to Rome, he made him selfe to be chosen Consul, whether the Senate would or not, when he was yet but a strippling or springal of twenty yeare old, as him selfe reporteth in his own *Commentaries*. So when he was Consul, he presently appoynted Judges to accuse Brutus and his companions, for killing of the noblest person in Rome, and chiefest Magistrate, without law or judgement: and made L. Cornificius accuse Brutus, and M. Agrippa, Cassius. So, the parties accused were condemned, bicause the Judges were compelled to give such sentence.[2] The voyce went, that when the Herauld (according to the custom after sentence given) went up to the chair or pulpit for orations, and proclaymed Brutus with a lowd voyce, summoning him to appeare in person before the Judges: the people that stoode by sighed openly, and the noble men that were present honge downe their heads, and durst not speake a word. Among them, the teares fell from Publius Silicius eyes: who shortly after, was one of the proscripts or outlawes appoynted to be slayne. After that, these three Octavius Cæsar, Antonius, and Lepidus, made an agreement betwene them selves.[3] and by those articles devided the provinces belonging to the Empire of Rome amonge them selves, and did set up billes of proscription and outlawry, condemning two hundred of the noblest men of Rome to suffer death, and among that number, Cicero was one.[4] Newes being brought thereof into Macedon, Brutus being then inforced to it, wrote unto Hortensius, that he should put Caius Antonius to death,[5] to be revenged of the death of

[1] *In margin:* 'Octavius Cæsar joyneth with Antonius.'

[2] *In margin:* 'Brutus accused, and condemned, by Octavius Cæsars meanes, for the death of Julius Cæsar.'

[3] *In margin:* 'The Triumvirate.' IV.1.1–51.

[4] IV.3.176–9.

[5] *In margin:* 'C. Antonius murdered.'

Cicero, and of the other Brutus, of the which the one was his friend, and the other his kinseman. For this cause therefore, Antonius afterwards taking Hortensius at the battell of Philippes, he made him to be slayne upon his brothers tombe. But then Brutus sayd, that he was more ashamed of the cause for the which Cicero was slayne, then he was otherwise sory for his death: and that he could not but greatly reprove his friendes he had at Rome, who were slaves more through their owne fault, then through their valliantnes or manhood which usurped the tyranny: considering that they were so cowardly and faynt hearted, as to suffer the sight of those things before their eyes, the report whereof should onely have grieved them to the hart. Nowe when Brutus had passed over his army (that was very great) into Asia, he gave order for the gathering of a great number of shippes together, aswell in the coast of Bithynia, as also in the citie of Cyzicum, bicause he would have an army by sea: and him selfe in the meane time went unto the cities, taking order for all things, and giving audience unto Princes and noble men of the contry that had to doe with him. Afterwards, he sent unto Cassius in Syria, to turne him from his jorney into Ægypt, telling him that it was not for the conquest of any kingdom for them selves, that they wandred up and downe in that sort, but contrarily, that it was to restore their contry againe to their libertie: and that the multitude of souldiers they gathered together, was to subdue the tyrannes that would keepe them in slavery and subjection. Wherefore regarding their chiefe purpose and intent, they should not be farre from Italy, as neare as they could possible, but should rather make all the haste they could, to helpe their contry men. Cassius beleved him, and returned. Brutus went to meete him, and they both met at the citie of Smyrna,[1] which was the first time that they saw together, since they tooke leave eche of other, at the haven of Piræa in Athens: the one going into Syria, and the other into Macedon. So they were marvelous joyfull, and no lesse coragious, when they saw the great armies together which they had both leavied: considering that they departing out of Italy, like naked and poore banished men, without armor and money, nor having any shippe ready, nor souldier about them, nor any one towne at their commaundement: yet notwithstanding, in a short time after they were now met together, having shippes, money and souldiers enowe, both footemen and horsemen, to fight for the Empire of Rome. Now Cassius would have done Brutus as much honor, as Brutus did unto him: but Brutus most commonly prevented him, and went

[1] *In margin:* 'Brutus and Cassius doe joyne armies together.'

first unto him, both bicause he was the elder man,[1] as also for that he was sickly of bodye. And men reputed him commonly to be very skilfull in warres, but otherwise marvelous chollerick[2] and cruell, who sought to rule men by feare, rather then with lenitie: and on the other side he was too familiar with his friends, and would jest too brodely with them. But Brutus in contrary manner, for his vertue and valliantnes, was well-beloved of the people and his owne, esteemed of noble men, and hated of no man, not so much as of his enemies[3] : bicause he was a marvelous lowly and gentle person, noble minded, and would never be in any rage, nor caried away with pleasure and covetousnes, but had ever an upright mind with him, and would never yeeld to any wronge or injustice, the which was the chiefest cause of his fame, of his rising, and of the good will that every man bare him: for they were all perswaded that his intent was good.[4] For they did not certainly beleve, that if Pompey him selfe had overcome Cæsar, he would have resigned his authoritie to the law: but rather they were of opinion, that he would still keepe the soverainty and absolute government in his hands, taking onely, to please the people, the title of Consul or Dictator, or of some other more civill office. And as for Cassius, a hot, chollerick, and cruell man, that would oftentymes be caried away from justice for gayne[5]: it was certainly thought that he made warre, and put him selfe into sundry daungers, more to have absolute power and authoritie, then to defend the libertie of his contry. For, they that will also consider others, that were elder men then they, as Cinna, Marius, and Carbo: it is out of doubt that the ende and hope of their victorie, was to be Lordes of their contry: and in manner they did all confesse that they fought for the tyranny, and to be Lordes of the Empire of Rome. And in contrary manner, his enemies them selves did never reprove Brutus, for any such chaunge or desire. For, it was sayd that Antonius spake it openly divers tymes, that he thought, that of all them that had slayne Cæsar, there was none but Brutus only that was moved to doe it, as thinking the acte commendable of it selfe: but that all the other conspirators did conspire his death, for some private malice or envy, that they otherwise did beare unto him.[6] Hereby it appeareth, that Brutus did not trust so much to the power of his army, as he did to his owne vertue: as is to be seene by his writings. For approaching neare to the instant

[1] Cf. IV.3.30–6, 56.

[2] *In margin:* 'The sharpe and cruell condicions of Cassius.' IV.3.39–54.

[3] *In margin:* 'Brutus gentle and fayer condicions.'

[4] *In margin:* 'Brutus intent good, if he had overcomen.'

[5] Hence the quarrel in IV.3.

[6] *In margin:* 'Antonius testimonie of Brutus.' V.5.68–75.

daunger, he wrote unto Pomponious Atticus, that his affayres had the best happe that could be. For, sayd he, eyther I will set my contry at libertie by battell, or by honorable death rid me of this bondage.[1] And furthermore, that they being certeine and assured of all things els, this one thing onely was doubtfull to them: whether they should live or dye with libertie. He wrote also that Antonius had his due paiment for his folly. For where he might have bene a partner equally of the glory of Brutus, Cassius, and Cato, and have made one with them: he liked better to choose to be joyned with Octavius Cæsar alone: with whome, though now he be not overcome by us, yet shall he shortly after also have warre with him.[2] And truely he proved a true Prophet, for so came it in deede to passe. Now whilest Brutus and Cassius were together in the citie of Smyrna: Brutus prayed Cassius to let him have some part of his money whereof he had great store, bicause all that he could rappe and rend of his side, he had bestowed it in making so great a number of shippes, that by meanes of them they should keepe all the sea at their commaundement. Cassius friends hindered this request, and earnestly disswaded him from it: perswading him, that it was no reason that Brutus should have the money which Cassius had gotten together by sparing, and leavied with great evil will of the people their subjects,[3] for him to bestowe liberally uppon his souldiers, and by this meanes to winne their good willes, by Cassius charge. This notwithstanding, Cassius gave him the thirde parte of his totall summe. So Cassius and Brutus then departing from eche other, Cassius tooke the citie of Rhodes, where he too dishonestly and cruelly used him selfe[4]: although when he came into the citie, he aunswered some of the inhabitants, who called him Lord and king, that he was nether Lord nor king, but he onely that had slaine him, that would have bene Lord and king. Brutus departing from thence, sent unto the Lycians, to require money, and men of warre. But there was a certaine Orator called Naucrates, that made the cities to rebell against him, insomuch that the contry men of that contry kept the straights and litle mountaines, thinking by that meanes to stoppe Brutus passage. Wherefore Brutus sent his horsemen against them, who stale uppon them as they were at dinner, and slue six hundred of them: and taking all the small townes and villages, he did let all the prisoners he tooke, goe without payment of ransome, hoping by this his great curtesie to winne them, to drawe all the

[1] *In margin:* 'Brutus noble mind to his contry.'

[2] *In margin:* 'Brutus, a true Prophet of Antonius.'

[3] IV.3.69–84.

[4] *In margin:* 'Cassius wanne the citie of Rhodes.' Shakespeare omits this cruelty.

rest of the contry unto him.[1] But they were so fierce and obstinate, that they would mutyne for every small hurt they receyved as they passed by their contry, and did despise his curtesie and good nature: untill that at length he went to beseege the citie of the Xanthians, within the which were shut uppe the cruellest and most warrelikest men of Lycia. There was a ryver that ranne by the walls of the citie, in the which many men saved them selves, swymming betweene two waters, and fledde: howbeit they layed nettes overthwart the ryver, and tyed litle bells on the toppe of them, to sownd when any man was taken in the nettes. The Xanthians made a salye out by night, and came to fire certaine engynes of battery that bette downe their walls: but they were presently driven in agayne by the Romanes, so soone as they were discovered. The winde by chaunce was marvelous bygge, and increased the flame so sore, that it violently caried it into the cranewes of the wall of the citie, so that the next houses unto them were straight set a fire thereby.[2] Wherefore Brutus beeing affrayde that all the citie woulde take of a fire, he presently commaunded his men to quenche the fire, and to save the towne if it might be. But the Lycians at that instant fell into such a frensie, and straunge and horrible dispayre, that no man can well expresse it: and a man can not more rightly compare or lyken it, then to a franticke and moste desperate desire to dye.[3] For all of them together, with their wives and children, Maisters and servaunts, and of all sortes of age whatsoever, fought uppon the ramper of their walles, and did cast downe stones and fierworkes on the Romanes, which were very busie in quenching the flame of the fire, to save the citie. And in contrary manner also, they brought fagotts, drye wodde, and reedes, to bringe the fire further into the citie asmuch as might bee, increasing it by suche thinges as they brought. Nowe when the fire had gotten into all the partes of the citie, and that the flame burnt bright in every place: Brutus beeing sorye to see it, gotte uppon his horse, and rode rownde about the walles of the citie, to see if it were possible to save it, and helde uppe his handes to the inhabitants, praying them to pardon their citye, and to save them selves. Howbeit they woulde not be perswaded, but did all that they coulde possible to cast them selves away, not onely men and women, but also litle children. For some of them weeping and crying out, did cast them selves into the fire: others headlong throwing them selves downe from the walles, brake their neckes: others also made their neckes bare, to the naked swordes of their fathers, and undid their

[1] *In margin:* 'Brutus jests [gestes] in Lycia.'
[2] *In margin:* 'The citie of Xanthus set a fire.'
[3] *In margin:* 'The desperat ende of the Xanthians.'

clothes, praying them to kill them with their owne handes. After the citye was burnt, they founde a woman hanged uppe by the necke, holding one of her children in her hande deade by her, hanged uppe also: and in the other hande a burning torche setting fire on her house. Some woulde have had Brutus to have seene her, but he woulde not see so horrible and tragicall a sight: but when he heard it, he fell a weeping, and caused a Herauld to make proclamation by sownd of trompet, that he woulde give a certaine summe of money, to every souldier that coulde save a Xanthian. So there were not (as it is reported) above fiftye of them saved, and yet they were saved against their willes. Thus the Xanthians having ended the revolution of their fatall destinie, after a longe continuance of tyme: they did through their desperation, renue the memorie of the lamentable calamities of their Auncestors. Who in like manner, in the warres of the Persians, did burne their citie, and destroyed them selves. Therefore Brutus likewise beseeging the citie of the Patareians, perceyving that they stowtly resisted him: he was also affrayde of that, and could not well tell whether he should give assault to it, or not, least they woulde fall into the dispayre and desperation of the Xanthians. Howbeit having taken certaine of their women prisoners, he sent them backe agayne, without payment of ransome. Nowe they that were the wives and Daughters of the noblest men of the citie, reporting unto their parents, that they had founde Brutus a mercifull, juste, and curteous man: they perswaded them to yeelde them selves and their citie unto him, the which they did.[1] So after they had thus yeelded them selves, divers other cities also followed them, and did the like: and founde Brutus more mercifull and curteous, then they thought they should have done, but specially farre above Cassius. For Cassius, about the selfe same tyme, after he had compelled the Rhodians every man to deliver all the ready money they had in gold and silver in their houses, the which being brought together, amounted to the summe of eyght thowsande talents: yet he condemned the citie besides, to paye the summe of five hundred talents more,[2] Where Brutus in contrary manner, after he had leavyed of all the contrye of Lycia but a hundred and fiftye talents onely: he departed thence into the contrye of Ionia, and did them no more hurt.[3] Nowe Brutus in all this jorney, did many notable actes and worthy of memorie, bothe for rewarding, as also in punishing those that had deserved it. [Plutarch tells how Brutus punished Theodotus who caused the murder of Pompey.]

[1] *In margin:* 'The Patareians doe yeld them selves unto Brutus.'
[2] *In margin:* 'The extreme covetousnes and crueltie of Cassius to the Rhodians.'
[3] *In margin:* 'Brutus clemency unto the Lycians.'

About that tyme, Brutus sent to praye Cassius to come to the citye of Sardis, and so he did. Brutus, understanding of his comming, went to meete him with all his friendes.[1] There, both their armies being armed, they called them both Emperors. Nowe, as it commonly hapneth in great affayres betwene two persons, both of them having many friends, and so many Captaines under them: there ranne tales and complaints betwixt them. Therefore, before they fell in hand with any other matter, they went into a litle chamber together, and bad every man avoyde, and did shut the dores to them.[2] Then they beganne to powre out their complaints one to the other, and grew hot and lowde, earnestly accusing one another, and at length fell both a weeping.[3] Their friends that were without the chamber hearing them lowd within, and angry betwene them selves, they were both amased, and affrayd also lest it would grow to further matter: but yet they were commaunded, that no man should come to them. Notwithstanding, one Marcus Phaonius, that had bene a friend and follower of Cato while he lived,[4] and tooke upon him to counterfeate a Philosopher, not with wisedom and discretion, but with a certaine bedlem and frantick motion: he would needes come into the chamber, though the men offered to keepe him out. But it was no boote to let Phaonius, when a mad moode or toye tooke him in the head: for he was a hot hasty man, and sodaine in all his doings, and cared for never a Senator of them all. Now, though he used this bold manner of speeche after the profession of the Cynick Philosophers, (as who would say, doggs)[5] yet this boldnes did no hurt many times, bicause they did but laugh at him to see him so mad. This Phaonius at that time, in despite of the doorekeepers, came into the chamber, and with a certaine scoffing and mocking gesture which he counterfeated of purpose, he rehearsed the verses which old Nestor sayd in Homer:

> My Lords, I pray you harken both to mee,
> For I have seene moe yeares than suchye three.[6]

Cassius fel a laughing at him: but Brutus thrust him out of the chamber, and called him dogge, and counterfeate Cynick.[7] Howbeit his comming in brake their strife at that time, and so they left eche other. The selfe same night Cassius prepared his supper in his

[1] *In margin:* 'Brutus and Cassius doe meete at the citie of Sardis.' IV.2.
[2] Cf. IV.2.37ff.
[3] *In margin:* 'Brutus and Cassius complaints one unto the other.' IV.3.1–122.
[4] *In margin:* 'M. Phaonius a follower of Cato.' In IV.3.123–36 he is a poet.
[5] *In margin:* 'Cynick Philosophers [ac]counted doggs.'
[6] [Iliad, i.259] IV.3.129–31.
[7] IV.3.132–6.

chamber, and Brutus brought his friendes with him. So when they were set at supper, Phaonius came to sit downe after he had washed. Brutus tolde him alowd, no man sent for him, and bad them set him at the upper end: meaning in deede at the lower ende of the bed. Phaonius made no ceremonie, but thrust in amongest the middest of them, and made all the companye laugh at him: so they were merry all supper tyme, and full of their Philosophie. The next daye after,[1] Brutus, upon complaynt of the Sardians, did condemne and noted Lucius Pella for a defamed person, that had bene a Prætor of the Romanes, and whome Brutus had given charge unto: for that he was accused and convicted of robberie, and pilferie in his office. This judgement much misliked Cassius: bicause he him selfe had secretly (not many dayes before) warned two of his friends, attainted and convicted of the like offences, and openly had cleered them: but yet he did not therefore leave to employ them in any manner of service as he did before. And therefore he greatly reproved Brutus, for that he would shew him selfe so straight and seveare in such a tyme, as was meeter to beare a litle, then to take thinges at the worst. Brutus in contrary manner aunswered, that he shoulde remember the Ides of Marche, at which tyme they slue Julius Cæsar: who nether pilled nor polled the contrye, but onely was a favorer and suborner of all them that did robbe and spoyle, by his countenaunce and authoritie. And if there were any occasion whereby they might honestly sette aside justice and equitie: they should have had more reason to have suffered Cæsars friendes, to have robbed and done what wronge and injurie they had would, then to beare with their owne men. For then sayde he, they could but have sayde they had bene cowards: and nowe they may accuse us of injustice, beside the paynes we take, and the daunger we put our selves into. And thus may we see what Brutus intent and purpose was.[2] But as they both prepared to passe over againe, out of Asia into Europe: there went a rumor that there appeared a wonderfull signe unto him. Brutus was a carefull man, and slept very litle, both for that his dyet was moderate, as also bicause he was continually occupied. He never slept in the day tyme, and in the night no lenger, then the tyme he was driven to be alone, and when every bodye els tooke their rest.[3] But nowe whilest he was in warre, and his heade ever busily occupied to thinke of his affayres, and what would happen: after he had slumbered a litle after supper, he spent all the rest of the night in dispatching of his waightiest causes, and

[1] Previously, in IV.3.1–8.

[2] *In margin:* 'The wonderfull constancy of Brutus, in matters of justice and equitie.' IV.3.18–28.

[3] *In margin:* 'Brutus care and watching.' Cf. IV.3.237–60.

after he had taken order for them, if he had any leysure left him, he would read some booke till the third watche of the night, at what tyme the Captaines, petty Captaines and Colonells, did use to come unto him.[1] So, being ready to goe into Europe, one night very late (when all the campe tooke quiet rest) as he was in his tent with a litle light, thinking of waighty matters: he thought he heard one come in to him, and casting his eye towards the doore of his tent, that he saw a wonderfull straunge and monstruous shape of a body comming towards him, and sayd never a word. So Brutus boldly asked what he was, a god, or a man, and what cause brought him thither. The spirit aunswered him, I am thy evill spirit, Brutus: and thou shalt see me by the citie of Philippes.[2] Brutus beeing no otherwise affrayd, replyed againe unto it: Well, then I shall see thee agayne. The spirit presently vanished away: and Brutus called his men unto him, who tolde him that they heard no noyse, nor sawe any thinge at all.[3] Thereuppon Brutus returned agayne to thinke on his matters as he did before: and when the daye brake, he went unto Cassius, to tell him what vision had appeared unto him in the night. Cassius beeing in opinion an Epicurian, and reasoning thereon with Brutus, spake to him touching the vision thus. In our secte, Brutus, we have an opinion, that we doe not alwayes feele, or see, that which we suppose we doe both see and feele: but that our senses beeing credulous, and therefore easily abused (when they are idle and unoccupied in their owne objects) are induced to imagine they see and conjecture that, which they in truth doe not.[4] For, our minde is quicke and cunning to worke (without eyther cause or matter) any thinge in the imagination whatsoever. And therefore the imagination is resembled to claye, and the minde to the potter: who without any other cause than his fancie and pleasure, chaungeth it into what facion and forme he will. And this doth the diversitie of our dreames shewe unto us.[5] For our imagination doth uppon a small fancie growe from conceit to conceit, altering both in passions and formes of thinges imagined. For the minde of man is ever occupied, and that continuall moving is nothing but an imagination. But yet there is a further cause of this in you. For you being by nature given to melancholick discoursing, and of late continually occupied: your wittes and sences having bene overlabored, doe easilier yeelde to such imaginations. For, to say that there are spirits or angells, and

[1] Hence IV.3.240–5.

[2] *In margin:* 'A spirit appeared unto Brutus in the citie of Sardis.' IV.3.274–83.

[3] IV.3.284–302.

[4] *In margin:* 'Cassius opinion of spirits, after the Epicurians sect.' Cf. Horatio in *Hamlet*.

[5] *In margin:* 'The cause of dreames.'

if there were, that they had the shape of men, or such voyces, or any power at all to come unto us: it is a mockerye. And for myne owne parte, I would there were suche, bicaûse that we shoulde not onely have souldiers, horses, and shippes, but also the ayde of the goddes, to guide and further our honest and honorable attempts. With these words Cassius did somewhat comfort and quiet Brutus. When they raysed their campe, there came two Eagles that flying with a marvelous force, lighted uppon two of the foremoste enseignes,[1] and alwayes followed the souldiers, which gave them meate, and fedde them, untill they came neare to the citie of Philippes: and there one daye onely before the battell, they bothe flewe awaye. Now Brutus had conquered the moste parte of all the people, and nations of that contry: but if there were any other citie or Captaine to overcome, then they made all cleere before them, and so drewe towards the coasts of Thassos. There Norbanus lying in campe in a certaine place called the straights, by another place called Symbolon: (which is a port of the sea) Cassius and Brutus compassed him in in such sort, that he was driven to forsake the place which was of great strength for him, and he was also in daunger beside to have lost all his armye. For, Octavius Cæsar could not followe him bicause of his sicknes, and therefore stayed behind: whereuppon they had taken his army, had not Antonius ayde bene, which made such wonderful speede, that Brutus could scant beleve it. So Cæsar came not thether of ten daies after: and Antonius camped against Cassius, and Brutus on thother side against Cæsar.[2] The Romanes called the valley betweene both campes, the Philippian fields: and there were never seene two so great armies of the Romanes, one before the other, ready to fight. In truth, Brutus army was inferior to Octavius Cæsars, in number of men: but for bravery and rich furniture, Brutus army farre excelled Cæsars.[3] For the most part of their armors were silver and gilt, which Brutus had bountifully given them: although in all other things he taught his Captaines to live in order without excesse. But for the bravery of armor, and weapon, which souldiers should cary in their hands, or otherwise weare upon their backes: he thought that it was an encoragement unto them that by nature are greedy of honor, and that it maketh them also fight like devills that love to get, and be affrayd to lose: bicause they fight to keepe their armor and weapon, as also

[1] *In margin:* 'A wonderfull signe by two Eagles.' V.1.77–92.

[2] *In margin:* 'Brutus and Cassius camps before the citie of Philippes: against Octavius Cæsar, and Antonius.'

[3] *In margin:* 'Brutus souldiers bravely armed.'

their goods and lands.[1] Now when they came to muster their armies, Octavius Cæsar tooke the muster of his army within the trenches of his campe, and gave his men onely a little corne, and five silver Drachmas to every man to sacrifice to the gods, and to pray for victory. But Brutus skorning this miserie and niggardlines, first of all mustered his armie, and did purifie it in the fields, according to the manner of the Romanes: and then he gave unto every band a number of wethers to sacrifice, and fiftie silver Drachmas to every souldier. So that Brutus and Cassius souldiers were better pleased, and more coragiously bent to fight at the daye of the battell, then their enemies souldiers were. Notwithstanding, being busily occupied about the ceremonies of this purification, it is reported that there chaunced certaine unlucky signes unto Cassius.[2] For one of his Sergeaunts that caried the roddes before him, brought him the garland of flowers turned backwards, the which he should have worne on his head in the tyme of sacrificing. Moreover it is reported also, that at another tyme before, in certaine sportes and triumphe where they caried an image of Cassius victorie of cleane gold, it fell by chaunce, the man stumbling that caried it. And yet further, there were seene a marvelous number of fowles of praye, that feede upon dead carkasses[3]: and beehives also were founde, where bees were gathered together in a certaine place within the trenches of the campe: the which place the Soothsayers thought good to shut out of the precinct of the campe, for to take away the superstitious feare and mistrust men would have of it. The which beganne somewhat to alter Cassius minde from Epicurus opinions,[4] and had put the souldiers also in a marvelous feare. Thereuppon Cassius was of opinion not to trye this warre at one battell, but rather to delay tyme, and to drawe it out in length, considering that they were the stronger in money, and the weaker in men and armors.[5] But Brutus in contrary manner, did alway before, and at that tyme also, desire nothing more, then to put all to the hazard of battell, assoone as might be possible: to the ende he might either quickely restore his contry to her former libertie, or rid him forthwith of this miserable world, being still troubled in following and mainteyning of such great armies together. But perceiving that in the dayly skirmishes and byckerings they made, his men were alway the stronger, and ever had the better: that yet quickned his spirits againe, and did put him in better hart. And furthermore, bicause that some of their

[1] *In margin:* 'Brutus opinion for the bravery of souldiers, in their armor and weapons.'

[2] *In margin:* 'Unlucky signes unto Cassius.'

[3] V.1.85–9.

[4] V.1.77–9.

[5] *In margin:* 'Cassius and Brutus opinions about battell.'

owne men had already yelded them selves to their enemies, and that it was suspected moreover divers others would doe the like: that made many of Cassius friendes, which were of his minde before, (when it came to be debated in counsell whether the battell shoulde be fought or not) that they were then of Brutus minde. But yet was therc one of Brutus friendes called Atellius, that was against it, and was of opinion that they should tary the next winter.[1] Brutus asked him what he should get by tarying a yeare lenger? If I get nought els, quoth Attellius agayne, yet have I lived so much lenger. Cassius was very angry with this aunswer: and Atellius was maliced and esteemed the worse for it of all men. Thereuppon it was presently determined they should fight battell the next daye. So Brutus all supper tyme looked with a cheerefull countenaunce, like a man that had good hope, and talked very wisely of Philosophie, and after supper went to bed. But touching Cassius, Messala reporteth that he supped by him selfe in his tent with a fewe of his friendes, and that all supper tyme he looked very sadly, and was full of thoughts, although it was against his nature: and that after supper he tooke him by the hande, and holding him fast (in token of kindnes as his manner was) tolde him in Greeke: Messala, I protest unto thee, and make thee my witnes, that I am compelled against my minde and will (as Pompey the great was) to jeopard the libertie of our contry, to the hazard of a battel. And yet we must be lively, and of good corage, considering our good fortune, whome we shoulde wronge too muche to mistrust her, although we followe evill counsell.[2] Messala writeth, that Cassius having spoken these last wordes unto him, he bad him farewell, and willed him to come to supper to him the next night following, bicause it was his birth day. The next morning by breake of day, the signall of battell was set out in Brutus and Cassius campe, which was an arming scarlet coate: and both the Chiefetaines spake together in the middest of their armies.[3] There Cassius beganne to speake first, and sayd: The gods graunt us, O Brutus, that this day we may winne the field, and ever after to live all the rest of our life quietly, one with another.[4] But sith the gods have so ordeyned it, that the greatest and chiefest things amongest men are most uncertaine, and that if the battell fall out otherwise to daye then we wishe or looke for, we shall hardely meete againe: what art thou then determined to doe, to flye, or dye?[5] Brutus aunswered him, being yet but a young man,

[1] *In margin:* 'Atellius opinion for the battell.'

[2] *In margin:* 'Cassius words unto Messala, the night before the battell.'

[3] *In margin:* 'Brutus and Cassius talke before the battell.'

[4] V.I.93–100.

[5] *In margin:* 'Brutus aunswer to Cassius.'

and not overgreatly experienced in the world: I trust, (I know not how) a certaine rule of Philosophie, by the which I did greatly blame and reprove Cato for killing of him selfe, as being no lawfull nor godly acte, touching the gods, not concerning men, valliant, not to give place and yeld to divine providence, and not constantly and paciently to take whatsoever it pleaseth him to send us, but to drawe backe, and flie: but being nowe in the middest of the daunger, I am of a contrary mind. For if it be not the will of God, that this battell fall out fortunate for us: I will looke no more for hope, neither seeke to make any new supply for warre againe, but will rid me of this miserable world, and content me with my fortune.[1] For, I gave up my life for my contry in the Ides of Marche, for the which I shall live in another more glorious worlde.[2] Cassius fell a laughing to heare what he sayde, and imbracing him, Come on then sayde he, let us goe and charge our enemies with this mynde. For eyther we shall conquer, or we shall not neede to feare the Conquerors. After this talke, they fell to consultacion amonge their friendes for the ordering of the battell. Then Brutus prayed Cassius he might have the leading of the right winge, the which men thought was farre meeter for Cassius: both bicause he was the elder man, and also for that he had the better experience.[3] But yet Cassius gave it him, and willed that Messala (who had charge of one of the warrelikest legions they had) shoulde be also in that winge with Brutus. So Brutus presently sent out his horsemen, who were excellently well appoynted, and his footemen also were as willing and readye to give charge.[4] Nowe Antonius men did cast a trenche from the marishe by the which they laye, to cutte of Cassius way to come to the sea: and Cæsar, at the least his armye, styrred not. As for Octavius Cæsar him selfe, he was not in his campe, bicause he was sicke.[5] And for his people, they litle thought the enemies would have given them battell, but onely have made some light skirmishes to hinder them that wrought in the trenche, and with their darts and slings to have kept them from finishing of their worke: but they taking no heede to them that came full upon them to give them battell, marvelled much at the great noyse they heard, that came from the place where they were casting their trenche. In the meane tyme Brutus that led the right winge, sent litle billes to the Colonells and Captaines of private bandes, in the which he wrote the worde of the battell[6]: and he him selfe riding a horse backe by all the

[1] V.1.100–8.
[2] Cf. V.1.113–15.
[3] Cf. Antony and Octavius, V.1.16–20.
[4] *In margin:* 'The battell at Philippes, against Octavius Cæsar, and Antonius.'
[5] Octavius is present in V.1.
[6] V.2.1–2.

trowpes, did speake to them, and incoraged them to sticke to it like men. So by this meanes very fewe of them understoode what was the worde of the battell, and besides, the moste parte of them never taryed to have it tolde them, but ranne with greate furie to assayle the enemies: whereby through this disorder, the legions were marvelously scattered and dispersed one from the other. For first of all, Messalaes legion, and then the next unto them, went beyond the left winge of the enemies, and did nothing, but glawnsing by them, overthrewe some as they went, and so going on further, fell right upon Cæsars campe, out of the which (as him selfe writeth in his *Commentaries*) he had bene conveyed away a litle before, thorough the counsell and advise of one of his friendes called Marcus Artorius: who dreaming in the night, had a vision appeared unto him, that commaunded Octavius Cæsar should be caried out of his campe. Insomuch as it was thought he was slayne, bicause his lytter (which had nothing in it) was thrust through and through with pykes and darts. There was great slaughter in this campe. For amongest others, there were slayne two thowsand Lacedæmonians, who were arrived but even a litle before, comming to ayde Cæsar. The other also that had not glaunsed by, but had given a charge full upon Cæsars battell: they easily made them flie, bicause they were greatly troubled for the losse of their campe, and of them there were slayne by hand, three legions. Then being very earnest to followe the chase of them that fled, they ranne in amongest them hand over head into their campe, and Brutus among them. But that which the conquerors thought not of, occasion shewed it unto them that were overcome: and that was, the left wing of their enemies left naked, and ungarded of them of the right wing, who were strayed too far of, in following of them that were overthrowen. So they gave a hot charge upon them. But notwithstanding all the force they made, they coulde not breake into the middest of their battell, where they founde men that received them, and valliantlie made head against them. Howbeit they brake and overthrewe the left wing where Cassius was, by reason of the great disorder among them, and also bicause they had no intelligence how the right wing had sped. So they chased them beating them into their campe, the which they spoyled,[1] none of both the Chieftaines being present there. For Antonius, as it is reported, to flie the furie of the first charge, was gotten into the next marish: and no man coulde tell what became of Octavius Cæsar, after he was caried out of his campe. Insomuche that there were certaine souldiers that shewed their swords bloodied, and sayd that they had slaine him, and did describe his face, and

[1] V.3.1–8.

shewed what age he was of.[1] Furthermore the voward, and the middest of Brutus battell, had alreadie put all their enemies to flight that withstoode them, with great slaughter: so that Brutus had conquered all of his side, and Cassius had lost all on the other side.[2] For nothing undid them, but that Brutus went not to helpe Cassius, thinking he had overcome them, as him selfe had done: and Cassius on the other side taried not for Brutus, thinking he had bene overthrowen, as him selfe was. And to prove that the victorie fell on Brutus side, Messala confirmeth it: that they wanne three Eagles, and divers other ensignes of their enemies, and their enemies wanne never a one of theirs. Now Brutus returning from the chase, after he had slaine and sacked Cæsars men: he wondred muche that he coulde not see Cassius tent standing up high as it was wont, neither the other tentes of his campe standing as they were before, bicause all the whole campe had bene spoiled, and the tentes throwen downe, at the first comming in of the enemies. But they that were about Brutus, whose sight served them better, tolde him that they sawe a great glistering of harnes, and a number of silvered targets, that went and came into Cassius campe, and were not (as they tooke it) the armors, nor the number of men that they had left there to gard the campe: and yet that they saw not such a number of dead bodies, and great overthrow, as there should have bene, if so many legions had bene slaine. This made Brutus at the first mistrust that which had hapned. So he appointed a number of men to keepe the campe of his enemie which he had taken, and caused his men to be sent for that yet followed the chase, and gathered them together, thinking to leade them to aide Cassius, who was in this state as you shall heare.[3] First of all he was marvelous angrie, to see how Brutus men ranne to geve charge upon their enemies, and taried not for the word of the battell, nor commaundement to geve charge: and it grieved him beside, that after he had overcome them, his men fell straight to spoyle, and were not carefull to compasse in the rest of the enemies behinde. But with tarying too long also, more then through the valliantnesse or foresight of the Captaines his enemies: Cassius founde him selfe compassed in with the right wing of his enemies armie.[4] Whereuppon his horsemen brake immediatly, and fled for life towardes the sea. Furthermore, perceiving his footemen to geve ground, he did what he could to kepe

[1] *In margin:* 'Octavius Cæsar falsely reported to be slaine at the battell of Philippes.'

[2] *In margin:* 'Cassius misfortune.'

[3] *In margin:* 'Cassius offended with the sundrie errors Brutus and his men committed in battell.' V.3.5–7.

[4] V.3.8.

them from flying, and tooke an ensigne from one of the ensigne bearers that fled, and stucke it fast at his feete[1]: although with much a do he could scant keepe his owne gard together. So Cassius him selfe was at length compelled to flie, with a few about him, unto a litle hill, from whence they might easely see what was done in all the plaine: howebeit Cassius him selfe sawe nothing, for his sight was verie bad,[2] saving that he saw (and yet with much a doe) how the enemies spoiled his campe before his eyes.[3] He sawe also a great troupe of horsemen, whom Brutus sent to aide him, and thought that they were his enemies that followed him: but yet he sent Titinnius, one of them that was with him, to goe and know what they were. Brutus horsemen sawe him comming a farre of, whom when they knewe that he was one of Cassius chiefest frendes, they showted out for joy: and they that were familiarly acquainted with him, lighted from their horses, and went and imbraced him. The rest compassed him in rounde about a horsebacke, with songs of victorie and great rushing of their harnes, so that they made all the field ring againe for joy. But this marred all.[4] For Cassius thinking in deede that Titinnius was taken of the enemies, he then spake these wordes: Desiring too much to live, I have lived to see one of my best frendes taken, for my sake, before my face. After that, he gotte into a tent where no bodie was, and tooke Pyndarus with him, one of his freed bondmen, whom he reserved ever for suche a pinche, since the cursed battell of the Parthians, where Crassus was slaine, though he notwithstanding scaped from that overthrow[5]: but then casting his cloke over his head, and holding out his bare neck unto Pindarus, he gave him his head to be striken of. So the head was found severed from the bodie: but after that time Pindarus was never seene more.[6] Whereupon, some tooke occasion to say, that he had slaine his master without his commaundement. By and by they knew the horsemen that came towards them, and might see Titinnius crowned with a garland of triumphe, who came before with great speede unto Cassius. But when he perceived by the cries and teares of his frends which tormented them selves, the misfortune that had chaunced to his Captaine Cassius, by mistaking: he drew out his sword, cursing him selfe a thowsand times that he had taried so long, and so slue him selfe presentlie in the fielde.[7] Brutus in the meane time came forward still, and understoode also

[1] *In margin:* 'Cassius valliantnes in warres.' V.3.1–4.

[2] V.3.21.

[3] V.3.12–13.

[4] *In margin:* 'The importance of error and mistaking in warres.' V.3.14–35.

[5] *In margin:* 'Cassius slaine by his man Pindarus.' V.3.36–46.

[6] V.3.49–50.

[7] *In margin:* 'The death of Titinnius.' V.3.51–90.

that Cassius had bene overthrowen: but he knew nothing of his death, till he came verie neere to his campe. So when he was come thither, after he had lamented the death of Cassius, calling him the last of all the Romanes, being unpossible that Rome should ever breede againe so noble and valliant a man as he: he caused his bodie to be buried, and sent it to the citie of Thassos,[1] fearing least his funerals within the campe should cause great disorder. Then he called his souldiers together, and did encorage them againe. And when he saw that they had lost all their cariage, which they could not brooke well: he promised everie man of them two thowsand Drachmas in recompence. After his souldiers had heard his Oration, they were al of them pretily cheered againe, wondering much at his great liberalitie, and waited upon him with great cries when he went his way, praising him, for that he only of the foure Chieftaines, was not overcome in battell. And to speake the trueth, his deedes shewed that he hoped not in vaine to be conqueror. For with fewe legions, he had slaine and driven all them away, that made head against him: and yet if all his people had fought, and that the most of them had not outgone their enemies to runne to spoyle their goods: surely it was like enough he had slaine them all, and had left never a man of them alive.[2] There were slaine of Brutus side, about eight thowsand men, counting the souldiers slaves, whom Brutus called Brigas: and of the enemies side, as Messala wryteth, there were slaine as he supposeth, more then twise as many moe. Wherefore they were more discoraged then Brutus, untill that verie late at night, there was one of Cassius men called Demetrius, who went unto Antonius, and caried his maisters clothes, whereof he was stripped not long before, and his sword also. This encoraged Brutus enemies, and made them so brave, that the next morning betimes they stoode in battell ray againe before Brutus. But on Brutus side, both his campes stoode wavering, and that in great daunger. For his owne campe being full of prisoners, required a good garde to looke unto them: and Cassius campe on the other side tooke the death of their Captaine verie heavilie, and beside, there was some vile grudge betwene them that were overcomen, and those that did overcome. For this cause therefore Brutus did set them in battell ray, but yet kept him selfe from geving battell. Now for the slaves that were prisoners, which were a great number of them, and went and came to and fro amongst the armed men, not without suspicion: he commaunded they shoulde kill them. But for the freemen, he sent them freely home, and said, that they were better prisoners

[1] V.3.104.

[2] *In margin:* 'The number of men slaine, at the battel of Philippes.'

with his enemies, then with him. For with him, they were slaves and servauntes: and with him, they were free men, and citizens. So when he saw that divers Captaines and his frendes did so cruelly hate some, that they would by no meanes save their lives: Brutus him selfe hid them, and secretlie sent them away.[1] Among these prisoners, there was one Volumnius a jeaster, and Sacculio a common player, of whom Brutus made no accompt at all. Howbeit his frends brought them unto him, and did accuse them, that though they were prisoners, they did not let to laugh them to scorne, and to jeast broadly with them. Brutus made no aunswere to it, bicause his heade was occupied otherwayes. Whereupon, Messala Corvinus sayd: that it were good to whippe them on a skaffold, and then to sende them naked, well whipped, unto the Captaines of their enemies, to shewe them their shame, to keepe suche mates as those in their campe, to play the fooles, to make them sport. Some that stoode by, laughed at his devise. But Publius Casca, that gave Julius Cæsar the first wounde when he was slaine, sayd then: It doth not become us to be thus merie at Cassius funeralls: and for thee, Brutus, thou shalt showe what estimacion thou madest of suche a Captaine thy compere, by putting to death, or saving the lives of these bloodes, who hereafter will mocke him, and defame his memorie. Brutus aunswered againe in choller: Why then doe you come to tell me of it, Casca, and doe not your selves what you thinke good? When they hearde him say so, they tooke his aunswere for a consent against these poore unfortunate men, to suffer them to doe what they thought good: and therefore they caried them away, and slue them. Afterwards Brutus performed the promise he had made to the souldiers, and gave them the two thowsand Drachmas a peece, but yet he first reproved them, bicause they went and gave charge upon the enemies at the first battell, before they had the word of battell geven them: and made them a new promise also, that if in the second battell they fought like men, he would geve them the sacke and spoyle of two cities, to wit, Thessalonica, and Lacedæmon. In all Brutus life there is but this only fault to be found, and that is not to be gainesaid[2]: though Antonius and Octavius Cæsar did reward their souldiers farre worse for their victory. For when they had driven all the naturall Italians out of Italie, they gave their souldiers their landes and townes, to the which they had no right: and moreover, the only marke they shot at in all this warre they made, was but to overcome, and raigne. Where in contrarie

[1] *In margin:* 'Brutus clemency and curtesie.'

[2] *In margin:* 'Brutus fault wisely excused by Plutarke.' And ignored by Shakespeare.

manner they had so great an opinion of Brutus vertue, that the common voyce and opinion of the world would not suffer him, neither to overcome, nor to save him selfe, otherwise then justlie and honestly, and speciallie after Cassius death: whome men burdened, that oftentimes he moved Brutus to great crueltie. But nowe, like as the mariners on the sea after the rudder of their shippe is broken by tempest, do seeke to naile on some other peece of wodde in liew thereof, and doe helpe them selves to keepe them from hurt, as much as may be upon that instant daunger: even so Brutus, having such a great armie to governe, and his affaires standing verie tickle, and having no other Captaine coequall with him in dignitie and authoritie: he was forced to imploy them he had, and likewise to be ruled by them in many things, and was of mind him selfe also to graunt them any thing, that he thought might make them serve like noble souldiers at time of neede. For Cassius souldiers were verie evill to be ruled, and did shewe them selves verie stubborne and lustie in the campe, bicause they had no Chieftaine that did commaund them: but yet rancke cowards to their enemies, bicause they had once overcome them. On the other side Octavius Cæsar, and Antonius, were not in much better state: for first of all, they lacked vittells. And bicause they were lodged in low places, they looked to abide a hard and sharpe winter, being camped as they were by the marish side, and also for that after the battell there had fallen plentie of raine about the autumne, where through, all their tents were full of myre and durt, the which by reason of the colde did freeze incontinentlie. But beside all these discommodities, there came newes unto them of the great losse they had of their men by sea. For Brutus shippes met with a great aide and supplie of men, which were sent them out of Italie, and they overthrewe them in suche sorte, that there scaped but few of them[1]: and yet they were so famished, that they were compelled to eate the tackle and sailes of their shippes.[2] Thereuppon they were verie desirous to fight a battell againe, before Brutus should have intelligence of this good newes for him: for it chaunced so, that the battell was fought by sea, on the selfe same day it was fought by lande. But by ill fortune, rather then through the malice or negligence of the Captaines, this victory came not to Brutus eare, till twentie dayes after.[3] For had he knowen of it before, he would not have bene brought to have fought a second battell, considering that he had excellent good provision for his armie for a long time, and besides, lay in a place of

[1] *In margin:* 'Brutus victorie by sea.'

[2] *In margin:* 'Wonderfull famine among Cæsars souldiers by sea.'

[3] *In margin:* 'The ignorance of Brutus victorie by sea, was his utter destruction.'

great strength, so as his campe could not be greatly hurt by the winter, nor also distressed by his enemies: and further, he had bene a quiet Lord, being a conqueror by sea, as he was also by land. This would have marvelously encoraged him. Howbeit the state of Rome (in my opinion) being now brought to that passe, that it could no more abide to be governed by many Lordes, but required one only absolute Governor: God, to prevent Brutus that it should not come to his government, kept this victorie from his knowledge, though in deede it came but a litle too late. For the day before the last battell was geven, verie late in the night, came Clodius, one of his enemies into his campe, who told that Cæsar hearing of the overthrow of his armie by sea, desired nothing more then to fight a battell before Brutus understoode it. Howebeit they gave no credit to his words, but despised him so muche, that they would not vouchsafe to bring him unto Brutus, bicause they thought it was but a lye devised, to be the better welcome for this good newes. The selfe same night, it is reported that the monstrous spirit which had appeared before unto Brutus in the citie of Sardis, did now appeare againe unto him in the selfe same shape and forme,[1] and so vanished away, and sayd never a word. Now Publius Volumnius, a grave and wise Philosopher, that had bene with Brutus from the beginning of this warre, he doth make mencion of this spirite, but sayth: that the greatest Eagle and ensigne was covered over with a swarme of bees, and that there was one of the Captaines,[2] whose arme sodainly fell a sweating, that it dropped oyle of roses from him, and that they oftentimes went about to drie him, but all would doe no good. And that before the battell was fought, there were two Eagles fought betwene both armies, and all the time they fought, there was a marvelous great silence all the valley over, both the armies being one before the other, marking this fight betwene them: and that in the end, the Eagle towardes Brutus gave over, and flew away. But this is certaine, and a true tale: that when the gate of the campe was open, the first man the standerd bearer met that caried the Eagle, was an Æthiopian, whome the souldiers for ill lucke mangled with their swordes. Now, after that Brutus had brought his armie into the fielde, and had set them in battell ray, directlie against the voward of his enemie[3]: he pawsed a long time, before he gave the signall of battell. For Brutus riding up and downe to view the bands and companies: it came in his head to mistrust some of them, besides, that some came to tell him so muche as he

[1] *In margin:* The evill spirit appeared againe unto Brutus.' V.5.17–19.
[2] *In margin:* 'Straunge sightes before Brutus second battell.'
[3] *In margin:* 'Brutus second battell.'

thought. Moreover, he sawe his horsemen set forward but faintly, and did not goe lustely to geve charge: but still stayed, to see what the footemen woulde doe. Then sodainly, one of the chiefest Knightes he had in all his armie called Camulatius, and that was alway marvelously esteemed of for his valliantnes, untill that time: he came hard by Brutus a horsebacke, and roade before his face to yeeld him selfe unto his enemies. Brutus was marvelous sorie for it, wherefore partely for anger, and partely for feare of greater treason and rebellion, he sodainly caused his armie to marche, being past three of the clocke in the after noone.[1] So in that place where he him selfe fought in person, he had the better: and brake into the left wing of his enemies, which gave him way, through the helpe of his horsemen that gave charge with his footemen, when they saw the enemies in a maze, and affrayed. Howbeit the other also on the right wing, when the Captaines would have had them to have marched: they were affraid to have bene compassed in behinde, bicause they were fewer in number then their enemies, and therefore did spred them selves, and leave the middest of their battell. Wherby they having weakened them selves, they could not withstande the force of their enemies, but turned taile straight, and fled. And those that had put them to flight, came in straight upon it to compasse Brutus behinde, who in the middest of the conflict, did all that was possible for a skilfull Captaine and valliant souldier: both for his wisedom, as also for his hardinesse, for the obtaining of victorie.[2] But that which wanne him the victorie at the first battell, did now lose it him at the seconde. For at the first time, the enemies that were broken and fled, were straight cut in peeces: but at the seconde battell, of Cassius men that were put to flight, there were fewe slaine: and they that saved them selves by speede, being affrayed bicause they had bene overcome, did discourage the rest of the armie when they came to joyne with them, and filled all the army with feare and disorder. There was the sonne of M. Cato slaine, valliantly fighting amongst the lustie youths.[3] For, notwithstanding that he was verie wearie, and overharried, yet would he not therefore flie, but manfully fighting and laying about him, telling alowde his name, and also his fathers name, at length he was beaten downe amongest many other dead bodies of his enemies, which he had slaine rounde about him. So there were slaine in the field, all the chiefest gentlemen and nobilitie that were in his armie: who valliantlie ranne into any daunger, to save Brutus life. Amongest

[1] V.3.109.

[2] *In margin:* 'Brutus valliantnes and great skilll in warres.'

[3] *In margin:* 'The death of the valliant young man Cato, the sonne of Marcus Cato.' V.3.107: V.4.2–9.

them there was one of Brutus frendes called Lucilius,[1] who seeing a troupe of barbarous men making no reckoning of all men else they met in their way, but going all together right against Brutus, he determined to stay them with the hazard of his life, and being left behinde, told them that he was Brutus: and bicause they should beleve him, he prayed them to bring him to Antonius, for he sayd he was affrayed of Cæsar, and that he did trust Antonius better. These barbarous men being very glad of this good happe, and thinking them selves happie men: they caried him in the night, and sent some before unto Antonius, to tell him of their comming. He was marvelous glad of it, and went out to meete them that brought him. Others also understanding of it, that they had brought Brutus prisoner: they came out of all parts of the campe to see him, some pitying his hard fortune, and others saying, that it was not done like him selfe so cowardlie to be taken alive of the barbarous people, for feare of death. When they came neere together, Antonius stayed a while, bethinking him selfe how he should use Brutus. In the meane time Lucilius was brought to him, who stowtly with a bold countenaunce sayd: Antonius, I dare assure thee, that no enemie hath taken, nor shall take Marcus Brutus alive: and I beseech God keepe him from that fortune. For wheresoever he be found, alive or dead: he will be found like him selfe. And nowe for my selfe, I am come unto thee, having deceived these men of armes here, bearing them downe that I was Brutus: and doe not refuse to suffer any torment thou wilt put me to. Lucilius wordes made them all amazed that heard him. Antonius on the other side, looking upon all them that had brought him, sayd unto them: My companions, I thinke ye are sorie you have failed of your purpose, and that you thinke this man hath done you great wrong: but I doe assure you, you have taken a better bootie, then that you followed. For, in steade of an enemie, you have brought me a frend: and for my parte, if you had brought me Brutus alive, truely I can not tell what I should have done to him. For, I had rather have suche men my frendes, as this man here, then enemies. Then he embraced Lucilius, and at that time delivered him to one of his frendes in custodie, and Lucilius ever after served him faithfullie, even to his death. Nowe Brutus having passed a litle river[2], walled in on either side with hie rockes, and shadowed with great trees, being then darke night, he went no further, but stayed at the foote of a rocke with certaine of his Captaines and frends that followed him[3]: and looking

[1] *In margin:* 'The fidelitie of Lucilius unto Brutus.' V.4.9–29.
[2] *In margin:* 'Brutus flying.'
[3] V.5.1.

up to the firmament that was full of starres, sighing, he rehearsed two verses, of the which Volumnius wrote the one, to this effect:

> Let not the wight from whom this mischiefe went
> (O Love) escape without dew punishment.[1]

And sayth that he had forgotten the other. Within a litle while after, naming his frendes that he had seene slaine in battell before his eyes, he fetched a greater sigh then before: specially, when he came to name Labio, and Flavius,[2] of the which the one was his Lieutenant, and the other, Captaine of the pioners of his campe. In the meane time, one of the companie being a thirst, and seeing Brutus a thirst also: he ranne to the river for water, and brought it in his sallet. At the selfe same time they heard a noyse on the other side of the river. Whereupon Volumnius tooke Dardanus, Brutus servaunt with him, to see what it was: and returning straight againe, asked if there were any water left. Brutus smiling, gentlie tolde them all was dronke, but they shall bring you some more. Thereuppon he sent him againe that went for water before, who was in great daunger of being taken by the enemies, and hardly scaped, being sore hurt. Furthermore, Brutus thought that there was no great number of men slaine in battell, and to know the trueth of it, there was one called Statilius, that promised to goe through his enemies (for otherwise it was impossible to goe see their campe) and from thence if all were well, that he woulde lift up a torche light in the ayer, and then returne againe with speede to him. The torche light was lift up as he had promised, for Statilius went thither. Nowe Brutus seeing Statilius tarie long after that, and that he came not againe, he sayd: If Statilius be alive, he will come againe. But his evill fortune was suche, that as he came backe, he lighted in his enemies hands, and was slaine.[3] Now, the night being farre spent, Brutus as he sate bowed towards Clitus one of his men, and told him somewhat in his eare, the other aunswered him not, but fell a weeping.[4] Thereupon he proved Dardanus, and sayd somwhat also to him[5]: at length he came to Volumnius him selfe, and speaking to him in Græke, prayed him for the studies sake which brought them acquainted together, that he woulde helpe him to put his hande to his sword, to thrust it in him to kill him. Volumnius denied his request,[6] and so did many others: and amongest the rest, one of them sayd, there was no tarying for them there. but that they must needes flie.[7] Then Brutus rising up,[8] We must flie in deede sayd he,

[1] *In margin:* 'Appian meaneth this by Antonius.' [2] Cf. V.3.108.
[3] *In margin:* 'The death of Statilius.' V.5.2–3. [4] V.5.4–7.
[5] V.5.8.14. [6] V.5.15–29. [7] V.5.30.
[8] *In margin:* 'Brutus saying of flying with hands, and not with feete.'

but it must be with our hands, not with our feete. Then taking every man by the hand, he sayd these words unto them with a cheerefull countenance: It rejoyceth my hart that not one of my frends hath failed me at my neede, and I do not complaine of my fortune, but only for my contries sake: for, as for me, I thinke my selfe happier than they that have overcome, considering that I leave a perpetuall fame of our corage and manhoode, the which our enemies the conquerors shall never attaine unto by force nor money, neither can let their posteritie to say, that they being naughtie and unjust men, have slaine good men, to usurpe tyrannical power not pertaining to them. Having sayd so, he prayed everie man to shift for them selves, and then he went a litle aside with two or three only, among the which Strato was one, with whom he came first acquainted by the studie of Rethoricke. He came as neere to him as he coulde, and taking his sword by the hilts with both his hands, and falling downe upon the poynt of it, ran him selfe through.[1] Others say, that not he, but Strato[2] (at his request) held the sword in his hand, and turned his head aside, and that Brutus fell downe upon it: and so ranne him selfe through, and dyed presently. Messala, that had bene Brutus great frend, became afterwards Octavius Cæsars frend. So, shortly after, Cæsar being at good leasure, he brought Strato, Brutus frende unto him, and weeping sayd[3]: Cæsar, beholde, here is he that did the last service to my Brutus. Cæsar welcomed him at that time, and afterwards he did him as faithfull service in all his affaires, as any Græcian els he had about him, untill the battell of Actium. It is reported also, that this Messala him selfe aunswered Cæsar one day, when he gave him great praise before his face, that he had fought valliantlie, and with great affection for him, at the battell of Actium: (notwithstanding that he had bene his cruell enemy before, at the battell of Philippes, for Brutus sake) I ever loved, sayd he, to take the best and justest parte.[4] Now, Antonius having found Brutus bodie, he caused it to be wrapped up in one of the richest cote armors he had.[5] Afterwards also, Antonius understanding that this cote armor was stollen, he put the theefe to death that had stollen it, and sent the ashes of his bodie unto Servilia his mother. And for Porcia, Brutus wife: Nicolaus the Philosopher, and Valerius Maximus doe wryte, that she determining to kill her selfe (her parents and frendes carefullie looking to her to kepe her from it) tooke hotte burning coles,

[1] *In margin:* 'Brutus slue him selfe.' V.5.27–8.

[2] *In margin:* 'Strato, Brutus familiar and frend.' V.5.33–51.

[3] *In margin:* 'Strato received into Cæsars frendship.' V.5.52–67.

[4] *In margin:* 'Messala Corvinus, Brutus frend.'

[5] *In margin:* 'Brutus funeralls.' V.5.76–9.

and cast them into her mouth, and kept her mouth so close, that she choked her selfe.[1] There was a letter of Brutus found wrytten to his frendes, complayning of their negligence, that his wife being sicke, they would not helpe her, but suffred her to kill her selfe, choosing to dye, rather then to languish in paine. Thus it appeareth, that Nicolaus knewe not well that time, sith the letter (at the least if it were Brutus letter) doth plainly declare the disease and love of this Lady, and also the maner of her death.

THE COMPARISON OF DION WITH BRUTUS

To come nowe to compare these two noble personages together, it is certaine that both of them having had great gifts in them (and specially Dion) of small occasions they made them selves great men: and therfore Dion of both deserveth chiefest praise. For, he had no cohelper to bring him unto that greatnesse, as Brutus had of Cassius: who doubtlesse was not comparable unto Brutus, for vertue and respect of honor, though otherwise in matters of warre, he was no lesse wise and valliant then he. For many doe impute unto Cassius, the first beginning and originall of all the warre and enterprise: and sayd it was he that did encourage Brutus, to conspire Cæsars death. Where Dion furnished him selfe with armor, shippes and souldiers and wanne those frendes and companions also that did helpe him, to prosecute his warre. Nor he did not as Brutus, who rose to greatnesse by his enterprises, and by warre got all his strength and riches. But he in contrarie maner, spent of his owne goods to make warre for the libertie of his contrie and disbursed of his owne money, that should have kept him in his banishment. Furthermore, Brutus and Cassius were compelled of necessity to make warres, bicause they coulde not have lived safelie in peace, when they were driven out of Rome: for that they were condemned to death, and pursued by their enemies. And for this cause therefore they were driven to hazard them selves in warre, more for their owne safetie, then for the libertie of their contrie men. Whereas Dion on the other side, living more merily and safelie in his banishment, then the tyranne Dionysius him selfe that had banished him: did put him selfe to that daunger, to deliver Sicile from bondage. Nowe the matter was not a like unto the Romanes, to be delivered from the government of Cæsar: as it was for the Syracusans, to be ridde of Dionysius tyrannie. For Dionysius denyed not, that he was not a tyranne, having filled Sicile with suche miserie and calamitie.

[1] *In margin:* 'Porcia, Brutus wife, killed her selfe with burning coles.' IV.3.145–56.

Howebeit Cæsars power and government when it came to be established, did in deede much hurt at his first entrie and beginning unto those that did resist him: but afterwardes, unto them that being overcome had received his government, it seemed he rather had the name and opinion onely of a tyranne, then otherwise that he was so in deede. For there never followed any tyrannicall nor cruell act,[1] but contrarilie, it seemed that he was a mercifull Phisition, whom God had ordeyned of speciall grace to be Governor of the Empire of Rome, and to set all thinges againe at quiet stay, the which required the counsell and authoritie of an absolute Prince. And therefore the Romanes were marvelous sorie for Cæsar after he was slaine, and afterwardes would never pardon them that had slaine him. On the other side, the cause why the Syracusans did most accuse Dion, was: bicause he did let Dionysius escape out of the castell of Syracusa, and bicause he did not overthrow and deface the tombe of his father. Furthermore, towching the warres: Dion alway shewed him selfe a Captaine unreprovable, having wiselie and skilfullie taken order for those things, which he had enterprised of his owne head and counsell: and did amende the faults others committed, and brought things to better state then he found them. Where it seemeth, that Brutus did not wisely to receive the second battell: considering his rest stoode upon it. For, after he had lost the battell, it was unpossible for him ever to rise againe: and therefore his hart failed him, and so gave up all, and never durst strive with his evill fortune as Pompey did, considering that he had present cause enough in the field to hope of his souldiers, and being beside a dreadfull Lorde of all the sea over. Furthermore, the greatest reproache they could object against Brutus, was: that Julius Cæsar having saved his life, and pardoned all the prisoners also taken in battell, as many as he had made request for, taking him for his frende, and honoring him above all his other frends.[2] Brutus notwithstanding had imbrued his hands in his blood, wherewith they could never reprove Dion. For on the contrarie side, so long as Dion was Dionysius frende and kinseman, he did alway helpe him to order and governe his affaires. But after he was banished his contrie, and that his wife was forciblie maried to an other man, and his goodes also taken from him: then he entred into just and open warres against Dionysius the tyranne. But in this poynt, they were contrarie together.[3] For wherein their chiefest praise consisted, to witte, in hating of tyrannes and wicked men: it is most true that Brutus desire was most sincere of both. For having no private cause

[1] Cf. Brutus, II.1.18–21. [2] Not used by Shakespeare.

[3] *In margin:* 'In what things Dion was inferior unto Brutus.'

of complaint or grudge against Cæsar,[1] he ventred to kill him, onely to set his contrie againe at libertie. Where if Dion had not received private cause of quarrell against Dionysius: he woulde never have made warre with him. The which Plato proveth in his *Epistells*, where is plainlie seene: that Dion being driven out of the tyrans Court against his will, and not putting him selfe to voluntarie banishment, he drave out Dionysius. Furthermore, the respect of the common wealth caused Brutus, that before was Pompeys enemie, to become his frende, and enemie unto Cæsar, that before was his frend: only referring his frendshippe and enmitie, unto the consideracion of justice and equitie. And Dion did many things for Dionysius sake and benefit, all the while he trusted him: and when he beganne to mistrust him, then for anger he made warre with him. Wherefore all his frendes did not beleve, but after he had driven out Dionysius, he would stablish the government to him selfe, flattering the people with a more curteous and gentle title then the name of a tyranne. But for Brutus, his verie enemies them selves confessed, that of all those that conspired Cæsars death, he only had no other ende and intent to attempt his enterprise, but to restore the Empire of Rome againe, to her former state and government.[2] And furthermore, it was not all one thing to deale with Dionysius, as it was to have to doe with Julius Cæsar. For no man that knew Dionysius, but would have despised him, considering that he spent the most parte of his time in drinking, dycing, and in haunting lewde womens company. But to have undertaken to destroy Julius Cæsar, and not to have shroncke backe for feare of his great wisedom, power, and fortune, considering that his name only was dreadfull unto everie man, and also not to suffer the kings of Parthia and India to be in rest for him: this could not come but of a marvelous noble minde of him, that for feare never fainted, nor let fall any part of his corage. And therfore, so sone as Dion came into Sicilia, many thowsands of men came and joyned with him, against Dionysius. But the fame of Julius Cæsar did set up his frends againe after his death, and was of suche force, that it raised a young stripling, Octavius Cæsar, (that had no meanes nor power of him selfe) to be one of the greatest men of Rome: and they used him as a remedie to encounter Antonius malice and power. And if men will say, that Dion drave out the tyran Dionysius with force of armes, and sundrie battells: and that in contrarie maner Brutus slue Cæsar, being a naked man, and without gard: then doe I aunswere againe, that it was a noble parte, and of a wise Captaine, to choose so apt a time and place, to come uppon a man of so great power, and to finde him

[1] Cf. II.1.11: 'I know no personal cause to spurn at him.' [2] V.5.71–2.

naked without his gard. For he went not sodainlie in a rage, and alone, or with a small companie, to assaile him: but his enterprise was long time before determined of, and that with divers men, of all the which, not a man of them once fayled him: but it is rather to be thought, that from the beginning he chose them honest men, or else that by his choyse of them, he made them good men. Whereas Dion, either from the beginning made no wise choyse in trusting of evill men, or else bicause he could not tell how to use them he had chosen: of good men he made them become evill, so that neither the one nor the other coulde be the parte of a wise man. For Plato him selfe reproveth him, for that he had chosen suche men for his frendes, that he was slaine by them, and after he was slaine, no man woulde then revenge his death. And in contrarie maner, of the enemies of Brutus, the one (who was Antonius) gave his bodie honorable buriall: and Octavius Cæsar the other, reserved his honors and memories of him.[1] For at Millayne, (a citie of Gaule on Italie side) there was an image of his in brasse, verie like unto him: the which Cæsar afterwardes passing that way, behelde verie advisedly, for that it was made by an excellent workeman, and was verie like him, and so he went his way.[2] Then he stayed sodainly againe, and called for the Governors of the citie, and before them all tolde them, that the citizens were his enemies and traitors unto him, bicause they kept an enemie of his among them. The Governors of the citie at the first were astonied at it, and stowtlie denyed it: and none of them knowing what enemie he ment, one of them looked on an other. Octavius Cæsar then turning him unto Brutus statue, bending his browes, sayd unto them: This man you see standing up here, is he not our enemie? Then the Governors of the citie were worse affrayed then before, and could not tel what answere to make him. But Cæsar laughing, and commending the Gaules for their faithfulnes to their frendes, even in their adversities: he was contented Brutus image should stand still as it did.

[1] *In margin:* 'Brutus honored of his enemies after his death.

[2] *In margin:* 'Brutus image or statue standing in brasse in Millaine, was preserved and kept by Octavius Cæsar.'

III. Source

PLUTARCH'S LIVES OF THE NOBLE GRECIANS AND ROMANES

translated by Sir Thomas North (1579)

FROM THE LIFE OF MARCUS TULLIUS CICERO

Cicero was dogge leane, a litle eater, and woulde also eate late, bicause of the greate weakenesse of his stomacke[1]: but yet he had a good lowde voyce, though it was somewhat harshe, and lacked grace and comelynesse. Furthermore he was so earnest and vehement in his Oration that he mounted still with his voyce into the highest tunes: insomuche that men were affrayed it woulde one daye put him in hazard of his life. When he came to Athens, he went to heare Antiochus of the citie of Ascalona,[2] and fell in greate likinge with his sweete tongue, and excellent grace, though otherwise he misliked his newe [Stoic] opinions in Philosophie . . . Cicero had most affection unto the Academickes, and did studie that sect more then all the rest . . . [Cicero's Consulship was praised by Cato.] For by decree of the people he was called, father of the contry, as Cato him selfe had called him in his oration: the which name was never given to any man, but onely unto him,[3] and also he bare greater swaye in Rome at that time, than any man beside him. This notwithstanding, he made him selfe envyed and misliked of many men, not for any ill acte he did, or ment to doe: but onely bicause he did too much boast of him selfe.[4] For he never was in any assembly of people, Senate, or judgement, but every mans head was full still to heare the sound of Catulus and Lentulus brought in for sporte, and filling the bookes and workes he compiled besides full of his owne prayses: the which made his sweete and pleasant stile, tedious, and troublesom to those that heard them, as though this misfortune ever followed him to take away his excellent grace.

[Cicero's last days.]

[1] *In margin:* 'Cicero a weake man.'
[2] *In margin:* 'Cicero, Antiochus scholler.'
[3] *In margin:* 'Cicero the first man called, Father of the contry.'
[4] *In margin:* 'Cicero too much given to praise him self.'

Nowe touching the conspiracie against Cæsar, he was not made privie to it, although he was one of Brutus greatest frendes, and that it grieved him to see thinges in that state they were brought unto, and albeit also he wished for the time past, as much as any other man did.[1] But in deede the conspirators were affrayed of his nature, that lacked hardinesse: and of his age, the which oftentimes maketh the stowtest and most hardiest natures, faint harted and cowardly. Notwithstanding, the conspiracie being executed by Brutus and Cassius, Cæsars frendes being gathered together, everie man was afrayed that the citie woulde againe fall into civill warres. And Antonius also, who was Consul at that time, did assemble the Senate, and made some speache and mocion then to draw things againe unto quietnes. But Cicero having used divers perswasions fit for the time, in the end he moved the Senate to decree (following the example of the Athenians) a generall oblivion of thinges done against Cæsar, and to assigne unto Brutus and Cassius some governmentes of provinces. Howbeit nothing was concluded: for the people of them selves were sorie, when they sawe Cæsars bodie brought through the market place. And when Antonius also did shew them his gowne all bebloodied, cut, and thrust through with swordes: then they were like madde men for anger, and sought up and downe the market place if they coulde meete with any of them that had slaine him: and taking fire brandes in their handes, they ranne to their houses to set them a fire. But the conspirators having prevented this daunger, saved them selves: and fearing that if they taried at Rome, they should have many such alaroms, they forsooke the citie. Then Antonius began to looke aloft, and became fearefull to all men, as though he ment to make him selfe king: but yet most of all unto Cicero, above all others. For Antonius perceiving that Cicero began againe to increase in credit and authoritie, and knowing that he was Brutus very frend: he did mislike to see him come neere him, and besides, there was at that time some gealousie betwext them, for the diversitie and difference of their manners and disposicions,[2] Cicero being affrayed of this, . . . tooke sea alone, to goe into Græce.[3] But as it chaunceth oftentimes, there was some let that kept him he could not saile, and newes came to him daily from Rome, as the manner is, that Antonius was wonderfully chaunged, and that nowe he did nothing any more without the authoritie and consent of the Senate, and that there lacked no thing but his person, to make all things well. Then Cicero condemning his dastardly

[1] *In margin:* 'Cicero not made privy to the conspiracie against Cæsar.'

[2] *In margin:* 'Private grudge betwext Antonius and Cicero.'

[3] *In margin:* 'Cicero saileth into Greece.'

feare, returned foorthwith to Rome, not being deceived in his first hope. For there came suche a number of people out to meete him, that he coulde doe nothing all day long, but take them by the handes, and imbrace them: who to honor him, came to meete him at the gate of the citie, as also by the way to bring him to his house. The next morning Antonius assembled the Senate, and called for Cicero by name. Cicero refused to goe, and kept his bedde, fayning that he was werie with his jorney and paines he had taken the day before: but in deede, the cause why he went not, was, for feare and suspicion of an ambushe that was layed for him by the way, if he had gone, as he was informed by one of his verie good frends. Antonius was marvelously offended that they did wrongfully accuse him, for laying of any ambush for him: and therefore sent souldiers to his house, and commaunded them to bring him by force, or else to sette his house a fire. After that time, Cicero and he were alwayes at jarre, but yet coldly enough, one of them taking heede of an other[1]: untill that the young Cæsar returning from the citie of Apollonia, came as lawfull heire unto Julius Cæsar Dictator, and had contention with Antonius for the summe of two thowsande five hundred Myriades, the which Antonius kept in his handes of his fathers goodes. Thereuppon, Philip who had maried the mother of this young Cæsar, and Marcellus, who had also maried his sister, went with young Cæsar unto Cicero, and there agreed together, that Cicero should helpe young Cæsar with the favour of his authoritie, and eloquence, as well towardes the Senate, as also to the people[2]: and that Cæsar in recompence of his good will should stande by Cicero, with his money and souldiers. For this young Cæsar, had many of his fathers old souldiers about him, that had served under him. [For a time Cicero had great power in Rome, drove Antony out, and helped Octavius to become Consul.] But there was Cicero finely colted, as old as he was, by a young man, when he was contented to sue for the Consulship in his behalfe, and to make the Senate agreable to it: wherefore his frendes presently reproved him for it, and shortly after he perceived he had undone him selfe, and together also lost the libertie of his contrie. For this young man Octavius Cæsar being growen to be verie great by his meanes and procurement: when he saw that he had the Consulshippe upon him, he forsooke Cicero, and agreed with Antonius and Lepidus.[3] Then joyning his armie with theirs, he devided the Empire of Rome with them, as if it had bene lands left in common

[1] *In margin:* 'Ill will betwext Cicero and Antonius.'

[2] *In margin:* 'Cicero and Octavius Cæsar joyned in frendship.'

[3] *In margin:* 'Octavius Cæsar forsaketh Cicero. Note the fickelnes of youth.'

betwene them: and besides that, there was a bill made of two hundred men and upwards, whom they had appointed to be slaine.[1] But the greatest difficultie and difference that fell out betwene them, was about the outlawing of Cicero. For Antonius woulde hearken to no peace betwene them, unlesse Cicero were slaine first of all: Lepidus was also in the same mind with Antonius: but Cæsar was against them both. Their meeting was by the citie of Bolonia, where they continued three dayes together, they three only secretly consulting in a place environned about with a litle river. Some say that Cæsar stuck hard with Cicero the two first dayes, but at the third, that he yeelded and forsooke him. The exchaunge they agreed upon betwene them, was this. Cæsar forsooke Cicero[2]: Lepidus, his owne brother Paulus: and Antonius, Lucius Cæsar, his uncle by the mothers side. Such place tooke wrath in them, as they regarded no kinred nor blood, and to speake more properly, they shewed that no brute or savage beast is so cruell as man if with his licentiousnes he have liberty to execute his will. While these matters were a brewing, Cicero was at a house of his in the contrie, by the city of Thusculum, having at home with him also his brother Quintus Cicero. Newes being brought them thither of these proscriptions or outlawries, appointing men to be slaine: they determined to goe to Astyra, a place by the sea side where Cicero had an other house, there to take sea, and from thence to goe into Macedon unto Brutus. . . . [The two brothers parted and Quintus Cicero was soon slain. The servants of Marcus Tullius sought to save his life and] partely by intreatie, and partely by force, they put him againe into his litter to carie him to the sea. But in the meane time came the murderers appointed to kill him, Herennius a Centurion, and Popilius Læna, Tribune of the souldiers (to wit, Colonell of a thowsande men, whose cause Cicero had once pleaded before the Judges, when he was accused for the murther of his owne father) having souldiers attending upon them.[3] So Ciceroes gate being shut, they entred the house by force, and missing him, they asked them of the house what was become of him. They aunswered, they could not tell. Howbeit there was a young boy in the house called Philologus, a slave infranchised by Quintus Cicero, whom Tullius Cicero had brought up in the Latin tongue, and had taught him the liberall sciences: he told this Herennius, that his servauntes caried him in a litter towards the sea, through darke narrowe lanes,

[1] *In margin:* 'The meeting of the Triumviri: Antonius, Lepidus, Octavius Cæsar.'

[2] *In margin:* 'Cicero appointed to be slaine.' IV.1.1–6

[3] *In margin:* 'Herennius, and Popilius, sent to kill M. T. Cicero.'

shadowed with wodde on either side. Popilius the Colonell taking some souldiers with him, ranne about on the outside of the lanes to take him at his comming out of them: and Herennius on thother side entred the lanes. Cicero hearing him comming, commaunded his men to set downe his litter, and taking his beard in his left hande, as his manner was, he stowtly looked the murderers in the faces, his heade and beard being all white, and his face leane and wrinckled, for the extreame sorowes he had taken: divers of them that were by, helde their handes before their eyes, whilest Herennius did cruelly murder him.[1] So Cicero being three score and foure yeares of age, thrust his necke out of the litter, and had his head cut of by Antonius commaundement, and his hands also, which wrote the Orations (called the Philippians) against him. For so did Cicero call the Orations he wrote against him, for the malice he bare him: and do yet continue the same name untill this present time. When these poore dismembred members were brought to Rome, Antonius by chaunce was busily occupied at that time about the election of certaine officers: who when he heard of them and saw them, he cried out alowde that now all his outlawries and proscriptions were executed: and thereuppon commaunded his head and his hands should straight be set up over the pulpit for Orations, in the place called Rostra.[2] This was a fearefull and horrible sight unto the Romanes, who thought they saw not Ciceroes face, but an image of Antonius life and disposicion: who among so many wicked deedes as he committed, yet he did one act only that had some shew of goodnes, which was this. He delivered Philologus into the handes of Pomponia, the wife of Quintus Cicero: and when she had him, besides other cruell tormentes she made him abide, she compelled him to cut his owne flesh of by litle morsells, and to broyle them, and then to eate them.[3] Some historiographers doe thus reporte it. But Tyro who was a slave infranchised by Cicero, made no mencion of the treason of this Philologus. Howbeit I understoode that Cæsar Augustus, long time after that, went one day to see one of his Nephewes, who had a booke in his hande of Ciceroes: and he fearing least his Uncle woulde be angrie to finde that booke in his handes, thought to hide it under his gowne. Cæsar saw it, and tooke it from him, and red the most parte of it standing, and then delivered it to the young boy, and sayd unto him: He was a wise man in deede, my childe, and loved his contrie well.[4]

[1] *In margin:* 'M. T. Cicero slaine by Herennius.'

[2] *In margin:* 'Ciceroes head and hands set up over the pulpit for Orations.'

[3] *In margin:* 'A straunge and cruell punishment taken by Pomponia (Quintus Ciceroes wife) of Philologus for betraying of his maister.'

[4] *In margin:* 'Augustus Cæsars testimony of Cicero.'

IV. Translation of Analogue

From THE HISTORIES OF SALLUST translated by Thomas Heywood (1608)

The two most worthy and notable Histories which remaine unmaimed to posterity: viz. the conspiracie of Cateline, undertaken against the government of the Senate of Rome, and the warre which Jugurth for many yeares maintained against the same state. Both written by C. C. Salustius. *Historia est testis Temporum, Lux veritatis: Magistra vitae: Nuncia vetustatis.* For J. Jaggard.

A Comparison of M. Cato, and Ca. Cæsar

In discent, in yeares, and eloquence they were almost equall: in greatnesse of mind and popular commendation alike, but diversly. Cæsar affected the Sir-name of Great, by Largesse and Bountie: Cato by Integritie of life. Cæsar became famous for his curtesie and gentlenesse; Cato for his sterne carriage and severity. Cæsar grew popular by giving, by forgiving, by releeving: Cato by contraries. The one profest refuge to the oppressed: the other, inexorable to offenders. The one was praised for affability: the other for gravity. Cæsars chiefest felicity was, to labor, to watch, to prefer the suits of his favourites, to be careles of his own, to deny nothing worth giving: of command, of Soldiery, of difficult wars (wherein valor and good conduct shewed the man) very desirous: But Catoes studies were modesty, grave carriage, and above all, severity. With the rich, he contended not for Riches, neither with the factious, for followers; but with the valourous, by imitation: with the modest, in Conscience, and with the good man, in abstinence. He coveted to be, not to seem. The lesse he sought praise, the more it followed him. Thus much for this.

V. Translation of Analogue

From THE ROMAN HISTORY OF VELLEIUS PATERCULUS
translated by Sir R. LeGrys (1632)

Velleius Paterculus, his Romane Historie: in two Bookes. Exactly trans. out of the Latine Edition supervised by Janus Gruterus . . . and rendred English by Sr. Robert Le Grys K^nt^. London. M.F. for R. Swaine. MDCXXXII.

Lib. 2—Chap. 56
[The death of Cæsar]

Cæsar being absolute victor of all his enemies, returning to the Citie (which no mortal man could believe) granted a general pardon to all that had borne armes against him, and with most magnificent showes of fencers at the sharpe, representations of Sea fights, of horse and foote, with fight of Elephants, and feasts many dayes together, did give it full content. He entred in five Triumphs and the setting out of that of *Gallia* was of Lymon wood; that of Pontus, of Brasile; that of Africa, of Ivory; that of Alexandria of Tortoyses; and that of Spaine, of Silver polished. The money brought in of the spoyles was somewhat more then sixe-hundred Millions of Sesterces. Yet could not this man, so great, and who with so much clemency to all men had caryed himselfe in his victory, enjoy himselfe in perfect quiet, above five months. For having made his returne to the City in the month of October, in the Ides of March following by conspiracie, of which *Brutus & Cassius* were the Authors, one of whom by promising him the Consulship he had not obliged, and on the other side, by putting him off he had offended *Cassius*: they having also joyned to their designe complices in the murder, the neerest of all his friends, and who by the support of his party were raised to the highest honors, *Decius Brutus*, and *Caius Trebonius*, with other men of noble qualitie, he was slaine. To whom indeed *Marcus Antonius*, a man that was most ready to dare any thing, had procured much dislike, being his fellow Consull, by putting upon his head a Royall diademe, as in the Lupercalian games he sate in the pleading place, which *Cæsar* refused, but so as it appeared he was not offended with it.

Chap. 57

Experience makes it appeare that the advice of *Pansa* and *Hirtius* was to be commended, who alwaies had perswaded *Cæsar*, that the command which by force he had obtained, he should in the same sort retaine. To whom he replying, that he had rather dye then live in feare while he expects to finde the same gentlenesse in his owne case which he had shewed to others; he was seized upon by those ingratefull men: when indeed the immortal gods had given him very many presages, and tokens of the future danger; for both the Soothsayers had forewarned him, that he should most carefully take heed of the Ides of March; and his wife *Calphurnia*, affrighted with a vision in the night had earnestly intreated him, that day not to goe out of his house: And besides certaine writings which were delivered to him, discovering the whole plot of the conspiracy, he did not presently reade. But truly the force of the destinies is unresistable, the fortune whereof while he resolved to change, he spoiled the intendments thereof. . . .

Chap. 70

[The defeat of Brutus and Cassius]

Whiles these passages are on foot in Italy, *Cassius* with a sharpe and very fortunate warre had (an action of mighty import) taken Rhodes, and *Brutus* had conquered the Lycians: from whence they had passed their armies over into Macedonia: when *Cassius* in everything running a contrary course to the nature of *Brutus*, had in the end also mastered his clemency. Neither do I finde any upon whom a more indulgent fortune did once attend: or whom, as if she had beene tryed, she did with more speed abandon, then *Brutus* and *Cassius*. *Cæsar* then and *Antonius*, passing their armies into Macedonia, neere the City of *Philippi*, came to fight a battaile with *Marcus Brutus* and *Cassius*. The wing that *Brutus* commanded, having beaten their opposites, did take *Cæsars* campe; For himselfe, though extreamely sicke, did yet discharge all the duties of a Generall, and was also earnestly intreated by his Physitian *Artorius*, that he should not tarry in his quarter, he being frighted in his sleepe with a manifest threatning of danger toward him. The wing in which *Cassius* commanded, was on the other side forced to fall off and, shrewdly plagued, had retyred to a higher ground. *Cassius* then by his owne fortune guessing at the successe of his consort, when he had sent one whom he had called out, for that purpose, and commanded him to bring him word what the number and force of those men was which were comming toward him: he returned an account thereof somewhat slowly, and they being now neere him, and upon their full speed, and for the dust neither their faces nor their ensignes could be discerned, beleeving that they were enemies that were rushing upon him, he wrapped his coat about his head, and feare-lessly yelded his necke to his freed man. The head of *Cassius* was but fallen to the ground, when he that was sent came and brought word, that *Brutus* was Victor, who seeing his Generall lying dead, I will, said he, follow him, whom my dulnesse hath slaine, and with that fell upon his sword. A few dayes after *Brutus* fought another battaile, and in that being overthrowne, when he had fled to a knolle by night he intreated *Strato* the Ægeatian his neerest friend to lend him a hand in his death: and lifting his left arme up to his head when he held the hilts in his right hand, he guided the point to his left pappe where the heart doth pant, and pressing on the same, with one blow ended his life.

Chap. 72

This end was fortune pleased to appoint to the faction of *Marcus Brutus*, when he was thirtie seven yeares old; His mind being depraved in that day which with his rashnesse of his fact, did blot out all his other vertues. As for *Cassius* he was as much a better Captaine then *Brutus*, as *Brutus* was a better man then he: of whom thou wouldest rather love *Brutus* for a friend, and more redoubt *Cassius* if thy enemy[1]: in the one there was more violence, in the other more vertue. Who if they had beene Conquerors, as much as it was better to have *Cæsar* for our Prince then *Antonius*, so much had it beene to have had *Brutus* then *Cassius*....

VI. Possible Source

From THE FIRST BOOKE OF THE ANNALES OF CORNELIUS TACITUS translated by R. Grenewey (1598)

The Proeme of Tacitus, containing the forme of government untill Augustus time.

The citie of Rome was in the beginning governed by Kings. Libertie and the Consulship *L. Brutus* brought in. The Dictators were chosen

[1] Cf. the Epilogue to *Cæsar Interfectus* [*inf.* 195].

but for a time: the *Decemviri* passed not two yeeres: neither had the Consularie authoritie of the Tribune of the soldiers any long continuance: nor *Cinna* nor *Sillaes* dominion: *Pompey* and *Crassus* quickly yeelded to *Cæsars* forces: *Lepidus* and *Antonie* to *Augustus*; who entiting himselfe by the name of Prince, brought under his obedience the whole Romane state, wearied and weakened with civill disorders . . .

1. The meanes by which Augustus came to the Empire: and whom he chose to succeed

After that *Brutus* and *Cassius* were slaine, and no armes now publikely borne: *Pompey* defeated in Sicilie; *Lepidus* disarmed; *Antonie* killed; and no chiefe leader of *Julius Cæsars* faction left, but onely *Augustus*; he would no longer be called *Triumvir*, but in shew contented with the dignitie of a Tribune to defend the people, bearing himselfe as Consul: after he had wound into the favour of the soldier by giftes; of the people by provision of sustenance; and of all in generall with the sweetenes of ease and repose; by little and little taking upon him, he drew to himselfe the affaires of Senate, the dutie of magistrates and lawes, without contradiction of any: the stowtest by war or proscriptions alreadie spent, and the rest of the nobilitie, by how much the more serviceable, by so much the more bettered in wealth, and advanced in honors: seeing their preferment to growe by new government, did rather choose the present estate with securitie, than strive to recover their olde with danger. The forme of government the provinces disliked not, as mistrusting the Senates and peoples regiment by reason of noble mens factions; covetousness of magistrates: the lawes affoording no securitie, being swaied hither and thither by might, ambition, and corruption.

2. Tacitus tells how Augustus advanced his relatives to ensure the succession

Wars there were none at that time, but onely against the Germans . . . All was quiet in the citie; the old names of the magistrates unchanged; the yoong men borne after the victorie of *Actium*, and the greatest part of the old, during the Civill wars: how many were there which had seene the ancient forme of government of the free Common-wealth. Thus then the state of the citie turned upside downe, there was no signe of the olde laudable customes to be seene: but contrarie, equalitie taken away, every man endevored to obey the prince; misdoubting nothing whilest *Augustus* yet strong in bodie, was able to defend himselfe, his house, and peace . . .

3. The solemnities of Augustus funerals, and the censure which men gave of him

[People discussed Augustus—often trivially.]

But among the better sort his life was diversly commended or discommended: Some sayd, that the love of his father, and the care of the Common-wealth, at that time when all lawes were dasht drove him to civill warres, which can never be begun or prosecuted by any good meanes: and that he had yeelded in many things to *Antony*, and to *Lepidus* in like maner, because he would revenge his fathers death. For seeing the one grew carelesse with age, and the other wasted with lasciviousnes, there was no other meanes left to redresse all discords in the Common-wealth, then to bring her under the obedience of one alone, who should governe; neverthelesse not as King or Dictator, but as Prince. The Empire he had bounded with the Ocean, and other Rivers farre off: the Legions, Provinces and Navie were linked and knit in peace and unitie: justice was ministred in the cities: the allies intreated with modestie: the citie beautified with sumptuous building: and if any rigorous dealing had bene used against some few, it was for setling of quietnes in the whole. Contrarily some sayd, that the love of his father, the corruption of times, served him but for a cloake and colour: and that he had stirred up the old souldyers by gifts and bribery, through ambition and desire of rule; that being but yong and a private person, he had gathered a power; corrupted the legions of the Consuls. . .

Indeede, the revenge and pursuing his fathers death upon *Cassius* and *Brutus* may be tolerated (albeit it had bene convenient for a publick benefit to have layd aside private grudges) but he deceived *Pompey* under colour of peace, and *Lepidus* under a shadow of friendship. Afterward he tolled on *Antony* with the treatie of Tarentum and Brundusium, and mariage of his sister, which deceitfull alliance he payed with the losse of his life. Doubtlesse a peace ensued this, but a bloudie one, as may witnes the death of *Lollius* and *Varus*, and in *Rome* itselfe, of *Varro*, *Egnatius*, and *Julus* . . . There was no honor left for the gods, seeing hee would himselfe by the Priests and Flamines be worshipped in the temples, with all the ornaments belonging to the gods. . . .

VII. Translation of Analogue

From THE HISTORIE OF TWELVE CÆSARS

by Suetonius, translated by Philemon Holland (1606)

The Historie of Twelve Cæsars Emperours of Rome Written in Latine by C. Suetonius Tranquillus and newly translated into English by Philemon Holland Doctor in Physicke. Together with a Marginall Glosse, and other briefe Annotations there-upon. Printed for Matthew Lownes. 1606.

[Julius Cæsar's appearance and habits]

§ 45

Of stature he is reported to have beene tall; of complexion white and cleare; with limbs well trussed and in good plight; somewhat full faced; his eies black, lively, and quick; also very healthfull, saving that in his latter daies he was given to faint and swoune sodainly; yea, and as he dreamed, to start and be affrighted: twice also in the midst of his martiall affaires,[1] he was surprized with the falling sicknes. About the trimming of his body, he was over-curious[2]: so as he would not onely be notted and shaven very precisely, but also have his haire plucked, in so much as some cast it in his teeth, and twitted him therewith. Moreover, finding by experience, that the deformity of his bald head was oftentimes subject to the scoffes and scornes of back-biters and slaunderers, hee tooke the same exceedingly to the heart: and therefore he both had usually drawne downe his haire that grew but thin, from the crowne toward his forehead: and also of all honours decreed unto him from the Senate and People, he neither received nor used any more willingly, than the priviledge to weare continually the triumphant Lawrel guirland. Men say also, that in his apparel he was noted for singularity,[3] as who used to goe in his Senatours purple studded robe,

[1] *In margin:* '*Inter res gerendas vel agendas*, that is, *cum aciem ordinaret*, Plutarch. Whiles he was setting his Armie in battaile ray.'

[2] *In margin:* 'Or fantasticall.'

[3] *In margin:* 'His attire different from others, or of a new [Greek] fashion.'

trimmed with a jagge or frindge at the sleeve hand: and the same so, as hee never was but girt over it, and that very slack and loose: whereupon, arose (for certaine) that saying of Sulla, who admonished the Nobles oftentimes, To beware of the boy that went girded so dissolutely.

§ 50

An opinion there is constantly received, that he was given to carnall pleasures, and that way spent much: also that he dishonoured many Dames, and those of noble houses . . . But above the rest, he cast affection to Servilia the mother of M. Brutus . . .

§ 52

He was enamoured also upon Queenes, and among them he loved Eunoe, the Moore, wife of Bogudes (King of Mauritania) upon whom, as also upon her husband, he bestowed very many gifts and of infinite value, as Naso hath left in writing: but most especially hee fancied Cleopatra: For, with her, hee both sate up many times and feasted all night long even untill the breake of day; and also in the same Barge or Galley[1] called *Thalamegos*, had passed into Ægypt, almost as farre as to Æthiopia, but that his Armie refused to followe: and in the end having trained her into the Citie of Rome, he sent her back againe, not without exceeding great honours, and enriched with many rewards: yea, and suffered her to call the sonne she bare, after his owne name.[2] Whom verily, some Greek writers have recorded, to have been very like unto Cæsar both in shape and also in gate[3] . . .

§ 53

That he was a most sparie drinker of wine, his very enemies would never denie. Whereupon arose this Apophthegm of M. Cato, That of all that ever were, Cæsar alone came sober to the overthrow of the State. For, about his foode and diet C. Oppius sheweth hee was so indifferent and without curiosity, that when upon a time his Host set before him upon the bord olde ranke oile[4] in steed of greene, sweet, and fresh, so that other guests refused it, he onely (by his saying) fell to it and eate therof the more liberally; because he

[1] *In margin:* 'Of which the Ægyptians Kings had alwaies ready rigged 800, as Appian writeth.'

[2] *In margin:* 'That is Ptolomæus Cesario.'

[3] *In margin:* '*Incessu*, in his gang or manner of going.'

[4] *In margin:* '*Conditum oleum penult. cor.* or *conditum product. id est unguentum*, an ointment.'

would not be thought to blame his Host[1] either for negligence or rusticitie . . .

§ 59

No religious feare of divine prodigies could ever fray him from any enterprise, or stay him if it were once in hand. As he sacrificed upon a time, the beast made an escape and ran away: yet for all that differred not he his journey against Scipio and Juba. He fortuned also to take a fall then, even as hee went forth of the ship to land: but turning this foretoken to the better presage, 'I take possession,' quoth hee, 'of thee, O Afrike.' Moreover, in verie skorne, and to make but a mockerie of those prophesies, whereby the name of Scipions was fatall to that province, and held luckie and invincible there, he had with him in his Campe the most base and abject fellow of all the Cornelian family, and who in reproch of his life was surnamed Saluito.[2]

§ 76

Howbeit, the rest of his deedes and words overweigh and depresse his good parts downe: so as he might be thought both to have abused his soveraintie, and worthily to have beene murthered. For, he not only tooke upon him excessive honours, to wit, continued Consulship, perpetuall Dictature, and Presidency of Manners[3]; and more than so, the forename of Emperour,[4] the Surname Father of his Countrie; his statue among the Kings, an eminent seate of Estate raised above the rest in the *Orchestra*, among the Senatours: but hee suffered also more stately dignities than beseeming the condition of a mortall wight to bee decreed and ordained for him: namely, a golden Throne in the Curia, and before the Tribunal[5]: a sacred Chariot and therein a frame carrying an Image,[6] at the solemne pomp of his Games *Circenses*: Temples, Altars, his owne Images placed neere unto the Gods: a sacred Bedloft for such Images to be bestowed upon: a *flamin*, certaine *Luperci*: and thed enomination of one moneth after his owne name.[7] Besides, no honourable offices there were but he tooke and gave at his owne pleasure. His third and fourth Consulship in name onely and title he bare: contenting himselfe with the absolute power of Dictatourship decreed

[1] *In margin:* 'Or friend.'

[2] *In margin:* 'Or Salutio. Read Plinie, *Natur. Hist.* lib. 7. cap. 12.'

[3] *In margin:* '*i.e.* Censorship in deed though not in name.'

[4] *In margin:* '*Imperatoris*, *i.* Soveraine and absolute commander.'

[5] *In margin:* 'In the forum.'

[6] *In margin:* 'Of himselfe, as a God.'

[7] *In margin:* 'Juliani.'

unto him with his Consulares all at one time: and in both yeeres, he substituted two Consuls under him for the three last moneths: so as, in the meane time, he held no Election but of Tribunes and Ædiles of the Commons. In steed of Pretours he ordained Provosts, who should administer the affaires of the Citie even whiles he was present.[1] And upon the very last day of the yeare, to wit next before the Kalends of Januarie,[2] the place of a Consulship being vacant by the suddaine death of a Consull he conferred uppon one that made suite to enjoy the same but a few houres. With semblable licentiousnesse despising the custome of his Countrie, he ordained majestrates to continue in office many yeares together. To x. men of Pretours degree he graunted the Consulare Ornaments. Such as were but enfranchized Citizens, and divers mungrell Gaules no better then halfe Barbarians, he admitted Senatours.[3] Furthermore, over the Mint and receipt of the City-revenewes, he set certaine peculiar servants of his owne to be rulers. The charge and commaund of three Legions which he left in Alexandria, he committed wholly to a sonne of Rufinus his freed man, a stale youth and Catanite of his owne.

§ 77

Neither did some words of his which he openly delivered, bewraie lesse presumptuous Lordlines, as T. Ampius writeth. For example, That the Commonwealth was now no more any reall thing, but a name onely, without forme and shape: That Sulla was altogether unlettered and no Grammarian,[4] in giving over his Dictature. That men ought now to speake with him more considerately, and to hold every word that he saith for a Law. Nay he proceeded to this point of Arrogancie, that when upon a time in a certaine Sacrifice, the South-sayer brought him word of unlucky Inwards in the beast; and such as had no heart at all, he made answere and said, That those which were to follow afterwards should prove more joyfull and fortunate if it pleased him[5]: neither was it to be taken for a prodigious and strange token, if a beast wanted an heart.

§ 78

But the greatest envie and inexpiable hatred he drew upon himselfe by this occasion most of all.[6] What time as al the Senatours in

[1] *In margin: 'Etiam præsente se:* some read *absente te*: cleane contrarie.'

[2] *In margin:* 'The last of December.'; A.U.C. 709

[3] *In margin:* 'Made free Citizens of Rome.'

[4] *In margin: 'Nam Grammatici est dictare.'*

[5] *In margin:* 'Should signifie better fortune.'

[6] *In margin: 'In expiabilem* or *exitiabilem, i.e.* deadly, and that which brought him to mischeife.'

generall came unto him with many and those most honourable decrees, he received them sitting still[1] before the Temple of Venus Genitrix. Some thinke, that when he was about to rise up, Cornelius Balbus stayed and helde him backe: others are of the mind, that he never went about it. But when C. Trebatius advertised him to arise unto them,[2] he looked backe upon him with a strang kind of looke: Which deede of his was thought so much the more intollerable, for that himselfe, when Pontius Aquila one of the Colledge of Tribunes, stood not up nor did reverence to him as he rode in Tryumph and passed by the Trybunes Pues, tooke such snuffe and indignation therat, that he brake out alowd into these words: 'Well done Tribune Aquila, recover thou then, the common-welth out of my hands': and for certaine dayes togither, never promised ought unto any man without this Proviso and Exception, 'If Pontius Aquila will give me leave.'

§ 79

To this contumelious and notorious behaviour[3] of his toward the Senate thus despised, he adjoyned a deede much more arrogant: For when as in his returne from the solemne Sacrifice of the Latine Holie dayes, among other immoderate and new acclamations of the people, one out of the multitude had set upon his Statue, a Coronet of Laurell tied about with a white band[4]; and Epidius Marullus, a Tribune of the Commons together with his colleague Cæsetius Flavus commanded the said band to be plucked of, and the man to be had away to prison, he taking it to heart, either that this overture to a kingdome sped no better, or, (as he made semblance and pretended himselfe) that he was put by the glorie of refusing it, sharpely rebuked the Tribunes, and deprived them both of their authoritie. Neither for all this, was he willing afterwards to put away the infamous note of affecting and seeking after the title of a King: albeit he both made answere unto a Commoner saluting him by the name of a King, That he was Cæsar and no King: and also at the *Lupercalia*, when Antonius the Consul imposed the Diademe oftentimes upon his head before the *Rostra*, did put it backe againe, and send it into the Capitoll to Jupiter Optimus Maximus. Moreover sundrie rumours ran rife abroad, that he would depart (for ever) to Alexandria or to Ilium, having at once translated and remooved thither the puissance and wealth of the Empire: dispeopeld Italie

[1] *In margin:* 'Not so much as rising up unto them.'

[2] *In margin:* 'Saying with all, What, Sir. Remember you are Cæsar.'

[3] *In margin:* 'Or gesture.'

[4] *In margin:* 'Resembling a Diademe.'

with mustring of soldiers; and withall betaken the administration of Rome-Citie unto his friends: as also, that in the next Session of the Senate, L. Cotta one of the Quindecimvirs would move the house to this effect, That for as much as it was contained in the Fatall bookes of Sybilla, that the Parthians could not possiblie be vanquished but by a King, therfore Cæsar should be stiled King.

§ 80

This gave occasion to the Conspiratours for to hasten the execution of their designe, least of necessitie they should be driven to assent thereto. Their counsuls therefore and conferences about this matter, which before time they held dispersed here and there, and projected oftentimes by two and three in a companie, they now complotted altogither, for that by this time the very people joyed not in the present state, seeing how things went; but both in secret and openly also distasted such soveraintie, and called earnestly for protectors and maintainers of their liberties. . . .

After that Cæsetius and Marullus the Tribunes aforesaid, were removed out of their office, at the next Solemne assembly, held for Election, verie many voices were found declaring them ii. Consuls. Some there were who subscribed under the Statue of L. Brutus these words, 'Would God thou were alive'. Likewise under the Statue of Cæsar himselfe,

Brutus for expelling the Kings, was created Consul the first.
This man for expelling the Consuls is become King, the last,[1]

There conspired against him more than three-score, the heads of which conspiracie were C. Cassius, Marcus[2] and Decimus Brutus; who having made doubt at first whether by dividing themselves into partes,[3] they should cast him downe the bridge, as he called the Tribes to give their voices at the Election in Mars fielde, and so take him when hee was downe and kill him right out: or set uppon him in the high streete called *Sacra via*[4]: or else in the very entrance to the Theater; after that the Senate had summons to meete in Counsell within the Court of Pompeius upon the Ides of March,[5] they soone agreed of this time and place before all others.

§ 81

But Cæsar surely had faire warning of his death before it came, by many evident prodigies and strang foretokens. Some few moneths

[1] *In margin:* '*Postremus* or *Postremo*, at last.' [2] *In margin:* 'M. Brutus.'
[3] *In margin:* 'Some upon the bridge others under it.'
[4] *In margin:* 'In which Cæsar dwelt after he had beene high priest.'
[5] *In margin:* '15 of March in honor of Anna Perenna. And because the plaies were exhibited in Pompeis Theatre. Therfore the Senate met also in his *Curia*.'

before, when certaine new inhabitants, brought by vertue of the Law Julia[1] to dwell in the Colonie Capua, overthrew most auncient Sepulchers for to builde them houses to their landes; and did the same so much the more diligently and with better will, for that in searching they light upon manufactures and vessels good store of Antique worke: there was found in that verie monument, wherein by report, Capys the founder of Capua lay buried, a brasen Table with a writing upon it in Greeke words and Greeke letters to this effect: 'When the bones and reliques of Capys happen to be discovered, it shall come to passe, that one descended from Julus shall be murdered by the hands of his neere kinsfolke, and his death soone after revenged with the great calamities and miseries of all Italie.' And least any man should thinke this to be a fabulous tale and forged matter, know he that Cornelius Balbus a verie inward and familiar friend of Cæsar is the author thereof. And the verie day next preceeding his death, those troupes of horses which in his passage over the River Rubicon hee had consecrate and let go loose ranging here and there without a keeper, (as he understood for certaine) forbare their meat and would not to die for it, touch any, yea, and shed teares aboundantly. Also, as he offered sacrifice, the Soothsayer Spurina warned him to take heede of danger toward him. and which would not be differred after the Ides of March. Now, the verie day before the said Ides, it fortuned that as the birde *Regaliolus*[2] was flying with a little branch of Lawrell, into the Court of Pompeius, a sort of other birdes of diverse kindes from out of the grove hard by, pursued after and there pulled it in peeces. But that night next before the day of his murder, both himselfe dreamed as he lay a sleepe, one while, that he was flying above the clouds: another while, that Jupiter and he shooke hands: and also his wife Calpurnia, imagined, that the Finiall of his house fell downe, and that her husband was stabbed in her verie bosome: and sodainely withall the chamber doore of it selfe flew open. Hereupon, as also by reason of sickelinesse, he doubted a good while whether he should keepe at home and put off those matters which he had purposed to debate before the Senate, or no? At the last, being counselled and perswaded by Decius Brutus, not to disappoint the Senatours who were now in frequencie assembled and stayed for his comming long since, he went forth when it was well neere eleven of the clocke. And when one met him by the way,[3] and offered him a written pamphlet, which layd open the conspiracie,

[1] *In margin:* 'Which him selfe promulged.'

[2] *In margin:* 'Or *Regaviolus*, quasi *rex avium.*'

[3] *In margin:* '*Ab Obvio quodam, vel Ovio, i.e.* one Ovius.'

and who they were that sought his life, he shuffled the same among other skroes and writings which he held in his left hand as if he would have red it anone. After this when he had killed many beasts for sacrifices and could speede of the Gods favour in none, he entred the *Curia*[1] in contempt of all Religion; and therewith laughed Spurina to scorne: charging him to bee a false Prophet, for that the Ides of March were come: and yet noe harme befell unto him; albeit hee aunswered, That come indeede they were, but not yet past.

§ 82

When they saw once that he had taken his place,[2] and was set, they stood round about him as serviceable attendants readie to do him honor: and then immediatly Cimber Tullus[3]: who had undertaken to begin first, stepped neerer unto him, as though he would have made some request. When Cæsar seemed to mislike and put him backe, yea and by his gesture to post him of unto another time, he caught hold of his gowne at both shoulders: whereupon as he cried out, 'This is violence,' Cassius[4] came in too, full afront, and wounded him a little beneth the throat.[5] Then Cæsar catching Cassius by the arme thrust it through with his stile or writing punches; and with that being about to leape forward[6] he was met with another wound and stayed. Now when he perceived himselfe beset on everie side and assailed with drawne daggers he wrapped and covered his head with his gowne: but withall he let downe the large lap[7] with his left hand to his legges beneath, hiding thereby the inferiour part also of his bodie, that he might fall more decently: and so, with 3 and 20 wounds he was stabbed: during which time he gave but one grone, without any worde uttered, and that was at the first thrust; although some have written, that as M. Brutus came running upon him he said, *καὶ σὺ τέκνον*,[8] *i.* 'And thou my sonne'. When all others fled sundrie waies, there lay he a good while dead, untill three of his owne pages bestowed him in a licter: and so with one arme hanging downe,[9] carried him home. Neither in so many

[1] *In margin:* 'Of Pompeius.'

[2] *In margin:* '*Conspicati*, or *conspirati*, *i.e.* the conspirators stood round about him.'

[3] *In margin:* 'Who before had beene his great friend and sided with him.'

[4] *In margin:* '*Alter Cassius* or *alter e Cassiis* one of the *Cassi, vel alter, Cascæ.*'

[5] *In margin:* '*Jugulum*, or the chanell bone.'

[6] *In margin:* 'Out of his chaire.'

[7] *In margin:* 'Which they were wont to cast over their shoulders. Senec. *de Benefico*. Or tucke up slack above the wast.'

[8] *In margin:* 'Some read: *καί σὺ ει ἐκνὼν*'

[9] *In margin:* 'Some expound this of the licter as if one corner thereof hung downe, carried as it was by three.'

wounds, was there, as Antistius his Physitian deemed, any one found mortall, but that which he received second, in his breast.[1] The conspiratours were minded to have dragged his Corps, after hee was thus slaine, into the River Tiberis; confiscated his goods, and repealed all his acts: but for feare of M. Antonius the Consul and Lepidus, Maister of the Horsemen, they held their hands and gave over those courses.

§ 83

At the demand therefore of L. Piso whose daughter he married, his last will and Testament was opened and red in the house of Antonius: which will, upon the Ides of September[2] next before, he had made in his owne house at Lavicium and committed to the keeping of the chiefe vestal Virgin. Q. Tubero writeth, that from his first Consulship unto the beginning of the Civill war, he was ever wont to write downe for his heire, Cn. Pompeius, and to reade the saide will unto his soldiers in their publike assemblie. But in this last Testament of his, he ordained three Coheires, the nephewes all of his sisters.[3] To wit C. Octavius,[4] of three fourth parts, L. Pinarius, and Q. Pedius of one fourth part remaining. In the latter end and bottome of this Testamentarie Instrument, he adopted also C. Octavius into his house and name; and many of those that afterwards murdered him, he nominated for guardiers to his sonne,[5] if it fortuned he had any borne. Yea and Decimus Brutus to be one of his second heires in remainder. Hee bequeathed in his legacies unto the people[6] his hortyards about Tiberis to ly common; and three hundred Sesterces[7] to them by the Poll.

§ 85

The common people streight after his funerall obsequies went with burning fire-brands and torches to the dwelling houses of Brutus and Cassius: From whence being hardly repelled, they meeting with Helvius Cinna by the way, and mistaking his name, as if he had beene Cornelius Cinna (one who the day before had made a bitter invective as touching Cæsar and whom they sought for) him they slew: set his head upon a speare, and so carried it about with

[1] *In margin:* 'Whereby it seemeth he had one given him in his neck before: which the Author hath omitted.'

[2] *In margin:* '13 of September.'

[3] *In margin:* 'So hee was there great Unkle.'

[4] *In margin:* 'Afterwards Augustus, sonne of Atia Julius Cæsars sisters daughter.'

[5] *In margin:* 'As *Posthumus, i.e.* borne after his death.'

[6] *In margin:* 'Of Rome.'

[7] *In margin:* '46s. 10d. ob. starling.'

them. After this they erected in the Forum a solide Columne[1] almost 20 foote high, of Numidian Marble: with this title graven therupon; PARENTI PATRIÆ. 'To the father of his Countrie.' At which piller for a long time they used still to sacrifice, to make vowes and prayers, to determine and end certaine controversies interposing alwaies their oth by the name of Cæsar. . . .

§ 89

Of these murderers, there was not one in manner that either survived him above three yeares, or died of his naturall death. All stood condemned: and by one mishap or other perished: some by ship-wracke, others in battaile: and some againe,[2] shortened their own daies, with the verie same dagger, wherewith they had wounded Cæsar.

VIII. Possible Source

From THE CIVIL WARS
by Appian of Alexandria, translated by W.B. (1578)

An auncient Historie and exquisite Chronicle of the Romanes warres, both Civile and Foren. Written in Greeke by the noble Orator and Historiographer, *Appian* of *Alexandria*, one of the learned Counsell to the most mightie Emperoures, *Trajane* and *Adriane*. . . . Imprinted at London by Raufe Newbery, and Henrie Bynniman. Anno. 1578.

[Antony's speech at Cæsar's funeral and its effects]

Book II

Piso brought forth *Cæsars* body, to the which, infinit numbers in armes ran, to kepe it, and with much noyse and pompe, brought it to the place of speech. There was much lamentation and weeping, ther was rushing of harnesse togither, with repentaunce of the forgetting of revengeance. *Antony* marking how they were affected, did

[1] *In margin:* 'Or Piller.'

[2] *In margin:* 'Cassius: as Plutarch reporteth, and Brutus according to Dion, and the ii. Cascaes. A notable judgement of Almightie God upon the unnatural murderers of their Soveraine.'

not let it slippe, but toke upon him to make *Cæsars* funeral sermon, as Consul, of a Consul, friend, of a friend, and kinsman, of a kinsman (for *Antony* was partly his kinsman) and to use craft againe. And thus he said[1]:

> I do not thinke it meete (O Citizens) that the buriall praise of suche a man, should rather be done by me, than by the whole country. For what you have altogither for the love of hys vertue given him by decree, aswell the Senate as the people, I thinke your voice, and not *Antonies*, oughte to expresse it.

This he uttered with sad and heavy cheare, and wyth a framed voice, declared every thing, chiefly upon the decree, whereby he was made a God, holy and inviolate, father of the country, benefactor and governor, and suche a one, as never in al things they entituled other man to the like. At every of these words *Antonie* directed his countenance and hands to *Cæsars* body, and with vehemencie of words opened the fact. At every title he gave an addition, with briefe speach, mixte with pitie and indignation. And when the decree named him father of the Country, then he saide: *This is the testimony of our duety.*

And at these wordes, *holy*, *inviolate* and *untouched*, and *the refuge of all other*, he said:

> None other made refuge of hym. But, he, *this holy and untouched*, is kylled, not takyng honoure by violences whiche he never desired, and then be we verye thrall that bestowe them on the unworthy, never suing for them. But you doe purge your selves (O Citizens) of this unkindnesse, in that you nowe do use suche honoure towarde hym being dead.

Then rehearsing the othe, that all shoulde keepe *Cæsar* and *Cæsars* body, and if any one wente about to betraye hym, that they were accursed that would not defende him: at this he extolled hys voice, and helde up his handes to the Capitoll, saying:

> O *Jupiter* Countries defendour, and you other Gods, I am ready to revenge, as I sware and made execration, and when it seemes good to my companions to allowe the decrees, I desire them to aide me.

At these plaine speeches spoken agaynst the Senate, an uproare being made, *Antony* waxed colde, and recanted hys wordes.

> It seemeth (O Citizens) (saide hee) that the things done have not bin the worke of men but of Gods, and that we ought to have

[1] *In margin:* '*Antony* of *Cæsar*.'

more consideration of the present, than of the past, bycause the thyngs to come, maye bring us to greater danger, than these we have, if we shall returne to oure olde, and waste the reste of the noble men that be in the Cittie. Therfore let us send thys holy one to the number of the blessed, and sing to him his due hymne and mourning verse.

When he had saide thus, he pulled up his gowne lyke a man beside hymselfe, and gyrded it, that he might the better stirre his handes[1]: he stoode over the Litter, as from a Tabernacle, looking into it, and opening it, and firste sang his Himne, as to a God in heaven. And to confirme he was a God, he held up his hands, and with a swift voice, he rehearsed the warres, the fights, the victories, the nations that he had subdued to his Countrey, and the great booties that he had sent, making every one to be a marvell. Then with a continuall crie,

> This is the only unconquered of all that ever came to hands with hym. Thou (quoth he) alone diddest revenge thy countrey being injured .300. years, and those fierce nations that onely invaded *Rome*, and only burned it, thou broughtest them on their knees.

And when he had made these and many other invocations, he tourned hys voice from triumphe to mourning matter, and began to lament and mone him as a friend that had bin unjustly used, and did desire that he might give hys soule for *Cæsars*. Then falling into moste vehement affections, uncovered *Cæsars* body, holding up his vesture with a speare, cut with the woundes, and redde with the bloude of the chiefe Ruler, by the which the people lyke a Quire, did sing lamentation unto him, and by this passion were againe repleate with ire. And after these speeches, other lamentations wyth voice after the Country custome, were sung of the Quires, and they rehearsed again his acts and his hap.

Then made he *Cæsar* hymselfe to speake as it were in a lamentable sort, to howe many of his enemies he hadde done good by name, and of the killers themselves to say as in an admiration, *Did I save them that have killed me*? This the people could not abide, calling to remembraunce, that all the kyllers (only *Decimus* except) were of *Pompeys* faction, and subdued by hym, to whom, in stead of punishment, he had given promotion of offices, governments of provinces and armies, and thought *Decimus* worthy to be made his heyre and son by adoption, and yet conspired hys death. While the matter was thus handled, and like to have come to a fray, one shewed out of

[1] *In margin:* '*Antonies* gesture in the time of the funerall of *Cæsar*.'

the Litter the Image of *Cæsar*, made of waxe,[1] for hys body it selfe lying flat in the Litter, could not be seene. Hys picture was by a devise turned about, and .xxiii. wounds wer shewed over al his body, and his face horrible to behold. The people seeing this pittifull picture, coulde beare the dolour no longer,[2] but thronged togyther, and beset the Senate house, wherein *Cæsar* was kylled, and set it a fyre,[3] and the kyllers that fledde for their lives, they ranne and sought in every place, and that so outragiouslye both in anger and dolour, as they kylled *Cynna* the Tribune being in name lyke to *Cynna* the Pretor that spake evill of *Cæsar*, and wold not tarry to heare the declaration of his name, but cruelly tore him a peeces, and lefte not one parte to be put in grave.[4] They caried fire against other mens houses, who manlye defending themselves, and the neighbours entreating them, they refrayned from fyre, but threatned to be in armes the next day.[5] Wherefore the strikers hid themselves, and fled out of the Citie. The people returned to the Litter, and caried it as an holye thing, to be buried in an holy place among the Gods, but bicause the Priests did deny it, they brought hym againe into the common place, where the Pallaice of the old Kings were, and there, with al the bourds and tymber, which they could find in the place, which was muche, beside that every man broughte of himselfe, with garlandes and other gifts of private persons, makyng a solemne shew, they buryed the body, and abode al night about the fyre,[6] In the whiche place, at the first was made an Altare, but nowe there is a temple of *Cæsar*, where he is thought worthy divine honors.[7] For his son by election, *Octavius*, taking the name of *Cæsar*, and disposing the state after his example, which then takyng the beginning, and he exceedingly advancing to the degree it is now did thinke his father to deserve honors equall with the Gods, the which at this time having their originall, the Romaines now use to give the same to hym that ruleth the estate, unlesse he be a Tyranne, or diffamed at his death, that in olde tyme could not suffer the name of a Kyng alyve.[8]

[1] *In margin:* '*Cæsars* shape shewed in waxe.'
[2] *In margin:* 'Change of peoples mindes.'
[3] *In margin:* 'The Senate house set a fire wherein *Cæsar* was killed.'
[4] *In margin:* 'One *Cynna* killed [for] another.'
[5] *In margin:* 'Tumulte and rage of people.'
[6] *In margin:* '*Cæsars* funerall.'
[7] *In margin:* 'A Temple to *Cæsar*.'
[8] *In margin:* 'The *Romaines* used to give divine honours to their princes.'

IX. Translation of Analogue

From THE ROMAN HISTORIES OF FLORUS

translated by E. M. B[olton] [1619]

Florus. The Roman Histories of Lucius Julius Florus, from the foundation of Rome, till Cæsar Augustus, for above DCC. yeares, & from thence to Trajan near CC. yeares, divided by Florus into IV ages. Translated into English. London by William Stansby for Tho: Dewe. [Colophon]... translated into English by E.M.B.

Lib. 3—Chap. XII

The recapitulation [after the death of Crassus]

This is that third transmarine age of the people of *Rome*, in which employing themselves upon exploits out of *Italy*, they displayed their adventurous armes over the whole earth. Of which age, the first hundred yeeres were holy, pious, and (as we have alreadie said) the age of gold, voide of hainous fact, or foule black deed, all the while the simplenesse, and puritie of that shepherdish originall continued, and the imminent feare of the *Pænish*-men maintained among us ancient discipline. The other hundred yeeres (which we reckon from the destruction of *Carthage*, *Corinth*, *Numance*, and from the date of the last will, and testament of *King Attalus* (in which hee devised his kingdome in *Asia*) up to *Cæsar*, and *Pompey*, and to *Augustus*, who followed them) as the glorie of martial acts made stately great, if so vast domestick mischiefes made wretched, and worthie to bee blushed at. For as it was noble, and goodly to have conquer'd *Gallia*, *Thrace*, and *Cilicia*, most fertil, and most powrfull provinces, the *Armenians* also, & *Britans*, great names, but more for the honour of the empire, than for the uses thereof: So was it a brutish, and a shamefull thing to fight, and bicker at home, at the same time, with our owne citizens, associates, bondmen, fencers, and the whole Senate with it selfe. And I know not, whether it had not beene better for the people of *Rome* to have rested content with *Sicilia*, and *Africk*, yea, or to have wanted them also, having *Italie* at command, then to growe to such greatnesse as to bee consumed with their proper strengths. For what other things else bred civill furies, but the too much rankness of prosperitie? The first thing which corrupted us, was the conquest of *Syria*, & next after that, the heritage of the king of *Pergamus* in *Asia*. The wealth, and riches *of those countries* were the things which crusht under them the morall vertues of that age, and overthrew the commonweal drownd in her owne vices as in a common sinke. For what cause was there why the people of *Rome* should stand so hard for fields, or foode, but as they were driven by the hunger which prodigalitie had procured? From hence therefore sprang the first, and second *Gracchan* seditions, & that third *Appuleian*. And out of what other ground did it growe, that the knights and gentlemen *of Rome* separated themselves from the Lords, to have soveraigne power in seats of judgement, but *meerly* out of covetousnes, that so they might convert to private lucre the customarie paiments due to the State, and even judgement in law itself? This brought in the promise of making all *Latium* free of *Rome*, from whence rose the war with associats. And what bred the warre with bondmen? what? but the great number of them in families? whence came the armies of fensers against their owners, but for the excessive prodigality used in showes for gaining popular favour? while the *Romans* gave themselves over to showes of sword-players, they brought that to bee a profession, and Arte, which was before those times the punishment of enemies. And, to touch on more gallant vices, was it not over-much wealth which stirr'd *among us* rivalities in honours? Or did not the stormes of *Marius*, and *Sylla*, and the magnificent furniture of feasts, & sumptuous presents, rise out of that abundance, which ere long would bring forth beggerie? This was it which made *Catiline* fall foule upon his countrey. To bee briefe, what other fountaine had that very desire *in some* of soveraigntie, & to rule alone, but too much store of wealth? But that desire did mutually arme *Cæsar* and *Pompey* with those mortall enmities, which like the furies fire-brands, set *Rome* on a bright blaze. Our purpose therefore is, to handle these civill quarrels, distinguished from just, and foreine warres, in order as they fall.

Lib. 4—Chap. II

[After vanquishing the Pompeians, Cæsar returned to Rome]

Heere, for a while, were weapons layd aside, the following calme without blood, and *the cruelties of* warre were made amends for with goodenesse . . .

His countrey therefore not ingratefull, all sorts of honours were heaped upon this one prime man; images about the temples; in the theater a crowne deckt with rayes; a chaire of state in the Senate-house; a pinacle upon his house top; a month in the Zodiac; and besides all these himselfe proclaimed Father of his countrey, and perpetuall *Dictator*; last of all (and it was unknowne whether it were with his good liking) [by] *Antonius*, Consull, the ornaments of a king were offred: all which prooved but as ribbands, or trimmings of an host ordayned to be slaine in sacrifice. For the mildnesse of this prince was lookt upon with envious eyes, and the power itselfe, which conferred benefits, was to free mindes cumbersome. Nor was the forbearance of him an acquitall any longer: for *Brutus*, and *Cassius*, and other *Patricians*, *Lords of the highest ranke*, conspired to assassinate him. How great is the force of fate! the conspiracy was knowne far abroade; a scroll was given also to *Cæsar* himselfe, upon the very day *of the fact*; & though an hundred beasts were sacrificed, yet not one of them had any signe of luckines. He came into the Senate-house with a meaning to advance a warre against the *Parthians*: there the Senators stabd at him, as he sat in his court-chair, & with twenty three wounds he was driven to the ground. So, he who had embrewed the whole earth with civill bloud, did with his owne bloud overflow the Senat-house.

Chap. III

Cæsar Octavianus

Cæsar, and *Pompey* slaine, the people of *Rome* seem'd to have returnd to the state of the ancient libertie, and had returnd indeed, if *Pompey* had left no children, nor *Cæsar* an heire; or, which was more pestilent then both, if once his fellow *in office*, and then his rivall *in honour*, that firebrand of *Cæsars* power, and whirlewind of the ensuing age, *Antonius* had not over-lived. For, while *Sextus Pompeius* seekes to recover his fathers estate, no part of the sea was free from feare *of him*; while *Octavius* revengeth his fathers bloud, *Thassalia* was againe to be stirred: while *Antonius*, variable-witted, either disdained that *Octavius* should succeed to *Cæsar*, or for love to *Cleopatra*, takes upon him to bee a king: for hee had no other way to be safe, but by turning vassall. In so great perturbation we are to be glad notwithstanding, that the whole power *of Rome* came to be setled upon *Octavius*, first *Cæsar Augustus*, who by his wisedome, and dexteritie reduced into order the body of the Empire, shaken, and distempred on all sides, which without all doubt could never have been brought together, and made to agree, unlesse it had been governed by the authoritie of some *worthy* one, as with a soule, or mind. *Marcus Antonius*, & *Publius Dolobella*, consuls, fortune now *busie* in transferring the empire to the *house of the Cæsars*, the troubles of the citie were various, and manifold: that as in the change of yeerly seasons the stirred heavens doe thunder, and signifie their turnings by the weather; so in the change of the government of the *Romans*, that is to say, of all mankind, the world troubled throughout, and the whole body of the empire was turmoiled with all sorts of perils, and with civill warrs both at land, and sea.

Chap. IIII

The Mutinensian Warre

The first cause of civill breach was *Cæsars* last will, and testament, in which Antonius being named *but* in the second place, he grew starke mad, that *Octavius* was preferred, and *for that cause* opposed the adoption of that most spiritfull young-man with an inexpiable warre. For seeing him not fully eighteene yeeres old, tender, & fit to be wrought upon, and open to abuse, both defaced the dignitie of *Cæsar's* name with reviling termes, and diminisht his inheritance with privie thefts, disgraced him with foule phrases, and gave not over, by all the wayes hee could invent, to impeach his adoption into the *Julian* family: lastly, enterprised a warre for over-bearing the yong *noble gentleman*, and with an armie, raised in *Gall* on this side the *Alpes*, besieged *Decimus Brutus* for resisting his practices. *Octavius Cæsar*, pitied for his youth, and wrongs, & gracious for the majestie of that name which hee assumed, calling his *adoptive fathers* old souldiers to arms, hee then a private person (who would give credit to it?) sets upon the Consull, delivers *Brutus* from siege, and strips *Antonius* out of his campe: at that time hee did nobly with his owne hand: for bloudy, & wounded as hee was, hee carried upon his owne shoulders the eagled ensigne into the campe, which the eagle-bearer deliverd to him, dying slaine.

Chap. V

The Triumvirate

Antonius, of his owne nature, troublesom to peace, and troublesome to commonweale, *Lepidus* comes in like fire to flame: [*omitted from trans.*: 'what could be done against 2 consuls and 2 armies? because'] there was a necessitie of entring into the bond of a most bloudy league against two armies. The intentions of the *boutefeus* were severall in kindling these firie-blazes: *Lepidus*, covetous of riches, the hope whereof stood upon troubling the state, *Antonius* desirous to be revenged upon them, who proclaymed him traitor, *and Cæsar for* the death of his *adoptive* father upon *Cassius* and *Brutus*, offensive to his unrevenged ghost. Upon these termes of as it were a league,[1] peace was established among the three captaines, and at *Confluents* betweene *Perusia* and *Bononia* they joyne hands, and their armies embrace: *so* the triumvirate is entred upon with no good fashion. The common-weale opprest with force, *Sulla's* proscriptions returne, the hideous crueltie whereof containd no lesse then the number of one hundred and fortie *Senatours*: the ends of such as fledde for their lives over all the world, were gastly, foule, and miserable.

Chap. VI

The warre with Cassius *and* Brutus

Brutus, and *Cassius* seemed to have put by *Julius Cæsar* from the tyrannie, as *another Tarquinius Superbus*. But common libertie, the restitution whereof they principally aymed at, was lost by this assassinate of *the common Father*. So soone therefore as the fact was committed, they fled out of the Senate house, or *Curia*, into the *Capitoll*, as fearing *Cæsars* old souldiers, not without cause, who wanted not the minde to take revenge, but a captain for it. And when it now appeared what destruction hung over the state: the murther was disliked, & by the *Consuls* consent a decree of oblivion was enacted: yet to bee out of the eye of the publike griefe, they departed into *Syria*, and *Macedonia*, provinces given them even by *Cæsar* himselfe, whom they slue; revenge was rather defferred then buried. The commonweale therfore being setled upon *the pleasure of the Triumvirs*, rather as it might be then as it were fit, and *Lepidus one of the three*, left at home for defence of *Rome*, *Cæsar* addresseth himselfe, with *Antonius* against *Cassius* and *Brutus*. They having drawne huge forces to an head, took the selfe-same field which was fatall to *Cnæus Pompeius*, where the tokens of their destinated overthrow were not obscure: for the birds which used to gorge themselves upon carion, hoverd about the campe as if it were already theirs. As they marcht out to batel, a black Moore meeting them, was too too plainely a sign foreboding dire successe: and to *Brutus* himselfe at night, when light beeing brought in, he meditated somewhat, as his maner was, all alone, a certain gloomie Image appeared to him, which being by him demanded what it was, I AM (it said) THINE EVILL SPIRIT, and therewithall vanished out

[1] *In margin:* 'A.U.C. DCCXI.'

of his admiring sight. In *Cæsars* campe all presages were as much for good, as they were in the other for the bad; birds, & beasts promising alike faire fortune: but nothing was in present more luckie, then that *Cæsars* physician was warnd in his sleepe, that *Cæsar* should not stay in his owne campe, for that it would be surprised, accordingly as it fel out. For the battels joyning, and the fight maintain'd on both sides with equal manhood for a while, although the Generals were not present, the one withdrawne through sicknesse of bodie[1] and the other for sloth, and feare[2]; yet the unvanquisht fortune both of the revenger, and hee for whom the revenge was undertaken, stood for the side. The danger was as doubtfull at first, and as equal on both parts, as the event of the fight declared: *Cæsars* campe taken heere, and *Cassius* his campe there. But how much more forceable is fortune then virtue! and how true is that speech in which hee breathed out his last! THAT VERTUE WAS ONLY A VERBAL THING, AND NOT A REAL. Meere mistaking gave away that battell: for when *Cassius*, a wing of his armies shrinking, saw his owne troops of horse gallop back upon the spurre, after they had taken *Cæsars* campe, supposing they fled, got himselfe to an hillocke; from whence not being able to discerne what was done by reason of the dust, noise, & night at hand; and when the scout whom hee had emploid for discoverie, staid somewhat long before he returnd, he verily thought the day was lost; and thereupon caused one of them who was next him, to strike off his head. *Brutus*, when he had in *Cassius* lost his own life also, not to breake in any point that faith which each of them had plighted to the other, for otherwise they meant not to over-live the battel, laid his side open to the deadly blow of one of his owne companions. Who would not wonder that those most wise men used not their own hands at their last? unlesse in this point also they had a joynt perswasion, not to distaine their hands, but in letting out their most pure, and pious soules they meant the direction should be theirs, but the heinous execution other mens.

[1] Augustus.

[2] Plutarch says that some writers declared that Antony did not 'reach the field until his men were already in pursuit of the enemy.'

X. Analogue

From THE GOVERNOUR
by Sir Thomas Elyot (1531)

(a) [The cause of Julius Cæsar's death]

[II.v] *Of affabilitie and the utilitie therof in every astate.*

But I had almost forgoten Julius Cesar, who, beinge nat able to sustaine the burden of fortune, and envienge his owne felicitie, abandoned his naturall disposition, and as it were, beinge dronke with over moche welth, sought newe wayes howe to be advaunced above the astate of mortall princes. Wherfore litle and litle he withdrewe from men his accustomed gentilnesse, becomyng more sturdy in langage, and straunge in countenance, than ever before had ben his usage. And to declare more plainely his entent, he made an edict or decre, that no man shulde prease to come to hym uncalled, and that they shuld have good awaite, that they spake not in suche familiar facion to hym as they before had ben accustomed; wherby he so dyd alienate from hym the hartis of his most wise and assured adherentis, that, from that tyme forwarde, his life was to them tedious, and abhorring him as a monstre or commune enemie, they beinge knitte in a confederacy slewe hym sitting in the Senate; of which conspiracie was chiefe capitaine, Marcus Brutus, whome of all other he beste loved, for his great wisedome and prowesse. And it is of some writers suspected that he was begoten of Cesar, for as moche as Cesar in his youth loved Servilia, the mother of Brutus, and, as men supposed, used her more familiarly than honestie required. Thus Cesar, by omittinge his olde affabilitie, dyd incende his next frendes and companions to sle hym.

But nowe take hede what domage insued to hym by his decre, wherin he commanded that no man shuld be so hardy to approche or speke to hym. One whiche knewe of the conspiracie agayne hym, and by al lykelyhode did participate therin, beinge meved either with love or pitie, or other wise his conscience remording agayne the destruction of so noble a prince, consideringe that by Cesars decre he was prohibited to have to hym any familiar accesse, so that he might nat plainly detect the conspiraci; he, therto vehemently meved, wrate in a byll all the forme therof, with the meanes howe it myght be espied, and sens he mought fynde none other oportunitie, he delyvered the byll to Cesar the same day that his dethe was prepared, as he wente towarde the place where the Senate was holden. But he beinge radicate in pride, and neglecting to loke on that bil, not esteminge the persone that delivered it, whiche perchance was but of a mean haviour, continued his way to the Senate, where he incontinently was slaine by the said Brutus, and many mo of the Senate for that purpose appoynted.

Who beholdinge the cause of the dethe of this moste noble Cesar, unto whom in eloquence, doctrine, martiall prowesse, and gentilnesse, no prince may be comparid, and the acceleration or haste to his confusion, causid by his owne edict or decre, will nat commende affabilite and extolle libertie of speche? Wherby onely love is in the hartis of people perfectly kendled, all feare excluded, and consequently realmes, dominions and all other autorites consolidate and perpetuelly stablisshed. The sufferaunce of noble men to be spoken unto is not onely to them an incomparable suretie, but also a confounder of repentance, enemie to prudence, wherof is ingendred this worde, *Had I wist*, whiche hath ben ever of all wise men reproved.

(b) [Pompey and Cæsar slaves of ambition]

[III.xvi] *Of an other vyce folowing Magnanimitie, called Ambition.*

Also Pompei, and Julius Cesar, the one suffrynge no piere, the other no superior, by their ambycion caused to be slaine betwene them people innumerable, and subverted the best and mooste noble publyke weale of the worlde, and fynally havynge lyttell tyme of rejoysinge theyr unlefull desire, Pompeie, shamefully fleinge, had his heed striken of, by the commaundement of Ptolomee, king of Egipt, unto whome as unto his frende he fledde for succour. Cesar, the vainquyssher, was murdred in the Senate with daggers, by them, whome he mooste specially favoured.

I could occupie a great volume with histories of them whiche, coveytynge to mount into excellent dignities, dyd therby bringe in to extreme perylles bothe them selves and their countreys. For as Tacitus saith, wonderfull elegantly, with them whyche desire soveraygnetie, there is no meane place betwene the toppe and the stepe downe. To the which wordes Tulli agreinge, sayeth that hygh autorities shulde nat moche be desired, or rather nat to be taken at some tyme, and often tymes to be left and forsaken.

(c) [Brutus and Cassius examples of disloyalty]

[III.vi] *Of faythe or fidelitie, called in latyne* FIDES *which is the fundation of justyce.*

This one thinge I wolde were remembred, that by the juste

providence of god, disloyalte or treason seldome escapeth great vengeaunce, all be it that it be pretended for a necessary purpose. Example we have of Brutus and Cassius, two noble Romaynes, and men of excellent vertues, whiche, pretendinge an honorable zeale to the libertie and commune weale of their citie, slewe Julius Cesar (who trusted them moste of all other) for that he usurped to have the perpetuall dominion of the empire, supposinge thereby to have brought the senate and people to their pristinate libertie. But it dyd nat so succede to their purpose. But by the dethe of so noble a prince hapned confusion and civile batayles. And bothe Brutus and Cassius, after longe warres vanquisshed by Octavian, nevewe and hiere unto Cesar, at the last falling in to extreme desperation, slewe them selfes. A worthy and convenient vengeaunce for the murder of so noble and valyaunt a prince.

XI. Analogue

From THE MIRROR FOR MAGISTRATES

(1587 edition)

Caius Julius Cæsar, by John Higgins

The Mirour for Magistrates, wherein may bee seene, by examples passed in this Realme, with how greevous plagues vices are punished in great Princes and Magistrates, and how fraile and unstable worldly prosperity is found, where Fortune seemeth most highly to favour: Newly imprinted, and with the addition of divers Tragedies enlarged. At London in Fleete streete, by Henry Marsh, being the assigne of Thomas Marsh. 1587. Cum Privilegio.

How Caius Julius Cesar which first made
this Realme tributary to the Romaynes,
was slayne in the Senate house,
about the yeare before
Christ, 42.

Although by *Bocas* I have whilom told my mind,
And *Lydgate* have likewise translated wel the same:
Yet sith my place in order here againe I find,
And that my factes deserv'd in *Britayne* worthy fame:
Let me againe renue to memory my name.
Recite my mind, which if thou graunt to mee,
Thou shalt therefore receive a friendly fee,
And for my tale, perhaps commended thou shalt bee.

But least thou seeme to doubt what Prince thou seest appeare,
And wotst not well which way to winde or wrest his talke,
As may both sound to like a perfect *English* eare,
And eke direct thy dreadfull pen which way to walke:
Lest thou on this shouldst long divine, or muse, or calke,
I will thee tell: but take in hand thy pen,
First set thy selfe to write my wordes, and then
A mirrour make yet more for Magistrates agen.

If ever erst the fame of auncient *Romayne* facts
Have come to pearce thine eares before this present time,
I thinke amongst the rest, likewise my noble actes
Have shewde them selves in sight, as *Phoebus* fayre in prime.
When first the *Romayne* state began aloft to clime,
And wanne the wealth of all the worlde beside,
When first their force in warlike feates were tryde,
My selfe was victour hee that did the *Romaynes* guyde.

I *Caius Julius Cæsar Consull* had to name,
That worthie *Romayne* borne, renownde with noble deeds:
What neede I here recyte the linage whence I came,
Or else my great exploytes? perdy 'tis more then needes:
But onely this to tell, of purpose now proceedes:
Why I a *Romayne* Prince, no *Britayne*, here
Amongst these *Britayne* Princes now appeere,
As if amongst the rest a *Britayne* Prince I were.

And yet because thou maist perceyve the story all
Of all my life, and so deeme better of the end:
I will againe the same to mind yet briefly call,
To tell thee how thou maist me prayse or discommend.
Which when thou hast, perdy, as I recyte it, pend,
Thou shalt confesse that I deserved well,
Amongst them here my tragedie to tell,
By conquest sith I wanne this Ile before I fell.

Of stature high and tall, of colour fayre and white,
Of body spare and leane, yet comely made to see:
What neede I more of these impertinent recyte,
Sith *Plutarch* hath at large describde it all to thee.
And eke thy selfe that thinkst thou seest and hearest me,
Maist well suppose the rest, or take the viewe
Thou maist by talke of those which erst me knewe,
And by my statures tell of my proportion true.

In journey swift I was, and prompte and quicke of witte,
My eloquence was likte of all that hearde me pleade,
I had the grace to use my tearmes, and place them fitte,
My roling Rhetoricke stoode my Clients oft in steade:
No fine conveyance past the compasse of my heade.
I wan the spurres, I had the laud and prayse,
I past them all that pleaded in those dayes,
I had of warlike knowledge, Keasar, all the keyes.

At seventeene yeeres of age, a *Flamin* was I chose,
An office great in *Rome* of priesthoode Princely hie,
I married eke *Cossutia* whereof much mischiefe rose,
Because I was divorc'st from her so speedily.
Divorcement breeds despite, defame is got thereby.
For such as fancies fond by chaunge fulfil,
Although they thinke it cannot come to ill,
The wrong they shew doth cry to God for vengeance still.

Of these the stories tell, what neede I more recyte,
Or of the warres I waged *Consul* with the *Galles*?
The worthiest writers had desire of me to write,
They plac'st my life amongst the worthies and their falles.
So Fame me thinks likewise amids the *Britaynes* calles
For *Cæsar* with his sword, that bare with them the sway,
And for the cause that brought him into such decay,
Which by his noble acts did beare their freedome first away.

When I in *Fraunce* had brought the *Galles* to bende,
And made them subject all obaysant unto mee:
Mee thought I had unto the worlde his ende
By west subdued the Nations whilome free.
There of my warres I wrot an historye
By nights, at leisure times so from my Countrey far:
I did describe the places and the sequelles of my war
The Commentaryes calde of *Cæsars* acts that ar.

At length I did perceave there was an Island yet
By west of *Fraunce*, which in the *Ocean* sea did lye:
And that there was likewise no cause or time to let,
But that I might with them the chance of Fortune trye.
I sent to them for hostage of assuraunce, I,
And wild them tribute pay unto the *Romayne* stoute,
Or else I woulde both put theyr lives & goods in doubte,
And also reave away the best of all theyr route.

But they a people fearce and recklesse of my powres,
Abused those which brought th'ambassage that I sent:
Now sith (quod they) the land and region here is oures,
Wee will not *Cæsar* to thy rightlesse hestes assent.
By dome of frendly Goddes first this Ile wee hent,
Of *Priames* bloud wee ar, from *Greece* we *Trojanes* came.
As *Brutus* brought us thence, & gave this land his name,
So for our fredome we will freely fight to keepe the same.

. . . .

[Cæsar describes his invasions of Britain and
the wars against Pompey and his sons]

But glory won, the way to holde and keepe the same,
To holde good Fortune fast, a worke of skill:
Who so with prudent arte can stay that stately dame
Which sets us up so high upon her hauty hill,
And constant aye can keepe her love and favour still,
Hee winnes immortall fame and high renowne:
But thrise unhappy hee that weres the stately crowne,
Yf once misfortune kicke and cast his scepter downe.

For when in *Rome* I was *Dictator* chose,
And Emperour or Captayne sole for aye:
My glory did procure mee secret foes,
Because above the rest I bare the sway.
By sundry meanes they sought my deepe decaye.
For why, there coulde no *Consuls* chosen bee,
No *Pretor* take the place, no sentence have decree,
Unlesse it likte mee first, and were approvde by mee.

This they envide that sude aloft to clime,
As *Cassius*, which the *Pretorship* did crave,
And *Brutus* eke his friende which bare the crime
Of my dispatch, for they did first deprave

My life, mine actes,[1] and sought my bloud to have,
Full secretly amongst them selves conspirde, decreede
To bee attemptors of that cruell bloudy deede,
When *Cæsar* in the *Senate* house from noble hart should bleede.

But I forewarned was by *Capis* tombe,
His *Epitaph* my death did long before forshowe:
Cornelius Balbus sawe mine horses headlesse ronne
Without a guide, forsakeing foode for woe.
Spurina warned mee that sooth of thinges did knowe,
A wrenne in beake with Laurell greene that flewe
From woods to *Pompeys* Court, whom birdes there slew,
Forshowde my dolefull death, as after all men knew.

The night before my slaughter, I did dreame
I caried was, and flewe the clouds above:
And sometime hand in hand with *Jove* supreame
I walkte mee thought, which might suspitions move.
My wife *Calphurnia*, *Cæsars* only love,
Did dreame shee sawe her crest of house to fall,
Her husband thrust through breast a sword withall,
Eke that same night her chamber dores themselves flewe open all.

These thinges did make mee doubte that morning much,
And I accrazed was and thought at home to stay:
But who is hee can voyde of destnyes such,
Where so great number seekes hym to betray.
The traytour *Brutus* bad mee not delay,
Nor yet to frustrate there so great assembly sate:
On which to heare the publique pleas I gate,
Mistrusting naught mine end and fatall fate.

There met mee by the way a *Romayne* good,
Presenting mee a scrole of every name:
And all their whole devise that sought my bloud,
That presently would execute the same.
But I supposde that for some suit hee came,
I heedelesse bare this scrole in my left hand,
And others more, till leasure, left unscand,
Which in my pocket afterwards they fand.

[1] As Cassius and Casca do in Act I.

Spurina as I came at sacrifizes was,
Nere to the place where I was after slayne:
Of whose divinings I did litle passe,
Though hee to warne mee oft before was fayne.
My hauty hart these warnings all disdayne.
(Quod I) the Ides of Marche bee come, yet harme is none.
(Quod hee) the Ides of Marche be come, yet th'ar not gone.
And reckelesse so to Court I went, and tooke my throne.

Assoone as I was set, the traytors all arose,
And one approached nere, as to demaund some thing:
To whom as I layd eare, at once my foes
Mee compast round, their weapons hid they bring.
Then I to late perceiv'd the fatall sting.
O this (quoth I) is violence: then *Cassius* pearst my breast:
And *Brutus* thou my sonne (quoth I) whom erst I loved best?
Hee stabde mee in, and so with daggers did the rest.

You Princes all, and noble men beware of pride,
And carefull will to warre for Kingdomes sake:
By mee, that set my selfe aloft the world to guide,
Beware what bloudsheds you doe undertake.
Ere three & twenty wounds had made my hart to quake,
What thousands fell for *Pompeys* pride and mine?
Of *Pompeys* life that cut the vitall line,
My selfe have told what fate I found in fine.

Full many noble men, to rule alone, I slewe,
And some themselves for griefe of hart did slay:
For they ne would mine Empyre stay to vewe.
Some I did force to yeelde, some fled away
As loth to see theyr Countryes quite decay.
The world in *Aphrike*, *Asia*, distant far,
And *Europe* knew my bloudsheds great in war,
Recounted yet through all the world that ar.

But sith my whole pretence was glory vayne,
To have renowne and rule above the rest,
Without remorce of many thousands slayne,
Which, for their owne defence, their warres addrest:
I deeme therefore my stony harte and brest
Receiv'd so many wounds for just revenge, they stood
By justice right of *Jove*, the sacred sentence good,
That who so slayes, hee payes the price, is bloud for bloud.

XII. Translation of Possible Source

From IL CESARE

by Orlando Pescetti (1594)

Il Cesare. Tragedia D'Orlando Pescetti Dedicata Al Sereniss. Principe Donno Alfonso II D'Este Duca di Ferrara. In Verona. Nella Stamparia di Girolamo Discepolo. MDXCIIII.

[The Dedicatory Epistle links the family of Alfonso d'Este with that of Julius Cæsar, likens the Duke's great deeds to Cæsar's, and asserts that if Brutus and Cassius lived today they would not rebel but rejoice to be governed by Alfonso.]

Prologue [in Heaven]
Mars. Venus. Jove.

MARS O Joy of earthly men and of the gods,
Fair mother of young Love, alas, what cause
O'erclouds that face in which, as in a shrine,
Gladness and smiles are wont to have their seat? . . .
Alas, what new, what strange mishap is this?
Laughter itself weeps? pleasure grieves? the fount
Of happiness is all perturb'd and sad? . . .

VENUS The man who yet in arms had never a peer
By whom Disdain might blindly forge a weapon,
The man who fear has never known, the hero
Whose back in battle no foe ever saw,
Whose zeal burned for all greatness and who brought
Whate'er he burned for to a happy end;
He who hath made more wars than other men
Have fled; he who the more things perilous showed,
More hard the enterprise, so grew more venturous;
He who imposed the curb on rebel Gaul,
On the proud German and the horrific Briton,
He who in Thessaly, conquering the great Pompey,
Transferred the latter's honours to himself;
He, through whose efforts thy proud city, Rome,
Rears up her head to the stars and rules the world;

He finally, O Mars, the man who's now
The sole surviving scion of my stock,
In whom alone lives, who upholds, the name
Of my Dardanian Julius and his race,
Today must be in sacred place destroyed
Most cruelly by sacrilegious hands.
See now if I've not only cause to grieve,
Reason for tears, but also to desire
To end my life together now with his—
If it were possible for Gods to die.

MARS Cæsar be killed today? He who on earth
Doth represent my power? in whom doth rest
Whatever I have had of force and valour,
Must lose his life today? What do I hear?
And Jove allows it? Jove, how can it be
That thou permittest such impiety? . . .

[Venus inveighs against the Father of the Gods.]

VENUS He sleeps, O Mars, he has grown old; O Mars
He sees no more, he hears no more, for he
Is blind and deaf; maybe he's childish grown.
Now anyone 's allowed to do him shame
And he will not resent, nor more be moved
Than if he were of wood or marble made . . .

[She recalls the immoralities of Jove's youth, and declares that he has forgotten justice.]

While he's reverting to such vanities
So long without a ruler rests the realm;
And human kind, left without fear's restraint,
Runs headlong into every wickedness.
Nor doth this end the evil, since his own
Life's dissolute and lascivious and this
Vicious example hath corrupted all
His court until there's neither God nor Goddess
Who is not either adulterer or whore;
For a King's court follows the King's example
As soldiers do the blare of the shrill brass. . . .

[Their lengthy complaints are interrupted by Jove's approach.]

VENUS But he comes towards us; silence lest he hear.

JOVE Banish from you, my children, these ill thoughts
About your father, this indecent talk,
These dreadful blasphemies. Nothing is done by Him
Except with sovereign Providence and Wisdom.
And if at times quite otherwise it seems
To mortal eyes, that is because, weighed down
By weight of bodily members and by mists
Of passion, they can never penetrate
The secret chambers of my mind. All things
That I perform, permit, or hinder, work
Towards the maintenance and benefit
Of the universe, for every thought I have,
My every action, turns to jovial use.
Hence was I namèd Jove. I am the fount
And head of every good—nay, that same good
I am, nor is there good in the universe
Derives not from me nor to me returns,
As from the sea all rivers have their birth,
And all the rivers to the sea return.
How then can I be source of any evil?
For every good that men possess is there . . .
Is it not all my gift? that man's alive,
That he has discourse, joys in heav'ns bright look,
And lords it o'er the animals, to his use
Converts whatever's covered by the sky;
Is it not all my bounty? Often indeed
Men are oppressed by ills and sore afflicted.
But wars, calamities, and fell diseases,
Floods, famines, and the score of other evils
(To call them so as doth the erring world)
With which at times now this, now another part
Of the world I torment, are, if judged aright
And without passion, benefits, not ills;
Both since they emanate from me, from whom
Nothing can come that is not good, and since
To holy ends they are ordained by me
Because my end is naught but happiness.
When man I castigate, 'tis as a father
His son chastises but to make him good. . . .
Dost thou not know that not to punish only
Sinners I order whips and fling down fire,
But even more to exercise the good,
To purify and render them more perfect,
As in a furnace gold is purified? . . .

So Julius, for whose death you feel such grief,
Such anguish, and for whom you sigh and moan,
Will shine resplendent in the heav'ns tomorrow
Among the stars his peers. Beneath his feet
The clouds you'll see, and tempests; this because
Jove's promises stand firm, and ere they fail
The elements and Nature herself will fail.
And those who steep their arms in sacred blood
Within a little time shall all be slain
In bloody death and quite extinguished.
So with an adamantine firm resolve,
With letters irremovable and eternal,
Within the impenetrable and profound abyss
Of my unchanging mind is fixed and written. . . .

[He bids Venus be consoled.]

VENUS To what thou willest, Father, I'm reconciled.
JOVE And thou, Mars, whom I see so much to yearn
To please thy goddess, do thou scatter hate,
Discord, disdain and fury among Romans,
Desire for blood and vengeance, whence in fine
All impious men in the world shall draw the sword.
MARS For me to carry out thy bidding needs
No spur to incite, and no encouragement.

Act I.

Brutus. Cassius.

BRU. Most noble shade, lo here I plight my troth
And gird myself to the high task you set me.
This day the Tyrant's blood, or else my own,
Shall dew thy sacred ground. Today thy death
Shall be avenged upon impiety,
And freedom be restored to the fatherland.
O turn thyself to watch, where'er thou art.
Today it shall be known in Rome that I
Am no unworthy seed of that great Brutus
Who, driving out the kings from Rome, did high
And memorable vengeance for Lucretia's rape.
Today, O Rome, this dagger in this hand
Must break and loose the chains whereby thou'rt bound,
Must draw thee from a shameful, grievous life
Ev'n though I perish. Jove, if thou art just,

If it be right to set the City free
From Tyrants proud . . .
do not disdain that I
Although unworthy, be thy minister
And instrument of justice. . . .

[Cassius enters in soliloquy.]

CASS. The loftiest power and the highest wisdom
Cannot but be superlatively just;
And so considering with what great order
And providence is governed this great World,
Perforce all intellects not blind or stubborn
[Must realise God's justice, fear to offend Him;]
. . . yet one there is
(O foolish greed, whither dost drive thyself?)
Who not one man alone, but entire Cities,
Against humanity and every law
Divine and human, 'gainst the natural order,
Oppresses fiercely and o'erthrows in ruin.
And this O Rome thou provest, now thou art
By the proud Tyrant basely trampled on. . . .

BRU. Rise, golden God in the East,
Though wan as yet, arise!
And with thy vital ray
Clear the dark air; lend speed
To thy for once too tardy steed,
For thou shalt see today
The happiest and most joyous feast
That e'er has met thine eyes.

CASS. If in this not yet dissipated dark
My sight deceives me not, 'tis my friend Brutus.
'Tis he indeed. Maybe he's urged from home
By the same thoughts with which I am impelled.
O Brutus, sovereign price, glory of Rome,
In whom shines ancient virtue, whom Heav'n calls
To glorious and immortal enterprise,
What care molests thee and so early makes
Thee thus abandon thy bed's feathery down
To wander here alone (when in soft sleep
Lies buried almost every other mortal)
Discoursing with the breezes and thyself?

BRU. 'The trophies of Miltiades', replied
The Greek when asked a similar question,
'Keep me from sleep and will not let me rest.'
Grief holds me wide awake to see our Mother
Placed in base servitude. The great desire
I have to lift from her the bitter yoke
Has grown until I can no more restrain it,
And I must let it lead me where it will.
Today, my Cassius, I have resolved to make
An end of that which you and I have planned.
The Tyrant who has robbed me of repose
Must close his eyes in everlasting sleep
Before the Sun in Ocean hides himself.

CASS. O now indeed I call thee man, and true
Branch of that heavenly, glorious stock which erst
Lifted from Rome the ignominious yoke.
And O, what a bright beam of truly Roman
Spirit is locked up, enclosed in thee!
The valour dwells in thee that now in vain
I yearn for in our people, seek in vain.
In this way, Brutus, we ascend to Heaven,
By killing Tyrants, rescuing the oppressed,
Purging the world of cruel monsters....

BRU. Hear that which hath
Fresh fuel added to the all-burning fire.
Last night when at my body's ease in bed,
As soon as I had closed my eyes in sleep,
Behold, before me stood great Pompey's shade
With angry mien and stern; in these words called me:
'Can Brutus be a slave? Thou who dost draw
Thy source from him who first to this great City
Gave liberty? Yet thou canst serve the Tyrant?
Thou who descend'st from him who could not brook
Even a lawful lord? This thou hast learnt
From Rome, most sacred and most venerable
Mistress of life and manners.
Now in her bitter age thou turn'st from her,
Abandoning thy country where have flowered
All honoured studies, gentle arts, good habits?'

[The ghost called on Brutus to let his mind correspond to his name]

... This said, he vanished,
And as I followed him he waved his hand,

And as he went from sleep I started up,
And with such fury felt my heart to burn
That, quite unable to control myself
I was obliged to rise up from my bed,
And having wandered long about the house
In rage like that of Athamas or Orestes,
Finding those walls too narrow for my frenzy,
Not waiting till the dawn rose up the sky
I issued forth, meaning to walk about
Until the guards opened the temple doors,
Then go within, pay honour to the gods
And supplicate their help in my great task.

[With Cassius he awaits the Priest who goes to offer sacrifice for the peace and happiness of Rome. The Chorus prays. Brutus tells Cassius that Heaven is propitious, and that 'after many divided opinions' it has been decided to kill Cæsar in the Senate as 'an offering and sacrifice to liberty.']

CAS. Thou know'st he's fierce. No matter what the danger
He's ne'er disheartened; rather he becomes
More bold and full of heart when greater seems
The peril.

BRU. Let it be so; all his boldness
Will help him not, nor will his strength; for were
He made of steel, he cannot overcome
The force of thirty men who've set their lives
At stake to free their land. Believ'st thou, Cassius,
That I know not as great a courage hides
In thy breast as in Cæsar's? That thine arm
Is no less muscular and strong than his?
Naught of myself I'll say, but be assured,
Four times or more deep in his breast this steel
Shall hide itself. With heart renewed in courage
I feel a vigour unaccustomed rise
Into my limbs, and with desire I pine
These hands to ensanguine in the impious blood.

CASS. Methinks I have perceived in Antony
Desire for power; hence, if we would secure
Our land in every way, let us despatch him
Together with the Tyrant; from our eyes
Remove this mote which could in future days
Give us no little trouble. Well thou know'st,

How friendly to him are the soldiers and
How skilled he is to inflame the crowd's mad mind.

BRU. But if we slay others besides the Tyrant,
The mob (which things distorts and ever gives
Interpretations false) will deem't not zeal
To free our land, but private hate and vengeance.
Let it be moved by this, then for the work
Whence we anticipate eternal glory,
Dishonour we should gain, eternal blame;
And where we seek a name for piety,
We'd be notorious for impiety.
Nor should we have accomplished very much;
For Antony is not greatly to be feared,
A man vowed to his belly, sleep and lust,
Weakened by dissolute acts and drunkenness,
A broken man; will he dare take up arms
'Gainst those who ne'er made friends with ease and pleasure,
But passed their lives entire in hard pursuits,
In exercise laborious and harsh?
The sight of the end administered to those
Who seek to take the liberty of others,
And the Tyrant's recent death, will terrify
Him so that, had he any wish for power,
'Twould quickly be extinguished.

CASS. Antony
Is certainly to ease and pleasure vowed,
But on the other hand no man exists
Stronger or more courageous, more enduring
In toils and troubles that concern himself.
Of what the vulgar say, the foolish mob,
We should take small account, for he that's moved
By the voices of the mob is than the mob
Himself more light, inconstant.

BRU. We must not punish
A man who has not sinned. I have no mind
To deal out death to one who has not harmed me
Or done me injury.

CASS. More like am I
To him who kills his enemy before
He offends, than him who waits to avenge the harm
Until he's been offended.

BRU. Not the mere thought, only the deed is punishable.
Besides, what dost thou say of him who assures me
That he's of such a mind? For who can reach
The bottom of his heart, see what hides there?
Only Jove understands the thoughts of men.

CASS. Brutus thou art too scrupulous. Heav'n grant
That these thy scruples be not harmful to us
Some coming day.
To cure a body of a growing ulcer
The knife and fire are needed. Well thou know'st,
The tender-hearted doctor swells the abscess
And the whole body often thus infects.

BRU. To cut the head off from the other members
Cuts off all vigour and all power from them.

CASS. When from the Hydra one head is removed
Immediately there grow another seven.

BRU. Yet in the end she lies there, life extinct.

CASS. Indeed; but slain by a son of eternal Jove.

BRU. Whoe'er loves virtue is a son of Jove.
But let us leave such questions; rather turn
Our every thought and will towards Cæsar's death . . .

[Brutus describes how Cæsar is to be surrounded and killed. While they are talking Portia enters from Brutus's house.]

Portia. Cassius. Brutus.

PORT. Not without cause my husband went this morning
So early from the house. Great things engage
Him surely, and, if my thoughts do not err,
He's planning soon to give the evil Tyrant
His just reward (if just reward indeed
Can be accorded one so unjust and impious).
O why does not my sex let me put on
Masculine robes and mingle in men's councils,
Discussing the Republic, and with hard
Steel toughening the body for its sake
The spear and sword to wield? For with the glory
Of such illustrious action I should wish
To adorn myself, and I should like to dye
My weapon in the foul blood of the Tyrant,

In blood of that proud man by whom my unconquered
Father (than whom Rome never had a man
More wise and firm to seek the liberty
That criminal took from her) twice was forced
To rend his mortal veil. Therefore I wish
To show myself a worthy child of Cato,
And prove that freedom is to me as dear
As life to others; that a generous
And manly heart dwells in this female breast.
And if it were not that I do not wish
To rob my husband of so great a glory,
I could dare things that women dare no more,
Bring it about that by a feminine hand
The ruthless one should be destroyed, by whom
So many famed and noble citizens
Have died. I see my Brutus there with Cassius
Before the temple; they have been to pray
Help of the gods.

CASS. Early indeed thou com'st
From home, O Portia, rare embodiment
Of modesty, clear spotless mirror of
Matronly prudence, image live of him
Whose wisdom made the wisest Greeks seem foolish,
And with whose death liberty died, as if
She wished to lie beside him in the grave.
What business draws thee here against thy wont
So early?

[He lectures her on the duty of a wife to stay at home.]

POR. Now by the love ye bear our dead Republic,
Faithful companions, I conjure you, on whom
Alone rests what small hope remains for our
Declining Roman state, that you unveil
Your thoughts to me and solemnly entrust
To these my ears what vainly you have striven
To hide. Who can deceive a loving woman?
What can be hidden from a loving eye?
The Lynx's eye is not more sharp, nor that
Of Jove's bird, than the eye of a true lover,
Though some may feign love's blind. These eyes of mine
Penetrate, friends, your hearts' most secret depths,
And read within your face what in your breast
You seal in vain; in vain you hide from me
Your schemes and thoughts.

CASS. 'Tis not that any doubt of thy good faith
And taciturnity—a virtue rare
In female soul,—O Portia, enters our minds,
Because we know thee the true child of Cato,
To whom belonged all constancy and judgement.
But since to discourse e'en with oneself of things
Which others wish kept private and occult
Is a great peril, we have concealed from thee
Till now what thou desirest much to know.
Sometimes a glance of the eyes, a swift expression,
A wordless sigh, a little word cut off,
Discovers that which others hide within them.
So great the load we bear upon our lives
That little reck we of them, only fear
Lest we may not achieve our grand design.
But since thou seek'st so much to know it, listen.

POR. Without more prologue tell me what you plan.

CAS. Without more prologue then. In a few words,
Know, we intend to lift the yoke from Rome
And to restore her to the state whence greed
And impious will in some have dragged her down . . .

[He tells her to pray for their success. She would sooner bear arms, but is persuaded to go home.]

POR. Go forth, ye strong and wise. Go forth, ye are
Worthy of your high lineage. May Heav'n
Second your wishes. May Jove, benign, support
And govern right your footsteps and your hands.

[She will prepare for death if need be, preferring]

Rather to perish than to live a slave.
Then may all generous and masculine spirits
Arm this my feminine breast and steel thy heart
So that a last act worthy of thy birth
And of thy life so far thy life may end.

[A Chorus of Roman matrons begs Romulus to bring back peace to Rome.]

ACT II

Calpurnia. Waiting Woman.

[They discuss Calpurnia's evil dreams, during which Cæsar appeared as if dead.]

CAL. I do not know whether 'twas Julius' body
Or else his shade; alas how sick and doleful,

How ugly, bloodless, pale, alas, how changed
From Cæsar as he entered Rome but now,
Triumphing in his honours with the spoils
Of enemies adorned . . .

[The Waiting Woman vainly tries to console Calpurnia. The Chorus sings both of the baseness of the human heart and of its ability to rise above afflictions. Brutus and Portia enter. Portia has cut herself, and Brutus, thinking she got it doing servant's work, chides her.]

BRU. Thou should'st not in base ministry employ those hands
Which suited are to wield, not razors, distaffs,
Spindles and other instruments of vulgar housewives,
But royal sceptres, reins of kingdoms, empires.
If mishap thou hast met, 'tis well for thee
Not to thrust sickle into other people's corn,
Nor put thy hand to other people's steel.

POR. Imprudence it was not, nor chance, but conscious
Choice that this hand wounded, and to wound
My hand, not cut my nails, was my intent. . . .
I wished to prove whether in me there dwelt
The firmness and resolve to kill myself
With my own hand, should fit occasion rise
To make death beautiful or necessary.

BRU. The antique valour's not entirely lost
To the female sex, while women such as this
Live. If our lost Republic had but four
Souls like to thine, which had more fear of shame
Than fear of death, Rome would not stay for long
Enslaved . . .

[He tells her not to cut short her life whatever happens to him. They argue the point at great length.]

POR. . . . And thou canst think
So little of my love, as to believe
I'd cling one hour to life, deprived of thee?
BRU. I know thou lov'st me,
And know besides that thou art no less wise
Than loving.
POR. Never did Love and Wisdom go
Together. Therefore Pallas was ne'er a lover,
And Cupid plays the child and ne'er grows old.

BRU. Where wisdom's lacking, granted that no lover
Can be a wise man also, yet his love
Will give him strength and constancy.

POR. There's nothing can resist the force of Love.

BRU. But loving me, thou shouldst obey my will.

POR. I yearn for nothing save to satisfy thee.

BRU. I will that thou live on until it please
The Supreme King to summon thee to Heav'n.

POR. Yet if thou lov'st me that cannot be true.

BRU. Why not?

POR. Since if thou lovedst me thou couldst
Not wish me evil.

BRU. Do I wish thee evil,
Wishing to save thy life?

POR. 'Tis hell for me
And torments thou desirest, wishing to keep me
Living, once thou'rt dead. If by Love's miracle
Two souls are in his furnace liquefied,
And in his fire through wondrous tempering
By the divine craftsman one soul's made,
Fusing the will of both, compelling them
To will or to reject the selfsame things,
How canst thou then desire what I do not?

BRU. And thou, if what thou sayst of Love be true,
How canst thou not desire whate'er I wish?

POR. Ill to thyself thou wishest, willing mine
And I whose will could never wish thee evil,
Tell me, if e'er thou knewst that I endured
A life most miserable and unhappy,
Wouldst thou not, Brutus, feel a grief extreme
For all my sufferings and my languishing?

BRU. Thy woe would burden me more than thyself.

POR. I therefore, lest thou feel grief at my grief,
Would wish by death to extricate myself,
Not simply to escape from ills which I
Believe I have the spirit to endure,
But so that thou, within the Fortunate Fields,
Should not feel pain to see me suffering.

BRU. Who could reply to such keen reasoning,
So eloquent and prompt a tongue? But Jove
Will not allow that a woman so courageous,
So beautiful and apt to bring salvation
To a thousand others should herself destroy . . .

[Calpurnia comes from the temple, and they overhear her conversation with her Waiting Woman. Calpurnia ascribes most human suffering to men's desire for power. She will try to prevent Cæsar from going to the Senate. Brutus prays Jove to make Cæsar go, and leaves his wife, to rejoin Cassius. The Chorus sings that human happiness is short-lived.]

Act III

Cæsar. Mark Antony.

CÆSAR Magnificent the dinner was, superb,
And fit for a High Priest, that Lepidus
Gave us last night, and no less sumptuous
The chamber that he gave us and the bed
Where afterwards he placed us to repose;
Delightful above all, and gracious, was
The conversation livening our food.
Good talk's the condiment of any table,
And that's the truest feast which feeds at once
The flesh with pleasant foods, the mind with glad
And knowledgeable discourse. These the meals
That next day still delight us. Such were those
Of the great Plato: What delight it is,
And what inestimable happiness
When four or five wise and familiar souls
Together at a splendid feast can talk
Of many things in gay and honest fashion!

[They discuss the alternating joys and sorrows of life.]

CÆSAR This instability, this mutability
Of earthly things bids me remember that
The present state in which I have been placed
By excellence or fortune, is not ordained
For ever. Though I feel and am secure
It can be changed whenever that must be so.

MARK Respecting Fortune, I assure thee, it
Can never prove contrary while thy hands

Are twisted in its mane. And yet I urge,
Guard thyself well from wiles of enemies.
Many there are offended by thee, many
Are envious of thy glory. Some indeed
Are dazzled by thy splendour, others cannot
Endure that thou art their superior.

CÆSAR Tomorrow I shall choose from the Tenth Legion
Fifty of the most strong and faithful men
To stand continually at my side and be
My shield against all guile or open force.
Indeed I am not destitute of sense,
Nor am I so intoxicate with all
The sweetness of success as not to know
How much good reason I may have to fear.
Hints of some plot unknown as yet are whispered
Into my ears; but I shall laugh to scorn
The schemes of any who seek to do me injury.
And little this oppresses and disturbs me;
Much more it grieves and pains me to recall
The deaths of Crassus and his son who still
Are unavenged . . .

[He wishes to march against the Parthians. Antony praises Cæsar, who takes it all with dignity.]

CÆSAR This sovereign praise with which thou dost adorn me
Greatly I prize, dear Antony, with reason,
Because it comes from one who, as he sees,
Ever habitually will speak the truth,
And his mouth utters what is in his heart,
For he's so wise and candid that, as he
Cannot in making judgements be deceived,
So he in speech wills no deceit to others.
I wish to go indoors. Meanwhile do thou
Begin the preparations needful for
Our expedition, for in eight or ten
Days' time I mean to march against the Parthians.
[*Exit Cæsar.*]

[Antony soliloquizes about Cæsar's glory. He would be happy to possess such power.]

MARK So much I cannot hope. Yet who can know
What is ordained in the celestial realm?

I am resolved never to fail myself
Should heaven present the opportunity
And show me such a way to follow as
Could make of me another Jove on earth
And place within my hand the reins of the world.
Meanwhile I'll seek in every way I can
To curry favour with the populace
And make the soldiers well disposed to me,
So that should Cæsar be removed by death
Whether through nature's curse or violence,
By them I'll set my foot upon the step
Whither my kind star hath directed me.

[A Priest tells of prodigious omens (taken from many classical sources) prophesying woe.]

PRIEST ... But what above all else made me afraid
Was that the entrails of each victim showed
Unlucky events, atrocious, horrible ills;
For within some of them no heart is found;
In some the liver or the lungs are spoiled;
Others were all bespattered with black gall,
All signs prognosticating mighty woes ...

[Enter Calpurnia and Cæsar. Cæsar is entreated to remain at home, but refuses.]

CÆSAR If of some evil touching my own life
These auguries are signs, 'tis needful I
Must meet whate'er they show. If otherwise,
They're false, and he who gives them heed is foolish.
But if indeed they threaten us with ill,
Who can oppose or stay Necessity?
Who can elude the inevitable? ...

[Cæsar goes off; the Priest tells Calpurnia to importune him to stay at home. The Chorus declares that Rome's troubles are caused by the decay of religion.]

Act IV

Brutus. Cassius.

[Brutus says that if Cæsar obeys his wife's prayers their design will fail, since Cæsar intends to surround himself from tomorrow with a guard of fifty soldiers.]

CASSIUS . . . Liberty is none other
Than rule and mastery over oneself.
A man has nothing dearer than himself.
Thus he who takes another's liberty
Robs him of the most dear, most prized thing
That he could e'er possess. Wherefore how great
The injustice of the Tyrant is here seen.

BRUTUS A Tyrant's viler than a murderer.
A murderer only takes away one's life,
But the Tyrant takes not only dignity
But the lordship of one's life: and he who lives
Not for himself but at another's will
Leads a life worse than death; therefore wise Cato,
Sage and courageous, chose rather death than live
A slave.

CASSIUS Base cowards we, who until now
Could bear to live in servitude so vile.

BRUTUS Believe me, Cassius, 'tis not fear nor baseness
But only zeal to liberate our land
Which has until today bound me to life . . .

[Decimus Brutus enters, and announces that Cæsar has decided not to go to the Senate. Enter Cæsar.]

CÆSAR Whoso by women's counsels lets himself
Be governed is more foolish far than they.
Nevertheless I needs must condescend
To my own wife today, if I'd have peace,
And free myself from this vexation.
But the so great and unaccustomed fear
Wherewith she is so grievously tormented,
Is not without a cause; and though no fear
In me can find a place, yet I suspect
Some treason is afoot against my life.
Some cause I have to think it. Let it be so.
If it be doomed in Heaven that I must die,
Then let me die; I bow to Heaven's will,
Accepting death which cannot be but glorious.

[He speaks of his glories and triumphs.]

The memory of my name will stay immortal.
In nature's course and glory's long enough

Now have I lived. In my remaining days
How further to enhance my name's great honour
I do not see . . .

BRUTUS Let us accost him. Cæsar, may the Heavens
Fulfil thy every wish! Thou art awaited.
Why goest thou not to the Senate? For today
All Senators are met together there.

CÆSAR Must I now tell him, or be silent? For
My wife's strong prayers and plaints have had the power
To make me otherwise resolve. Moreover
I am afraid; my fear is based on no
Delusions and vain dreams, but evidence,
Clear signs that plots are laid against my life.

[Decimus Brutus mingles praise and exhortation.]

CÆSAR I do not fear; no; fear can have no place
Within my breast. Never my heart has known
What fear might be: also I now have reached
To such an age, and such things have performed
In arms, that I should have no fear of death.
Indeed death shall—that every thing husks off—
This body lay in earth, yet the eternal
Memory of my name shall not be quenched.
Yet I believe (and upon credible
And certain signs is based my firm belief)
That several plots are spread against my life,
From which I shall protect myself so well
I need not fear for that, nor in my breast
Need quiet be disturbed. Do thou go find
Mark Antony and tell him to dismiss
The Senate, telling them that today
I cannot come to meet them; excuse me so
That none suspect they are by me despised.

DECIMUS If personally thou goest not to do
This duty, be assured they'll take it with
A sinister interpretation; others
Will learn from them that in contempt and pride
Thou did'st it. They will say thy habits are
Transformed by fortune, that from being humble
And mild thou art become lofty and arrogant.

CÆSAR Thy counsel Brutus I intend to follow.
Call back the fellow whom I sent to Antony.

Let someone have my litter brought me here;
For in a litter I will go, because
I'm tired and weak. I shall return at once.
First to my wife within I'll say a word.

[Marcus Brutus thanks God for changing Cæsar's mind and begs Him to help them, since human wisdom is blind folly unless illumined by Divine light.]

Cæsar. Calpurnia. Decimus Brutus.

[Cæsar returns to the stage with Calpurnia, who still begs him not to go. Decimus Brutus flatters Cæsar until he decides to go. On his way to the Senate he is accosted by Lenate. This makes Cassius think their plot will be discovered.]

LEN. Behold the Emperor going to the Senate
I reach here just in time. Before he leaves
I'll greet him. 'May the Heavens, O highest Emperor,
Thy every wish fulfil!'

CÆSAR And thee, Lenatus,
Give full content. What dost thou ask of me?
In what can Cæsar serve thee? Tell
What need thou hast of Cæsar's offices?

CASSIUS Brutus, we are undone! for see, Lenatus
Converses privately with Cæsar.

BRUTUS Well,
What matters it to us?

CASSIUS What matters it?
Thou know'st not if he tells him of our plot!

BRUTUS I understand. Where fortune lends support
Valour avails not. Let us be prepared
If need be, to provide for our escape,
And let us make a road to liberty
If all else fails, by stabbing each the other
With daggers in the side and in the breast.

[Soon it is clear that all is well. Lenatus is only asking Cæsar for a military post for Quintus Fulvius.]

BRUTUS Breathe freely, Cassius, for he speaks not of us,
As I perceive from here by his looks and gestures.

[Cæsar passes on. Lenatus is indignant when Cassius tells him of his fears. Calpurnia and the Chorus of court ladies end the Act.]

Act V

Brutus. The Conspirators. Chorus of Court Ladies. Calpurnia.

BRUTUS Citizens hear, the Tyrant with his blood
Has paid due penalty, and satisfied
The spirits of the many noble men
Who by his crimes are laid beneath the soil.
Henceforth our Rome is free!
The yoke is shaken from our necks, and he,
Befitting his deserts, in his own blood,
Which through a hundred wounds spills in abundance,
Lies at the foot of the great Leader's statue
Ne'er to be seen again in these high walls . . .

[He calls on Cicero to use his eloquence in rejoicing and to call all Rome to joy.]

Away now, run through the land, you who have been
My comrades in the honoured enterprise,
With steel in hand still dripping Tyrant's blood,
With javelins on poles, to liberty
We'll call the populace of Roman Mars.

CONSPIRATORS Liberty, liberty, dead is the Tyrant!
Now Rome is free, and broken the vile yoke!

[The Chorus expresses horror, and grief for Calpurnia, who laments. A Messenger enters and describes Cæsar's murder. Calpurnia and the Chorus renew their lamentations.]

CAL. O Brutus, Brutus, brutal sure thou art
No less in mind and deeds than in thy name!
How couldst thou have the heart to kill the man
Who life had granted thee, and taken thee
Unto him as a son? Ah criminal!
Enemy of all humanity, with soul
More fierce than bear or the Hircanian tiger!
How, when thou woundedst that most sacred flesh,
Did horrid frost not seal thy cruel limbs?

[The Chorus of male Citizens and the female Chorus sing, the one of liberty, the other of the fear of war. A Chorus of soldiers sings Cæsar's praises and demands vengeance. A second Messenger describes the confusion in the city and the fires started by vengeful friends of Cæsar.]

2ND MESSENGER . . . Antony, whom Trebonius had held
Chatting outside the door while the other plotters
Fulfilled their task, now must I call him pious
Or impious? He has fled to his house, where, fearing
Himself also condemned to die, he girds
His house with strong protection and prepares
To guard himself against whoever tries
To do him shame or injury. Lepidus
With four strong legions has retired to the Island,
And sent to tell Mark Antony that he's ready
To do whatever's asked of him and his;
Whence it is thought that he, his friend to avenge,
Will soon advance upon the conspirators,
Cut them to pieces, and their houses burn,
Razing them down to their foundations.
O Rome, O lofty realm, till now the sure
Rock of the entire world, where hast thou sunk?
Surely the gods were envious of thy greatness . . .

[He bewails the state of affairs. The Chorus ends, advising patience.]

XIII. Analogue

From CÆSAR INTERFECTUS

by Richard Eedes[1]

Epilogus Caesaris interfecti, quomodo in scenam prodiit ea res acta in ecclesia Xr̄i Oxon̄, qui epilogus a M^{ro} Ricardo Eedes et scriptus et in proscenio ibidem dictus fuit.

Egit triumphum Cæsar de repub. Brutus de Cæsare; nihil ille magis potuit, nihil iste magis voluit; nihil aut ille, aut iste minus debuit: Est quod utrique laudi tribuam; est quod utrique vitio vertam; malè Cæsar qui occupavit Rep.; benè, qui sine cæde & sanguine occupavit: rectè Brutus qui libertatem restituit; improbè, qui interfecto Cæsare, restituendam censuit; illius facinoris turpitudini Victoriæ moderatio quasi Velum obduxit; huius facti gloriae ingrata crudelitas tenebras offudit; ille se gessit optimè in

[1] *Bodleian MS Top. Oxon. e. 5, f. 359.* Text from F. S. Boas, *University Drama in the Tudor Age*, pp. 164–5.

causa pessima; hic pessimè in optima. Sed neque defuerunt qui hos tam illustres viros, alterum regni, alterum libertatis studiosum, velut admotis facibus concitarunt. Antonius Cæsari subiecit igniculos, Bruto Cassius: Cæsari Antonius regium diadema ita optavit ut offerret; Cæsar ita recusavit ut cuperet. Quicquid voluit, valde voluit Brutus; nimium Cassius: tanto certè quedem Dux melior quanto Vir Brutus: in altero maior Vis, in altero Virtus: Brutum amicum habere malles; mágis inimicum timeres Cassium: odio habuit ille tyrannidem, hic tyrannum: Cæsarem secuta est fortuna iusta, si tyrannidem spectemus; iniusta si hominem: sed neque tyrannos Dii immortales licet optimos ferunt; et illi quasi in mercedem tantae Virtutis datum est, ut videret, non ut caveret interitum.

[Translation of the above.]

The Epilogue of Cæsar Murdered, *as the piece went on the stage when it was acted at Christ Church, Oxford, which epilogue was both written and spoken on the stage by Master Richard Eedes*

Cæsar triumphed forcibly over the Republic; Brutus over Cæsar. The former could do no more, the latter wished for nothing more; neither of them was more at fault than the other. There is something for me to praise in both; there is something in both for me to regard as vicious. It was evil that Cæsar seized the Republic; good that he seized it without slaughter or bloodshed. Brutus acted rightly when he restored its liberty; but wickedly when he thought to restore it by killing Cæsar. The former's moderation in victory almost veiled the vileness of his crime; the ungrateful cruelty of the latter darkened the glory of his achievement. The former behaved admirably in the worst, the latter reprehensibly in the best, of causes.

Men were not lacking who as if they had applied firebrands, inflamed these illustrious heroes, the one eager for power, the other for liberty. Antony placed his kindling fire under Cæsar; Cassius did so to Brutus. Just as Antony longed for the royal diadem while offering it to Cæsar, so Cæsar refused it while longing for it. What he wanted, Brutus wanted intensely; Cassius excessively. Cassius was as much the better General as Brutus was the better Man; in one Force was greater, in the other Virtue. You would prefer to have Brutus as a friend, but you would fear more to have Cassius as an enemy. The former hated tyranny, the latter the tyrant. Cæsar's fate seems just if we consider his tyranny, but unjust if we consider the man he was. But the Gods do not suffer tyrants, however excellent they be; and to Cæsar it was given as if in reward for so much virtue that he might see, but not avoid, his ruin.

XIV. Summary of Possible Source

From CÆSAR'S REVENGE

Anon (1607)

The Tragedie of Cæsar and Pompey. Or Cæsars Revenge. Privately acted by the Studentes of Trinity Colledge in Oxford. At London. Imprinted for Nathaniel Fosbrooke and John Wright, and are to be sould in Paules Church-yard at the signe of the Helmet. 1607

The Tragedie of Cæsar and Pompey begins with a prologue in which Discord, as Chorus, rejoices over the carnage at Pharsalia and the confusion of Rome. In I.1 after Titinius has declared that with Pompey's defeat 'The liberty and commonweale is lost', Brutus and Pompey enter, each in turn lamenting the collapse of their hopes. Brutus urges Pompey not to give way to 'weake effeminate passion'

> Why do we use of vertues strength to vant,
> If every crosse a Noble mind can daunt (142–3)

Pompey has lost all hope, but bids Brutus live 'To free thy country from a Tyrants yoke'. Brutus remains when the others go off, encounters Cæsar pursuing the fleeing foe (I.2), and invites the conqueror to slay him. This Cæsar refuses to do, forgiving Brutus for opposing him, since 'True setled love can neere be turn'd to hate.' Brutus shows no gratitude though he admits:

> To what a pitch would this mans vertues so[a]re,
> Did not ambition clog his mounting fame. (210–11)

In I.6 Cæsar and Antony are both deeply in love with Cleopatra, Antony secretly, Cæsar openly, as he promises to replant her in the Egyptian throne. Their admiration for her is couched in swelling Marlovian terms.

The second Act begins with Discord reminding us that 'Though *Cæsar* be as great as great may be, / Yet *Pompey* once was even as great as he.' This Act is devoted to events in Egypt, where Pompey is murdered by Achillas and Sempronius (II.1) and Cornelia mourns his death (II.2). In II.3 Cæsar has killed the murderers and proud Ptolemy; he mourns Pompey's 'princely vertues and . . .

noble minde.' (808). Antony's grief however is caused by his love for Cleopatra. She cheers Cæsar by offering to show him the wonders of Egypt. Cæsar declares that for her sake he will

> change his armes, and deadly sounding droms,
> For loves sweet Laies, and Lydian harmony (872–3)

Dolabella and another Lord comment disapprovingly on the dangers of such voluptuous enchantments. Antony's secret passion makes him abstracted; he explains it as due to thoughts of returning to Rome, but in an aside he confesses that his real desire is to 'spend my life in this sweete paradise'.

With II.4 the scene changes to Rome, where Cicero, Brutus, Casca, Cimber and Trebonius, awaiting Cæsar's arrival from Egypt, discuss the downfall of liberty and lament the death of Pompey. Brutus fears that '*Cæsar* the *Senates* deadly enimie' will triumph 'Upon poore conquered *Rome* and commonwealth'. Cicero, after speaking a noble epitaph on Pompey, believes that Cæsar may be pacified, since

> *Cæsar* although of high aspiring thoughtes,
> And uncontrould ambitious Majesty,
> Yet is of nature faire and courteous.

In II.5 Cato Senior commits suicide.

In Act III Discord in a third Chorus notes Cæsar's triumph in Rome: in him 'Ambition now doth vertues seat usurp'. She invokes the Furies to kindle rage 'In discontented *Brutus* boyling brest', and, looking forward to Cæsar's death, calls on Cassius (who is afflicted with bad dreams) to wake. Accordingly in III.1 Cassius describes the rejoicings of the 'Cæsarians' at the leader's triumph, and declares that, moved by the loss of Roman liberty, he will undertake the task of overthrowing Cæsar:

> *Cassius* hath vowed it to dead Pompeys soule,
> *Cassius* hath vowed it to afflicted *Rome*,
> *Cassius* hath vowed it, witnes Heaven and Earth.

III.2 introduces Cæsar, who having 'shaked off these womanish linkes / In which my capturd thoughts were chayned afore' speaks pompously of his military glory, 'And *Cæsar* ruling over all the world' (1226). His officers repeat the theme, but Antony still longs for Cleopatra. After representative Romans have sung his praises, Cæsar boasts of his conquests.

In the next scene (III.3) Antony is reproached by his Good Genius and told that he will not long be idle,

> Yet must *Philippi* see thy high exploytes,
> And all the world ring of thy Victories (1326–7).

But his love for Cleopatra 'shall end with bloud and shame'. He rouses himself from his stupor.

Brutus in III.3 reproaching himself for his 'ignoble patience' finds in his chair accusations: '*O utinam Brute viveres*'; '*Brutus mortuus es*'. Cassius, seeing his melancholy, stirs him to action against Cæsar, who in the next scene is preparing to make war on the Parthians. Antony offers him a kingly diadem, and a Lord asserts that Rome submits to his rule. But Cæsar refuses to undo the work of the old Romans who expelled the Tarquins. Dolobella praises this moral victory.

> That thou has conquerd thy owne climing thoughts,
> And with thy vertue beat ambition downe. (1489–90)

Antony tries to persuade him, but Cæsar is resolved not to take the odius name of King.

That the conspirators have mistaken Cæsar's character is clear in III.5 when Cassius kneels and invokes Revenge, and Brutus cries

> Another *Tarquin* is to bee expeld,
> Another *Brutus* lives to act the deede (1551–2)

Cimber explains that although Cæsar has refused the title of a King, 'wee do see hee doth usurp the thing', and the scene ends with Cassius uttering bloodthirsty threats.

The scene (III.6) in which Calphurnia tells her dream and begs her husband not to go to the Senate is rather less turgid than most. Cæsar replies that he fears derision if he give way to her, and is resolved to go. He meets the Augur who tells him of the unfavourable auguries and other omens. Cæsar, perturbed, decides to go and dismiss the Senate and return home. A Priest (?) gives him a paper with the names of the plotters. Cæsar laughs in ridicule, but when Cassius comes to take him to Pompey's Court where the Senate waits, his indecision returns. Cassius persuades him to go.

The scene changes to the place of murder and we see Cassius and others stabbing Cæsar, who calls on blackest hell and Pluto to avenge him. Brutus [not Decius Brutus] has been holding Antony 'with a vaine discourse'; he enters, and finding Cæsar still alive, stabs him.

CÆSAR What Brutus too? nay, nay, then let me die,
Nothing wounds deeper then ingratitude (1727–8)

Antony arrives to find Cæsar butchered, and with real eloquence execrates the deed and promises revenge. He goes out carrying Cæsar in his arms.

Discord in Chorus IV calls Brutus 'the author of Rome's liberty, / Proud in thy murthering hand and bloody knife', mentions the grief of Octavian and foresees his military actions. Calphurnia, Cicero, and other friends mourn by Cæsar's hearse (IV.1). Antony makes a formal speech blaming the Romans for Cæsar's death, and Octavian addresses the murderers accusing them of ingratitude (1877–85). In IV.2 Brutus and Cassius, learning that the people, urged by Antony's 'exhorting to revenge', are murdering 'All those that caused *Cæsars* overthrowe', leave Rome for their provinces, intending to meet the enemy in Thessaly. Brutus rejoices that he has killed Cæsar ('And blesse the Heavens for favoring my attempts'); united with Cassius he will continue his endeavours to free Rome. Cæsar's Ghost next appears (IV.4) lamenting his fall, and regretting the dissensions between Antony and Octavian. These two are about to lead their armies against each other when the Ghost appears to them, bids them sheathe their swords and wreak revenge on Brutus. They are reconciled, swear vengeance, and unite their armies to meet the enemy in Macedon.

Act V begins with Discord gleefully foreboding ill to Brutus and bidding the Stygian fiends leave their dwelling places, 'And come into the world and make it hell'. Cassius and Brutus in V.1 describe their Conquests (Rhodes, Zanthus, etc.), though Trebonius has been slain by Dolabella. When Titinius declares that the enemy are approaching, Cassius prays for victory, but Brutus' vexed soul 'Misgives me this wilbe a heavy day' (2229), and is not cheered by Cassius' encouragement. Left alone he realises his 'sad ingratitude' to Cæsar, whose Ghost appears and exults over his approaching death. Brutus' imagination conjures up other avenging spirits and he goes to meet 'death, the guerdon that my deeds deserve' (2325). Young Cato dies, crying out against Stoic virtue; Cassius declares that the battle is going against him; Titinius goes to find out what has happened to Brutus. Cassius despairs when he hears shouts of triumph, and kills himself just before Titinius returns with news of Brutus' success. Titinius commits suicide with Cassius' sword. Brutus enters pursued by the Ghost, and kills himself to satisfy its thirst for his blood. The Ghost rejoices. Discord enters exultant over so much strife and bloodshed, and will go down to hell ('And laugh to thinke I caused such endlesse woe'). Cæsar's Ghost will go to 'sweete *Elysium* pleasure', and dwell 'with the mighty champions of old time.'

The following passages will illustrate the quality of this play:

Act. 3. Sc. 3

[Brutus resolves to slay Cæsar]

Enter Brutus.

BRU. How long in base ignoble patience,
Shall I behold my Countries wofull fall,
O you brave *Romains*, and among'st the rest
Most Noble *Brutus*, faire befall your soules:
Let Peace and Fame your Honored graves awaite,
Who through such perils, and such tedious warres,
Won your great labors prise sweete liberty,
But wee that with our life did freedoms take,
And did no sooner Men, then free-men, breath:
To loose it now continuing so long,
And with such lawes, such vowes, such othes confirm'd
Can nothing but disgrace and shame expect:
But soft what see I written on my seate,
O utinam Brute viveres.
What meaneth this, thy courage dead,
But stay, reade forward, *Brute mortuus es.*
I thou art dead indeed, thy courrage dead
Thy care and love thy dearest Country dead,
Thy wonted spirit and Noble stomack dead.

Enter Cassius

CASSI. The times drawe neere by gratious heavens assignd
When *Philips* Sonne must fall in *Babilon*,
In his triumphing proud persumption:
But see where melancholy *Brutus* walkes,
Whose minde is hammering on no meane conceit:
Then sound him *Cassius*, see how hee is inclined,
How fares young *Brutus* in this tottering state.

BRU. Even as an idle gaser, that beholdes,
His Countries wrackes and cannot succor bring.

CASSI. But wil *Brute* alwaies in this dreame remaine,
And not bee mooved with his Countries mone.

BRU. O that I might in *Lethes* endles sleepe,
And neere awaking pleasant rest of death
Close up mine eyes, that I no more might see,
Poore *Romes* distresse and Countries misery.

CASSI. No *Brutus* live, and wake thy sleepy minde,
Stirre up those dying sparkes of honors fire,
Which in thy gentle breast weare wont to flame:
See how poore *Rome* opprest with Countries wronges,
Implores thine ayde, that bred thee to that end,
Thy kins-mans soule from heaven commandes thine aide:
That lastly must by thee receive his end,
Then purchas honor by a glorious death,
Or live renown'd by ending *Cæsars* life.

BRU. I can no longer beare the Tirants pride,
I cannot heare my Country crie for ayde,
And not bee mooved with her pitious mone,
Brutus thy soule shall never more complaine:
That from thy linage and most vertuous stock,
A bastard weake degenerat branch is borne,
For to distaine the honor of thy house.
No more shall now the *Romains* call me dead,
Ile live againe and rowze my sleepy thoughts:
And with the Tirants death begin this life.
Rome now I come to reare thy states decayed,
When or this hand shall cure thy fatall wound,
Or else this heart by bleeding on the ground.

CASSI. Now heaven I see applaudes this enterprise,
And *Rhadamanth* into the fatall Urne,
That lotheth death, hath thrust the Tirants name,
Cæsar the life that thou in bloud hast led:
Shall heape a bloudy vengance on thine head. *Exeunt.*

Actus 3. Scena 6.

[Cæsar goes to his death]

Enter Cæsar, Calphurnia.

CÆS. Why thinkes my love to fright me with her dreames? 1591
Shall bug-beares feare *Cæsars* undaunted heart,
Whome *Pompeys* Fortune never could amaze,
Nor the *French* horse, nor *Mauritanian* boe,
And now shall vaine illusions mee affright:
Or shadowes daunt, whom substance could not quell?

CALPHUR. O dearest *Cæsar*, hast thou seene thy selfe,
(As troubled dreames to me did faine thee seene:)
Torne, Wounded, Maymed, Blood-slaughtered, Slaine,
O thou thy selfe, wouldst then have dread thy selfe:
And feard to thrust thy life to dangers mouth.

CÆS. There you bewray the folly of your dreame,
For I am well, alive, uncaught, untoucht.

CALPHUR. T'was in the Senate-house I sawe thee so,
And yet thou dreadles thither needes will go.

CÆS. The Senate is a place of peace, not death,
But these were but deluding visions.

CALPHUR. O do not set so little by the heavens,
Dreames ar divine, men say they come from *Jove*,
Beware betimes, and bee not wise to late:
Mens good indevours change the wills of Fate.

CÆS. Weepe not faire love, let not thy wofull teares
Bode mee, I knowe what thou wouldest not have to hap
It will distaine mine honor wonne in fight
To say a womans dreame could me affright.

CAL. O *Cæsar* no dishonour canst thou get,
In seeking to prevent unlucky chance:
Foole-hardy men do runne upon their death,
Bee thou in this perswaded by thy wife:
No vallour bids thee cast away thy life.

CÆS. Tis dastard cowardize and childish feare,
To dread those dangers that do not appeare:

CAL. Thou must sad chance by fore-cast, wise resist,
Or being done say boote-les had I wist.

CÆS. But for to feare wher's no suspition,
Will to my greatnesse be derision.

CAL. There lurkes an adder in the greenest grasse,
Daungers of purpose alwayes hide their face:

CÆS. Perswade no more; *Cæsar's* resolv'd to go.

CAL. The Heavens resolve that hee may safe returne,
For if ought happen to my love but well:
His danger shalbe doubled with my death. *Exit.*

Enter Augur.

AUGUR. I, come they are, but yet they are not gon.[1]

CÆS. What hast thou sacrifiz'd, as custome is,
Before wee enter in the Senat-house.

AUGUR. O stay those steeps that leade thee to thy death,
The angry heavens with threeatning dire aspect,
Boding mischance, and balfull massacers,
Menace the overthrowe of *Cæsars* powre:
Saturne sits frowning on the God of Warre,
Who in their sad conjunction do conspire,
Uniting both their bale full influences,
To heape mischance, and danger to thy life:
The Sacrificing beast is heart-les found:
Sad ghastly sightes, and raysed Ghostes appeare,
Which fill the silent woods, with groning cries:
The hoarse Night-raven tunes the chearles voyce,
And calls the bale-full Owle, and howling Doge,
To make a consort. In whose sad song is this,
Neere is the overthrow of *Cæsars* blisse. *Exit.*

CÆSAR. The world is set to fray mee from my wits,
Heers harteles Sacrifice and visions,
Howlinge and cryes, and ghastly grones of Ghosts,
Soft *Cæsar* do not make a mockery,
Of these Prodigious signes sent from the Heavens,
Calphurnias Dreame Jumping with[2] *Augurs* words,
Shew (if thou markest it *Cæsar*) cause to feare:
This day the Senate there shalbe dissolved,
And Ile returne to my *Calphurnia* home, *One gives him*
What hast thou heare that thou presents us with. *a paper.*

PRE. A thing my Lord that doth concerne your life.
Which love to you and hate of such a deed,
Makes me reveale unto your excellence. *Cæsar laughs.*
Smilest thou, or think'st thou it some idle toy,
Thou[l]t frowne a non to read so many names.
That have conspird and sworne thy bloody death, *Exit.*

Enter Cassius.

CASSIUS. Now must I come, and with close subtile girdes,
Deceave the prey that Ile devoure anon,

[1] A line is missing here in which Cæsar must tell the Augur, 'The Ides of March are come.'
[2] Which *1607*.

My Lord the Sacred Senate doth expect,
Your royall presence in *Pompeius* court:

CÆSAR. *Cassius* they tell me that some daungers nigh,
And death pretended in the Senate house.

CASSI. What danger or what wrong can be,
Where harmeles gravitie and vertue sits,
Tis past all daunger present death it is,
Nor is it wrong to render due desert.
To feare the Senators without a cause,
Will bee a cause why theile be to be feared,

CÆSA. The Senate stayes for me in *Pompeys* court.
And *Cæsars* heere, and dares not goe to them,
Packe hence all dread of danger and of death,
What must be must be; *Cæsars* prest for all.

CASSI. Now have I sent him headlong to his ende,
Vengance and death awayting at his heeles,
Cæsar thy life now hangeth on a twine,
Which by my Poniard must bee cut in twaine,
Thy chaire of state now turn'd is to thy Beere,
Thy Princely robes to make thy winding sheete:
The Senators the Mourners ore the Hearse,
And *Pompeys* Court, thy dreadfull grave shalbe.

Senators crie all at once.

OMNES. Hold downe the Tyrant stab him to the death:

CASSI. Now doth the musick play and this the song
That *Cassius* heart hath thirsted for so long:
And now my Poniard in this mazing sound,
Must strike that touch that must his life confound.
Stab on, stab on, thus should your Poniards play,
Aloud deepe note upon this trembling Kay. *stab him.*

BUCO. *Bucolian* sends thee this. *stab him.*

CUM. And *Cumber* this. *stab him.*

CAS. Take this from *Casca* for to quite *Romes* wronges.

CÆS. Why murtherous villaines know you whom you strike,
Tis *Cæsar*, *Cæsar*, whom your Poniards pierce:
Cæsar whose name might well afright such slaves:
O Heavens that see and hate this haynous guilt,
And thou Immortall *Jove* that Idle holdest
Deluding Thunder in thy faynting hand,
Why stay'st thy dreadfull doome, and dost with-hold,

Thy three-fork'd engine to revenge my death:
But if my plaintes the Heavens cannot moove,
Then blackest hell and *Pluto* bee thou judge:
You greesly daughters of the cheereles night,
Whose hearts, nor praier nor pitty, ere could lend,
Leave the black dungeon of your *Chaos* deepe:
Come and with flaming brandes into the world,
Revenge, and death, bringe seated in your eyes:
And plague these villaynes for their trecheries.

Enter Brutus.

BRU. I have held *Anthony* with a vaine discourse,
The whilst the deed's in execution,
But lives hee still, yet doth the Tyrant breath?
Chalinging Heavens with his blasphemies,
Heere *Brutus* maketh a passage for thy Soule,
To plead thy cause for them whose ayde thou cravest,

CÆS. What *Brutus* to? nay nay, then let me die,
Nothing wounds deeper then ingratitude,

BRU. I bloody *Cæsar*, *Cæsar*, *Brutus* too,
Doth geeve thee this, and this to quite *Romes* wrongs,

CASSIUS. O had the Tyrant had as many lives.
As that fell *Hydra* borne in *Lerna lake*,
That heare I still might stab and stabing kill,
Till that more lives might bee extinguished,
Then his ambition, *Romanes* Slaughtered.

TRE. How heavens have justly on the authors head,
Returnd the guiltles blood which he hath shed,
And *Pompey*, he who caused thy Tragedy,
Here breathles lies before thy Noble Statue,

Enter Anthony.

ANTH. What cryes of death resound within my eares,
Whome I doe see great *Cæsar* buchered thus?
What said I great? I *Cæsar* thou wast great,
But O that greatnes was that brought thy death:
O unjust Heavens, (if Heavens at all there be,)
Since vertues wronges makes question of your powers,
How could your starry eyes this shame behold,
How could the sunne see this and not eclipze?
Fayre bud of fame ill cropt before thy time:
What *Hyrcan* tygar, or wild savage bore,

(For he more heard then Bore or Tyger was,)
Durst do so vile and execrate a deede,
Could not those eyes so full of majesty,
Nor priesthood (o not thus to bee prophand)
Nor yet the reverence to this sacred place,
Nor flowing eloquence of thy goulden tounge,
Nor name made famous through immortall merit,
Deter those murtherors from so vild a deed?
Sweete friend accept these obsequies of mine,
Which heare with teares I doe unto thy hearse,
And thou being placed among the shining starrs.
Shalt downe from Heaven behold what deepe revenge
I will inflict upon the murtherers, *Exit with Cæsar, in his armes.*

Act. 5. Sce. 1.

[At Philippi]

Enter Discord.

DIS. The balefull harvest of my joy, thy woe
Gins ripen *Brutus*, Heavens commande it so.
Pale sad *Avernus* opes his yawning Jawes,
Seeking to swallow up thy murtherous soule,
The furies have proclaym'd a festivall:
And meane to day to banquet with thy bloud,
Now Heavens array you in your clowdy weedes:
Wrap up the beauty of your glorious lamp,
And dreadfull *Chaos*, of sad drery night,
Thou Sunne that climest up to the easterne hill:
And in thy Chariot rides with swift steedes drawne,
In thy proud Jollity and radiant glory:
Go back againe and hide thee in the sea,
Darkenesse to day shall cover all the world:
Let no light shine, but what your swords can strike,
From out their steely helmes, and fiery shildes:
Furies, and Ghosts, with your blue-burning lampes,
In mazing terror ride through *Roman* rankes:
With dread affrighting those stout Champions hearts,
All stygian fiendes now leave whereas you dwell:
And come into the world and make it hell.

Enter Cassius, Brutus, Cato Junior,
with an army marching

. . . . . .

CAS. And now to thee *Phillipi*, are wee come,
Whose fields must twise feele *Roman* cruelty,
And flowing blood like to *Dærcean* playnes,
When proud *Eteocles* on his foaming steede,
Rides in his fury through the *Argean* troopes,
Now making great *Ærastus* give him way,
Now beating back *Tidæus* puissant might:
The ground not dry'd from sad *Pharsalian* blood,
Will now bee turned to a purple lake:
And bleeding heapes and mangled bodyes slayne,
Shall make such hills as shall surpasse in height
The Snowy Alpes and aery *Appenines*.

TITI. A Scout brought word but now that he descryd,
Warlike *Anthonius* and young *Cæsars* troopes,
Marching in fury over *Thessalian* playnes.
As great *Gradinus* when in angry moode,
He drives his chariot downe from heavens top,
And in his wheels whirleth reveng and death:
Heere by *Phillippi* they will pich their tents,
And in these fieldes (fatall to *Roman* lives)
Hazard the fortune of the doubtfull fight,

CATO. O welcome thou this long expected day,
On which dependeth *Romane* liberty,
Now *Rome* thy freedom hangeth in suspence,
And this the day that must assure thy hopes.

CASSI. Great *Jove*, and thou *Trytonyan* warlike Queene:
Arm'd with thy amazing deadly *Gorgons* head.
Strengthen our armes that fight for *Roman* welth:
And thou sterne *Mars*, and *Romulus* thy Sonne,
Defend that Citty which your selfe begun.
All heavenly powers assist our rightfull armes,
And send downe silver winged victory,
To crowne with Lawrells our triumphant Crests.

BRU. My minde thats troubled in my vexed soule,
(Opprest with sorrow and with sad dismay,)
Misgives me this wilbe a heavy day.

CASSI. Why faynt not now in these our last extremes,
This time craves courage not dispayring feare,

TITIN. Fie, twill distayne thy former valiant acts.
To say thou faintest now in this last act,

BRU. My mind is heavy, and I know not why,
But cruell fate doth sommon me to die,

CATO. Sweet *Brute*, let not thy words be ominous signes,
Of so mis-fortunnate and sad event,
Heaven and our Vallour shall us conquerours make.

CASSI. What Bastard feare hath taunted our dead hearts,
Or what unglorious unwounted thought,
Hath changed the vallour of our daunted mindes.
What are our armes growne weaker then they were?
Cannot this hand that was proud *Cæsars* death,
Send all *Cæsarians* headlong that same path?
Looke how our troups in Sun-bright armes do shine,
With vaunting plumes and dreadfull bravery.
The wrathfull steedes do check their iron bits,
And with a well grac'd terror strike the ground,
And keeping times in warres sad harmony.
And then hath *Brutus* any cause to feare,
My selfe like valiant *Peleus* worthy Sonne,
The Noblest wight that ever *Troy* beheld,
Shall of the adverse troopes such havock make,
As sad *Phillipi* shall in blood bewayle,
The cruell massacre of *Cassius* sword,
And then hath *Brutus* any cause to feare?

BRU. No outward shewes of puissance or of strength,
Can helpe a minde dismayed inwardly,
Leave me sweete Lordes a while unto my selfe.

CASSI. In the meane time take order for the fight,
Drums let your fearefull mazing thunder playe.
And with their sound peirce Heavens brazen Towers,
And all the earth fill with like fearefull noyse,
As when that *Boreas* from his Iron cave.
With boysterous furyes Striving in the waves,
Comes swelling forth to meet his blustering foe,
They both doe runne with feerce tempestuous rage,
And heaves up mountaynes of the watry waves.
The God *Oceanus* trembles at the stroke,

BRU. What hatefull furyes vex my tortured mind?
What hideous sightes appalle my greeved soule,
As when *Orestes* after mother slaine.
Not being yet at *Scithians* Alters purged,
Behould the greesly visages of fiends

And gastly furies which did haunt his steps,
Cæsar upbraves my sad ingratitude,
He saved my life in sad *Pharsalian* fieldes,
That I in *Senate* house might worke his death.
O this remembrance now doth wound my soule,
More then my poniard did his bleeding heart,

Enter Ghost.

GHO. *Brutus*, ingratefull *Brutus* seest thou mee:
Anon in field againe thou shalt me see,

BRU. Stay what so ere thou art, or fiend below,
Rays'd from the deepe by inchanters bloody call,
Or fury sent from *Phlegitonticke* flames,
Or from *Cocytus* for to end my life,
Be then *Megera* or *Tysiphone*,
Or of *Eumenides* ill boading crue.
Fly me not now, but end my wretched life,
Come greesly messenger of sad mishap,
Trample in blood of him that hates to live,
And end my life and sorrow all at once.

GHO. Accursed traytor damned *Homicide*,
Knowest thou not me, to whome for forty honors
Thou three and twenty Gastly wounds didst give?
Now dare no more for to behould the Heavens,
For they to-day have destyned thine end:
Nor lift thy eyes unto the rising sunne,
That nere shall live for to behould it set,
Nor looke not downe unto the Hellish shades,
There stand the furyes thursting for thy blood,
Flie to the field but if thou thither go'st,
There *Anthonyes* sword will peirce thy trayterous heart.
Brutus to daie my blood shalbe revenged,
And for my wrong and undeserved death,
Thy life to thee a torture shall become,
And thou shalt oft amongest the dying grones,
Of slaughtered men that bite the bleeding earth.
Wish that like balefull cheere might thee befall,
And seeke for death that flies so wretched wight,
Untill to shunne the honour of the fight,
And dreadfull vengeance of supernall ire.
Thine owne right hand shall worke my wish'd reveng,
And so Fare ill, hated of Heaven and Men.

BRU. Stay *Cæsar* stay, protract my greife no longer,
Rip up my bowells glut thy thirsting throte,
With pleasing blood of *Cæsars* guilty heart:
But see hee's gon, and yonder Murther stands:
See how he poynts his knife unto my hart.
Althea raveth for her murthered Sonne,
And weepes the deed that she her-selfe hath done:
And *Meleager* would thou livedst againe,
But death must expiate. *Altheas* come.
I, death the guerdon that my deeds deserve:
The drums do thunder forth dismay and feare,
And dismall triumphes sound my fatall knell,
Furyes I come to meete you all in Hell,

Enter Cato wounded.

CATO. Bloodles and faynt; *Cato* yeelde up thy breath;
While strength and vigour in these armes remayned,
And made me able for to wield my sword,
So long I fought; and sweet *Rome* for thy sake
Fear'd not effusion of my blood to make.
But now my strength and life doth fayle at once,
My vigor leaves my could and feeble Joynts,
And I my sad soule, must power forth in blood.
O vertue whome *Phylosophy* extols.
Thou art no essence but a naked name,
Bond-slave to Fortune, weake, and of no power.
To succor them which alwaies honourd thee:
Witnesse my Fathers and mine owne sad death,
Who for our country spent our latest breath:
But oh the chaines of death do hold my toung,
Mines eyes wax dim I faynt, I faynt, I die.
O Heavens help *Rome* in this extremity.

. . . . . .

[The end of Brutus]

Enter Brutus the Ghost following him.

BRU. What doest thou still persue me ugly fiend,
Is this it that thou thirsted for so much?
Come with thy tearing clawes and rend it out,
Would thy appeaseles rage be slacked with blood,
This sword to day hath crimsen channels made,
But heare's the blood that thou woulds drinke so fayne,
Then take this percer, broch this trayterous heart.

Or if thou thinkest death to small a payne,
Drag downe this body to proud *Erebus*,
Through black *Cocytus* and infernall *Styx*,
Lethean waves, and fiers of *Phlegeton*,
Boyle me or burne, teare my hatefull flesh,
Devoure, consume, pull, pinch, plague, paine this hart,
Hell craves her right, and heere the furyes stand,
And all thc hell-hounds compasse me a round
Each seeking for a parte of this same prey,
Alasse this body is leane, thin, pale and wan,
Nor can it all your hungery mouthes suffice,
O tis the soule that they stand gaping for,
And endlesse matter for to prey upon.
Renewed still as *Titius* pricked heart.
Then clap your hands, let Hell with Joy resound?
Here it comes flying through this aery round.

GHO. Hell take their hearts, that this ill deed have done
And vengeance follow till they be overcome:
Nor live t'applaud the justice of this deed.
Murther by her owne guilty hand doth bleed.

ANTONY AND CLEOPATRA

INTRODUCTION

THE PLAY was entered in the Stationers' Register to Edward Blount on 20 May, 1608, along with *Pericles*, but whereas *Pericles* was printed in 1609 by William White for Henry Gosson, *Antony and Cleopatra* was not printed before the First Folio of 1623, when it was registered by Blount and Isaak Jaggard with fifteen other plays (including *Timon* and *Coriolanus*) 'not formerly entred to other men'. The previous registration was either forgotten or ignored.

How long before May, 1608 it had been written is uncertain, but there is evidence to suggest that it was written late in 1606 or early in 1607. Samuel Daniel, whose *Civile Wars* (1595) probably influenced *Richard II* had later used Shakespeare's play in revising his poem. He probably did the same with his *Cleopatra* (first published in 1594), which when remodelled in his *Certain Small Workes* in 1607 shows possible influence by Shakespeare's tragedy.[1] A few verbal resemblances in the anonymous *Nobody and Somebody* (entered 1606) and Barnabe Barnes's *The Divil's Charter* (first played 2 February, 1607), make it likely that Shakespeare wrote *Antony and Cleopatra* in 1606.

It is hard to believe that by the time Shakespeare finished *Julius Cæsar* he was not already thinking of writing another play describing the break-up of the triumvirate (already shown as shakily founded in *JC*.IV.1), the fall of Antony and the triumph of Octavius. Though Shakespeare did not in *Julius Cæsar* suggest, with Plutarch and other historians, that the gods and the survival of Rome insisted on a monarchical government, yet the end of that play left much undecided, and Brutus' last words,

> I shall have glory by this losing day
> More than Octavius and Mark Antony
> By this vile conquest shall attain unto, (V.5.36–8)

[1] Cf. M. R. Ridley, *New Arden* (1954), xxvii–xxxii.

look forward to further action, as does Antony's earlier prophecy of Lepidus' dismissal (IV.1.19–27). Why then did the dramatist let several years go by before carrying on with a subject so rich in dramatic intensity as the tragedy of Antony and Cleopatra? We can only speculate; but I suggest that the postponement was due to political, theatrical and personal causes.

Shakespeare's acquaintance with Essex was probably not close, but that he admired the Earl is apparent in the Chorus to *Henry V*, Act V, in which the Irish expedition of 1599 is hailed and a victorious outcome anticipated. Essex failed however, and *Julius Cæsar* was performed on 21 September, 1599 shortly before the general returned in disgrace. '*Julius Cæsar* was a play from which Essex might have learned much, had he been teachable.'[1]

Essex remained in disgrace until in February 1601 he made his foolish attempt to rouse the City against the Queen's ministers, and was shortly condemned and executed (25 February). The Queen did not object to *Julius Cæsar* as she did to the performance of *Richard II* on 7 February, 1601, when the deposition scene was applauded by Essex's friends. But no doubt Shakespeare and his company were careful about what they played after the rising, when Southampton was pent in the Tower (where he remained until 1603) and the morale of the country was shaken by revelations of division in high places. Essex's popularity was shown in ballads lamenting his death and expressing dislike of 'little Cecil' and the proud fox Raleigh. The Queen was accused of having betrayed the Earl, and she grieved for him.

'I am Richard II, know ye not that?' she had said to the antiquary, William Lambarde. Had occasion been given she might well have said, 'I am Cleopatra'—who had also forsaken and caused the death of a great general in decline. Fulke Greville, who was near to her, certainly thought so, for he later related that he had written three tragedies,

'Whereof *Antonie* and *Cleopatra*, according to their irregular passions, in forsaking Empire to follow sensuality, were sacrificed to the fire. The executioner, the author himselfe. Not that he conceived it to be a contemptible younger brother to the

[1] J. D. Wilson, *The Essential Shakespeare*, 1932, p. 98.

rest: but lest while he seemed to looke over much upward, hee might stumble into the Astronomers pit. Many members in that creature (by the opinion of those few eyes which saw it) having some childish wantonnesse in them, apt enough to be construed, or strained to a personating of vices in the present Governors, and government. . . . And again in the practice of the world, seeing the like instance not poetically, but really fashioned in the Earle of *Essex* then falling; and ever till then worthily beloved, both of *Queen*, and people: This sudden descent of such greatnesse, together with the quality of the Actors in every Scene, stir'd up the Authors second thoughts, to bee carefull (in his owne case) of leaving faire weather behind him.'[1]

If Greville, who never meant his tragedies to be performed, destroyed his *Antony and Cleopatra*, is it surprising that Shakespeare, whose Company had only just escaped grave censure, forbore to write a play from which invidious conclusions would almost certainly be drawn, until the circumstances changed?

About this time, however, Shakespeare *did* write a play about a man possessed by love against a background of great historical events. But this was *Troilus and Cressida* (entered on 7 February, 1603) and probably written in 1602. Now although this play had an erotic theme not unlike that of the Antony-Cleopatra story, its tone was entirely opposed to Plutarch's, being bitter, satiric against love and war, even hostile towards the Greek and Trojan heroes. As has often been suggested, the change in tone may have been due to a theatrical fashion of realism, to a desire to satirize other writers (Chapman among them), and to the bitterness about contemporary political life felt by Essex's friends in their disgrace. For all these reasons Shakespeare switched from the Roman theme to one which enabled him to mock at Chapman's *Homer* and political and erotic idealism all at the same time. We may be glad that Shakespeare did not write *Antony and Cleopatra* in the same mood as *Troilus*, for that would not only have spoiled the tragedy but robbed us of the miracle of art in which he entered into the consuming passion of a middle-aged love and set it against a political order marred by self-interest yet full of imperial grandeur.

[1] *Sir Fulke Greville's Life of Sir Philip Sidney* . . . ed. Nowell Smith, Oxford, 1907, pp. 155–7.

Returning in 1606 to Roman history after writing in *Lear* and *Macbeth* about early British and Scottish legends, he was perhaps encouraged by the popularity of classical themes in drama during the first years of James I's reign, which saw the performance or publication of such works as Alexander's *Darius* (pubd. 1603) and *Crœsus* (pubd. 1604), Jonson's *Sejanus* (pubd. 1605), Daniel's *Philotas* (pubd. 1605), Marston's *Sophonisba* (pubd. 1606) and the anonymous *Cæsar's Revenge* (entd. 1606).

As for *Julius Cæsar* Shakespeare's main source for *Antony and Cleopatra* was North's Plutarch, and it has been declared that he looked no farther for any of his material. Certainly he could have developed all his plot and characterization from Plutarch's *Life of Antony* and the *Comparison of Demetrius and Antony*; and there is here less of the ambiguity of attitude shown towards Julius Cæsar down the ages. Nevertheless it is not unprofitable to consider briefly the Cleopatra-legend as it affected literature before Shakespeare.

Cleopatra played an important part in the story of Julius Cæsar's last years and of events after his death; for long before Antony gave up Rome for Alexandrian pleasures Cæsar had vivid adventures in Egypt and a liaison with the Queen which resulted in the birth of a son. So Cleopatra was the seducer of two great Romans, the enemy of *gravitas*, and as such she was treated harshly by Roman poets and historians.[1] For Horace she was the 'mad Queen' who shackled Antony in servile bondage (*Epode* ix); in Virgil's *Æneid* (VIII) Æneas foresees on Venus' shield the Battle of Actium in which Antony is followed by his Egyptian mistress. Lucan, ever hostile to Julius, told in *Pharsalia*, Bk. X, how Cæsar went to Alexandria after defeating Pompey, and ended his campaign when Cleopatra came and begged him to help her regain her throne. Lucan described her evil beauty, which did no less damage to Rome than Helen's did to Troy, the magnificence of her palace, the variety of her servants, her jewels, and the banquet she gave the conqueror, who discussed with the High Priest of Isis the mystery of the Nile's flood [Text III]. The poem broke off after the execution of Pothinus and Achillas while Cæsar was still in great danger.

[1] Cf. F. M. Dickey, *Not Wisely but Too Well*, San Marino, 1957, Ch. X–XI.

Flavius Josephus had much to say of Antony's friendship with Herod I, King of the Jews, who helped him at Samosata by the Euphrates, and Antony 'entertained him very kindly, and could not but admire his courage. Antony also embraced him as soon as he saw him, and saluted him in a most affectionate manner.' After Herod married Mariamne, he had her brother Aristobulus drowned 'accidentally'. The boy's mother, a friend of Cleopatra's, complained of this, and Cleopatra ordered Antony to punish Herod, but Herod, knowing that Antony had fallen in love with Mariamne, commanded that she should be killed if Antony slew him. He won Antony over with presents, so that when Cleopatra wanted to have Judæa for herself Antony would not allow it. Josephus asserted that Cleopatra tried to seduce Herod but that he withstood her wiles [Text IV]. Shakespeare refers to Herod several times in the play, and it is probable that he knew this tradition.[1]

To L. Annæus Florus Cleopatra seemed an ambitious schemer who sold her favours to win an empire; Antony, 'always in his own nature a most wicked man', was also a vain contemptible fool enslaved by passion [Text V]. Plutarch was one of the few Roman historians to treat the lovers with any sympathy. He recounted Julius Cæsar's Egyptian adventure briefly, commenting that he made war there 'for the love of Cleopatra: wherein he won little honour, and besides did put his person in great danger' by his delight in 'her sweet conversation and pleasant entertainment' (*supra* 73). What Plutarch made of her spell over Antony may be read below in North's colourful version [Text I]. By his vigorous movement and adroit use of significant incident, his reporting or invention of apt speech, Plutarch created the fascinating, capricious Cleopatra of the Elizabethans, and traced the bemused degeneration of Antony in such a way as to bring out the pathos and dignity as well as the folly of the tragic pair.

Dion Cassius followed Plutarch in emphasizing the attractions and guile of Cleopatra:

> For she was a woman of surpassing beauty, and at that time, when she was in the prime of youth, she was most striking; she also possessed a most charming voice, and a

[1] *E.g.* I.2.28–9; III.3.2–7; III.6.73; IV.6.13–15.

> knowledge of how to make herself agreeable to everyone. Being brilliant to look upon and to listen to, with the power to subjugate everyone, even a love-sated man already past his prime, she thought it would be in keeping with her role to meet Cæsar, and she reposed in her beauty all her claims to the throne.[1]

Cæsar's soldiers jested broadly about his love-affair with her when he invited her to Rome with her husband Ptolemy and settled her in his own house, 'so that he derived an ill repute on account of both of them' (Bk. XLIII). Her husband died, probably poisoned. After Cæsar's murder she fled from Rome, helped Dolabella against Cassius, and later captured the affections of Antony, who 'thereafter gave not a thought to honour but became the Egyptian woman's slave and devoted his time to his passion for her'. She killed herself only when she realized that Octavius was impervious to her wiles.

From the thirteenth century onwards there were many prose and verse accounts of Cæsar's life based on Lucan and supplemented from other sources. Thus the compiler of the French *Li Faits des Romains* drew largely on Lucan and Suetonius, using the *De Bello Alexandro* for the Egyptian phase, added a long account of Cleopatra's beauty and made a romantic story of Arsinoe and Ganimede. In J. de Tuim's *Li hystoire de Julius Cesar* (c. 1240) the love affair is described in terms of courtly love, and Cæsar expresses his passion like any chivalric youth:

> 'O God, how happy would he be who could hold that lady naked and willing in his arms . . . for you know well that no man can have delight so great as the joy and youthfulness that follow when he who loves a beautiful lady and is well loved by her, can hold her at his sweet will.'[2]

A shift in attitude to Cleopatra is apparent here, as also in the fourteenth century *I Fatti di Cesare* where the writer expands Lucan's description of her palace and her beauty [Text VII]. 'For love of her he remained in Egypt for two years; he loved her greatly, and often went with her on the Nile as far as Syria in a boat covered with silk' (Ch. XXXIII). Cæsar loved many

[1] *Roman History*, Bk. XLII. Loeb, iv, 167–9.

[2] Cf. F. Settegast, *Li hystoire de J.C. eine alt-französische Erzählung in prosa von Jehan de Tuim, zum ersten mal herausgegeben*, Halle, 1881.

women, 'but Cleopatra, Queen of Egypt, he loved more than any other queen. He ordered her to come and see him in Rome, which she did, and she lived there for a long time. In the end he sent her home, after giving her great gifts and honour. A male child which she had by him she named Cæsarion for love of him.'

Since the tradition of Cæsar's love for Cleopatra was so vivid and well-known, it is remarkable that Shakespeare omitted all reference to it from *Julius Cæsar*, though he mentioned it several times in *Antony and Cleopatra*.[1] But to allude to Cæsar's Egyptian liaison would have detracted from his relation with Calpurnia and distracted attention from the domestic politics which are the main theme of *Julius Cæsar*. On the other hand the omission may merely indicate that Shakespeare was closely following Plutarch, who made little of the affair.

Dante placed 'the luxurious Cleopatra' in the second circle of Hell among the carnal sinners, with Semiramis, Dido, Helen, Tristan, and Paolo and Francesca (Canto V). Boccaccio had no good to say of either Antony or Cleopatra. The former, in *De Casibus Illustrium Virorum*, is depicted as naturally cruel and ambitious, but under her influence he let himself be drawn into the utmost infamy. Cleopatra was a whore who deserved her fate. Similarly in *De claris mulieribus* Boccaccio described her as extravagant and promiscuous.

After this it is strange to find Chaucer (who drew so much on Boccaccio) giving a favourable picture of Cleopatra in his *Legend of Good Women*.

In the Prologue to this poem Chaucer is accused by Love of misogyny for translating the *Romance of the Rose* and writing ill of Criseyde. Alcestis defends him but commands him to write 'Of wommen trewe in lovyng al hire lyf,' and Love says:

> At Cleopatre I wole that thou begynne . . .
> For lat see now what man that lover be,
> Wol doon so stronge a peyne for love as she.

So the legend of Cleopatra is a tale of true love. Antony is a man 'of discrecion and of hardynesse' who was so filled with love for her 'That all the worlde he sette at no value'. He married Cleopatra, and no mention is made of Octavia; but

[1] E.g. II.2.232–3; II.6.70; III.11.82–5, 116–17.

Octavian 'that woode was of this dede,' came with a host of 'stoute Romaynes, crewel as lyoun'. The Battle of Actium is described at some length, and how Antony fled.

> Fleeth ek the queene with al hir purpre sayle,
> For strokes which that wente as thik as hayle;
> No wonder was she myght it nat endure.

But Antony went mad with despair and stabbed himself to the heart. Cleopatra built a shrine and had the body embalmed, and next to the tomb she made a snake-pit. Lamenting over her lover she declared that she had sworn never to let him out of her mind, but to follow him in life or death:

> And with that worde, naked, with ful good herte,
> Amonge the serpents in the pit she sterte;
> And ther she chees to han hir buryinge.
> Anon the neddres gonne hir for to stynge,
> And she hir deeth receveth with good chere,
> For love of Antony that was hir so dere.
> And this is storial sooth, it is no fable.

This tale of a martyr for love immediately precedes that of Pyramus and Thisbe. Shakespeare probably knew it, but he made no use of its 'storial sooth'. Other poets occasionally praised the lovers for their fidelity, but Lydgate treated them as horrid examples:

> Folwyng ther lustis foul and abhominable,
> She desiryng to have be emperesse;
> And he, alas, of froward wilfulnesse;

and Spenser put them in the dungeon of the House of Pride for their 'wastfull Pride and wanton Riotise' (*F.Q.*, I.v.46).

A new turn however was provided by the rise of drama in Europe. Italy, which came first in the attempt to create a new drama based on classical precept and practice, was also first to see the possibilities inherent for pity and horror in the Cleopatra story; and the writer who did more than anyone else to popularize Senecan drama on the Italian stage, G. B. Giraldi Cinthio, wrote a tragedy, *Cleopatra*,[1] in or about the year 1542,

[1] *Cleopatra Tragedia di M. Gio Battista Giraldi Cinthio Nobile Ferrarese. In Venetia. Appresso Giulio Cesare Cagnacini*, MDLXXXIII.

although it was not published till much later. Cinthio's theory of tragedy as providing a moral purge through pity and horror is briefly expressed in the Prologue, which is given below with a summary of the piece [Text VIII]. The horrors are less frequent in this play than in some of Cinthio's others, the pity more pervasive. Cinthio also illustrates his belief in the importance of 'sentences', by which he means passages of ethical commentary on the action.[1] His *Cleopatra* begins just after the land-battle in which Antony was decisively defeated. A servant brings the news to Cleopatra and her Nurse, telling them that Antony has been abandoned by his trusted men and that he blames Cleopatra for her flight at Actium. In Sc. IV a Captain bewails his leader's downfall. In Sc. V Antony laments his evil Fortune, upbraids his absent mistress and asks his slave to kill him. The Nurse (Sc. VI) announces Cleopatra's death, and Antony goes out to commit suicide. Then we learn from Cleopatra (Sc. VIII) that 'I feigned death so as to know if he was really angry with me'. Thus the first Act is concerned, as Sc. IX emphasizes, with the destructive power of Cleopatra. In Act II (Sc. I–IV) Antony dies and is lamented. Another topic is now introduced (Sc. V) when Octavius with Agrippa and Mæcenas—ignorant of what has happened—discuss what should be done with Antony. Mæcenas is for clemency, Agrippa for removing Antony once and for all. This ethical debate is continued in Act III, Sc. III, before they learn of Antony's death, but after this it turns on the question whether Octavius will pardon Cleopatra or take her to Rome to walk in his Triumph (Sc. V, VI, VII).

Act IV continues this theme in a discussion between Agrippa and Cleopatra's doctor Olimpus (Sc. II) who is unable to see the Queen (Sc. IV). Cleopatra's seizure in her 'proud Pyramid' by Gallus and Proculeius (Sc. VII) is described at length. In her interview with Cæsar she ascribes her behaviour first to Antony's demands on her, then to her wifely obedience. She will accept death as a punishment, but wishes to be buried with Antony; she will come to Rome if he wishes it.

At the beginning of Act V Olimpus, taken in by Cleopatra's pretences, is amazed at her changed attitude, but her long

[1] On Cinthio's aims see H. B. Charlton, *The Senecan Tradition in Renaissance Tragedy*, Manchester U.P., 1946, pp. lxxix–xciv.

soliloquy in Scene II proves that 'though Octavius has conquered Egypt he has not conquered Cleopatra'. Octavius tries to take precautions, but too late; in Scene VI Proculeius tells how he found Cleopatra dead; an Egyptian priest describes how she killed herself with poison from a phial. Attributing the fall of Antony and Cleopatra to 'immoderate love', Octavius says that the bodies of such lovers should not be sundered; they must be buried together; then he will go to Rome.

The final Chorus points out the perils of Fortune, most to be feared when she seems most favourable.

Cinthio's play is notable for the large number of minor characters, such as the Captain who laments Antony's downfall (I.4), the Nurse (Cleopatra's confidante) who misleads Antony in thinking his mistress dead, Mæcenas and Agrippa (Cæsar's advisers), the doctor Olimpus who has little to do but reflect on the way things seem to be going, Gallus and Proculeius who capture the Queen and are afterwards too late to prevent her suicide. Cleopatra uses no asps but another method mentioned in Plutarch. The downfall of the noble pair is variously ascribed to Fortune, to innate destiny, to Cleopatra's cowardice and Antony's base servitude, above all to the immoderate passion against which the Chorus frequently warns us and which Octavius mentions at the last. There are some excellent passages of dialogue and monologue, but the action moves slowly, with overmuch pause for comment and speculation.

An important Italian *Life* of Cleopatra was written in 1551 by Count Giulio Landi.[1] After outlining the history of Egypt since Roman times Landi described Egypt, its fertility and dependence on the waters of the Nile: 'if the Nile rises only twelve hands, that means famine; if it rises thirteen, this means that Egypt will not go hungry; if fourteen, this brings universal joy', etc. He told of Cleopatra's youth, of Julius Cæsar's coming, of his astonishment at her beauty, and invented a long speech in which she craved his protection. Landi gave a favourable account of Cleopatra, of her intelligence and prudence: e.g. 'She preserved the utmost dignity in public and never showed herself to the people save in great majesty and with venerable ceremony.' Captivated by her, Cæsar gave himself up to

[1] *La Vita di Cleopatra Reina d'Egitto. Dell'Illustre S. conte Giulio Landi. In Vinegia, MDLI.*

pleasure for a time, until duty recalled him. For the story of Antony, Landi supplemented Plutarch from other sources and his own invention. He ascribed the quarrel between Antony and Octavian not to Cleopatra's spell but to Octavian's jealous dislike of sharing the rule with another man; but Antony's extravagant presents of Roman territory to Cleopatra made an excellent excuse, and Antony's divorce of his wife Octavia added fuel to the fire. In describing how Antony fell in love with Cleopatra Landi kept close to Plutarch's account of the barge on the river Cydnus.[1] He omitted some of the less favourable traits of Antony and Cleopatra and their less dignified pastimes, but told of their fishing and of the pearl dissolved in wine. When Antony awoke to the need to march against the Parthians Landi introduced a long internal debate between his warring impulses. But finally love, appetite, desire and blinded will prevailed and, parting from Cleopatra very tardily, Antony could not carry out what he had planned against the Parthians. After the Battle of Actium he went to Cleopatra's galley, and 'like a man lost in love and dishonour, he stood without speaking, and regarded her, holding both his hands to his face, as if for shame he did not dare to speak to her.'

Landi expanded the mission of Thyreus [Tirreus] to win her over to Octavian from Antony, and added an incident when Cleopatra, becoming suspicious of Antony, poisoned his wine, but stopped him drinking in time. After Antony's death Cleopatra in a long speech tries to make Octavian think she has no intention of killing herself.

Though closely modelled on Plutarch, Landi's *Life* is more sympathetic to Cleopatra, and more suffused with emotion. In its expansion of key-incidents it also comes nearer to drama. His version was used in a Senecan play by Cesare de' Cesari whose *Cleopatra* in the following year (1552) departed considerably from Cinthio's handling of the theme, and in particular develops the passionate grief of the Queen after Antony's death. When the play opens she is already in Octavius' power, and closely guarded. Her sorrow for Antony is increased by the realization that she cannot end her own life. Ermafrodite urges

[1] Of the silver oars Landi wrote that 'they were fashioned with such wonderful art that when they struck the water they gave out a musical sound, various and sweeter than flutes or other such instruments'.

her to control her grief and to placate Cæsar, and this she tries to do, begging for pity and calling attention to her streaming, disordered hair which no longer wears a diadem. Her right hand, which used to carry the sceptre, is now clasped with her left in supplication. Octavius is affected to tears. When he asks why she was hostile to Rome for so long she answers with humble flattery.

In Act II her waiting-woman Cherimonia soliloquizes on the cruelties of Fortune through which

> That voice and that so deeply reverenced head,
> That overlofty soul with which till now
> She made a show to reign alone in pride,
> Must humbly bow before the boy Octavius,
> Until that he, half-weeping too for pity,
> Consent to let her live again in freedom
> Loosed wholly from the fear of servitude.

Eras tells how in a distant part of the palace she heard the child Cleopatra shrieking and crying that she has had a vision of her father Antony,

> And as the fearsome shade came from the door
> To lean over the bed where frequently
> Antony with Cleopatra had reposed in love,
> It bowed three times, embraced the crown laid there
> Since the hour when grieving Cleopatra took
> It from her hair dishevelled. Then at last
> He vanished from the sight of the little girl
> But first he said with sad and tearful voice,
> 'O Cleopatra, hasten now thy steps,
> For 'tis not given to me to await thee long.'

Cornelio enters and informs them that in three days Cleopatra is to be taken to Rome to await Cæsar's triumph.

In Act III the Queen begs Cæsar to spare her this indignity, and at least to let her die where she was born. Cæsar explains that her presence is the necessary climax of his glory, that without her he would seem to his citizens to have been vanquished by her sweet and subtle wiles. Cleopatra rages, wishing that he would let the forest beasts take pity on her and kill her. They argue about the laws of Nature and self-interest.

Act IV opens to show the child Cleopatra mourning with Cherimonia. The Queen enters and bids her daughter live on in hopes of revenge. The child cannot believe that Antony would wish her mother to die, but Cleopatra longs to join him and addresses him:

> But since the miser Heav'ns
> Grant not that souls which to the other shore
> Have passed may to this living light return . . .
> More harsh to thee I'd be than to myself,
> However short the time I kept aloof
> From thee, my lord . . .
> Therefore, my lord, open thy loving arms,
> Since, having furnished thee with every rite
> That's possible, it only now remains
> For me to see thee again, my light. O light
> Of these my eyes, 'tis time for thee to bless
> With joyous calm thy Cleopatra's heart
> Which now is wandering in cloudy night.

In a touching scene she bids her daughter good-bye:

> And thou my daughter rest, if not content,
> At least in peace that's promised by thy youth.
> My daughter, be thou happier every hour;
> Thy every age be happy, happy in years,
> Happy the months, the days, the hours, the minutes
> That will conduct thee to thy blossoming time . . .

She asks Eras and Cherimonia to stay with her till she dies, and bids them prepare her bath.

In Act V a Servant describes her death, and the Chorus relates how Cæsar's men found her lying naked in her bed, as lovely as in life save for the asp's bite on her arm. Cæsar regrets her fate and orders her to be buried with Antony:

> With funeral pomp not ever elsewhere seen,
> For in them both there reigned one selfsame soul,
> With perfect love, perhaps unique in the world.
> But I go home my people to prepare
> For enterprises new and greater tasks.

In this play sympathy with the characters in their emotional predicaments prevails over moral judgement.

With the *Cléopatre Captive* of Estienne Jodelle the dramatic cult of Cleopatra reached France. Presented in 1552 this play was much admired until the seventeenth-century classicists turned against its style. It was printed in 1574, in the *Œuvres et meslanges poétiques* of Jodelle, and again in 1583 and 1597. Largely based on the manner of Muret's *Cæsar*, the *Cléopatre* may also show the influence of De Baïf's translation of Euripides' *Hecuba* (1544), and of Cesare de' Cesari's *Cleopatra*. A follower of the Pléiade, Jodelle on the whole followed out their theories. His play is filled with inversions, long periods, confused syntax, repetition of words, phrases, frequent alliteration, a mixture of elaborate figures and allusions to classical myths with down-to-earth expressions and 'sententiae'.[1] The five Acts of the piece occupy 1616 lines of which 608 go to the Chorus. The Unities are kept, but decorum is somewhat broken in Act III where tragic dignity is lost.

The play limits itself to the last day of Cleopatra's life after she has been captured. In I.1 Antony's Ghost soliloquizes, and in the next scene Cleopatra declares that it has appeared to her in a dream and summoned her to join him. The main action concerns Octavius' desire to keep her alive for his triumph and her desire to be with Antony. Act III in which Cleopatra meets Octavius is largely devoted to her unwillingness to reveal all her treasures, the treachery of Seleucus, and her anger with him. Act IV however makes it clear that Cleopatra intends to die after completing Antony's obsequies; and in Act V Proculeius tells how she and her ladies killed themselves.

Jodelle is more interested in moral comment than in characterization. Octavius is cold and unsympathetic. Antony was a victim of love but his Ghost is vengeful towards his mistress. Cleopatra still loves him but her suicide is also caused by her fear of servitude. The tragedy is one of pride rather than love: Cleopatra's rage with Seleucus is meant to be regal; her death spells the victory of her will over Cæsar's. There are several references to the fickleness of Fortune and the Chorus's general reflections are to the effect that no man is happy until he is dead. Of the two lovers Cleopatra was the more to blame.

A similar mixture of motifs marks the *Marc Antoine* of Robert

[1] Cf. *Cléopatre Captive. A critical edition*, by L. B. Ellis, University of Pennsylvania, Philadelphia, 1946. Introduction.

Garnier (1578) which affords 'a tangle of ancient ideas of Fate, Christian ideas of punishment for sin, ancient and mediæval ideas of the power of Fortune over men, and Renaissance ideas of the power of man to shape his own fortune.'[1]

This last element however predominates in the piece and makes it a tragedy of passionate aberration. *Marc Antoine* has some importance for English literature since by translating it in 1590 Mary Sidney, Countess of Pembroke, initiated the courtly Senecan movement which led several members of her circle to write Roman tragedies within the next ten or fifteen years. I give it below from the 1595 edition[2] [Text IX].

The Garnier-Pembroke play opens, like Cinthio's, when Antony is still alive. In soliloquy he blames Cleopatra for seducing him by 'sweete baites' which have turned him from 'Launces and Pikes to daunces and to feastes' and made him neglect the Parthian wars

> In haste to runne about her necke to hang
> Languishing in her armes thy Idoll made.

He broke away 'as one encharm'd / Breakes from th'enchaunter that him strongly helde', but, besotted by her absence, soon returned misled by wanton love, only to be betrayed by her at Actium.

This depiction of Antony closely resembles Shakespeare's, and the resemblance is increased when in Act II Philostratus the philosopher (like Philo in Shakespeare) bewails the decline of the 'great Emperor! . . . whom worlds did fear.' Love has destroyed Egypt as it did Troy. Entering with her women Eras and Charmion, Cleopatra declares that she has loved Antony 'more deare than Scepter, children, freedome, light'. Admitting that her beauty has ruined Antony she blames herself as 'sole cause' of his overthrow (447–8), and asserts that we wrongly blame the gods for the consequences of our errors:

> We may them not to their high majesties
> But to our selves impute, whose passions
> Plunge us each day in all afflictions.' (476–8)

[1] W. Farnham, *Shakespeare's Tragic Frontier*, Berkeley, 1950, pp. 148–56.
[2] It was edited by Alice Luce (Weimar, 1897) from the 1592 edition.

When Charmion urges her to abandon '*Antonies* wracke, lest it your wracke procure' (524), she indignantly refuses. She would rather die as a 'wife kindhearted' than live for her children or for herself.

In Act III the moral theme is reiterated when Antony shows himself in despair and jealousy yet still bound to Cleopatra, and Lucilius (once Brutus' friend, now Antony's) states that Fortune is fickle and 'nothing is dureable / Vertue except, our never failing host' (988–9). He tries to turn his master from thoughts of suicide. The latter inveighs against the Machiavellian weakling Octavius ('In *Mars* his schole who never lesson learn'd'). The 'one disordred act at Actium' which has destroyed him was brought about by his own fault:

> Pleasure, nought else, the plague of this our life . . .
> Alone hath me this strange disastre spunne. (1150–2)

Cæsar in Act IV gloats over his own vast power. He pities Antony's passion and folly but is determined to keep himself supreme:

> Murther we must, until not one we leave
> Which may hereafter us of rest bereave. (1499–1500)

When the messenger Dircetus has told at great length how Antony died Cæsar reflects

> I cannot but his tearefull chaunce lament,
> Although not I, but his owne pride the cause,
> And unchast love of this Aegiptian. (1692–4)

In the last Act Cleopatra bids a moving farewell to her children, invokes Antony at his tomb, and dies of grief on his body.

Mary Sidney's translation, besides capturing much of Garnier's moral earnestness and rhetorical sentiment, brought into England the insistence on political theorizing which henceforth influenced the academic Senecans. As Dr E. Schanzer points out,[1] the play is remarkable for its sympathetic treatment of the Queen, who is scarcely blamed (save by Antony and Cæsar) and accuses herself only of failing him at Actium, not of debasing his manhood. 'She is all heav'nlie' says Diomede, and in her virtues she anticipates Dryden's Cleopatra, being

[1] E. Schanzer, *The Problem Plays of Shakespeare*, 1963, pp. 150–2.

less the mistress than the wife ('our holy marriage' (1947)) and the mother. A simple, faithful creature, she does not deserve Antony's resentment, and we never see them together. Shakespeare probably knew the *Antonie*, and he may have taken from it a few words and images. Thus J. D. Wilson has pointed out that the Countess's *Argument*, saying that Antony 'for knitting a straiter bonde of amitie betweene them, had taken to wife *Octavia*' probably produced Shakespeare's

> To hold you in perpetual amity,
> To make you brothers, and to knit your hearts
> With an unslipping knot, take Antony
> Octavia to his wife. (II.2.130–3)

Shakespeare's reference to the flooding of the Nile (II.7.21–4) may possibly have been suggested by the 'fat slime' in the Chorus 754–64; and the 'many thousand kisses' of Shakespeare's dying Antony (IV.13.20) may be a reminiscence of the 'thousand kisses, thousand thousand more' of Cleopatra's farewell to him in *Antonie*, 1997. These and other trivial echoes are quite in accord with Shakespeare's habit of floating to the surface of his memory details from works read sometimes years before.

It is highly probable that he owed much more to Samuel Daniel's *Cleopatra*, first published in *Delia and Rosamond augmented* (1594), and slightly revised in *The Poeticall Essayes of Samuel Danyel. Newly corrected and augmented* (1599). The drama was largely remodelled before its reappearance in *Certaine Small Workes Heretofore Divulged by Samuel Daniel . . . and now againe by him corrected and augmented.*[1] Most critics have believed that this major reshaping was made after seeing a play (probably Shakespeare's) in the theatre. Recently Dr E. Schanzer has shown that Daniel got his new material from the Countess of Pembroke's *Antonie* though he tried to adapt it for possible

[1] In 1607 events previously described in narration are presented on the stage (e.g. Cleopatra's death), and the boy Cesario is given a bigger part in the action. In I.1 Cleopatra sends him away with Rodon. In I.2 Dircetus informs Octavius of Antony's death. IV.2 expands the same scene in 1594/9. A new IV.3 shows Cesario going to his death. In V.2 Cleopatra and her women kill themselves. The several editions were collated by M. Lederer in *Daniel's The Tragedie of Cleopatra nach dem Drucke von 1611* (Bang's Materialien, 31), Louvain, 1911.

stage-production.[1] I am not however convinced by the further argument, based on the few verbal parallels with *Antony and Cleopatra*, that Shakespeare studied the 1607 as well as the 1594/9 version of Daniel's tragedy. The 1599 text is given below [Text X].

Dedicating his tragedy to the Countess of Pembroke, Daniel calls it 'the worke the which she did impose', for she bade him 'To sing of State, and tragicke notes to frame.' Her 'well-grac'd *Anthony* . . . Requir'd his *Cleopatras* company'. His task, like hers and Sir Philip Sidney's, is cultural, 'To chase away this tyrant of the North / Grosse Barbarisme.'

Daniel begins his play after Antony's burial, when Cleopatra, in her monument, is temporizing with Cæsar in order to save her children's lives. The first Act opens with a long soliloquy in which she moralizes on her own faults, for she will not blame Antony

> My *Atlas*, and supporter of my pride,
> That did the world of all my glory sway. (15–16)

She refuses to live a prisoner, to be bound, and to see Octavia gloating over her misery. She speaks of herself and Antony as 'grappling in the Ocean of our pride' and sinking together. She must pretend to Cæsar, 'Seeming to suit my mind unto my fortune' (190).

The Chorus of Egyptians moralizes on the torments of those 'who by their doing ill, / Have wrought the worlds unrest'.

In Act II Cæsar observes to Proculeius that though he can conquer territories he cannot conquer hearts, 'Free is the heart, the temple of the minde' (262). Proculeius describes how he carried out Cæsar's command 'To win her forth alive (if that I might) / From out the Monument', and how Cleopatra, prevented from suicide, mingled a long complaint against Cæsar with prayers for her children, especially Cesario. Proculeius thinks that she will be 'content to live'. Cæsar, out of his high esteem for princes, doubts this. She must be well guarded.

The Chorus sings of Opinion and the vain imaginations of men who, like Antony and Cleopatra, follow ambition, lust and honour.

[1] E. Schanzer, 'Daniel's Revision of his *Cleopatra*', *RES*, n.s. VIII, No. 32, 375–81.

Act III has two scenes. The first is based upon the passage in Plutarch [*inf.* 312] which relates that after the seizure of Cleopatra and the capture of Alexandria Octavius honoured the great philosopher Arrius and pardoned the orator Philostratus although he disliked the latter's pretence to be an Academic philosopher. In Daniel Philostratus thanks Arrius for saving his life and expatiates on the failure of consolatory eloquence in man's hour of need,

> For when this ship of life pale Terror boords,
> Where are our precepts then, where is our art?

Like all other men he sought, however shamefully, to avoid death. Arrius bids him not to grieve, and declares that the age is so evil as to make men tired of life, and that moral decay has caused the downfall of Egypt. He preaches a cyclical theory of history

> Thus doth the ever-changing course of things
> Runne a perpetuall circle, ever turning:
> And that same day that hiest glory brings,
> Brings us unto the poynt of backe-returning (555–8)

Arrius fears that Cæsar will kill Cleopatra's children, including Cesario, since 'Plurality of *Cæsars* are not good' (576).

In Scene 2 Cleopatra defends her acts of war by blaming Antony's will and her loving obedience. Cæsar rejects this explanation; she has always hated Rome. She gives him written testimony of Julius Cæsar's love for her and hands him a note of her treasures. Seleucus interrupts to say that the list is not complete. She attacks him and explains that she kept some as gifts for Livia and Octavia to win their mediation. Cæsar promises to treat her kindly. Dolabella says that if she can be so beautiful and persuasive now when no longer young, and in grief, how wonderful she must have been in her youth. Cæsar bids Dolabella not to be taken in by Cleopatra's wiles.

> Time now hath altred all, for neither is
> She as she was, nor we as she conceives.

He wishes merely to get her to Rome and his triumph, and he intends to send her there direct while he goes round by Syria.

The Chorus celebrates Nemesis and the doom of the gods,

and asks why 'The innocent poore multitude / For great mens faults should punished be'.

Act IV opens with a dialogue between Seleucus and Rodon. Seleucus laments his betrayal of Cleopatra's secrets, for he has found no favour with Cæsar. Rodon confesses that his fault is greater than Seleucus'. He had been given charge of Cesario to take him to India in the hope that the offspring of Julius Cæsar might some day 'come to guide / The Empire of the world, as his by right'. Cleopatra's grief at parting is dramatized quite sensitively. Rodon tells how he betrayed his trust, bringing Cesario back to Rhodes; he gives the thoughts of the boy looking forward to the time when descendants of Antony shall be emperors [cf. Plutarch, *inf.* 317]. Now Rodon is as infamous as Seleucus and expects to be slain. The two unhappy wretches retire as Cleopatra enters with a letter from Dolabella stating that Cæsar means her to grace his triumph in Rome. She pays her last respects to Antony's tomb in terms based on Plutarch and promises that 'with speede / My selfe will bring my soule to Antony'. She refers to the man she has sent to fetch the means of death,

> So shall I act the last of life with glory,
> Die like a Queene, and rest without controule.

The Chorus regards the decay of Egypt as typical of the changes inevitable in human affairs. Maybe Rome will go the same way.

In Act V.1 Dolabella hears from Titius that Cleopatra has sent a letter to Cæsar, and after dressing richly and dining sumptuously has sent all from the tomb 'But her two maids and one poore countreyman'. Dolabella goes to beg Cæsar not to humiliate Cleopatra. In Scene 2 the countryman, as Nuntius, tells the Chorus of Cleopatra's death. Cleopatra had sent him to get two asps. Her address to the snake is given,

> And here I sacrifice these armes to Death,
> That lust late dedicated to Delights.

After some hesitation she nerved herself and died drowsily and smiling. Charmian's last act, the straightening of her diadem, is celebrated, 'That all the world may know she dide a Queene'. Cæsar's messengers rushed in, too late.

The Chorus sings the return of Egypt to desert, and the evils of luxury, the destructive power of greatness.

Daniel's drama differs from the *Antonie* of Garnier and Mary Sidney in the narrower scope of its plot, its more detailed following of Plutarch's *Life*, and the attempts intermittently made to set it in a wider frame of reference. The causes of Antony's fall are naturally not stressed; Cleopatra's tragedy is one of pride and grief. Like the Countess, Daniel gets pathos from her sufferings as a mother, substituting for the child Cleopatra the sad history of Cesario, and using it to introduce the theme of betrayal in the neat scene between Seleucus and Rodon. The play is more varied in its detail than Garnier's, but still untheatrical, for Daniel was a reflective poet rather than a dramatist. The philosopher Philostratus is here made to moralize on general moral and historical implications—human fear of death, perpetual recurrence, and the decay of nations. The fourth and fifth Choruses apply this last idea to Egypt and Rome. So far we find little connection with Shakespeare.

There can be little doubt however that Shakespeare remembered Daniel's drama, or that he had recently read it in the 1599 version. Like Shakespeare Daniel contrasts the austerity of Rome with the luxury of Egypt, though he suggests that Antony was ignorant of women until he met Cleopatra:

Thou comming from the strictnesse of thy citty
And never this loose pomp of monarchs learnest,
Inur'd to warrs, in womens wiles unwitty.

Shakespeare's middle-aged heroine ('Wrinkled deep in time') is anticipated by Daniel's in her 'beauties waine' with 'new-appearing wrinkles of declining'.

Senecan Cleopatras usually had mixed motives for their behaviour after Antony's death: love of him and their children, hatred of servitude; but Shakespeare and Daniel alone agree in adding to her fear of being led bound in Cæsar's triumph fear of Octavia's scorn:

Know sir, that I
Will not wait pinion'd at your master's court,
Nor once be chastis'd with the sober eye
Of dull Octavia. (*AC* V.2.52–5, cf. Daniel 63–70)

Shakespeare's Proculeius, like Daniel's, advises Cleopatra to beg Cæsar for mercy, and both dramatists make her send to Cæsar stating her desire to die. Both follow Plutarch closely in the incident of Seleucus and the treasure, but when Shakespeare's Cleopatra declares

> 'That I some lady trifles have reserv'd,
> Immoment toys . . .'

hoping to give them to Livia and Octavia 'to induce / Their mediation' (V.2.164–9) she is probably echoing Daniel's 'little toyes . . . That . . . they / Might mediate'.

Whereas Plutarch's Dolabella 'did beare no evill will unto Cleopatra', Daniel's is in love with her and exposes Cæsar's intentions in a love-letter. Shakespeare is more theatrical and more subtle; he shows Dolabella falling in love with her on the stage (V.2.67–101) and obeying her command ('Which my love makes religion to obey'). 'I must die his debtor' in Daniel (1078–84) is echoed by Shakespeare's heroine: 'I shall remain your debtor' (V.2.204).

Cleopatra meets death as a lover, and dresses for it as for her first meeting with Antony. Here Shakespeare, in Cleopatra's words as she sends for her best attire: 'I am again for Cydnus, / To meet Mark Antony' (V.2.227–8), repeats Daniel's description of her waiting for the rustic

> Even as she was when on thy cristall streames,
> Cleere *Cydnos* she did shew what earth could shew
> (1460–1).

In contemplating suicide both Cleopatras associate ideas of hands and resolution, e.g.:

> 'My resolution and my hands I'll trust' (*AC* IV.15.49)

> But what have I save these bare hands to doe it? . . .
> For who can stay a minde resolv'd to die? (*Cleo.* 1162–71)

Other examples could be given which suggest Shakespeare's debt.[1]

[1] I am indebted here to W. Farnham, *Shakespeare's Tragic Frontier* (1950), pp. 158–73; F. M. Dickey, *Not Wisely but Too Well* (1957), pp. 163–73; K. Muir *Shakespeare's Sources*, Vol. I, 1957, pp. 207–16; E. Schanzer, *The Problem Plays of Shakespeare*, 1963, pp. 167–81.

Shakespeare may also have known 'A Letter from Octavia to Marcus Antonius' which in Daniel's *Poeticall Essayes* (1599) preceded *Cleopatra*. Daniel writes in the Argument that though Antony married Octavia, she 'met not with that integritie she brought',

> 'For Antonie having yet upon him the fetters of Aegypt,[1] layde on by the power of a most incomparable beautie, could admit no new lawes into the state of his affection, or dispose of himself being not himselfe, but as having his heart turned Eastwarde[2] whither the point of his desires were [*sic*] directed, touchte with the strongest allurements that ambition, and a licentious soveraintie could draw a man unto: could not trulie descend to the private love of a civill nurtred Matrone, whose entertainment bounded with modestie and the nature of her education, knew not to cloth her affections in any other colours then the plain habit of truth.'

Her letter, supposedly written after Antony has gone back to Egypt while she was making peace between him and Octavius, is a dignified protest against his maltreatment of her. She protests also against the false estimation of women as fickle and against the double standard in morality ('What? are there bars for us, no bounds for you?' (St. 20).) It comes closest to Shakespeare in St. 2 where she imagines Cleopatra as mocking at the letter when Antony receives it:

> Although, perhaps these my complaints may come
> Whilst thou in th' armes of that incestuous Queene
> The staine of *Aegypt*, and the shame of *Rome*
> Shalt dallying sit, and blush to have them seene:
> Whilst proud disdainefull she, gessing from whome
> The message came, and what the cause hath beene,
> Wil skorning saie, faith, this comes from your Deere,
> Now sir you must be shent for staying heere.

Later she imagines how Antony was won back by the 'Inchantress':

> She armes her teares, the ingins of deceit
> And all her batterie, to oppose my love:
> And bring thy comming grace to a retraite

[1] Cf. I.2.120. 'These strong Egyptian fetters I must break.'
[2] Cf. II.3.40. 'I' th' East my pleasure lies.'

The powre of all her subtiltie to prove:
Now pale and faint she languishes, and straight
Seemes in a sound, unable more to move:
Whilst her instructed followers plie thine eares
With forged passions, mixt with fained teares. (36)

She calls on him to redeem himself, reconcile his warring passions, 'And be thine owne, and then thou wilt be mine' (42).

It is possible as Professor Dickey says (p. 172) that St. 2 suggested Shakespeare's opening scene in which Cleopatra mocks at Fulvia's letters, but for the account of Cleopatra's wiles Plutarch and human nature would be enough.

Before Shakespeare wrote his play Samuel Brandon, in imitation of Daniel and the Countess, had written his *Virtuous Octavia* (1598) a tragedy built up by expanding the truism that reason should overcome the rebel passions:

The instinct of nature, which doth all things move,
Bids love whereas you like without regarde,
But pietie saith, where 'tis lawfull love,
Or else hells torments shall be your rewarde (2084–8)

Shakespeare drew nothing from this dull pedagogy unless it were a determination to make his virtuous Octavia as reticent as Brandon's is loquacious.

The Senecan dramatists on the whole balanced their moral judgements on the lovers with considerable sympathy for their fates, and Daniel is typical when he makes Cleopatra hope, 'Though life were bad my death may yet be praised.' These Senecans recognized the mixed nature of mankind; they could demand pity for the lovers without condoning their faults; hence the Choruses usually lamented the sadness of their fall, the weakness of human nature, and the necessity of moral standards in princes as in lesser mortals.

In rehandling the story after writing *Lear* and *Macbeth* Shakespeare was not tempted to be didactic or sentimental, nor to attribute overmuch to Fortune. Antony and Cleopatra are not star-crossed lovers, but prisoners of their own characters. Shakespeare may have learned a little from the moral antinomies of some earlier dramas on the theme, but his theatrical genius and chronicle-technique led him to explore the process of decline, to represent the principal incidents of several years, the vacillations of Antony and the caprices of Cleopatra, and to enact the many turns of their struggle against the fate they brought on themselves.

The play starts in 40 B.C., some little time after Antony and Cleopatra have met at Tarsus, and ends with their deaths in 30 B.C.

The first Act, while revealing the hold which Cleopatra has over Antony and his shameful neglect of his colleagues in Rome, shows him hearing of his wife Fulvia's death, breaking away from the Egyptian and going home, leaving her longing for him. Shakespeare modifies Plutarch, since Antony left Cleopatra in order to war against the Parthians, and had got as far as Phoenicia before he heard about his wife's difficulties with Cæsar, then made for Rome, but was told of her death long before he got there. Shakespeare makes the crisis in Antony's emotions more sudden and devastating by combining with the more private matter news of the peril to Rome caused by Sextus Pompeius. The public peril is decisive (I.2.180–97), although to Cleopatra he makes Fulvia's death 'more particular' (I.3.54–56), and despite Cleopatra's tantrums he leaves her.

Into the first three scenes Shakespeare has crammed a great deal of expository material bearing on character rather than plot. Our first view of Antony is unfavourable, through Philo's moral disapproval. Yet after Philo has said that we shall see

> The triple pillar of the world transformed
> Into a strumpet's fool,

what we actually see is a magnificent pair of lovers, the woman jealous and waspish yet regal, 'a wrangling queen', the man extravagant in feeling and language ('Let Rome in Tiber melt' . . . 'the nobleness of life / Is to do thus . . .') so that in him as well as in her

> every passion fully strives
> To make itself . . . fair and admir'd. (I.1.50–1)

Demetrius may be dismayed by the slighting of Cæsar's messengers; we are attracted, and this continues through I.2 when Cleopatra's ladies, Charmian and Iras, have their fortunes told, merrily but with ironic undertones, revealing in their daring repartee the freedom of Cleopatra's court. With them Shakespeare introduces Alexas, a Greek who according to Plutarch helped Cleopatra to seduce Antony's affections, and who later betrayed him [*inf.* 306]. She is furious at Antony's 'Roman thought' on hearing Cæsar's messenger. Antony himself, aware of the disrepute into which he is falling, realizes that a crisis is upon him:

> These strong Egyptian fetters I must break,
> Or lose myself in dotage. (I.2.119–20)

The bluff Enobarbus in this scene shares Antony's admiration for his mistress, though he mocks at her posing (I.2.143–58) and he feels no sorrow at the death of Fulvia, who, Plutarch relates, had already 'taught Antonius . . . obedience to women', and 'was somewhat sour and crooked of disposition'. The effect of Antony's resolve on Cleopatra's capricious, contrary disposition is violent (I.3.1–10). He wants her advice but she refuses to hear him and taunts him till he leaves in anger; but at the last moment she surrenders and wishes him success ('Your honour calls you hence . . .' (97–101)). So the question of Antony's departure has been used by the dramatist to evoke a superb display of diverse emotions, and Antony has revealed that he is still not lost to honour.

Rome's need of Antony appears in I.4 when Cæsar, always anxious to prove that he was blameless for the split with his colleague, expresses abhorrence of Antony's light and irresponsible behaviour in a puritanic way (I.4.16–33). Whereas Lepidus pities Antony's decline, Octavius is bitter, recalling his past feats of endurance. Note that Cæsar is not beloved nor does he love the common people (40–7). Next, in a fine scene (I.5) scarcely needed for the plot, Cleopatra displays the longing which makes her continually send messengers after Antony. She rejoices in the love she has excited in three great men, but prefers Antony to Julius Cæsar or Pompey. She makes no attempt to hide that she is ageing (27–29).

Act II extends from Antony's arrival in Rome (40 B.C.) to the peace made with Sextus Pompeius, and includes the reconciliation between Antony and Octavius and Antony's marriage to Octavia.

The scene at Messina between Pompey and the pirate Menas

shows Pompey's mean opinion of Octavius and Lepidus (II.1.8–16) and his respect for Antony ('his soldiership / Is twice the other twain') and hope that he will remain in Egypt. That this hope is unfounded appears in II.2, for Antony is now in Rome. His meeting with Octavius opens with a quarrel less 'brotherly' than that between Brutus and Cassius. Lepidus makes ineffectual attempts to pacify them, but Mecænas and Enobarbus (with his blundering sense) bring them to the need for immediate alliance, and Agrippa suggests that Octavia should be married to Antony, who readily agrees. Yet even at this moment of Roman reunion Cleopatra intrudes when Enobarbus first describes (from Plutarch) her meeting with Antony and her customary behaviour in such terms as to win admiration from Agrippa and Mecænas, and then prophesies that Antony will not abandon her. The scene ends with a contrast between her and Octavia which puts clearly the sexual alternatives before Antony: 'Age cannot wither her . . .' or 'beauty, wisdom, modesty.'

Significantly, II.3 begins with Antony telling Octavia that he will sometimes have to leave her, though he promises amendment of life. The Soothsayer, sorry to have left Egypt, urges Antony to quit Cæsar since his genius is overborne by Cæsar's. Antony, recognizing his inferiority, declares that he will return to Egypt and sends Ventidius against the Parthians. But first (II.4) he goes with Lepidus to meet Pompey. Shifting to Egypt, II.5 shows how Cleopatra, enjoying memories of her conquest of Antony, receives news of his marriage with the utmost rage and violence, torn between love and jealous pride. Meanwhile (II.6) the triumvirate parleys with Pompey, who ascribes his warlike moves to revenge for his father and equalitarian zeal (like Brutus and Cassius to 'Have one man but a man' (II.6.19)). Antony's rash challenge to a sea-combat nearly prevents agreement, but Pompey agrees to take Sicily and Sardinia and shows his friendly feelings towards Antony and Enobarbus.

The feast on Pompey's galley (II.7) portrays the ill-assorted nature of the triumvirate, Lepidus as inept and sottish (1–54, 90), Cæsar as cold and unsociable, Antony as a likeable roisterer. Pompey (as in Plutarch) is willing for his henchman to do the basest treachery for him but not to do it himself (66–85). The greatest men in the world are not seen in a favourable light.

The eleven scenes of Act III are packed with important action, for it extends from Ventidius' triumph over the Parthians and Antony's departure from Rome with Octavia to the embassy of Thyreus (after Antony's defeat at Actium) which causes a violent quarrel and reconciliation with Cleopatra. Ventidius' victory is the occasion of a cold glance at Antony's reluctance to allow much glory to a subordinate ('Who does in the wars more than his captain can / Becomes his captain's captain.' III.1.21–2). According to Plutarch, Antony did not leave Rome for Greece until Octavia had borne him a daughter, and the news from Ventidius was told him when with her at Athens (hence III.1.29–37). III.2 shows their departure, with Agrippa and Enobarbus mocking at Lepidus, Cæsar's affection for his sister, and her shy gentleness. Octavia's reticence makes a sharp contrast with Cleopatra's jealous badgering of the Messenger in III.3 (which recalls the similar queries at the end of II.5). Some time elapses before III.4, in which Octavia is leaving Athens to smoothe over fresh dissensions between her husband and her brother. (In Plutarch she was 'great with child'.) Antony's complaints, that Octavius had treated him coldly and renewed the war against Pompey come from later in Plutarch [*inf.* 291]. Their parting is most affectionate, although Antony will prepare for war. Shakespeare omits Octavia's success in bringing the rivals together, Antony's expedition into Asia and his bitter and unsuccessful Parthian campaign (36 B.C.), which occupies a fifth of the *Life*. Instead the dramatist leaps ahead in III.5 to the later quarrel, briefly explained in conversation between Enobarbus and Eros, when Cæsar's imprisonment of Lepidus (36 B.C.) and Antony's preparation of a fleet are mentioned [cf. *inf.* 291]. Octavia's arrival in Rome in III.6 also refers historically to a later stage, for after she had reconciled Octavius and Antony, the latter went into Asia, but, driven by 'the unreined lust of concupiscence', had Cleopatra come to him in Syria where he gave her many provinces, thus exciting resentment in Rome. The 'sweet poison of her love' made him begin his Parthian war 'out of due time', in the winter of 36 B.C. He suffered great losses and privations, but having won eighteen indecisive battles he gave himself a triumph in Alexandria and met Cleopatra near

Sidon. Plutarch has a vivid account of his 'running many times to the sea side to see if she were coming'. When Octavia wished to come to him he bade her wait in Athens (35 B.C.), but Cleopatra kept him with her by starving herself and continual weeping; and he returned to Egypt. It was after this that Octavia returned to Rome, where Cæsar ordered her to leave her faithless husband's house, but she refused. Her love and constancy made men hate him the more for his unkindness; but they hated especially his public honouring of his bastards by Cleopatra and his gifts to her of rich kingdoms. Antony's final abandonment of his wife came in 31 B.C. when he sent to Rome 'to put [her] out of his house'.

When III.6 opens Octavius is telling Mecænas and Agrippa of Antony's misdeeds and of his own efforts to keep peace. Octavia enters unexpectedly. Shakespeare combines here two comings, that with Antony's permission, to make peace, and that after he kept her waiting vainly in Athens. Hence ll. 54–64 her belief that he was in Athens, and Cæsar's contradiction of it (65–90, 'You are abus'd / Beyond the mark of thought', and 'The adulterous Antony . . . turns you off'). Thus many months are omitted in the scene which gives Cæsar a legitimate reason for war and proves the extent of Octavia's patience.

III.7.3 refers to Antony's command that Cleopatra should not go to the wars with him but go to Egypt. As in Plutarch, Domitius Enobarbus is responsible for this rapidly changed decision, but Shakespeare omits Cleopatra's bribery of Canidius to alter Antony's mind, and makes her refuse to stay. In Plutarch Canidius changed his advice later and urged Antony to send Cleopatra away and to fight on the mainland in Macedonia [*inf.* 298]. Here Canidius enters with Antony and joins Enobarbus in advising against a sea-battle when Antony and Cleopatra wish it (27–49). The inadequate preparations (34–53) are described in a well-chosen selection of details from Plutarch: the untrained mariners, the heavy ships, the burning of all but sixty Egyptian vessels. Cæsar's incredible speed and the veteran soldier's warning, the separation of Canidius with the land-army, are also taken from Plutarch.

III.8 combines events at Actium in 31 B.C. by land and sea. First Cæsar orders Taurus not to fight until the sea-battle is over, while Antony sets forces to face them. The sea-fight is seen through the eyes of Enobarbus and Scarus, who tell of Cleopatra's flight at the critical moment, followed by Antony in his own galley, forsaking his men. The dismal effects of the defeat on Antony's generals are illustrated in Canidius' despair and decision to surrender. Shakespeare does not describe the gallantry of the fleet, which fought on for hours, and his soldiers' loyalty, who kept together for seven days, hoping 'that he would come by some means or other unto them.' This is perhaps symbolized by the continued fidelity of Enobarbus.

III.9 which most editors set in Alexandria is probably one of many examples of 'indeterminate setting'. (No places are given in F1 for this play.) It combines what in Plutarch happened 'at the head of Tænarus' (Cape Matapan in Southern Greece) with what was done later in Alexandria. On Tænarus, Antony, intending to go to Africa, dismissed his friends with a ship richly laden (III.9.1–21). There also 'Cleopatra's women first brought Antonius and Cleopatra to speak together, and afterwards to lie together' (25–74). In Plutarch Antony then went to Libya, sent Cleopatra to Egypt and, following after her, found her trying to move her ships and treasures over the Isthmus of Suez to escape the Romans. Antony then built a house by the sea and played Timon for a time, until, learning that his allies and armies had deserted him, he plunged desperately into a gay life and sent the schoolmaster Euphronius as ambassador to Octavius. This is referred to at III.9.61–5, 71–2. So a considerable time is compressed in this scene.

In III.10 Euphronius gets short shrift from Cæsar, who wants Cleopatra to drive her lover out or kill him, and sends Thyreus to tempt her with promises (19–36). The next scene shows Antony receiving Cæsar's reply with boasts and a personal challenge, the puerility of which makes Enobarbus decide to abandon his master. Thyreus' courtship of Cleopatra excites Antony's jealousy, so the man is whipped and sent back with insults. Antony vents his fury on Cleopatra too, until, appeased by her protestations, he resolves to fight again, and speaks in a boasting manner which finally convinces Enobarbus of 'the diminution in our captain's brain'.

The third Act therefore bears the main burden of Antony's fall. At its start he was still powerful, triumphant (if vicariously), and careful of his honour, reconciled to Octavius and blest with a good wife. By the end he is a man doomed by his own fault, raging vainly against superior power and competence. The concupiscible elements in his nature have now drowned both his valour and his common sense. Seen with the cold eyes of Cæsar he is ridiculous, as we realize at the beginning of Act IV, though even Octavius can say 'Poor Antony!' (IV.1.16). The pathos of his decline is brought out again in IV.2 where he bids farewell to his servants and even Enobarbus stands 'onion-ey'd'. Here and in the next scene, where soldiers hear music underground and take it for a sign:

> 'Tis the god Hercules, whom Antony lov'd,
> Now leaves him (IV.3.16–17)

Shakespeare is still following Plutarch closely, but the arming of Antony in IV.4 is invented to bring Cleopatra on the stage and to suggest their doubts about the issue of the day's battle. In IV.5 Antony meets the soldier whose advice to fight only on land he had previously ignored, then learns that Enobarbus has forsaken him, heartsick no doubt but not 'sick of an ague' like Domitius [*inf.* 298]. Antony's characteristic generosity appears when he has the deserter's treasure sent after him. Whereas in Plutarch this desertion occurred before Actium, Shakespeare makes it more poignant by placing it just before the catastrophe, and adds to it by having Antony send a kindly letter without overt reproach. 'O! my fortunes have / Corrupted honest men', he cries in a flash of moral perception.

Enobarbus (IV.6) realizes that from Octavius he will have 'No honourable trust' and repents of his infidelity even before he learns of his master's magnanimity. 'I will go seek / Some ditch wherein to die.'

The successful sally of IV.7, and Antony's triumphant return to Cleopatra, provide a short hopeful phase—a sort of lightning before death, but he plunges into feasting instead of preparing for 'the next day's fate'. In this euphoria he and Cleopatra reward a gallant soldier—whose behaviour seems to contrast with Enobarbus'. The latter however dies of grief in IV.9. In Plutarch (and Cinthio) the soldier deserts next day. Before battle is joined (IV.10) Antony misjudges the situation. He is not leading his men but, watching from a hill, sees his fleet desert to the enemy. All is lost and, blaming Cleopatra for betraying him, he drives her away and raves like his ancestor Hercules in the shirt of Nessus.

Shakespeare omits Plutarch's details of the monuments Cleopatra had built near the temple of her goddess Isis and filled with her treasures. Retiring thither (IV.11), she sends to tell Antony that she is dead: 'and bring me how he takes my death'. Antony's rage quickly turns to grief at Mardian's piteous report, and he prepares for death. The scene (IV.12) in which Eros commits suicide and Antony gives himself a mortal wound is only equalled in splendour by IV.13, where he is hoisted into the monument and dies, and is lamented by Cleopatra, who promises to die 'after the high Roman fashion'.

Act V begins when Octavius, unaware of Antony's death, sends Dolabella to demand his surrender. (This is not in Plutarch). But immediately Dercetas enters with Antony's blood-stained sword and announces his suicide. All present are greatly moved, Cæsar in particular. A message from Cleopatra declares that she awaits Cæsar's bidding. He sends Proculeius and Gallus to comfort her and prevent her suicide, 'for her life in Rome / Would be eternal in our triumph'. V.2 shows, without clear indication of the method [cf. *inf.* 311], the capture of Cleopatra by Proculeius with Gallus' help. She tries to kill herself. Handed over to Dolabella she utters a superb panegyric on Antony. Dolabella tells her that she will be taken to Rome, and when Cæsar enters she is prepared for the worst. She appears to submit completely when Cæsar under kind words cloaks reproaches and threats to her children (116–32). When Seleucus reveals that her proffered list of treasure is incomplete, she attacks him, then admits that she kept something back out of vanity and also as gifts 'For Livia and Octavia to induce / Their mediation' (V.2.167–9). Giving her back her possessions Cæsar takes his leave, asserting,

> . . . we intend so to dispose you as
> Yourself shall give us counsel.

Cleopatra sees through him:

> He words me, girls, he words me, that I should not
> Be noble to myself. (190–1)

When Dolabella brings Cæsar's order to leave for Rome within three days, both Cleopatra and her ladies are resolved on suicide. She sends for her 'best attires' and the 'rural fellow' comes in with the asps in his basket. He jests warningly about them. Dressing in her royal robes Cleopatra makes her dying speech, says farewell to Iras (who falls and dies) and applies the asps to her breast and arm. She sinks into the sleep of death and Charmian is adjusting the crown on her mistress' head when the Guard rushes in, followed by Dolabella, sent to prevent the suicide. Charmian dies. Cæsar enters and cannot but admire the nobility of Cleopatra's death. There is discussion about the manner of it, and Cæsar, ordering her to be buried with Antony, utters their epitaph.

All this is close to Plutarch, even in the discussion about the way she died. There seems no reason to doubt the constancy of Cleopatra's resolve to die after Antony's death. Shakespeare makes less of Dolabella's revelation than did Daniel, who greatly expanded Plutarch's, 'He sent her word secretly (as she had requested him)' [*inf.* 314, 433, 438]. But from this moment to her grief over Antony is added fear of public humiliation. There is likewise no doubt (as J. D. Wilson does in *Camb.*, 238) that Shakespeare meant her to take the threat to her children seriously (128–31). Although they receive little mention in the play she knew that she could not trust Cæsar in anything. (In the event Cæsarion was killed, but Octavia, charitable as ever, adopted her rival's children and in time married them off well.)

Shakespeare may have found in Simon Goulart's *Life of Augustus* translated by North for the 1603 edition of Plutarch confirmation of Plutarch's description of Octavius' aloof efficiency [Text II]. The dramatist seems to have been dissatisfied with Plutarch's account of the wars of Fulvia, Lucius Antonius and Sextus Pompeius, and to have consulted the 1578 translation of Appian's *Bella Civilia*. Appian clears up some obscurities about the war between Fulvia and Lucius and then between them and Octavius. Fulvia stirred up trouble in hope 'To have me out of Egypt', as Antony declares (II.2.98–9), whereas Lucius Antonius was an aristocratic republican opposed to the dictatorship of the triumvirate and to his brother as a member of it [Text VI]. That explains why when Octavius accuses him of being the cause of the wars (II.2.46–8), Antony protests:

> Did he not rather
> Discredit my authority with yours, etc. (*ibid.*, 49–65)

The reference to Pompey's commanding 'the empire of the sea' (I.2.187–8) also comes from Appian's 'Pompey being Lorde of the Sea'; likewise the statement that the Romans began 'to throw / Pompey the Great and all his dignities / Upon his son' (I.2.190–2) is from Appian's 'So was he most profitable to hys afflicted Countrey, and wonne greate glory to hymselfe, not inferioure to that he hadde of hys father.' Plutarch did not mention Pompey's death. Goulart declared it to be 'by Antonius' commandment'. Appian however had 'There bee that saye that Plancus, and not Antony, did commaunde hym to dye, whyche beeyng president of Syria had Antonyes signet, and in great causes wrote letters in hys name.' This explains III.5.18–19, where Antony 'Threats the throat of that his officer / That murder'd Pompey.' So in this play as so often, Shakespeare supplemented his main source with material from elsewhere.[1]

The political situation of *Julius Cæsar* is continued in *Antony and Cleopatra*, though not immediately following the events at the end of that play. Antony has met Cleopatra and become besotted with her, the triumvirate exists still, but it is divided. Lepidus is a nonentity, scorned by his partners, and he disappears after showing his credulity, drunkenness and unfitness for serious work; as the servant declares: 'To be called into a huge sphere, and not to be seen to move in't, are the holes where eyes should be, which pitifully disaster the cheeks' (II.7.17–19). Antony is forgetting his duties, leaving Octavius to bear the burden of the state and to consolidate his position as the only leader suited to the needs of the time. Against Cæsar's single-minded, cold devotion to duty and self-interest the others cannot stand, and he deserves to be Emperor not merely because, as Plutarch writes, heaven wished it so, but by his politic shrewdness and mastery of events. As in *Julius Cæsar*, however, Shakespeare does not make much of political theory in *Antony and Cleopatra*. For Professor J. E. Phillips Pompey

[1] These and other parallels were noted by M. W. MacCallum, *Shakespeare's Roman Plays*, 1910, Appendix D., and E. Schanzer, *Shakespeare's Appian*, 1956, pp. xxiii–xxviii.

represents 'the last aristocratic threat to Roman monarchy, the last conflict of the old order with the new',[1] and this is true, but does Shakespeare depict him in this light? He declares that he makes war for revenge and because he agrees with Brutus and Cassius who 'would / Have one man but a man' (II.6.14–23). But 'freedom' is not explicitly equated with aristocracy or republicanism.

Octavius has developed since *Julius Cæsar*. There he had little to do but agree with Antony's plans which overthrew Brutus and Cassius. For Antony in *Julius Cæsar*, though a 'masker and a reveller' was yet a man with a mission, personal rather than political. Once that was completed and Cæsar was avenged he relapsed into the man of pleasure, and thought it not

> Amiss to tumble on the bed of Ptolemy,
> To give a kingdom for a mirth,

and to confound the time 'That drums him from his sport'. Now Octavius has the reasonableness, the steadfastness, the public spirit that Antony lacks. Sir Thomas Elyot praised him for his 'magnanimity, nobility, tolerance, frugality and sobriety'—and these qualities or most of them are to be found in Shakespeare's two plays. But he is not lovable; he is political man at his most efficient, and if we recall his affection for Octavia (III.2), we also remember his attempt to deceive Cleopatra. Shakespeare wants us to think well of him and so diminishes his calculating coldness, making him tolerant towards Cleopatra when she tries to trick him over the treasure. His personal ambition is not stressed by Shakespeare; he is in the right even though we admire his enemies more. He regards himself as the minister of the high gods (III.6.87–9) and is able to promise that if he defeats Antony

> The time of universal peace is near.
> Prove this a prosperous day, the three-nook'd world
> Shall bear the olive freely. (IV.6.5–7)

He is the future Augustus, the man fit to rule. Yet he is priggish in his censures on Antony and ruthless in his determination to have Cleopatra grace his triumph.

[1] J. E. Phillips, *op. cit.*, pp. 192–3.

Shakespeare's interest is less in political theory than in the pattern of events, in the people concerned, and in the emotional implications of the theme. The play is organized carefully. Contrary to Dr Johnson's view that unity was sacrificed to variety, the events being 'produced without any art of connection or care of disposition', H. Granville-Barker (*Prefaces to Shakespeare*, 2nd Series, 1930) found the play well balanced and closely constructed provided that we consider the play as not divided into scenes but flowing on continuously. 'The play is now seen to be a careful pattern of interwoven and contrasting episodes, all duly subordinate to the main design: the presentation of Antony and Cleopatra in the broad context of the Roman Empire' [1]—and, we may add, the Roman Empire is seen mainly in relation to Antony and Cleopatra. We may agree with Granville-Barker that the play is about great actions rather than psychology—for there is an epic element about the structure and feeling, but few of Shakespeare's plays give a more definite idea of the characters of the chief personages. In a sense there may be too much characterization, for some critics are troubled by inconsistencies due to fullness of detail. L. L. Schücking saw too broad a contrast between the 'great courtesan whom Shakespeare shows us in the first acts of his play' and the woman 'inwardly as well as outwardly a queen' whom he portrays in the last two acts. Shakespeare indeed, Schücking declares, has made the early Cleopatra inferior to Plutarch's—for whereas in North she is cultured, learned in languages, a diplomat, capable of ruling a great kingdom, in Shakespeare she is vulgar, lazy, sensual, hysterical, shrewish, and calculating.[2] This view springs from a narrow knowledge of human nature; but there can be no doubt that Shakespeare intended us to see Cleopatra at first not as the noble Queen but as the royal seductress full of feminine trickery, wiles and perverseness, the opposite of Octavia, appealing to Antony's concupiscible nature as he appeals to hers. They bring out the worst in each other—the worst for a Roman triumvir and a Queen, that is. But Shakespeare's conception of human nature was not Ben Jonson's; his characters are not humours but com-

[1] S. L. Bethell, *Shakespeare and the Popular Dramatic Tradition*, 1944, p. 116.
[2] L. L. Schücking, *Character Problems in Shakespeare's Plays*, 1922, pp. 119–44.

posed of many opposite qualities.[1] In this conception of 'the union of opposites' he was aided by Plutarch, who loved to portray the diversity of motives warring in the same man. So Julius Cæsar may be deaf and epileptic and uxorious, yet bestride the world like a Colossus, and Brutus may be a perfect man yet make sorry misjudgements of the political situation and of his fellows. Similarly, Cleopatra, the royal harlot, may, when her pride and love are in question, rouse herself to nobility, her lust turn to 'air and fire', purged by grief.[2] And though Antony is a falling star, some sparks of his former greatness yet burn to the last. He cannot put up much of a struggle against his sensual cravings, but he is aware of his own decline.

What binds together the several sides of these characters is the sense of true life which they give us throughout, the immense vitality that burns in them, through their actions and words. The vital energy given to immoral behaviour helped to make Richard III more than a mere monster of evil through his wit and scheming and resourcefulness; it kept Falstaff from becoming a bore or just a 'hoary iniquity'. It preserves through all the evidences of irresponsibility and decline in Antony and Cleopatra a continual implication of greatness through the saving grace of vivacity, of 'personality'. There is a magic in Cleopatra at her worst which will 'make defect perfection' (II.2.236), so that 'vilest things / Become themselves in her, that the holy priests / Bless her when she is riggish' (II.2.244). We cannot understand the play unless we can comprehend this kind of personality.

The late S. L. Bethell wrote: 'To do justice to Shakespeare we must . . . begin—and end—with the poetry itself.'[3] This is true provided that we do not consider only the poetry but sec it in relation to the action and the personages. For the poetry emerged in the first place from the action and the personages; and from these as largely ready made in North's *Plutarch*. North gave to the story some splendid prose which kindled Shakespeare's imagination.

[1] This affects the rhetoric. Cf. B. T. Spencer, '*AC* and the Paradoxical Metaphor', *ShQ* IX. 3. 1958, 373–8.

[2] Just as, to compare small things with great, Bessie Burgess in Sean O'Casey's *The Plough and the Stars*, at first a slum-harridan, is also capable of being a heroine who cares for Nora Clitheroe in distress.

[3] Bethell, *Shakespeare and the Popular Dramatic Tradition*, p. 117.

Consequently whereas Shakespeare in *Romeo and Juliet* had found Brooke's verse so dull that he drew scarcely any of his poetry from the poem, in *Antony and Cleopatra* he found it easy often to keep close to North's version, and not only in the celebrated description of the Queen on the Cydnus. But behind this the antitheses implied in the story, the Rome-Egypt, Love-Empire and Pleasure-Honour themes, the contrast between Octavius-Octavia and Antony-Cleopatra, set up a poetic ferment in Shakespeare's mind such as neither *Julius Cæsar* nor *Coriolanus* provided. Roman history, in those two plays somewhat austere and cold, suddenly burst into flaming images when involved with the luxury of Egypt and its voluptuous queen so that Shakespeare could make his play both a tragedy of state and a tragedy of love and honour. More than in *Julius Cæsar* Plutarch gave him the means and incentive to combine moral judgement with a glowing sympathy which perceived grandeur in the most deplorable sins of passion and the inevitable dooms they brought.

As Dr Schanzer and others have asserted, the play is built up on a constant oscillation between attraction and repulsion to and from the two chief characters. But the breadth and intensity of Shakespeare's vision are such as to make us accept both moral judgements against and passionate approval of Antony and Cleopatra in their desire for each other which leads them to self-destruction. 'The nobleness of life is to do thus' exclaims Antony. We know that he is wrong, yet we are led to see it as fitting for the man he is, and to balance our colder political and ethical reasoning with participation in his sexual (and spiritual) obsession. That the world is *not* well lost for love Shakespeare reminds us again and again, and the 'exultation' which critics such as Bradley and J. D. Wilson rightly experience at Cleopatra's death is not, I think, because 'she has foiled Cæsar' (Bradley), but because 'the nobleness of death is to do thus'. The lesser grandeur of Antony's suicide is a prelude to the glory of Cleopatra's, which consists in the triumph of spirit over flesh and the sublimation of selfishness in the act of self-immolation. Morality is not defied but transcended, and previous errors are purged in the rightness of the end and its fitness to the personages. It is a tragedy of beings 'Born under one Law, to another bound', which we can join because we share in what Greville called the 'wearisome condition of humanity'. The final impression, given by Cæsar, is of dignity, lasting fame, pity, a distancing of the tragic intensity, a sense of 'High order in this great solemnity'.

I. Source

PLUTARCH'S LIVES OF THE NOBLE GRECIANS AND ROMANES

translated by Sir Thomas North (1579)

THE LIFE OF MARCUS ANTONIUS

Antonius grandfather was that famous Orator whome Marius slue, bicause he tooke Syllaes parte.[1] His father was an other Antonius surnamed Cretan,[2] who was not so famous, nor bare any great sway in the common wealth: howbeit otherwise he was an honest man, and of a very good naure, and specially very liberall in giving, as appeareth by an acte he did.[3] He was not very wealthie, and therefore his wife would not let him use his liberalitie and francke nature. One day a friend of his comming to him to praye him to helpe him to some money, having great neede: Antonius by chaunce had no money to give him, but he commaunded one of his men to bringe him some water in a silver basen, and after he had brought it him, he washed his beard as though he ment to have shaven it, and then found an arrant for his man to send him out, and gave his friend the silver basen, and bad him get him money with that. Shortly after, there was a great sturre in the house among the servaunts, seeking out this silver basen. Insomuch as Antonius seeing his wife marvelously offended for it, and that she would examine all her servaunts, one after another about it, to know what was become of it: at length he confessed he had given it away, and prayed her to be contented. His wife was Julia, of the noble house and familie of Julius Cæsar[4]: who for her vertue and chastitie, was to be compared with the noblest Lady of her time. M. Antonius was brought up under her, being married after her first husbands death, unto Cornelius Lentulus, whom Cicero put to death with Cethegus,

[1] *In margin:* 'Antonius parentage.'

[2] *In margin:* 'Bicause that by his death he ended the warre which he unfortunately made against those of Creta.'

[3] *In margin:* 'The liberalitie of Antonius father.'

[4] *In margin:* 'Julia, the mother of M. Antonius.'

and others, for that he was of Catilines conspiracie against the common wealth. And this seemeth to be the originall cause and beginning of the cruell and mortall hate Antonius bare unto Cicero. For Antonius selfe sayth, that he would never give him the body of his father in law to bury him, before his mother went first to intreat Ciceroes wife: the which undoubtedly was a flat lye. For Cicero denied buriall to none of them, whom he executed by law. Now Antonius being a fayer younge man, and in the pryme of his youth: he fell acquainted with Curio, whose friendship and acquaintance (as it is reported) was a plague unto him.[1] For he was a dissolute man, given over to all lust and insolencie, who to have Antonius the better at his commaundement, trayned him on into great follies, and vaine expences upon women, in rioting and banketing. So that in short time, he brought Antonius into a marvelous great det, and too great for one of his yeres, to wete: of two hundred and fifty talents, for all which summe Curio was his suretie. His father hearing of it, did put his sonne from him, and forbad him his house. Then he fell in with Clodius, one of the desperatest and most wicked Tribunes at that time in Rome. Him he followed for a time in his desperate attempts, who bred great sturre and mischiefe in Rome: but at length he forsooke him, being weary of his rashnes and folly, or els for that he was affraid of them that were bent against Clodius. Thereuppon he left Italy, and went into Græce, and there bestowed the most parte of his tyme, sometime in warres, and otherwhile in the studie of eloquence. He used a manner of phrase in his speeche, called Asiatik, which caried the best grace and estimation at that time, and was much like to his manners and life: for it was full of ostentation, foolishe braverie, and vaine ambition.[2] After he had remayned there some tyme, Gabinius Proconsul going into Syria, perswaded him to goe with him. Antonius tolde him he would not goe as a private man: wherefore Gabinius gave him charge of his horsemen, and so tooke him with him.[3] So, first of all he sent him against Aristobulus, who had made the Jewes to rebell, and was the first man him selfe that got up to the wall of a castell of his, and so drave Aristobulus out of all his holds[4]: and with those few men he had with him, he overcame al the Jewes in set battel, which were many against one, and put all of them almost to the sword, and

[1] *In margin:* 'Antonius corrupted by Curio.'

[2] *In margin:* 'Antonius used in his pleading the Asiatik phrase.' Shakespeare ignores its faults.

[3] *In margin:* 'Antonius had charge of horsemen, under Gabinius Proconsul, going into Syria.'

[4] *In margin:* 'Antonius acts against Aristobulus.'

furthermore, tooke Aristobulus him selfe prisoner with his sonne.[1] Afterwards Ptolomy king of Ægypt, that had bene driven out of his contry, went unto Gabinius to intreate him to goe with his armie with him into Ægypt, to put him againe into his kingdom: and promised him if he would goe with him, tenne thowsand talents. The most part of the Captaines thought it not best to goe thither, and Gabinius him selfe made it daintie to enter into this warre: although the covetousnes of these tenne thowsand talents stucke sorely with him. But Antonius that sought but for oportunitie and good occasion to attempt great enterprises, and that desired also to gratifie Ptolomyes request: he went about to perswade Gabinius to goe this voyage. Now they were more affrayd of the way they should goe, to come to the citie of Pelusium, then they feared any daunger of the warre besides: bicause they were to passe through deepe sandes and desert places, where was no freshe water to be had all the marisses thorough, which are called the marisses Serbonides, which the Ægyptians call the exhalations or fume, by the which the Gyant Typhon breathed. But in truth it appeareth to be the overflowing of the red sea, which breaketh out under the ground in that place, where it is devided in the narrowest place from the sea on this side. So Antonius was sent before into Ægypt with his horsemen,[2] who did not onely winne that passage, but also tooke the citie of Pelusium, (which is a great citie) with all the souldiers in it: and thereby he cleared the way, and made it safe for all the rest of the armie, and the hope of the victorie also certaine for his Captaine. Nowe did the enemies them selves feele the frutes of Antonius curtesie, and the desire he had to winne honor. For when Ptolomy (after he had entred into the citie of Pelusium) for the malice he bare unto the citie, would have put all the Ægyptians in it to the sword: Antonius withstoode him, and by no meanes would suffer him to doe it. And in all other great battells and skirmishes which they fought, and were many in number, Antonius did many noble actes of a valliant and wise Captaine: but specially in one battell, where he compassed in the enemies behind, giving them the victorie that fought against them, whereby he afterwards had such honorable reward, as his valliantnes deserved. So was his great curtesie also much commended of all, the which he shewed unto Archelaus.[3] For having bene his very friend, he made warre with him against his will while he lived: but after his death he sought for his bodye, and gave it honorable buriall. For these respects he wanne him selfe

[1] *In margin:* 'Antonius tooke Aristobulus prisoner.'
[2] *In margin:* 'Antonius acts in Ægypt under Gabinius.'
[3] *In margin:* 'Antonius curtesie unto Archelaus being dead.'

great fame of them of Alexandria, and he was also thought a worthy man of all the souldiers in the Romanes campe. But besides all this, he had a noble presence, and shewed a countenaunce of one of a noble house: he had a goodly thicke beard, a broad forehead, crooke nosed, and there appeared such a manly looke in his countenaunce, as is commonly seene in Hercules pictures, stamped or graven in mettell.[1] Now it had bene a speeche of old time, that the familie of the Antonii were discended from one Anton, the sonne of Hercules, whereof the familie tooke name.[2] This opinion did Antonius seeke to confirme in all his doings: not onely resembling him in the likenes of his bodye, as we have sayd before, but also in the wearing of his garments. For when he would openly shewe him selfe abroad before many people, he would alwayes weare his cassocke gyrt downe lowe upon his hippes, with a great sword hanging by his side, and upon that, some ill favored cloke. Furthermore, things that seeme intollerable in other men, as to boast commonly, to jeast with one or other, to drinke like a good fellow with every body, to sit with the souldiers when they dine, and to eate and drinke with them souldier-like: it is incredible what wonderfull love it wanne him amongest them. And furthermore, being given to love: that made him the more desired, and by that meanes he brought many to love him. For he would further every mans love, and also would not be angry that men should merily tell him of those he loved. But besides all this, that which most procured his rising and advauncement, was his liberalitie,[3] who gave all to the souldiers, and kept nothing for him selfe: and when he was growen to great credit, then was his authoritie and power also very great, the which notwithstanding him selfe did overthrowe by a thowsand other faults he had. . . .

Nowe the Romanes mainteyning two factions at Rome at that tyme, one against the other, of the which, they that tooke part with the Senate, did joyne with Pompey being then in Rome: and the contrary side taking part with the people, sent for Cæsar to ayde them, who made warres in Gaule. Then Curio Antonius friend, that had chaunged his garments, and at that tyme tooke parte with Cæsar, whose enemie he had bene before: he wanne Antonius, and so handled the matter, partly through the great credit and swaye he bare amongest the people, by reason of his eloquent tongue: and partly also by his exceeding expence of money he made which Cæsar gave him: that Antonius was chosen Tribune, and afterwards made Augure.[4] But this was a great helpe and furtheraunce to

[1] *In margin:* 'Antonius shape and presence.'
[2] *In margin:* 'The house of the Antonii discended from Hercules.'
[3] *In margin:* 'Antonius liberalitie.'
[4] *In margin:* 'Antonius Tribune of the people and Augure.'

Cæsars practises. For so soone as Antonius became Tribune he did oppose him selfe against those thinges which the Consul Marcellus preferred. . . . [Finally] Lentulus, one of the Consuls drave Antonius by force out of the Senate, who at his going out made grevous curses against him. After that, he tooke a slaves gowne, and speedily fled to Cæsar, with Quintus Cassius, in a hyered coch.[1] When they came to Cæsar, they cryed out with open mouth, that all went hand over head at Rome: for the Tribunes of the people might not speake their mindes, and were driven away in great daunger of their lives, as many stoode with lawe and justice. Hereuppon Cæsar incontinently went into Italy with his army, which made Cicero say in his *Philippides*: that as Hellen was cause of the warre of Troy, so was Antonius the author of the civill warres, which in deede was a starke lye.[2] For Cæsar was not so fickle headed, nor so easily caried away with anger, that he would so sodainly have gone and made warre with his contry, upon the sight onely of Antonius and Cassius, being fled unto him in miserable apparell, and in a hyered coche: had he not long before determined it with him selfe. But sith in deed Cæsar looked of long time but for some culler, this came as he wished, and gave him just occasion of warre. But to say truely, nothing els moved him to make warre with all the world as he did, but one selfe cause, which first procured Alexander and Cyrus also before him: to wit, an insatiable desire to raigne,[3] with a senseles covetousnes to be the best man in the world, the which he could not come unto, before he had first put downe Pompey, and utterly overthrowen him.[4] Now, after that Cæsar had gotten Rome at his commaundement, and had driven Pompey out of Italy, he purposed first to goe into Spayne, against the legions Pompey had there: and in the meane time to make provision for shippes and marine preparacion, to follow Pompey. In his absence, he left Lepidus that was Prætor, governor of Rome: and Antonius that was Tribune, he gave him charge of all the souldiers, and of Italy.[5] Then was Antonius straight marvelously commended and beloved of the souldiers, bicause he commonly exercised him self among them, and would oftentimes eate and drinke with them, and also be liberall unto them, according to his abilitie. But then in contrary manner, he purchased divers other mens evill willes, bicause that through negligence he would not doe them justice that were injuried, and delt very churlishly with them that had any sute unto him: and besides all this, he had

[1] *In margin:* 'Antonius flyeth from Rome unto Cæsar.'
[2] *In margin:* 'Cicero reproved for lying.'
[3] *In margin:* 'Alexander, Cyrus, and Cæsar: all contended to raigne.'
[4] *In margin:* 'Cæsars ambition the onely cause of the civill warre.'
[5] *In margin:* 'Cæsar gave the charge of Italy unto Antonius.'

an ill name to intise mens wives.[1] To conclude, Cæsars friends that governed under him, were cause why they hated Cæsars government (which in deede in respect of him selfe was no lesse then a tyrannie) by reason of the great insolencies and outragious parts that were committed: amongst whom Antonius, that was of greatest power, and that also committed greatest faultes, deserved most blame. But Cæsar notwithstanding, when he returned from the warres of Spayne, made no reckoning of the complaints that were put up against him: but contrarily, bicause he found him a hardy man, and a valliant Captaine, he employed him in his chiefest affayres, and was no whit deceived in his opinion of him. So he passed over the Ionian sea unto Brundusium, being but slenderly accompanied: and sent unto Antonius, and Gabinius, that they should imbarke their men as soone as they could, and passe them over into Macedon. Gabinius was affrayd to take the sea, bicause it was very roughe, and in the winter time: and therefore fetched a great compasse about by land. But Antonius fearing some daunger might come unto Cæsar, bicause he was compassed in with a great number of enemies: first of all he drave away Libo, who roade at ancker with a great armie, before the haven of Brundusium. For he manned out such a number of pynnasies, barks, and other small boates about every one of his gallies, that he drave them thence. After that, he imbarked into shippes twenty thowsand footemen, and eyght hundred horsemen, and with this armie he hoysed sayle.[2] When the enemies sawe him, they made out to followe him: but the sea rose so highe, that the billowes put backe their gallies that they could not come neare him, and so he scaped that daunger. But withall he fell uppon the rockes with his whole fleete, where the sea wrought very highe: so that he was out of all hope to save him selfe. Yet by good fortune, sodainely the winde turned Southwest, and blewe from the gulffe, driving the waves of the river into the mayne sea. Thus Antonius loosing from the lande, and sayling with safetie at his pleasure, soone after he sawe all the coastes full of shippewracks. For the force and boysterousnes of the winde, did cast away the gallies that followed him: of the which, many of them were broken and splitted, and divers also cast away, and Antonius tooke a great number of them prisoners, with a great summe of money also. Besides all these, he tooke the citie of Lyssus, and brought Cæsar a great supplie of men, and made him coragious, comming at a pynche with so great a power to him. Nowe there were divers hotte skyrmishes and en-

[1] *In margin:* 'Antonius vices.'

[2] *In margin:* 'Antonius taketh sea with his army at Brundisium, and goeth unto Cæsar.'

cownters, in the which Antonius fought so valliantly, that he caried the prayse from them all[1]: but specially at two severall tymes, when Cæsars men turned their backes, and fled for life. For he stepped before them, and compelled them to returne againe to fight: so that the victorie fell on Cæsars side. For this cause he had the seconde place in the campe amonge the souldiers, and they spake of no other man unto Cæsar, but of him: who shewed playnely what opinion he had of him, when at the last battell of Pharsalia (which in deede was the last tryall of all, to give the Conqueror the whole Empire of the worlde) he him selfe did leade the right wing of his armie, and gave Antonius the leading of the left wing, as the valliantest man, and skilfullest souldier of all those he had about him. [2] After Cæsar had wonne the victorie, and that he was created Dictator, he followed Pompey steppe by steppe: howbeit before, he named Antonius generall of the horsemen, and sent him to Rome. The generall of the horsemen is the second office of dignitie, when the Dictator is in the citie[3]: but when he is abroad, he is the chiefest man, and almost the onely man that remayneth, and all the other officers and Magistrates are put downe, after there is a Dictator chosen. Notwithstanding, Dolabella being at that tyme Tribune, and a younge man desirous of chaunge and innovation: he preferred a law which the Romanes call *Novas tabulas* (as much to saye, as a cutting of and cancelling of all obligacions and specialties, and were called the newe tables, bicause they were driven then to make bookes of daily receit and expense) and perswaded Antonius his friend (who also gaped for a good occasion to please and gratifie the common people) to aide him to passe this lawe. But Trebellius and Asinius disswaded from it all they could possible. So by good hap it chaunced that Antonius mistrusted Dolabella for keeping of his wife, and tooke suche a conceite of it, that he thrust his wife out of his house being his Cosin Germane, and the daughter of C. Antonius, who was Consul with Cicero: and joyning with Asinius, he resisted Dolabella, and fought with him.[4] Dolabella had gotten the market place where the people doe assemble in counsel, and had filled it ful of armed men, intending to have this law of the newe tables to passe by force. Antonius by commaundement of the Senate, who had given him authoritie to leavy men, to use force against Dolabella: he went against him, and fought so valliantly, that men were

[1] *In margin:* 'Antonius manhood in warres.'

[2] *In margin:* 'Antonius led the left wing of Cæsars battell at Pharsalia where Pompey lost the field.'

[3] *In margin:* 'The dignitie of the general of the horsemen.'

[4] *In margin:* 'Dissention betwixt Antonius and Dolabella.'

slaine on both sides. But by this meanes, he got the il will of the common people, and on the other side, the noble men (as Cicero saith) did not only mislike him, but also hate him for his naughty life: for they did abhor his banckets and dronken feasts he made at unseasonable times, and his extreme wastful expences upon vaine light huswives, and then in the day time he would sleepe or walke out his dronkennes, thinking to weare away the fume of the aboundaunce of wine which he had taken over night. In his house they did nothing but feast, daunce, and maske: and him selfe passed away the time in hearing of foolish playes, or in marrying these plaiers, tomblers, jeasters, and such sort of people.[1] As for proofe hereof it is reported, that at Hippias mariage, one of his jeasters, he drank wine so lustely all night, that the next morning when he came to pleade before the people assembled in counsel, who had sent for him: he being quesie stomaked with his surfet he had taken, was compelled to lay all before them, and one of his friends held him his gowne in stead of a basen.[2] He had another pleasaunt player called Sergius, that was one of the chiefest men about him, and a woman also called Cytheride, of the same profession, whom he loved derely: he caried her up and downe in a litter unto all the townes he went, and had as many men waiting apon her litter, she being but a player, as were attending upon his owne mother.[3] It greved honest men also very much, to see that when he went into the contry, he caried with him a great number of cubbords ful of silver and gold plate, openly in the face of the world, as it had ben the pompe or shewe of some triumphe: and that eftsoones in the middest of his jorney he would set up his hales and tents hard by some greene grove or pleasaunt river, and there his Cookes should prepare him a sumptuous dinner. And furthermore, Lyons were harnesed in trases to drawe his carts: and besides also, in honest mens houses in the cities where he came, he would have common harlots, curtisans, and these tumbling gillots lodged. Now it greved men much, to see that Cæsar should be out of Italy following of his enemies, to end this great warre, with such great perill and daunger: and that others in the meane time abusing his name and authoritie, should commit such insolent and outragious parts unto their Citizens. This me thinkes was the cause that made the conspiracie against Cæsar increase more and more, and layed the reynes of the brydle uppon the souldiers neckes, whereby they durst boldlier commit many extorsions, cruelties and robberies. And therefore Cæsar after his returne

[1] *In margin:* 'Antonius abominable life.' Contrast *JC* I.2.202–3.
[2] *In margin:* 'Antonius laid up his stomack before the whole assembly.'
[3] *In margin:* 'Antonius insolency.'

pardoned Dolabella, and being created Consul the third time, he tooke not Antonius, but chose Lepidus, his colleague and fellow Consul.[1] Afterwards when Pompeys house was put to open sale, Antonius bought it[2]: but when they asked him money for it, he made it very straung, and was offended with them, and writeth him selfe that he would not goe with Cæsar into the warres of Africk, bicause he was not well recompenced for the service he had done him before. Yet Cæsar did somewhat bridle his madnes and insolencie, not suffering him to passe his faulte so lightly away, making as though he sawe them not. And therefore he left his dissolute manner of life, and married Fulvia that was Clodius widowe,[3] a woman not so basely minded to spend her time in spinning and housewivery, and was not contented to master her husband at home, but would also rule him in his office abroad,[4] and commaund him, that commaunded legions and great armies: so that Cleopatra was to give Fulvia thankes for that she had taught Antonius this obedience to women, that learned so well to be at their commaundement. Nowe, bicause Fulvia was somewhat sower, and crooked of condition, Antonius devised to make her pleasaunter, and somewhat better disposed: and therefore he would playe her many prety youthfull partes to make her mery. As he did once, when Cæsar returned the last time of all Conqueror out of Spayne, every man went out to meete him: and so did Antonius with the rest. But on the sodeine there ranne a rumor through Italy, that Cæsar was dead, and that his enemies came againe with a great armie. Thereuppon he returned with speede to Rome, and tooke one of his mens gownes, and so apparelled came home to his house in a darke night, saying that he had brought Fulvia letters from Antonius. So he was let in, and brought to her muffled as he was, for being knowen: but she taking the matter heavily, asked him if Antonius were well. Antonius gave her the letters, and sayd never a word. So when she had opened the letters, and beganne to read them: Antonius ramped of her necke, and kissed her. We have told you this tale for examples sake onely, and so could we also tell you of many such like as these. Nowe when Cæsar was returned from his last warre in Spayne, all the chiefest nobilitie of the citie road many dayes jorney from Rome to meete him, where Cæsar made marvelous much of Antonius, above all the men that came unto him. For he alwayes tooke him into his coche with him, through out all Italy: and behind him,

[1] *In margin:* 'Cæsar, and Lepidus, Consuls.'
[2] *In margin:* 'Antonius byeth Pompeys house.' II.6.26-9
[3] *In margin:* 'Antonius married Fulvia, Clodius widow.'
[4] *In margin:* 'Fulvia ruled Antonius, at home, and abroad.' I.1.31–2.

Brutus Albinus, and Octavius, the sonne of his Nece, who afterwards was called Cæsar, and became Emperor of Rome long time after. So Cæsar being afterwards chosen Consul the fift time, he immediatly chose Antonius his colleague and companion[1]: and desired by deposing him selfe of his Consulship, to make Dolabella Consul in his roome, and had already moved it to the Senate. But Antonius did stowtly withstand it, and openly reviled Dolabella in the Senate: and Dolabella also spared him as litle. Thereuppon Cæsar being ashamed of the matter he let it alone. Another time also when Cæsar attempted againe to substitute Dolabella Consul in his place, Antonius cryed out, that the signes of the birdes were against it: so that at length Cæsar was compelled to give him place, and to let Dolabella alone, who was marvelously offended with him. Now in truth, Cæsar made no great reckoning of either of them both. For it is reported that Cæsar aunswered one that did accuse Antonius and Dolabella unto him for some matter of conspiracie: Tushe said he, they be not those fat fellowes and fine comed men that I feare, but I mistrust rather these pale and leane men, meaning by Brutus and Cassius, who afterwards conspired his death, and slue him.[2] Antonius unwares afterwards, gave Cæsars enemies just occasion and culler to doe as they did: as you shall heare.[3] The Romanes by chaunce celebrated the feast called Lupercalia, and Cæsar being apparelled in his triumphing robe, was set in the Tribune where they use to make their orations to the people, and from thence did behold the sport of the runners. The manner of this running was this. On that day there are many young men of noble house, and those specially that be chiefe Officers for that yeare: who running naked up and downe the citie annointed with the oyle of olyve, for pleasure do strike them they meete in their way, with white leather thongs they have in their hands. Antonius being one amonge the rest that was to ronne, leaving the auncient ceremonies and old customes of that solemnitie: he ranne to the Tribune where Cæsar was set, and caried a laurell crowne in his hand, having a royall band or diademe wreathed about it, which in old time was the auncient marke and token of a king. When he was come to Cæsar, he made his fellow ronners with him lift him up, and so he did put this laurell crowne upon his head,[4] signifying thereby that he had deserved to be king. But Cæsar making as though he refused it, turned away his heade. The people were so rejoyced at it, that they

[1] *In margin:* 'Cæsar, and Antonius, Consuls.' [2] Cf. *JC.* I.2.189–95.

[3] *In margin:* 'Antonius unwittingly gave Cæsars enemies occasion to conspire against him.'

[4] *In margin:* 'Antonius Lupercian putteth the diademe upon Cæsars head.'

all clapped their hands for joy. Antonius againe did put it on his head: Cæsar againe refused it, and thus they were striving of and on a great while together. As oft as Antonius did put this laurell crowne unto him, a fewe of his followers rejoyced at it: and as oft also as Cæsar refused it, all the people together clapped their hands. And this was a wonderfull thing, that they suffered all things subjects should doe by commaundement of their kings: and yet they could not abide the name of a king, detesting it as the utter destruction of their liberty. Cæsar in a rage rose out of his seate, and plucking downe the choller of his gowne from his necke, he shewed it naked, bidding any man strike of his head that would. This laurel crowne was afterwards put upon the head of one of Cæsars statues or images, the which one of the Tribunes pluckt of. The people liked his doing therein so well, that they wayted on him home to his house, with great clapping of hands. Howbeit Cæsar did turne them out of their offices for it. This was a good incoragement for Brutus and Cassius to conspire his death,[1] who fel into a consort with their trustiest friends, to execute their enterprise: but yet stood doubtful whether they should make Antonius privy to it or not. Al the rest liked of it, saving Trebonius only. He told them, that when they rode to meete Cæsar at his returne out of Spayne, Antonius and he alwaies keping company, and lying together by the way, he felt his mind a farre of: but Antonius finding his meaning, would harken no more unto it, and yet notwithstanding never made Cæsar acquainted with this talke, but had faithfully kept it to him self.[2] After that they consulted whether they should kil Antonius with Cæsar.[3] But Brutus would in no wise consent to it, saying: that ventring on such an enterprise as that, for the maintenance of law and justice, it ought to be clere from all villanie.[4] Yet they fearing Antonius power, and the authoritie of his office, appointed certain of the conspiracy, that when Cæsar were gone into the Senate, and while others should execute their enterprise, they should keepe Antonius in a talke out of the Senate house. Even as they had devised these matters, so were they executed: and Cæsar was slaine in the middest of the Senate. Antonius being put in a feare withall, cast a slaves gowne upon him, and hid him selfe. But afterwards when it was told him that the murtherers slue no man els, and that they went onely into the Capitoll: he sent his sonne unto them for a pledge, and bad them boldly come downe upon his word. The selfe same day he did bid

[1] *In margin:* 'Brutus and Cassius conspire Cæsars death.'

[2] Hence perhaps Trebonius' suggestion II.1.190–1.

[3] *In margin:* 'Consultation about the murther of Antonius with Cæsar.'

[4] *JC*.II.1.155–89.

Cassius to supper, and Lepidus also bad Brutus. The next morning the Senate was assembled, and Antonius him selfe preferred a lawe that all things past should be forgotten, and that they should appoint provinces, unto Cassius and Brutus: the which the Senate confirmed, and further ordeyned, that they should cancell none of Cæsars lawes. Thus went Antonius out of the Senate more praysed, and better esteemed, than ever man was: bicause it seemed to every man that he had cut of all occasion of civill warres, and that he had shewed him selfe a marvelous wise governor of the common wealth, for the appeasing of these matters of so great waight and importance. But nowe, the opinion he conceived of him selfe after he had a litle felt the good will of the people towards him, hoping thereby to make him selfe the chiefest man if he might overcome Brutus: did easily make him alter his first mind.[1] And therefore when Cæsars body was brought to the place where it should be buried, he made a funeral oration in commendacion of Cæsar, according to the auncient custom of praising noble men at their funerals. When he saw that the people were very glad and desirous also to heare Cæsar spoken of, and his praises uttered: he mingled his oration with lamentable wordes, and by amplifying of matters did greatly move their harts and affections unto pitie and compassion.[2] In fine to conclude his oration, he unfolded before the whole assembly the bloudy garments of the dead, thrust through in many places with their swords, and called the malefactors, cruell and cursed murtherers.[3] With these words he put the people into such a fury, that they presently toke Cæsars body, and burnt it in the market place, with such tables and fourmes as they could get together. Then when the fire was kindled, they toke firebrands, and ran to the murtherers houses to set them afire, and to make them come out to fight. Brutus therfore and his accomplices, for safety of their persons were driven to fly the city. Then came all Cæsars friends unto Antonius, and specially his wife Calpurnia putting her trust in him,[4] she brought the moste part of her money into his house, which amounted to the summe of foure thowsand talents, and furthermore brought him al Cæsars bokes and writings, in the which were his memorials of all that he had done and ordeyned. Antonius did daily mingle with them such as he thought good, and by that meanes he created newe officers, made newe Senators, called home some that were banished, and delivered those that were prisoners, and then he sayde that all those thinges were so appoynted

[1] *In margin:* 'Antonius maketh uprore among the people, for the murther of Cæsar.'

[2] Cf. *JC.* III.2.75ff.

[3] *JC.* III.2.171–99. Contrast 211–17.

[4] *In margin:* 'Calpurnia, Cæsars wife.'

and ordeyned by Cæsar. Therefore the Romanes mocking them that were so moved, they called them Charonites[1]: bicause that when they were overcome, they had no other helpe but to saye, that thus they were found in Cæsars memorialls, who had sayled in Charons boate, and was departed. Thus Antonius ruled absolutely also in all other matters, bicause he was Consul, and Caius one of his brethren Prætor, and Lucius the other, Tribune.[2] Now thinges remayning in this state at Rome, Octavius Cæsar the younger, came to Rome, who was the sonne of Julius Cæsars Nece, as you have heard before, and was left his lawefull heire by will, remayning at the tyme of the death of his great Uncle that was slayne, in the citie of Apollonia. This young man at his first arrivall went to salute Antonius, as one of his late dead father Cæsars friendes, who by his last will and testament had made him his heire: and withall, he was presently in hande with him for money and other thinges which were left of trust in his handes, bicause Cæsar had by will bequeathed unto the people of Rome, three score and fifteene silver Drachmas to be given to every man, the which he as heire stoode charged withall. Antonius at the first made no reckoning of him, bicause he was very younge:[3] and sayde he lacked witte, and good friendes to advise him, if he looked to take such a charge in hande, as to undertake to be Cæsars heire.[4] But when Antonius saw that he could not shake him of with those wordes, and that he was still in hande with him for his fathers goods, but specially for the ready money: then he spake and did what he could against him. And first of all, it was he that did keepe him from being Tribune of the people: and also when Octavius Cæsar beganne to meddle with the dedicating of the chayer of gold, which was prepared by the Senate to honor Cæsar with: he threatned to send him to prison, and moreover desisted not to put the people in an uprore. This young Cæsar seeing his doings, went unto Cicero and others, which were Antonius enemies, and by them crept into favor with the Senate[5]: and he him self sought the peoples good will every manner of way, gathering together the olde souldiers of the late deceased Cæsar, which were dispersed in divers cities and colonyes. Antonius being affrayd of it, talked with Octavius in the capitoll, and became his friend.[6] But

[1] *In margin:* 'Charonites, why so called.'

[2] *In margin:* 'M. Antonius Consul. Caius Antonius Prætor. Lucius Antonius Tribune: all three brethren.'

[3] Hence *JC.* III.1.288–90.

[4] *In margin:* 'Variance betwixt Antonius and Octavius Cæsar, heire unto Julius Cæsar.'

[5] *In margin:* 'Octavius Cæsar joyned in friendship with Cicero.'

[6] *In margin:* 'Antonius and Octavius became friends.'

the very same night Antonius had a straunge dreame, who thought that lightning fell upon him, and burnt his right hand.[1] Shortly after word was brought him, that Cæsar lay in waite to kil him. Cæsar cleered him selfe unto him, and told him there was no such matter: but he could not make Antonius beleve the contrary. Whereuppon they became further enemies then ever they were: insomuch that both of them made friends of either side to gather together all the old souldiers through Italy, that were dispersed in divers townes: and made them large promises, and sought also to winne the legions of their side, which were already in armes. Cicero on the other side being at that time the chiefest man of authoritie and estimation in the citie, he stirred up al men against Antonius: so that in the end he made the Senate pronounce him an enemy to his contry,[2] and appointed young Cæsar Sergeaunts to cary axes before him, and such other signes as were incident to the dignitie of a Consul or Prætor: and moreover sent Hircius and Pansa, then Consuls, to drive Antonius out of Italy.[3] These two Consuls together with Cæsar, who also had an armye, went against Antonius that beseeged the citie of Modena, and there overthrew him in battell: but both the Consuls were slaine there.[4] Antonius flying upon this overthrowe, fell into great miserie all at once: but the chiefest want of all other, and that pinched him most, was famine. Howbeit he was of such a strong nature, that by pacience he would overcome any adversitie, and the heavier fortune lay upon him, the more constant shewed he him selfe.[5] Every man that feleth want or adversitie, knoweth by vertue and discretion what he should doe: but when in deede they are overlayed with extremitie, and be sore oppressed, few have the harts to follow that which they praise and commend, and much lesse to avoid that they reprove and mislike. But rather to the contrary, they yeld to their accustomed easie life: and through faynt hart, and lacke of corage, doe chaunge their first mind and purpose. And therefore it was a wonderfull example to the souldiers, to see Antonius that was brought up in all finenes and superfluitie, so easily to drinke puddle water, and to eate wild frutes and rootes[6]: and moreover it is reported, that even as they passed the Alpes, they did eate the barcks of trees, and such

[1] *In margin:* 'Antonius dreame.'

[2] *In margin:* 'Antonius judged an enemy by the Senate.'

[3] *In margin:* 'Hircius and Pansa Consuls.'

[4] *In margin:* 'Antonius overthrowen in battell by the citie of Modena.' *AC* I.4.56–8.

[5] *In margin:* 'Antonius patient in adversitie.'

[6] *In margin:* 'Antonius hardnes in adversitie, notwithstanding his fine bringing up.' *AC* I.4.59–61.

beasts, as never man tasted of their flesh before.[1] Now their intent was to joyne with the legions that were on the other side of the Mountaines, under Lepidus charge: whom Antonius tooke to be his friend, bicause he had holpen him to many things at Cæsars hand, through his meanes. When he was come to the place where Lepidus was, he camped hard by him: and when he saw that no man came to him to put him in any hope, he determined to venter him selfe, and to goe unto Lepidus. . . . When he was come into their campe, and that he had all the army at his commaundement[2]: he used Lepidus very curteously, imbraced him, and called him father: and though in deede Antonius did all, and ruled the whole army, yet he alway gave Lepidus the name and honor of the Captaine.[3] Munatius Plancus, lying also in campe hard by with an armye: understanding the report of Antonius curtesie, he also came and joined with him. Thus Antonius being a foote againe, and growen of great power, repassed over the Alpes, leading into Italy with him seventeene legions, and tenne thowsand horsemen, besides six legions he left in garrison amonge the Gaules, under the charge of one Varius, a companion of his that would drinke lustely with him, and therefore in mockery was surnamed Cotylon[4]: to wit, a bibber. So Octavius Cæsar would not leane to Cicero, when he saw that his whole travail and endevor was onely to restore the common wealth to her former libertie. Therefore he sent certaine of his friends to Antonius, to make them friends againe: and thereuppon all three met together, (to wete, Cæsar, Antonius, and Lepidus)[5] in an Iland envyroned round about with a litle river, and there remayned three dayes together. Now as touching all other matters, they were easily agreed, and did devide all the Empire of Rome betwene them, as if it had bene their owne inheritance. But yet they could hardly agree whom they would put to death: for every one of them would kill their enemies, and save their kinsmen and friends. Yet at length, giving place to their gredy desire to be revenged of their enemies, they spurned all reverence of bloud, and holines of friendship at their feete.[6] For Cæsar left Cicero to Antonius will, Antonius also forsooke Lucius Cæsar, who was his Uncle by his mother[7]: and both of them together suffred Lepidus to kill his owne brother Paulus. Yet some writers affirme, that Cæsar and Antonius requested Paulus

[1] *AC* I.4.61–8.
[2] *In margin:* 'Antonius wan all Lepidus army from him.'
[3] Contrast *JC* IV.1.7–15.
[4] *In margin:* 'Varius, surnamed Cotylon.'
[5] *In margin:* 'The conspiracie and meeting of Cæsar, Antonius, and Lepidus.'
[6] *JC.* IV.1 starts here. *In margin:* 'The proscription of the Triumviri.'
[7] Shakespeare invented a nephew, Publius, instead of Lucius Cæsar.

might be slain, and that Lepidus was contented with it. In my opinion there was never a more horrible, unnatural, and crueller chaunge then this was. For thus chaunging murther for murther, they did aswel kill those whom they did forsake and leave unto others, as those also which others left unto them to kil: but so much more was their wickednes and cruelty great unto their friends, for that they put them to death being innocents, and having no cause to hate them. After this plot was agreed upon betwene them: the souldiers that were thereabouts, would have this friendship and league betwixt them confirmed by mariage, and that Cæsar should mary Claudia, the daughter of Fulvia, and Antonius wife. This mariage also being agreed upon, they condemned three hundred of the chiefest citizens of Rome, to be put to death by proscription. And Antonius also commaunded them to whom he had geven commission to kil Cicero, that they should strike of his head and right hand, with the which he had written the invective Orations (called *Philippides*) against Antonius.[1] So when the murtherers brought him Ciceroes head and hand cut of, he beheld them a long time with great joy, and laughed hartily, and that oftentimes for the great joy he felt. Then when he had taken his pleasure of the sight of them, he caused them to be set up in an open place, over the pulpit for Orations (where when he was alive, he had often spoken to the people) as if he had done the dead man hurt, and not bleamished his owne fortune, shewing him selfe (to his great shame and infamie) a cruell man, and unworthie the office and authoritie he bare. His uncle Lucius Cæsar also, as they sought for him to kill him, and followed him hard, fledde unto his sister. The murtherers comming thither, forcing to breake into her chamber, she stoode at her chamber dore with her armes abroadc, crying out still: You shall not kill Lucius Cæsar, before you first kill me, that bare your Captaine in my wombe. By this meanes she saved her brothers life.[2] Now the government of these Triumviri grewe odious and hatefull to the Romanes, for divers respects: but they most blamed Antonius, bicause he being elder then Cæsar, and of more power and force then Lepidus, gave him selfe againe to his former riot and excesse, when he left to deale in the affaires of the common wealth.[3] But setting aside the ill name he had for his insolencie, he was yet much more hated in respect of the house he dwelt in, the which was the house of Pompey the great[4]: a man as famous for his temperaunce, modestie, and civill life, as for his three triumphes.[5] For it grieved

[1] *In margin:* 'Antonius cruelty unto Cicero.'
[2] *In margin:* 'Lucius Cæsars life saved, by his sister.'
[3] *In margin:* 'Antonius riot in his Triumvirate.'
[4] Cf. *AC.* II.6.26–9.
[5] *In margin:* 'The praise of Pompey the great.'

them to see the gates commonly shut against the Captaines, Magistrates of the citie, and also Ambassadors of straunge nations, which were sometimes thrust from the gate with violence: and that the house within was full of tomblers, anticke dauncers, juglers, players, jeasters, and dronkards, quaffing and goseling, and that on them he spent and bestowed the most parte of his money he got by all kind of possible extorcions, briberie and policie. For they did not onely sell by the crier, the goods of those whom they had outlawed, and appointed to murther, slaunderously deceived the poore widowes and young orphanes, and also raised all kind of imposts, subsidies, and taxes: but understanding also that the holy vestall Nunnes had certaine goods and money put in their custodie to keepe, both of mens in the citie, and those also that were abroade: they went thither, and tooke them away by force. Octavius Cæsar perceiving that no money woulde serve Antonius turne, he prayed that they might devide the money betwene them, and so did they also devide the armie, for them both to goe into Macedon to make warre against Brutus and Cassius: and in the meane time they left the government of the citie of Rome unto Lepidus. When they had passed over the seas, and that they beganne to make warre, they being both camped by their enemies, to wit, Antonius against Cassius, and Cæsar against Brutus: Cæsar did no great matter, but Antonius had alway the upper hand, and did all.[1] For at the first battell Cæsar was overthrowen by Brutus, and lost his campe, and verie hardly saved him selfe by flying from them that followed him. Howebeit he writeth him selfe in his *Commentaries*, that he fled before the charge was geven, bicause of a dreame one of his frends had. Antonius on the other side overthrewe Cassius in battell, though some write that he was not there him selfe at the battell, but that he came after the overthrowe, whilest his men had the enemies in chase. So Cassius at his earnest request was slaine by a faithfull servaunt of his owne called Pindarus, whom he had infranchised: bicause he knewe not in time that Brutus had overcomen Cæsar.[2] Shortly after they fought an other battell againe, in the which Brutus was overthrowen, who afterwardes also slue him selfe.[3] Thus Antonius had the chiefest glorie of all this victorie, specially bicause Cæsar was sicke at that time. Antonius having found Brutus body after this battel, blaming him muche for the murther of his brother Caius, whom he had put to death in Macedon for revenge of Ciceroes cruell death, and yet laying the fault more in Hortensius then in him: he made Hortensius to be slaine on his brothers tumbe.

[1] *In margin:* 'The valliantnes of Antonius against Brutus.'
[2] *In margin:* 'The death of Cassius.' [3] *In margin:* 'Brutus slue him selfe.'

Furthermore, he cast his coate armor (which was wonderfull rich and sumptuous) upon Brutus bodie, and gave commaundement to one of his slaves infranchised, to defray the charge of his buriall.[1] But afterwards, Antonius hearing that his infranchised bondman had not burnt his coate armor with his bodie, bicause it was verie riche, and worth a great summe of money, and that he had also kept backe much of the ready money appointed for his funerall and tombe: he also put him to death. After that Cæsar was conveied to Rome, and it was thought he would not live long, nor scape the sickenes he had. Antonius on thother side went towardes the East provinces and regions, to leavie money: and first of all he went into Græce, and caried an infinite number of souldiers with him. Now, bicause everie souldier was promised five thowsande silver Drachmas, he was driven of necessitie to impose extreame tallages and taxacions. At his first comming into Græce, he was not hard nor bitter unto the Græcians,[2] but gave him selfe onely to heare wise men dispute, to see playes, and also to note the ceremonies and sacrifices of Græce, ministring justice to everie man, and it pleased him marvelously to heare them call him Philellen, (as much to say, a lover of the Græcians) and specially the Athenians, to whom he did many great pleasures. . . . But when he was once come into Asia, having left Lucius Censorinus Governor in Græce, and that he had felt the riches and pleasures of the East partes, and that Princes, great Lordes and Kinges, came to waite at his gate for his comming out, and that Queenes and Princesses to excell one an other, gave him verie riche presentes, and came to see him, curiously setting forth them selves, and using all art that might be to shewe their beawtie, to win his favor the more: (Cæsar in the meane space turmoyling his wits and bodie in civill warres at home, Antonius living merily and quietly abroad) he easely fell againe to his old licentious life. For straight one Anaxenor a player of the citherne, Xoutus a player of the flutes, Metrodorus a tombler, and such a rabble of minstrells and fit ministers for the pleasures of Asia, (who in finenes and flattery passed all the other plagues he brought with him out of Italie)[3] all these flocked in his court, and bare the whole sway: and after that, all went awry. For every one gave them selves to riot and excesse, when they saw he delighted in it: and all Asia was like to the citie Sophocles speaketh of in one of his tragedies:

> Was full of sweete perfumes, and pleasant songs,
> With woefull weping mingled thereamongs.

[1] *In margin:* 'Antonius gave honorable buriall unto Brutus.'

[2] *In margin:* 'Antonius great curtesie in Græce.'

[3] *In margin:* 'The plagues of Italie, in riot.'

For in the citie of Ephesus, women attyred as they goe in the feastes and sacrifice of Bacchus, came out to meete him with such solemnities and ceremonies, as are then used: with men and children disguised like Fawnes and Satyres. Moreover, the citie was full of Ivey, and darts wreathed about with Ivey, psalterions, flutes and howboyes, and in their songes they called him Bacchus, father of mirth, curteous, and gentle: and so was he unto some, but to the most parte of men, cruell, and extreame. For he robbed noble men and gentle men of their goods, to geve it unto vile flatterers: who oftentimes begged mens goods living, as though they had bene dead, and would enter their houses by force.[1] As he gave a citizens house of Magnesia unto a cooke, bicause (as it is reported) he dressed him a fine supper. In the ende he doubled the taxacion, and imposed a seconde upon Asia. But then Hybræas the Orator sent from the estates of Asia, to tell him the state of their contrie, boldly sayd unto him[2]: If thou wilt have power to lay two tributes in one yere upon us, thou shouldest also have power to geve us two sommers, two autumnes, and two harvests. This was gallantly and pleasauntly spoken unto Antonius by the Orator, and it pleased him well to heare it: but afterwardes amplifying his speache, he spake more boldly, and to better purpose: Asia hath payed the two hundred thowsand talents. If all this money be not come to thy cofers, then aske accompt of them that leavied it: but if thou have received it, and nothing be left of it, then are we utterly undone. Hybræas words nettled Antonius roundly. For he understoode not many of the thefts and robberies his officers committed by his authoritie, in his treasure and affaires: not so muche bicause he was carelesse, as for that he oversimply trusted his men in all things. For he was a plaine man, [3] without suttletie, and therefore overlate founde out the fowle faultes they committed against him: but when he heard of them, he was muche offended, and would plainly confesse it unto them whome his officers had done injurie unto, by countenaunce of his authoritie. He had a noble minde, as well to punish offendors, as to reward well doers: and yet he did exceede more in geving, then in punishing.[4] Now for his outragious manner of railing he commonly used, mocking and flouting of everie man: that was remedied by it selfe. For a man might as boldly exchaunge a mocke with him, and he was as well contented to be mocked, as to mock others. But yet it oftentimes marred all. For he thought that those which told

[1] *In margin:* 'Antonius crueltie in Asia.'

[2] *In margin:* 'Hybræas words unto Antonius, touching their great payments of money unto him.'

[3] *In margin:* 'Antonius simplicity.' Cf. III.2.220 'a plain blunt man'.

[4] *In margin:* 'Antonius maners.'

him so plainly, and truly in mirth: would never flatter him in good earnest, in any matter of weight. But thus he was easely abused by the praises they gave him, not finding howe these flatterers mingled their flatterie, under this familiar and plaine manner of speach unto him, as a fine devise to make difference of meates with sharpe and tart sauce, and also to kepe him by this franke jeasting and bourding with him at the table, that their common flatterie should not be troublesome unto him, as men do easely mislike to have too muche of one thing: and that they handled him finely thereby, when they would geve him place in any matter of waight, and follow his counsell, that it might not appeare to him they did it so muche to please him, but bicause they were ignoraunt, and understoode not so muche as he did. Antonius being thus inclined, the last and extreamest mischiefe of all other (to wit, the love of Cleopatra) lighted on him, who did waken and stirre up many vices yet hidden in him, and were never seene to any: and if any sparke of goodnesse or hope of rising were left him, Cleopatra quenched it straight, and made it worse then before. The manner how he fell in love with her was this.[1] Antonius going to make warre with the Parthians, sent to commaunde Cleopatra to appeare personally before him, when he came into Cilicia, to aunswere unto suche accusacions as were layed against her, being this: that she had aided Cassius and Brutus in their warre against him. The messenger sent unto Cleopatra to make this summons unto her, was called Dellius: who when he had throughly considered her beawtie, the excellent grace and sweetenesse of her tongue, he nothing mistrusted that Antonius would doe any hurte to so noble a Ladie, but rather assured him selfe, that within few dayes she should be in great favor with him. Thereupon he did her great honor, and perswaded her to come into Cilicia, as honorably furnished as she could possible, and bad her not to be affrayed at all of Antonius, for he was a more curteous Lord, then any that she had ever seene. Cleopatra on thother side beleving Dellius wordes, and gessing by the former accesse and credit she had with Julius Cæsar,[2] and Cneus Pompey (the sonne of Pompey the great) only for her beawtie: she began to have good hope that she might more easely win Antonius. For Cæsar and Pompey knew her when she was but a young thing, and knew not then what the worlde ment[3]: but nowe she went to Antonius at the age when a womans beawtie is at the prime, and she also of best judgement. So, she furnished her selfe with a world of gifts, store of gold and silver, and of riches and other sumptuous ornaments, as is

[1] *In margin:* 'Antonius love to Cleopatra whom he sent for into Cilicia.'
[2] Cf. II.2.232–3; I.5.31–2 'great Pompey'.
[3] I.5.73–5.

credible enough she might bring from so great a house, and from so wealthie and rich a realme as Ægypt was.[1] But yet she caried nothing with her wherein she trusted more then in her selfe, and in the charmes and inchauntment of her passing beawtie and grace. Therefore when she was sent unto by divers letters, both from Antonius him selfe, and also from his frendes, she made so light of it, and mocked Antonius so much, that she disdained to set forward otherwise, but to take her barge in the river of Cydnus,[2] the poope whereof was of gold, the sailes of purple, and the owers of silver, which kept stroke in rowing after the sounde of the musicke of flutes, howboyes, citherns, violls, and such other instruments as they played upon in the barge. And now for the person of her selfe: she was layed under a pavillion of cloth of gold of tissue, apparelled and attired like the goddesse Venus, commonly drawen in picture: and hard by her, on either hand of her, pretie faire boyes apparelled as painters doe set forth god Cupide, with litle fannes in their hands, with the which they fanned wind upon her. Her Ladies and gentlewomen also, the fairest of them were apparelled like the nymphes Nereides (which are the mermaides of the waters) and like the Graces, some stearing the helme, others tending the tackle and ropes of the barge, out of the which there came a wonderfull passing sweete savor of perfumes, that perfumed the wharfes side, pestered with innumerable multitudes of people. Some of them followed the barge all alongest the rivers side: others also ranne out of the citie to see her comming in. So that in thend, there ranne such multitudes of people one after an other to see her, that Antonius was left post alone in the market place, in his Imperiall seate to geve audience: and there went a rumor in the peoples mouthes, that the goddesse Venus was come to play with the god Bacchus, for the generall good of all Asia. When Cleopatra landed, Antonius sent to invite her to supper to him. But she sent him word againe, he should doe better rather to come and suppe with her. Antonius therefore to shew him selfe curteous unto her at her arrivall, was contented to obey her, and went to supper to her: where he found such passing sumptuous fare, that no tongue can expresse it. But[3] amongest all other thinges, he most wondered at the infinite number of lightes and torches hanged on the toppe of the house, geving light in everie place, so artificially set and ordered by devises, some

[1] *In margin:* 'The wonderfull sumptuousnes of Cleopatra, Queene of Ægypt, going unto Antonius.'

[2] *In margin:* 'Cydnus fl.' Cf. Enobarbus' description II.2.196ff.

[3] *In margin:* 'The sumptuous preparations of the suppers of Cleopatra and Antonius.' II.2.219–26.

round, some square: that it was the rarest thing to behold that eye could discerne, or that ever books could mencion. The next night, Antonius feasting her, contended to passe her in magnificence and finenes: but she overcame him in both. So that he him selfe began to skorne the grosse service of his house, in respect of Cleopatraes sumptuousnes and finenesse. And when Cleopatra found Antonius jeasts and slents to be but grosse, and souldier like, in plaine manner: she gave it him finely, and without feare taunted him throughly.[1] Now her beawtie[2] (as it is reported) was not so passing, as unmatchable of other women, nor yet suche, as upon present viewe did enamor men with her: but so sweete was her companie and conversacion, that a man could not possiblie but be taken. And besides her beawtie, the good grace she had to talke and discourse, her curteous nature that tempered her words and dedes, was a spurre that pricked to the quick.[3] Furthermore, besides all these, her voyce and words were marvelous pleasant: for her tongue was an instrument of musicke to divers sports and pastimes, the which she easely turned to any language that pleased her. She spake unto few barbarous people by interpreter, but made them aunswere her selfe, or at the least the most parte of them: as the Æthiopians, the Arabians, the Troglodytes, the Hebrues, the Syrians, the Medes, and the Parthians, and to many others also, whose languages she had learned. Whereas divers of her progenitors, the kings of Ægypt, could scarce learne the Ægyptian tongue only, and many of them forgot to speake the Macedonian. Nowe, Antonius was so ravished with the love of Cleopatra, that though his wife Fulvia had great warres, and much a doe with Cæsar for his affaires, and that the armie of the Parthians, (the which the kings Lieutenauntes had geven to the onely leading of Labienus) was now assembled in Mesopotamia readie to invade Syria: yet, as though all this had nothing touched him, he yeelded him selfe to goe with Cleopatra into Alexandria, where he spent and lost in childish sports, (as a man might say) and idle pastimes, the most pretious thing a man can spende, as Antiphon sayth: and that is, time. For they made an order betwene them,[4] which they called Amimetobion (as much to say, no life comparable and matcheable with it) one feasting ech other by turnes, and in cost, exceeding all measure and reason.[5] And for proofe hereof, I have heard my grandfather Lampryas report, that one Philotas a Physition, born in the citie of Amphissa,

[1] As she does in *AC*.
[2] *In margin:* 'Cleopatraes beawtie.'
[3] Shakespeare built on these hints.
[4] *In margin:* 'An order set up by Antonius and Cleopatra.'
[5] *In margin:* 'The excessive expences of Antonius and Cleopatra in Ægypt.'

told him that he was at that present time in Alexandria, and studied Physicke: and that having acquaintance with one of Antonius cookes, he tooke him with him to Antonius house, (being a young man desirous to see things) to shew him the wonderfull sumptuous charge and preparation of one only supper. When he was in the kitchin, and saw a world of diversities of meates, and amongst others, eight wild boares rosted whole[1]: he began to wonder at it, and sayd, Sure you have a great number of ghests to supper. The cooke fell a laughing, and answered him, No (quoth he) not many ghestes, nor above twelve in all: but yet all that is boyled or roasted must be served in whole, or else it would be marred straight. For Antonius peradventure will suppe presently, or it may be a pretie while hence, or likely enough he will deferre it longer, for that he hath dronke well to day, or else hath had some other great matters in hand: and therefore we doe not dresse one supper only, but many suppers, bicause we are uncerteine of the houre he will suppe in. Philotas the Phisition[2] tolde my grandfather this tale. . . . But now againe to Cleopatra. Plato wryteth that there are foure kinds of flatterie[3]: but Cleopatra devided it into many kinds.[4] For she, were it in sport, or in matter of earnest, still devised sundrie new delights to have Antonius at commaundement, never leaving him night nor day, nor once letting him go out of her sight. For she would play at dyce with him, drinke with him, and hunt commonly with him, and also be with him when he went to any exercise or activity of body. And somtime also, when he would goe up and downe the citie disguised like a slave in the night, and would peere into poore mens windowes and their shops,[5] and scold and brawle with them within the house: Cleopatra would be also in a chamber maides array, and amble up and downe the streets with him, so that oftentimes Antonius bare away both mockes and blowes. Now, though most men misliked this maner, yet the Alexandrians were commonly glad of this jolity, and liked it well, saying verie gallantly, and wisely: that Antonius shewed them a commicall face, to wit, a merie countenaunce: and the Romanes a tragicall face, to say, a grimme looke. But to reckon up all the foolishe sportes they made, revelling in this sorte: it were too fond a parte of me, and therefore I will only tell you one among the rest. On a time he went to angle for fish, and when he could take none, he was as angrie as

[1] *In margin:* 'Eight wilde boares rosted whole.'

[2] *In margin:* 'Philotas a Phisition, borne in Amphissa, reporter of this feast. Philotas, Phisition to the younger Antonius.'

[3] *In margin:* 'Plato writeth of foure kinds of flatterie.'

[4] *In margin:* 'Cleopatra Queene of all flatterers.'

[5] I.1.53–4 gloss over this.

could be, bicause Cleopatra stoode by.[1] Wherefore he secretly commaunded the fisher men, that when he cast in his line, they should straight dive under the water, and put a fishe on his hooke which they had taken before: and so snatched up his angling rodde, and brought up fish twise or thrise. Cleopatra found it straight, yet she seemed not to see it, but wondred at his excellent fishing: but when she was alone by her selfe among her owne people, she told them howe it was, and bad them the next morning to be on the water to see the fishing. A number of people came to the haven, and got into the fisher boates to see this fishing. Antonius then threw in his line and Cleopatra straight commaunded one of her men to dive under water before Antonius men, and to put some old salte fish upon his baite, like unto those that are brought out of the contrie of Pont. When he had hong the fish on his hooke, Antonius thinking he had taken a fishe in deede, snatched up his line presently. Then they all fell a laughing. Cleopatra laughing also, said unto him: Leave us (my Lord) Ægyptians (which dwell in the contry of Pharus and Canobus) your angling rodde: this is not thy profession: thou must hunt after conquering of realmes and contries.[2] Nowe Antonius delighting in these fond and childish pastimes,[3] verie ill newes were brought him from two places. The first from Rome, that his brother Lucius, and Fulvia his wife, fell out first betwene them selves, and afterwards fell to open warre with Cæsar, and had brought all to nought, that they were both driven to flie out of Italie. The seconde[4] newes, as bad as the first: that Labienus conquered all Asia with the armie of the Parthians, from the river of Euphrates, and from Syria, unto the contries of Lydia and Ionia.[5] Then began Antonius with much a doe, a litle to rouse him selfe as if he had bene wakened out of a deepe sleepe, and as a man may say, comming out of a great dronkennes.[6] So, first of all he bent him selfe against the Parthians, and went as farre as the contrie of Phœnicia: but there he received lamentable letters from his wife Fulvia.[7] Whereuppon he straight returned towards Italie, with two hundred saile: and as he went, tooke up his frends by the way that fled out of Italie, to come to him. By them he was informed, that his wife Fulvia was the only cause of this warre: who being of a peevish, crooked, and troublesome nature,[8] had purposely raised this uprore in Italie, in hope thereby to withdraw him from Cleopatra. But by

[1] *In margin:* 'Antonius fishing in Ægypt.' II.5.10–18.
[2] Cf. II.5.18–23.
[3] Developed in I.1.18–55.
[4] *In margin:* 'The warres of Lucius Antonius and Fulvia, against Octavius Cæsar.' I.2.91–96.
[5] I.2.96–105.
[6] I.2.112–33; 125; 174–86.
[7] Cf. I.1.20ff.
[8] As Cleopatra hints in I.2.

good fortune, his wife Fulvia going to meete with Antonius, sickened by the way, and dyed in the citie of Sicyone[1]: and therefore Octavius Cæsar, and he were the easelier made frendes together. For when Antonius landed in Italie, and that men saw Cæsar asked nothing of him, and that Antonius on the other side layed all the fault and burden on his wife Fulvia: the frendes of both parties would not suffer them to unrippe any olde matters, and to prove or defend who had the wrong or right, and who was the first procurer of this warre, fearing to make matters worse betwene them: but they made them frendes together, and devided the Empire of Rome betwene them,[2] making the sea Ionium the bounds of their division. For they gave all the provinces Eastward, unto Antonius: and the contries Westward, unto Cæsar: and left Africke unto Lepidus: and made a law, that they three one after an other should make their frendes Consuls, when they would not be them selves. This seemed to be a sound counsell, but yet it was to be confirmed with a straighter bonde, which fortune offered thus. There was Octavia[3] the eldest sister of Cæsar, not by one mother, for she came of Ancharia, and Cæsar him self afterwards of Accia. It is reported, that he dearly loved his sister Octavia, for in deede she was a noble Ladie, and left the widow of her first husband Caius Marcellus, who dyed not long before: and it seemed also that Antonius had bene widower ever since the death of his wife Fulvia. For he denied not that he kept Cleopatra, but so he did not confesse that he had her as his wife: and so with reason he did defend the love he bare unto this Ægyptian Cleopatra. Thereuppon everie man did set forward this mariage, hoping thereby that this Ladie Octavia, having an excellent grace, wisedom, and honestie, joined unto so rare a beawtie, that when she were with Antonius (he loving her as so worthy a Ladie deserveth) she should be a good meane to keepe good love and amitie betwext her brother and him. So when Cæsar and he had made the matche betwene them, they both went to Rome about this mariage, although it was against the law,[4] that a widow should be maried within tenne monethes after her husbandes death. Howbeit the Senate dispensed with the law, and so the mariage proceeded accordingly.[5] Sextus Pompeius at that time kept in Sicilia, and so made many an inrode into Italie with a great number of pynnasies and other pirates shippes, of the which were Captaines two notable

[1] *In margin:* 'The death of Fulvia Antonius wife.' I.2.110–24.

[2] *In margin:* 'All the Empire of Rome devided betwene the Triumviri.'

[3] *In margin:* 'Octavia, the halfe sister of Octavius Cæsar, and daughter of Ancharia which was not Cæsars mother.'

[4] *In margin:* 'A law at Rome for marying of widowes.'

[5] *In margin:* 'Antonius maried Octavia, Octavius Cæsars halfe sister.'

pirats, Menas, and Menecrates, who so scoored all the sea thereabouts, that none durst peepe out with a sayle.[1] Furthermore, Sextus Pompeius had delt verie frendly with Antonius, for he had curteously received his mother, when she fled out of Italie with Fulvia: and therefore they thought good to make peace with him.[2] So they met all three together by the mount of Misena, upon a hill that runneth farre into the sea: Pompey having his shippes ryding hard by at ancker, and Antonius and Cæsar their armies upon the shoare side, directly over against him. Now, after they had agreed that Sextus Pompeius should have Sicile and Sardinia, with this condicion, that he should ridde the sea of all theeves and pirats, and make it safe for passengers, and withall that he should send a certaine [quantity] of wheate to Rome[3]: one of them did feast an other, and drew cuts who should beginne.[4] It was Pompeius chaunce to invite them first. Whereupon Antonius asked him: And where shall we suppe? There, said Pompey, and shewed him his admirall galley which had six bankes of owers: That (sayd he) is my fathers house they have left me. He spake it to taunt Antonius, bicause he had his fathers house, that was Pompey the great.[5] So he cast ankers enowe into the sea, to make his galley fast, and then built a bridge of woode to convey them to his galley, from the heade of mount Misena: and there he welcomed them, and made them great cheere. Now in the middest of the feast, when they fell to be merie with Antonius love unto Cleopatra[6]: Menas the pirate came to Pompey, and whispering in his eare, said unto him: Shall I cut the gables of the ankers, and make thee Lord not only of Sicile and Sardinia, but of the whole Empire of Rome besides? Pompey having pawsed a while upon it, at length aunswered him: Thou shouldest have done it, and never have told it me, but now we must content us with that we have. As for my selfe, I was never taught to breake my faith, nor to be counted a traitor.[7] The other two also did likewise feast him in their campe, and then he returned into Sicile. Antonius after this agreement made, sent Ventidius before into Asia to stay the Parthians, and to keepe them they should come no further[8]: and he him selfe in the meane time, to gratefie Cæsar, was contented to be

[1] I.2.186–8; II.1; II.2.164–8.

[2] *In margin:* 'Antonius and Octavius Cæsar, doe make peace with Sextus Pompeius.' II.6.1–82.

[3] II.6.35–9. [4] II.6.60–1.

[5] *In margin:* 'Sextus Pompeius taunt to Antonius.' Cf. II.6.26–7.

[6] In *AC* they mock Lepidus.

[7] *In margin:* 'Sextus Pompeius being offered wonderfull great fortune: for his honestie and faithes sake, refused it.' II.7.42–85.

[8] By III.1.1–3 Ventidius has beaten Parthia.

chosen Julius Cæsars priest and sacrificer, and so they joyntly together dispatched all great matters, concerning the state of the Empire. But in all other maner of sportes and exercises, wherein they passed the time away the one with the other: Antonius was ever inferior unto Cæsar, and alway lost, which grieved him much. With Antonius there was a soothsayer or astronomer of Ægypt, that coulde cast a figure, and judge of mens nativities, to tell them what should happen to them. He, either to please Cleopatra, or else for that he founde it so by his art, told Antonius plainly, that his fortune (which of it selfe was excellent good, and very great) was altogether bleamished, and obscured by Cæsars fortune: and therefore he counselled him utterly to leave his company, and to get him as farre from him as he could.[1] For thy Demon said he, (that is to say, the good angell and spirit that kepeth thee) is affraied of his: and being coragious and high when he is alone, becometh fearefull and timerous when he commeth neere unto the other. Howsoever it was, the events ensuing proved the Ægyptians words true. For, it is said, that as often as they two drew cuts for pastime, who should have any thing, or whether they plaied at dice, Antonius alway lost. Oftentimes when they were disposed to see cockefight, or quailes that were taught to fight one with an other: Cæsars cockes or quailes did ever overcome,[2] The which spighted Antonius in his mind, although he made no outward shew of it: and therefore he beleved the Ægyptian the better. In fine, he recommended the affaires of his house unto Cæsar, and went out of Italie with Octavia his wife, whom he caried into Græce, after he had had a daughter by her. So Antonius lying all the winter at Athens, newes came unto him of the victories of Ventidius, who had overcome the Parthians in battel, in the which also were slaine, Labienus, and Pharnabates, the chiefest Captaine king Orodes had.[3] For these good newes he feasted all Athens, and kept open house for all the Græcians, and many games of price were plaied at Athens, of the which he him selfe would be judge. Wherfore leaving his gard, his axes, and tokens of his Empire at his house, he came into the show place (or listes) where these games were played, in a long gowne and slippers after the Græcian facion, and they caried tippestaves before him, as marshalls men do cary before the Judges to make place: and he him selfe in person was a stickler to part the young men, when they had fought enough. After that, preparing to go to the warres, he made him a garland of the holy Olive, and caried a vessell with him

[1] *In margin:* 'Antonius told by a Soothsayer, that his fortune was inferior unto Octavius Cæsar.' II.3.16–30.

[2] *In margin:* 'Antonius unfortunate in sport and earnest, against Octavius Cæsar.'

[3] *In margin:* 'Orodes king of Parthia.'

of the water of the fountaine Clepsydra, bicause of an Oracle he had received that so commaunded him. In the meane time, Ventidius once againe overcame Pacorus, (Orodes sonne king of Parthia) in a battell fought in the contrie of Cyrrestica, he being come againe with a great armie to invade Syria: at which battell was slaine a great number of the Parthians, and among them Pacorus, the kings owne sonne slaine. This noble exployt as famous as ever any was, was a full revenge to the Romanes, of the shame and losse they had received before by the death of Marcus Crassus[1]: and he made the Parthians flie, and glad to kepe them selves within the confines and territories of Mesopotamia, and Media, after they had thrise together bene overcome in severall battells. Howbeit Ventidius durst not undertake to follow them any further, fearing least he should have gotten Antonius displeasure by it.[2] Notwithstanding, he led his armie against them that had rebelled, and conquered them againe: amongest whome he besieged Antiochus, king of Commagena, who offered him to give a thowsand talentes to be pardoned his rebellion, and promised ever after to be at Antonius commaundement. But Ventidius made him aunswere, that he should send unto Antonius, who was not farre of, and would not suffer Ventidius to make any peace with Antiochus, to the end that yet this litle exployt should passe in his name, and that they should not thinke he did any thing but by his Lieutenaunt Ventidius. The siege grew verie long, bicause they that were in the towne, seeing they coulde not be received upon no reasonable composition: determined valliantly to defende them selves to the last man. Thus Antonius did nothing, and yet received great shame, repenting him much that he tooke not their first offer.[3] And yet at last he was glad to make truce with Antiochus, and to take three hundred talentes for composition. Thus after he had set order for the state and affaires of Syria, he returned againe to Athens[4]: and having given Ventidius suche honors as he deserved, he sent him to Rome, to triumphe for the Parthians. Ventidius was the only man that ever triumphed of the Parthians untill this present day,[5] a meane man borne, and of no noble house nor family: who only came to that he attained unto, through Antonius frendshippe, the which delivered him happie occasion to achieve to great matters. And yet to say truely, he did so well quit him selfe in all his enterprises, that he confirmed that which was spoken of Antonius and Cæsar: to wit,

[1] *In margin:* 'Ventidius notable victorie of the Parthians. The death of Pacorus, the king of Parthiaes sonne.' III.1.1–5.

[2] III.2.5–37.

[3] Not made clear in III.1.

[4] III.1.35.

[5] *In margin:* 'Ventidius the only man of the Romanes, that triumphed for [over] the Parthians.' III.1.30–4.

that they were alway more fortunate when they made warre by their Lieutenants, then by them selves.[1] For Sossius, one of Antonius Lieutenauntes in Syria, did notable good service: and Canidius, whom he had also left his Lieutenaunt in the borders of Armenia, did conquer it all.[2] So did he also overcome the kinges of the Iberians and Albanians, and went on with his conquests unto mount Caucasus. By these conquests, the fame of Antonius power increased more and more, and grew dreadfull unto all the barbarous nations. But Antonius notwithstanding, grewe to be marvelously offended with Cæsar, upon certaine reportes that had bene brought unto him: and so tooke sea to go towards Italie with three hundred saile.[3] And bicause those of Brundusium, would not receive his armie into their haven, he went further unto Tarentum. There his wife Octavia that came out of Græce with him, besought him to send her unto her brother: the which he did.[4] Octavia at that time was great with child, and moreover had a second daughter by him, and yet she put her selfe in jorney, and met with her brother Octavius Cæsar by the way, who brought his two chiefe frendes, Mæcenas and Agrippa with him. She tooke them aside, and with all the instance she could possible, intreated them they would not suffer her that was the happiest woman of the world, to become nowe the most wretched and unfortunatest creature of all other.[5] For now, said she, everie mans eyes doe gaze on me, that am the sister of one of the Emperours and wife of the other. And if the worst councell take place, (which the goddes forbidde) and that they growe to warres: for your selves, it is uncertaine to which of them two the goddes have assigned the victorie, or overthrowe. But for me, on which side soever victorie fall, my state can be but most miserable still.[6] These words of Octavia so softned Cæsars harte, that he went quickely unto Tarentum. But it was a noble sight for them that were present, to see so great an armie by lande not to sturre, and so many shippes aflote in the roade, quietly and safe: and furthermore, the meeting and kindenesse of frendes, lovinglie imbracing one an other.[7] First, Antonius feasted Cæsar, which he graunted unto for his sisters sake. Afterwardes they agreed together, that Cæsar should geve Antonius two legions to go against the Parthians: and that Antonius should

[1] III.1.16–17.

[2] *In margin:* 'Canidius conquests.'

[3] *In margin:* 'Newe displeasures betwext Antonius and Octavius Cæsar.' Cf. III.4.1–10.

[4] III.4.24–32.

[5] *In margin:* 'The wordes of Octavia unto Mæcenas and Agrippa.' III.6.38ff.

[6] Octavia says this to Antony. III.4.10–20.

[7] *In margin:* 'Octavia pacifieth the quarrell betwixt Antonius, and her brother Octavius Cæsar.' Omitted by Shakespeare.

let Cæsar have a hundred gallies armed with brasen spurres at the prooes. Besides all this, Octavia obteyned of her husbande, twentie brigantines for her brother: and of her brother for her husbande, a thowsande armed men. After they had taken leave of eache other, Cæsar went immediatly to make warre with Sextus Pompeius, to gette Sicilia into his handes.[1] Antonius also leaving his wife Octavia and litle children begotten of her, with Cæsar, and his other children which he had by Fulvia: he went directlie into Asia. Then beganne this pestilent plague and mischiefe of Cleopatraes love (which had slept a longe tyme, and seemed to have bene utterlie forgotten, and that Antonius had geven place to better counsell) againe to kindle, and to be in force, so soone as Antonius came neere unto Syria. And in the ende, the horse of the minde as Plato termeth it,[2] that is so hard of rayne (I meane the unreyned lust of concupiscence) did put out of Antonius heade, all honest and commendable thoughtes: for he sent Fonteius Capito to bring Cleopatra into Syria.[3] Unto whome, to welcome her, he gave no trifling things: but unto that she had already, he added the provinces of Phœnicia, those of the nethermost Syria, the Ile of Cyprus, and a great parte of Cilicia, and that contry of Jurie where the true balme is, and that parte of Arabia where the Nabatheians doe dwell, which stretcheth out towardes the Ocean. These great giftes muche misliked the Romanes.[4] But now, though Antonius did easely geve away great seigniories, realmes, and mighty nations unto some private men, and that also he tooke from other kings their lawfull realmes: (as from Antigonus king of the Jewes, whom he openly beheaded, where never king before had suffred like death)[5] yet all this did not so much offend the Romanes, as the unmeasurable honors which he did unto Cleopatra. But yet he did much more aggravate their malice and il wil towards him, bicause that Cleopatra having brought him two twinnes, a sonne and a daughter, he named his sonne Alexander, and his daughter Cleopatra, and gave them to their surnames, the Sunne to the one, and the moone to the other.[6] This notwithstanding, he that could finely cloke his shamefull deedes with fine words, said that the greatnes and magnificence of the Empire of Rome appeared most, not where the Romanes tooke, but where they gave much: and nobility was multiplied amongest men, by the posterity of kings, when they left of their seede in divers

[1] Referred to in III.4.1–4; III.5.4.

[2] *In margin:* 'Plato calleth concupiscence: the horse of the minde.'

[3] *In margin:* 'Antonius sent for Cleopatra into Syria.'

[4] *In margin:* 'Antonius gave great provinces unto Cleopatra.' III.6.8–16.

[5] *In margin:* 'Antigonus king of Jurie, the first king beheaded by Antonius.'

[6] *In margin:* 'Antonius twinnes by Cleopatra, and their names.'

places: and that by his meanes his first auncester was begotten of Hercules, who had not left the hope and continuance of his line and posterity, in the wombe of one only woman, fearing Solons lawes, or regarding the ordinaunces of men touching the procreacion of children: but that he gave it unto nature, and established the fundacion of many noble races and families in divers places. Nowe when Phraortes had slaine his father Orodes, and possessed the kingdom[1]: many gentlemen of Parthia forsooke him, and fled from him. Amongst them was Monæses, a noble man, and of great authority among his contry men, who came unto Antonius, that received him, and compared his fortune unto Themistocles, and his owne riches and magnificence, unto the kings of Persia. For he gave Monæses three cities, Larisa, Arethusa, and Hierapolis, which was called before Bombyce. Howbeit the king of Parthia shortly after called him home againe, upon his faith and word. Antonius was glad to let him go, hoping thereby to steale upon Phraortes unprovided. For he sent unto him, and told him that they would remaine good frends, and have peace together, so he would but only redeliver the standerds and ensignes of the Romanes, which the Parthians had wonne in the battell where Marcus Crassus was slaine, and the men also that remained yet prisoners of this overthrow. In the meane time he sent Cleopatra backe into Ægypt, and tooke his way towards Arabia and Armenia, and there tooke a general muster of all his army he had together, and of the kings his confederats, that were come by his commaundement to aide him, being a marvelous number[2]: of the which, the chiefest was Artavasdes, king of Armenia, who did furnish him with six thowsande horsemen, and seven thowsand footemen. There were also of the Romanes about three score thowsand footmen, and of horsemen (Spaniards and Gaules reckoned for Romanes) to the number of ten thousand, and of other nations thirty thowsand men, reckoning together the horsemen and light armed footemen. This so great and puisant army which made the Indians quake for feare, dwelling about the contry of the Bactrians, and all Asia also to tremble: served him to no purpose, and all for the love he bare to Cleopatra.[3] For the earnest great desire he had to lye all winter with her, made him begin his warre out of due time, and for hast, to put all in hazard, being so ravished and enchaunted with the sweete poyson of her love, that he had no other thought but of her, and how he might quickly returne againe: more then how he might overcome

[1] *In margin:* 'Phraortes slue his father Orodes king of Persia.'
[2] *In margin:* 'Antonius great and puisant army.'
[3] *In margin:* 'Antonius dronke with the love of Cleopatra.'

his enemies. For first of all, where he should have wintered in Armenia to refresh his men, wearied with the long jorney they had made, having comen eight thowsand furlongs, and then at the beginning of the spring to go and invade Media, before the Parthians should stirre out of their houses and garrisons: he could tary no lenger, but led them forthwith unto the province of Atropatene, leaving Armenia on the left hand, and forraged al the contry. Furthermore, making all the hast he coulde, he left behinde him engines of battery which were caried with him in three hundred carts, (among the which also there was a ramme foure score foote long) being things most necessary for him, and the which he could not get againe for money if they were once lost or marred. For the hie provinces of Asia have no trees growing of such height and length, neither strong nor straight enough to make such like engines of battery. This notwithstanding, he left them all behind him, as a hinderance to bring his matters and intent speedily to passe: and left a certaine number of men to keepe them, and gave them in charge unto one Tatianus. Then he went to besiege the citie of Phraata, being the chiefest and greatest citie the king of Media had, where his wife and children were.[1] Then he straight founde his owne fault, and the want of his artillerie he left behinde him, by the worke he had in hande: for he was fayne for lacke of a breache (where his men might come to the sworde with their enemies that defended the walle) to force a mount of earth hard to the walles of the citie, the which by litle and litle with greate labour, rose to some height. In the meane time king Phraortes came downe with a great armie, who understanding that Antonius had left his engines of batterie behind him, he sent a great number of horsemen before, which environed Tatianus with all his cariage, and slue him, and ten thowsand men he had with him. After this, the barbarous people tooke these engines of battery and burnt them, and got many prisoners, amongst whom they tooke also king Polemon.[2] This discomfiture marvelously troubled all Antonius army, to receive so great an overthrow (beyond their expectacion) at the beginning of their jorney: insomuche that Artabazus, king of the Armenians, dispairing of the good successe of the Romanes: departed with his men, notwithstanding that he was him selfe the first procurer of this warre and jorney. On the other side, the Parthians came coragiously unto Antonius campe, who lay at the siege of their chiefest citie, and cruelly reviled and threatned him. . . . [Antony suffered many setbacks.]

[1] *In margin:* 'Antonius besiegeth the city of Phraata in Media.'
[2] *In margin:* 'The Parthians tooke Antonius engines of battery.'

Then seeing him selfe environned of all sides, he sent unto the army, that they should come and aide him: but there the Captaines that led the legions (among the which Canidius, a man of great estimacion about Antonius made one) committed many faults. For where they should have made head with the whole army upon the Parthians, they sent him aide by small companies: and when they were slaine, they sent him others also. So that by their beastlinesse and lacke of consideracion, they had like to have made all the armie flie, if Antonius him selfe had not come from the front of the battell with the third legion, the which came through the middest of them that fled, untill they came to front of the enemies, and that they stayed them from chasing any further. Howbeit at this last conflict there were slaine no lesse then three thowsand men, and five thowsande besides brought sore hurt into the campe, and amongest them also Flavius Gallus, whose body was shot through in foure places, whereof he died.[1] Antonius went to the tents to visite and comfort the sicke and wounded,[2] and for pities sake he could not refraine from weeping: and they also shewing him the best countenaunce they coulde, tooke him by the hand, and prayed him to go and be dressed, and not to trouble him selfe for them, most reverently calling him their Emperour and Captaine: and that for them selves, they were whole and safe, so that he had his health. For in deede to say truly, there was not at that time any Emperour or Captaine that had so great and puisant an army as his together, both for lusty youths, and corage of the souldiers, as also for their pacience to away with so great paines and trouble. Furthermore, the obedience and reverence they shewed unto their captaine,[3] with a marvelous earnest love and good wil, was so great: and all were indifferently (as wel great as smal, the noble men, as meane men, the Captaines and souldiers) so earnestly bent to esteeme Antonius good will and favor, above their owne life and safety: that in this point of marshall discipline, the auncient Romanes could not have don any more. But divers things were cause therof, as we have told you before[4]: Antonius nobility and ancient house, his eloquence, his plaine nature, his liberality and magnificence, and his familiarity to sport and to be mery in company: but specially the care he tooke at that time to help, visite, and lament those that were sicke and wounded, seing every man to have that which was meete for him: that was of such force and effect, as it made them that were sicke and wounded to love him better, and were more desirous to do him

[1] *In margin:* 'Flavius Gallus slaine.'
[2] *In margin:* 'Antonius care of them that were wounded.'
[3] *In margin:* 'The love and reverence of the souldiers unto Antonius.'
[4] *In margin:* 'The rare and singular gifts of Antonius.'

service, then those that were whole and sound. [After undergoing many privations Antony withdrew.]

There Antonius mustring his whole army, found that he had lost twenty thowsand footemen, and foure thowsand horsemen, which had not all bene slayne by their enemies: for the most part of them dyed of sicknes, making seven and twenty dayes jorney, comming from the citie of Phraata into Armenia, and having overcome the Parthians in eighteene severall battells.[1] But these victories were not throughly performed nor accomplished, bicause they followed no long chase: and thereby it easily appeared, that Artabazus king of Armenia, had reserved Antonius to end this warre.[2] . . . Therefore, all those that were of any credit and countenaunce in the army, did perswade and egge Antonius to be revenged of this Armenian king. But Antonius wisely dissembling his anger, he told him not of his trechery, nor gave him the worse countenaunce, nor did him lesse honor then he did before: bicause he knew his armie was weake, and lacked things necessary, Howbeit afterwards he returned againe into Armenia with a great army, and so with fayer wordes, and sweete promises of Messengers, he allured Artabazus to come unto him: whome he then kept prisoner, and led in triumphe in the citie of Alexandria.[3] This greatly offended the Romanes, and made them much to mislike it: when they saw that for Cleopatraes sake he deprived his contry of her due honor and glory, onely to gratifie the Ægyptians. But this was a prety while after. Howbeit then, the great haste he made to returne unto Cleopatra, caused him to put his men to so great paines, forcing them to lye in the field all winter long when it snew unreasonably, that by the way he lost eight thowsand of his men, and so came downe to the sea side with a small companye, to a certaine place called Blancbourg, which standeth betwixt the cities of Berytus and Sidon, and there taried for Cleopatra. And bicause she taried longer then he would have had her, he pined away for love and sorrow.[4] So that he was at such a straight, that he wist not what to doe, and therefore to weare it out, he gave him selfe to quaffing and feasting. But he was so drowned with the love of her, that he could not abide to sit at the table till the feast were ended: but many times while others banketted, he ranne to the sea side to see if she were comming. At length she came, and brought with her a worlde of apparell and money to

[1] *In margin:* '18 severall battels fought with the Parthians.'

[2] *In margin:* 'The trechery of Artabazus king of Armenia, unto Antonius.' *Reserved*, restrained, prevented [by not pursuing the foe].

[3] *In margin:* 'Antonius triumphed of Artabazus king of Armenia, in Ægypt.'

[4] *In margin:* 'Antonius pined away looking for Cleopatra.'

give unto the souldiers.[1] But some saye notwithstanding, that she brought apparell, but no money, and that she tooke of Antonius money, and caused it to be given amonge the souldiers in her owne name, as if she had given it them. In the meane time it chaunced, that the king of the Medes, and Phraortes king of the Parthians, fell at great warres together,[2] the which began (as it is reported) for the spoyles of the Romanes: and grew to be so hot betwene them, that the king of Medes was no lesse affrayd, then also in daunger to lose his whole Realme. Thereuppon he sent unto Antonius to pray him to come and make warre with the Parthians, promising him that he would ayde him to his uttermost power. This put Antonius againe in good comfort, considering that unlooked for, the onely thing he lacked, (which made him he could not overcome the Parthians, meaning that he had not brought horsemen, and men with darts and slings enough) was offred him in that sort: that he did him more pleasure to accept it, then it was pleasure to the other to offer it. Hereuppon, after he had spoken with the king of Medes at the river of Araxes, he prepared him selfe once more to goe through Armenia, and to make more cruell warre with the Parthians, then he had done before. Now whilest Antonius was busie in this preparation, Octavia his wife, whome he had left at Rome, would needes take sea to come unto him. Her brother Octavius Cæsar was willing unto it, not for his respect at all (as most authors doe report) as for that he might have an honest culler to make warre with Antonius if he did misuse her, and not esteeme of her as she ought to be. But when she was come to Athens, she received letters from Antonius, willing her to stay there untill his comming, and did advertise her of his jorney and determination.[3] The which though it grieved her much, and that she knewe it was but an excuse: yet by her letters to him of aunswer, she asked him whether he would have those thinges sent unto him which she had brought him, being great store of apparell for souldiers, a great number of horse, summe of money, and gifts, to bestow on his friendes and Captaines he had about him: and besides all those, she had two thowsand souldiers chosen men, all well armed, like unto the Prætors bands. When Niger, one of Antonius friends whome he had sent unto Athens, had brought these newes from his wife Octavia, and withall did greatly prayse her, as she was worthy, and well deserved: Cleopatra knowing that Octavia would have Antonius from her, and fearing also that if with her vertue and honest behavior, (besides the great power of her

[1] *In margin:* 'Cleopatra came to Blancbourg unto Antonius.'

[2] *In margin:* 'Warres betwixt the Parthians and Medes.'

[3] *In margin:* 'Octavia, Antonius wife, came to Athens to meete with him.'

brother Cæsar) she did adde thereunto her modest kind love to please her husband, that she would then be too stronge for her, and in the end winne him away: she suttelly seemed to languish for the love of Antonius, pyning her body for lacke of meate. Furthermore, she every way so framed her countenaunce, that when Antonius came to see her, she cast her eyes upon him, like a woman ravished for joy.[1] Straight againe when he went from her, she fell a weeping and blubbering, looked rufully of the matter, and still found the meanes that Antonius should oftentymes finde her weeping: and then when he came sodainely uppon her, she made as though she dryed her eyes, and turned her face away, as if she were unwilling that he should see her weepe. All these tricks she used, Antonius being in readines to goe into Syria, to speake with the king of Medes. Then the flatterers that furthered Cleopatraes mind, blamed Antonius, and tolde him that he was a hard natured man, and that he had small love in him, that would see a poore Ladye in such torment for his sake, whose life depended onely upon him alone. For, Octavia, sayd they, that was maryed unto him as it were of necessitie, bicause her brother Cæsars affayres so required it: hath the honor to be called Antonius lawefull spowse and wife: and Cleopatra, being borne a Queene of so many thowsands of men, is onely named Antonius Leman, and yet that she disdayned not so to be called, if it might please him she might enjoy his company, and live with him: but if he once leave her, that then it is unpossible she should live. To be short, by these their flatteries and enticements, they so wrought Antonius effeminate mind, that fearing least she would make her selfe away: he returned againe unto Alexandria, and referred the king of Medes to the next yeare following, although he receyved newes that the Parthians at that tyme were at civill warres amonge them selves. This notwithstanding, he went afterwardes and made peace with him. For he maried his Daughter which was very younge, unto one of the sonnes that Cleopatra had by him: and then returned, beeing fully bent to make warre with Cæsar.[2] When Octavia was returned to Rome from Athens, Cæsar commaunded her to goe out of Antonius house, and to dwell by her selfe, bicause he had abused her.[3] Octavia aunswered him againe, that she would not forsake her husbands house, and that if he had no other occasion to make warre with him, she prayed him then to take no thought for her: for sayd she, it were too shamefull a thinge, that two so famous Captaines should bringe in civill warres among

[1] *In margin:* 'The flickering enticements of Cleopatra unto Antonius.' Cf.I.3.
[2] *In margin:* 'The occasion of civil warres betwixt Antonius and Cæsar.'
[3] Cf. III.6.86–7.

the Romanes, the one for the love of a woman, and the other for the jelousy betwixt one an other. Now as she spake the worde, so did she also performe the deede.[1] For she kept still in Antonius house, as if he had bene there, and very honestly and honorably kept his children, not those onely she had by him, but the other which her husband had by Fulvia. Furthermore, when Antonius sent any of his men to Rome, to sue for any office in the common wealth: she received him very curteously, and so used her selfe unto her brother, that she obtained the thing she requested. Howbeit thereby, thinking no hurt, she did Antonius great hurt. For her honest love and regard to her husband, made every man hate him, when they sawe he did so unkindly use so noble a Lady: but yet the greatest cause of their malice unto him, was for the division of lands he made amongst his children in the citie of Alexandria.[2] And to confesse a troth, it was too arrogant and insolent a part, and done (as a man would say) in derision and contempt of the Romanes. For he assembled all the people in the show place, where younge men doe exercise them selves, and there upon a high tribunall silvered, he set two chayres of gold, the one for him selfe, and the other for Cleopatra, and lower chaires for his children: then he openly published before the assembly, that first of all he did establish Cleopatra Queene of Ægypt, of Cyprus, of Lydia, and of the lower Syria, and at that time also, Cæsarion king of the same Realmes. This Cæsarion was supposed to be the sonne of Julius Cæsar, who had left Cleopatra great with child.[3] Secondly he called the sonnes he had by her, the kings of kings, and gave Alexander for his portion, Armenia, Media, and Parthia, when he had conquered the contry: and unto Ptolomy for his portion, Phenicia, Syria, and Cilicia.[4] And therewithall he brought out Alexander in a long gowne after the facion of the Medes, with a high copped tanke hat on his head, narrow in the toppe, as the kings of the Medes and Armenians doe use to weare them: and Ptolomy apparelled in a cloke after the Macedonian manner, with slippers on his feete, and a broad hat, with a royall band or diademe. Such was the apparell and old attyre of the auncient kinges and successors of Alexander the great. So after his sonnes had done their humble duties, and kissed their father and mother: presently a company of Armenian souldiers set there of purpose, compassed the one about, and a like company of the

[1] *In margin:* 'The love of Octavia to Antonius her husband, and her wise and womanly behavior.'

[2] *In margin:* 'Antonius arrogantly devideth divers provinces unto his children by Cleopatra.' III.6.1–16.

[3] *In margin:* 'Cæsarion, the supposed sone of Cæsar, by Cleopatra.'

[4] *In margin:* 'Alexander and Ptolomy, Antonius sonnes by Cleopatra.'

Macedonians the other. Now for Cleopatra, she did not onely weare at that time (but at all other times els when she came abroad) the apparell of the goddesse Isis, and so gave audience unto all her subjects, as a new Isis.[1] Octavius Cæsar reporting all these thinges unto the Senate, and oftentimes accusing him to the whole people and assembly in Rome[2]: he thereby stirred up all the Romanes against him. Antonius on thother side sent to Rome likewise to accuse him, and the chiefest poyntes of his accusations he charged him with, were these: First, that having spoyled Sextus Pompeius in Sicile, he did not give him his parte of the Ile. Secondly, that he did deteyne in his hands the shippes he lent him to make that warre. Thirdly, that having put Lepidus their companion and triumvirate out of his part of the Empire, and having deprived him of all honors: he retayned for him selfe the lands and revenues thereof, which had bene assigned unto him for his part.[3] And last of all, that he had in manner devided all Italy amongest his owne souldiers, and had left no part of it for his souldiers. Octavius Cæsar aunswered him againe: that for Lepidus, he had in deede deposed him, and taken his part of the Empire from him, bicause he did overcruelly use his authoritie. And secondly, for the conquests he had made by force of armes, he was contented Antonius should have his part of them, so that he would likewise let him have his part of Armenia. And thirdly, that for his souldiers, they should seeke for nothing in Italy, bicause they possessed Media and Parthia, the which provinces they had added to the Empire of Rome, valliantly fighting with their Emperor and Captaine.[4] Antonius hearing these newes, being yet in Armenia, commaunded Canidius to goe presently to the sea side with his sixteene legions he had: and he him selfe with Cleopatra, went unto the citie of Ephesus, and there gathered together his gallies and shippes out of all parts, which came to the number of eight hundred, reckoning the great shippes of burden,[5] and of those Cleopatra furnished him with two hundred, and twenty thowsand talents besides and provision of vittells also to mainteyne al the whole army in this warre. So Antonius, through the perswasions of Domitius, commaunded Cleopatra to returne againe into Ægypt, and there to understand the successe of this warre. But Cleopatra, fearing least Antonius should againe be made friends with Octavius Cæsar, by the meanes of his wife Octavia: she so plyed Canidius with money, and filled his purse, that he became her spokes man unto Antonius, and told him there was no reason to

[1] III.6.16–18.

[2] *In margin:* 'Accusasions betwixt Octavius Cæsar, and Antonius.' III.6.19–21.

[3] III.6.22–30. [4] III.6.30–7.

[5] *In margin:* 'Antonius came with eight hundred saile against Octavius Cæsar.'

send her from this warre, who defraied so great a charge: neither that it was for his profit, bicause that thereby the Ægyptians would then be utterly discoraged, which were the chiefest strength of the army by sea: considering that he could see no king of all the kings their confederats, that Cleopatra was inferior unto, either for wisedom or judgement, seeing that longe before she had wisely governed so great a realme as Ægypt, and besides that she had bene so long acquainted with him, by whom she had learned to manedge great affayres.[1] These fayer perswasions wan him: for it was predestined that the government of all the world should fall into Octavius Cæsars handes. Thus, all their forces being joyned together, they hoysed sayle towards the Ile of Samos, and there gave them selves to feasts and sollace.[2] For as all the kings, Princes, and communalties, peoples and cities from Syria, unto the marishes Mæotides, and from the Armenians to the Illyrians, were sent unto, to send and bringe all munition and warlike preparation they could: even so all players, minstrells, tumblers, fooles, and jeasters, were commaunded to assemble in the Ile of Samos. So that, where in manner all the world in every place was full of lamentations, sighes and teares: onely in this Ile of Samos there was nothing for many dayes space, but singing and pyping, and all the Theater full of these common players, minstrells, and singing men. Besides all this, every citie sent an oxe thither to sacrifice, and kings did strive one with another who should make the noblest feasts, and give the richest gifts. So that every man sayd, What can they doe more for joy of victorie, if they winne the battell? when they make already such sumptuous feasts at the beginning of the warre? When this was done, he gave the whole rabble of these minstrells, and such kind of people, the citie of Priene to keepe them withal, during this warre. Then he went unto the citie of Athens, and there gave him selfe againe to see playes and pastimes, and to keepe the Theaters. Cleopatra on the other side, being jelous of the honors which Octavia had received in this citie, where in deede she was marvelously honored and beloved of the Athenians: to winne the peoples good will also at Athens, she gave them great gifts: and they likewise gave her many great honors, and appointed certain Ambassadors to cary the decree to her house, among the which Antonius was one, who as a Citizen of Athens reported the matter unto her, and made an oration in the behalfe of the citie. Afterwards he sent to Rome to put his wife Octavia out

[1] Cf. Cleopatra's talk with Enobarbus, III.7.1–19.

[2] *In margin:* 'Antonius carieth Cleopatra with him to the warres, against Octavius Cæsar: and kept great feasting at the Ile of Samos together.' Shakespeare omits the feasting.

of his house,[1] who (as it is reported) went out of his house with all Antonius children, saving the eldest of them he had by Fulvia, who was with her father, bewailing and lamenting her cursed hap that had brought her to this, that she was accompted one of the chiefest causes of this civill warre.[2] The Romanes did pitie her, but much more Antonius, and those specially that had seene Cleopatra: who nether excelled Octavia in beawtie, nor yet in young yeares. Octavius Cæsar understanding the sodain and wonderful great preparation of Antonius, he was not a litle astonied at it, (fearing he should be driven to fight that sommer) bicause he wanted many things, and the great and grievous exactions of money did sorely oppresse the people.[3] For all manner of men els, were driven to pay the fourth part of their goods and revenue: but the Libertines, (to wete, those whose fathers or other predecessors had some time bene bond men) they were sessed to pay the eight part of all their goods at one payment. Hereuppon, there rose a wonderfull exclamation and great uprore all Italy over: so that among the greatest faults that ever Antonius committed, they blamed him most, for that he delayed to give Cæsar battell. For he gave Cæsar leysure to make his preparacions, and also to appease the complaints of the people. When such a great summe of money was demaunded of them, they grudged at it, and grewe to mutinie upon it: but when they had once paied it, they remembred it no more. Furthermore, Titius and Plancus (two of Antonius chiefest friends and that had bene both of them Consuls) for the great injuries Cleopatra did them, bicause they hindered all they could, that she should not come to this warre: they went and yelded them selves unto Cæsar, and tolde him where the testament was that Antonius had made, knowing perfitly what was in it.[4] The will was in the custodie of the Vestall Nunnes: of whom Cæsar demaunded for it. They aunswered him, that they would not give it him: but if he would goe and take it, they would not hinder him. Thereuppon Cæsar went thither, and having red it first to him self, he noted certaine places worthy of reproch: so assembling all the Senate, he red it before them all.[5] Whereuppon divers were marvelously offended, and thought it a straunge matter that he being alive, should be punished for that he had appoynted by his will to be done after his death. Cæsar chiefly tooke hold of this that he ordeyned touching his buriall: for he willed that his bodie, though he dyed at Rome, should be brought in funerall

[1] *In margin:* 'Antonius put his wife Octavia out of his house at Rome.'
[2] III.6.76–8.
[3] *In margin:* 'Octavius Cæsar exacteth grievous payments of the Romanes.'
[4] *In margin:* 'Titius and Plancus revolt from Antonius, and doe yeld to Cæsar.'
[5] Contrast III.4.4–6.

pompe through the middest of the market place, and that it should be sent into Alexandria unto Cleopatra. Furthermore, among divers other faultes wherewith Antonius was to be charged, for Cleopatraes sake: Calvisius, one of Cæsars friends reproved him, bicause he had franckly given Cleopatra all the libraries of the royall citie of Pergamum, in the which she had above two hundred thowsand bookes.[1] Againe also, that being on a time set at the table, he sodainly rose from the borde, and trode upon Cleopatraes foote, which was a signe given betwene them, that they were agreed of. That he had also suffred the Ephesians in his presence to call Cleopatra, their soveraine Ladye. That divers times sitting in his tribunall and chayer of state, giving audience to all kings and Princes: he had received love letters from Cleopatra, written in tables of onyx or christall, and that he had red them, sitting in his imperial seate. That one day when Furnius, a man of great accompt, and the eloquentest man of all the Romanes, pleaded a matter before him: Cleopatra by chaunce comming through the market place in her litter where Furnius was pleading: Antonius straight rose out of his seate, and left his audience to followe her litter.[2] This notwithstanding, it was thought Calvisius devised the most part of all these accusations of his owne head. Nevertheles they that loved Antonius, were intercessors to the people for him, and amongest them they sent one Geminius unto Antonius, to pray him he would take heede, that through his negligence his Empire were not taken from him, and that he should be counted an enemie to the people of Rome.[3] This Geminius being arrived in Græce, made Cleopatra jelous straight of his comming: bicause she surmised that he came not but to speake for Octavia. Therefore she spared not to tawnt him all supper tyme, and moreover to spyte him the more, she made him be set lowest of all at the borde, the which he tooke paciently, expecting occasion to speake with Antonius. Now Antonius commaunding him at the table to tell him what wind brought him thither: he aunswered him, that it was no table talke, and that he would tell him to morrow morning fasting: but dronke or fasting, howsoever it were, he was sure of one thing, that all would not go well on his side, unles Cleopatra were sent backe into Ægypt. Antonius tooke these wordes in very ill part. Cleopatra on the other side aunswered him, Thou doest well Geminius, sayd she, to tell the truth before thou be compelled by torments: but within fewe dayes

[1] *In margin:* 'A famous librarie in the citie of Pergamum.'

[2] *In margin:* 'Furnius, an eloquent Orator among the Romanes.'

[3] *In margin:* 'Geminius sent from Rome to Antonius, to bid him take heede to him selfe.'

after, Geminius stale away, and fled to Rome. The flatterers also to please Cleopatra, did make her drive many other of Antonius faithfull servaunts and friends from him, who could not abide the injuries done unto them[1]: amonge the which these two were chiefe, Marcus Syllanus, and Dellius the Historiographer: who wrote that he fled, bicause her Phisitian Glaucus tolde him, that Cleopatra had set some secretly to kill him. Furthermore he had Cleopatraes displeasure, bicause he sayde one night at supper, that they made them drinke sower wine, where Sarmentus at Rome drancke good wine of Falerna. This Sarmentus was a pleasaunt younge boye, such as the Lordes of Rome are wont to have about them to make them pastyme, which they call their joyes, and he was Octavius Cæsars boye. Nowe, after Cæsar had made sufficient preparation, he proclaymed open warre against Cleopatra, and made the people to abolishe the power and Empire of Antonius, bicause he had before given it uppe unto a woman.[2] And Cæsar sayde furthermore, that Antonius was not Maister of him selfe, but that Cleopatra had brought him beside him selfe, by her charmes and amorous poysons: and that they that should make warre with them should be Mardian the Euenuke, Photinus, and Iras, a woman of Cleopatraes bedchamber, that friseled her heare, and dressed her head, and Charmion, the which were those that ruled all the affaires of Antonius Empire.[3] Before this warre, as it is reported, many signes and wonders fel out.[4] First of all, the citie of Pisaurum which was made a colony to Rome, and replenished with people by Antonius, standing upon the shore side of the sea Adriatick, was by a terrible earthquake sonck into the ground.[5] One of the images of stone which was set up in the honor of Antonius, in the citie of Alba, did sweate many dayes together: and though some wyped it away, yet it left not sweating still. In the citie of Patras, whilest Antonius was there, the temple of Hercules was burnt with lightning. And at the citie of Athens also, in a place where the warre of the gyants against the goddes is set out in imagerie: the statute of Bacchus with a terrible winde was throwen downe in the Theater. It was sayd that Antonius came of the race of Hercules, as you have heard before, and in the manner of his life he followed Bacchus: and therefore he was called the new Bacchus. Furthermore, the same blustering storme of wind, overthrew the great monstrous images at Athens, that were made

[1] *In margin:* 'Many of Antonius friends doe forsake him.'

[2] *In margin:* 'Antonius Empire taken from him.'

[3] Cf. III.7.12–17.

[4] *In margin:* 'Signes and wonders before the civill warres betwixt Antonius and Oct. Cæsar.'

[5] *In margin:* 'Pesaro, a citie in Italy, sonck into the ground by an earthquake.'

in the honor of Eumenes and Attalus, the which men had named and intituled, the Antonians, and yet they did hurt none of the other images which were many besides. The Admirall galley of Cleopatra, was called Antoniade, in the which there chaunced a marvelous ill signe. Swallowes had bred under the poope of her shippe,[1] and there came others after them that drave away the first, and plucked downe their neasts. Now when all things were ready, and that they drew neare to fight: it was found that Antonius[2] had no lesse then five hundred good ships of warre, among the which there were many gallies that had eight and ten bancks of owers, the which were sumptuously furnished, not so meete for fight, as for triumphe: a hundred thowsand footemen, and twelve thowsand horsemen, and had with him to ayde him these kinges and subjects following: Bocchus king of Lybia, Tarcondemus king of high Cilicia, Archelaus king of Cappadocia, Philadelphus king of Paphlagonia, Mithridates king of Comagena, and Adallas king of Thracia. All the which were there every man in person.[3] The residue that were absent sent their armies, as Polemon king of Pont, Manchus king of Arabia, Herodes king of Jury: and furthermore, Amyntas king of Lycaonia, and of the Galatians: and besides all these, he had all the ayde the king of Medes sent unto him. Now for Cæsar, he had two hundred and fifty shippes of warre, foure score thowsand footemen, and well neare as many horsemen as his enemy Antonius.[4] Antonius for his part, had all under his dominion from Armenia, and the river of Euphrates, unto the sea Ionium and Illyricum.[5] Octavius Cæsar had also for his part, all that which was in our Hemisphære, or halfe part of the world, from Illyria, unto the Occean sea upon the west: then all from the Occean, unto Mare Siculum: and from Africk, all that which is against Italy, as Gaule, and Spayne.[6] Furthermore, all from the province of Cyrenia, unto Æthiopia, was subject unto Antonius. Now Antonius was made so subject to a womans will,[7] that though he was a great deale the stronger by land, yet for Cleopatraes sake, he would needes have this battell tryed by sea[8]: though he sawe before his eyes, that for

[1] *In margin:* 'An ill signe, foreshewed by swallowes breding in Cleopatraes shippe.'

[2] *In margin:* 'Antonius power against Oct. Cæsar.'

[3] *In margin:* 'Antonius had eyght kings, and their power to ayde him.' Cf. III.6.67–76 where some titles are confused.

[4] *In margin:* 'The army and power of Octavius Cæsar against Antonius.'

[5] *In margin:* 'Antonius dominions.'

[6] *In margin:* 'Octavius Cæsars dominions.'

[7] *In margin:* 'Antonius too much ruled by Cleopatra.' III.7.27–8.

[8] II.7.40,48.

lacke of water men, his Captaines did presse by force all sortes of men out of Græce that they could take up in the field, as travellers, muletters, reapers, harvest men, and younge boyes, and yet could they not sufficiently furnishe his gallies: so that the most part of them were empty, and could scant rowe, bicause they lacked water men enowe.[1] But on the contrary side, Cæsars shippes were not built for pompe, highe, and great, onely for a sight and bravery, but they were light of yarage,[2] armed and furnished with water men as many as they needed, and had them all in readines, in the havens of Tarentum, and Brundusium. So Octavius Cæsar sent unto Antonius, to will him to delay no more time, but to come on with his army into Italy: and that for his owne parte he would give him safe harber, to lande without any trouble, and that he would withdraw his armie from the sea, as farre as one horse could runne, until he had put his army a shore, and had lodged his men. Antonius on the other side bravely sent him word againe, and chalenged the combate of him man to man, though he were the elder: and that if he refused him so, he would then fight a battell with him in the fields of Pharsalia, as Julius Cæsar, and Pompey had done before.[3] Now whilest Antonius rode at anker, lying idely in harber at the head of Actium, in the place where the citie of Nicopolis standeth at this present:[4] Cæsar had quickly passed the sea Ionium, and taken a place called Toryne, before Antonius understoode that he had taken shippe. Then began his men to be affraid, bicause his army by land was left behind. But Cleopatra making light of it: And what daunger, I pray you, said she, if Cæsar keepe at Toryne?[5] The next morning by breake of day, his enemies comming with full force of owers in battell against him, Antonius was affraid that if they came to joyne, they would take and cary away his shippes that had no men of warre in them. So he armed all his water men, and set them in order of battell upon the forecastell of their shippes, and then lift up all his rancks of owers towards the element, as well of the one side, as the other, with the prooes against the enemies, at the entry and mouth of the gulfe, which beginneth at the point of Actium, and so kept them in order of battell, as if they had bene armed and furnished with water men and souldiers. Thus Octavius Cæsar beeing finely deceyved by this strastageame, retyred presently, and there-

[1] III.7.34–6. [2] III.7.36–8. [3] III.7.29–34.

[4] *In margin:* 'Antonius rode at anker at the head of Actius: where the citie of Nicopolis standeth.'

[5] *In margin:* 'The grace of this tawnt can not properly be expressed in any other tongue, bicause of the equivocation of this word Toryne, which signifieth a citie of Albania, and also, a ladell to scoome the pot with: as if she ment, Cæsar sat by the fire side, scomming of the pot.' Shakespeare ignores the pun. III.7.20–3.

withall Antonius very wisely and sodainely did cut him of from fresh water. For, understanding that the places where Octavius Cæsar landed, had very litle store of water, and yet very bad: he shut them in with stronge ditches and trenches he cast, to keepe them from salying out at their pleasure, and so to goe seeke water further of. Furthermore, he delt very friendely and curteously with Domitius, and against Cleopatraes mynde. For, he being sicke of an agewe when he went and tooke a litle boate to goe to Cæsars campe, Antonius was very sory for it, but yet he sent after him all his caryage, trayne, and men: and the same Domitius, as though he gave him to understand that he repented his open treason, he died immediatly after.[1] There were certen kings also that forsooke him, and turned on Cæsars side: as Amyntas, and Deiotarus.[2] Furthermore, his fleete and navy that was unfortunate in all thinges, and unready for service, compelled him to chaunge his minde, and to hazard battell by land. And Canidius also, who had charge of his army by land, when time came to follow Antonius determination: he turned him cleane contrary, and counselled him to send Cleopatra backe againe, and him selfe to retyre into Macedon, to fight there on the maine land. And furthermore told him, that Dicomes king of the Getes, promised him to ayde him with a great power: and that it should be no shame nor dishonor to him to let Cæsar have the sea, (bicause him selfe and his men both had bene well practised and exercised in battels by sea, in the warre of Sicilia against Sextus Pompeius) but rather that he should doe against all reason, he having so great skill and experience of battells by land as he had, if he should not employ the force and valliantnes of so many lusty armed footemen as he had ready, but would weaken his army by deviding them into shippes.[3] But now, notwithstanding all these good perswasions, Cleopatra forced him to put all to the hazard of battel by sea: considering with her selfe how she might flie, and provide for her safetie, not to helpe him to winne the victory, but to flie more easily after the battel lost. Betwixt Antonius campe and his fleete of shippes, there was a great hie point of firme lande that ranne a good waye into the sea, the which Antonius often used for a walke, without mistrust of feare or daunger. One of Cæsars men perceived it, and told his Maister that he would laugh and they could take up Antonius in the middest of his walke.[4] Thereuppon Cæsar sent some

[1] *In margin:* 'Domitius forsaketh Antonius, and goeth unto Octavius Cæsar.' Cf. Enobarbus III.11.194–200; IV. 5; IV.7.30ff.

[2] *In margin:* 'Amyntas, and Deiotarus, do both revolt from Antonius, and goe unto Cæsar.'

[3] Cf. Enobarbus in III.7.

[4] *In margin:* 'Antonius in daunger of taking at Actium.'

of his men to lye in ambush for him, and they missed not much of taking of him: for they tooke him that came before him, bicause they discovered to soone, and so Antonius scaped verie hardly. So when Antonius had determined to fight by sea, he set all the other shippes a fire, but three score shippesof Ægypt, and reserved onely but the best and greatest gallies, from three bancks, unto tenne bancks of owers. Into them he put two and twenty thowsand fighting men, with two thowsand darters and slingers. Now, as he was setting his men in order of battel, there was a Captaine, and a valliant man, that had served Antonius in many battels and conflicts, and had all his body hacked and cut: who as Antonius passed by him, cryed out unto him, and sayd: O noble Emperor, how commeth it to pass that you trust to these vile brittle shippes? what, doe you mistrust these woundes of myne, and this sword? let the Ægyptians and Phænicians fight by sea, and set us on the maine land, where we use to conquer, or to be slayne on our feete.[1] Antonius passed by him, and sayd never a word, but only beckoned to him with his hand and head, as though he willed him to be of good corage, although in deede he had no great corage him selfe. For when the Masters of the gallies and Pilots would have let their sailes alone, he made them clap them on, saying to culler the matter withall, that not one of his enemies should scape. All that day, and the three dayes following, the sea rose so high, and was so boysterous, that the battel was put of. The fift day the storme ceased, and the sea calmed againe, and then they rowed with force of owers in battaile one against the other[2]: Antonius leading the right wing with Publicola, and Cælius the left, and Marcus Octavius, and Marcus Justeius the middest.[3] Octavius Cæsar on thother side, had placed Agrippa in the left winge of his armye, and had kept the right winge for him selfe. For the armies by lande, Canidius was generall of Antonius side, and Taurus of Cæsars side[4]: who kept their men in battell raye the one before the other, uppon the sea side, without stirring one agaynst the other.[5] Further, touching both the Chieftaynes: Antonius being in a swift pinnase, was caried up and downe by force of owers through his army, and spake to his people to encorage them to fight valliantly, as if they were on maine land, bicause of the steadines and heavines of their ships: and commaunded the Pilots and masters of the gallies, that they should not sturre, none otherwise then if they were at anker, and so to receive the first charge of their enemies, and that

[1] *In margin:* 'Antonius regardeth not the good counsell of his souldier.' III.7.61–70.

[2] *In margin:* 'Battail by sea at Actium, betwixt Antonius and Cæsar.'

[3] Alluded to at III.7.72–3.

[4] III.7.70–1; 74; 77–8.

[5] Cf. Octavius, III.8.3–4; and 10 *s.d.*

they should not goe out of the straight of the gulfe. Cæsar betymes in the morning going out of his tent, to see his ships thorough out: met a man by chaunce that drave an asse before him. Cæsar asked the man what his name was. The poore man told him, his name was Eutychus, to say, fortunate: and his asses name Nicon, to say, Conquerer.[1] Therefore Cæsar after he had wonne the battell, setting out the market place with the spurres of the gallies he had taken, for a signe of his victorie: he caused also the man and his asse to be set up in brasse. When he had visited the order of his armie thorough out, he tooke a litle pinnase, and went to the right wing, and wondered when he sawe his enemies lye stil in the straight, and sturred not. For, decerning them a farre of, men would have thought they had bene shippes riding at anker, and a good while he was so perswaded: so he kept his gallies eight furlong from his enemies. About noone there rose a litle gale of winde from the sea, and then Antonius men waxing angry with tarying so long, and trusting to the greatnes and height of their shipps, as if they had bene invincible: they began to march forward with their left wing. Cæsar seeing that, was a glad man, and began a litle to give backe from the right wing, to allure them to come further out of the straight and gulfe: to thend that he might with his light shippes well manned with water men, turne and environe the gallies of the enemies, the which were heavy of yarage, both for their biggenes, as also for lacke of watermen to row them. When the skirmish began, and that they came to joyne, there was no great hurt at the first meeting, neither did the shippes vehemently hit one against the other, as they doe commonly in fight by sea. For on the one side, Antonius shippes for their heavines, could not have the strength and swiftnes to make their blowes of any force: and Cæsars shippes on thother side tooke great heede, not to rushe and shocke with the forecastells of Antonius shippes, whose proues were armed with great brasen spurres. Furthermore they durst not flancke them, bicause their points were easily broken, which way soever they came to set upon his shippes, that were made of great mayne square peeces of tymber, bounde together with great iron pinnes: so that the battel was much like to a battel by land, or to speake more properly, to the assault of a citie. For there were alwaies three or foure of Cæsars shippes about one of Antonius shippes, and the souldiers fought with their pykes, halberds, and darts, and threw pots and darts with fire. Antonius ships on the other side bestowed among them, with their crosbowes and engines of battery, great store of shot from their highe towers of wodde, that

[1] *In margin:* 'A lucky signe unto Octavius Cæsar. Eutychus Nicon, fortunate Conqueror.'

were apon their shippes. Now Publicola seing Agrippa put forth his left wing of Cæsars army, to compasse in Antonius shippes that fought: he was driven also to loose of to have more roome, and going a litle at one side, to put those further of that were affraid, and in the middest of the battel. For they were sore distressed by Aruntius. Howbeit the battell was yet of even hand, and the victorie doubtfull, being indifferent to both: when sodainely they saw the three score shippes of Cleopatra busie about their yard masts, and hoysing saile to flie.[1] So they fled through the middest of them that were in fight, for they had bene placed behind the great shippes, and did marvelously disorder the other shippes. For the enemies them selves wondred much to see them saile in that sort, with ful saile towards Peloponnesus.[2] There Antonius shewed plainely, that he had not onely lost the corage and hart of an Emperor, but also of a valliant man, and that he was not his owne man: (proving that true which an old man spake in myrth, that the soule of a lover lived in another body, and not in his owne)[3] he was so caried away with the vaine love of this woman, as if he had bene glued unto her, and that she could not have removed without moving of him also. For when he saw Cleopatraes shippe under saile, he forgot, forsooke, and betrayed them that fought for him, and imbarked upon a galley with five bankes of owers, to follow her that had already begon to overthrow him, and would in the end be his utter destruction.[4] When she knew this galley a farre of, she lift up a signe in the poope of her shippe, and so Antonius comming to it, was pluckt up where Cleopatra was, howbeit he saw her not at his first comming, nor she him, but went and sate down alone in the prowe of his shippe, and said never a word, clapping his head betwene both his hands. In the meane time came certaine light brigantynes of Cæsars that followed him hard. So Antonius straight turned the prowe of his shippe, and presently put the rest to flight, saving one Eurycles Lacedæmonian, that followed him neare, and prest upon him with great corage, shaking a dart in his hand over the prow, as though he would have throwen it unto Antonius. Antonius seing him, came to the fore castell of his ship, and asked him what he was that durst follow Antonius so neare? I am, aunswered he, Eurycles, the sonne of Lachares, who through Cæsars good fortune seketh to revenge the death of my father. This Lachares was condemned of fellonie, and beheaded by Antonius. But yet Eurycles durst not venter on Antonius shippe, but set upon the other Admirall galley (for there were two)

[1] *In margin:* 'Cleopatra flyeth.' III.8.11–25. [2] III.8.40.
[3] *In margin:* 'The soule of a lover liveth in another body.'
[4] *In margin:* 'Antonius flyeth after Cleopatra.' III.8.27–38.

and fell with him with such a blowe of his brasen spurre, that was so heavy and bigge, that he turned her round, and tooke her, with another that was loden with very rich stuffe and cariage. After Eurycles had left Antonius, he returned againe to his place, and sate downe, speaking never a word as he did before: and so lived three dayes alone, without speaking to any man. But when he arrived at the head of Tænarus, there Cleopatraes women first brought Antonius and Cleopatra to speake together, and afterwards, to suppe and lye together.[1] Then beganne there agayne a great number of Marchaunts shippes to gather about them, and some of their friends that had escaped from this overthrow: who brought newes, that his army by sea was overthrowen, but that they thought the army by land was yet whole. Then Antonius sent unto Canidius, to returne with his army into Asia, by Macedon. Now for him self, he determined to crosse over into Africk, and toke one of his carects or hulks loden with gold and silver, and other rich cariage, and gave it unto his friends: commaunding them to depart, and to seeke to save them selves. They aunswered him weeping, that they would nether doe it, nor yet forsake him. Then Antonius very curteously and lovingly did comfort them, and prayed them to depart[2]: and wrote unto Theophilus governor of Corinthe, that he would see them safe, and helpe to hide them in some secret place, until they had made their way and peace with Cæsar.[3] This Theophilus was the father of Hipparchus, who was had in great estimation about Antonius. He was the first of all his infranchised bondmen that revolted from him, and yelded unto Cæsar, and afterwardes went and dwelt at Corinthe. And thus it stoode with Antonius. Now for his armie by sea, that fought before the head or foreland of Actium: they helde out a longe tyme, and nothing troubled them more then a great boysterous wind that rose full in the prooes of their shippes, and yet with much a doe, his navy was at length overthrowen, five howers within night.[4] There were not slaine above five thowsand men: but yet there were three hundred shippes taken, as Octavius Cæsar writeth him selfe in his *Commentaries*. Many plainely sawe Antonius flie, and yet could hardly beleeve it, that he that had nyneteene legions whole by lande, and twelve thowsand horsemen upon the sea side, would so have forsaken them, and have fled so cowardly: as if he had not oftentimes proved both the one and the other fortune, and that he had not bene throughly acquainted with the divers chaunges and fortunes of battells. And yet his souldiers

[1] III.9.25–74.

[2] *In margin:* 'Antonius lycenceth his friends to depart, and giveth them a shippe loden with gold and silver.' III.9.1–24.

[3] III.9.15–17.

[4] *In margin:* 'Antonius navy overthrowen by Cæsar.'

still wished for him, and ever hoped that he would come by some meanes or other unto them. Furthermore, they shewed them selves so valliant and faithfull unto him, that after they certainly knewe he was fled, they kept them selves whole together seven daies. In the ende Canidius, Antonius Lieuetenant, flying by night, and forsaking his campe: when they saw them selves thus destitute of their heads and leaders, they yelded themselves unto the stronger.[1] This done, Cæsar sailed towards Athens, and there made peace with the Græcians, and devided the rest of the corne that was taken up for Antonius army, unto the townes and cities of Græce, the which had bene brought to extreme misery and poverty, cleane without money, slaves, horse, and other beastes of cariage. So that my grandfather Nicarchus tolde, that all the Citizens of our citie of Chæronea, (not one excepted) were driven them selves to cary a certaine measure of corne on their shoulders to the sea side, that lieth directly over against the Ile of Anticyra, and yet were they driven thether with whippes. They caried it thus but once: for, the second tyme that they were charged againe to make the like cariage, all the corne being ready to be caried, newes came that Antonius had lost the battel, and so scaped our poore city. For Antonius souldiers and deputies fled immediatly, and the citizens devided the corne amongst them. Antonius being arrived in Libya, he sent Cleopatra before into Ægypt from the citie of Paraetonium: and he him selfe remained very solitary, having onely two of his friends with him, with whom he wandred up and down, both of them orators, the one Aristocrates a Græcian, and the other Lucilius a Romane. Of whom we have written in an other place,[2] that at the battell where Brutus was overthrowen, by the citie of Philippes, he came and willingly put him self into the hands of those that followed Brutus, saying that it was he: bicause Brutus in the meane time might have liberty to save him selfe. And afterwards bicause Antonius saved his life, he still remained with him: and was very faithfull and frendly unto him till his death.[3] But when Antonius heard, that he whom he had trusted with the government of Libya, and unto whom he had geven the charge of his armie there, had yelded unto Cæsar: he was so madde withall, that he would have slaine him selfe for anger, had not his frendes about him withstoode him, and kept him from it. So he went unto Alexandria, and there found Cleopatra about a wonderfull enterprise, and of great

[1] *In margin:* 'Antonius legions doe yeld them selves unto Octavius Cæsar.' III.8.42–4.

[2] *In margin:* 'Lucilius spoken of in Brutus life.' *supra*, 129; and *JC.* V.4.

[3] *In margin:* 'The fidelitie of Lucilius unto Antonius.'

attempt.[1] Betwixt the redde sea, and the sea betwene the landes that poynt upon the coast of Ægypt, there is a litle peece of land that devideth both the seas, and separateth Africke from Asia: the which straight is so narrow at the end where the two seas are narrowest, that it is not above three hundred furlonges over. Cleopatra went about to lift her shippes out of the one sea, and to hale them over the straight into the other sea: that when her shippes were come into this goulfe of Arabia, she might then carie all her gold and silver away, and so with a great companie of men goe and dwell in some place about the Ocean sea farre from the sea Mediterranium, to scape the daunger and bondage of this warre. But now, bicause the Arabians dwelling about the citie of Petra, did burne the first shippes that were brought alande, and that Antonius thought that his armie by lande, which he left at Actium was yet whole: she left of her enterprise, and determined to keepe all the portes and passages of her realme. Antonius, he forsooke the citie and companie of his frendes,[2] and built him a house in the sea, by the Ile of Pharos, upon certaine forced mountes which he caused to be cast into the sea, and dwelt there, as a man that banished him selfe from all mens companie: saying that he would lead Timons life, bicause he had the like wrong offered him, that was affore offered unto Timon: and that for the unthankefulnes of those he had done good unto, and whom he tooke to be his frendes, he was angry with all men, and would trust no man. [For Plutarch's account of Timon see the next volume.] But now to returne to Antonius againe. Canidius him selfe came to bring him newes, that he had lost all his armie by land at Actium. On thother side he was advertised also, that Herodes king of Jurie, who had also certeine legions and bandes with him, was revolted unto Cæsar, and all the other kings in like maner[3]: so that, saving those that were about him, he had none left him. All this notwithstanding did nothing trouble him, and it seemed that he was contented to forgoe all his hope, and so to be ridde of all his care and troubles. Thereupon he left his solitarie house he had built in the sea which he called Timoneon, and Cleopatra received him into her royall pallace. He was no sooner comen thither, but he straight set all the city of rioting and banketing againe, and him selfe, to liberalitie and giftes.[4] He caused the sonne of Julius Cæsar and Cleopatra, to be enrolled (according to the maner of the Romanes) amongest the

[1] *In margin:* 'The wonderful attempt of Cleopatra.'

[2] *In margin:* 'Antonius followeth the life and example of Timon Misanthropus the Athenian.'

[3] Cf. Canidius, III.8.43–4.

[4] *In margin:* 'Antonius rioting in Alexandria after his great losse and overthrow.'

number of young men: and gave Antyllus, his eldest sonne he had by Fulvia, the mans gowne, the which was a plaine gowne, without gard or imbroderie of purple.[1] For these things, there was kept great feasting, banketing, and dauncing in Alexandria many dayes together. In deede they did breake their first order they had set downe, which they called Amimetobion, (as much to say, no life comparable) and did set up an other which they called Synapothanumenon (signifying the order and agreement of those that will dye together) the which in exceeding sumptuousnes and cost was not inferior to the first.[2] For their frendes made them selves to be inrolled in this order of those that would dye together, and so made great feastes one to an other: for everie man when it came to his turne, feasted their whole companie and fraternitie. Cleopatra in the meane time was verie carefull in gathering all sorts of poysons together to destroy men.[3] Now to make proofe of those poysons which made men dye with least paine, she tried it upon condemned men in prison. For when she saw the poysons that were sodaine and vehement, and brought speedy death with grievous torments: and in contrary maner, that suche as were more milde and gentle, had not that quicke speede and force to make one dye sodainly: she afterwardes went about to prove the stinging of snakes and adders, and made some to be applied unto men in her sight, some in one sorte, and some in an other. So when she had dayly made divers and sundrie proofes, she found none of all them she had proved so fit, as the biting of an Aspicke, the which only causeth a heavines of the head, without swounding or complaining, and bringeth a great desire also to sleepe, with a litle swet in the face, and so by litle and litle taketh away the sences and vitall powers, no living creature perceiving that the pacientes feele any paine.[4] For they are so sorie when any bodie waketh them, and taketh them up: as those that being taken out of a sound sleepe, are very heavy and desirous to sleepe. This notwithstanding, they sent Ambassadors unto Octavius Cæsar in Asia, Cleopatra requesting the realme of Ægypt for her children, and Antonius praying that he might be suffered to live at Athens like a private man, if Cæsar would not let him remaine in Ægypt.[5] And bicause they had no other men of estimacion about

[1] *In margin:* '*Toga virilis.* Antillus, the eldest sonne of Antonius by his wife Fulvia.'

[2] *In margin:* 'An order erected by Antonius, and Cleopatra, called Synapothanumenon, revoking the former called Amimetobion.'

[3] *In margin:* 'Cleopatra verie busie in proving the force of poyson.' V.2.351–3.

[4] *In margin:* 'The property of the biting of an Aspick.' Cf. V.2.242–56; 307–9.

[5] *In margin:* 'Antonius and Cleopatra send Ambassadors unto Octavius Cæsar.' III.10.6–19.

them, for that some were fledde, and those that remained, they did not greatly trust them: they were inforced to sende Euphronius the schoolemaister of their children.[1] For Alexas Laodician, who was brought into Antonius house and favor by meanes of Timagenes, and afterwards was in greater credit with him, then any other Grecian: (for that he had alway bene one of Cleopatraes ministers to win Antonius, and to overthrow all his good determinations to use his wife Octavia well) him Antonius had sent unto Herodes king of Jurie, hoping still to keepe him his frend, that he should not revolt from him. But he remained there, and betrayed Antonius. For where he should have kept Herodes from revolting from him, he perswaded him to turne to Cæsar: and trusting king Herodes, he presumed to come in Cæsars presence. Howbeit Herodes did him no pleasure: for he was presently taken prisoner, and sent in chaines to his owne contrie, and there by Cæsars commaundement put to death. Thus was Alexas in Antonius life time put to death, for betraying of him.[2] Furthermore, Cæsar would not graunt unto Antonius requests: but for Cleopatra, he made her aunswere, that he woulde deny her nothing reasonable, so that she would either put Antonius to death, or drive him out of her contrie.[3] Therewithall he sent Thyreus one of his men unto her, a verie wise and discreete man, who bringing letters of credit from a young Lorde unto a noble Ladie, and that besides greatly liked her beawtie, might easely by his eloquence have perswaded her.[4] He was longer in talke with her then any man else was, and the Queene her selfe also did him great honor: insomuch as he made Antonius gealous of him.[5] Whereupon Antonius caused him to be taken and well favoredly whipped, and so sent him unto Cæsar[6]: and bad him tell him that he made him angrie with him, bicause he shewed him selfe prowde and disdainfull towards him, and now specially when he was easie to be angered, by reason of his present miserie. To be short, if this mislike thee said he, thou hast Hipparchus one of my infranchised bondmen with thee: hang him if thou wilt, or whippe him at thy pleasure, that we may crie quittaunce.[7] From thenceforth, Cleopatra to cleere her selfe of the suspicion he had of her, she made more of him then ever she did. For first of all, where she did solemnise the day of her birth very meanely and sparingly, fit for her present misfortune: she now in contrary maner did keepe it with such solemnitie, that she exceeded all measure of sumptuousnes and magnificence: so that the ghests that were bidden to the feasts, and came poore, went

[1] III.10.1–10. [2] *In margin:* 'Alexas treason justly punished.' IV.6.12–16.
[3] III.10.19–24. [4] III.10.26ff. [5] III.11.46–86.
[6] III.11.88–139. [7] III.11.139–52.

away rich.[1] Nowe things passing thus, Agrippa by divers letters sent one after an other unto Cæsar, prayed him to returne to Rome, bicause the affaires there did of necessity require his person and presence. Thereupon he did deferre the warre till the next yeare following[2]: but when winter was done, he returned againe through Syria by the coast of Africke, to make warres against Antonius, and his other Captaines. When the citie of Pelusium was taken,[3] there ran a rumor in the citie, that Seleucus, by Cleopatraes consent, had surrendered the same. But to cleere her selfe that she did not, Cleopatra brought Seleucus wife and children unto Antonius, to be revenged of them at his pleasure. Furthermore, Cleopatra had long before made many sumptuous tombes and monumentes, as well for excellencie of workemanshippe, as for height and greatnes of building, joyning hard to the temple of Isis.[4] Thither she caused to be brought all the treasure and pretious things she had of the auncient kings her predecessors: as gold, silver, emerods, pearles, ebbanie, ivorie, and sinnamon, and besides all that, a marvelous number of torches, faggots, and flaxe. So Octavius Cæsar being affrayed to loose suche a treasure and masse of riches, and that this woman for spight would set it a fire, and burne it every whit: he alwayes sent some one or other unto her from him, to put her in good comfort, whilest he in the meane time drewe neere the citie with his armie. So Cæsar came, and pitched his campe hard by the city, in the place where they runne and manage their horses. Antonius made a saly upon him, and fought verie valliantly, so that he drave Cæsars horsemen backe, fighting with his men even into their campe.[5] Then he came againe to the pallace, greatly boasting of this victorie, and sweetely kissed Cleopatra, armed as he was, when he came from the fight, recommending one of his men of armes unto her, that had valliantly fought in this skirmish. Cleopatra to reward his manlines, gave him an armor and head peece of cleane gold[6]: howbeit the man at armes when he had received this rich gift, stale away by night, and went to Cæsar. Antonius sent againe to chalenge Cæsar, to fight with him hande to hande. Cæsar aunswered him, that he had many other wayes to dye then so.[7] Then Antonius seeing there was no way more honorable for him to dye, then fighting valliantly: he determined to sette up his rest, both by sea and lande.[8] So being at supper, (as it is reported) he commaunded his officers and household servauntes that waited on him at his bord, that they

[1] III.11.152–93. [2] Cf. Mecænas, IV.1.8: 'Give him no breath.'
[3] *In margin:* 'Pelusium was yeelded up to Octavius Cæsar.'
[4] *In margin:* 'Cleopatraes monuments set up by the temple of Isis.'
[5] IV.7; IV.8.1. [6] IV.8.2–27. [7] IV.1.1–6. [8] IV.2.1–5.

should fill his cuppes full, and make as muche of him as they could: for said he, you know not whether you shall doe so much for me to morrow or not, or whether you shall serve an other maister: and it may be you shall see me no more, but a dead bodie. This notwithstanding, perceiving that his frends and men fell a weeping to heare him say so: to salve that he had spoken, he added this more unto it, that he would not leade them to battell, where he thought not rather safely to returne with victorie, then valliantly to dye with honor.[1] Furthermore, the selfe same night within litle of midnight, when all the citie was quiet, full of feare and sorrowe, thinking what would be the issue and ende of this warre: it is said that sodainly they heard a marvelous sweete harmonie of sundrie sortes of instrumentes of musicke, with the crie of a multitude of people, as they had bene dauncing, and had song as they use in Bacchus feastes, with movinges and turninges after the maner of the Satyres: and it seemed that this daunce went through the city unto the gate that opened to the enemies, and that all the troupe that made this noise they heard, went out of the city at that gate.[2] Now, such as in reason sought the depth of the interpretacion of this wonder, thought that it was the god unto whom Antonius bare singular devotion to counterfeate and resemble him, that did forsake them.[3] The next morning by breake of day, he went to set those few footemen he had in order upon the hills adjoyning unto the citie: and there he stoode to behold his gallies which departed from the haven, and rowed against the gallies of his enemies, and so stoode still, looking what exployte his souldiers in them would do. But when by force of rowing they were come neere unto them, they first saluted Cæsars men: and then Cæsars men resaluted them also, and of two armies made but one,[4] and then did all together row toward the citie. When Antonius sawe that his men did forsake him, and yeelded unto Cæsar, and that his footemen were broken and overthrowen: he then fled into the citie, crying out that Cleopatra had betrayed him unto them, with whom he had made warre for her sake.[5] Then she being affraied of his fury, fled into the tombe which she had caused to be made, and there locked the dores unto her, and shut all the springes of the lockes with great boltes, and in the meane time sent unto Antonius to tell him that she was dead.[6] Antonius

[1] IV.2.9ff.

[2] *In margin:* 'Straunge noises heard, and nothing seene.' Cf. IV.3.3–22.

[3] IV.3.16–17.

[4] *In margin:* 'Antonius navie doe yeeld them selves unto Cæsar.' IV.10.1–9; 22–6.

[5] *In margin:* 'Antonius overthrowen by Octavius Cæsar.' IV.10.22–62.

[6] *In margin:* 'Cleopatra flieth into her tombe or monument.' IV.11.

beleving it, said unto him selfe: What doest thou looke for further, Antonius, sith spitefull fortune hath taken from thee the only joy thou haddest, for whom thou yet reservedst thy life? When he had sayd these words, he went into a chamber and unarmed him selfe,[1] and being naked said thus: O Cleopatra, it grieveth me not that I have lost thy companie, for I will not be long from thee[2]: but I am sory, that having bene so great a Captaine and Emperour, I am in deede condemned to be judged of lesse corage and noble minde, then a woman. Now he had a man of his called Eros, whom he loved and trusted much, and whom he had long before caused to sweare unto him, that he should kill him when he did commaunde him: and then he willed him to keepe his promise. His man drawing his sworde, lift it up as though he had ment to have striken his maister: but turning his head at one side, he thrust his sword into him selfe, and fell downe dead at his maisters foote.[3] Then said Antonius, O noble Eros, I thanke thee for this, and it is valliantly done of thee, to shew me what I should doe to my selfe, which thou couldest not doe for me. Therewithall he tooke his sword, and thrust it into his bellie, and so fell downe upon a litle bed. The wounde he had killed him not presently, for the blood stinted a litle when he was layed: and when he came somwhat to him selfe againe, he praied them that were about him to dispatch him.[4] But they all fled out of the chamber, and left him crying out and tormenting him selfe: untill at last there came a secretarie unto him called Diomedes, who was commaunded to bring him into the tombe or monument where Cleopatra was.[5] When he heard that she was alive, he verie earnestlie prayed his men to carie his bodie thither, and so he was caried in his mens armes into the entry of the monument. Notwithstanding, Cleopatra would not open the gates,[6] but came to the high windowes, and cast out certaine chaines and ropes, in the which Antonius was trussed: and Cleopatra her owne selfe, with two women only, which she had suffered to come with her into these monumentes, trised Antonius up.[7] They that were present to behold it, said they never saw so pitiefull a sight.[8] For, they plucked up poore Antonius all bloody as he was, and drawing on with pangs of death, who holding up his hands to Cleopatra, raised up him selfe as well as he could.

[1] IV.12.35–43. [2] IV.12.44–50.

[3] *In margin:* 'Eros Antonius servant, slue him selfe.' IV.12.54–95.

[4] *In margin:* 'Antonius did thrust his sword into him selfe, but died not presently.' IV.12.95–107.

[5] *In margin:* 'Antonius caried unto Cleopatraes tombe.' IV.12.114ff.

[6] IV.13.21–3. [7] IV.13.29–37.

[8] *In margin:* 'A lamentable sight to see Antonius and Cleopatra.' IV.13.40, 'A heavy sight!'

It was a hard thing for these women to do, to lift him up: but Cleopatra stowping downe with her head, putting to all her strength to her uttermost power, did lift him up with much a doe, and never let goe her hold, with the helpe of the women beneath that bad her be of good corage, and were as sorie to see her labor so, as she her selfe. So when she had gotten him in after that sorte, and layed him on a bed: she rent her garments upon him, clapping her brest, and scratching her face and stomake. Then she dried up his blood that had berayed his face, and called him her Lord, her husband, and Emperour, forgetting her owne miserie and calamity, for the pitie and compassion she tooke of him. Antonius made her ceasse her lamenting, and called for wine, either bicause he was a thirst, or else for that he thought thereby to hasten his death.[1] When he had dronke, he earnestly prayed her, and perswaded her, that she would seeke to save her life, if she could possible, without reproache and dishonor: and that chiefly she should trust Proculeius above any man else about Cæsar. And as for him selfe, that she should not lament nor sorowe for the miserable chaunge of his fortune at the end of his dayes: but rather that she should thinke him the more fortunate, for the former triumphes and honors he had received, considering that while he lived he was the noblest and greatest Prince of the world, and that now he was overcome, not cowardly, but valiantly, a Romane by an other Romane.[2] As Antonius gave the last gaspe, Proculeius came that was sent from Cæsar.[3] For after Antonius had thrust his sworde in him selfe, as they caried him into the tombes and monuments of Cleopatra, one of his gard called Dercetæus, tooke his sword with the which he had striken him selfe, and hidde it: then he secretly stale away, and brought Octavius Cæsar the first newes of his death, and shewed him his sword that was bloodied.[4] Cæsar hearing these newes, straight withdrewe him selfe into a secret place of his tent, and there burst out with teares, lamenting his hard and miserable fortune, that had bene his frende and brother in law, his equall in the Empire, and companion with him in sundry great exploytes and battells.[5] Then he called for all his frendes,[6] and shewed them the letters Antonius had written to him, and his aunsweres also sent him againe, during their quarrell and strife: and how fiercely and prowdly the other answered him, to all just and reasonable matters he wrote unto him. After this, he sent Proculeius, and commaunded him to doe what he

[1] IV.13.42. [2] IV.13.45–58. [3] *In margin:* 'The death of Antonius.'
[4] IV. 12.111–13; V.1.5–13.
[5] *In margin:* 'Octavius Cæsar lamenteth Antonius death.' V.1.14–48.
[6] Here Shakespeare breaks off (V.1.48–9) until 73–7.

could possible to get Cleopatra alive, fearing least otherwise all the treasure would be lost: and furthermore, he thought that if he could take Cleopatra, and bring her alive to Rome, she would marvelously beawtifie and sette out his triumphe.[1] But Cleopatra would never put her selfe into Proculeius handes, although they spake together. For Proculeius came to the gates that were very thicke and strong, and surely barred, but yet there were somc cranewes through the which her voyce might be heard, and so they without understoode, that Cleopatra demaunded the kingdome of Ægypt for her sonnes: and that Proculeius aunswered her, that she should be of good cheere, and not be affrayed to referre all unto Cæsar. After he had viewed the place verie well, he came and reported her aunswere unto Cæsar. Who immediatly sent Gallus to speake once againe with her, and bad him purposely hold her with talke, whilest Proculeius did set up a ladder against that high windowe, by the which Antonius was trised up, and came downe into the monument with two of his men hard by the gate, where Cleopatra stoode to heare what Gallus sayd unto her.[2] One of her women which was shut in her monuments with her, saw Proculeius by chaunce as he came downe, and shreeked out: O, poore Cleopatra, thou art taken.[3] Then when she sawe Proculeius behind her as she came from thc gate, she thought to have stabbed her selfe in with a short dagger she ware of purpose by her side. But Proculeius came sodainly upon her, and taking her by both the hands,[4] said unto her: Cleopatra, first thou shalt doe thy selfe great wrong, and secondly unto Cæsar: to deprive him of the occasion and oportunitie, openly to shew his bountie and mercie, and to geve his enemies cause to accuse the most curteous and noble Prince that ever was, and to appeache him, as though he were a cruell and mercielesse man, that were not to be trusted. So even as hc spake the word, he tooke her dagger from her, and shooke her clothes for feare of any poyson hidden about her. Afterwardes Cæsar sent one of his infranchised men called Epaphroditus,[5] whom he straightly charged to looke well unto her, and to beware in any case that she made not her selfe away: and for the rest, to use her with all the curtesie possible. And for him selfe, he in the meane time entred the citie of Alexandria, and as he went, talked with the Philosopher Arrius, and helde him by the hande, to the end that his contrie men should reverence him the more, bicause

[1] *In margin:* 'Proculeius sent by Octavius Cæsar to bring Cleopatra alive.' V.1.61–9.

[2] This may throw light on V.2.34–6, where F has no *s.d.*

[3] Charmian, V.2.38.

[4] *In margin:* 'Cleopatra taken.' V.2.39–64.

[5] Dolabella in V.2.64ff.

they saw Cæsar so highly esteeme and honor him.[1] Then he went into the show place of exercises, and so up to his chaire of state which was prepared for him of a great height: and there according to his commaundement, all the people of Alexandria were assembled, who quaking for feare, fell downe on their knees before him, and craved mercie. Cæsar bad them all stande up, and told them openly that he forgave the people, and pardoned the felonies and offences they had committed against him in this warre. First, for the founders sake of the same citie, which was Alexander the great: secondly, for the beawtie of the citie, which he muche esteemed and wondred at: thirdly, for the love he bare unto his verie frend Arrius. Thus did Cæsar honor Arrius, who craved pardon for him selfe and many others, and specially for Philostratus, the eloquentest man of all the sophisters and Orators of his time, for present and sodaine speech: howbeit he falsly named him selfe an Academicke Philosopher.[2] Therefore, Cæsar that hated his nature and condicions, would not heare his sute. Thereupon he let his gray beard grow long, and followed Arrius steppe by steppe in a long mourning gowne, still bussing in his eares this Greeke verse:

> A wise man if that he be wise in deede,
> May by a wise man have the better speede.

Cæsar understanding this, not for the desire he had to deliver Philostratus of his feare, as to ridde Arrius of malice and envy that might have fallen out against him: he pardoned him. Now touching Antonius sonnes, Antyllus, his eldest sonne by Fulvia was slaine, bicause his schoolemaister Theodorus did betray him unto the souldiers, who strake of his head.[3] And the villaine tooke a pretious stone of great value from his necke, the which he did sowe in his girdell, and afterwards denied that he had it: but it was founde about him, and so Cæsar trussed him up for it. For Cleopatraes children, they were verie honorablie kept, with their governors and traine that waited on them.[4] But for Cæsarion, who was sayd to be Julius Cæsars sonne: his mother Cleopatra had sent him unto the Indians through Æthiopia, with a great summe of money. But one of his governors also called Rhodon, even such an other as Theodorus, perswaded him to returne into his contrie, and told him that

[1] *In margin:* 'Cæsar tooke the citie of Alexandria. Cæsar greatly honored Arrius the Philosopher.'

[2] *In margin:* 'Philostratus, the eloquentest Orator in his time, for present speech upon a sodaine.' Cf. Mary Sidney's Act II and Daniel's Act III.

[3] *In margin:* 'Antyllus, Antonius eldest sonne by Fulvia, slaine.'

[4] Cf. V.2.129–32.

Cæsar sent for him to geve him his mothers kingdom. So, as Cæsar was determining with him selfe what he should doe, Arrius sayd unto him:

Too Many Cæsars is not good[1]:

alluding unto a certaine verse of Homer that sayth:

Too Many Lords doth not well.

Therefore Cæsar did put Cæsarion to death, after the death of his mother Cleopatra.[2] Many Princes, great kings and Captaines did crave Antonius body of Octavius Cæsar, to give him honorable burial: but Cæsar would never take it from Cleopatra, who did sumptuously and royally burie him with her owne handes, whom Cæsar suffred to take as much as she would to bestow upon his funeralls. [3] Now was she altogether overcome with sorow and passion of minde, for she had knocked her brest so pitiefully, that she had martired it, and in divers places had raised ulsers and inflamacions, so that she fell into a fever withal: whereof she was very glad, hoping thereby to have good colour to absteine from meate, and that so she might have dyed easely without any trouble. She had a Phisition called Olympus, whom she made privie of her intent, to thend he shoulde helpe her to ridde her out of her life: as Olympus wryteth him selfe, who wrote a booke of all these thinges.[4] But Cæsar mistrusted the matter, by many conjectures he had, and therefore did put her in feare, and threatned her to put her children to shameful death.[5] With these threats, Cleopatra for feare yelded straight, as she would have yelded unto strokes: and afterwards suffred her selfe to be cured and dieted as they listed. Shortly after, Cæsar came him selfe in person to see her, and to comfort her.[6] Cleopatra being layed upon a litle low bed in poore estate, when she sawe Cæsar come in to her chamber, she sodainly rose up, naked in her smocke, and fell downe at his feete marvelously disfigured: both for that she had plucked her heare from her head, as also for that she had martired all her face with her nailes, and besides, her voyce was small and trembling, her eyes sonke into her heade with continuall blubbering: and moreover, they might see the most parte of her stomake torne in sunder.[7] To be short, her bodie was not much

[1] *In margin:* 'The saying of Arrius the Philosopher.' Cf. Daniel, l. 576.

[2] *In margin:* 'Cæsarion Cleopatraes sonne, put to death.'

[3] *In margin:* 'Cleopatra burieth Antonius.'

[4] *In margin:* 'Olympus Cleopatraes Phisition.'

[5] V.2.127–32.

[6] *In margin:* 'Cæsar came to see Cleopatra.'

[7] *In margin:* 'Cleopatra, a martired creature, through her owne passion and fury.'

better then her minde: yet her good grace and comelynes, and the force of her beawtie was not altogether defaced. But notwithstanding this ougly and pitiefull state of hers, yet she showed her selfe within, by her outward lookes and countenance. When Cæsar had made her lye downe againe, and sate by her beddes side: Cleopatra began to cleere and excuse her selfe for that she had done, laying all to the feare she had of Antonius. Cæsar, in contrarie maner, reproved her in every poynt. Then she sodainly altered her speache, and prayed him to pardon her, as though she were affrayed to dye, and desirous to live.[1] At length, she gave him a breefe and memoriall of all the readie money and treasure she had. But by chaunce there stoode Seleucus[2] by, one of her Treasorers, who to seeme a good servant, came straight to Cæsar to disprove Cleopatra, that she had not set in al, but kept many things back of purpose. Cleopatra was in such a rage with him, that she flew upon him, and tooke him by the heare of the head, and boxed him wellfavoredly. Cæsar fell a laughing, and parted the fray.[3] Alas, said she, O Cæsar: is not this a great shame and reproche, that thou having vouchesaved to take the peines to come unto me, and hast done me this honor, poore wretche, and caitife creature, brought into this pitiefull and miserable estate: and that mine owne servaunts should come now to accuse me, though it may be I have reserved some juells and trifles meete for women, but not for me (poore soule) to set out my selfe withall, but meaning to geve some pretie presents and gifts unto Octavia and Livia, that they making meanes and intercession for me to thee, thou mightest yet extend thy favor and mercie upon me?[4] Cæsar was glad to heare her say so, perswading him selfe thereby that she had yet a desire to save her life. So he made her answere, that he did not only geve her that to dispose of at her pleasure, which she had kept backe, but further promised to use her more honorably and bountifully then she would thinke for: and so he tooke his leave of her, supposing he had deceived her, but in deede he was deceived him selfe.[5] There was a young gentleman Cornelius Dolabella, that was one of Cæsars very great familiars, and besides did beare no evil will unto Cleopatra. He sent her word secretly as she had requested him, that Cæsar determined to take his jorney through Suria, and that within three dayes he would sende her away before with her children.[6]

[1] Cf. V.2.116–22.

[2] *In margin:* 'Seleucus, one of Cleopatraes Treasorers.' In V.2.137–47 she asks him to support her.

[3] *In margin:* 'Cleopatra bet her treasorer before Octavius Cæsar.' V.2.148–57.

[4] *In margin:* 'Cleopatraes wordes unto Cæsar.' V.2.158–70.

[5] *In margin:* 'Cleopatra finely deceiveth Octavius Cæsar, as though she desired to live.' V.2.178–91: 'He words me, girls.'

[6] V.2.196–205.

When this was tolde Cleopatra, she requested Cæsar that it would please him to suffer her to offer the last oblations of the dead, unto the soule of Antonius. This being graunted her, she was caried to the place where his tombe was, and there falling downe on her knees, imbracing the tombe with her women, the teares running downe her cheekes, she began to speake in this sorte[1]: 'O my deare Lord 'Antonius, not long sithence I buried thee here, being a free woman: 'and now I offer unto thee the funerall sprinklinges and oblations, 'being a captive and prisoner, and yet I am forbidden and kept 'from tearing and murdering this captive body of mine with blowes, 'which they carefully gard and keepe, onely to triumphe of thee: 'looke therefore henceforth for no other honors, offeringes, nor sacri-'fices from me, for these are the last which Cleopatra can geve thee, 'sith nowe they carie her away. Whilest we lived together, nothing 'could sever our companies: but now at our death, I feare me they 'will make us chaunge our contries. For as thou being a Romane, 'hast bene buried in Ægypt: even so wretched creature I, an 'Ægyptian, shall be buried in Italie, which shall be all the good that 'I have received by thy contrie. If therefore the gods where thou art 'now have any power and authoritie, sith our gods here have forsaken 'us: suffer not thy true frend and lover to be caried away alive, that 'in me, they triumphe of thee: but receive me with thee,[2] and let me 'be buried in one selfe tombe with thee. For though my griefes and 'miseries be infinite, yet none hath grieved me more, nor that I 'could lesse beare withall: then this small time, which I have bene 'driven to live alone without thee.' Then having ended these doleful plaints, and crowned the tombe with garlands and sundry nosegayes, and marvelous lovingly imbraced the same: she commaunded they should prepare her bath, and when she had bathed and washed her selfe, she fell to her meate, and was sumptuously served.[3] Nowe whilest she was at dinner, there came a contrieman, and brought her a basket. The souldiers that warded at the gates, asked him straight what he had in his basket. He opened the basket, and tooke out the leaves that covered the figges, and shewed them that they were figges he brought. They all of them marvelled to see so goodly figges. The contrieman laughed to heare them, and bad them take some if they would. They beleved he told them truely, and so bad him carie them in.[4] After Cleopatra had dined, she sent a certaine table written and sealed unto Cæsar,[5] and commaunded them all to go out of the tombes where she was, but the two women, then she

[1] *In margin:* 'Cleopatraes lamentation over Antonius tombe.'

[2] Hence V.2.281–5.

[3] Cf. V.2.225–8; 278.

[4] V.2.232ff.

[5] Shakespeare omits this.

shut the dores to her. Cæsar when he received this table, and began to read her lamentation and petition, requesting him that he would let her be buried with Antonius, founde straight what she ment, and thought to have gone thither him selfe: howbeit he sent one before in all hast that might be, to see what it was.[1] Her death was very sodaine.[2] For those whom Cæsar sent unto her ran thither in all hast possible, and found the souldiers standing at the gate, mistrusting nothing, nor understanding of her death. But when they had opened the dores, they founde Cleopatra starke dead, layed upon a bed of gold, attired and araied in her royall robes, and one of her two women, which was called Iras, dead at her feete: and her other woman called Charmion halfe dead, and trembling, trimming the Diademe which Cleopatra ware upon her head.[3] One of the souldiers seeing her, angrily sayd unto her: Is that well done Charmion? Verie well sayd she againe, and meete for a Princes discended from the race of so many noble kings. She sayd no more, but fell downe dead hard by the bed. Some report that this Aspicke was brought unto her in the basket with figs, and that she had commaunded them to hide it under the figge leaves, that when she shoulde thinke to take out the figges, the Aspicke shoulde bite her before she should see her: howbeit, that when she would have taken away the leaves for the figges, she perceived it, and said, Art thou here then? And so, her arme being naked, she put it to the Aspicke to be bitten.[4] Other say againe, she kept it in a boxe, and that she did pricke and thrust it with a spindell of golde, so that the Aspicke being angerd withall, lept out with great furie, and bitte her in the arme. Howbeit fewe can tell the troth. For they report also, that she had hidden poyson in a hollow raser which she caried in the heare of her head: and yet was there no marke seene of her bodie, or any signe discerned that she was poysoned, neither also did they finde this serpent in her tombe. But it was reported onely, that there were seene certeine fresh steppes or trackes where it had gone, on the tombe side toward the sea, and specially by the dores side.[5] Some say also, that they found two litle pretie bytings in her arme, scant to be discerned: the which it seemeth Cæsar him selfe gave credit unto, bicause in his triumphe he caried Cleopatraes image, with an Aspicke byting of her arme[6]. And thus goeth the report of her death.

[1] Dolabella, V.2.326. [2] *In margin:* 'The death of Cleopatra.'

[3] *In margin:* 'Cleopatraes two waiting women dead with her.' V.2.290; 316–26; 337–41.

[4] *In margin:* 'Cleopatra killed with the biting of an Aspicke.' Cf. V.2.301–10.

[5] V.2.341–50.

[6] *In margin:* 'The image of Cleopatra, caried in triumphe at Rome, with an Aspicke biting of her arme.'

Now Cæsar, though he was marvelous sorie for the death of Cleopatra, yet he wondred at her noble minde and corage, and therefore commaunded she should be nobly buried, and layed by Antonius[1]: and willed also that her two women shoulde have honorable buriall. Cleopatra dyed being eight and thirtie yeare olde, after she had raigned two and twenty yeres, and governed above foureteene of them with Antonius. And for Antonius, some say that he lived three and fiftie yeares: and others say, six and fiftie.[2] All his statues, images, and mettalls, were plucked downe and overthrowen, saving those of Cleopatra which stoode still in their places, by meanes of Archibius one of her frendes, who gave Cæsar a thowsande talentes that they should not be handled, as those of Antonius were. Antonius left seven children by three wives, of the which, Cæsar did put Antyllus, the eldest sonne he had by Fulvia, to death. Octavia his wife tooke all the rest, and brought them up with hers, and maried Cleopatra, Antonius daughter, unto Juba, a marvelous curteous and goodly Prince. And Antonius, the sonne of Fulvia came to be so great, that next unto Agrippa, who was in greatest estimacion about Cæsar, and next unto the children of Livia, which were the second in estimacion: he had the third place. Furthermore, Octavia having had two daughters by her first husband Marcellus, and a sonne also called Marcellus: Cæsar maried his daughter unto that Marcellus, and so did adopt him for his sonne. And Octavia also maried one of her daughters unto Agrippa. But when Marcellus was deade, after he had bene maried a while, Octavia perceiving that her brother Cæsar was very busie to choose some one among his frends, whom he trusted best to make his sonne in law: she perswaded him, that Agrippa should mary his daughter, (Marcellus widow) and leave her owne daughter. Cæsar first was contented withall, and then Agrippa: and so she afterwards tooke away her daughter and maried her unto Antonius, and Agrippa married Julia, Cæsars daughter. Now there remained two daughters more of Octavia and Antonius. Domitius Ænobarbus maried the one: and the other, which was Antonia, so fayer and vertuous a young Ladie, was maried unto Drusus the sonne of Livia, and sonne in law of Cæsar. Of this mariage, came Germanicus and Clodius: of the which, Clodius afterwards came to be Emperour.[3] And of the sonnes of Germanicus, the one whose name was Caius, came also to be Emperour: who, after he had licentiously raigned a time, was slaine, with his wife and daughter. Agrippina also, having a sonne by her

[1] V.2.353–7.

[2] *In margin:* 'The age of Cleopatra and Antonius.'

[3] *In margin:* 'Of Antonius issue came Emperors.'

first husbande Ænobarbus called Lucius Domitius: was afterwardes maried unto Clodius, who adopted her sonne, and called him Nero Germanicus. This Nero was Emperour in our time, and slue his owne mother, and had almost destroyed the Empire of Rome, through his madnes and wicked life, being the fift Emperour of Rome after Antonius.

THE COMPARISON OF DEMETRIUS WITH ANTONIUS

Now, sithence it falleth out, that Demetrius and Antonius were one of them much like to the other, having fortune a like divers and variable unto them: let us therefore come to consider their power and authoritie, and how they came to be so great.[1] First of all, it is certaine that Demetrius power and greatnes fell unto him by inheritance from his father Antigonus: who became the greatest and mightiest Prince of all the successors of Alexander, and had won the most parte of Asia, before Demetrius came of full age. Antonius in contrary maner, borne of an honest man, who otherwise was no man of warre, and had not left him any meane to arise to such greatnes; durst take upon him to contend for the Empire with Cæsar, that had no right unto it by inheritaunce, but yet made him selfe successor of the power, the which the other by great paine and travell had obteyned, and by his owne industrie became so great, without the helpe of any other: that the Empire of the whole worlde being devided into two partes, he had the one halfe, and tooke that of the greatest countenaunce and power. Antonius being absent, oftentimes overcame the Parthians in battell by his Lieutenaunts, and chased away the barbarous people dwelling about mount Caucasus, unto the sea Hyrcanium: insomuche as the thing they most reprove him for, did most witnes his greatnes. For, Demetrius father made him gladly marrie Phila, Antipaters daughter, although she was too old for him: bicause she was of a nobler house then him selfe. Antonius on thother side was blamed for marying of Cleopatra, a Queene that for power and nobilitie of blood, excelled all other kings in her time, but Arsaces: and moreover made him selfe so great, that others thought him worthie of greater things, then he him selfe required. Now for the desire that moved the one and the other to conquer realmes[2]: the desire of Demetrius was unblameable and just, desiring to raigne over people,

[1] *In margin:* 'The power of Demetrius and Antonius.' Demetrius of Macedonia d. 286 B.C.

[2] *In margin:* 'Demetrius and Antonius ambition to governe.'

which had bene governed at all times, and desired to be governed by kings. But Antonius desire was altogether wicked and tyrannicall: who sought to keepe the people of Rome in bondage and subjection, but lately before rid of Cæsars raigne and government. For the greatest and most famous exployte Antonius ever did in warres (to wit, the warre in the which he overthrew Cassius and Brutus) was begon to no other ende, but to deprive his contriemen of their libertie and freedom. Demetrius in contrarie maner, before fortune had overthrowen him, never left to set Græce at libertie, and to drive the garrisons away, which kept the cities in bondage: and not like Antonius, that bosted he had slaine them that had set Rome at libertie. The chiefest thing they commended in Antonius, was his liberalitie and bountie[1]: in the which Demetrius excelled him so farre, that he gave more to his enemies, then Antonius did to his frends: although he was marvelously well thought of, for the honorable and sumptuous funerall he gave unto Brutus bodie. Howbeit Demetrius caused all his enemies be buried that were slaine in battel, and returned unto Ptolomy all the prisoners he had taken, with great giftes and presentes he gave them. They were both in their prosperitie, verie riotouslie and licentiouslie geven[2]: but yet no man can ever say, that Demetrius did at any time let slippe any oportunitie or occasion to followe great matters, but onelie gave him selfe in deede to pleasure, when he had nothing else to doe. And further, to say truely, he tooke pleasure of Lamia, as a man woulde have a delight to heare one tell tales, when he hath nothing else to doe, or is desirous to sleepe: but in deede when he was to make any preparation for warre, he had not then Ivey at his darts end, nor had his helmet perfumed, nor came not out of Ladies closets, picked and princt to go to battell: but he let all dauncing and sporting alone, and became as the Poet Euripides saith,

The souldier of Mars, cruell, and bloodie.

But to conclude, he never had overthrowe or misfortune through negligence, nor by delaying time to followe his owne pleasure: as we see in painted tables, where Omphale secretlie stealeth away Hercules clubbe, and tooke his Lyons skinne from him. Even so Cleopatra oftentimes unarmed Antonius, and intised him to her, making him lose matters of great importaunce, and verie needeful jorneys, to come and be dandled with her, about the rivers of Canobus, and Taphosiris. In the ende, as Paris fledde from the battell, and went to hide him selfe in Helens armes: even so did he in Cleopatraes

[1] *In margin:* 'The liberalitie and bountie of Demetrius and Antonius.'
[2] *In margin:* 'Demetrius and Antonius riots.'

armes, or to speake more properlie, Paris hidde him selfe in Helens closet, but Antonius to followe Cleopatra, fledde and lost the victorie. Furthermore, Demetrius had many wives that he had maried, and all at one time[1]: the which was not dissalowable or not forbidden by the kinges of Macedon, but had bene used from Philippe and Alexanders time, as also king Lysimachus and Ptolomy had, and did honor all them that he maried. But Antonius first of all maried two wives together, the which never Romane durst doe before, but him selfe.[2] Secondly, he put away his first Romane wife, which he had lawfully maried: for the love of a straunge woman, he fondly fell in fancy withall, and contrarie to the lawes and ordinaunces of Rome. And therefore Demetrius mariages never hurt him, for any wrong he had done to his wives: but Antonius contrarily was undone by his wives. Of all the lascivious partes Antonius played, none were so abhominable, as this onely fact of Demetrius.[3] For the historiographers write, that they would not suffer dogges to come into the castell of Athens, bicause of all beastes he is too busie with bitcherie[4]: and Demetrius, in Minervaes temple it selfe lay with Curtisans, and there defiled many citizens wives. And besides all this, the horrible vice of crueltie, which a man would thinke were least mingled with these wanton delightes, is joyned with Demetrius concupiscence: who suffered, (or more properly compelled) the goodliest young boy of Athens, to dye a most pitiefull death, to save him selfe from violence, being taken. And to conclude, Antonius by his incontinencie, did no hurte but to him selfe:[5] and Demetrius did hurte unto all others. Demetrius never hurte any of his frendes: and Antonius suffered his Uncle by his mothers side to be slaine, that he might have his will of Cicero to kill him: a thing so damnable, wicked, and cruell of it selfe, that he hardlie deserved to have bene pardoned, though he had killed Cicero, to have saved his Uncles life. Nowe where they falsefied and brake their othes, the one making Artabazus prisoner, and the other killing of Alexander: Antonius out of doubt had best cause, and justest colour. For Artabazus had betrayed him, and forsaken him in Media. But Demetrius (as divers doe reporte) devised a false matter to accuse Alexander, to cloke the murther he had committed: and some thinke he did accuse him, to whom he him selfe had done injurie unto: and was not revenged of him, that woulde doe him

[1] *In margin:* 'Demetrius and Antonius wives.'

[2] *In margin:* 'Antonius the first Romane that ever maried two wives together.'

[3] *In margin:* 'Demetrius lasciviousnes.'

[4] *In margin:* 'Dogges not suffred in Athens castle, bicause of bitcherie.'

[5] *In margin:* 'The love and impietie: the faith and falsehoode of Demetrius and Antonius.'

injurie. Furthermore, Demetrius him selfe did many noble feates in warre, as we have recited of him before[1]: and contrarilie Antonius, when he was not there in person, wanne many famous and great victories by his Lieutenauntes: and they were both overthrowen being personallie in battell, but yet not both after one sorte. For the one was forsaken of his men being Macedonians, and the other contrarily forsooke his that were Romanes: for he fled, and left them that ventred their lives for his honor. So that the fault the one did was, that he made them his enemies that fought for him: and the fault in the other, that he so beastlie left them that loved him best, and were most faithfull to him. And for their deathes, a man can not praise the one nor the other, but yet Demetrius death the more reproachefull. For he suffered him selfe to be taken prisoner, and when he was sent away to be kept in a straunge place, he had the hart to live yet three yeare longer, to serve his mouth and bellie, as brute beastes doe. Antonius on the other side slue him selfe, (to confesse a troth) cowardly, and miserably, to his great paine and griefe: and yet was it before his bodie came into his enemies hands.

II. Probable Source

From THE LIFE OF OCTAVIUS CÆSAR AUGUSTUS IN NORTH'S PLUTARCH (1603 edition) [by S. Goulart]

The Lives of Epaminondas, of Philip of Macedon, of Dionysius the Elder, and of Octavius Cæsar Augustus: collected out of good Authors . . . Also the lives of nine excellent chieftaines of warre, taken out of Latine from Enybius Probus by S.G.S. . . . And now translated into English, by Sir Thomas North Imprinted at London by Richard Field 1603

[The Character of Octavius Cæsar Augustus]

He was very modest and continent in all the parts of his life, saving that he was somewhat given to women and play: for the rest, he liked not great pallaces, but was contented with meane lodgings:

[1] *In margin:* 'Demetrius and Antonius acts in warres.'

and if there were any ornament, it was in porches and parkes. His household-stuffe and apparell was nothing sumptuous nor costly. It pleased him well to make feasts; he very carefully made choise of his guests, and oftentimes he sate downe at the table a long time after every bodie, and would rise before others, which remained after he was up. In his ordinarie diet he banished superfluity of meates; he delighted to be merry and pleasant among his friends, or to bring in pleasant players of comedies to passe the time away. And he did not tie himselfe to any certaine howres to eate his meate, but when his stomacke served him he tooke something. So that somtimes he supped not at al, and then when every man was gone, he made them bring him meate, neither dainty nor delicate. Also he drunke very litle wine, he slept in the day, and by times in the night, talking with some, or reading: so that oftentimes he slept not till the breake of day, and for that he tooke no rest in the night, he might chaunce to sleepe in his litter as they caried him in the streetes in the day time up and downe Rome. He was a goodly Prince, and that kept himselfe in good state from the beginning of his life to the latter end: not curious to set himselfe out, as litle caring to be shaven, as to weare long haire: and in stead of a looking-glasse, reading in his booke, or writing, even whilest the Barber was trimming of him. Whether he spake or held his peace, he had so comely a face, that many of his enemies bent to do him hurt, their hearts would not serve them so soone as ever they looked on him. He had very cleare and lively eyes, but with time he was subject to many diseases and infirmities, the which he remedied with great care. As for his exercises, he left armes and horses immediatly after the civill warres: for he was never any great souldier. He would play at tennis, at the ballone, he would go abroad in his coach to walke and stirre himselfe. Sometimes he would go a fishing, or play at the bones, or at nuts with yong children of the Moores and Syrians that had some prety maner and behaviour with them, and alwayes spake words to move laughter. He was learned in the liberall sciences, very eloquent, and desirous to learne: insomuch that during the warre of Mutine, in the middest of all his infinite affaires, he did reade, he wrote, and made orations amongst his familiars. He never spake unto the Senate nor people, nor to his souldiers, but he had first written and premeditated that he would say unto them, although he had speech at commaundement, to propound or aunswer to any thing in the field. And because he would not deceive his memory, or lose time in superfluous speech: he determined ever to write all that he would say: and he was the first inventer of it. If he had to conferre with any man, or with his wife in any matters of importance: he would put that downe in his writing tables, because he would speake neither more nor lesse. And he tooke pleasure to pronounce his words with a sweete voyce and good grace, having continually about him for this purpose a fine man to frame his voyce. But one day having a paine in his mouth, he made his oration to the people by an Herauld. He made many bookes and verses of diverse sorts: but all is dead with time. His speech was as the rest of his life, eloquent, well couched together, and sententious. He delighted to reade good authors, but he gathered nothing other then the sentences teaching good maners: and having written them out word by word, he gave out a copie of them to his familiars: and sent them about to the governours of provinces and to the magistrates of Rome and of other cities. He was somewhat, and too much given to divinations: he was marvellously afraid of thunder and lightning: he had a great confidence in dreames, and in such like vanities. But peradventure we are too curious searching out his private life: yet that may sometime discover great personages more then their publicke actions, in the which they are more carefull to frame their countenances, and do counterfeit most.

Now, as we have lightly runne over his private life before spoken of: so shall the memorable deedes done by his authoritie be briefly represented: being unpossible to comprehend in a few lines so many notable things, unlesse a man would make a great book of them. This is to be noted in him, that so young a man having so small beginnings, coming out of a meane house in comparison of others, hath excelled all other young and old men in wisedome and greatnesse of courage: should rise so high, that before he had bene Prætor the Senate gave him the name of *Augustus*, created him maister of the horse, when as yet he never had charge of a company of men at armes: proclaimed him Emperour and Soveraigne captaine, afore he had bene placed in any publicke office by authoritie of the Senate. Furthermore, for the first time he was chosen Consull when he was but twentie yeares old: and he was thirteene times Consull, and twentie times called Soveraigne captaine. Afterwards, when he was not yet foure and thirtie yeares old, the Senate and people of Rome gave him this goodly name of father of his country, because he had maintained and preserved the commonwealth. It is a wonderfull thing that he could winde himselfe out of so many great affaires and warres, that he could within foure and twenty yeares of age, restore againe into so good estate the commonwealth of Rome, turmoiled and troubled with so many proscriptions and civill warres as it was. And that afterwards so long as he commanded alone, he did so firmely establish this Monarchie, that notwithstanding the infinite troubles received under other Emperours, yet it stood upright and in so great prosperitie for so many hundred yeares.

III. Analogue

From LUCAN'S PHARSALIA
translated by Thomas May (1627)
The tenth Booke

Lucans Pharsalia. The whole ten bookes. Englished by T. May. For T. Jones and J. Marriott. 1627.

THE ARGUMENT

Cæsar *in Ægypt fearlesse walkes, and sees*
Their temples, tombes, and fam'd antiquityes.
Before his feete faire Cleopatra *kneeles,*
Whom to her brother king he reconciles.
With sumptuous feasts this peace they celebrate,
To Cæsars *eare* Achoreus *doth relate*
Niles ebbes, and flowes, and long concealed spring.
Within the pallace Cæsar, *and the King*
By sterne Achillas *are besieg'd by night.*
Cæsar *to Pharos takes a secret flight*;
There from his ship he leapes into the waves,
And his endanger'd life by swimming saves.

When *Cæsar* first, possest of *Pompey's* head,
Arrived there; and those dire sands did tread:
His fortune strove with guilty Ægypts fate,
Whether that Rome that land should captivate;
Or Ægypts sword take from the world the head
Both of the Conquerer, and the conquered.
Pompey, thy ghost prevailes, thy *Manes* free
Cæsar from death least Nile should after thee
Be by the Romans lov'd. He goes from thence
To Alexandria arm'd with confidence
In this dire mischiefes pledge, following along
His Fasces. But, perceiving that the throng
Of people murmur'd that in Ægypt hee
Bore th'Ensignes up of Romes authority,
He findes their wavering faiths, perceiving plaine
That for his sake great *Pompey* was not slaine.
Then with a looke still hiding feare goes he

The stately temple of th'old god to see,
Which speakes the ancient Macedonian greatnesse.
But there delighted with no objects sweetnesse,
Not with their gold, nor gods majestike dresse,
Nor lofty city walls, with greedinesse
Into the burying vault goes *Cæsar* downe.
There Macedonian *Philip's* mad-brain'd son
The prosperous theife lyes buryed: whom just fate
Slew in the worlds revenge: vaults consecrate
Containe those limbs, which through the world 'twere just
To cast abroad: but fortune spar'd his dust,
And to that Kingdomes end his fate remain'd.
If ere the world her freedome had attaind,
He for a mocke had beene reserv'd, whose birth
Brought such a dire example to the earth,
So many lands to be possest by one,
Scorning the narrow bounds of Macedon,
And Athens, which his father had subdew'd:
Through Asian lands, with human slaughter strew'd,
Led by too forward fates he rushes on,
Driving his sword through every nation:
Rivers unknowne, Euphrates he distaines
With Persians blood, Ganges with Indians:
Th'earths fatall mischiefe, lightning dire, that rent
All people, and a star malevolent
To nations. To invade the South-east sea
He built a fleete. Not barren Libya,
Water, nor heat, nor Ammons desart sands
Could stop his course. Upon the Westerne lands
(Following the worlds devexe) he meant to tread,
To compasse both the poles, and drinke Niles head.
But death did meete his course; that checke alone
Could nature give this Kings ambition;
Who to his grave the worlds sole Empire bore,
With the same envy, that 'twas got before;
And wanting heires left all he did obtaine
To be divided by the sword againe.
But fear'd in Parthia; and his Babylon
He dy'd. Oh shame, that Easterne nation
Then trembled at the Macedonian speare
Farre more, then now the Roman pile they feare.
Though all the North, the West, and South be ours,
In th'East the Parthian King contemnes our powers.
That, which to *Crassus* proov'd a fatall place,

A secure province to small *Pella* was.
Now the yong King come from Pelusium
Had pacify'd the peoples wrath: in whom
As hostage of his peace, in Ægypts court
Cæsar was safe; when loe from Pharos port,
Bribing the keeper to unchaine the same,
In a small galley *Cleopatra* came
Unknowne to *Cæsar* entering the house;
The staine of Ægypt, Romes pernicious
Fury, unchast to Italyes disgrace,
As much as *Helena's* bewitching face
Fatall to Troy, and her owne Greekes did proove,
As much Romes broiles did *Cleopatra* moove,
Our Capitall she with her Sistrum fearr'd,
With Ægypts base effeminate rout prepar'd
To seize Romes Eagles, and a triumph get
Ore captiv'd *Cæsar*: when at *Leucas* fleet
It doubtfull stood, whether the world that day
A woman, and not Roman should obey.
Her prides first spring that impious night had been,
That with our chiefes mixt that incestuous queene.
Who would not pardon *Anthonyes* mad love,
When *Cæsars* flinty breast desires could move
In midst of war, when heat of fight rag'd most,
And in a court haunted by *Pompey's* ghost?
Embrew'd with blood from dire Pharsaliaes field
Could he unto adultrous *Venus* yeild?
And mixe with warlike cares (oh harmelesse head)
A bastard issue, and unlawfull bed;
Forgetting *Pompey*, to beget a brother
To thee, fare *Julia*, on a strumpet mother:
Suffring the forces of his scattered foes
To joyne in Affrike, basely he bestowes
Time in Egyptian love, a conquerer
Not for himselfe, but to bestow on her;
Whom, trusting to her beauty, without teares,
Though gesture sad, with loose, as if rent haires,
Drest in a beautious, and becomming woe
Did *Cleopatra* meete bespeaking so:
If, mighty *Cæsar*, noblenesse there be,
Ægyptian *Lagus* royall issue I,
Depos'd and banisht from my fathers state,
If thy great hand restore my former fate,
Kneele at thy feet a queene, unto our nation

Thou dost appeare a gratious constellation.
I am not the first woman that hath sway'd
The Pharian scepter: Ægypt has obay'd
A queene; not sexe excepted: I desire
Thee read the will of my deceased Sire,
Who left me there a partner to enjoy
My brothers crowne, and marriage bed. The boy
(I know) would love his sister were he free:
But all his power, will, and affections be
Under *Photinus* girdle. To obtaine
The crowne I beg not; *Cæsar* from this staine
Free thou our house: command the King to be
A King, and free from servants tyranny.
Shall slaves so proud of *Pompey's* slaughter be,
Threatning the same (which fates avert) to thee?
Cæsar, 'tis shame enough to th'earth, and thee
His death *Photinus* gift, and guilt should be.
  Her suite in *Cæsars* eares had found small grace,
But beauty pleades, and that incestuous face
Prevailes, the pleasures of a wanton bed
Corrupt the judge. The King had purchased
His peace with weighty summes of gold; which done,
With sumptuous feasts this glad accord they crowne.
Her riot forth in highest pompe (not yet
Transferr'd to Rome) did *Cleopatra* set.
The house excell'd those temples, which men build
In wicked'st times; the high-arch'd roofes were fill'd
With wealth; high tressells golden tables bore:
Nor did carv'd marble only cover ore
The house; alone th'unmixt *Achates* stood,
And pillars of red marble: their feet troad
On pavements of rich Onyx: pillars there
Not coverd with Ægyptian Eben were;
Eben was timber there, and that rich wood
Not to adorne, but prop the Pallace stood.
The roomes with Ivory glister'd, and each dore
Inlay'd with Indian shels, embellish'd ore
With choisest Emeraulds: the beds all shone
With richest gems, and yellow Jasper stone.
Coverlids rich, some purple dy'd in graine,
Whose tincture was not from one Caldron tane,
Part wove of glittering gold, part scarlet dy,
As is th'Ægyptian use of Tapestry:
The servitours stood by, and waiting pages,

Some different in complexions, some in ages;
Some of blacke Libyan hew, some golden haires,
That *Cæsar* yeilds in all his German warres
Hee nere had seene so bright a yellow haire:
Some stiffe curl'd lockes on Sun-burnt fore heads weare.
Besides th'unhappy strength-robb'd company
The Eunuch'd youths: neere these were standing by
Youths of a stronger age, yet those so young
Scarse any downe darkning their cheekes was sprung.
  Downe sate the princes, and the higher power
Cæsar; her hurtfull face all painted ore
Sate *Cleopatra*, not content alone
T'enjoy her brothers bed, nor Ægypts crowne:
Laden with pearles, the red seas spoiled store
On her rich haire, and weary'd necke shee wore.
Her snowy breasts their whitenesse did display
Thorough the thinne Sidonian tiffenay
Wrought, and extended by the curious hand
Of Ægypts workemen. Citron tables stand
On Ivory tressells, such as *Cæsars* eyes
Saw not, when hee King *Juba* did surprise.
O blinde ambitious madnesse to declare
Your wealth to him, that makes a civill warre,
And tempt an armed guest. For though that hee
Sought not for wealth by warres impiety,
And the worlds wracke: suppose our chiefes of old
Were there, compos'd of that poore ages mould,
Fabritii, *Curii* grave, or that plaine man
That Consull from th'Etrurian plowes was tane,
Were sitting at those tables, whom to Rome
With such a tryumph he would wish to come.
  In golden plate they fill their feasting bords
With what the aire, the earth, or Nile affords,
What luxury with vaine ambition had
Sought through the world, and not as hunger badd,
Beasts, foules, the gods of Ægypt are devour'd:
From christall ewers is Niles water powr'd
Upon their hands: studded with gemms that shine
Their bowles conteine no Mareotike wine,
But strong, and sparkling wines of Meroë,
To whom few yeares give full maturity.
With fragrant Nard, and never-fading rose
Their heads are crown'd: their haire anointed flowes
With sweetest cinnamon, that has not spent

His favour in the aire, nor lost his sent
In forreine climes: and fresh Amomum brought
From harvests neere at hand, there *Cæsar's* taught
The riches of the spoiled world to take;
And is asham'd that hee a warre did make
With his poore Sonne in law, desiring now
Some quarell would twixt him, and Ægypt grow.
When wine, and cares had tir'd their glutted pleasure,
Cæsar beginns with long discourse to measure
The howers of night, bespeaking gently thus
The linnen-vested grave *Achoreus*:
Old man devoted to religion,
And, (which thine age confirmes) despis'd by none
Of all the gods, to longing eares relate
Ægypts originall, her site, and state,
Worshipp of gods, and what doth ere remaine
In your old temples charactere'd, explaine.
The gods, that would bee knowne, to us unfold,
If your forefathers their religion told
T'Athenian *Plato* once, when had you ere
A guest more worthy, or more fitt to heare?
Rumor of *Pompey* drew our march thus farre,
And fame of you, for still in midd'st of warre
I leasure had of heaven, and gods to heare,
And the starres course: nor shall *Eudoxus* yeare
Excell my Consulshipp. But though so much
My vertue bee, my love of truth bee such,
There's nought I more desire to know at all
Then Niles hid head, and strange originall
So many yeares unknowne: grant but to mee
A certaine hope the head of Nile to see,
Ile leave of civill warre. *Cæsar* had done,
When thus divine *Achoreus* begunne:
  Lett it bee lawfull, *Cæsar* to unfold
Our great forefathers secretts hid of old
From the lay people. Lett who ere suppose
It piety to keepe these wonders close:
I thinke the gods are pleas'd to bee made knowne;
And have their sacred lawes to people showne:
Planetts, which crosse, and slacke the tenth sphæres course,
Had from the worlds first law their different powers.
The Sunne divides the yeares, makes nights, and dayes,
Dimmes other starrs with his resplendent rayes.
And their wilde courses moderates; the tides

Of Thetis *Phœbes* growth, and waning guides.
Saturne cold ice, and frozen zones obtaines;
Mars ore the windes, and winged lightning reignes;
Quiett well temper'd aire doth *Love* possesse;
The seedes of all things *Venus* cherishes;
Cyllenius rules ore waters which are great;
Hee when hee enters, where the doggestarres heat,
And burning fire's display'd, there where the signe
Of *Cancer* hott doth with the Lion joine,
And where the Zodiacke holds his *Capricorne*,
And *Cancer*, under which Niles head is borne:
Ore which when *Mercuryes* proud fires doo stand,
And in a line direct, (as by command
Of Phœbe the obeying Ocean growes)
So from his open'd fountaine Nilus flowes;
Nor ebbs againe till night have from the Sunne
Those howers recover'd, which the summer wonne.
  Vaine was the old opinion, that Niles flow
Was caus'd, or help'd by Æthiopian snow.
For on those hills cold Boreas never blowes,
As there the natives Sunburnt visage showes,
And moist hott Southerne windes. Besides the head
Of every streame, that from thaw'd ice is bred,
Swells then, when first the spring dissolves the snowes.
But Nile before the doggdayes never flowes,
Nor is confin'd within his bankes againe
Till the Autumnal æquinoctian:
Thence tis hee knowes no lawes of other streames,
Nor swells in winter, when *Sols* scorching beames
Are farre remote, his waters want their end:
But Nile comes forth in summer time to lend
A cooler temper to the sweltring aire.
Under the torrid zone, least fire impaire
The earth, unto her succour Nilus drawes,
And swells against the Lions burning jawes.
And when hott *Cancer* his *Siene* burnes,
Unto her aide implored Nilus turnes:
Nor till the sunne to Autumne doo descend,
And that hott Meroë her shades extend,
Doth he restore againe the drowned feild:
Whoo can the causes of this flowing yeild?
Even so our mother nature hath decreed
That Nile should flow, and so the world hath neede. . .

[Lucan, X, 1–239]

IV. Translation of Analogue

From THE ANTIQUITIES OF THE JEWS By FLAVIUS JOSEPHUS translated by T. Lodge 1602

The Famous and Memorable Workes of Josephus . . . Faithfully translated out of the Latin, and French, by T. Lodge. At the charges of G. Bishop, S. Waterson, P. Short and T. Adams. (Colophon: Printed by P. Short) 1602

[After Cleopatra 'entangled Antony in her loves' she frequently tried to get possession of lands governed by Herod of Judæa. But Antony, who had been helped by Herod at the siege of Samosata, rejected her demands.]

Book XV. Chap. IV.

About the same time there grew certaine troubles and alterations in Syria: for that *Cleopatra* continually sollicited and importuned *Anthony*, and whetted on his displeasure against all, perswading him to remoove all from their governments, and to bestow the same on her selfe.[1] And for that *Anthony* loved her extremely, she was in great estimation and credit with him: and being in her owne nature inclined to covetousnesse, shee abstained from no kinde of corrupt dealing and wickednesse. For knowing that the kingdome should descend unto her brother, she caused him to be poisoned, when he was but fifteene yeeres olde: as for her sister *Arsinoe*, she caused her to be slaine by *Anthonies* meanes at such time, as she made her prayers in the temple of Diana at Ephesus.[2] Moreover in what place soever she understood that there was any hope to get money, whether it were in robbing of temples, or in breaking open sepulchers; she would be possessed thereof: neither was there any religious place so sacred, from whence she tooke not away the ornaments. Furthermore there was not any thing so prophane and interdicted, which she laid not hands on to satisfie her unbridled avarice.[3] Neither was the whole world sufficient enough to content this magnificent Ladie, who was made slave to her owne desires; and her disordinate appetite was such, that all the riches in the world were not able to saciate

[1] *In margin:* 'Hedio & Ruffinus, chap. 4.'

[2] *In margin:* 'Cleopatra verie covetous. Cleopatra murthereth her brother and sister.'

[3] *In margin:* '*The yeare of the world, 3932, before Christs birth 32.*'

and fill the same. For this cause she incessantly importuned *Antonius* to take from others, to be liberall towards her: and therefore intring into Syria with him, she presently bethought her selfe how she might get it into her possession. For she caused *Lysanias Ptolomeies* sonne to be put to death, objecting against him that he had private intelligence with the Parthians.[1] She begged Jury also at *Antonius* hands, and required him besides that to dispossesse the kings of Arabia. He was in such sort possessed by this woman that he seemed not only to be bewitched with her words, but also inchanted by her poisons, to obey her in whatsoever she thought meet: yet was he ashamed to commit so manifest an iniquity, for feare least being so farre overruled by her, he should happen to offend in matters of more consequence. Least therefore either by denying her, he should draw her to discontent; or by condiscending to her demands, he should seeme to be the wickeddest man alive, he deducted a severall portion of both their dominions, & presented her with the same. He gave her likewise those cities that are scituate between the floud Eleutherius & Ægypt, except Tyre and Sydon, which he knew to be free cities of long continuance: although by earnest sollicitation she sought to be seazed of these also.[2]

Chap. V.

Cleopatras *progresse into Judæa.*

After that *Cleopatra* had obtained all these things, and had accompanied *Antonius* as farre as Euphrates, who at that time went to make warre in Armenia: she returned backe againe, and by the way visited Apamea and Damasco, and at last tooke her progresse into Jury: Where King *Herode* met with her, and assured that portion which had beene given unto her in Arabia, with all the revenewes of Jericho unto her.[3] This countrey bringeth forth that balme, which of all other oyntments is the most precious, and onely groweth in that place, and no other, to the bignes of great Dates. Being arrived in that place, and growen inwardly familiar with *Herode*, she sought to allure and draw him to her lust, being of her selfe naturally addicted to such pleasures and intemperance;[4] and happely also being somewhat touched with love, or rather (as it seemeth most likely) she in this sort laid the foundation to intrap him under colour to revenge

[1] *In margin:* 'Cleopatra contriveth Lysanias death.'

[2] *In margin:* 'Antonius giveth Cleopatra a portion deducted out of Jury and Arabia.'

[3] *In margin:* 'Cleopatra cometh to Herode who enstateth hir in that the part of Arabia & these revenewes of Jericho that were given her.'

[4] *In margin:* 'An intemperate woman given to lust.'

her selfe of some outrage by that meanes. But in effect she generally manifested, that she was overcome by her desire and sensuall lust. But *Herode* was not over kindly bent towards *Cleopatra*, knowing of long time how badly she was enclined towards al men; and at that time he conceived the greater hatred against her, because by that intemperance of hers she pretended to destroy him: and although that from the beginning he had rejected her sollicitations; yet determined he to revenge himselfe on her, if so be by these her subtill underminings she should prosecute and continue her subtil pollicies to betray him. He asked counsaile also of his friends, whether having her in his possession, he should put her to death.[1] For in so doing all those should be delivered from divers evils, whom either in time past she had molested, or hereafter should bring in trouble. Moreover that it would be profitable for *Antonius* also, whom without all doubt she would forsake, if any occasion or necessitie should enforce him to make triall of her friendship. But whilest he debated and discoursed upon this resolution, his friends restrained and disswaded him, assuring him that it was a great indignitie for him, who was a Prince of high thoughts and hautie resolutions, to cast himselfe into manifest perill, beseeching him to attempt nothing rashly: For that *Antonius* would not endure the same, notwithstanding it might be approved that it stood with his profit: nay rather that by this meanes he should increase his desire, for that by force & subtilty he might seem to have lost her. Further, that no one colour of excuse should be left him, in that she was the woman of greatest note & nobility of that time; & that what soever profit might redound unto him by her death, should be annexed with *Antonius* injurie. Wherby it most evidently appeared, how great & remediles domages would befall both to the kingdome & the kings family also; whereas nothing letted him by repulsing her unlawfull demand to dispose allthings for the present state with great discretion. By these & such like reasons and probable conjectures, they deterred and disswaded him from adventuring upon his apparant daunger, and attempting so hainous an act; so that contrariwise they induced him to offer *Cleopatra* many rich presents, and to conduct her onward on her way towards Ægypt.[2]

As soone therefore as *Antonius* was seazed of Armenia he sent *Artabazes Tigranes* sonne, with all his children, who were great princes, prisoners into Ægypt, and presented them to *Cleopatra* with all those precious Jewels likewise, which were taken by him or

[1] *In margin:* 'Herode goeth about to put Cleopatra to death, and is disswaded by his friends.'

[2] *In margin:* 'Herode bringeth Cleopatra onward off her way towards Egypt.' 'Antonius conquereth Armenia.'

found in the kingdome. But *Artaxias* his elder sonne (who at that time had saved himselfe by flight) raigned in Armenia, whom *Archelaus* and *Nero* the Emperour drove out of his kingdome, and placed his younger brother *Tigranes* in his roome, as it shall be declared hereafter.[1] As for the tributes of the countries which *Herode* was bound to pay unto *Cleopatra*, for the lands bestowed on her by *Antonius*, he without deceit justly paid them, supposing it to be verie incident to his securitie, to continue himselfe in her good favour. As for the Arabians, they seeing that *Herode* had the levying of such a tribute, paied him for some little time two hundreth talents a yeere; but afterwards they grew slow and negligent in their paiments, and scarcely satisfied the halfe, and that also verie negligently.

Chap. VI.

Herode *maketh warre with* Aretas *at the same time that* Antonius *is overthrowne by* Augustus Cæsar *in his Actian warre.*

Aretas demeasning himselfe thus ungratefully, and refusing to doe that which in right he ought to performe; *Herode* made a shew to take armes against him, but deferred his revenge in regard of the contentions amongst the Romans. For at that time nought else was expected then the Actian warre (which fell in the hundreth, eightie and seventh Olympiade) in which *Augustus Cæsar* determined to trie his title with *Antonius* for the Monarchie. In the meane while *Herode*, who had alreadie for many yeeres beene master of a peaceable and fruitfull country, from whence he drew rich revenues & many forces, gathered divers companies of men, with the greatest expedition that he might, to succour *Antonius*. But he by letters signified unto him, that he had no need of his assistance: notwithstanding he commaunded him to make a road upon the Arabian, whose perfidious dealing *Antonius* had not only understood by *Herode* himselfe, but also by *Cleopatras* advertisements. For she verie cunningly conceived, that it woulde redound unto her profit, if one of these two should overthrow the other. *Herode* according to these instructions from *Antonius*, returned backe into his countrey, and retained his armie alwaies readie about him, and incontinently with the same invaded Arabia, and with his forces both horsemen and footmen came directly to Diospolis, where the Arabians (having notice of his intended warre against them) came out to meete him. In this place fought they a most cruell battell, wherein at the last the Jewes had the upper hand . . .[2]

[After Antony's defeat at Actium Herod's position was precarious.]

[1] *In margin: 'The yeare of the world 3933, before Christs birth 31.'*

[2] *In margin: 'The yeare of the world 3934, before Christ's birth 30.'*

Chap. X.

How Herode *obtained the kingdome of Judæa at* Cæsars *hands.*[1]

After he had in this sort given order for all his affairs, he withdrew himselfe unto Rhodes, intending there to meete with *Cæsar*. And as soone as he arrived in that citie, he tooke the Diademe from his head and laid it apart; but as for his other princely ornaments, he chaunged them in no sort; and being admitted to *Cæsars* presence, he at that time gave a more ample testimony of the greatnes of his magnanimitie and courage: for neither addressed he his speech to intreat his favour (according to the custome of suppliants) neither presented he any request, as if he had in any sort offended him, but gave account of al that which he had done, without concealing or mistrusting any thing. For he freely confessed before *Cæsar*, that he had intirely loved *Antonius*, and that to the utmost of his power he had done him service, to the end that he might obtaine the soveraigntie and monarchie; not by annexing his forces unto his, in that he was otherwaies imployed in the Arabian warre; but in furnishing him both with wheat and money, and that this was the least office which it behooved him to performe towards *Antonius*; for that being once his professed friend, it behooved him not onely to imploy his best endevours on his so princely benefactor, but also to hazard both his head and happines to deliver him from perils. All which (said he) I have not performed according as I ought to have done, yet notwithstanding I know that at such time as he was overcome in the Actian battell, I did not alter my affection with his fortune: neither did I restraine my selfe: for although I befriended not *Antonius* with my presence and assistance in his Actian warre, yet at leastwise I assisted him with my counsaile, certifying him that he had but one onely meanes left him for his securitie, and prevention of his utter ruine, which was, to put *Cleopatra* to death, for that by cutting her off hee might enjoy her estate, and might more easily obtaine his peace, and pacifie thy displeasure against him. And for that he gave but slender regard for these mine admonitions by his owne sottishnesse and indiscretion, he hath hurte himselfe and profited you, because, as I said, he did not follow my counsaile. Now therefore (O *Cæsar*) in regard of the hate which you beare unto *Anthony*, you condemne my friendship also, I will not denie that which I have done; neither am I affraid freely and publikely to protest how much I have loved him: but if without regard of persons, you consider how kindly I am affected towards my benefactors, and how resolute and constant a friend I am, and how mindefull of kindnesse, the effect of that which

[1] *In margin: 'The yeare of the world, 3935, before Christs Nativitie, 29.'*

I have done, may make me knowne unto thee. For if the name be onely changed, the friendship notwithstanding may remaine, and deserve a due praise.

By these words (which were manifest testimonies of his resolute and noble courage) he so inwardly indeered himselfe unto *Cæsar*, who was a magnificent and worthy monarcke, that hee converted this his accusation into an occasion to winne and worke him to be his friend: for which cause *Cæsar* in setting the diademe upon his head, exhorted him that he should no lesse respect his friendship, then he had in former time *Anthonies*: and withall did him much honour . . .[1]

V. Analogue

FROM THE ROMAN HISTORIES OF LUCIUS FLORUS

translated by E.M.B[olton]. [1619]

[Aspects of Marcus Antonius]

[Lib. 4. Chap. VIII]

. . . Though in *Cassius*, and *Brutus*, *Cæsar* had ridded the power of the faction out of the world, and in *Pompey* had abolished the whole name, and title of it, yet could not hee settle a sound peace, while *Antonius* the rocke, the knot, and the common let of assured quiet, was alive, and there was no want in him why vices made not an end of him: nay his pride, and riot having made triall of all things, hee first overcame enemies, then citizens, and lastly the times with the terrour hee had raised of himselfe.

Lib. 4, Chap. XI. *The* Actian *war with* Antonie *and* Cleopatra.

The furie of *Antonie* which ambition could not kill, was quencht with wanton lust, and riot, for after his *Parthian* journey growing into hatred with warre, he gave himselfe over to rest, and surprised with the love of Queene *Cleopatra*, solaced on her bosome, as freely as if all other matters had succeeded well. This *Egyptian* woman did value her companie at no lesse a rate to *Antonie* drunken with love, then the *whole Roman* empire. & he promised it as if the *Romans* were more easily to be dealt with then the *Parthians*. Therefore hee began

[1] *In margin:* 'Hedio & Ruffinus, chap. 8. Cæsar confirmeth Herodes authoritie.'

to plot a tyrannie, nor that covertly, but forgetting his countrey, his name, his gowne, his *fasces*, hee absolutely degenerated into no lesse a monster in his understanding, then he did in his affection, and fashion. hee went with a staffe of gold in his hand, a *Persian* sword by his side, a purple robe buttond with huge precious stones, and a diadem in readinesse, that a king might enjoy a Queene. At the first bruite of these stirres, *Cæsar* crosseth over from *Brundisium*, that hee might give warre the meeting; and, pitching his tents in *Epirus*, did beset the iland *Leucades*, and the rocke *Leucades*, and the points or nesses of the *Ambracian* bay, with his ships of warre, hee had aboute foure hundred soule; the enemies not fewer then two hundred, but what they wanted in number, was made up in bulke: for they had from sixe to nine bankes of oares, besides that, their fights were raised so high with decks, and turrets, as they resembled castles, and cities, making the very sea grone under, & the windes out of breath to carry them: which hugenesse of theirs was it selfe their bane. *Cæsar's* navie had not in it any vessell but from three bankes of oares, to sixe, and nine above: therefore they are yare, & ready for all the needes of service, whether to charge, recharge, or turne about. Those of the other side were meere slugges, and unwieldie for all worke: upon every of which many of ours setting, and plying them what with darts; and all sorts of flingings, what with beak-heads, or prows, and castings of fire, scattred them all at pleasure. Nor did the greatnesse of the enemies preparations appeare at any time more then after the victorie: for the huge armada, bulged, & split in the fight, was carryed in the wracks thereof, up, and downe over the whole sea, containing the spoiles of *Arabia*, and *Saba*, and of thousand other nations of *Asia*, and the waves stirred with the winds, did daily belch up gold, and purple upon the shores. The first who led the way to running away, was the Queen, who in a galleon whose poope was of gold, and saile of purple, thrust into the deepes, *Antonius* forthwith following her: but *Cæsar* was at his heels. So that neither the preparations which he had made to fly into the *Indian Ocean*, nor *Parastonium*, and *Pelusium*, the two corner coasts of Ægypt, stuft by him with garrisons, stood him in any stead, all were so quickly seized. *Antonius* was the first of the two who slew himselfe. The Queene kneeling at the feete of *Cæsar*, laid baits for his eyes; but in vaine; her beauties were beneath that princes chastitie. Nor was life her suit, for that was offered, but her care was for a part of the kingdome: which when she despaired to obtaine of the prince, and saw her selfe reserved for triumph, the guard put about her being negligent, she betooke herselfe to the Mausolie (so cal they the sepulchres of their kings) where attired in most pompous habit, as her custome was, shee seated herselfe in a throne, sweetned with rich perfumes, close to her *Lord Antonius*, and clapping serpents to her veines, died away in a slumber.

Chapt. XII *Warres against foraine nations*

Here ended the civill wars, the rest were against strangers, who, while the empire was turmoild with these intestine miseries, sallied out against us in divers quarters of the world: [Describes the progress of Octavius Cæsar's conquests.]

For these so many, and so wondrous great deeds of his, hee was called *perpetual Dictator*, and *Father of his Countrey*. It was also debated in the Senate, whether, because hee had founded the empire, hee should be styled *Romulus*. But the name *Augustus* seemed to be a more holy, and venerable word then the other, that so even now while hee lived on the earth, hee might bee as it were deifide by the name itselfe, and title.

VI. Source

From THE ROMAN CIVIL WARS OF APPIAN OF ALEXANDRIA

translated by W.B. (1578)

Book V, Section 18

[Lucius and Fulvia made war against Octavius.]

The Citie in the meane time, was in great penurie, their provision of corne beyng stopped by *Pompey*. In *Italie*, tillage beyng almost lefte for the continuaunce of warre, and that there was, being consumed of the Soldiours: and in the Citie, theeves and murderers by night, were unpunished, for what soever was done, was imputed to the Souldiour. The commons shutte up theyr shoppes, and were withoute officers, whiche woulde not serve where thefte was suffred.

But *Lucius*, beyng well affected to the common wealth, and greeved with the power of the three Princes, continuyng longer than the time appoynted, contended with *Cæsar*: for he onely promised helpe to the olde possessioners, making supplication to all the officers, and they promised their service to him.[1] Wherby, bothe *Antonies* Soldiours, and *Cæsar* himself, accused him as an enimy to him, and *Fulvia* also, as stirrers of warre out of time. But a devise of *Manius*

[1] *In margin:* '*Lucius* taketh parte with the old husbande-men.'

prevayled, which persuaded *Fulvia*, that if *Italie* were in quiet, *Antony* woulde remayne with *Cleopatra* in *Aegipt*, but if warres were styrred, hee woulde come quickly.[1] Then *Fulvia* of a womannishe passion, incensed *Lucius*,[2] and when *Cæsar* wente to place the newe inhabitancies, *Antonies* chyldren and *Lucius* wente with them, that *Cæsar* shoulde not have the whole thankes, by goyng alone. *Cæsars* horsemenne scoured the coaste towarde *Sicelie*, that *Pompey* shoulde not spoyle it. *Lucius* eyther afrayde in deede, or fayning to bee afrayde, that these horsemen were sente agaynst him and *Antonies* children, wente in haste to the inhabitauncies of *Antonie*, to gette a garde about him, accusing *Cæsar*, as unfaithfull to *Antony*.[3] But he answered, that he kept faith and friendship with *Antonie*, and that *Lucius* sought to move warre, for that he was offended with the rule of them three. . . .

Book V, Sections 41–2

[Lucius explains to Octavius why he took up arms against him.]

When it was tolde *Cæsar* that *Lucius* was comming to hym, he went straight to meete him, and they bothe came in sight, accompanied with their friends, in the habite of a General.[4] Then *Lucius* sending aside all hys friends, wente on with two Sergeants, signifying what he meant: and *Cæsar* following that benevolence, shewed the lyke token of modestie. And when he saw *Lucius* come within his trenche, that so he might shew himselfe to be in his power, he firste wente oute of the Trenche, that *Lucius* might be free to save hymselfe. Thys they dyd outwardly by tokens of courtesy, and when they were come to the ditche, and had saluted eche other, *Lucius* thus began.[5]

'If I had made this warre with straungers, I would have bin ashamed (O *Cæsar*) to have bin overcome, and more ashamed to yeelde myselfe: from the whiche ignominie, I woulde easilye have delivered my life: But bicause I have dealt with a Citizen of lyke authoritie, and that for my country, I thinke it no shame for such a cause to be overcome of such a manne, which I speake, not that I refuse to suffer any thyng that thou wilt put upon mee, beyng come to this campe, wythout an Herauld, but to aske pardon for other, juste and commodious for thyne estate. Whych, that thou mayste understande the more playnly, I wyll separate theyr cause from mine, that after thou shalt understand that I am the onelye cause,

[1] *In margin:* '*Manius*' counsel.' Cf. II.2.98–9.

[2] *In margin:* '*Fulvia Antonies* wife stirreth warre.'

[3] *In margin:* 'Begynnyng of suspition.'

[4] *In margin:* '*Cæsar* meeteth with *Lucius*.'

[5] *In margin:* '*Lucius* to *Cæsar*.'

thou mayste exercise thine anger uppon me. Thinke not that I will invey againste thee licentiously, which now were oute of tyme, but wyll onelye tell the truth, which I cannot dissemble.

'I tooke thys warre agaynste thee, not that I woulde bee a Prince, if I hadde dispatched thee: but that I myghte have broughte the Common wealth to the rule of the Senate, whyche is nowe taken awaye by the power of three, as thou thy selfe canste not denye.[1]

'For when you begunne it, confessyng it unlawfull, you sayde it was necessarye for a tyme, *Cassius* and *Brutus* beyng alyve, who coulde not be reconciled unto you. They being taken awaye, the reste, (if any rest there be) being afraide of you, and takyng armes, not agaynste the Common wealth, and youre tyme beeyng ended, I requyred that the oppressed Senate myghte be restored,[2] not regardyng my brother before my Countrey. For I hoped to have perswaded him at his retourne, and I made haste to doe it in the tyme of myne offyce. If thou wouldest have doone so, thou shouldest have hadde the glorye alone, but bycause I could not perswade thee, I wente to the Cittye, and thought to gette it by strength and force, being a Senatoure, and a Consull.

'These were the onelye causes of this warre, not my brother,[3] not *Manius*, not *Fulvia*, nor the landes divided to the Souldyoures, that wanne the fielde at *Philippi*: not the pitie of the olde possessioners cast out of the landes: for by myne authoritie, some were appoynted to landes for my brothers Legions, the olde owners spoyled. But thys calumniation thou dyddest devise, that thou myghtest putte the faulte of the warre from thy selfe to me, and the newe inhabiters. And by thys arte, wynnyng the heartes of the olde Souldyoures, thou hast wonne also the victory: for it was persuaded them, that I woulde putte them out by violence. These devices were to be used, when thou madest warre agaynste me. Nowe beeyng Conqueroure, if thou bee an ennimie of thy Countrey, make mee an enimie also, that coulde not remedie it, beeyng lette by famyne. And thys I speake freelie, gyving my selfe (as I sayde) into thy handes, shewyng what I thought of thee before, and nowe also, beeyng with thee alone. Thus much of my selfe. . . .'

Book V, Sections 67–8

[New taxes caused riots in Rome.]

In the meane tyme the cytie was oppressed with famine,[4] for neyther durst the Merchauntes bring any corne from the East

[1] Cf. II.2.52–5.
[2] Cf. Pompey too, II.6.14–19.
[3] II.2.48–50.
[4] *In margin:* 'Famine in Rome.'

bicause of *Pompeis* being in *Sicelie*, nor from the Weast of *Corsica* and *Sardinia*, where *Pompeis* shippes also lay: nor from *Africa*, where the navies of the other conspiratours kepte their stations. Being in this distresse, they alleaged, that the discorde of the rulers was the cause, and therefore required that peace might be made with *Pompey*, unto the whiche when *Cæsar* woulde not agree,[1] *Antonie* thought warre was needfull for necessitie, and bycause mony wanted, a decree was made by *Antonies* advise, that every maister should pay the half of .xxv. drammes, for every slave that he had, which was determined to have bene done in the war of *Cassius*, and that somewhat also shoulde be payde of every mans heritage.[2] The people tore the decree with great furie, and objected the consuming of treasure publike, the spoylyng of provinces, the sacking of *Italie*, and all for private displeasure, and yet all woulde not serve, but muste nowe put newe impositions upon them that have nothing left.[3] They assembled and murmured, and compelled them that would not, and with threatnings to spoyle and burne theyr houses, gathered all the people. Then *Cæsar* with a fewe of his freends and garde, came to them to excuse themselves, but they threw stones and drove him away,[4] which when *Antonie* heard, he came to help him. To him comming the holy way, the people did nothing, bycause he was willing to agree with *Pompey*, but prayde him to departe, which when he would not do, they threw stones at him.[5] Then he brought in his soldiours that were without the walles, and not about him, into the citie, being divided into market places and streates, wounded and set upon the multitude and killed them in the streates as they came. And they could not easily flee for the multitude, nor breake through by runnyng, so that many were hurte and killed, crying and yellyng from their houses.

So *Antonie* hadde muche ado to escape and *Cæsar* by him was evidently preserved and got away.[6] Thus did *Antonie* delyver *Cæsar* from present perill.

[1] *In margin:* '*Cæsar* wyll not agree to peace with *Pompey*.'
[2] *In margin:* 'A payment put upon the people.'
[3] *In margin:* 'The people resist the decree of *Cæsar* and *Antony*.'
[4] *In margin:* 'The people resist *Cæsar*.'
[5] *In margin:* 'Who buyeth friendship to deere shal smart as *Antony* did.'
[6] *In margin:* '*Cæsar* escapeth by *Antonies* meanes.'

VII. Translation of Analogue

From THE DEEDS OF CÆSAR[1]

[1] *I Fatti di Cesare*, ed. L. Banchi, Bologna, 1863.

Anon. [13th century]

Chapter XXXI

How [Julius] Cæsar went to the Castle of Paluse where Ptolemy was; and how Cleopatra, having learned of his coming, went to him and begged him to give her back her kingdom; and how Cæsar was enamoured of the beautiful Queen and dined in the marvellous palace of Ptolemy; and while feasting spoke with Achoreus, the priest of Alexandria, about the customs of the country and the sources of the Nile.

Then he went to the Castle of Paluse, where Ptolemy was; and Cleopatra the Queen was in prison, and hearing of Cæsar's coming cunningly sought speech with him; and Cæsar, who had heard talk about her great beauty, had her brought to the palace. She was very beautiful, and she exerted herself greatly to deck herself out to please Cæsar. Coming to the palace she spoke to Cæsar and said: 'My father made no distinction between women and men, and left me the kingdom in his will; but those false counsellors Pothinus and Achillas have taken away my right.'

With such words Cleopatra addressed Cæsar in that wonderful palace, which was all in plates of gold and encrusted with gems. The overlay was of onyx and chalcedony; the statues by the gates, some were of ivory and some of fine gold and very lovely, and some were of purest silver. The eyes of the images were the finest of sapphires. The attendants and the slaves were as various as the flowers of the fields: some blonde as gold, others black beyond measure, some young, some old, some small, some tall.

Cleopatra sat in Cæsar's view as well adorned and decked out as any lady in the world. Her hair she had surrounded with precious stones, the best ever found in the Red Sea. She had at her throat a circlet of splendid gold, which heightened the whiteness of her neck. She was clad in cloth of gold with figures in relief, marvellous to see. She had a belt of snakeskin ornamented with bright gold; also a covering of curious samite [?] lined with white ermine. The buckle was of fine gold in which were fixed two pure rubies worth two great cities.

The beauteous Cleopatra endeavoured to allure Cæsar, and Cæsar gazed on her clear brow, broad and level above the eyebrows, which were fine and well turned; her eyes shining and lovely; her nose straight, delicate and well-formed; her mouth small and pouting with the lips crimson and the teeth white and small; her hair chestnut; her shoulders smooth and well-shaped; her breasts full and jutting out on her body; her hands long and fine; the fingers and the wrists likewise, in the finest of coverings; the hips plump and wide; the feet small, shod in a silken material.

The appurtenances were noble. The water was in crystal vases. There were urns full of flowery nard, cinnamon and balsams. They ate delicate meats of wild beasts; peacocks and other birds were served dressed in diverse ways. Cleopatra, Ptolemy and Cæsar ate together at one table. Cæsar spoke with Achoreus the high priest of Alexandria, who was at the feast and by the table, of the customs of the country, and the ways of the river, and the diversity of that great land. This Achoreus, who was an astrologer, spoke in answer to Cæsar's questions and told him everything, the order of the planets, and how in Ethiopia there are black men; he told of the Nile and how it grows and how it diminishes through the virtue of the planet called Mercury, and how the King of Persia and of Macedonia wished to know the source of the Nile and how King Alexander sought to know it. . . .

[The Death of Cleopatra] [1]

[Cleopatra killed herself to avoid being kept in prison to satisfy Octavius's sister who hated her.] She called a faithful slave and bade him find a live serpent. She went to the tomb where Antony was buried (and where all the noble kings and famous men of Egypt were interred), telling her slave that she wished to make a sacrifice to God by the body of Antony her lord.

She undressed herself naked as she was born and went into the tomb with the serpent, making the slave close her up in the tomb, and thrust him out sorrowing. Then she placed that snake to her left breast near her heart. And thus died Cleopatra, and this was her final end. Praise be to God.

VIII. Summary of Analogue

CLEOPATRA

by G. B. Giraldi Cinthio (1583 edition)

Cleopatra Tragedia di M. Gio Battista Giraldi Cinthio

[1] Added in a manuscript of *I Fatti di Cesare*.

Nobile Ferrarese. In Venetia. Appresso Giulio Cesare Cagnacini. MDLXXXIII.

Prologue

Among the things invented by the ancients
To inculcate good manners to the world
Nothing there is gives more delight and joy
Than fables well presented on the stage.
And though the kinds of these are various,
Among them certainly the foremost place
And greatest praise is held by Tragedy,
Whether it have a doleful end or happy;
A poem that in gravity exceeds
Whatever was composed in Greece or Rome.
In it are imitated real actions
With such solemnity and such decorum
As pity springs from them and also horror,
Purging our mortal souls from every vice
And making us towards virtue only yearn
By seeing how those persons meet their end
Who are not either wholly good or bad.
  Thus, howsoever difficult it seem
To the most excellent and noble minds,
Today the Poet nonetheless has tried
(As well as he is able) to present
For common use on stage a Tragedy
In which is told the end of Cleopatra,
To whom the whole of Egypt once was subject,
The end of Antony, too, who fought Octavius
To subject to his rule the world entire.
  Here now, Spectators, you shall see how little
True happiness can be got from Empires, Wealth,
Power and all other human attributes
When the pursuit of pleasure outruns virtue;
Pleasure which draws a man beyond his scope.
For greater war against imperial rule
Is made by pleasures and delights beyond
The customary rule of human reason
Than many squadrons of armed enemies,
And he alone can reign for long and well
Who, taking light of reason for his guide,
Knows to command and rule over himself.
  This place is Alexandria; that is Egypt

Made fertile by the waters of the Nile.
The story here befell of which I spake,
Which could to many give examples good.
  I would say more, but I see Cleopatra
Waiting to enter, and my duty is
To give way to her. 'Tis enough for now
T'have shown you what the subject is to be
Of this our Tragedy. So at the end
Of my discourse, I ask a gracious hearing
In the Poet's name, who thinks and cares for naught
But to provide by pleasing that delight
Which is most apt to royal fables. Hence
I pray you listen most attentively
To these grave happenings. Thus never may
Desires vain afflict you, but your life
Be ever happy, happy too your end,
And glory eternal in this world attend you.

Act I.

Scene I.

[Cleopatra, awaiting the outcome of Antony's land-battle against Octavius Cæsar, expresses dark forebodings to her Nurse.]

CLEO. Where ever may I turn my afflicted mind,
Alas? I'm so opposed by Fortune that
I know not what to hope in any matter.

[The Nurse says that Fortune may change again. Cleopatra tells how she fled at Actium and destroyed Antony who followed her, 'Rapt in the singular love he felt for me'. She fears that, if he loses today's battle, she may be carried off to Rome. The Nurse thinks he may win but Cleopatra cannot hope for a happy outcome since Fortune appears so contrary.]

Scene 2.

[An Attendant enters and declares that Antony has been betrayed by men he trusted, e.g.]

ATT. But yesterday because a soldier showed
High valour 'gainst the enemy, Mark Antony,
The more to encourage him, gave him in the field
Remarkable presents, as did Cleopatra.
At night the unfaithful wretch to Cæsar fled,
And took up arms today 'gainst Antony
His noble benefactor (caring naught

For gifts or faith), thus giving ample proof
That souls towards evil turned cannot be changed
By benefits received . . .

[The Attendant brings worse news:]

Alas,
Poor Cleopatra, to what hour of grief
Have you been led! O how unhappy was
That day when in the barges made of gold,
With oars of silver and with purple sails,
You went to meet Mark Antony, so decked
That Venus' self resembled you exactly
When out she went Bacchus to meet. That day
The miserable ruin was declared
Of you yourself and also of your realm.

[Antony has been defeated. He is still alive, but hopeless, and blames Cleopatra for betraying him at Actium.]

Scene 3.

[Cleopatra soliloquises, bitterly lamenting that the reward of her faithful love is to be accused of treachery. She says that when Thyreus came from Octavius Antony became suspicious of her. She will go to her tomb.]

For I've no wish
(Since Heaven has made me Antony's wife) to live
Without his love, nor do I wish to survive him
—Not by one hour—once he is alive no more.

Scene 4.

[One of Antony's Captains mourns the downfall of Antony ('honour erst of the Romans') and wishes that his general would die with him, sword in hand, a 'noble death'.]

Scene 5.

[Antony enters with a Servant, and utters his despair:]

ANT. Fortune, alas, woe's me, Fortune where have you
Now borne Mark Antony?
. . . O Cleopatra, wicked,
Evil one, unfaithful, villainous!
Through you, through you alone, am I, who brought
Terror to all the world, now given up
Into my enemy's power . . .

[He asks his faithful Slave to kill him with his sword. The Captain bids him not let his glorious life have so vile an end. Antony says that he has betrayed his soldiers. The Captain begs him not to despair. Antony thinks it folly to go on hoping:]

ANT. I had of the future a clear prophecy
As far back as the opening of the war,
In dreaming that a burning thunderbolt
Had struck my right hand fiercely . . .

[Cleopatra is now his enemy. The Captain recalls previous setbacks —in Italy, at Modena, and in the Alps, but Antony is not consoled.]

Scene 6.

[The Nurse announces that Cleopatra has killed herself to prove her good faith:]

. . . She took up in her hand a knife
And said: 'May this my blood bear witness to
My innocence and my fidelity';
And having spoken thus, woe's me, unhappy,
She struck herself to the heart and fell down dead . . .

[Antony declares that he will kill himself to be with her, and goes off.]

Scene 7.

[The Nurse, left alone, says that she lied because Cleopatra wished to test Antony's love.]

Scene 8.

[Cleopatra enters and the Nurse tells her that Antony still loves her. Cleopatra bids her tell him that she is alive and feigned death only to know if he was angry with her. Exeunt.]

Scene 9

[The Captain enters, regretting that great men let themselves be enslaved by women:]

So the great Captain, when he gave himself
Entire to Cleopatra's will became,
From man of courage, like the vilest slave,
Fearing one glance of the lady as
Children are wont to fear the teacher's rod.

[Now he has killed himself.]

Cruel indeed the influence of the stars
(If stars it were that brought him to this death

And not Tesiphone or Megara)
That led him to Cleopatra here in Egypt.

[The Chorus ends the Act explaining that God holds men in his power, but his ways are various.]

God did not bind
The will of man but with true freedom made him
The lord of his own actions.

[If man is misled blindly by vain desires God has mercy, but if he voluntarily strays, loving the shackles of sin better than a free and serene life, then man is truly afflicted by the bondage he chooses for himself. In this way Antony and Cleopatra are suffering.]

Act II

Scene I.

[Learning that Antony is bleeding to death, Cleopatra mourns over him. He bids her remain alive, for he will be happy if she, the most lovely and faithful lady ever married to a man, will keep his memory green.]

Scene 2.

[A Eunuch and the Lady-in-Waiting describe Antony's death.]

Scene 3.

[Cleopatra enters and laments:]

While you were living, Antony, you were
My life. Now you my death also shall be
Since you, alas, are dead . . .

[She wishes to die and be buried in the same tomb. Her Lady entreats her for all their sakes not to die, but she is determined, repeating]

I cannot live now that my Lord is dead.
He was my life; without him life is death.

[In vain the Eunuch tells her that she will master her grief and hostile Fortune. Exeunt.]

Scene 4.

[Cleopatra's secretary enters; he expatiates on her grief. She has sent him to fetch Olimpus her faithful doctor.]

Scene 5.

[Octavius enters with Agrippa, Mæcenas, and a Standard-bearer. Ignorant of Antony's death he asks his friends for their views on how he should treat the defeated general. Mæcenas advises moderation and clemency. Little honour comes by killing a fallen foe, much by pardoning him. Agrippa is for excuting Antony so as to end all danger. They have a long debate on mercy and severity.

The Chorus ends the Act.]

Act III

Scene 1.

[Olimpus has tried to reason with Cleopatra:]

I thought that just as I have faithfully cured
The infirmities of bodies, so I might
Take also from her heart by fruitful words
The grief which pierces her like sharpest knife.

[She would not listen to him, but ordered him to prepare a poison 'by which she might die painlessly.' When he answered that it was his duty to save life, not to take it, she drove him out with bitter words.]

Scene 2.

[The Nurse calls Olimpus back to Cleopatra.]

Scene 3.

Mæcenas and Agrippa continue their debate, Mæcenas saying that Octavius must not kill Antony or he will become unpopular in Rome. Agrippa disagrees. Mæcenas says that at worst Octavius should not stain his fingers with blood, but keep Antony in prison.]

Scene 4.

[The Captain enters saying that such strange things have happened]

That I believe Fortune had seized on Antony
At the beginning of this bitter war
To make a jest and sport upon his woe.

[Mæcenas says that Antony was so enslaved to Cleopatra]

That he who 'mid the lances and the swords
Had walked secure, has met his death through her
He loved more than his eyes, nay more than life,
After her vile and most blameworthy flight.

[The Captain is taking to Octavius the sword which killed Mark Antony, hoping thereby to win pardon for fighting against him.]

Scene 5.

[The Nurse tells the Lady-in-Waiting her fears for Cleopatra:]

Happy indeed can we call Antony
Who died a free man on the loved breast
Of Cleopatra, has not had to see her
(As I fear well we may) in servile yoke
Under the power of Roman women.

[She believes that all we do is fated:]

Daughter, our first day brings our final one,
For all our destiny is born with us.

Scene 6.

[Mæcenas tells a Servant of Mark Antony that Octavius had a thousand reasons to hate Antony and wish him dead,]

And yet when he beheld the sword all stained
With Antony's blood and learned that he was dead,
He was not able to withhold his tears,
Sign of a generous and noble heart,
A true example of the Roman soul.

[By pardoning Antony's soldiers]

Well showest thou, Octavius, only need
It was and not thy wish brought thee to arms.

[The Servant, bearing letters from Antony to Cæsar, describes Cleopatra as representing grief in human form. She will die of sorrow unless some hope comes from Octavius to keep her alive. Mæcenas wishes that he could persuade Octavius to pardon Cleopatra as he got him to pardon Antony's men.]

For mercy
Descended has, I think, from heaven to earth
So that by it man may resemble God;
But yet I fear to urge it will be vain,
For I imagine that, insane for glory,
He'll want her to adorn his Roman triumph.

Scene 7.

[Mark Antony's servant says that if Octavius really means what he says he will treat Cleopatra honourably, but 'I greatly fear the snake lurks in the flowers.' Cleopatra should pretend to believe Cæsar's fair words. If they are true, all will be well; if not, at the worst she can kill herself.]

Scene 8.

[Octavius tells Mæcenas and Agrippa of his grief at Antony's death. Antony's letters show him to have been wiser and more thoughtful in dying than ever before in his life. He sends Agrippa to persuade Cleopatra that all will be well.

The Chorus reflects on the evils of blind desire and passion, and the need for men to rule their lives by reason.]

Act IV

Scene 1.

[Agrippa soliloquises. A great lord should not tempt Fortune as Antony and Cleopatra have done. Not content with Egypt Cleopatra has taken up arms with Antony in hope of ruling the universe with him.]

Scene 2.

[Cleopatra's doctor Olimpus enters, reflecting on the ill worked by Fortune:]

I know not what a man may hold as certain
In this our mortal state, when we behold
Kingdoms which among human things are so
Momentous, girt with strength, such great defences,
Are oft by Fortune toppled upside down.

[He and Agrippa discuss whether Octavius will be merciful.]

OLIMP. A conqueror neither thinks nor cares of aught
But to display supremacy, imagining
That he will never see it turn against him.

[Cleopatra will have to suffer the will of Octavius, who will try to keep her alive whatever she may wish.]

Scene 3.

[Going to Cleopatra's tomb Agrippa soliloquises. Death is the natural way out for anyone cast down from high rank; Olimpus probably knows Cleopatra's mind and that she will die.]

Scene 4.

[Returning from a vain attempt to see Cleopatra Olimpus tells Agrippa that she refuses to reply as yet to Octavius's advances.]

Scene 5.

[Left alone Olimpus ruminates on the evils of courts and the miseries of those who serve in them.]

Scene 6.

[Proculeius and Gallus discuss how to take Cleopatra alive. Proculeius knows how to get into the 'proud Pyramid' which she has built to be her sepulchre. If Gallus will hold her in conversation he will mount to the window by which she admitted Antony.]

Scene 7.

[Cleopatra. Gallus. Lady-in-Waiting. Proculeius. Olimpus. Olimpus tries to persuade Cleopatra to come to the gate and talk to Gallus.]

CLEO. Merely to see him whom Octavius made
Cut off the head of Antilus, moves me much
To fear that he may also soon extend
A like fate to my sons . . .

[Since Octavius has seized them she will promise to remain alive if he will set them free, and to live with them henceforth as a private person. Olimpus says that if she will come out and listen to Gallus she need fear no enemy.]

CLEO. No enemy? I only have two ladies,
The noblest and most faithful that I've known
Ever at court. Bid him rather, Olimpus,
Come hither first, and lest you think I fail
To come and hear him speak, I'll stand within here
And come out further when you summon me.

OLIMPUS [to Gallus] I beg you be content to wait till I
See if she'll give you audience.

GALLUS I'll wait.
(*aside*) I think that Proculeius must by now
Have placed the ladders. Maybe he has entered.

OLIMPUS Come, sir; she waits you at the entrance; but
She asks you not to approach her nearer than
Here where I stand.

GALLUS So that I speak to her,
I care not whether I am near or far,
Nothing I have to bring her but means well.
O Queen, my lord Octavius sends to you
Greetings.

CLEO. Alas that I have need of them.

GALLUS My lord has nothing in his thoughts except
To give you proof, O Queen, of his great mercy.

LADY Woe, Majesty! here in the sepulchre

Are enemies, and you are ta'en alive!
See, Majesty, behold them at your side!

CLEO. Ah traitors! Even so, you shall not have
What you expect, if this sword fail me not!

PROCUL. Do it not, Majesty!

CLEO. Is this the way
Cæsar intends to send me hopes of good?

OLIMPUS Ah traitors! Criminals! Release the Queen!

PROCUL. What can you hope to do, Olimpus? 'Twere
More wise to stand there quiet, not seek death.

OLIMPUS I kill myself because I would not see
My Queen in servitude.

PROCUL. Will someone take
This madman's sword?
Your Majesty, all's done for your own good.
Our lord and master feared that grief might prove
Stronger in you than reason . . .

[Cleopatra is taken out under guard.]

Scene 8.

[Olimpus, left alone, thinks that Cæsar will want Cleopatra's treasure.]

Scene 9.

[Octavius has a long interview with Cleopatra in which she tries to deceive him about her intentions.]

OCT. All reason would suggest that Cleopatra
Should come to meet her conqueror, but since
I seek to give her every reassurance
And since she's called for me, I'll go to her
In order to remove her deep suspicion.

[Gallus brings Cæsar to meet Cleopatra. She makes a long speech of submission and self-defence, referring to Julius Cæsar, 'Who held you as his son and made me Queen / Of Egypt'. She was forced to join Antony against Octavius.]

That was not, Sir, result of my own wish,
Nor could I do aught else, unhappy woman,
Timid by nature, inexpert in affairs,
When Antony came upon me with such power,
So numerous a host . . .
I was not fitted to resist him then,
Nor was I able to refuse to obey him.

[She joined Antony to preserve her throne. When Octavius asks why she let Thyreus be ill-treated, she answers that, having become Antony's wife, she did his bidding,]

And since I had become his wife, I should
Have been devoid of honesty and justice
Had I not wished to share in common with him
All happinesses, griefs, all good and evil.

[She could not break faith with her husband. Now, she admits]

Ashamed I feel to know myself alive,
Because I have betrayed him . . .

[She does not want to escape punishment but begs to be buried with Mark Antony. Octavius declares that he will treat her well if she will not die. Cleopatra says that her life now becomes dear to her, since it is dear to him. She wishes to perform Antony's exequies]

ere I leave Egypt
And come to Rome as I desire to do,
Octavia and your Livia to honour.

[Octavius agrees to her request.]
Chorus.

Act V

Scene I.

[Olimpus, in soliloquy, says that unhappy people find it hard to believe promises of good, but Cleopatra has believed Octavius:]

Nevertheless, my Queen, than whom was ne'er
A woman more unhappy, who herself
Might well have freed, giving herself to death
To fly dishonour and escape from pain,
Four little words which Cæsar has said to her,
Giving her thus I know not what of hope,
Have left her ripe to think that, loosed from care,
She may regain her kingdom and her sons,
Nay, hope yet better things and not fear evil.
But if she lets herself accompany Cæsar
To Rome, she'll see, she'll know, true misery;
For that which she has suffered has been nothing
Beside the anguish she will have to endure
When she is led in bonds to the Capitol,
As I foresee she will be . . .

Scene 2.

[In a long soliloquy Cleopatra shows that she is not deceived by Octavius's fair words.]

And so you think, Octavius, that I am
Void of intelligence, nay out of my wits,
And that I've not perceived why you so long
For me to stay alive; and that I fail
To see your promises and your deceits
Are all so many snares you put around me
To bring me bound unto the Capitol.

[Had Antony been alive and victorious she would have liked to go to Rome, to do to Cæsar, Octavia and Livia what they now think to do to her. She will not go alive to Rome,]

. . . but to end
Under the sky where I was born, let now
My life depart.

[She prays the gods of Egypt to ensure that she be buried with Mark Antony.]

Scene 3.

[Gallus has been sent by Octavius to ensure that Cleopatra does not 'dispose of herself as she pleases' while performing Antony's obsequies.]

Scene 4.

[An Attendant of Cleopatra enters.]

ATT. 'Tis often said that no man can be sure
Whether he's happy or unhappy while
He is alive, nor if his life be good
Or guilty; since his dying day is that
Gives final blame and praise to every man.

[Cleopatra has gone to perform the last rites adorned with her sceptre and crown. It is a pity that when great ones fall they do not become humble:]

It seems this proud Queen, being ill content
To have sunk Mark Antony to the lowest rung,
Not only does not shed her regal heart,
But fills her mind with loftier desires,

Because the memory of what has been
(To the end self-asking, 'What am I?', 'What was I?')
Brings double grief and doubly grieves itself.
So must it be with Cleopatra . . .

[He is carrying a letter from her to Octavius.]

Scene 5.

[Gallus informs Octavius that Cleopatra is firmly guarded in her palace, along with her two Ladies. The letter brought by the Attendant however declares that she is about to kill herself.]

Scene 6.

[Proculeius now enters, bringing news of Cleopatra's death. He relates that he went to Cleopatra's chamber and found a Priest with a torch standing outside.]

PROC. Arriving at the chamber, in the entrance
I saw one of her waiting-ladies, dead,
Standing at foot of the couch, and saw the other
Who o'er the Queen (reposing on the couch
Clad in a cloth of gold) the crown adjusted
Upon her head, and placed the royal sceptre
In her right hand. I said, 'Why do you this?'
''Tis done', she said, 'in order to escape
Servitude and deep shame.'—and thereupon
Fell dead. I quickly to the bed advanced
And set myself to shake the Queen Cleopatra,
Calling her loudly, but she hearing naught
And not responding, I saw she was dead
And that too late you sent to warn me end
The liberty which you had given her.

OCT. How true the saying, that a woman is
The breeding-place of lying and the nest
Of all deceits! Who ever would have thought,
Seeing her smiles, her promises and gestures,
That she concealed within her heart desire
Of death? How did she kill herself?

PROC. I do not know, my lord. She had no dagger
(I turned her over in my search for one)
Nor had she any instrument in sight
By which she could have given herself to death.

[The Priest describes the rites for Antony and recites her speech over his body, telling how she bent over the bier and kissed her lover saying 'Alas, how great a change in Fortune / Had you and I'. Octavius is moved. The Priest describes Cleopatra's end:]

And having spoken thus, turning in tears
To her ladies, she instructed them to bring
A silver vessel. From her right temple
She took a golden tube round which she'd twined
Her hair, and placed it in the bowl. At once
Over the bowl she laid her naked arm,
And taking up the tube she touched her flesh
And, as if happy, said: 'See now, Mark Antony,
Your Cleopatra comes to you, no more
To be divided ever from you. Welcome
Her gaily as you used to do when you
Were with her in this life which now she leaves
To be with you!' Then as by gentle sleep
Borne down, without another word or breath
She lay still on the couch like one just dead;
And dead also with her the two fair ladies,
Using the same means she herself had used.
This have I seen and heard, and so much can
I tell you of the passing of our Queen.

OCT. Immeasurable was the love of both
Of these; and though they were my bitter enemies
And her death is as dangerous to me
As anything could be, I do not wish
To separate these bodies, since their souls
Such perfect love has joined . . .

[He orders them to be buried together. The Priest says that it is the sign of a 'Roman soul' thus to honour great enemies.]

OCT. And when this task is finished, Proculeius,
Come to the fleet together with your host
For we'll have settled all we must in Egypt,
And, our task ended, we'll proceed to Rome.

[The Chorus sings that Fortune is most to be feared when she shows herself most favourable.]

IX. Analogue

THE TRAGEDIE OF ANTONIE[1]

by Robert Garnier

translated by Mary Herbert (Sidney) (1595 edition)

The Tragedie of Antonie. Doone into English by the Countesse of Pembroke. Imprinted at London for William Ponsonby. 1595.

The Tragedie of Antonie

THE ARGUMENT

After the overthrowe of Brutus *and* Cassius, *the libertie of* Rome *being now utterly opressed, and the Empire setled in the hands of* Octavius Cæsar *and* Marcus Antonius, (*who for knitting a straiter bonde of amitie betweene them, had taken to wife* Octavia *the sister of* Cæsar)[2] Antonius *undertooke a journey against the Parthians, with intent to regaine on them the honor won by them from the Romanes, at the discomfiture and slaughter of* Crassus. *But comming in his journey into Siria the places renewed in his remembrance the long intermitted love of* Cleopatra, *Queene of Aegipte: who before time had both in Cilicia and at Alexandria, entertained him with all the exquisite delightes and sumptuous pleasures, which a great Prince and voluptuous lover could to the uttermost desire. Whereupon omitting his enterprice, he made his returne to Alexandria, againe falling to his former loves, without any regarde of his vertuous wife* Octavia, *by whom nevertheles he had excellent children. This occation* Octavius *toke of taking armes against him: & preparing a mighty fleet, encountred him at Actium, who also had assembled to that place a great number of Gallies of his own, beside 60 which* Cleopatra *brought with her from Aegipt. But at the very beginning of the battel* Cleopatra *with all her Gallies betooke her to flight, which* Antony *seeing could not but follow: by his departure leaving to* Octavius *the greatest victory which in any Sea battell hath beene hard off. Which he not negligent to pursue, followes them the next spring and besiedgeth them within Alexandria, where* Antony *finding al that he trusted to faile him, beginneth to growe jealouse and to suspect* Cleopatra. *She thereupon enclosed her selfe with two of her women in a monument she had before caused to be built, thence sends*

[1] Called *Antonius* in the first edition, 1592.
[2] Cf. *AC.* II.2.130–3.

him worde she was dead: which he beleeving for truth, gave himselfe with his Sworde a deadly wound: but died not until a messenger came from Cleopatra *to have him brought to her to the tombe. Which she not daring to open least she should bee made a prisoner to the Romaines, & carried in* Cæsars *triumph, cast downe a cord from an high window, by the which (her women helping her) she trussed up* Antonius *halfe dead, & so got him into the monument. The stage supposed Alexandria: the chorus first Egiptians, & after Romane souldiors: The history to be read at large in* Plutarch *in the life of* Antonius.

The Actors

Antonius.
Cleopatra.
Eras *and* Charmion } Cleopatras *women*
Philostratus *a Philosopher.*
Lucilius.
Diomede *Secretarie to* Cleopatra.
Octavius Cæsar.
Agrippa.
Euphron, *teacher of* Cleopatras *children.*
Children *of* Cleopatra,
Dircctus *the Messenger.*

[Act 1.]

Antonius

Since cruell Heav'ns against me obstinate,
Since all mishappes of the round engin doo
Conspire my harme: since men, since powers divine
Aire, earth, and Sea are all injurious:
And that my Queene her selfe, in whome I liv'd,
The Idoll of my harte, doth me pursue;
It's meete I dye. For her have I forgone
My Country, *Cæsar* unto warre provok'd
(For just revenge of Sisters wrong, my wife,
Who mov'de my Queene (ay me!) to jealousie)
For love of her, in her allurements caught,
Abandon'd life, I honor have despisde,
Disdain'd my freends, and of the statelye Rome
Despoilde the Empire of her best attire,
Contemn'd that power that made me so much fear'd,
A slave become unto her feeble face.

O cruell, traitres, woman most unkinde,
Thou dost, forsworne, my love and life betraie:
And giv'st me up to ragefull enemie,
Which soone (o foole!) will plague thy perjurye.
 Yeelded *Pelusium* on this countries shore,
Yeelded thou hast my Shippes and men of warre,
That nought remaines (so destitute am I)
But these same armes which on my back I weare.
Thou should'st have had them too, and me unarm'de
Yeelded to *Cæsar* naked of defence.
Which while I beare let *Cæsar* never thinke
Triumph of me shall his proud chariot grace
Not thinke with me his glory to adorne,
On me alive to use his victorie.
 Thou only *Cleopatra* triumph hast,
Thou only hast my fredome servile made,
Thou only hast me vanquisht: not by force
(For forste I cannot be) but by sweete baites
Of thy eyes graces, which did gaine so fast
Upon my libertie, that nought remain'd.
None els henceforth, but thou my dearest Queene,
Shall glorie in commaunding *Antonie*.
 Have *Cæsar* fortune and the Gods his freends,
To him have love and fatall sisters given
The Scepter of the earth: he never shall
Subject my life to his obedience.
But when that death, my glad refuge, shall have
Bounded the course of my unstedfast life,
And frosen corps under a marble colde
Within tombes bosome widdowe of my soule:
Then at his will let him it subject make:
Then what he will let *Cæsar* doo with me:
Make me limme after limme be rent: make me
My buriall take in sides of *Thracian* wolfe.
 Poore *Antonie*! alas what was the day,
The daies of losse that gained thee thy love!
Wretch *Antonie*! since *Mægæra* pale
With Snakie haires enchain'd thy miserie.
The fire thee burnt was never *Cupids* fire
(For Cupid beares not such a mortall brand)
It was some furies torch, *Orestes* torche,
Which somtimes burnt his mother-murdering soule
(When wandring madde, rage boiling in his bloud,
He fled his fault which folow'd as he fled)

Kindled within his bones by shadow pale
Of mother slaine return'd from Stygian lake.
  Antony, poore *Antony*! since that daie
Thy olde good hap did faire from thee retire.
Thy vertue dead: thy glory made alive
So ofte by martiall deeds is gone in smoke:
Since then the Baies so well thy forehead knewe
To Venus mirtles yeelded have their place:
Trumpets to pipes: field tents to courtly bowers:
Launces and Pikes to daunces and to feastes.
Since then, o wretch! instead of bloudy warres
Thou shouldst have made upon the Parthian Kings
For Romain honor filde by *Crassus* foile,
Thou threw'st thy Curiace off, and fearfull healme,
With coward courage unto *Aegipts* Queene
In haste to runne, about her necke to hang
Languishing in her armes thy Idoll made:
In summe given up to *Cleopatras* eies.
Thou breakest at length from thence, as one encharm'd
Breakes from th'enchaunter that him strongly helde.[1]
For thy first reason (spoyling of their force
The poisned cuppes of thy faire Sorceres)
Recur'd thy sperit: and then on every side
Thou mad'st again the earth with Souldiours swarme.
All Asia hidde: Euphrates bankes do tremble
To see at once so many Romanes there
Breath horror, rage, and with a threatning eye
In mighty squadrons crosse his swelling streames.
Nought seene but horse, and fiery sparkling armes:
Nought heard but hideous noise of muttring troups.
The *Parth*, the *Mede*, abandoning their goods
Hide them for feare in hilles of *Hircanie*,
Redoubting thee. Then willing to besiege
The great *Phraate* head of *Media*,
Thou campedst at her walles with vaine assault,
Thy engins fit (mishap!) not thither brought,
  So long thou stai'st, so long thou dost thee rest,
So long thy love with such things nourished
Reframes, reformes it selfe and stealingly
Retakes his force and rebecomes more great.
For of thy Queene the lookes, the grace, the words,
Sweetnes, alurements, amorous delights,

[1] Cf. I.2.131.

Entred againe thy soule, and day and night,
In watch, in sleepe, her Image follow'd thee:
Not dreaming but of her, repenting still
That thou for warre hadst such a goddes left.
  Thou car'st no more for *Parth*, nor *Parthian* bow,
Sallies, assaults, encounters, shocks, alarmes,
For ditches, rampiers, wards, entrenched grounds:
Thy only care is sight of *Nilus* streames,
Sight of that face whose gilefull semblant doth
(Wandring in thee) infect thy tainted hart.
Her absence thee besottes: each hower, each hower
Of staie, to thee impatient seemes an age.
Enough of conquest, praise thou deem'st enough,
If soone enough the bristled fields thou see
Of fruitfull *Aegipt*, and the stranger floud
Thy Queenes faire eyes (another *Pharos*) lights.
  Returned loe, dishonoured, despisde,
In wanton love a woman thee misleades
Sunke in foule sinke: meanewhile respecting nought
Thy wife *Octavia* and her tender babes,
Of whome the long contempt against thee whets
The sword of *Cæsar* now thy Lord become.
  Lost thy great Empire, all those goodly townes
Reverenc'd thy name as rebells now thee leave:
Rise against thee, and to the ensignes flocke
Of conqu'ring *Cæsar*, who enwalles thee round
Cag'd in thy hold, scarse maister of thy selfe,
Late maister of so many Nations.
  Yet, yet, which is of griefe extreamest griefe,
Which is yet of mischiefe highest mischiefe,
It's *Cleopatra* alas! alas, it's she,
It's she augments the torment of thy paine,
Betraies thy love, thy life alas! betraies,
Cæsar to please, whose grace she seekes to gaine:
With thought her crowne to save and fortune make
Onely thy foe which common ought have beene.
  If her I alwaies lov'd, and the first flame
Of her heart-killing love shall burne me last:
Justly complaine I she disloyall is,
Nor constant is, even as I constant am,
To comfort my mishap, despising me
No more, then when the heavens favour'd me.
  But ah! by nature women wav'ring are,
Each moment changing and rechanging mindes.

Unwise, who blinde in them, thinkes loyaltie
Ever to finde in beauties companie.

Chorus

The boyling tempest still
  makes not Sea waters fome:
  nor still the Northern blast
  disquiets quiet streames:
  Nor who his chest to fill
  sayles to the morning beames,
  on waves winde tosseth fast,
  still kepes his ship from home.
Nor *Jove* still downe doth cast
  inflam'd with bloudie ire
  on man, on tree, on hill,
  his darts of thundring fire.
  nor still the heat doth last
  on face of parched plaine
  nor wrinkled colde doth still
  on frozen furrowes raigne.
But still as long as we
  in this low world remaine,
  mishapps our daily mates
  our lifes doe intertaine:
  and woes which beare no dates
  still pearch upon our heads;
  none go but straight will be
  some greater in their steads.
Nature made us not free
  When first she made us live:
  When we began to be,
  To be began our woe:
  Which growing evermore
  As dying life doth growe,
  Do more and more us greeve,
  And tire us more and more.
No stay in fading states,
  For more to height they retch,
  Their fellow miseries
  The more to height do stretch.
  They cling even to the crowne,
  And threatning furious wise
  From tirannizing pates

Do often pull it downe.
In vaine on waves untride
To shun them go we should
To *Scythes* and *Massagetes*
Who neere the Pole reside:
In vaine to boiling sandes
Which *Phœbus* battry beates,
For with us still they would
Cut seas and compasse landes.
The darknes no more sure
To joyne with heavy night:
The light which guildes the days
To follow *Titan* pure:
No more the shadow light
The body to ensue:
Than wretchednes alwaies
Us wretches to pursue.
O blest who never breath'd,
Or whome with pittie mov'de,
Death from his cradle reav'de,
And swadled in his grave:
And blessed also he
(As curse may blessing have)
Who low and living free
No princes charge hath prov'de.
By stealing sacred fire
Prometheus then unwise,
provoking Gods to ire,
the heape of ills did sturre,
and sicknes pale and colde
our ende which onward spurre,
to plague our hands too bolde
to filch the wealth of skies.
In heavens hate since then
of ill with ill enchain'd
we race of mortall men
ful fraught our brests have borne
and thousand thousand woes
our heav'nly soules now thorne,
which free before from those
no earthly passion pain'd.
Warre and warrs bitter cheare
now long time with us staie,
and feare of hated foe

still still encreaseth sore:
our harmes worse dayly grow:
lesse yesterday they were
then now, and will be more
to morrow then to day.

Act 2.

Philostratus.

What horrible furie, what cruell rage,
O *Aegipt* so extremely thee torments?
Hast thou the Gods so angred by thy fault?
Hast thou against them some such crime conceiv'd,
That their engrained hand lift up in threats
They should desire in thy heart bloud to bathe?
And that their burning wrath which noght can quench
Should pittiles on us still lighten downe?
We are not hew'n out of the monst'rous masse
Of *Giantes* those, which heavens wrack conspir'd:
Ixions race, false prater of his loves:
Nor yet of him who fained lightnings found:
Nor cruell *Tantalus*, nor bloudy *Atreus*,
Whose cursed banquet for *Thyestes* plague
Made the beholding Sunne for horrour turne
His backe, and backward from his course returne:
And hastning his wing-footed horses race
Plunge him in sea for shame to hide his face:
While sulleine night upon the wondring world
For mid-daies light her starrie mantle cast.
But what we be, what ever wickednesse
By us is done, Alas! with what more plagues,
More eager torments could the Gods declare
To heaven and earth that us they hatefull holde?
With souldiors, strangers, horrible in armes
Our land is hidde, our people drown'd in teares.
But terror here and horror, nought is seene:
And present death prising our life each hower.
Hard at our ports and at our porches waites
Our conquering foe: harts faile us, hopes are dead:
Our Queene laments: and this great Emperour
Somtime (would now they did) whom worlds did fear
Abandoned, betraid, now mindes no more
But from his evils by hast'ned death to passe.
Come you poore people tirde with ceasles plaints,

With teares and sighes make mournfull sacrifice
On *Isis* altars: not our selves to save,
But soften *Cæsar* and him piteous make
To us, his praie: that so his lenitie
May change our death into captivitie.
  Strange are the evils the fates on us have brought;
O but alas! how far more strange the cause!
Love, love (alas, who ever would have thought?)
Hath lost this Realme inflamed with his fire.
Love, playing love, which men say kindles not
But in soft hearts, hath ashes made our townes.
And his sweet shafts, with whose shot none are kill'd,
Which ulcer not, with deaths our lands have fill'd.
  Such was the bloudie, murdring, hellish love
Possest thy hart, faire false guest *Priams* sonne,
Firing a brand which after made to burne
The *Trojan* towers by *Græcians* ruinate.
By this love, *Priam*, *Hector*, *Troilus*,
Memnon, *Deiphœbus*, *Glaucus*, thousands mo
Whome redd *Scamanders* armor clogged streames
Roll'd into Seas, before their dates are dead.
So plaguie he, so many tempests raiseth,
So murdring he, so many Citties raseth,
When insolent, blinde, lawles, orderles,
With mad delights our sence he entertaines.
  All knowing Gods our wracks did us fortell
By signes in earth, by signes in starry Sphæres,
Which should have mov'd us, had not destinie
With too strong hand warped our miserie.
The *Comets* flaming through the scat'red clouds
With fiery beames, most like unbroaded haires:
The fearfull dragon whistling at the bankes:
And holy *Apis* ceasles bellowing
(As never erst) and shedding endles teares:
Bloud raining down from heav'n in unknow'n showers:
Our Gods darke faces overcast with woe,
And dead mens Ghosts appearing in the night.
Yea, even this night while all the Cittie stood
Opprest with terror, horror, servile feare,
Deepe silence over all: the sounds were heard
Of divers songs, and diverse instruments,
Within the voide of aire: and howling noise,
Such as madde *Bacchus* priests in *Bacchus* feasts
On *Nisa* make: and (seem'd) the company,

Our Cittie lost, went to the enemie.
So we forsaken both of Gods and men,
So are we in the mercy of our foes:
And we henceforth obedient must become
To lawes of them who have us overcome.

Chorus.

Lament we our mishaps,
Drowne we with teares our woe:
For Lamentable happes
Lamented easie growe:
and much lesse torment bring
then when they first did spring.
We want that wofull song,
wherwith wood-musiques Queen
doth ease her woes, among
fresh springtimes bushes greene,
on pleasant branch alone
renewing auntient mone.
We want that monefull sound,
that pratling *Progne* makes
on fields of *Thracian* ground,
or streames of *Thracian* lakes:
to empt her brest of paine
for *Itys* by her slaine.
Though *Halcyons* do still,
bewailing *Ceyx* lot,
the Seas with plainings fill
which his dead limmes have got,
not ever other grave
then tombe of waves to have:
And though the bird in death
that most *Meander* loves
so sweetly sighes his breath
when death his fury proves,
as almost softs his heart,
and almost blunts his dart:
Yet all the plaints of those,
nor all their tearfull larmes,
cannot content our woes,
nor serve to waile the harmes,
in soule which we, poore we,
to feele enforced be.
Nor they of *Phœbus* bredd

in teares can doo so well,
they for their brother shedd,
who into *Padus* fell,
rash guide of chariot cleere
surveiour of the yeare.
Nor she whom heav'nly powers
to weping rocke did turne,
whose teares distill in showers,
and shew she yet doth mourne,
wherewith his toppe to Skies
mount *Sipylus* doth rise.
Nor weping drops which flowe
from barke of wounded tree,
that *Mirrhas* shame doth showe
with ours compar'd may be,
to quench her loving fire
who durst embrace her sire.
Nor all the howlings made
on *Cybels* sacred hill
By Eunukes of her trade,
who *Atys*, *Atys* still
with doubled cries resound,
which *Eccho* makes rebound.
Our plaints no limits stay,
nor more then do our woes:
both infinitely straie
and neither measure knowes.
In measure let them plaine:
Who measur'd griefes sustaine.

Act 2

Cleopatra. Eras. Charmion. Diomede.
Cleopatra.

That I have thee betraide, deare *Antonie*,
My life, my soule, my sunne? I had such thought?
That I have thee betraide my Lord, my King?
That I would breake my vowed faith to thee?
Leave thee? deceive thee? yeelde thee to the rage
Of mightie foe? I ever had that hart?
Rather sharpe lightning lighten on my head:
Rather may I to deepest mischiefe fall:
Rather the opened earth devoure me:

Rather fierce *Tigers* feed them on my flesh:
Rather, ô rather let our *Nilus* send,
To swallow me quicke, some weeping *Crocodile.*
  And didst thou then suppose my royall heart
Had hatcht, thee to ensnare, a faithles love?
And changing minde, as Fortune changed cheare,
I would weake thee, to winne the stronger, loose.
O wretch! ô caitive! ô too cruell happe!
And did not I sufficient losse sustaine
Loosing my Realme, loosing my libertie,
My tender of-spring, and the joyfull light
Of beamy Sunne, and yet, yet loosing more
Thee *Antony* my care, if I loose not
What yet remain'd? thy love alas! thy love,
More deare then Scepter, children, freedome, light.
  So readie I to row in *Charons* barge,
Shall leese the joy of dying in thy love:
So the sole comfort of my miserie
To have one tombe with thee is me bereft.
So I in shady plaines shall plaine alone,
Not (as I hop'd) companion of thy mone,
O height of griefe! ERAS. Why with continuall cries
Your griefull harmes doo you exasperate?
Torment your selfe with murthering complaints;
Straine your weake brest so oft, so vehemently?
Water with teares this faire alablaster?
With sorrowes sting so many beauties wound?
Come of so many Kings, want you the hart
Bravely, stoutly, this tempest to resist?
  CL. My ev'lls are wholy unsupportable,
No humain force can them withstand, but death.
  ERAS. To him that strives nought is impossible.
  CL. In striving lyes no hope of my mishapps.
  ERAS. All things do yeelde to force of lovely face.
  CL. My face too lovely caus'd my wretched case.
My face hath so entrap'd, to cast us downe,
That for his conquest *Cæsar* may it thanke,
Causing that *Antonie* one army lost,
The other wholy did to *Cæsar* yeld.
For not induring (so his amorouse sprite
Was with my beautie fir'de) my shamefull flight,
Soone as he saw from ranke wherein he stoode
In hottest fight, my Gallies making saile:
Forgetfull of his charg (as if his soule

Unto his Ladies soule had beene enchain'd)
He left his men, who so couragiously
Did leave their lives to gaine him victorie,
And carelesse both of fame and armies losse
My oared Gallies follow'd with his ships,
Companion of my flight, by this base parte
Blasting his former flourishing renowne.

ERAS. Are you therefore cause of his overthrow?

CL. I am sole cause: I did it, only I.

ER. Feare of a woman troubled so his sprite?

CL. Fire of his love was by my feare enflam'd.

ER. And should he then to warre have led a Queene?

CL. Alas! this was not his offence, but mine.
Antony (ay me! who else so brave a chiefe!)
Would not I should have taken Seas with him:
But would have left me fearefull woman farre
From common hazard of the doubtfull warre.
O that I had beleev'd! now, now of *Rome*
All the great Empire at our beck should bende.
All should obey, the vagabonding *Scythes*,
The feared *Germaines*, back-shooting *Parthians*,
Wandring *Numidians*, *Brittons* farre remov'd,
And tawny nations scorched with the Sunne.
But I car'd not: so was my soule possest,
(To my great harme) with burning jealousie:
Fearing least in my absence *Antony*
Should leaving me retake *Octavia*.

CHAR. Such was the rigour of your desteny.

CL. Such was my errour and obstinacie.

CH. But since Gods would not, could you do withall?

CL. Alwaies from Gods good haps, not harms, do fall.

CH. And have they not all power on mens affaires?

CL. They never bow so low as worldly cares,
But leave to mortall men to be dispos'd
Freely on earth what ever mortall is.
If we therein sometimes some faults commit,
We may them not to their high majesties,
But to our selves impute; whose passions
Plunge us each day in all afflictions.
Wherwith when we our soules do thorned feele,
Flatt'ring our selves we say they dest'nies are:
That gods would have it so, and that our care
Could not empeach but that it must be so.

CHAR. Things here below are in the heav'ns begot,

Before they be in this our worlde borne:
And never can our weaknesse turne awry
The stailesse course of powerfull destenie.
Nought here, force, reason, humaine providence,
Holie devotion, noble bloud prevailes:
And Jove himselfe whose hand doth heavens rule,
Who both to gods and men as King commands,
Who earth (our firme support) with plenty stores,
Moves aire and sea with twinckling of his eie,
Who all can doe, yet never can undoe
What once hath beene by their hard lawes decreed.
When *Troyan* walles, great *Neptunes* workmanship.
Environ'd were with *Greekes*, and Fortunes whele
Doubtfull ten yeares now to the campe did turne,
And now againe towards the towne return'd,
How many times did force and fury swell
In *Hectors* veines egging him to the spoile
Of conquer'd foes, which at his blowes did fly,
As fearefull sheepe at feared wolves approch:
To save (in vaine: for why? it would not be)
Poore walles of *Troy* from adversaries rage,
Who dyed them in bloud, and cast to ground
Heap'd them with bloudie burning carcases.
No, Madame, thinke, that if the ancient crowne
Of your progenitors that *Nilus* rul'd,
Force take from you; the Gods have will'd it so,
To whome oft times Princes are odious.
They have to every thing an end ordain'd;
All worldly greatnes by them bounded is:
Some sooner, later some, as they thinke best:
None their decree is able to infringe.
But, which is more, to us disastred men
Which subject are in all things to their will,
Their will is hid: nor while we live, we know
How, or how long we must in life remaine.
Yet must we not for that feede on dispaire,
And make us wretched ere we wretched be:
But alwaies hope the best, even to the last,
That from our selves the mischiefe may not grow.
Then, Madame, helpe your selfe, leave of in time
Antonies wracke, lest it your wracke procure:
Retire you from him, save from wrathfull rage
Of angry *Cæsar* both your Realme and you.
You see him lost, so as your amitie

Unto his evills can yeeld no more reliefe.
You see him ruin'd, so as your support
No more henceforth can him with comfort raise.
With-draw you from the storme: persist not still
To loose your selfe: this royall diademe
Regaine of *Cæsar*. CL. Sooner shining light
Shall leave the day, and darknes leave the night:
Sooner moist currents of tempestuous seas
Shall wave in heaven, and the nightly troopes
Of starres shall shine within the foming waves,
Then I thee, *Antony*, leave in deepe distres.
I am with thee, be it thy worthy soule
Lodge in thy brest, or from that lodging parte
Crossing the joyles lake to take her place
In place prepared for men Demy-gods.[1]
Live, if thee please, if life be lothsome die:
Dead and alive, *Antony*, thou shalt see
Thy princesse follow thee, follow, and lament
Thy wrack, no lesse her owne then was thy weale.
CHAR. What helps his wrack this ever-lasting love?
CL. Help, or help not, such must, such ought I prove.
CH. Ill done to loose your selfe, and to no end.
CL. How ill thinke you to follow such a frend?
CH. But this your love nought mitigates his paine.
CL. Without this love I should be inhumaine.
CH. Inhumaine he, who his owne death pursues.
CL. Not inhumaine who miseries eschues.
CH. Live for your sonnes. CL. Nay for their father die.
CH. Hardharted mother! CL. Wife, kindhearted, I.
CH. Then will you them deprive of royall right?
CL. Do I deprive them? no, it's dest'nies might.
CH. Do you not them deprive of heritage,
That give them up to adversaries hands,
A man forsaken fearing to forsake,
Whome such huge numbers hold invironned?
T'abandon one gainst whome the frowning world
Banded with *Cæsar* makes conspiring warre?
CL. The lesse ought I to leave him lest of all.
A frend in most distresse should most assist.
If that when *Antonie* great and glorious
His legions led to drinke *Euphrates* streames,
So many Kings in traine redoubting him;

[1] Cf. IV.12.51–4.

In triumph rais'd as high as highest heav'n;
Lord-like disposing as him pleased best,
The wealth of *Greece*, the wealth of *Asia*:
In that faire fortune had I him exchaung'd
For *Cæsar*, then, men would have counted me
Faithles, unconstant, light: but now the storme,
And blustring tempest driving on his face,
Readie to drowne, *Alas*! what would they say?
What would himselfe in *Plutos* mansion say?
If I, whome alwaies more then life he lov'de,
If I, who am his heart, who was his hope,
Leave him, forsake him (and perhaps in vaine)
Weakly to please who him hath overthrowne?
Not light, unconstant, faithlesse should I be,
But vile, forsworne, of treachrous cruelty.

CH. Crueltie to shunne you selfe-cruell are:
CL. Selfe-cruell him from cruelty to spare.
CH. Our first affection to ourselfe is due.
CL. He is my selfe. CH. Next it extends unto
Our children, frends, and to our country soile.
And you for some respect of wively love,
(Albee scarce wively) loose your native land,
Your children, frends, and (which is more) your life.
With so strong charmes doth love bewitch our witts:
So fast in us this fire once kindled flames.
Yet if his harme by yours redresse might have, —
CL. With mine it may be clos'de in darksome grave.
CH. And that, as *Alcest* to her selfe unkind,
You might exempt him from the lawes of death.
But he is sure to die: and now his sword
Already moisted is in his warme bloud,
Helples for any succour you can bring
Against deaths sting, which he must shortly feele.
Then let your love be like the love of olde
Which *Carian* Queene did nourish in hir heart
Of hir Mausolus: builde for him a tombe
Whose statelinesse a wonder new may make.
Let him, let him have sumptuous funeralls:
Let grave thereon the horror of his fights:
Let earth be buri'd with unburied heaps.
Frame the *Pharsaly*, and discoulour'd streams
Of deepe *Enipeus*: frame the grassie plaine,
Which lodg'd his campe at siege of *Mutina*.
Make all his combats, and couragious acts:

And yearely plaies to his praise institute:
Honor his memory: with doubled care
Breed and bring up the children of you both
In *Cæsars* grace: who as a noble Prince
Will leave them Lords of this most glorious realme.
  CL. What shame were that! ah Gods! what infemie!
With *Antony* in his good haps to share,
And overlive him dead: deeming enough
To shed some teares upon a widdow tombe!
The after-livers justly might report
That I him only for his Empire lov'd,
And high estate: and that in hard estate
I for another did him lewdly leave.
Like to those birds wafted with wandring wings
From foraine lands in spring-time here arrive:
And live with us so long as Somers heate,
And their foode lasts, then seeke another soile.
And as we see with ceaslesse fluttering
Flocking of seelly flies a brownish cloud
To vintag'd wine yet working in the tonne:
Not parting thence while they sweete liquor taste:
After, as smoke, all vanish in the aire,
And of the swarme not one so much appeare.
  ERAS. By this sharpe death what profit can you winne?
  CL. I neither gaine nor profit seeke therein.
  ER. What praise shall you of after-ages get?
  CL. Nor praise, nor Glory in my cares are set.
  ERAS. What other end ought you respect, then this?
  CL. My only end my onely duty is.
  ERAS. Your duty must upon some good be founded!
  CL. On vertue it, the onely good, is grounded.
  ER. What is that *vertue*? CL. That which us beseemes.
  ER. Outrage our selves? who that beseeming deemes?
  CL. Finish I will my sorrowes dieng thus.
  ER. Minish you will your glories doing thus.
  CL. Good frends I pray you seeke not to revoke
My fix'd intent of folowing *Antony*.
I will die. I will die: must not his life,
His life and death by mine be followed?
  Meane while, deare sisters, live: and while you live,
Do often honor to our loved Tombes.
Straw them with flowers: and sometimes happely
The tender thought of *Antony* your Lord
And me poore soule to teares shall you invite,

And our true loves your dolefull voice commend.
CH. And thinke you Madame, we from you will part?
Thinke you alone to feele deaths ougly darte?
Thinke you to leave us? and that the same sunne
Shall see at once you dead, and us alive?
Weele die with you: and *Clotho* pittilesse
Shall us with you in hellish boate imbarque.
CL. Ah live, I praie you: this disastred woe
Which racks my heart, alone to me belongs:
My lot longs not to you: servants to be
No shame, no harme to you, as is to me.
Live sisters, live, and seing his suspect
Hath causlesse me in sea of sorrowes drown'd,
And that I cannot live, if so I would,
Nor yet would leave this life, if so I could,
Without his love: procure me, *Diomed*,
That gainst poore me he be no more incensd.
Wrest out of his conceit that harmefull doubt,
That since his wracke he hath of me conceiv'd
Though wrong conceiv'd: witnes you reverent Gods,
Barking *Anubis*, *Apis* bellowing.
Tell him, my soule burning, impatient,
Forlorne with love of him, for certaine seale
Of her true loialtie my corpse hath left,
T'encrease of dead the number numberlesse.
Go then, and if as yet he me bewaile,
If yet for me his heart one sigh forth breathe
Blest shall I be: and far with more content
Depart this world, where so I me torment.
Meane season us let this sad tombe enclose,
Attending here till death conclude our woes.
DIOM. I will obey your will. CL. So the desert
The Gods repay of thy true faithfull heart.

Diomed.

And is't not pittie, Gods, ah Gods of heav'n!
To see from love such hatefull frutes to spring?
And is't not pittie that this firebrand so
Laies waste the trophes of *Phillippi* fieldes?
Where are those sweet allurements, those sweet lookes,
Which gods themselves right hart sick wuld have made?
What doth that beautie, rarest guift of heav'n,
Wonder of earth? Alas! what do those eies?

And that sweete voice all *Asia* understoode,
And sunburnt *Africke* wide in deserts spred?
Is their force dead? have they no further power?
Can not by them *Octavius* be surpriz'd?
Alas! if *Jove* in middst of all his ire,
With thunderbolt in hand some land to plague,
Had cast his eies on my Queene, out of hand
His plaguing bolte had falne out of his hand:
Fire out of his wrath into vaine smoke should turne,
And other fire within his brest should burne.
  Nought lives so faire. Nature by such a worke
Her selfe, should seeme, in workmanship hath past.
She is all heav'nly: never any man
But seeing hir was ravish'd with her sight.
The Allablaster covering of her face,
The corall coullor hir two lips engraines,
Her beamy eies, two Sunnes of this our world,
Of hir faire haire the fine and flaming golde,
Her brave streight stature, and her winning partes
Are nothing else but fiers, fetters, dartes.
  Yet this is nothing [to] th'enchaunting skilles
Of her celestiall Spirite, hir training speach,
Her grace, hir majesty, and forcing voice,
Whether she it with fingers speach consorte,
Or hearing sceptred kings embassadors
Answere to each in his owne language make.
  Yet now at neede it aides her not at all
With all these beauties, so her sorrow stinges.
Darkned with woe her only study is
To weepe, to sigh, to seeke for lonelines.
Careles of all, hir haire disordred hangs:
Hir charming eies whence murthring looks did flie,
Now rivers grown, whose wellspring anguish is,
Do trickling wash the marble of hir face.
Hir faire discover'd brest with sobbing swolne
Selfe cruell she still martirith with blowes.
  Alas! It's our ill hap, for if hir teares
She would convert into her loving charmes,
To make a conquest of the conqueror,
(As well she might, would she hir force imploie)
She should us safetie from these ills procure,
Hir crowne to hir, and to hir race assure.
Unhappy he, in whome selfe-succour lies,
Yet selfe-forsaken wanting succour dies

Chorus.

O sweete fertile land, wherein
Phœbus did with breth inspire
man who men did first begin,
formed first of *Nilus* mire,
whence of *Artes* the eldest kindes,
earths most heavenly ornament,
were as from their fountaine sent
to enlight our misty mindes.
whose grose sprite from endles time
as in darkned prison pente,
never did to knowledge clime.
Wher the *Nile*, our father good,
father-like doth never misse
yearely us to bring such food,
as to life required is:
visiting each yeare this plaine,
and with fat slime cov'ring it,[1]
which his seaven mouthes do spit,
as the season comes againe,
making therby greatest growe
busie reapers joyfull paine,
when his flouds do highest flow.
Wandring Prince of rivers thou,
honor of the *Aethiops* lande,
of a Lord and maister now
thou a slave in awe must stand.
now of *Tiber* which is spred
lesse in force, and lesse in fame
reverence thou must the name,
whome all other rivers dread,
for his children swolne in pride,
who by conquest seeke to treade
round this earth on every side.
Now thou must begin to send
tribute of thy watry store,
as sea pathes thy steps shall bend,
yearely presents more and more.
thy fat skumme, our fruitfull corne,
pill'd from hence with thevish hands
all uncloth'd shal leave our lands

[1] Cf. I.3.69; II.7.21–4.

into forraine country borne,
which puft up with such a pray
shall thereby the praise adorne
of that scepter *Rome* doth sway.
Nought thee helps thy hornes to hide
far from hence in unknown grounds,
that thy waters wander wide,
yerely breaking banks, and bounds.
and that thy Skie-coullor'd brooks
through a hundred peoples passe,
drawing plots for trees and grasse
with a thousand turnes and crookes,
whome all weary of their way
thy throats which in widenesse passe
powre into their mother Sea.
"Nought so happie haplesse life
"in this world as freedome findes:
"nought wherin more sparkes are rife
"to inflame couragious mindes.
"but if force must us inforce
"needes a yoke to undergo,
"under foraine yoke to go,
"still it proves a bondage worse,
"and doubled subjection
"see we shall, and feele, and know
"subject to a stranger growne.
From hence forward for a King,
whose first being from this place
should his brest by nature bring
care of country to imbrace,
We at surly face must quake
of some *Romaine* madly bent:
who our terrour to augment
his *Proconsuls* axe will shake,
driving with our Kings from hence
our establish'd government,
justice sword, and lawes defence.
Nothing worldly of such might
but more mighty *Destiny*,
by swift *Times* unbridled flight,
makes in end his end to see.
Every thing *Time* overthrowes,
nought to end doth steadfast staie.
his great sithe mowes all away

as the stalke of tender rose.
onely immortalitie
of the heavens doth it oppose
gainst his powrefull *Deitie.*
One day there will come a day
which shall quaile thy fortunes flower
and thee ruinde low shall laie
in some barbarous Princes power,
when the pittie-wanting fire
shall, O *Rome*, thy beauties burne,
and to humble ashes turne
thy proud wealth and rich attire,
those guilt roofes which turretwise,
justly making envy mourne,
threaten now to pearce Skies.
As thy forces fill each land
harvests making here and there,
reaping all with ravening hand
they find growing any where:
from each land so to thy fall
multitudes repaire shall make,
from the common spoile to take
what to each mans share may fall.
fingred all thou shalt behold:
no iote left for tokens sake
that thou wert so great of olde.
Like unto the ancient *Troie*
whence deriv'd thy founders be,
conqu'ring foe shall thee enjoie,
and a burning praie in thee.
for within this turning ball
this we see, and see each daie:
all things fixed ends do staie,
ends to first beginnings fall.
& that nought, how strong or strange
chaungeles doth endure alwaie,
but endureth fatall change.

[Act 3]

M. Antonius. Lucilius.

M. Ant.

Lucill sole comfort of my bitter case,
The only trust, the only hope I have,

In last despaire: Ah is not this the daie
That death should me of life and love bereave?
What waite I for that have no refuge left,
But am sole remnant of my fortune left?
All leave me, flie me: none, noe not of them
Which of my greatnes greatest good receiv'd,
Stands with my fall: they seeme as now asham'd
That heretofore they did me ought regard:
They draw them backe, shewing they folow'd me,
Not to partake my harms, but coozen me.
LU. *In this our world nothing is stedfast found,*
In vaine he hopes, who here his hopes doth ground.
AN. Yet nought afflicts me, nothing killes me so,
As that I so my *Cleopatra* see
Practise with *Cæsar*, and to him transport
My flame, her love, more deare then life to me.
LU. Beleeve it not: Too high a heart she beares,
Too princely thoughts. AN. Too wise a head she weares
Too much enflam'd with greatnes, evermore
Gaping for our great Empires government.
LU. So long time you her constant love have tri'de.
AN. But still with me good fortune did abide.
LU. Her changed love what token makes you know?
AN. *Pelusium* lost, and *Actian* overthrow,
Both by her fraud: my well appointed fleet,
And trusty Souldiors in my quarrell arm'd,
Whome she, false she, in stede of my defence,
Came to perswade to yelde them to my foe:
Such honor *Thyre* done, such welcome given,
Their long close talkes I neither knew, nor would,
And trecherous wrong *Alexas* hath me donne,
Witnes too well her perjur'd love to me.
But you O Gods (if any faith regarde)
With sharpe revenge her faithlesse change reward.
LU. The dole she made upon our overthrow,
Her realme given up for refuge to our men,
Her poore attire when she devoutly kept
The solemne day of her nativitie,
Againe the cost and prodigall expence
Shew'd when she did your birth day celebrate,
Do plaine enough her heart unfained prove,
Equally toucht, you loving, as you love.
AN. Well, be her love to me or false, or true,
Once in my soule a cureles wound I feele.

I love: nay burne in fire of her love:
Each day, each night hir Image haunts my minde.
Her selfe my dreames: and still I tired am,
And still I am with burning pincers nipt.
Extreame my harme: yet sweeter to my sence
Then boiling Torch of jealous torments fire:
This griefe, nay rage, in me such sturre doth keepe,
And thornes me still, both when I wake and sleepe.
  Take *Cæsar* conquest, take my goods, take he
Th'onor to be Lord of the earth alone,
My sonnes, my life bent headlong to mishapps:
No force, so not my *Cleopatra* take.
So foolish I, I cannot her forget,
Though better were I banisht her my thought.
Like to the sicke whose throte the feavers fire
Hath vehemently with thirstie drought enflam'd,
Drinkes still, albee the drinke he still desires
Be nothing else but fewell to his flame.
He cannot rule himselfe: his health's respect
Yealdeth to his distempered stomacks heate.
  LU. Leave of this love, that thus renewes your woe.
  AN. I do my best, but ah! can not do so.
  LU. Thinke how you have so brave a captaine bene,
And now are by this vaine affection falne.
  AN. The ceasles thought of my felicitie
Plunges me more in this adversitie.
For nothing so a man in ill torments,
As who to him his good state represents.
This makes my rack, my anguish, and my woe
Equall unto the hellish passions growe,
When I to mind my happie puisance call
Which erst I had by warlike conquest wonne,
And that good ſortune which me never left,
Which hard disastre now hath me bereft.
  With terror tremble all the world I made
At my sole word, as Rushes in the streames
At waters will: I conquer'd Italie,
I conquer'd *Rome*, that nations so redoubt,
I bare (meane while besieging *Mutina*)
Two consuls armies for my ruine brought;
Bath'd in their bloud, by their deaths witnessing
My force and skill in matters Martiall.
  To wreake thy unkle, unkind *Cæsar*, I
With bloud of enemies the bankes embru'd

Of stain'd *Enipeus*, hindring his course
Stopped with heapes of piled carcases:
When *Cassius* and *Brutus* ill betide
Marcht against us, by us twise put to flight,
But by my sole conduct: for all the time
Cæsar hart-sicke with feare and feaver lay.
Who knowes it not? and how by every one
Fame of the fact was giv'n to me alone.
There sprang the love, the never changing love,
Wherin my heart hath since to yours bene bound:
There was it, my *Lucill*, you *Brutus* sav'de,
And for your *Brutus Antony* you found.
Better my hap in gaining such a frend,
Then in subduing such an enimie.
Now former vertue dead doth me forsake,
Fortune engulfes me in extreame distresse:
She turnes from me her smiling countenance,
Casting on me mishapp upon mishapp.
Left and betraide of thousand thousand frends,
Once of my sute, but you *Lucill* are left,
Remaining to me stedfast as a tower
In holy love, in spite of fortunes blastes.
But if of any God my voice be heard,
And be not vainely scatt'red in the heav'ns,
Such goodnes shall not glorilesse be loste.
But comming ages still thereof shall boste.
LU. Men in their frendship ever should be one,
And never ought with fickle Fortune shake,
Which still removes, nor will, nor knowes the way,
Her rowling bowle in one sure state to staie.
Wherfore we ought as borrow'd things receive
The goods light she lends us to pay againe:
Not hold them sure, nor on them build our hopes
As on such goods as cannot faile, and fall:
But thinke againe, nothing is dureable,
Vertue except, our never failing host:
So bearing saile when favoring windes do blow,
As frowning tempests may us least dismaie
When they on us do fall: not over-glad
With good estate, nor over-griev'd with bad,
Resist mishap. ANT. Alas! it is too strong.
Mishappes oft times are by some comfort borne:
But these, ay me! whose weights oppresse my hart,
Too heavie lie, no hope can them relieve.

There rests no more, but that with cruell blade
For lingring death a hastie waie be made.
LU. *Cæsar*, as heire unto his fathers state,
So will his Fathers goodnes imitate,
To you ward: whome he know's allied in bloud,
Allied in mariage, ruling equally
Th'Empire with him, and with him making warre
Have purg'd the earth of *Cæsars* murtherers.
You into portions parted have the world
Even like coheirs their heritages parte:
And now with one accord so many yeares
In quiet peace both have your charges rul'd.
ANT. Bloud and alliance nothing do prevaile
To coole the thirst of hote ambitious brests:
The sonne his Father hardly can endure,
Brother his brother, in one common Realme.
So fervent this desire to commaund:
Such jealousie it kindleth in our hearts,
Sooner will men permit another should
Love her they love, then weare the crowne they weare.
All lawes it breakes, turnes all things upside downe:
Amitie, kindred, nought so holy is
But it defiles. A monarchie to gaine
None cares which way, so he may it obtaine.
LU. Suppose he Monarch be and that this world
No more acknowledg sundry Emperours,
That *Rome* him only feare, and that he joyne
The east with west, and both at once do rule:
Why should he not permitt you peaceablie
Discharg'd of charge and Empires dignitie,
Private to live reading *Philosophy*,
In learned *Greece*, *Spaine*, *Asia*, any land?
AN. Never will he his Empire thinke assur'de
While in this world *Marke Antony* shall live.
Sleepeles Suspicion, Pale distrust, cold feare
Alwaies to princes companie do beare
Bred of reports: reports which night and day
Perpetuall guests from court go not away.
LU. He hath not slaine your brother *Lucius*,
Nor shortned hath the age of *Lepidus*,
Albeit both into his hands were falne,
And he with wrath against them both enflam'd.
Yet one, as Lord in quiet rest doth beare,
The greatest sway in great *Iberia*:

The other with his gentle Prince retaines
Of highest Priest the sacred dignitie.
AN. He feares not them, their feeble force he knowes.
LU. He feares no vanquisht overfill'd with woes.
AN. Fortune may chaunge againe. LU. A down-cast foe
Can hardly rise, which once is brought so low.
ANT. All that I can is donne: for last assay
(When all means fail'd) I to entreaty fell,
(Ah coward creature!) whence againe repulst
Of combate I unto him proffer made:
Though he in prime, and I by feeble age
Mightily weakned both in force and skill.
Yet could not he his coward heart advaunce
Basely affraide to trie so praisefull chaunce.
This makes me plaine, makes me my selfe accuse,
Fortune in this her spitefull force doth use
'Gainst my gray hayres: in this unhappy I
Repine at heav'ns in my happes pittiles.
A man, a woman both in might and minde,
In *Mars his* schole who never lesson learn'd,
Should me repulse, chase, overthrow, destroy,
Me of such fame, bring to so low an ebbe?
Alcides bloud, who from my infancy
With happy prowesse crowned have my praise,
Witnesse thou *Gaule* unus'd to servile yoke,
Thou valiant *Spaine*, you fields of *Thessalie*,
With millions of mourning cries bewail'd,
Twise watred now with bloud of *Italie*.
LU. Witnes may *Afrique*, and of conquer'd world
All fower quarters witnesses may be.
For in what part of earth inhabited,
Hungry of praise have you not ensignes spred?
ANT. Thou know'st rich *Aegipt* (*Aegipt* of my deedes
Faire and foule subject) *Aegypt* ah! thou know'st
How I behav'd me fighting for thy kinge,
When I regainde him his rebellious Realme:
Against his foes in battaile shewing force,
And after fight in victory remorse.
Yet if to bring my glory to the ground,
Fortune had made me overthrowne by one
Of greater force, of better skill then I:
One of those Captaines feared so of olde,
Camill, *Marcellus*, worthy *Scipio*,
This late great *Cæsar*, honor of our state,

Or that great *Pompei* aged growne in armes;
That after harvest of a world of men
Made in a hundred battailes, fights, assaults,
My body thorow pearst with push of pike
Had vomited my bloud, in bloud my life,
In midd'st of millions, felowes in my fall:
The lesse her wrong, the lesse should be my woe:
Nor she should paine, nor I complaine me so.
No, no, wheras I should have died in armes,
And vanquisht oft new armies should have arm'd,
New battailes given, and rather lost with me
All this whole world submitted unto me:
A man who never saw enlaced pikes
With bristled points against his stomake bent,
Who feares the field, and hides him cowardly
Dead at the very noise the souldiors make,
His vertue, fraud, deceit, malicious guile,
His armes the arts that false *Ulisses* us'de,
(Knowne at Modena, where the *Consuls* both
Death-wounded were, and wounded by his men
To get their armie, war with it to make
Against his faith, against his country soile.
Of *Lepidus*, which to his succours came,
To honor whome he was by dutie bound,
The Empire he usurpt: corrupting first
With baites and bribes the most part of his men)
Yet me hath overcome, and made his pray,
And state of *Rome* with me hath overcome.
Strange! one disordred act at *Actium*
The earth subdu'de, my glory hath obscur'd.
For since, as one whome heavens wrath attaints,
With furie caught, and more then furious
Vex'd with my evills, I never more had care
My armies lost, or lost name to repaire:
I did no more resist. LU. All warres affaires,
But battailes most, dayly have their successe
Now good, now ill: and though that fortune have
Great force and power in every worldly thing,
Rule all, do all, have all things fast enchaind
Unto the circle of hir turning wheele:
Yet seemes it more then any practise else
She doth frequent *Bellonas* bloudy trade:
And that hir favour, wavering as the wind,
Hir greatest power therein doth oftnest shewe.

Whence growes, we dailie see, who in their youth
Gatt honor ther, do loose it in their age,
Vanquisht by some lesse warlike then themselves:
Whome yet a meaner man shall overthrowe.
Hir use is not to lend us still her hande,
But sometimes headlong backe againe to throwe,
When by hir favor she hath us extolld
Unto the topp of highest happines.
ANT. Well ought I curse within my grieved soule,
Lamenting daie and night, this sencelesse love,
Whereby my faire entising foe entrap'd
My hedelesse *Reason*, could no more escape.
It was not fortunes ever chaunging face:
It was not Destnies chaungles violence
Forg'd my mishap. Alas! who doth not know
They make, nor marre nor anything can doe.
Fortune, which men so feare, adore, detest,
Is but a chaunce whose cause unknow'n doth rest,
Although oft times the cause is well perceiv'd,
But not th'effect the same that was conceiv'd.
Pleasure, nought else, the plague of this our life,
Our life which still a thousand plagues pursue,
Alone hath me this strange disastre spunne,
Falne from a souldior to a chamberer,
Careles of vertue, careles of all praise.
Nay, as the fatted swine in filthy mire
With glutted heart I wallowed in delights,
All thoughts of honor troden under foote.
So I me lost: for finding this sweet cupp
Pleasing my tast, unwise I drunke my fill,
And through the sweetnes of that poisons power
By steps I drave my former wits astraie.
I made my frends, offended, me forsake,
I holpe my foes against my selfe to rise.
I robd my subjects, and for followers
I saw my selfe beset with flatterers,
Mine idle armes faire wrought with spiders worke,
My scattred men without their ensignes strai'd:
Cæsar meane while who never would have dar'de
To cope with me, me sodainely despis'de,
Tooke hart to fight, and hop'de for victorie
On one so gone, who glorie had forgone.
LU. Enchaunting pleasure, *Venus* sweete delights
Weaken our bodies, over-cloud our sprights,

Trouble our reason, from our hearts out chase
All holie vertues lodging in their place:
Like as the cunning fisher takes the fishe
By traitor baite whereby the hooke is hid:
So *Pleasure* serves to vice in steede of foode
To baite our soules thereon too liquorishe.
This poison deadly is alike to all,
But on great kings doth greatest outrage worke,
Taking the roiall scepters from their hands,
Thence forward to be by some stranger borne:
While that their people charg'd with heavie loades
Their flatt'rers pill, and suck their mary[1] drie,
Not rul'd but left to great men as a pray,
While this fonde Prince himselfe in pleasures drowns
Who hears nought, sees nought, doth nought of a king
Seming himselfe against himselfe conspirde.
Then equall Justice wandreth banished,
And in her seat sitts greedie Tyrannie.
Confus'd disorder troubleth all estates,
Crimes without feare and outrages are done.
Then mutinous *Rebellion* shewes her face,
Now hid with this, and now with that pretence,
Provoking enimies, which on each side
Enter at ease, and make them Lords of all.
The hurtfull workes of pleasure here behold.
  AN. The wolfe is not so hurtfull to the folde,
Frost to the grapes, to ripened frutes the raine:
As pleasure is to princes full of paine.
  LU. There nedes no proofe, but by th'*Assirian* kinge,
On whom that Monster woefull wrack did bring.
  AN. There nedes no proofe, but by unhappie I,
Who lost my empire, honor, life thereby,
  LU. Yet hath this ill so much the greater force,
As scarcely any do against it stand:
No not the Demy-gods the olde world knew,
Who all subdu'de, could *Pleasures* power subdue.
  Great *Hercules*, *Hercules* once that was
Wonder of earth and heaven, matchles in might,
Who *Anteus*, *Lycus*, *Geryon* overcame,
Who drew from hell the triple-headed dogg,
Who *Hydra* kill'd, vanquishd *Achelous*,
Who heavens weight on his strong shoulders bare:

[1] marrow.

Did he not under *Pleasures* burthen bow?
Did he not Captive to this passion yelde,
When by his Captive, so he was inflam'd,
As now your selfe in *Cleopatra* burne?
Slept in hir lapp, hir bosome kist and kiste,
With base unseemely service bought her love,
Spinning at distaffe, and with sinewy hand
Winding on spindles threde, in maides attire?
His conqu'ring clubbe at rest on wal did hang:
His bow unstringd he bent not as he us'de:
Upon his shafts the weaving spiders spunne:
And his hard cloake the fretting mothes did pierce.
The monsters free and fearles all the time
Throughout the world the people did torment,
And more and more encreasing daie by daie
Scorn'd his weake heart become a mistresse play.

AN. In onely this like *Hercules* am I,
In this I prove me of his lignage right:
In this himselfe, his deedes I shew in this:
In this, nought else, my ancestor he is.
But goe we: die I must, and with brave end
Conclusion make of all foregoing harmes:
Die, die I must: I must a noble death,
A glorious death unto my succour call:
I must deface the shame of time abus'd,
I must adorne the wanton loves I us'de,
With some couragious act: that my last day
By mine owne hand my spots may wash away.
Come deare *Lucill*: alas! why weepe you thus!
This mortall lot is common to us all.
We must all die, each doth in homage owe
Unto that God that shar'd the Realmes belowe.
Ah sigh no more: alas! appeace your woes,
For by your greife my griefe more eager growes.

Chorus.

Alas, with what tormenting fire
Us martireth this blind desire
To stay our life from flieng!
How ceasleslie our minds doth rack,
How heavie lies upon our back
This dastard feare of dieng!
Death rather healthfull succour gives,
Death rather all mishapps relieves

That life upon us throweth:
And ever to us doth unclose
The dore whereby from curelesse woes
Our weary soule out goeth.
What Goddesse else more milde then she
To burie all our paine can be,
What remedie more pleasing?
Our pained hearts when dolor stings,
And nothing rest, or respite brings,
What help have we more easing?
Hope which to us doth comfort give,
And doth our fainting harts revive,
Hath not such force in anguish:
For promising a vaine reliefe
She oft us failes in midst of griefe,
And helples lets us languish.
But Death who call on her at neede
Doth never with vaine semblant feed,
But when them sorrow paineth,
So riddes their soules of all distresse
Whose heavie weight did them oppresse,
That not one griefe remaineth.
Who feareles and with courage bolde
Can *Acherons* black face behold,
Which muddie water beareth:
And crossing over in the way
Is not amaz'd at Perruque gray
Olde rusty *Charon* weareth?
Who voide of dread can looke upon
The dreadfull shades that roame alone,
On bankes where sound no voices:
Whome with hir fire-brands and her Snakes
No whit afraide *Alecto* makes,
Nor triple-barking noises:
Who freely can himselfe dispose
Of that last hower which all must close,
And leave this life at pleasure:
This noble freedome more esteemes,
And in his heart more precious deemes,
Then crowne and kinglie treasure.
The waves which *Boreas* blasts turmoile
And cause with foaming furie boile,
Make not his heart to tremble:
Nor brutish broile, when with strong head

A rebell people madly ledde
  Against their Lords assemble:
Nor fearefull face of Tirant wood,
Who breaths but threats, & drinks but bloud,
  No, nor the hand which thunder,
The hand of *Jove* which thunder beares,
And ribbs of rocks in sunder teares,
  Teares mountains sides in sunder:
Nor bloudy *Marses* butchering bands,
Whose lightnings desert laie the lands
  Whome dustie cloudes do cover:
From of whose armour sun-beames flie,
And under them make quaking lie
  The plaines wheron they hover:
Nor yet the cruell murth'ring blade
Warme in the moistie bowels made
  Of people pell-mell dieng
In some great Cittie put to sack,
By savage Tirant brought to wrack,
  At his colde mercie lieng.
How abject him, how base thinke I,
Who wanting courage can not dye
  When need him thereto calleth?
From whome the dagger drawne to kill
The cureles griefes that vexe him still
  For feare and faintnes falleth?
O *Antony* with thy deare mate
Both in misfortunes fortunate!
  Whose thoughts to death aspiring
Shall you protect from victors rage,
Who on each side doth you encage,
  To triumph much desiring.
That *Cæsar* may you not offend
Nought else but death can you defend,
  Which his weake force derideth.
And all in this round earth containd,
Pow'rles on them whome once enchaind
  Avernus prison hideth:
Where great *Psammetiques* ghost doth rest,
Not with infernall paine possest,
  But in sweete fields detained:
And olde *Amasis* soule likewise,
And all our famous *Ptolomies*
  That whilome on us raigned.

Act 4

Cæsar. Agrippa. Dircetus.
The Messenger.

Cæsar.

You ever-living Gods which all things holde
Within the power of your celestiall hands,
By whome heate, colde, the thunder, and the wind,
The properties of enterchaunging months
Their course and being have; which do set downe
Of Empires by your destinied decree
The force, age, time, and subject to no chaunge
Chaunge all, reserving nothing in one state:
You have advaunst, as high as thundring heav'n
The *Romaines* greatnes by *Bellonas* might:
Maistring the world with fearefull violence,
Making the world widdow of libertie.
Yet at this day this proud exalted *Rome*
Despoil'd, captiv'd, at one mans will doth bend:
Her Empire mine, her life is in my hand,
As Monarch I both world and *Rome* commaund;
Do all, can all; foorth my commandment cast
Like thundring fire from one to other Pole
Equall to Jove: bestowing by my word
Happs and mishappes, as Fortunes King and Lord.
No towne there is, but up my Image settes,
But sacrifice to me doth dayly make:
Whether where *Phæbus* joyne his morning steedes,
Or where the night them weary entertaines,
Or where the heat the *Garamante* doth scorch,
Or where the colde from *Boreas* breath is blowne:
All *Cæsar* do both awe and honor beare,
And crowned Kings his verie name doth feare.
Antony knowes it well, for whome not one
Of all the Princes all this earth do rule,
Armes against me: for all redoubt the power
Which heav'nly powers on earth have made me beare.
Antony, he poore man with fire inflam'de
A womans beauties kindled in his heart,
Rose against me, who longer could not beare
My sisters wrong he did so ill intreat:
Seing her left while that his leud delights

Her husband with his *Cleopatra* tooke
In *Alexandria*, where both nights and daies
Their time they pass'd in nought but loves and plaies.
  All *Asias* forces into one he drewe,
And forth he set upon the azur'd waves
A thousand and a thousand Shipps, which fill'd
With Souldiors, pikes, with targets, arrowes, darts,
Made *Neptune* quake, and all the watry troupes
Of *Glauques*, and *Tritons* lodg'd at *Actium*,
But mightie Gods, who still the force withstand
Of him, who causeles doth another wrong,
In lesse then moments space redus'd to nought
All that proud power by Sea or land he brought.
  AGR. Presumptuous pride of high and hawtie sprite,
Voluptuous care of fond and foolish love,
Have justly wrought his wrack: who thought he helde
(By overweening) Fortune in his hand.
Of us he made no count, but as to play,
So feareles came our forces to assay.
  So sometimes fell to Sonnes of mother earth,
Which crawl'd to heav'n warre on the Gods to make,
Olymp on *Pelion*, *Ossa* on *Olymp*,
Pindus on *Ossa* loading by degrees:
That at hand-strokes with mightie clubs they might
On mossie rocks the Gods make tumble downe:
When mightie *Jove* with burning anger chaf'd,
Disbraind with him *Gyges* and *Briareus*,
Blunting his darts upon their brused bones.
For no one thing the Gods can lesse abide
In deedes of men, then Arrogance and pride.
And still the proud, which too much takes in hand,
Shall fowlest fall, where best he thinkes to stand.
  CÆS. Right as some Pallace, or some stately tower,
Which over-lookes the neighbour buildings round
In scorning wise, and to the starres up growes,
Which in short time his owne weight overthrowes.
  What monstrous pride, nay what impietie
Incenst him onward to the Gods disgrace?
When his two children, *Cleopatras* bratts,
To *Phœbe* and her brother he compar'd,
Latonas race, causing them to be call'd
The Sunne and Moone? Is not this follie right
And is not this the Gods to make his foes?
And is not this himselfe to worke his woes?

AGR. In like proud sort he causd his hed to leese
The Jewish king *Antigonus*, to have
His Realme for balme, that *Cleopatra* lov'd,
As though on him he had some treason prov'd.
CÆS. *Lidia* to her, and *Siria* he gave,
Cyprus of golde, *Arabia* rich of smelles:
And to his children more *Cilicia*,
Parth's, *Medes*, *Armenia*, *Phænicia:*
The kings of kings proclaming them to be,
By his owne word, as by a sound decree.
AGR. What? Robbing his owne country of her due?
Triumph'd he not in *Alexandria*,
Of *Artabasus* the *Armenian* King,
Who yeelded on his perjur'd word to him?
CÆS. Nay, never *Rome* more injuries receiv'd,
Since thou, ô *Romulus*, by flight of birds
With happy hand the *Romain* walles did'st build,
Then *Antonyes* fond loves to it hath done.
Nor ever warre more holie, nor more just,
Nor undertaken with more hard constraint,
Then is this warre: which were it not, our state
Within small time all dignitie should loose:
Though I lament (thou Sunne my witnes art,
And thou great *Jove*) that it so deadly proves:
That *Romaine* bloud should in such plentie flowe,
Watring the fields and pastures where we go.
What *Carthage* in olde hatred obstinate,
What *Gaule* still barking at our rising state,
What rebell *Samnite*, what fierce *Pyrrhus* power,
What cruell *Mithridate*, what *Parth* hath wrought
Such woe to *Rome*? whose common wealth he had,
(Had he bene victor) into *Egypt* brought.
AGR. Surely the Gods, which have this cittie built
Steadfast to stand as long as time endures,
Which keepe the Capitoll, of us take care,
And care will take of those shall after come,
Have made you victor, that you might redresse
Their honor growne by passed mischieves lesse.
CÆS. The seelie man when all the Greekish Sea
His fleete had hid, in hope me sure to drowne,
Me battaile gave: where fortune in my stede,
Repulsing him his forces disaraied.
Himselfe tooke flight, soone as his love he saw
All wanne through feare with full sailes flie away.

His men, though lost, whome none did now direct,
With courage fought, fast grappled shipp with shipp,
Charging, resisting, as their oares would serve,
With darts, with swords, with pikes, with fiery flames.
So that the darkned night her starrie vaile
Upon the bloudy sea had over-spred,
Whilst yet they held: and hardly, hardly then
They fell to flieng on the wavie plaine,
All full of soldiors overwhelm'd with waves.
The aire throughout with cries & grones did sound:
The sea did blush with bloud: the neighbour shores
Groned, so they with shipwracks pestred were,
And floting bodies left for pleasing foode
To birds, and beasts, and fishes of the sea.
You know it well *Agrippa*. AG. Mete it was
The *Romain* Empire so should ruled be,
As heav'n is rul'd: which turning over us,
All under things by his example turnes.
Now as of heav'n one onely Lord we know:
One onely Lord should rule this earth below.
When one selfe pow're is common made to two
Their duties they nor suffer will, nor doe.
In quarell still, in doubt, in hate, in feare;
Meanewhile the people all the smart do beare.
CÆS. Then to the end none, while my daies endure,
Seeking to raise himselfe may succours find,
We must with bloud marke this our victory,
For just example to all memorie
Murther we must, until not one we leave,
Which may hereafter us of rest bereave.
AG. Marke it with murthers? Who of that can like?
CÆS. Murthers must use, who doth assurance seeke.
AG. Assurance call you enemies to make?
CÆS. I make no such, but such away I take.
AG. Nothing so much as rigour doth displease.
CÆS. Nothing so much doth make me live at ease.
AG. What ease to him that feared is of all?
CÆS. Feared to be, and see his foes to fall.
AG. Commonly feare doth brede and nourish hate.
CÆS. Hate without pow'r comes commonly too late.
AG. A feared Prince hath oft his death desir'd.
CÆS. A Prince not fear'd hath oft his wrong conspir'd.
AG. No guard so sure, no forte so strong doth prove,
No such defence, as is the peoples love.

CÆS. Nought more unsure, more weak, more like the winde,
Then *Peoples* favour still to change enclinde.
AG. Good Gods! what love to gratious prince men beare!
CÆS. What honor to the Prince that is severe!
AG. Nought more divine then is *Benignitie.*
CÆS. Nought likes the *Gods* as doth *Severity.*
AG. *Gods* all forgive. CÆS. On faults they paines do lay.
AG. And give their goods. CÆS. Oft times they take away.
AG. They wreake them not, ô *Cæsar,* at each time
That by our sinnes they are to wrath provok'd.
Neither must you (beleeve, I humblie praie)
Your victorie with crueltie defile.
The Gods it gave, it must not be abus'd,
But to the good of all men mildely us'd,
And they be thank'd that having giv'n you grace
To raigne alone, and rule this earthly masse,
They may hence-forward hold it still in rest,
All scattered power united in one brest.
CÆS. But what is he that breathles comes so fast,
Approching us, and going in such hast?
AG. He seemes affraid: and under his arme I
(But much I erre) a bloudy sword espie.
CÆS. I long to understand what it may be.
AG. He hither comes: it's best we stay and see.
DIRCE. What good God now my voice will reenforce,
That tell I may to rocks, and hilles, and woods,
To waves of sea, which dash upon the shore,
To earth, to heaven, the woefull newes I bring?
AG. What sodaine chance thee towards us hath broght?
DIR. A lamentable chance. O wrath of heav'ns!
O Gods too pittiles! CÆS. What monstrous hap
Wilt thou recount? DIR. Alas, too hard mishap!
When I but dreame of what mine eies beheld,
My hart doth freeze, my limmes do quivering quake,
I senceles stand, my brest with tempest tost
Killes in my throte my words, ere fully borne.
Dead, dead he is: be sure of what I say,
This murthering sword hath made the man away.
CÆS. Alas my heart doth cleave, pittie me rackes,
My brest doth pant to heare this dolefull tale.
Is *Antony* then dead? to death, alas!
I am the cause despaire him so compelld.
But soldior, of his death the manner showe,
And how he did this living light forgoe.

DIR. When *Antony* no hope remaining saw
How warre he might, or how agreement make,
Saw him betraid by all his men of warre
In every fight as well by sea, as land;
That not content to yeeld them to their foes
They also came against himselfe to fight:
Alone in court he gan himselfe torment,
Accuse the Queene, himselfe of hir lament,
Call'd hir untrue and traitresse, as who sought
To yeeld him up she could no more defend:
That in the harmes which for hir sake he bare,
As in his blisfull state, she might not share.
But she againe, who much his fury fear'd,
Gat to the tombes, darke horror's dwelling place:
Made lock the doores, and pull the hearses[1] downe.
Then fell she wretched, with hir selfe to fight.
A thousand plaints, a thousand sobbes she cast
From hir weake brest which to the bones was torne.
Of women hir the most unhappy call'd,
Who by hir love, hir woefull love, had lost
Hir realme, hir life, and more, the love of him
Who while he was, was all hir woes support.
But that she faultles was she did invoke
For witnes heav'n, and aire, and earth, and sea.
Then sent him word, she was no more alive,
But lay inclosed dead within her tombe.
This he beleev'd; and fell to sigh and grone,
And crost his armes, then thus began to mone.
CÆS. Poore hopeles man! DIR. What dost thou more attend
Ah *Antony*! why dost thou death deferre,
Since *Fortune* thy professed enimie,
Hath made to die, who only made thee live?
Soone as with sighes hee had these words up clos'd,
His armor he unlaste and cast it off,
Then all disarm'd he thus againe did say:
My Queene, my heart, the griefe that now I feele,
Is not that I your eies, my Sunne, do loose,
For soone againe one tombe shall us conjoyne:
I grieve, whome men so valorous did deeme,
Should now, then you, of lesser valor seeme.
So said, forthwith he *Eros* to him call'd,

[1] hearse-cloths, palls over the tomb.

Eros his man; summond him on his faith
To kill him at his nede. He tooke the sword,
And at that instant stab'd therwith his breast,
And ending life fell dead before his feete.
O *Eros* thankes (quoth *Antony*) for this
Most noble acte, who pow'rles me to kill,
On thee hast done, what I on mee should do.
  Of speaking thus he scarsce had made an end,
And taken up the bloudy sword from ground,
But he his bodie piers'd; and of red bloud
A gushing fountaine all the chamber fill'd.
He staggred at the blow, his face grew pale,
And on a couche all feeble downe he fell,
Swounding with anguish: deadly cold him tooke,
As if his soule had then his lodging left.
But he reviv'd, and marking all our eies
Bathed in teares, and how our breasts we beate
For pittie, anguish, and for bitter griefe,
To see him plong'd in extreame wretchednes,
He prai'd us all to haste his lingring death:
But no man willing, each himselfe withdrew.
Then fell he new to cry and vexe himselfe,
Untill a man from *Cleopatra* came,
Who said from hir he had commaundement
To bring him to hir to the monument.
  The poore soule at these words even rapt with joy
Knowing she liv'd, prai'd us him to convey
Unto his Lady. Then upon our armes
We bare him to the Tombe, but entred not.
For she who feared captive to be made,
And that she should to *Rome* in triumph goe,
Kept close the gate, but from a window high
Cast downe a corde, wherein he was impackt.
Then by hir womens help the corps she rais'd,
And by strong armes into hir window drew.
  So pittifull a sight was never seene.
Little and little *Antony* was pull'd,
Now breathing death: his beard was all unkempt,
His face and brest al bathed in his bloud.
So hideous yet, and dieng as he was,
His eies half-clos'd uppon the Queene he cast:
Held up his hands, and holpe himselfe to raise,
But still with weaknes back his bodie fell.
The miserable ladie with moist eies,

With haire which careles on hir forhead hong,
With brest which blowes had bloudily benumb'd,
With stooping head, and body down-ward bent,
Enlast hir in the corde, and with all force
This life-dead man couragiously uprais'd.
The bloud with paine into hir face did flowe,
Hir sinewes stiff, her selfe did breathles grow.
The people which beneath in flocks beheld,
Assisted her with gesture, speach, desire:
Cride and incourag'd her, and in their soules
Did sweate, and labor, no whit lesse then she,
Who never tir'd in labor, held so long
Helpt by her women, and hir constant heart,[1]
That *Antony* was drawne into the tombe,
And there (I thinke) of dead augments the summe.
The cittie all to teares and sighes is turn'd,
To plaints and outcries horrible to heare:
Men, women, children, hoary-headed age
Do all pell mell in house and streete lament,
Scratching their faces, tearing of their haire,
Wringing their hands, and martyring their brests:
Extreame their dole: and greater misery
In sacked townes can hardlie ever be.
Not if the fire had scal'de the highest towers:
That all things were of force and murther full;
That in the streets the bloud in rivers stream'd.
The sonne his sire saw in his bosome slaine,
The sire his sonne: the husband reft of breath
In his wives armes, who furious runnes to death.
Now my brest wounded with their piteouse plaints
I left their towne, and tooke with me this sworde,
Which I tooke up at what time *Antony*
Was from his chamber caried to the tombe:
And brought it you, to make his death more plaine,
And that thereby my words may credite gaine.
CÆS. Ah Gods what cruell hap! poore *Antony*,
Alas hast thou this sword so long time borne
Against thy foe, that in the end it should
Of thee his Lord the cursed murth'rer be?
O *Death* how I bewaile thee! we (alas!)
So many warres have ended, brothers, frends,
Companions, coozens, equalls in estate:

[1] Cf. IV.13.29–37.

And must it now to kill thee be my fate?
AG. Why trouble you your selfe with bootles griefe?
For *Antony* why spend you teares in vaine?
Why darken you with dole your victory?
Me seemes your selfe your glory do envie.
Enter the towne, give thanks unto the Gods.
CÆS. I cannot but his tearefull chaunce lament,
Although not I, but his owne pride the cause,
And unchast love of this *Aegiptian*.
AG. But best we sought into the tombe to get,
Lest she consume in this amazed case
So much rich treasure, with which happely
Despaire in death may make hir feede the fire:
Suffring the flames hir Jewells to deface,
You to defraud, hir funerall to grace.
Sende then to hir, and let some meane be us'd
With some devise so hold her still alive,
Some faire large promises: and let them marke
Whither they may by some fine cunning slight
Enter the tombes. CÆSAR. Let *Proculeius* goe,
And feede with hope hir soule disconsolate.
Assure hir soe, that we may wholy get
Into our hands hir treasure and her selfe.
For this of all things most I do desire
To keepe her safe until our going hence:
That by hir presence beautified may be
The glorious triumph *Rome* prepares for me.

Chorus of Romaine Souldiors

Shall ever civile bate
gnaw and devour our state?
shall never we this blade,
our bloud hath bloudy made,
lay downe? these armes downe lay
as robes we weare alway?
but as from age to age
so passe from rage to rage?
Our hands shall we not rest
to bath in our owne brest?
and shall thick in each land
our wretched trophees stand,
to tell posteritie,
what madd Impietie

our stonie stomacks led
against the place us bred?
Then still must heaven view
the plagues that us pursue,
and everywher descrie
heaps of us scattred lie,
making the stranger plaines
fat with our bleeding reines,
proud that on them their grave
so many legions have.
And with our fleshes still
Neptune his fishes fill
and dronke with bloud from blue
the sea take blushing hue:
as juice of *Tyrian* shell,
when clarified well
to wolle of finest fields
a purple glosse it yeeldes.
But since the rule of *Rome*,
to one mans hand is come,
who governes without mate
hir now united state,
late jointly rulde by three
envieng mutuallie,
whose triple yoke much woe
on *Latines* necks did throwe:
I hope the cause of jarre,
and of this bloudie warre,
and deadly discord gone
by what we last have done:
our banks shall cherish now
the branchie pale-hew'd bow
of *Olive*, *Pallas* praise,
in stede of barraine baies.
And that his temple dore,
which bloudy *Mars* before
held open, now at last
olde *Janus* shall make fast:
and rust the sword consume,
and, spoild of waving plume,
the useles morion shall
on crooke hang by the wall.
At least if warre returne
it shall not here sojourne,

to kill us with those armes
were forg'd for others harmes:
but have their points addrest,
against the *Germaines* brest,
the *Parthians* fayned flight,
the *Biscaines* martiall might.
Olde Memory doth there
painted on forehead weare
our Fathers praise: thence torne
our triumphs baies have worne:
therby our matchles *Rome*
whilome of Shepeheards come
rais'd to this greatnes stands,
the Queene of forraine lands.
Which now even seemes to face
the heav'ns, her glories place:
nought resting under skies
that dares affront her eies.
So that she needes but feare
the weapons *Jove* doth beare,
who angry at one blowe
may her quite overthrowe.

Act 5

Cleopatra. Euphron. Children of Cleopatra.
Charmion, Eras.

Cleop.

O cruell fortune! ô accursed lot!
O plaguy love! ô most detested brand!
O wretched joyes! ô beauties miserable!
O deadly state! ô deadly roialtie!
O hatefull life! ô Queene most lamentable!
O *Antony* by my faulte buriable!
O hellish worke of heav'n! alas! the wrath
Of all the Gods at once on us is falne.
Unhappie Queene! ô would I in this world
The wandring light of day had never seene?
Alas! of mine the plague and poison I
The crowne have lost my ancestors me left,
This Realme I have to strangers subject made,
And robd my children of their heritage.
Yet this is nought (alas!) unto the price

Of you deare husband, whome my snares intrap'd:
Of you, whome I have plagu'd, whom I have made
With bloudy hand a guest of mouldie tombe:
Of you, whome I destroied, of you, deare Lord,
Whome I of Empire, honor, life have spoil'd.
  O hurtfull woman! and can I yet live,
Yet longer live in this Ghost-haunted tombe?
Can I yet breathe! can yet in such annoy,
Yet can my soule within this body dwell?
O Sisters you that spin the thredes of death!
O *Styx*! ô *Plegethon*! you brookes of hell!
O Impes of *Night*! EUPH. Live for your childrens sake:
Let not your death of kingdome them deprive.
Alas what shall they do? who will have care?
Who will preserve this royall race of yours?
Who pittie take? even now me seemes I see
These little soules to servile bondage falne,
And borne in triumph. CL. Ah most miserable!
  EUPH. Their tender armes with cursed cord fast bound
At their weake backs. CL. Ah Gods what pitty more!
  EUPH. Their seely necks to ground with weaknes bend.
  CL. Never on us, good Gods, such mischiefe send.
  EUPH. And pointed at with fingers as they go.
  CL. Rather a thousand deaths. EUPH. Lastly his knife
Some cruell cative in their bloud embrue.
  CL. Ah my heart breaks. By shady banks of hell,
By fields whereon the lonely Ghosts do treade,
By my soule, and the soule of *Antony*
I you besech, *Euphron*, of them have care.
Be their good Father, let your wisedome lett
That they fall not into this Tyrants hands.
Rather conduct them where their freezed locks
Black *Aethiops* to neighbour Sunne do shew;
On wavie *Ocean* at the waters will;
On barraine cliffes of snowie *Caucasus*;
To Tigers swift, to Lions, and to Beares;
And rather, rather unto every coaste,
To ev'ry land and sea: for nought I feare
As rage of him, whose thirst no bloud can quench.
  Adieu deare children, children deare adieu:
Good *Isis* you to place of safety guide,
Farre from our foes, where you your lives may leade
In free estate devoid of servile dread.
  Remember not, my children, you were borne

Of such a Princely race: remember not
So many brave Kings which have *Egipt* rul'de
In right descent your ancestors have beene:
That this great *Antony* your father was,
Hercules bloud, and more then he in praise.
For your high courage such remembrance will,
Seing your fall with burning rages fill.
Who knowes if that your hands false *Destinie*
The Scepters promis'd of imperious *Rome*,
In stede of them shall crooked shepehookes beare,
Needles or forkes, or guide the carte, or plough?
Ah learne t'endure: your birth and high estate
Forget, my babes, and bend to force of fate.
Farwell, my babes, farwell my heart is clos'd,
With pittie and paine, my selfe with death enclos'd,
My breath doth faile. Farwell for evermore,
Your Sire and me you shall see never more.
Farwell sweet care, farwell. CHIL. Madame Adieu.
CL. Ah this voice killes me. Ah good Gods! I swound.
I can no more, I die. ERAS. Madame, alas!
And will you yeld to woe? Ah speake to us.
EU. Come Children. CHIL. We come. EU. Follow we our chance.
The Gods shall guide us. CHAR. O too cruell lot!
O too hard chaunce! Sister what shall we do,
What shall we do, alas! if murthring darte
Of death arrive while that in slumbring swound
Halfe dead she lie with anguish overgone?
ER. Her face is frozen. CH. Madame for Gods love
Leave us not thus: bid us yet first farwell.
Alas! wepe over *Antony*: Let not
His bodie be without due rites entomb'd.
CL. Ah, ah. CHAR. Madame. CL. Ay me! CH. How fainte she is!
CL. My Sisters, holde me up. How wretched I,
How cursed am: and was there ever one
By Fortunes hate into more dolours throwne?
Ah, weeping *Niobe*, although thy heart
Beholds it selfe enwrap'd in causefull woe
For thy dead children, that a sencelesse rocke
With griefe become, on *Sipylus* thou stand'st
In endles teares: yet didst thou never feele
The weights of griefe that on my heart do lie.
Thy Children thou, mine I poore soule have lost,

And lost their Father, more then them I waile,
Lost this faire realme; yet me the heavens wrath
Into a stone not yet transformed hath.
Phaetons sisters, daughters of the Sunne,
Which waile your brother falne into the streames
Of stately *Po*: the Gods upon the bankes
Your bodies to banke-loving Alders turn'd.
For me, I sigh, I ceasles wepe, and waile,
And heaven pittiles laughes at my woe,
Revives, renewes it still: and in the ende
(Oh cruelty!) doth death for comfort lend.
Die *Cleopatra* then, no longer stay
From *Antony*, who thee at *Styx* attends:
Go joyne thy Ghost with his, and sob no more
Without his love within these tombes enclos'd.
ERAS. Alas! yet let us wepe, lest sodaine death
From him our teares, and those last duties take
Unto his tombe we owe. CH. Ah let us wepe
While moisture lasts, then die before his feete.
CL. Who furnish will mine eies with streaming teares
My boiling anguish worthily to waile,
Waile thee *Antony*, *Antony* my heart?
Alas, how much I weeping liquor want!
Yet have mine eies quite drawne their Condits drie
By long beweeping my disastred harmes.
Now reason is that from my side they sucke
First vitall moisture, then the vitall bloud.
Then let the bloud from my sad eies outflowe,
And smoking yet with thine in mixture grow.
Moist it, and heat it newe, and never stop,
All watring thee, while yet remaines one drop.
CH. *Antony* take our teares: this is the last
Of all the duties we to thee can yelde,
Before we die. ER. These sacred obsequies
Take *Antony*, and take them in good parte.
CL. O Goddesse thou whom *Cyprus* doth adore,
Venus of *Paphos*, bent to worke us harme
For olde *Iulus* broode, if thou take care
Of *Cæsar*, why of us tak'st thou no care?
Antony did descend, as well as he,
From thine owne Sonne by long enchained line:
And might have rul'd by one and selfe same fate,
True *Trojan* bloud, the stately *Romain* state.
Antony, poore *Antony*, my deare soule,

Now but a blocke, the bootie of a tombe,
Thy life thy heat is lost, thy coullour gone,
And hideous palenes on thy face hath seaz'd.
Thy eies, two Sunnes, the lodging place of love,
Which yet for tents to warlike *Mars* did serve,[1]
Lock'd up in lidds (as faire daies cherefull light
Which darkeness flies) do winking hide in night.
  Antony by our true loves I thee beseeche,
And by our hearts sweete sparks have set on fire,
Our holy mariage, and the tender ruthe
Of our deare babes, knot of our amitie:
My dolefull voice they eare let entertaine,
And take me with thee to the hellish plaine,
Thy wife, thy frend: heare *Antony*, ô heare
My sobbing sighes, if here thou be, or there.
  Lived thus long, the winged race of yeares
Ended I have as *Destinie* decreed,
Flourish'd and raign'd, and taken just revenge
Of him who me both hated and despisde.
Happie, alas too happie: if of *Rome*
Only the fleete had hither never come.
And now of me an Image great shall goe
Under the earth to bury there my woe.
What say I? where am I? ô *Cleopatra*,
Poore *Cleopatra*, griefe thy reason reaves.
No, no, most happie in this happles case,
To die with thee, and dieng thee embrace:
My bodie joynde with thine, my mouth with thine,
My mouth, whose moisture burning sighes have dried
To be in one selfe tombe, and one selfe chest,
And wrapt with thee in one selfe sheete to rest.
  The sharpest torment in my heart I feele
Is that I stay from thee, my heart, this while.
Die will I straight now, now streight will I die,
And streight with thee a wandring shade will be,
Under the *Cypres* trees thou haunt'st alone,
Where brookes of hell do falling seeme to mone.
But yet I stay, and yet thee overlive,
That ere I die due rites I may thee give.
  A thousand sobbes I from my brest will teare,
With thousand plaints thy funeralls adorne:
My haire shall serve for thy oblations,

[1] Cf. I.1.2–4.

My boiling teares for thy effusions,
Mine eies thy fire: for out of them the flame
(Which burnt thy heart on me enamour'd) came.
  Weepe my companions, weepe, and from your eies
Raine downe on him of teares a brinish streame.
Mine can no more, consumed by the coales
Which from my brest, as from a furnace rise.
Martir your breasts with multiplied blowes,
With violent hands teare of your hanging haire,
Outrage your face: alas! why should we seeke
(Since now we die) our beauties more to keepe?
  I spent in teares, not able more to spende,
But kisse him now, what rests me more to doe?
Then let me kisse you, you faire eies, my light,
Front seat of honor, face most fierce, most faire!
O neck, ô armes, ô hands, ô breast where death
(O mischiefe) comes to choake up vitall breath.
A thousand kisses, thousand thousand more
Let you my mouth for honors farewell give:[1]
That in this office weake my limmes may growe,
Fainting on you, and forth my soule may flow.

At Ramsbury. 26 *of November.*
1590.

Printed at London by P. S. for William Ponsonby. 1595.

X. Probable Source

THE TRAGEDIE OF CLEOPATRA

by Samuel Daniel (1599 edition)[2]

THE ARGUMENT

After the death of *Antonius, Cleopatra,* (living still in the Monument shee had caused to be built,) could not, by any means be drawne foorth, although *Octavius Cæsar* very earnestly labored it: and sent *Proculeius,* to use al dilligence to bring hir unto him: for that he thought it would bee a great Ornament to his Triumphes, to get her alive to Rome. But never would she put her selfe into the hands of

[1] Cf. IV.13.19–21.
[2] In *The Poeticall Essayes of Sam. Danyel. Newly corrected and augmented. Printed by P. Short for S. Waterson.* 1599.

Proculeius, although on a time hee founde the meanes, (by a window that was at the toppe of the Monument,) to come downe unto her: where hee perswaded her (all hee might) to yeelde her selfe to *Cæsars* mercie. Which shee, (to be ridde of him,) cunningly seemed to grant unto. After that, *Octavius* in person went to visite her, to whom she excused her offence, laying all the fault upon the greatnes, and feare she had of *Antonius*, and withall, seemed very tractable, and willing to be disposed of by him.

Whereupon *Octavius*, (thinking himselfe sure) resolved presently to send her away to Rome. Whereof, *Dolabella*, a favourite of *Cæsars*, (and one that was growne into some good liking of her) having certified her, shee makes her humble petition to *Cæsar*, that he would suffer her to sacrifice to the ghost of *Antonius*: which being granted her, she was brought unto his sepulchre, where, after her rites performed, she returned to the Monument, and there dined with great magnificence. And in dinner time, came there one in the habite of a countryman, with a basket of Figs unto her, who (unsuspected) was suffered to carry them in. And in that Basket (among the Figges) were conveyed the Aspickes wherewith she did herselfe to death. Dinner being ended, she dispatched Letters to *Cæsar*, containing great lamentations with an earnest supplication, that shee might be intombed with *Antonius*. Whereupon *Cæsar* knowing what she intended, sent presently with all speede, Messengers to have prevented her death, which notwithstanding, before they came, was dispatched.

Cæsario her sonne, which she had by *Julius Cæsar* (conveyed before unto India, out of the danger of the warres) was about the same time of her death, murthered at Rhodes: trained thither by the falshoode of his Tutor, corrupted by *Cæsar*. And so, hereby came the race of the *Ptolomies* to be wholy extinct, and the flourishing rich kingdome of Egypt utterly overthrowne and subdued.

The Scæne supposed *Alexandria*.

The Actors

Cleopatra. Octavius Cæsar.
Proculeius. Dolabella.
Titius, servant to Dolabella.
Arius, } two Philosophers.
Philostratus, }
Seleucus, secretarie to Cleopatra.
Rodon, Tutor to Cæsario.
Nuntius.
The Chorus, all Egyptians.

THE TRAGEDIE
of Cleopatra

Actus Primus

Cleopatra.

Yet do I live, and yet doth breath extend
My life beyond my life? nor can my grave
Shut up my griefes, to make my end my end?
Will yet confusion have more then I have?
Is th'honor, wonder, glory, pompe, and all
Of *Cleopatra* dead, and she not dead?
Have I out-liv'd my selfe, and seene the fall
Of all upon me, and not ruined?
Can yet these endure the ghastly looke
Of Desolations darke and ougly face,
Wont but on Fortunes fairest side to looke,
Where nought was but applause, but smiles, and grace?
Whiles on his shoulders all my rest relide
On whom the burthen of m'ambition lay,
My *Atlas*,[1] and supporter of my pride
That did the world of all my glory sway,
Who now throwne downe, disgrac'd, confounded lies
Crusht with the weight of Shame and Infamie,
Following th'unlucky party of mine eies,
The traines of lust and imbecilitie,
Whereby my dissolution is become
The grave of Egypt, and the wracke of all;
My unforeseeing weakenesse must intoome
My Countries fame and glory with my fall.
  Now who would thinke that I were she who late
With all the ornaments on earth inrich'd,
Environ'd with delights, compast with state,
Glittering in pomp that harts and eies bewitch'd;
Should thus distrest, cast downe from off that height
Levell'd with low disgrac'd calamitie,
Under the weight of such affliction sigh,
Reduc'd unto th'extreamest miserie?
  Am I the woman whose inventive pride,
Adorn'd like *Isis*, scornd mortalitie?
Is't I would have my frailetie so belide,

[1] Cf. I.5.23, 'demi-Atlas.'

That flattery could perswade I was not I?
Well, now I see, they but delude that praise us,
Greatnesse is mockt, prosperitie betrayes us.
And we are but our selves, although this cloude
Of interposed smoakes make us seeme more:
These spreading parts of pomp wherof w'are prowd,
Are not our parts, but parts of others store:
Witnesse these gallant fortune-following traines,
These Summer Swallowes of felicitie
Gone with the heate. Of all, see what remaines,
This monument, two maides, and wretched I.
And I, t'adorne their triumphs am reserv'd
A captive, kept to honour others spoiles,
Whom *Cæsar* labors so to have preserv'd,
And seekes to entertaine my life with wiles.
But *Cæsar*, it is more then thou canst do,
Promise, flatter, threaten extreamitie,
Imploy thy wits and all thy force thereto,
I have both hands, and will, and I can die.[1]
Though thou, of both my country and my crowne,
Of powre, of meanes and all dost quite bereave me;
Though thou hast wholy Egypt made thine owne,
Yet hast thou left me that which will deceive thee.
That courage with my bloud and birth innated,
Admir'd of all the earth as thou art now,
Can never be so abjectly abated
To be thy slave that rul'd as good as thou.
Thinke *Cæsar*, I that liv'd and raign'd a Queene,
Doe scorne to buy my life at such a rate,
That I should underneath my selfe be seene,
Basely induring to survive my state:
That Rome should see my scepter-bearing hands
Behind me bound, and glory in my teares,
That I should passe whereas *Octavia* stands,
To view my miserie that purchas'd hers.[2]
No, I disdaine that head which wore a crowne,
Should stoope to take up that which others give;
I must not be, unlesse I be mine owne.
Tis sweete to die when we are forc'd to live,
Nor had I staide behinde my selfe this space,
Nor paid such int'rest for this borrow'd breath,
But that hereby I seeke to purchase grace

[1] Cf. IV.13.49.

[2] Cf. V.2.52–5.

For my distressed seede after my death.
It's that which doth my deerest bloud controule,
That's it alas detaines me from my tombe,
Whiles Nature brings to contradict my soule
The argument of mine unhappy wombe.
  You lucklesse issue of a wofull mother,
The wretched pledges of a wanton bed,
You, Kings design'd, must subjects live to other;
Or else, I feare, scarce live, when I am dead.
It is for you I temporize with *Cæsar*,
And stay this while to mediate your safetie:
For you I faine content, and soothe his pleasure,
Calamitie herein hath made me craftie.
But this is but to trie what may be done,
For come what will, this stands, I must die free,
And die my selfe uncaptiv'd, and unwonne.
Bloud, Children, Nature, all must pardon me.
My soule yeeldes Honor up the victory,
And I must be a Queene, forget a mother,
Though mother would I be, were I not I;
And Queene would not be now, could I be other.
  But what know I if th'heavens have decreed,
And that the sinnes of Egypt have deserv'd
The *Ptolomies* should faile and none succeed,
And that my weakenes was thereto reserv'd,
That I should bring confusion to my state,
And fill the measure of iniquitie,
Luxuriousnesse in me should raise the rate
Of loose and ill-dispensed libertie.
If it be so, then what neede these delaies?
Since I was made the meanes of miserie:
Why should I strive but to make death my praise,
That had my life but for my infamie?
And let me write in letters of my bloud
A fit memoriall for the times to come,
To be example to such Princes good
As please themselves, and care not what become.
  And *Antony*, because the world takes note
That my defects have onely ruin'd thee:
And my ambitious practises are thought
The motive and the cause of all to be:
Though God thou know'st, how just this staine is laide
Upon my soule, whom ill successe makes ill:
Yet since condemn'd misfortune hath no aide

Against prowd lucke that argues what it will,
I have no meanes to undeceive their mindes,
But to bring in the witnesse of my bloud,
To testifie the faith and love that bindes
My equall shame, to fall with whom I stood.
Defects I grant I had, but this was worst,
That being the first to fall I dy'd not first.
 Though I perhaps could lighten mine own side
With some excuse of my constrained case
Drawn down with powre: but that were to devide
My shame: to stand alone in my disgrace.
To cleere me so, would shew m'affections naught,
And make th'excuse more hainous then the fault.
Since if I should our errours disunite,
I should confound afflictions onely rest,
That from sterne death even steales a sad delight
To die with friends or with the like distrest;
And since we tooke of either such firme hold
In th'overwhelming seas of fortune cast,
What powre should be of powre to reunfold
The armes of our affections lockt so fast:
For grapling in the ocean of our pride,
We suncke each others greatnesse both together;
And both made shipwracke of our fame beside,
Both wrought a like destruction unto either:
And therefore I am bound to sacrifice
To death and thee, the life that doth reprove me:
Our like distresse I feele doth simpathize,
And even affliction makes me truely love thee.
Which *Antony*, I must confesse my fault
I never did sincerely untill now:
Now I protest I do, now am I taught
In death to love, in life that knew not how.
For whilst my glory in her greatnesse stoode,
And that I saw my state, and knew my beautie;
Saw how the world admir'd me, how they woo'd,
I then thought all men must love me of duetie;
And I love none: for my lascivious Court,
Fertile in ever fresh and new-choise pleasure,
Affoorded me so bountifull disport,
That I to stay on Love had never leisure:
My vagabond desires no limites found,
For lust is endlesse, pleasure hath no bound.
 Thou comming from the strictnesse of thy Citty,

And never this loose pomp of monarchs learnest,
Inur'd to warres, in womens wiles unwitty,
Whilst others faind, thou fell'st to love in earnest;
Not knowing how we like them best that hover,
And make least reckning of a doting lover.
  And yet thou cam'st but in my beauties waine,
When new appeering wrinckles of declining[1]
Wrought with the hand of yeeres, seem'd to detaine
My graces light, as now but dimly shining
Even in the confines of mine age, when I
Failing of what I was, and was but thus;
When such as we do deeme in jealousie
That men love for themselves, and not for us,
Then, and but thus, thou didst love most sincerely
O *Antony*, that best deserv'st it better,
This Autumne of my beauty bought so dearely,
For which in more then death, I stand thy debter,
Which I will pay thee with so true a minde,
(Casting up all these deepe accompts of mine)
That both our soules, and all the world shall find
All recknings cleer'd, betwixt my love and thine.
  But to the end I may prevent prowd *Cæsar*,
Who doth so eagerly my life importune,
I must prevaile me of this little leasure,
Seeming to sute my minde unto my fortune;
Thereby with more convenience to provide
For what my death and honor best shall fit:
An yeelding base content must wary hide
My last dissigne till I accomplish it,
That hereby yet the world shall see that I,
Although unwise to live, had wit to die.

Exit.

CHORUS

Behold what furies stil
Torment their tortur'd brest,
Who by their doing ill,
Have wrought the worlds unrest.
Which when being most distrest,
Yet more to vexe their sprite,
The hideous face of sinne,
(In formes they must detest)
Stands ever in their sight.

[1] Cf. I.5.29.

Their conscience still within
Th'eternall larum is
That ever-barking dog that calles upon their misse.

No meanes at all to hide
Man from himselfe can finde:
No way to start aside
Out from the hell of minde.
But in himselfe confin'd,
He still sees sinne before:
And winged-footed paine,
That swiftly comes behinde,
The which is ever-more,
The sure and certaine gaine
Impietie doth get,
And wanton loose respect, that doth it selfe forget.

And *Cleopatra* now,
Well sees the dangerous way
She tooke, and car'd not how,
Which led her to decay.
  And likewise makes us pay
For her disordred lust,
The int'rest of our blood:
Or live a servile pray,
Under a hand unjust,
As others shall thinke good.
This hath her riot wonne:
And thus she hath her state, herselfe and us undonne.

Now every mouth can tell,
What close was muttered:
How that she did not well,
To take the course she did.
  For now is nothing hid,
Of what feare did restraine.
No secret closely done,
But now is uttered.
The text is made most plaine
That flattry glos'd upon,
The bed of sinne reveal'd,
And all the luxurie that shame would have conceal'd.

The scene is broken downe,
And all uncov'red lyes,
The purple actors knowne
Scarce men, whom men despise.
  The complots of the wise,
Prove imperfections smoake:
And all what wonder gave
To pleasure-gazing eyes,
Lyes scattred, dasht, all broke.
Thus much beguiled have
Poore unconsiderate wights,
These momentaric pleasures, fugitive delights.

Actus secundus.

Cæsar. *Proculeius.*

Kingdoms I see we winne, we conquere Climates,
Yet cannot vanquish hearts, nor force obedience,
  Affections kept in close-concealed limits,
Stand farre without the reach of sworde or violence.
Who forc'd do pay us dutie, pay not love:
Free is the heart, the temple of the minde,
The Sanctuarie sacred from above,
Where nature keeps the keies that loose and bind.
No mortall hand force open can that doore,
So close shut up, and lockt to all mankind:
I see mens bodies onely ours, no more,
The rest, anothers right, that rules the minde.
  Behold, my forces vanquisht have this Land,
Subdu'd that strong Competitor of mine:
All Egypt yeelds to my all-conqu'ring hand,
And all their treasure and themselves resigne.
Onely this Queene, that hath lost all this all,
To whom is nothing left except a minde:
Cannot into a thought of yeelding fall,
To be dispos'd as Chance hath her assign'd.
  But *Proculei*, what hope doth she now give,
  Will shee be brought to condiscend to live?
  PROC. My Lord, what time being sent from you to try
  To win her forth alive (if that I might)
From out the Monument, where wofully
She lives inclos'd in most afflicted plight:
No way I found, no means how to surprize her,

But through a grate at th'entry of the place
Standing to treat, I labour'd to advise her,
To come to *Cæsar*, and to sue for grace.
She said, she crav'd not life, but leave to die,
Yet for her children, pray'd they might inherite,
That *Cæsar* would vouchsafe (in clemencie)
To pittie them, though she deserv'd no merite.
So leaving her for then; and since of late,
With *Gallus* sent to trie an other time,
The whilst he entertaines her at the grate,
I found the meanes up to the Tombe to clime.
Where, in descending in the closest wise,
And silent manner as I could contrive:
Her woman me descri'd, and out she cries,
Poore *Cleopatra*, thou art tane alive.
With that the Queene raught from her side her knife,
And even in act to stab her martred brest,
I stept with speede, and held, and sav'd her life,
And forth her trembling hand the blade did wrest.
Ah *Cleopatra*, why shouldst thou, (said I)
Both injurie thy selfe and *Cæsar* so?
Barre him the honour of his victorie,
Who ever deales most mildly with his foe?
Live, and relie on him, whose mercy will
To thy submission alwayes readie be.
 With that (as all amaz'd) she held her still,
Twixt majestie confuz'd and miserie.
Her proud griev'd eyes, held sorow and disdaine,
State and distresse warring within her soule:
Dying ambition dispossest her raigne,
So base affliction seemed to controule.
Like as a burning Lampe, whose liquor spent
With intermitted flames, when dead you deeme it,
Sends forth a dying flash, as discontent
That so the matter failes that should redeeme it:
So she (in spight) to see her low-brought state,
When all her hopes were now consum'd to nought)
Scornes yet to make an abject league with Fate,
Or once descend into a servile thought.
Th'imperious tongue unused to beseech,
Authoritie confounds with prayers, so
Words of command conjoyn'd with humble speech,
Shew'd she would live, yet scorn'd to pray her foe.
 Ah, what hath *Cæsar* heere to do, said she,

In confines of the dead in darknesse lying?
Will he not grant our sepulchres be free,
But violate the priviledge of dying?
What, must he stretch foorth his ambitious hand
Into the right of Death, and force us heere?
Hath Miserie no covert where to stand
Free from the storme of Pride, is't safe no where?
Cannot my land, my golde, my crowne suffise,
And all what I held deere, to him made common,
But that he must in this sort tyrannize,
Th'afflicted body of an wofull woman?
Tell him, my frailetie, and the gods have given
Sufficient glorie, could he be content:
And let him now with his desires make even,
And leave me to this horror, to lament.
Now he hath taken all away from mee,
What must he take me from my selfe by force?
Ah, let him yet (in mercie) leave me free
The kingdome of this poore distressed corse.
No other crowne I seeke, no other good.
Yet wish that *Cæsar* would vouchsafe this grace,
To favour the poore of-spring of my bloud.
Confused issue, yet of Roman race.
If bloud and name be linckes of love in Princes,
Not spurres of hate; my poore *Cæsario* may
Finde favour notwithstanding mine offences,
And *Cæsars* bloud, may *Cæsars* raging stay.
But if that with the torrent of my fall,
All must be rapt with furious violence,
And no respect, nor no regard at all,
Can aught with nature or with bloud dispence:
Then be it so, if needes it must be so.
There staies and shrinckes in horror of her state:
When I beganne to mittigate her woe,
And thy great mercies unto her relate;
Wishing her not despaire, but rather come
And sue for grace, and shake off all vaine feares:
No doubt she should obtaine as gentle doome
As she desir'd, both for her selfe and hers.
And so with much adoe, (well pacifide
Seeming to be) she shew'd content to live,
Saying she was resolv'd thy doome t'abide,
And to accept what favour thou would'st give,
And herewithall, crav'd also that shee might

Performe her last rites to her lost belov'd.
To sacrifice to him that wrought her plight:
And that she might not be by force remov'd.
  I granting from thy part this her request,
  Left her for then, seeming in better rest.
  CÆS. But dost thou thinke she will remaine so still?
  PRO. I thinke, and do assure my selfe she will.
  CÆS. Ah, private men sound not the harts of Princes,
Whose actions oft beare contrarie pretences.
  PRO. Why tis her safetie to come yeelde to thee.
  CÆS. But tis more honour for her to die free.
  PRO. She may thereby procure her childrens good.
  CÆS. Princes respect their honour more then blood.
  PRO. Can Princes powre dispence with nature than?
  CÆS. To be a prince, is more then be a man.
  PRO. There's none but have in time perswaded beene.
  CÆS. And so might she too, were she not a Queene.
  PRO. Divers respects will force her be reclaim'd.
  CÆS. Princes (like Lions) never will be tam'd.
A private man may yeelde and care not how,
But greater hearts will breake before they bow.
And sure I thinke sh'will never condiscend,
To live to grace our spoiles with her disgrace:
But yet let still a wary troupe attend,
To guard her person, and to watch the place.
And looke that none with her come to confer:
Shortly my selfe will go to visite her.

CHORUS.

Opinion, how doost thou molest
Th'affected minde of restlesse man?
Who following thee never can,
  Nor ever shall attaine to rest,
For getting what thou saist is best,
  Yet loe, that best he findes farre wide
  Of what thou promisedst before:
  For in the same he lookt for more,
  Which proves but small when once tis tride,
Then something else thou find'st beside,
  To draw him still from thought to thought:
  When in the end all prooves but nought.
  Farther from rest he findes him than,
  Then at the first when he began.

O malecontent seducing guest,
Contriver of our greatest woes:
Which borne of winde, and fed with showes,
Doost nurse thy selfe in thine unrest.
Judging ungotten things the best,
Or what thou in conceit design'st,
And all things in the world dost deeme,
Not as they are, but as they seeme:
Which shews, their state thou ill defin'st:
And liv'st to come, in present pin'st.
For what thou hast, thou still dost lacke:
O mindes tormentor, bodies wracke,
Vaine promiser of that sweete rest,
Which never any yet possest.

If we unto ambition tend,
Then doost thou drawe our weakenesse on,
With vaine imagination
Of that which never hath an end.
Or if that lust we apprehend,
How doth that pleasant plague infest?
O what strange formes of luxurie,
Thou strait dost cast t'intice us by?
And tell'st us that is ever best,
Which we have never yet possest.
And that more pleasure rests beside,
In something that we have not tride.
And when the same likewise is had,
Then all is one, and all is bad.

This *Antony* can say is true,
And *Cleopatra* knowes tis so,
By th'experience of their woe.
She can say, she never knew
But that lust found pleasures new,
And was never satisfide:
He can say by proofe of toile,
Ambition is a Vulture vile,
That feeds upon the hart of pride:
And findes no rest when all is tride.
For worlds cannot confine the one,
Th'other, lists[1] and bounds hath none.
And both subvert the minde, the state,
Procure destruction, envie, hate.

[1] limits.

And now when all this is prov'd vaine,
  Yet *Opinion* leaves not heere,
  But sticks to *Cleopatra* neere,
  Perswading now, how she shall gaine
Honour by death, and fame attaine.
  And what a shame it were to live,
  Her kingdome lost, her Lover dead:
  And so with this perswasion led,
  Dispaire doth such a courage give,
That nought else can her minde relieve,
  Nor yet divert her from that thought:
  To this conclusion all is brought.
  This is that rest this vaine world lends,
  To end in death that all things ends.

Actus tertius.

Philostratus. Arius.

How deepely *Arius* am I bound to thee,
That sav'dst from death this wretched life of mine:
Obtaining *Cæsars* gentle grace for mee,
When I of all helps else dispaird but thine?
Although I see in such a wofull state,
Life is not that which should be much desir'd:
Sith all our glories come to end their date,
Our Countries honour and our own expir'd
Now that the hand of wrath hath over-gone us,
Living (as 'twere) in th'armes of our dead mother,
With bloud under our feet, ruine upon us,
And in a Land most wretched of all other,
When yet we reckon life our deerest good.
And so we live, we care not how we live:
So deepe we feele impressed in our blood,
That touch which Nature with our breath did give.
And yet what blasts of words hath Learning found,
To blow against the feare of death and dying?
What comforts unsicke eloquence can sound,
And yet all failes us in the point of trying.
For whilst we reason with the breath of safety,
Without the compasse of destruction living:
What precepts shew we then, what courage lofty
In taxing others feares in councell giving?
When all this ayre of sweet-contrived wordes

Proves but weake armour to defend the hart.
For when this life, pale Feare and Terrour boords,
Where are our precepts then, where is our arte?
O who is he that from himselfe can turne,
That beares about the body of a man?
Who doth not toile and labour to adjorne
The day of death, by any meanes he can?
All this I speake to th'end my selfe t'excuse,
For my base begging of a servile breath,
Wherein I grant my selfe much to abuse,
So shamefully to seeke t'avoide my death.

ARIUS. *Philostratus*, that selfe same care to live,
Possesseth all alike, and grieve not then
Nature doth us no more then others give:
Though we speake more then men, we are but men.
And yet (in truth) these miseries to see,
Wherein we stand in most extreame distresse:
Might to our selves sufficient motives be
To loathe this life, and weigh our death the lesse:
For never any age hath better taught,
What feeble footing pride and greatnesse hath.
How improvident prosperitie is caught,
And cleane confounded in the day of wrath.
See how dismaid Confusion keepes those streetes,
That nought but mirth and musique late resounded,
How nothing with our eie but horror meetes,
Our state, our wealth, our pride and all confounded.
Yet what weake sight did not discerne from far
This black-arising tempest, all confounding?
Who did not see we should be what we are,
When pride and ryot grew to such abounding.
When dissolute impietie possest
Th'unrespective mindes of prince, and people:
When insolent Security found rest
In wanton thoughts, with lust and ease made feeble.
Then when unwary Peace with fat-fed pleasure,
New-fresh invented ryots still detected,
Purchac'd with all the *Ptolomies* rich treasure,
Our lawes, our gods, our mysteryes neglected.
Who saw not how this confluence of vice,
This inundation of disorders, must
At length of force pay backe the bloody price
Of sad destruction, (a reward for lust.)
O thou and I have heard, and read, and knowne

Of like proude states, as wofully incombred,
And fram'd by them, examples for our owne:
Which now among examples must be numbred.
For this decree a law from high is given,
An ancient Canon, of eternall date,
In Consistorie of the starres of heaven,
Entred the Booke of unavoyded Fate;
That no state can in height of happinesse,
In th'exaltation of their glory stand:
But thither once arriv'd, declining lesse,
Ruine themselves, or fall by others hand.
Thus doth the ever-changing course of things
Runne a perpetuall circle, ever turning:
And that same day that hiest glory brings,
Brings us unto the poynt of backe-returning.
For sencelesse sensualitie, doth ever
Accompany felicitie and greatnesse.
A fatall witch, whose charmes do leave us never,
Till we leave all in sorrow for our sweetnesse;
When yet our selves must be the cause we fall,
Although the same be first decreed on hie:
Our errors still must beare the blame of all,
This must it be; earth, aske not heaven why.
  Yet mighty men with wary jealous hand,
Strive to cut off all obstacles of feare:
All whatsoever seemes but to withstand
Their least conceit of quiet, held so deere;
And so intrench themselves with blood, with crimes,
With all injustice as their feares dispose:
Yet for all this we see, how oftentimes
The meanes they worke to keepe, are meanes to lose.
And sure I cannot see, how this can stand
With great *Augustus* safety and his honor,
To cut off all succession from our land,
For her offence that pulld the warres upon her.
  PHI. Why must her issue pay the price of that?
  ARI. The price is life that they are rated at.
  PHI. *Cæsario* too, issued of *Cæsars* blood?
  ARI. Pluralitie of Cæsars are not good.
  PHI. Alas, what hurt procures his feeble arme?
  ARI. Not for it doth, but that it may do harme.
  PHI. Then when it offers hurt, represse the same.
  ARI. Tis best to quench a sparke before it flame.
  PHI. Tis inhumane, an innocent to kill.

ARI. Such innocents seldome remaine so still.
And sure his death may best procure our peace.
Competitors the subject deerely buyes:
And so that our afflicton may surcease,
Let great men be the peoples sacrifice.
But see where *Cæsar* comes himselfe, to try
And worke the mind of our distressed Queene,
To apprehend some falsed hope: whereby
She might be drawn to have her fortune seene.
But yet I thinke, Rome will not see that face
(That queld her champions) blush in base disgrace.

Scena secunda.

Cæsar, Cleopatra, Seleucus, Dolabella.

Cæsar.

What *Cleopatra*, doost thou doubt so much
Of Cæsars mercy, that thou hid'st thy face?
Or dost thou thinke, thy'offences can be such,
That they surmount the measure of our grace?
CLE. O *Cæsar*, not for that I flie thy sight
My soule this sad retire of sorrow chose:
But that m'oppressed thoughts abhorring light
Like best in darkenes, my disgrace t'inclose.
And heere to these close limites of despaire,
This solitarie horror where I bide:
Cæsar, I thought no Roman should repaire,
More after him, who here oppressed dyde.
Yet now, here at thy conquering feete I lie,
Poore captive soul, that never thought to bow:
Whose happy foote of rule and Majestie
Stood late on the same ground thou standest now.
CÆS. Rise Queene, none but thy selfe is cause of al,
And yet, would all were but thine owne alone:
That others ruine had not with thy fall
Brought Rome her sorrowes, to my triumphs mone.
For breaking off the league of love and blood,
Thou mak'st my winning joy a gaine unpleasing:
Sith th'eye of grief must looke into our good,
Thorow the horror of our own bloodshedding.
And all, we must attribute unto thee.
CLE. To me? Cæsar, what should a woman doe
Opprest with greatnes? what was it for me

To contradict my Lord, being bent thereto?
I was by love, by feare, by weakenesse, made
An instrument to such disseignes as these.
For when the Lord of all the Orient bade,
Who but obey'd? who was not glad to please?
And how could I withdraw my succouring hand
From him that had my heart, and what was mine?
The int'rest of my faith in streightest band,
My love to his most firmely did combine.
  CÆS. Love? alas no, it was th'innated hatred
That thou and thine hast ever borne our people,
That made thee seeke all meanes to have us scattred,
To disunite our strength, and make us feeble.
And therefore did that breast nurse our dissention,
With hope t'exalte thy selfe, t'augment thy state:
To pray upon the wracke of our contention,
And (with the rest our foes,) to joy thereat.
  CLEO. O *Cæsar*, see how easie tis t'accuse
Whom Fortune hath made faulty by their fall,
The wretched conquered may not refuse
The titles of reproch hee's charg'd withall.
  The conquering cause hath right, wherein thou art,
  The vanquisht still is judgde the worser part.
Which part is mine, because I lost my part,
No lesser then the portion of a Crowne.
Enough for me, alas what needed Art
To gaine by others, but to keepe mine owne?
But heere let weaker powers note what it is,
To neighbour great Competitors too neere.
If wee take part, we oft do perish thus,
If neutrall bide, both parties we must feare.
  Alas, what shall the forst partakers doe,
  When following none, yet must they perish too?
But Cæsar, sith thy right and cause is such,
Be not a heavy weight upon calamitie:
Depresse not the afflicted over-much,
The chiefest glorie is the Victors lenitie.
Th'inheritance of mercie from him take,
Of whom thou hast thy fortune and thy name:
Great Cæsar me a Queene at first did make,
And let not Cæsar now confound the same,
Reade here these lines which stil I keepe with me,
The witnes of his love and favours ever:
And God forbid this should be said of thee,

That Cæsar wrong'd the favoured of Cæsar.
For looke what I have beene to *Antony*,
Thinke thou the same I might have beene to thee.
And here I do present thee with the note
Of all the treasure, all the jewels rare
That Egypt hath in many ages got;
And looke what *Cleopatra* hath, is there.

SELEU. Nay there's not all set downe within that roule,
I know some things she hath reserv'd apart.

CLE. What, vile ungrateful wretch, dar'st thou controule
Thy Queene and soveraigne, caitife as thou art.[1]

CÆS. Holde, holde; a poore revenge can worke so feeble hands

CLE. Ah *Cæsar*, what a great indignitie
Is this, that here my vassal subject stands
T'accuse me to my Lord of trecherie?
If I reserv'd some certaine womens toyes,
Alas it was not for my selfe (God knowes,)
Poore miserable soule, that little joyes
In trifling ornaments in outward showes.
But what I kept, I kept to make my way
Unto thy *Livia* and *Octavias* grace,
That thereby in compassion mooved, they
Might mediate thy favour in my case.[2]

CÆS. Well *Cleopatra*, feare not, thou shalt finde
What favour thou desir'st, or canst expect:
For *Cæsar* never yet was found but kinde
To such as yeeld, and can themselves subject.
And therefore give thou comfort to thy minde,
Relieve thy soule thus overcharg'd with care.
How well I will intreate thee thou shalt find,
So soone as some affaires dispatched are.
Til when farewel. CL. Thanks thrise renowned *Cæsar*,
Poore *Cleopatra* rests thine owne for ever.

DOL. No marvel *Cæsar* though our greatest spirits,
Have to the powre of such a charming beautie
Been brought to yeeld the honor of their merits:
Forgetting all respect of other dutie,
Then whilst the glory of her youth remain'd
The wondring object to each wanton eye:
Before her full of sweet (with sorrow wain'd,)
Came to the period of this miserie.

[1] Cf. V.2.137–57. [2] Cf. V.2.158–69.

If still, even in the midst of death and horror
Such beautie shines, thorow clouds of age & sorow,
If even those sweet decaies seeme to pleade for her,
Which from affliction moving graces borrow:
  If in calamitie she could thus move,
  What could she do adorn'd with youth and love?
What could she do then, whenas spreading wide
The pompe of beauty, in her glory dight?
When arm'd with wonder, she could use beside,
Th'ingines of her love, Hope and Delight?
  Beautie daughter of Mervaile, O see how
Thou canst disgracing sorrowes sweetly grace.
What power thou shew'st in a distressed brow,
That mak'st affliction faire, giv'st tears their grace.
What, can untressed locks, can torne rent haire,
A weeping eye, a wailing face be faire?
  I see then, artlesse feature can content,
  And that true beautie needes no ornament.
    CÆS. What, in a passion *Dolabella?* what, take heed:
Let others fresh examples be thy warning;
What mischiefes these so idle humors breed,
Whilst error keepes us from a true discerning.
In deed I saw she labour'd to impart
Her sweetest graces in her saddest cheere:
Presuming on the face that knew the arte
To move with what aspect so ev'r it were.
But all in vaine, she takes her ayme amisse,
The ground and marke her level much deceives;
Time now hath altred all, for neither is
She as she was, nor we as she conceives.
And therefore now, twere best she left such badnesse.
Folly in youth is sinne, in age, tis madnes.
  And for my part, I seeke but t'entertaine
In her some feeding hope to draw her forth;
The greatest Trophey that my travailes gaine,
Is, to bring home a prizall of such worth.
And now, sith that she seemes so well content
To be dispos'd by us, without more stay
She with her children shall to Rome be sent,
Whilst I by *Syria* thither take my way.

CHORUS

O fearefull frowning *Nemesis*,
  Daughter of Justice, most severe,

That art the worlds great arbitresse,
And Queene of causes raigning heere:
Whose swift-sure hand is ever neere
Eternall justice, righting wrong:
Who never yet deferrest long
The prowds decay, the weaks redresse:
But through thy power every where,
Dost raze the great, and raise the lesse.
The lesse made great dost ruine too,
To shew the earth what heaven can do.

Thou from darke-clos'd eternitie,
From thy blacke cloudy hidden seate,
The worlds disorders dost descry:
Which when they swel so prowdly great,
Reversing th'order nature set,
Thou giv'st thy all confounding doome,
Which none can know before it come.
Th'inevitable destinie,
Which neither wit nor strength can let,
Fast chain'd unto necessitie,
In mortall things doth order so,
Th'alternate course of weale or wo.

O how the powres of heaven doe play
With travailed mortalitie:
And doth their weakenesse still betray,
In their best prosperitie?
When being lifted up so hie,
They looke beyond themselves so farre,
That to themselves they take no care;
Whilst swift confusion downe doth lay
Their late prowd mounting vanitie:
Bringing their glorie to decay,
And with the ruine of their fall,
Extinguish people, state and all.

But is it Justice that all wee
The innocent poore multitude,
For great mens faults should punisht be,
And to destruction thus pursude?
O why should th'heavens us include,
Within the compasse of their fall,
Who of themselves procured all?

Or do the gods in close decree,
Occasion take how to extrude
Man from the earth with crueltie?
Ah no, the gods are ever just,
Our faults excuse their rigor must.

This is the period Fate set downe,
To Egypts fat prosperitie:
Which now unto her greatest growne,
Must perish thus, by course must die.
And some must be the causers why
This revolution must be wrought:
As borne to bring their state to nought:
To change the people and the crowne,
And purge the worlds iniquitie:
Which vice so farre hath over-growne.
As we, so they that treate us thus,
Must one day perish like to us.

Actus quartus.

Seleucus. Rodon.

SEL. Never friend *Rodon* in a better howre
Could I have met thee then ev'n now I do,
Having affliction in the greatest powre
Upon my soule, and none to tell it to.
For tis some ease our sorrowes to reveale,
If they to whom we shall impart our woes
Seeme but to feele a part of what we feele:
And meete us with a sigh but at a cloze.
ROD. And never (friend *Seleucus*) found'st thou one
That better could beare such a part with thee:
Who by his own, knows others cares to mone,
And can, in like accord of griefe, agree.
And therefore tell th'oppression of thy hart,
Tell to an eare prepar'd and tun'd to care:
And I will likewise unto thee impart
As sad a tale as what thou shalt declare.
So shall we both our mournefull plaints combine;
Ile waile thy state, and thou shalt pitty mine.
SEL. Well then, thou know'st how I have liv'd in grace
With *Cleopatra*, and esteem'd in Court
As one of Councell, and of chiefest place,

And ever held my credite in that sort.
Till now in this confusion of our state,
When thinking to have us'd a meane to climbe,
And fled the wretched, flowne unto the great,
(Following the fortune of the present time,)
Am come to be cast down and ruin'd cleene;
And in the course of mine own plot undonne.
For having all the secrets of the Queene
Reveald to *Cæsar*, to have favor wonne,
My trechery is quited with disgrace,
My falshood loath'd, and not without great reason.
Though good for him, yet Princes in this case
Do hate the Traitor, though they love the treason.
For how could he imagine I would be
Faithfull to him, being false unto mine owne?
And false to such a bounteous Queene as she,
That had me rais'd and made mine honor knowne.
He saw twas not for zeale to him I bare,
But for base feare, or mine owne state to settle.
Weakenesse is false, and faith in Cowards rare,
Feare findes out shifts, timiditie is subtle.
And therefore scorn'd of him, scorn'd of mine own,
Hatefull to all that looke into my state:
Despis'd *Seleucus* now is onely grown
The marke of infamy, that's pointed at.
ROD. Tis much thou saist, and O too much to feele,
And I do grieve and do lament thy fall:
But yet all this which thou doost heere reveale,
Compar'd with mine, wil make thine seem but small.
Although my fault be in the selfe-same kind,
Yet in degree far greater, far more hatefull;
Mine sprong of mischiefe, thine from feeble mind,
I staind with bloud, thou onely but ungratefull.
For unto me did *Cleopatra* give
The best and deerest treasure of her blood,
Lovely *Cæsario*, whom she would should live
Free from the dangers wherein Egypt stoode.
And unto me with him this charge she gave,
Here *Rodon*, take, convey from out this coast,
This precious Gem, the chiefest that I have,
The jewell of my soule I value most.
Guide him to *India*, leade him farre from hence,
Safeguard him where secure he may remaine,
Till better fortune call him backe from thence,

And Egypts peace be reconcil'd againe.
For this is he that may our hopes bring backe;
(The rising Sunne of our declining state:)
These be the hands that may restore our wracke,
And raise the broken ruines made of late.
He may give limits to the boundlesse pride
Of fierce *Octavius*, and abate his might:
Great *Julius* of-spring, he may come to guide
The Empire of the world, as his by right.
  O how he seemes the modell of his Syre?
O how I gaze my Cæsar in his face?
Such was his gaite, so did his lookes aspire;
Such was his threatning brow, such was his grace.
High shouldred, and his forehead even as hie.
And O, (if he had not beene borne so late,)
He might have rul'd the worlds great Monarchy,
And now have beene the Champion of our state.
  Then unto him, O my deere Sonne (she saies,)
Sonne of my youth, flie hence, O flie, be gone,
Reserve thy selfe, ordain'd for better daies,
For much thou hast to ground thy hopes upon.
Leave me (thy wofull Mother) to endure
The fury of this tempest heere alone:
Who cares not for her selfe, so thou be sure,
Thou mayst revenge, when others can but mone:
Rodon will see thee safe, *Rodon* will guide
Thee and thy wayes, thou shalt not need to feare.
Rodon (my faithfull servant) wil provide
What shal be best for thee, take thou no care.
And O good Rodon, looke well to his youth,
The waies are long, and dangers ev'rywhere.
I urge it not that I doe doubt thy truth,
Mothers will cast the worst, and alwaies feare.
  The absent danger greater still appeares,
  Lesse feares he, who is neere the thing he feares.
And O, I knowe not what presaging thought
My sprite suggests of lucklesse bad event:
But yet it may be tis but Love doth doate,
Or ydle shadowes with my feares present,
But yet the memory of mine owne fate
Makes me feare his. And yet why should I feare?
His fortune may recover better state,
And he may come in pompe to governe heere.
But yet I doubt the *Genius* of our race

By some malignant spirite comes overthrowne:
Our bloud must be extinct, in my disgrace,
Egypt must have no more Kings of their owne.
Then let him stay, and let us fall together,
Sith it is fore-decreed that we must fall.
Yet who knowes what may come? let him go thither,
What Merchaunt in one vessell venters all?
Let us divide our starres. Go, go my sonne,
Let not the fate of Egypt finde thee heere:
Try if so be thy destinie can shunne
The common wracke of us, by being there.
But who is he found ever yet defence
Against the heavens, or hid him any where?
Then what neede I to send thee so farre hence
To seeke thy death that mayst as well die heere?
And here die with thy mother, die in rest,
Not travelling to what will come to thee.
Why should we leave our bloud unto the East,
When Egypt may a Tombe sufficient be?
  O my divided soule, what shall I do?
Whereon shall now my resolution rest?
What were I best resolve to yeelde unto,
When both are bad, how shall I know the best?
Stay, I may hap so worke with *Cæsar* now,
That he may yeelde him to restore thy right.
Goe; *Cæsar* never will content that thou
So neere in bloud, shalt be so great in might.
Then take him *Rodon*, go my sonne, farewell.
But stay; there's something else that I would say:
Yet nothing now, but O God speede thee well,
Lest saying more, that more may make thee stay.
Yet let me speake: It may be tis the last
That ever I shall speake to thee my sonne.
Do Mothers use to part in such post haste?
What, must I end when I have scarce begunne?
Ah no (deere heart) tis no such slender twine
Wherewith the knot is tide twixt thee and me:
That bloud within thy veins came out of mine,
Parting from thee, I part from part of mee:
And therefore I must speake. Yet what O sonne?
  Here more she would, when more she could not say.
Sorrow rebounding backe whence it begunne,
Filld up the passage, and quite stopt the way:
When sweete *Cæsario* with a princely spirite,

(Though comfortlesse himselfe) did comfort give;
With mildest wordes, perswading her to beare it.
And as for him, she should not neede to grieve.
And I (with protestations of my part,)
Swore by that faith, (which sworne I did deceive)
That I would use all care, all wit and art
To see him safe. And so we tooke our leave.
Scarce had we travail'd to our journeies end,
When *Cæsar* having knowledge of our way,
His Agents after us with speed doth send
To labour me, *Cæsario* to betray.
Who with rewards and promises so large,
Assail'd me then, that I grew soone content;
And backe to *Rhodes* did reconvay my charge,
Pretending that *Octavius* for him sent,
To make him King of Egipt presently.
  And thither come, seeing himselfe betray'd,
And in the hands of death through trechery,
Wailing his state, thus to himselfe he said.
  Lo here brought backe by subtile traine to death
Betraide by Tutors faith, or traitors rather:
My fault my bloud, and mine offence my birth,
For being sonne of such a mighty Father.
  From *India*, (whither sent by mothers care,
To be reserv'd from Egipts common wracke,)
To *Rhodes*, (so long the armes of tyrants are,)
I am by *Cæsars* subtile reach brought backe:
Heere to be made th'oblation for his feares,
Who doubts the poor revenge these hands may do him:
Respecting neither bloud, nor youth, nor yeeres,
Or how small safety can my death be to him.
  And is this all the good of being borne great?
Then wretched greatnesse, prowd rich misery,
Pompous distresse, glittering calamitie.
Is it for this th'ambitious Fathers sweat,
To purchase bloud and death for them and theirs?
Is this the issue that their glories get,
To leave a sure destruction to their heires?
O how much better had it beene for me,
From low descent, deriv'd of humble birth,
T'have eat the sweete-sowre bread of povertie,
And drunke of *Nylus* streames in *Nylus* earth:
Under the cov'ring of some quiet Cottage,
Free from the wrath of heaven, secure in minde,

Untoucht when sad events of princes dottage
Confounds what ever mighty it doth finde;
And not t'have stoode in their way, whose condition
Is to have all made cleere, and all thing plaine
Betweene them and the marke of their ambition,
That nothing let the full sight of their raigne,
Where nothing stands, that stands not in submission;
Where greatnesse must all in it selfe containe.
Kings will be alone, Competitors must downe,
Neere death he stands, that stands too neere a Crowne.
  Such is my case, for *Cæsar* will have all.
My bloud must seale th'assurance of his state:
Yet ah weake state that bloud assure him shall,
Whose wrongfull shedding, gods and men do hate.
Injustice never scapes unpunisht stil,
Though men revenge not, yet the heavens will.
  And thou *Augustus* that with bloudie hand
Cut'st off succession from anothers race,
Maist find the heavens thy vowes so to withstand,
That others may deprive thine in like case.
When thou maist see thy prowde contentious bed
Yeelding thee none of thine that may inherite:
Subvert thy bloud, place others in their sted,
To pay this thy injustice her due merite.
  If it be true (as who can that deny
Which sacred Priests of *Memphis* doe fore-say)
Some of the of-spring yet of *Antony*,
Shall all the rule of this whole Empire sway;
And then *Augustus*, what is it thou gainest
By poore *Antillus* blood, or this of mine?
Nothing but this thy victorie thou stainest,
And pull'st the wrath of heaven on thee and thine.
  In vaine doth man contend against the starrs,
  For that he seekes to make, his wisedome marrs.
  Yet in the mean-time we whom Fates reserve,
The bloodie sacrifices of ambition,
We feele the smart what ever they deserve,
And we indure the present times condition.
  The justice of the heavens revenging thus,
  Doth onely satisfie it selfe, not us.
    Yet tis a pleasing comfort that doth ease
Affliction in so great extremitie,
To thinke their like destruction shall appease
Our ghosts, who did procure our miserie.

But dead we are, uncertaine what shall bee,
And living, we are sure to feele the wrong:
Our certaine ruine we our selves doe see.
They joy the while, and we know not how long.
But yet *Cæsario*, thou must die content,
For men will mone, and God revenge th'innocent.
Thus he complain'd, and thus thou hear'st my shame,
SEL. But how hath *Cæsar* now rewarded thee?
ROD. As he hath thee. And I expect the same
As fell to *Theodor* to fall to mee:
For he (one of my coate) having betraid
The yong *Antillus* sonne of *Anthonie*,
And at his death from off his necke convaid
A jewell: which being askt, he did denie:
Cæsar occasion tooke to hang him strait.
Such instruments with Princes live not long.
Although they need such actors of deceit,
Yet still our sight seemes to upbraid their wrong;
And therefore we must needes this daunger runne,
And in the net of our owne guile be caught:
We must not live to brag what we have done,
For what is done, must not appeare their fault.
But here comes *Cleopatra*, wofull Queene,
And our shame wil not that we should be seene.
Exeunt.

Cleopatra.

What, hath my face yet powre to win a Lover?
Can this torne remnant serve to grace me so,
That it can *Cæsars* secret plots discover
What he intends with me and mine to do?
Why then poore Beautie thou hast done thy last,
And best good service thou could'st do unto mee.
For now the time of death reveal'd thou hast,
Which in my life didst serve but to undoe me.
Heere *Dolabella*, far forsooth in love,
Writes, how that *Cæsar* meanes forthwith to send
Both me & mine, th'ayre of Rome to prove:
There his Triumphant Chariot to attend.
I thanke the man, both for his love & letter;
The one comes fit to warne me thus before,
But for th'other, I must die his debter,[1]

[1] Cf. V.2.204.

For *Cleopatra* now can love no more.
  But having leave, I must go take my leave
And last farewell of my dead *Anthonie:*
Whose deerly honour'd tombe must here receive
This sacrifice, the last before I die.
  O sacred ever-memorable stone,
That hast without my teares, within my flame,
Receive th'oblation of the wofull'st mone
That ever yet from sad affliction came.
And you deare reliques of my Lord and Love,
(The sweetest parcels of the faithfull'st liver,)
O let no impious hand dare to remove
You out from hence, but rest you here for ever.
Let Egypt now give peace unto you dead,
That living gave you trouble and turmoile:
Sleepe quiet in this ever-lasting bed,
In forraine land preferr'd before your soile.
And O, if that the sp'rits of men remaine
After their bodies, and do never die,
Then heare thy ghost, thy captive spouse complaine,
And be attentive to her miserie.
But if that laboursome mortallitie
Found this sweete error, onely to confine
The curious search of idle vanitie,
That would the deapth of darknes undermine:
Or rather to give rest unto the thought
Of wretched man, with th'after-comming joy
Of those conceived fields whereon we dote,
To pacifie the present worldes annoy.
If it be so, why speake I then to th'ayre?
But tis not so, my *Anthonie* doth heare:
His ever-living ghost attends my prayer,
And I do know his hovering sprite is neere.[1]
And I wil speake, and pray, and mourne to thee,
O pure immortall love that daign'st to heare:
I feele thou answer'st my credulitie
With touch of comfort, finding none elsewhere.
Thou know'st these hands intomb'd thee here of late,
Free and unforc'd, which now must servile be,
Reserv'd for bands to grace proud *Cæsars* state,
Who seekes in me to triumph over thee.
O if in life we could not severd be,

[1] Cf. V.2.228, 281–5.

Shall death divide our bodies now asunder?
Must thine in Egypt, mine in Italie,
Be kept the Monuments of Fortunes wonder?
If any powres be there whereas thou art,
(Sith our country gods betray our case,)
O worke they may their gracious helpe impart,
To save thy wofull wife from such disgrace.
Do not permit she should in triumph shew
The blush of her reproach, joyn'd with thy shame:
But (rather) let that hatefull tyrant know,
That thou and I had powre t'avoyde the same.
But what, do I spend breath and ydle winde,[1]
In vaine invoking a conceived ayde?
Why do I not my selfe occasion finde
To breake the bounds wherein my selfe am staide?
Words are for them that can complaine and live,
Whose melting hearts composd of baser frame,
Can to their sorrowes, time and leasure give,
But *Cleopatra* may not do the same.
No *Antony*, thy love requireth more:
A lingring death, with thee deserves no merite,
I must my selfe force open wide a dore
To let out life, and so unhouse my spirit.
These hands must breake the prison of my soule
To come to thee, there to enjoy like state,
As doth the long-pent solitarie Foule,
That hath escapt her cage, and found her mate.
This sacrifice to sacrifize my life,
Is that true incense that dooth best beseeme:
These rites may serve a life-desiring wife,
Who doing them, t'have done enough doth deeme.
My hart bloud should the purple flowers have beene,
Which heere upon thy Tombe to thee are offred,
No smoake but dying breath should here bin seene,
And this it had bin too, had I bin suffred.
But what have I save these bare hands to doe it?
And these weake fingers are not yron-poynted:
They cannot pierce the flesh be'ing put unto it,
And I of all meanes else am disappointed.
But yet I must a way and meanes seeke, how
To come unto thee, whatsoere I do.[1]
O Death, art thou so hard to come by now,

[1] Cf. V.2.285. 'husband I come'.

That we must pray, intreate, and seeke thee too?
But I will finde thee wheresoere thou lie,
For who can stay a minde resolv'd to die?[1]
  And now I goe to worke th'effect indeed,
Ile never send more words or sighes to thee:
Ile bring my soule my selfe, and that with speede,
My selfe will bring my soule to *Antony*.
Come go my Maides, my fortunes sole attenders,
That minister to miserie and sorrow:
Your Mistris you unto your freedom renders.
And will discharge your charge yet ere to morrow.
  And now by this, I thinke the man I sent,
Is neere return'd that brings me my dispatch.
God grant his cunning sort to good event,
And that his skill may well beguile my watch:
So shall I shun disgrace, leave to be sorrie,
Flie to my love, scape my foe, free my soule;
So shall I act the last of life with glorie,
Die like a Queene, and rest without controule. *Exit.*

CHORUS

Misterious Egypt, wonder breeder,
  strict Religions strange observer,
State-ordrer zeale, the best rule-keeper,
  Fostring still in temp'rate fervor:
O how cam'st thou to lose so wholy
  all religion, law and order?
And thus become the most unholy
  of all Lands, that *Nylus* border?
How could confus'd Disorder enter
  where sterne Law sate so severely?
How durst weake lust and riot venter
  th'eye of Justice looking neerely?
Could not those meanes that made thee great
Be still the meanes to keepe thy state?

Ah no, the course of things requireth
  change and alteration ever:
That same continuance man desireth,
  th'unconstant world yeeldeth never.
We in our counsels must be blinded,
  And not see what doth import us:

[1] Cf. IV.13.90–1.

And often-times the thing least minded
  is the thing that most must hurt us.
Yet they that have the sterne in guiding,
  tis their fault that should prevent it,
For oft they seeing their Country sliding,
  take their ease, as though contented.
We imitate the greater powres,
The Princes manners fashion ours.

Th'example of their light regarding,
  vulgar loosenesse much incences:
Vice uncontrold, growes wide inlarging,
  Kings small faults be great offences.
And this hath set the window open
  unto licence, lust, and riot:
This way confusion first found broken,
  whereby entred our disquiet,
Those lawes that olde *Sesostris* founded,
  and the *Ptolomies* observed,
Hereby first came to be confounded,
  which our state so long preserved.
The wanton luxurie of Court,
Did forme the people of like sort.

For all (respecting private pleasure,)
  universally consenting
To abuse their time, their treasure,
  in their owne delights contenting:
And future dangers nought respecting,
  whereby, (O how easie matter
Made this so generall neglecting,
  confus'd weakenesse to discatter?)
Cæsar found th'effect true tried,
  in his easie entrance making:
Who at the sight of armes, descryed
  all our people, all forsaking.
For ryot (worse then warre,) so sore
Had wasted all our strength before.

And thus is Egypt servile rendred
  to the insolent destroyer:
And all their sumptuous treasure tendred,
  all her wealth that did betray her.
Which poison (O if heaven be rightfull,)

may so farre infect their sences,
That Egypts pleasures so delightfull,
may breed them the like offences.
And Romans learne our way of weakenes,
be instructed in our vices:
That our spoiles may spoile your greatnes,
overcome with our devises.
Fill full your hands, and carry home
Enough from us to ruine Rome.

Actus quintus.

Dolabella. Titius.

DOL. Come tell me *Titius* ev'ry circumstance
How *Cleopatra* did receive my newes:
Tell ev'ry looke, each gesture, countenance,
That she did in my Letters reading, use.
TIT. I shall my Lord, so farre as I could note,
Or my conceit observe in any wise.
It was the time whenas she having got
Leave to her Deerest dead to sacrifise;
And now was issuing out the monument
With odors, incense, garlands in her hand,
When I approacht (as one from *Cæsar* sent,)
And did her close thy message t'understand.
She turnes her backe, and with her takes me in,
Reades in thy lines thy strange unlookt for tale:
And reades, and smiles, and staies, and doth begin
Againe to reade, then blusht, and then was pale.
And having ended with a sigh, refoldes
Thy Letter up: and with a fixed eie,
(Which stedfast her imagination holds)
She mus'd a while, standing confusedly:
At length. Ah friend, (saith she) tell thy good Lord,
How deere I hold his pittying of my case:
That out of his sweete nature can affoord
A miserable woman so much grace.
Tell him how much my heavy soule doth grieve
Mercilesse *Cæsar* should so deale with me:
Pray him that he would all the counsell give,
That might divert him from such crueltie.
As for my love, say *Antony* hath all,
Say that my hart is gone into the grave

With him, in whom it rests and ever shall:
I have it not my selfe, nor cannot have.
Yet tell him, he shall more command of me
Then any, whosoever living can.
Hee that so friendly shewes himselfe to be
A right kind Roman, and a Gentleman.
Although his Nation (fatall unto me,)
Have had mine age a spoile, my youth a pray,
Yet his affection must accepted be,
That favours one distrest in such decay.
Ah, he was worthy then to have beene lov'd,
Of *Cleopatra* whiles her glory lasted;
Before she had declining fortune prov'd,
Or seen her honor wrackt, her flowre blasted.
Now there is nothing left her but disgrace,
Nothing but her affliction that can move:
Tell *Dolabella*, one that's in her case,
(Poore soule) needs rather pity now then love,
But shortly shall thy Lord heare more of me.
And ending so her speech, no longer stai'd,
But hasted to the tombe of *Antonie*,
And this was all she did, and all she said.

DOL. Ah sweet distressed Lady. What hard hart
Could chuse but pity thee, and love thee too?
Thy worthines, the state wherein thou art
Requireth both, and both I vow to doo.
Although ambition lets not *Cæsar* see
The wrong he doth thy majesty and sweetnes,
Which makes him now exact so much of thee,
To adde unto his pride, to grace his greatnes,
He knowes thou canst no hurt procure us now,
Sith all thy strength is seiz'd into our hands:
Nor feares he that, but rather labours how
He might shew Rome so great a Queene in bands:
That our great Ladies (envying thee so much
That stain'd them all, and held them in such wonder,)
Might joy to see thee, and thy fortune such,
Thereby extolling him that brought thee under.
But I will seeke to stay it what I may;
I am but one, yet one that *Cæsar* loves,
And O if now I could doe more then pray,
Then should'st thou know how farre affection moves.
But what my powre and prayer may prevaile,
Ile joyne them both, to hinder thy disgrace:

And even this present day I will not faile
To doe my best with *Cæsar* in this case.
TIT. And sir, even now herselfe hath letters sent,
I met her messenger as I came hither,
With a dispatch as he to *Cæsar* went,
But know not what imports her sending thither.
Yet this he told, how *Cleopatra* late
Was come from sacrifice. How richly clad
Was serv'd to dinner in most sumptuous state,
With all the bravest ornaments she had.
How having din'd, she writes, and sends away
Him strait to *Cæsar*, and commanded than
All should depart the Tombe, and none to stay
But her two maides, and one poore countryman.
DOL. Why then I know she sends t'have audience now,
And meanes t'experience what her state can do:
To see if majesty will make him bow
To what affliction could not move him to.
And O, if now she could but bring a view
Of that fresh beauty she in youth possest,
(The argument wherewith she overthrew
The wit of *Julius Cæsar*, and the rest,)
Then happily *Augustus* might relent,
Whilst powrefull Love, (farre stronger then ambition)
Might worke in him, a minde to be content
To grant her asking, in the best condition.
But being as she is, yet doth she merite
To be respected, for what she hath beene:
The wonder of her kinde, of rarest spirit,
A glorious Lady, and a mighty Queene.
And now, but by a little weakenesse falling
To do that which perhaps sh'was forst to do:
Alas, an errour past, is past recalling,
Take away weakenesse, and take women too.
But now I goe to be thy advocate,
Sweete *Cleopatra*, now Ile use mine arte.
Thy presence will me greatly animate,
Thy face will teach my tongue, thy love my hart.

Scena secunda.

Nuntius.

Am I ordain'd the carefull Messenger,
And sad newes bringer of the strangest death,

Which selfe hand did upon it selfe inferre,
To free a captive soule from servile breath?
Must I the lamentable wonder shew,
Which all the world must grieve and marvel at?
The rarest forme of death in earth below,
That ever pitty, glory, wonder gat.
CHO. What news bringst thou, can Egipt yet yeeld more
Of sorrow than it hath? what can it adde
To the already overflowing store
Of sad affliction, matter yet more sad?
Have we not seene the worst of our calamity?
Is there behind yet something of distresse
Unseene, unknown? Tel if that greater misery
There be, that we waile not that which is lesse.
Tell us what so it be, and tell at first,
For sorrow ever longs to heare her worst.
NU. Well then, the strangest thing relate I will,
That ever eye of mortall man hath seene.
I (as you know) even from my youth, have still
Attended on the person of the Queene:
And ever in all fortunes good or ill,
With her as one of chiefest trust have beene.
And now in these so great extreamities,
That ever could to majesty befall,
I did my best in what I could devise,
And left her not, till now she left us all.
CHO. What, is she gone? Hath *Cæsar* forst her so?
NUN. Yea, she is gone, and hath deceiv'd him to.
CHO. What, fled to *India*, to go find her sonne?
NUN. No, not to *India*, but to finde her sonne.
CHO. Why then there's hope she may her state recover.
NUN. Her state? nay rather honour, and her Lover.
CHO. Her Lover? him shee can not have againe.
NUN. Wel, him she hath, with him she doth remaine.
CHO. Why then she's dead. Ist so? why speakst not thou?
NUN. You gesse aright, and I will tell you how.
When she perceiv'd all hope was cleane bereft,
That Cæsar meant to send her strait away,
And saw no meanes of reconcilement left,
Worke what she could, she could not worke to stay:
She calles me to her, and she thus began.
O thou, whose trust hath ever beene the same,
And one in all my fortunes, faithfull man,
Alone content t'attend disgrace and shame.

Thou, whom the fearefull ruine of my fall,
Never deterr'd to leave calamitie:
As did those others, smoothe state-pleasers all,
Who followed but my fortune, and not me.
Tis thou must do a service for thy Queene,
Wherein thy faith and skill must do their best:
Thy honest care and duty shal be seene,
Performing this, more then in all the rest.
For all what thou hast done, may die with thee,
Although tis pitty that such faith should die.
But this shall evermore remembred be,
A rare example to posterity.
And looke how long as *Cleopatra* shall
In after ages live in memory,
So long shall thy cleere fame endure withall,
And therefore thou must not my sute denie
Nor contradict my will. For what I will
I am resolv'd: and this now must it be:
Go find me out with all thy art and skill
Two Aspicks, and convay them close to me.
I have a worke to do with them in hand,
Enquire not what, for thou shalt soone see what,
If the heavens do not my disseignes withstand,
But do thy charge, and let me shift with that.
   Being thus conjur'd by her t'whom I'had vow'd
My true perpetuall service, forth I went,
Devising how my close attempt to shrowde,
So that there might no art my art prevent.
And so disguis'd in habite as you see,
Having found out the thing for which I went,
I soone return'd againe, and brought with me
The Aspickes, in a basket closely pent,
Which I had filld with Figges, and leaves upon.
And comming to the guard that kept the dore,
What hast thou there? said they, and lookt thereon.
Seeing the figges, they deem'd of nothing more,
But said, they were the fairest they had seene.
Taste some, said I, for they are good and pleasant.
No, no, said they, go beare them to thy Queene,
Thinking me some poore man that brought a present.
Well, in I went, where brighter then the Sunne,
Glittering in all her pompous rich aray,
Great *Cleopatra* sate, as if sh'had wonne
Cæsar, and all the world beside this day:

Even as she was when on thy cristall streames,
Cleere *Cydnos* she did shew what earth could shew,[1]
When *Asia* all amaz'd in wonder, deemes
Venus from heaven was come on earth below.
Even as she went at first to meete her Love,
So goes she now at last againe to find him.
But that first, did her greatnes onely prove,
This last her love, that could not live behind him.
Yet as she sate, the doubt of my good speed
Detracts much from the sweetnes of her looke:
Cheere-marrer Care, did then such passions breed,
That made her eie bewray the griefe shee tooke.
But she no sooner sees me in the place,
But strait her sorrow-clouded brow she cleeres,
Lightning a smile from out a stormie face,
Which all her tempest-beaten sences cheeres.
  Looke how a strai'd perplexed traveller,
When chasd by theeves, and even at poynt of taking,
Descrying sodainely some towne not far,
Or some unlookt for aide to him-ward making;
Cheeres up his tyred sprites, thrusts forth his strength
To meete that good, that comes in so good houre:
Such was her joy, perceiving now at length,
Her honour was t'escape so proude a powre.
Forth from hir seate she hastes to meete the present,
And as one over-joy'd, she caught it strait.
And with a smiling cheere in action pleasant,
Looking among the figs, findes the deceite.
And seeing there the ugly venemous beast,
Nothing dismaid, she stayes and viewes it well.
At length th'extreamest of her passion ceast,
When she began with wordes her joy to tell.
  O rarest beast (saith she) that Affrick breedes,
How deerly welcome art thou unto me!
The fairest creature that faire *Nylus* feedes
Methinks I see, in now beholding thee.
What though the ever-erring world doth deeme
That angred Nature fram'd thee but in spight?
Little they know what they so light esteeme,
That never learn'd the wonder of thy might.
Better then Death, Deaths office thou dischargest,
That with one gentle touch canst free our breath:

[1] Cf. V.2.226–8.

And in a pleasing sleepe our soule inlargest,[1]
Making our selves not privie to our death.
If Nature err'd, O then how happy error,
Thinking to make thee worst, she made thee best:
Sith thou best freest us from our lives worst terror,
In sweetly bringing soules to quiet rest.
When that inexorable Monster Death
That followes Fortune, flies the poore distressed,
Tortures our bodyes ere he takes our breath,
And loads with paines th'already weak oppressed.
How oft have I begg'd, prayd, intreated him
To take my life, which he would never do,
And when he comes, he comes so ugly grim,
Attended on with hideous torments to.
Therefore come thou, of wonders wonder chiefe
That open canst with such an easie key
The doore of life, come gentle cunning thiefe,
That from our selves so steal'st our selves away.
Well did our Priests discerne something divine
Shadow'd in thee, and therefore first they did
Offrings and worships due to thee assigne,
In whom they found such mysteries were hid,
Comparing thy swift motion to the Sunne,
That mov'st without the instruments that move:
And never waxing old, but alwayes one,
Doost sure thy strange divinitie approve.
And therefore too, the rather unto thee
In zeale I make the offring of my blood,
Calamitie confirming now in me
A sure beliefe that pietie makes good.
Which happy men neglect, or hold ambiguous,
And onely the afflicted are religious.
  And heere I facrifice these armes to Death,
That Lust late dedicated to Delights:
Offring up for my last, this last of breath,
The complement of my loves dearest rites.
With that she beares her arme, and offer makes
To touch her death, yet at the touch with-drawes,
And seeming more to speake, occasion takes,
Willing to die, and willing too to pause.
  Looke how a mother at her sonnes departing
For some farre voyage bent to get him fame,

[1] Cf. V.2.306–9.

Doth entertaine him with an ydle parling
And stil doth speake, and stil speakes but the same;
Now bids farewell, and now recalles him backe,
Telles what was told, and bids againe farewell,
And yet againe recalles; for stil doth lacke
Something that Love would faine and cannot tell.
Pleas'd he should go, yet cannot let him go.
So she, although she knew there was no way
But this, yet this she could not handle so
But she must shew that life desir'd delay.
Faine would she entertaine the time as now,
And now would faine that Death would seize upon her,
Whilst I might see presented in her brow,
The doubtfull combate tride twixt Life and Honor:
Life bringing Legions of fresh hopes with her,
Arm'd with the proofe of time, which yeeldes we say
Comfort and helpe, to such as doe referre
All unto him, and can admit delay.
But Honour scorning Life, loe forth leades hee
Bright Immortalitie in shining armour:
Thorow the rayes of whose cleere glorie, she
Might see lifes basenesse, how much it might harme her.
Besides shee saw whole armies of Reproches,
And base Disgraces, Furies feareful sad,
Marching with Life, and Shame that still incroches
Upon her face, in bloody colours clad.
Which representments seeing, worse then death
She deem'd to yeeld to Life, and therefore chose
To render al to Honour, heart and breath;
And that with speede, lest that her inward foes
False flesh and bloud, joyning with life and hope,
Should mutinie against her resolution.
And to the end she would not give them scope,
Shee presently proceedes to th'execution.
And sharpely blaming of her rebel powres,
False flesh (saith she) and what dost thou conspire
With Cæsar too, as thou wert none of ours,
To worke my shame, and hinder my desire?
Wilt thou retaine in closure of thy vaines,
That enemy Base life, to let my good?[1]
No, know there is a greater powre constraines
Then can be countercheckt with fearefull blood.

[1] Cf. V.2.288, 298, 301–3.

For to the minde that's great, nothing seemes great:
And seeing death to be the last of woes,
And life lasting disgrace, which I shall get,
What doe I lose, that have but life to lose?
  This having said, strengthned in her owne hart,
And union of herselfe, sences in one
Charging together, she performes that part
That hath so great a part of glorie wonne.
And so receives the deadly poys'ning touch;
That touch that tride the gold of her love, pure,
And hath confirm'd her honour to be such,
As must a wonder to all worlds endure.
Now not an yeelding shrinke or touch of feare,
Consented to bewray least sence of paine:
But still in one same sweete unaltred cheere,
Her honour did her dying thoughts retaine.
  Well, now this worke is done (saith she) heere ends
This act of Life, that part the Fates assign'd:
What glory or disgrace heere this world lends,
Both have I had, and both I leave behind.
And now O earth, the Theater where I
Have acted this, witnes I die unforst.
Witnesse my soule partes free to *Antony*,
And now prowde Tyrant *Cæsar* do thy worst.
  This said, she staies, and makes a sodaine pause,
As twere to feele whether the poyson wrought:
Or rather else the working might be cause
That made her stay, and intertain'd her thought.
For in that instant I might well perceive
The drowsie humor in her falling brow:
And how each powre, each part opprest did leave
Their former office, and did sencelesse grow.
Looke how a new pluckt branch against the Sunne,
Declines his fading leaves in feeble sort;
So her disjoyned joyntures as undone,
Let fall her weake dissolved limbes support.
Yet loe that face the wonder of her life,
Retaines in death, a grace that graceth death,
Colour so lively, cheere so lovely rife,
That none would thinke such beauty could want breath.
And in that cheere th'impression of a smile,
Did seeme to shew she scorned Death and *Cæsar*,
As glorying that she could them both beguile,
And telling Death how much her death did please her.

Wonder it was to see how soone she went,
She went with such a will, and did so haste it,
That sure I thinke shee did her paine prevent,
Fore-going paine, or staying not to taste it.
And sencelesse, in her sinking downe she wries
The Diademe which on her head shee wore,
Which *Charmion* (poore weake feeble maid) espies,
And hastes to right it as it was before.
For *Eras* now was dead, and *Charmion* too
Even at the poynt, for both would immitate
Their Mistresse glorie, striving like to doo.
But *Charmion* would in this exceede her mate,
For she would have this honour to be last,
That should adorne that head that must be seene
To weare a Crowne in death, that life held fast,
That all the world may know she dide a Queene.
And as she stoode setting it fitly on,
Loe, in rush *Cæsars* messengers in haste,
Thinking to have prevented what was done,
But yet they came too late, for all was past.
For there they found stretcht on a bed of golde,
Dcad *Cleopatra*, and that prowdly dead,
In all the rich attire procure she could,
And dying *Charmion* trimming of her head,
And *Eras* at her feete, dead in like case.
Charmion, is this well done? saide one of them.
Yea, well saide she, and her that from the race
Of so great Kings descends, doth best become.
And with that word, yeelds to her faithfull breath,
To passe th'assurance of her love with death.
CHO. But how knew *Cæsar* of her close intent?
NUN. By Letters which before to him she sent.
For when she had procur'd this meanes to die,
She writes, and earnestly intreates, she might
Be buried in one Tombe with *Antony*.
Whereby then *Cæsar* gess'd all went not right.
And forthwith sends, yet ere the message came
She was dispatcht, he crost in his intent.
Her providence had ordred so the same,
That she was sure none should her plot prevent.

Chorus

Then thus we have beheld
Th'accomplishment of woes

The ful of ruine and
The worst of worst of ills:
And seene al hope expeld,
That ever sweete repose
Shall repossesse the Land,
That Desolation fills,
And where Ambition spills
With uncontrouled hand,
All th'issue of all those
That so long rule have held:
To make us no more us,
But cleane confound us thus.

And canst O Nylus thou,
Father of floods indure,
That yellow Tyber should
With sandy streames rule thee?
Wilt thou be pleas'd to bow
To him those feete so pure,
Whose unknowne head we hold
A powre divine to be?
Thou that didst ever see
Thy free bankes uncontrould,
Live under thine owne care:
Ah wilt thou beare it now?
And now wilt yeelde thy streames
A prey to other Reames?

Draw backe thy waters flo
To thy concealed head:
Rockes, strangle up thy waves,
Stop *Cataractes* thy fall,
And turne thy courses so,
That sandy Desarts dead,
(The world of dust that craves
To swallow thee up all)
May drinke so much as shall
Revive from vastie graves
A living greene which spred
Far florishing, may gro
On that wide face of Death,
Where nothing now drawes breath.

Fatten some people there,
Even as thou us hast done,

With plenties wanton store,
And feeble luxurie:
And them as us prepare
Fit for the day of mone
Respected not before.
Leave levell'd Egypt drie,
A barren prey to lie,
Wasted for ever-more:
Of plenties yeelding none
To recompence the care
Of Victors greedy lust,
And bring forth nought but dust.

And so O leave to be,
Sith thou art what thou art:
Let not our race possesse
Th'inheritance of shame,
The fee of sin, that we
Have left them for their part:
The yoke of whose distresse
Must still upbraid our blame,
Telling from whom it came.
Our weight of wantonesse
Lies heavie on their hart,
Who never-more shall see
The glory of that worth
They left, who brought us forth.

O thou all-seeing light,
High President of heaven,
You Magistrates the Starres
Of that eternall Court
Of Providence and Right,
Are these the bounds y'have given
Th'untranspassable barres,
That limite Pride so short?
Is greatnesse of this sort,
That greatnesse greatnesse marres,
And wrackes it selfe, selfe driven
On Rockes of her owne might?
Doth Order order so
Disorders overthrow?

FINIS.

CORIOLANUS

INTRODUCTION

No Quarto appears to have been printed of this play, and the first Folio of 1623 (where it comes first of the Tragedies) is the sole authority for the text. The stage-directions are elaborate and some read like instructions to the producer. Since they occasionally seem to show knowledge of Plutarch, they were probably written by Shakespeare. 'There can be no doubt that behind F lies a very carefully prepared author's transcript.'[1]

There is no evidence of any performance before the Restoration, and the date of composition is doubtful. The play was certainly written after the publication of Camden's *Remaines of a Greater Worke concerning Britaine* in 1605, for Shakespeare took a point or two from that for Menenius' fable of the belly and its members [*inf.* 551]. Halliwell-Phillips believed that *Coriolanus* must have been written after the publication of the 1612 edition of Plutarch's *Lives* because in V.3.97: 'How more unfortunate than all living women', the word 'unfortunate' points to that edition, earlier editions having 'unfortunately'. But 'unfortunate' is simpler and fits the metre. MacCallum pointed out that 'spite' in IV.5.87 is used thus only in the editions of North published before 1603.[2] Georg Brandes[3] thought that this play about a mother's love was occasioned by the death of Shakespeare's mother (buried on 9 September, 1608). This is speculation, but 1608 is suggested by more cogent circumstantial evidence. There was a dearth of corn in 1607 and 1608; and the play departs from Plutarch's account of the unrest in Rome in a topical manner, as will be shown later. There was a great frost in the winter of 1607/8 when the Thames was frozen over and 'pans of coals' were to be seen on it [Text VI]. This

[1] W. W. Greg, *The Shakespeare First Folio*, 1955, p. 407. J. D. Wilson (*Camb.*, 1960, pp. 130–7) argues that F1 contained many Shakespearian spellings and abbreviations.

[2] MacCallum, p. 458

[3] *William Shakespeare, a Critical Study* (trans.), 1902, pp. 532–3.

was probably referred to in 'the coal of fire upon the ice' at I.1.174.

The play was certainly well known by the end of 1609 when Ben Jonson in *Epicœne* (V.4.227) made Truewit praise the cunning Dauphine thus: 'you have lurched your friends of the better half of the garland, by concealing this part of the plot'—obviously a jesting allusion to Shakespeare's Coriolanus, who in his many battles 'lurch'd all swords of the garland' (II.2.101). In style *Coriolanus* resembles somewhat *Antony and Cleopatra* and *Timon*, and we may accept Chambers' suggestion (*WSh* i, 480) that it was produced early in 1608.

What led Shakespeare to write this play on a comparatively minor and early figure in Roman history? By 1607 he had presented in *Julius Cæsar* and *Antony and Cleopatra* two studies of Rome at the end of the Republic. He may have wished to show something of Rome in its beginnings. Critics who deny that Shakespeare had any historical sense overlook the changes in his handling of English history. In the nineties he traced in two great sweeps the vicissitudes of the fifteenth century, and in so doing paid some attention to the different atmospheres of the various reigns. Recently he had turned in *King Lear* to the legendary history of Britain and had made in *Macbeth* a foray into medieval Scottish history. Soon he was to mingle romance with early British history in *Cymbeline*. He had only to glance into Livy and Florus or Plutarch to realize that Rome was not built in a day and that the story of Coriolanus illustrated its early state.

J. D. Wilson (*Camb.*, xvi–xix) has suggested other reasons: the story 'provided more exciting battle scenes than *Antony and Cleopatra* and a tumultuous riot as well'. The relationship between the hero and his mother may have attracted him, and their great interview 'originally fired his imagination to compose yet another Roman play'. Moreover Antony and Coriolanus 'were at once like and unlike', both victims of passion, but of very different passions.

This last is a valuable suggestion, and the peculiar contrast between their flawed natures may have contributed greatly. They exemplified the two complementary aspects of human nature defined by many ethical writers since Aristotle; for if Antony was a slave to the 'concupiscible' forces, Coriolanus was at the mercy of the 'irascible' elements in his personality. They are indeed parallel portraits, and the antithesis is not spoiled if, as I believe probable, *Timon of Athens* was drafted after *Antony* and before *Coriolanus*. *Timon* begins as a study in inordinate friendliness and ends as a study in insane wrath; and it may be that the play was not completed because the dramatist turned against the double-theme with its 'broken-backed' structure, its depiction of mere extremities, its hero saved from absurdity only by agonized rhetoric and unashamed didacticism. Maybe too he found it difficult to fit Alcibiades into the drama by inventing incidents which could be reconciled with Plutarch's elaborate *Life* of that benevolent traitor. Alcibiades was Plutarch's parallel to Coriolanus, and he probably was the final link in the chain which brought Shakespeare to discard *Timon* for *Coriolanus*. For Marcius had something of Timon in him, but he was a whole man with a life-history, not just the personification of ethical excess. He had more of the stuff of tragedy, and the wealth of circumstance with which Plutarch surrounded him encouraged the dramatist to present a Roman tragedy of a different sort from his others.

As Swinburne wrote, 'in *Julius Cæsar* the family had been . . . wholly subordinate to the state'.[1] In *Antony and Cleopatra* the individual was in conflict with the state and its responsibilities. In *Coriolanus* the individual saves the state, then revolts against it, and is finally brought to recognize his obligations, not however by awaking to his sense of public duty but out of reverence for the family. Swinburne went so far as to declare: 'The subject of the whole play is not the exile's revolt, the rebel's repentance, or the traitor's reward, but above all it is the son's tragedy.' This is an exaggeration, for the subject is all of these things, and the opportunity for this wealth of contrast was no doubt a principal reason for Shakespeare's choice of the theme.

'I cannot but think [wrote Swinburne also] that enough at least of time has been spent if not wasted . . . on examination of *Coriolanus* with regard to its political aspect or bearing upon social questions.' Nonetheless recent writers have made it seem

[1] *A Study of Shakespeare*, by A. C. Swinburne, 1918 edn., p. 187.

likely that Shakespeare's handling of the story, and perhaps his choice of it, were affected by topical social questions. There had been much unrest among the poor in the sixteenth century not only for religious reasons but also because of the social changes which accompanied the Reformation, the rapacity of the new landlords who gained the lands formerly held by the monasteries, the eviction of peasants to make agricultural land into sheep-pasture as wool became more and more profitable, and the enclosure of common land. Kett's rebellion in Norfolk and Suffolk in 1548–9 was economic in character, whereas the Devonshire insurrection in the same year was also religious, aiming to restore Roman Catholicism and the Mass. In both risings the rebels showed a grudge against the upper classes and the cry 'Kill the gentleman' was often heard. Thomas Lever in his *Sermon in the Shroudes* (1550) said: 'The greatest griefe that hathe been unto the people in thys realme, hath bene the inclosing of commons', and in the same year a Spanish merchant declared that 'the London Butchers laid the blame for the high meat prices during the scarcity on inclosures.'[1] The 1569 rebellion in the north was due partly to Catholic hostility to Elizabeth and partly to the decay of tillage. The Oxfordshire rising of 1596 was directed against enclosures and the gentry held responsible for them [Text Va].

Naturally unrest was particularly rife in times of dearth, and this recurred during the first years of James I's reign. In 1604 the people of Northamptonshire protested to Parliament through their MPs against 'the depopulation and daily excessive conversion of tillage into pasture'. Nothing was done, and three years later when food grew scarce and prices rose high a rebellion began in that county which spread to Warwickshire and Leicestershire [Text Vb]. The rebels declared that they did not rise against the King, 'but only for reformation of those late enclosures, which made them of the poorest sorte reddy to pyne for want' [Text Vc]. There were large gatherings—3,000 at Hillmorton in Shakespeare's home-county—and some of them, calling themselves Levellers, broke down enclosures and dug the land; but they were ill-led, and could not withstand the gentry and the forces sent by the sheriffs and justices after

[1] I am indebted here to E. F. Gay, 'The Midland Revolt and the Inquisitions of Depopulation of 1607', *Trans. of Royal Hist. Soc.*, New Series, XVIII, 1904.

Proclamations had been issued ordering them to go home. The gentry took a prominent part in restoring order. Thus at Newton in Northamptonshire on 8 June, 1607, mounted gentlemen routed a thousand levellers,

> 'furnished with many halfe pykes, pyked staves, long bills and bowes and arrowes and stones'. The mob withstood the first charge, 'and fought desperatlie; but at the second charge they ran away, in which there weare slaine som 40 or 50 of them, and a very great number hurt.'[1]

The ringleaders were swiftly punished, but discontent was not allayed, for although a Proclamation of 24 July, 1607, asserted that 'there was not so much as any necessitie of famine or dearth of corne . . . that might provoke them', prices were rising, and other Proclamations were made in 1607 and 1608 'for thamendyng of the dearth of graine and other victuall'.[2] In 1608 the people of Northampton asked that the King's Progress be cancelled. It was held, but curtailed to reduce costs.[3]

Popular literature touched on current abuses and according to a letter from Sir William Pelham to the Earl of Rutland[4] a ballad called 'The Poor Man's Friend and the Gentleman's Plague' was thrown into the church at Caistor, Northants, in July, 1607. It began, 'You gentlemen that rack your rents and throwe downe land for corne', and clearly exemplified the alienation of the common people from the upper classes. Another ballad of uncertain date, 'A Lanthorne for Landlords' shows how wealthy farmers were thought to hoard grain to make high profits. After one landlord had dispossessed a poor widow of her house and land, he found the house unlucky:

> Whereas this miserable wretch
>   Did turne it to a barne,
> And fild it full in harvest time
>   With good red wheat and corne,
> To keepe it safely from the poore

[1] Lodge, *Illustrations of British History*, iii, 196; quoted from E. F. Gay, *op. cit.*

[2] *Hist. MSS. Comm.*, ix, 1, 160, 268–9.

[3] *CSP* Venetian, ed. H. F. Brown, ii, 1607–10, 1904, p. 146. The Venetian Ambassador described the revolt as a rising of the peasants against the gentry.

[4] *Hist. MSS. Comm.*, Rutland MSS., i, 406.

Untill there came a yeare
That famine might oppresse them all,
And make all victuals deare.[1]

During Shakespeare's lifetime the resentment of the poor against the rich and privileged was never far from the surface, and the dramatist, who had represented mob-riot in *Henry VI, Pt.* 2, and regarded the Roman populace, in *Julius Cæsar*, with no great favour however much he pitied them as individuals, could have depicted the plebeians in *Coriolanus* much as Plutarch did, but his treatment in fact suggests that he interpreted the social conflict not only in English terms but somewhat in terms of the situation in 1607–8.

For example, Shakespeare ignores the secession of the people to the Sacred Mount. He makes much of 'the dearth', without giving Livy's explanation of it, but sets out the opposed views of it in a manner which his audience would understand after the rising of 1607. Menenius gives the attitude of the English 'establishment':

For the dearth
The gods, not the patricians, make it and
Your knees to them, not arms, must help. Alack!
You are transported by calamity,
Thither where more attend you. (I.1.72–6)

On the other hand, the First Citizen accuses the nobility:

> They ne'er cared for us yet: suffer us to famish, and their storehouses crammed with grain: make edicts for usury, to support usurers; repeal daily any wholesome act established against the rich, and provide more piercing statutes daily to chain up and restrain the poor. (I.1.80–4)

The Citizen's opening cry, 'You are all resolved rather to die than to famish?' was what leaders of the insurrection cried. The corn shortage is also mentioned in III.1.462–5 when Brutus charges Coriolanus with opposing free corn for the populace, and Coriolanus accepts the charge and defends his action (III.1.112–138).

Shakespeare's reduction of the grievances almost to the one

[1] *The Roxburghe Ballads*, ed. C. Hindley, 1873/4, ii, 188.

about dearth was surely topical, and as E. C. Pettet says, the elaboration he gives to Menenius' fable (shifted from its place in Plutarch) was to give him 'the opportunity of saying something that he very much wanted to say'.[1] How important it was and how deeply he must have pondered the parable of interdependence in degree is proved by the fact that he fused into Menenius' ample account memories of several versions which he had read at various times in Livy, North, Sidney, Camden, and, it seems, William Averell's *A Marvailous Combate of Contrarieties.*[2] Sidney's and Camden's are given in Text IV. The fable applies the notion of Degree expounded by Ulysses in *Troilus and Cressida* in a manner well suited to a time of unrest. Menenius believes in the interdependence of the social classes; all men are 'members one of another'. The genial parable embodies an ideal unknown to Marcius, who sets 'the counsellor heart, the arm our soldier' above the rest, and ruins the effect of Menenius' speech by his angry intolerance.

In the light of this topicality the first speeches of Marcius may have some relevance to Jacobean social differences, when he rails against the common people in a brutal manner, dismissing their complaints without examining their possible justice or showing the slightest sympathy with their plight (I.1.165–215). 'Hang 'em! They say!' he exclaims disdainfully. No doubt much of what he says was true to current views of the populace,[3] but is this the moment to show such arrogance? He is the enemy of the people, like the Lord in Robert Crowley's dialogue who cries 'We will teach them who are their betters'.

[1] E. C. Pettet, 'Coriolanus and the Midlands Insurrection of 1607', *Sh. Survey*, 3, 1950, 34–42. On enclosures and their effects see E. K. Chambers *WSh* ii. 145–6 and his references. Shakespeare was concerned in a movement in 1614–15 to prevent W. Combe from enclosing land in Welcombe, though Shakespeare's property was not threatened. The town-clerk of Stratford wrote in September 1615 'M. Shakespeares telling J. Greene that I was not able to bear the enclosure of Welcombe'. The 'I' may suggest quotation of an actual remark, but Greene was involved in the affair, and maybe Shakespeare was commenting on the effect on his friend. *WSh* ii, 141–6.

[2] K. Muir, 'Menenius's Fable', *N&Q* Vol. 198, June 1953, 240–2. He points out that versions are also found in Dionysius of Halicarnassus, Aesop, John of Salisbury's *Polycraticon* (Camden's source), and Camerarius. T. W. Baldwin, in *Shakspere's Small Latine and Lesse Greeke* (1944), suggests that Shakespeare first read the fable at school.

[3] Cf. J. E. Phillips, *The State in Shakespeare's Greek and Roman Plays*, 1940.

[4] Robert Crowley, *Select Works*, pp. 133–43.

He is the extreme aristocrat with a scathing contempt for the lower classes of a kind rarely found today but doubtless common enough among the young lords of James I's court.

If Marcius had been only this the play would have been no more successful than *Timon*. Colonel Blimp is not a tragic figure. Fortunately Shakespeare's intuition made Coriolanus a more complex person, and in this he was greatly helped by Plutarch.

Shakespeare knew Titus Livy's great history *Ab Urbe Condita* and used it for *The Rape of Lucrece*. In Book II he would read of the troubles afflicting Rome after the expulsion of the Tarquins and how the struggle against neighbouring tribes was accompanied by internal dissensions between patricians and plebeians, chiefly because of high taxation, usury and cruel laws concerning debtors. Failing other means, a debtor might bind himself to work out his debt as the slave of his creditor; and this often led to the kind of abuses illustrated in an incident in 495 B.C. when an old man rushed into the Forum 'covered with filth, pale, and half dead with emaciation'. A soldier in the Sabine War, he had lost his crops and flocks and had his cottage burned.

> 'Then taxes had been levied . . . and he had contracted debts. When these had been swelled by usury, they had first stripped him of the farm which had been his father's and his grandfather's, then of the remnants of his property, and finally like an infection they had attached his person, and he had been carried off by his creditors, not to slavery, but to the prison and the torture-chamber. He showed them his back, disfigured with the wales of recent scourging.' (Loeb, II, 23)

The result was uproar and riot and the Senate met with difficulty to pass a law (opposed by Appius Claudius, 'a headstrong man') that no Roman citizen should be held prisoner 'so that he could not give his name to the consuls', and that a soldier's property should be free from seizure in his absence. Only in this way could the Senate get volunteers to war against the Volsces. (II.23–4). When during his consulship Appius Claudius 'began to pronounce judgement with the utmost rigour in suits to recover debts' (II.27), there was further trouble and the plebeians refused to fight for a tyrannical Senate, until Marius Valerius (regarded as favourable to the people) was appointed Dictator. After he had won some victories he resigned his Dictatorship when the Senate would not ameliorate the treatment of debtors, and soon after this, in protest against the harsh cruelty of the patricians, the plebeians left Rome, fortified a camp on a hill by the river Anio three miles outside the city, and refused to return unless their grievances were remedied. What followed, and Gnæus Marcius' part in it, is told below [Text I] from Livy's succinct narrative as translated by Philemon Holland in 1600. Livy gives the apologue of Menenius Agrippa in terms which some critics have thought Shakespeare remembered [*inf.* 497]. The people were placated by Menenius ('an eloquent man and dear to the plebeians as being one of themselves by birth' (II.32)), and by the appointment of two 'tribunes of the people', who were empowered to co-opt three others. Of these last the chief was Sicinius; Brutus is not mentioned. Gnæus Marcius is first mentioned (II.33) as 'a youth of active mind and ready hand' who while the army was besieging Corioli under the consul, Postumus Cominius, repelled a sally by the Volsci, forced his way inside the town with a picked body of men, set fire to some buildings, and made possible the capture of the town. This was in 493 B.C.; Menenius died in that year and was buried at the expense of the common people.

The respite from Volscian attack brought by Marcius' courage soon led to further conflict in the city. 'First the price of corn went up, from men's failure to cultivate the fields during the withdrawal of the plebs, and this was followed by a famine.' (II.34.) The consuls sent agents to buy corn in Italy and Sicily, but little was brought back. Luckily a plague stopped the Volsci from attacking Rome, and colonists were sent to Velitræ and elsewhere.

When in the following year a large quantity of grain arrived from Sicily, the Senate had to fix prices. Here Marcius Coriolanus came to the fore as 'an enemy of the power of the tribunes'. He was against selling the corn cheap, believing that the opportunity had come to tame the tribunes, and that need would soon bring the plebeians to heel. Infuriated by the suggestion that starvation should be used as a weapon against them the populace raged against Coriolanus, who was saved only by the tribunes' promise to have him brought to trial. The Senate 'had to sacrifice one man to appease' the plebs, but did their best by intimidation to prevent the trial and to get Marcius acquitted. He however failed to appear and was condemned in his absence. Going over to the Volsci he was received kindly and with the Volscian leader Attius Tullius plotted to persuade the Volscians (weary of adverse war) once more to attack Rome. Their method was to get the Volscians unjustly banned from the Great Games and then to whet their anger. Made joint leader with Tullius, Marcius 'inspired rather more hope than did his colleague'. He took several Roman colonies and camped five miles from Rome, ravaging the countryside but sparing the farms of the patricians 'whether from anger at the plebs or to sow dissension between them and the Senate.'

In Rome the people wanted peace, and forced the Senate to send ambassadors to Marcius, who twice rejected their advances and also denied the supplications of priests. When however his mother Veturia, his wife Volumnia and his two little sons went out to appeal to him, he gave way to his mother's upbraidings (II.40) and the tears of the women, and 'withdrew his forces'. Livy was uncertain whether he was killed by the Volsci or lived on to old age. The temple of Fortuna Muliebris was built in memory of the women's deed. An alliance between the Volsci and the Æqui was afterwards crushed.

A contemporary of Livy, Dionysius of Halicarnassus (c. 66 B.C.–c. A.D. 10), came to Rome in 29 B.C. and wrote in Greek a history, *Roman Antiquities*, in twenty-nine books, of which only the first nine are extant.[1] His work is a treasure-house of information about Roman life and institutions, and while being based, like Livy's, on the ancient annals, goes more fully into questions of law, government and religion, develops the personalities involved in history, and supplies long speeches to reveal different points of view. There was no English version of the history in the sixteenth century, and Shakespeare is unlikely to have known it, but that Plutarch was greatly indebted to it the following account of the relevant portions will show. Moreover reference to Dionysius often makes clear

[1] References are to the Loeb translation, by E. Cary, 7 vols. 1939–50.

passages which remain somewhat obscure either in Plutarch's biography of Coriolanus or in Sir Thomas North's translation of Amyot. Certainly Dionysius more than Livy gave the basis for Plutarch's—and so indirectly Shakespeare's—portrayal of some important personalities.

Book VI of the *Roman Antiquities* begins when the plebeians had left Rome in 491 B.C. Dionysius tells how, with the help of Menenius Agrippa and his fable of the mutinuous members the people were persuaded to return. Menenius was 'a person of superior wisdom and was particularly commended for his political principles, since he pursued a middle course, being inclined neither to increase the arrogance of the aristocratic party, nor to permit the people to have their own way in everything' (VI.49). He was supported by Marius Valerius, the oldest envoy, who was 'most in sympathy with the common people', and opposed by Appius Claudius, 'leader of the faction that opposed the people'.

Throughout his narrative Dionysius brings out the split in the Senate between those who wished to placate the plebs, either through pity or through fear of civil war, and those who wished to crush them. The older patricians were mostly for Menenius, the younger ones against him. On the other side were Lucius Junius and Gaius Sicinius, leaders of the plebs. The former was 'a laughing-stock because of his vain pretentiousness, and when they wished to make sport of him, they called him by the nickname Brutus'. (VI.70.) He was 'a very turbulent and seditious man who had a shrewd mind . . . a great talker and babbler'. The commander of the plebeian camp, Sicinius, was less dangerous because less politic. At Brutus' suggestion the plebs demanded the creation of magistrates to defend them, and after the Senate had debated it (Valerius supporting, Appius opposing, the innovation) the first tribunes of the people were elected, their persons to be inviolable. Two *ædiles* were appointed to support them and 'to have the oversight of public places' (II.87–9).

When the city was peaceful the Romans directed their attention to enemies in neighbouring states, especially the Volsci and their allies the Antiates. Two forces went out, one against Corioli, the other against Antium. Gnæus Marcius now first came into prominence. Dionysius describes him as 'of patrician rank, of no obscure lineage', 'sober and restrained in his private life and had the spirit of a freeman in full measure' (VI.92). His great deeds began when at the siege of Corioli he was 'the chief cause of the victory'. His moderation in accepting only one warhorse with splendid trappings, and one captive 'who chanced to be a personal friend of his', instead of the greater prizes offered him, was as much praised as his bravery, which was commemorated in the name 'Coriolanus' now bestowed upon him.

The dearth is ascribed, as in Livy, to the secession of the plebs, who left Rome 'just about the beginning of seed-time', and there was no planting before the winter solstice when the reconciliation took place. So there was little corn next year and what was brought in from Sicily and Tyrrhenia soon went. Plague alone prevented the Volscians from attacking Rome. The plebs began to blame the patricians either for not avoiding the famine or for actually planning it, and when the Senate ordered colonists to go to Vellitræ there was opposition, voiced by the ædiles Sicinius and Brutus, who ascribed the worst motives to the patricians (VII.14).

The Senate was divided whether 'to court the populace by all possible expressions of kindness and by promises of deeds', or to take a firm line with 'a headstrong and ignorant multitude', defending the patrician order, promising remedies and warning the seditious.

To stage a diversion and to reduce the number of men in Rome the Senate sent out an expedition against Antium, led by Coriolanus. The plebs had refused to join, so the army was mainly composed of 'patrician volunteers and their clients'. Coriolanus captured much spoil, and shared it among his followers, exciting the envy of those who had not taken part.

In the next year the consuls obtained a great supply of corn from 'the maritime and inland markets', and 50,000 bushels from Sicily, half purchased at a low rate, and half given by the ruler of Sicily. The Senators debated what to do. Some were for distributing the free corn gratis and selling the rest very cheaply, to help the common people. 'On the other hand, those who were more arrogant and more zealous for the oligarchy', and wanted to suppress the plebs, wished all the corn to be sold as dear as possible. Marcius Coriolanus was an outspoken member of this party. Here Dionysius touches briefly on Coriolanus' candidature for the consulship, saying that Marcius was the more aggrieved against the people because they had opposed his election since they feared that he might try to overthrow the tribunes. Dionysius writes of his brilliance and daring, his 'large faction of young men of noble birth and of the greatest fortunes', his haughty air. A long speech against cheap provisions and the people's demagogues is ascribed to him. Its effect was to please the oligarchs, but those patricians friendly to the common people regarded it as 'madness, not frankness of speech or liberty'. When Coriolanus threatened violence against the tribunes, they rushed out of the Senate-house, gathered the people together, and summoned Coriolanus to defend himself. When he paid no attention they tried to arrest him; but the patricians drove the ædiles (Titus Junius Brutus and Visellius Ruga) away, and the consuls narrowly averted civil violence.

In tracing the several stages in the trial of Coriolanus, Dionysius suggests that the case was of considerable importance historically. The people were clamouring for relief from patrician exactions; they had just been given tribunes but their powers were as yet in their infancy, and the summons to Coriolanus to defend himself before a plebeian assembly called by the tribunes was a new venture, and the people's rights in the matter were unestablished. Next day the tribunes assembled the people and made charges against the patricians as a class (blaming them for the dearth, the colonization, and the attempted depopulation of Rome) and against Marcius in particular for ignoring their summons and for driving away the ædiles by force (VII.27). The elder consul, Minucius, made a spirited defence of his order and gave good reasons for not proceeding against Marcius, who had honestly stated his beliefs and was 'a man who loves his country and excels all others in the art of war' (VII.32). Marcius was present. The tribune Gaius Sicinius, 'a most bitter foe of the aristocracy', taunted Marcius with not answering the charges or asking forgiveness, knowing well that Marcius was too proud to do anything of the kind (VII.34). Marcius fell into the trap and neither denied nor defended what he had said in the Senate, but 'absolutely refused even to let them be his judges in any matter, as having no lawful authority; but if anyone should think fit to accuse him before the consuls', then he was prepared to stand trial (by the consuls). His speech showed 'the untempered wrath of an enemy fearlessly insulting those under his power with an implacable contempt for his victims' (VII.34).

The plebeians were enraged all the more, and Sicinius on behalf of the tribunes condemned Marcius to be thrown from the Tarpeian rock for insulting them through their ædiles. Violence broke out when the ædiles tried to seize Marcius, but the consuls prevented a riot, and Lucius Junius Brutus showed his skill 'in finding possible solutions in impossible situations' by disowning Sicinius' condemnation of Marcius without proper trial, and proposed that a trial should be held and 'let the citizens give their votes by tribes concerning him' (VII.36). This was agreed.

The consuls now tried to placate the people by selling the disputed corn at a very low price; also to distract them by enlisting all men of military age into an expedition against the Antiates. This device failed because the Antiates surrendered at once.

The next phase was occupied with arguments about procedure; for when Sicinius appointed a day for Coriolanus' trial the consuls sought to avoid allowing the plebs 'to get control of so great power'. Accordingly they declared that the Senate should first pass a preliminary decree which would empower the people to try Marcius. This was agreed to by the tribune Marcus Decius and others, despite Sicinius' opposition, but next day in the Senate Decius stated that no preliminary decree was necessary since there was a law 'permitting the plebeians, when oppressed by patricians, to appeal their causes to the people'. He accused Marcius of breaking the pact of unity between people and Senate made after the secession (VII.43) by using the corn shortage as a weapon of revenge against the poor; and he urged Marcius to appear before the plebs and in a conciliatory mood (VII.45). In a long speech Appius Claudius opposed the preliminary decree since the plebeians and their tribunes had already taken too much upon themselves (VII.48–53); but Marius Valerius, 'the greatest friend to the plebeians of all the senators', poured oil on the troubled waters, urging that the decree be passed and that Marcius should remove danger of civil war by 'submitting his person to the power of those who complained of being injured, and not decline to clear himself by a just defence of an unjust charge'. He ended by appealing for a more democratic government since 'If you admit the populace also to a share in the government, no evil will arise for you here' (VII.54–6). Moved by his words the Senate passed the preliminary decree. Then Marcius rose and demanded what precise charge would be made against him in the popular assembly—thinking 'that he was to be tried for the words he had spoken in the Senate'. But the tribunes declared that the charge would be the more general one of 'tyranny' (which would enable them to introduce other items). Marcius then agreed to the preliminary decree and submitted himself to the judgement of the people. At this most of the senators were pleased, thinking that 'to speak one's mind freely in the Senate was not going to render one liable to an accounting, and second, that Marcius, who had led a modest and irreproachable life, would easily clear himself of that accusation' (VII.58). On the third market day (two or three weeks later) the assembly was held with 'such a crowd of people from the country as had never before been known'. The people were grouped in their tribes. 'And this was the first time the Romans ever met in their tribal assembly to give their votes against a man, the patricians very violently opposing it and demanding that the centuriate assembly should be convened, as was their time-honoured custom.' (VII.59.)

A brief explanation here may throw light on the reference in Shakespeare:

SICINIUS Have you a catalogue
Of all the voices that we have procur'd,
Set down by the poll?
ÆDILE I have; 'tis ready.
SICINIUS Have you collected them by tribes?
ÆDILE I have.

(III.3.8–11)

The early history of Roman institutions is uncertain, and it may be that Dionysius, writing in the Augustan age about a dim and distant period before laws and constitution were written down, tended to read the struggles of the early Republic in terms of the Republic in its decadence. Nevertheless he had before him annals and traditions since lost, and his account is a major source for later classical and modern historians. There were three major Roman assemblies, the *Comitia curiata*, of patricians alone; the *Comitia centuriata*, including both orders; and the *Comitia plebis* consisting of plebeians alone. Until the time of Servius Tullius the *Comitia curiata* wielded all civil and religious powers for the people as a whole. It 'was the court of last appeal in all matters affecting the life or privileges of Patricians' (Ramsay, p. 115). Most of its functions were taken over by the *Comitia centuriata*, the more representative assembly instituted by Servius Tullius, but in the time of Coriolanus 'no measure passed by the *Comitia centuriata* was binding until it had received the sanction of the *Comitia curiata*.' Dionysius does not mention that body in Bk. VII, but perhaps it was the *Comitia curiata* rather than the Senate which passed the enabling bill allowing Marcius' trial by the people. His was a test case in more ways than one, for he was the first patrician against whom the tribunes tried their recently created powers; and his case was the first step towards establishing voting by tribes (in the *Comitia tributa*). There were great advantages for the tribunes in having voting by tribes rather than centuries. Servius Tullius organized the population into thirty tribes, each occupying a region (four in Rome and twenty-six outside); according to Livy there were only twenty-one in 495 B.C. Servius also divided the people for military purposes into *classes* (armies), each subdivided into *centuriæ*. This division depended on property qualifications, and each of the five classes of infantry had different armour and weapons, varying from the full defensive bronze armour of the first class to the fifth class which had no armour and was armed only with slings and stones. There were 193 centuries all told. Any question submitted to the *Comitia centuriata* was decided by a majority of votes, each century having one vote which was obtained by a poll of the members. Ninety-seven centuries would form a majority. But the first class, together with the eighteen centuries of Equites, made up ninety-eight centuries, so that if they were unanimous, they would alone decide any question. This class voted first, being followed by the others in descending order of property-owning until a majority was reached. The centuries were of greatly differing sizes. The vast majority of the people were in the lowest centuries and often did not get a chance to express their will. So the *Comitia centuriata* usually favoured the wishes of the patricians and richer classes.

Hence the desire of the tribunes for another system of voting which would avoid patrician domination. As the *Comitia tributa* developed, after the motion had been discussed the people divided into their tribes; lots were drawn to decide their order of voting; each tribe had one vote (decided by the majority in the tribe) and the question was decided according to the majority of tribal votes. The assembly called to try Coriolanus was apparently the first formal meeting of a *Comitia tributa*, and it was the first time a patrician was tried by a body containing a majority of plebeians. It is not surprising that many patricians objected and that a 'preliminary decree' authorizing the innovation was called for. When Dionysius writes of the great number of people coming in for the meeting from outside the city, he refers to the fact that by far the greater number of tribes dwelt in the country districts. In most of the tribes the poorer members would be in a majority, and in circumstances such as those obtaining in 491 B.C. could be relied on to oppose the patricians.

Dionysius is not very clear about what happened, nor indeed is Plutarch. So it is not surprising that Shakespeare is confused about Roman procedure. Although he mentions collecting votes 'by tribes', he also writes of 'voices' 'set down by the poll', which suggests the counting of individual heads. The individual voters however would not matter to the tribunes: they were interested only in the second stage, in getting a majority of simple tribal votes. This they had apparently got before ever Marcius appeared to defend himself. So the issue was never in doubt. Shakespeare however was probably misled by North, who, thinking that tribal voting meant counting heads, added to Plutarch that 'their voyces were numbered by the polle' [cf. *inf.* 525]. Had Shakespeare read Dionysius of Halicarnassus he might not have made this slip.

When the trial began the consul, Minucius, urged the assembly to acquit Marcius, 'remembering . . . how many battles he had won in fighting' for the commonwealth, despite his 'objectionable words' (VII.60). The Senate, he said, had acquitted Marcius for what he had said in the Senate; he must now be tried upon specific charges relating to the accusation of tyranny. On these lines Sicinius prosecuted Marcius. Marcius defended himself by telling of his military deeds, and brought as witnesses generals and citizens whom he had saved. He also showed his wounds in disproof of the charges against him. But Decius now accused him of appropriating to his friends' use the spoils captured in his expedition against the Antiates in the previous year. The voting was made on a proposal to banish him for ever. Nine tribes were for acquittal; the other twelve were against Marcius, who took the verdict calmly, went home, exhorted his mourning wife and mother 'to bear their misfortunes with firmness', and left the city, 'informing no one to what place he proposed to retire' (VII.67).

Most of Book VIII is occupied with the remainder of Coriolanus' story, telling how he went to Antium and was made a general by the Volscians. Tullus himself remained at home to defend Antium, while Marcius led a Volscian army to besiege Rome (VIII.13).

The interview with the Roman ambassadors, chosen from his former friends, started with a reasoned speech by Minucius, admitting the crimes of the plebeians against Marcius, but arguing that for him to destroy his friends along with his enemies would be wrong, offering to recall him home, declaring that in the end Rome and her allies would surely win any war, and warning Marcius that, even if he won, he would be deprived of his mother, his wife and his two children. ('You will be called the slayer of your mother, the murderer of your children, the assassin of your wife, and the evil genius of your country' (VIII.28).)

In reply Marcius defended his behaviour in refusing 'to put the whole power of the commonwealth into the hands of an ignorant and base multitude', and complained against the Senate

> 'which encouraged me at first with vain hopes while I was opposing the tribunes in their efforts to establish a tyranny, promising that it would itself provide for my security, and then, upon the first suspicion of any danger from the plebeians, abandoned me and delivered me up to my enemies.' (VIII.30)

He had agreed to be tried by the people only because he feared that he would be handed over to them. He rejected Minucius' pleas for moderation and mutual forgiveness and gave the Romans thirty days to reflect on his demand that the Volscians be given their lost territories. After this time, during which he captured seven Latin cities, he rebuffed the conciliatory proposals of the ex-consuls who next came as emissaries from Rome and turned away a third embassy of priests.

Dionysius differed from Livy in making the matron Valeria (sister of the hero Publicola) instigate the embassy of women. When she appeals to Coriolanus' mother Veturia to lead them, the latter in a moving speech says that she has little hope, 'for Marcius has turned away from us, Valeria, ever since the people passed that bitter sentence against him, and has hated his whole family together with his country' (VIII.41). Her moving story of Marcius' departure is followed by a vivid account of the Romans' fear for their women's safety and of their journey by 'mules, carts and many other conveyances' to the Volscian camp. In reverence for his mother Coriolanus went out to meet her and ordered his lictors to lay aside their axes and lower their rods ('a custom observed by the Romans when inferior magistrates meet those who are their superiors'). Coriolanus was swept away from his stern resolution by the sight of his mother and wife, but their interview was long, until at last Veturia appealed to Marcius as his mother, threatening to kill herself should he refuse to spare his country, and throwing herself down to kiss her son's feet ('and the Volscians who were present at the assembly could not bear the unusual sight, but turned away their eyes').

So she won her victory, and by so doing, as Marcius declared, 'ruined her dutiful and affectionate son'. The end was not long delayed. Tullus Attius, long since jealous of Coriolanus, had resolved to destroy him either secretly or (should he fail) as a traitor. He accused Marcius of treason and ordered a trial in the forum where his faction would not let Coriolanus speak; 'then with cries of "Hit him", "Stone him", the most daring surrounded him and stoned him to death' (VIII.59).

Dionysius adds a character-study of Coriolanus as a man ruined by his lack of charm and 'his passion for exact and severe justice', stating that his memory had endured for nearly

500 years and 'he is still praised and celebrated by all as a pious and just man' (VIII.60–62).

For Dionysius Coriolanus was the victim of a class-struggle between plebeians and aristocrats. Himself a supporter of the latter, whom he regarded as the best in mind as well as in birth, and therefore as the natural rulers of the nation, Marcius displayed a noble's valour in war and a noble's courage and integrity in civic life, following out his principles to the end no matter what animosity he excited. He saw the tribunes as enemies of the state and of his own caste, and the plebeians as an ignorant mob to be ruled with the same firmness and severity as his soldiers. Dionysius' curiosity about political institutions led him to describe (or invent) the several stages of the tribunes' campaign against Coriolanus. His trial by the tribes was the first step in a movement which gradually increased the power of the tribunes and the plebeians until the Republic was endangered, divided and destroyed.

Dionysius was also greatly interested in oratory and invented long speeches expounding the motives of parties and individuals. Above all however he accentuated the moments of intense conflict in a manner entirely alien to Livy's drier, succinct manner.

Dionysius was the main source for Plutarch's *Life of Coriolanus* [Text II] but, being a biographer, not a chronicler, Plutarch used the material differently. His chief aim, as he tells us in his *Pericles*, was to encourage his readers to emulate the virtuous deeds of great men, and (as a corollary) to avoid their mistakes. Preoccupied with conduct, he generously approved acts of dignity or courage (however misdirected) and 'his sympathy goes out spontaneously to noble words or deeds or minds' (MacCallum). His political ideal was 'the need of authority and the obligation of the few to maintain it—by a "natural grace" springing on the one hand from courage combined with forbearance, and leading, on the other, to harmony between the rulers and the ruled' (Wyndham). Unlike Dionysius he was not intent on showing the nature of Roman institutions. His aim was to trace, with regard to general qualities and particular anecdotes, the ethical qualities of individual men. Hence he coupled Alcibiades with Coriolanus as two different types brought into conflict with their own countrymen. Alcibiades was the seeker after popular favour, who could be all things to all men, and in spite of his greed and luxury he kept men's good opinions. Coriolanus, on the other hand, was unsociable, supercilious and self-willed, too proud to court popular favour, yet hurt and angry when he was disregarded. Out of Dionysius' copious narrative Plutarch drew a moral portrait of great clarity and force, while obscuring in his summary his predecessor's lucid account of the political forces involved in Marcius' tragedy.

For Plutarch Coriolanus' errors were the result of the early loss of his father which robbed him of the discipline he needed, made him the complete individualist, vehement in his passion, unable to work with others, austere in manners, overbearing and imperious, yet eager for praise, especially from his mother on whom he lavished all his affection and respect. Plutarch does not comment adversely on her or her rearing of the boy, nor is she depicted as a stern Roman matron; on the contrary she is described as weeping for joy in his embraces. She seems however to have encouraged him in his martial ardour from the first and she was delighted to hear him praised and see his triumphs. Marcius had a generous and noble nature, which though perverted into an inordinate pride and desire for glory, was never entirely lost. Plutarch has been accused of presenting the contradictions of his subjects without trying to harmonize them. In his portrait of Coriolanus however this is not true. The tormented genius of the young aristocrat is beautifully presented, and the material is set out in such a way that it was easy for later dramatists to organize it into tragedy for the stage.

Two hundred years after Dionysius, in the time of Hadrian, L. Annæus Florus wrote an *Epitome* of Livy which probably took from the elder Seneca the division of Roman history into four ages, infancy, youth, manhood and old age. Coriolanus came at the beginning of the second age, which lasted about 150 years after the expulsion of the Tarquins, while the Romans were subjugating the rest of Italy. Florus refers briefly to Coriolanus in two or three section of the first Book. Thus, relating the wars against neighbouring tribes, Florus looks back from imperial heights on the small beginnings of the nation, and is condescendingly surprised at the importance in those early days of feuds with minor towns, when the capture of Corioli was regarded as so glorious a feat that Gnæus Marcius took the name Coriolanus from the city as though he had conquered Numantia or Africa.

In a section on the civil discords occurring at a somewhat primitive period, Coriolanus reappears to illustrate the unruly wilfulness of the Roman people; and the fable of Menenius is briefly summarized [Text III]. Obviously for Florus all that was far away and long ago.

Before Shakespeare wrote his play Alexandre Hardy in France had composed his *Coriolan*, which, though not published until 1625, was written by 1600. A Senecan tragedy in the tradition of Jodelle and Garnier, *Coriolan* is largely a rhetorical exercise round events in Plutarch. The design is simple, emphasizing the infernal pride of the hero, contrasting him with his rival Amfidie, and representing his mother as innocently bringing doom upon her son by persuading him to spare Rome. 'Few subjects in Roman history', declares the Argument, 'are more worthy of the theatre than this.'

The play begins when Coriolan has been summoned to explain his conduct to the people. In Act I, Sc. 1 he rages because he has been victimized by the envious commons and almost condemned to the Tarpeian Rock. His pride rebels that he 'sprung of such a race, must await examination by Tribunes, the judgement of this populace'. His mother Volumnie begs him to have patience and to placate the people. 'Remember that pride brings solitude', she says. Licinie, the tribune, enters and accuses him of yearning to be a tyrant. Coriolan recalls that earlier he was kept from the Consulship 'by the ungrateful refusal of a popular vote because he could not stoop to show the mob his body full of scars. When Licinie says that he is condemned to lifelong exile Coriolan accepts the verdict quietly: 'I shall obey, indeed I shall take care to leave these ungrateful men before they have need of me.' A Chorus of Romans abuses him as an 'arrogant monster', but the Senate fears that its power has gone, and 'henceforth we carry the yoke of slavery on our necks.'

Act II moves to the Volscian city where Coriolan disguises himself to enter, expressing his desire for vengeance. In II.2 Amfidie, resentful of Rome's growing power, is told of the stranger's arrival. Coriolan reveals himself (III.3) in terms close to Plutarch and is welcomed. When Amfidie expresses surprise that the Senate allowed him to be exiled, Coriolan accuses the senators of timidity, of opposing the armed commons only with words.

By the opening of Act III Coriolan is besieging Rome, and the Roman ambassadors have been to plead with him after the first truce of thirty days. They describe to the Senate his obduracy and the hard conditions to be accepted within three days. III.2 presents Coriolan soliloquizing in the Volscian camp. He has twice rejected the Roman delegates; his vengeance is Justice. In III.3 the Ambassadors come again to him, but he refuses to abandon his Volscian friends.

AMB. Your country's honour will you give to plunder?
COR. My country's only where my fortune's good.
AMB. But it was Rome that gave you your existence.
COR. 'Twas Rome that sought to rob me of my life.
AMB. Oppose your love to her ingratitude.
COR. Importune me no more with pleadings vain.

In IV.1 Valerie suggests to the Roman Ladies that as a last resort they should persuade Coriolan's family to go to him as 'a pregnant token of love and pity'. IV.2 moves again to the Volscian lands where Amfidie in soliloquy accuses Coriolan of betraying them as he betrayed the Romans; for he has granted the enemy a truce instead of pushing on to victory. In Rome (IV.3) Volumnie fears that her son, who has always thought more of glory than of his family, will not be moved by her appeals any more than by those of ambassadors and priests. However, she cannot refuse to be the advocate of her afflicted country. Coriolanus in IV.4 is weighing the advantages of a direct assault against the city and of slower methods when he sees the Roman Ladies approaching. Despite his attempt to arm himself with inflexible constancy he is overcome by affection. He greets them warmly. When his mother prays him not to ruin his country he quickly agrees, but tells her that in winning a happy victory for Rome she has brought her son a fatal gift. When she looks forward to seeing him again he bids her 'Hope not to meet till in the hall of shades' and says farewell to her and his 'loyal wife'.

Act V begins in the Volscian city where Coriolan soliloquizes, his mind disturbed by gloomy apparitions that have haunted his sleep. Amfidie's ancient rancour has been roused. A page summons the hero to Council and he goes full of forebodings. In V.2 Amfidie accuses him of coming over to the Volscians in order to earn his recall 'by some treason or great injury done to the people who credulously received this serpent thrust out from Rome.' Coriolan first permitted a truce without consulting the Council, and now, moved by women's prayers, has made a shameful peace. Coriolan asserts that it was never the Volscian intention to destroy Rome, only to weaken her and regain their lost territories; and 'I know not one of you would not have given way, deflected from his task by piety'.

A Chorus of Volscians cries that he must be executed forthwith, and he is murdered. The Council wishes that forms of law had been observed. Back in Rome Volumnie (V.3) hears from a Messenger that Amfidie has had her son assassinated, fearing that 'deep-ingrained respect for his rare virtues would obtain forgiveness for his crimes'. Volumnie grieves, blaming herself for the murder of her noble son.

As MacCallum pointed out, the 'scaffolding' of Hardy's and Shakespeare's plays is somewhat similar, 'because both follow closely the excellent guidance of Plutarch'. MacCallum also noted resemblances not due to Plutarch: In both plays Volumnia is introduced early to advise her son to placate the people; in both the rivalry between Coriolanus and the Volscian leader is intensified.

Hardy's play is however much narrower in scope of plot; the thought is abstract and schematic; the characters are little individualized, and Coriolan is a personification of aristocratic pride with few other traits to enrich his nature. That Shakespeare's play comes nearer to French classical drama than any of his others is due, not to influence by any French writer, but to the neatness of Plutarch's presentation and to the moral intensity which Shakespeare brought to the theme. It is extremely unlikely that he knew Hardy's *Coriolan*.

Shakespeare's adaptation of Plutarch's narrative was obviously governed by three main considerations: first, to make a good play; second, to re-create the characters of the hero and his associates; third, to interpret the political situation in Rome in terms suited to early Jacobean England and the conditions of 1607–8.

The dramatist took over certain key-features of Plutarch's story: the unrest in Rome, the Corioli campaign, Marcius' candidature for the consulship, his opposition to the multitude and to the distribution of cheap corn, the people's rage and Coriolanus' trial and banishment, his alliance with Tullus and his harrying of Rome, the embassy of women, his surrender to his mother's pleading, and his withdrawal, the vengeance of the Volscians. In shaping this varied material, which in Plutarch covered many months, into what became perhaps his most unified play, Shakespeare kept very closely to North's version in many passages, but on the other hand re-ordered, omitted and transformed the material in a remarkable way, as the following analysis will show.[1]

The first scene plunges us at once into the mutinous state of Rome, and combines two distinct risings of the plebeians. The citizens want 'corn at our own price' (I.1.10–11); they claim that they are starving. Although there is a reference to usurers at I.1.83, the main cause of their unrest is dearth, for which they blame the rich patricians. This is not the secession to the Sacred Mount (494 B.C.), but the later trouble of c. 491. Menenius' mediation is accordingly shifted to the later date, by which time he was dead. For his fable of the belly and members Shakespeare drew not only on Plutarch but also on Livy [*inf.* 497] and the British historian William Camden, whose *Remaines of a greater worke concerning Britaine* (1605) contained a version of the allegory.

Marcius is already regarded by many as 'chief enemy to the people' (I.1.8), 'a very dog to the commonalty', but others consider 'what services he has done for his country' (29–30) and excuse his pride. On his first appearance he speaks opprobriously to the citizens, calling them 'dissentious rogues', cowards, untrustworthy, haters of nobility, and stands out as a supporter of

'the noble senate, who
Under the gods, keep you in awe, which else
Would feed on one another.' (I.1.165–89)

[1] I am indebted to several scholars who have previously examined in detail Shakespeare's use of his sources in this play; notably to N. Delius, *ShJb* xi.32, 1876; R. Büttner, *ShJb* xli. 1905, 45–53; M. W. MacCallum, *Roman Plays*, 1910; K. Muir, *Shakespeare's Sources*, I, 195, 219–24; E.A.J. Honigmann, *ShQ* x. 1959, 25–33.

In order that the election of tribunes may be mentioned by him as a dangerous innovation (to 'make bold power look pale') Shakespeare imagines another group of rebels, offstage, who have demanded and obtained the appointment of five tribunes, including Junius Brutus and Sicinius Velutus.

A more favourable impression of Marcius is given when Cominius, Titus Lartius and other Senators come to ask his help against the Volsces, whose leader Tullus Aufidius is warmly praised by Marcius, already his rival in war. In Plutarch Tullus Attius is not mentioned until Coriolanus has been banished. But a main object in this scene is to introduce as many principal personalities and motifs as possible. So the dearth of corn is anticipated because it is to be a decisive factor in making Coriolanus destroy himself; the plebeians are shown as deserving our pity yet as wild and rebellious against the order of the state, which Menenius expounds so that from the first we shall know the 'right' attitude to take up and shall not accept the views of popular extremists. Marcius has revealed his ruthless irascibility and contempt for the mob, but also his warlike valour and a comradeliness not found in Plutarch. The scene closes with a short dialogue between the new-made tribunes in which they speak much truth about Marcius' hostility to them, his desire for fame, but wrongly ascribe base motives to his willingness to serve under Cominius (I.1.256ff). This finely planned scene thus adumbrates several of the main themes of Plutarch's biography; it represents not only a city-state in turmoil but some of the chief personages and their contrasting attitudes; it shows Marcius as an enigmatic figure, to be interpreted in opposite ways by men of different parties. It reveals him in his weakness and strength and raises questions about his motives. Is he a patriot or a self-seeker? The First Citizen drops a hint about his feelings for his mother (I.1.35–9). We are left wondering whether he is as cunning as Brutus believes.

I.2 gives a glimpse of the Volscian city of Corioli, where Aufidius is departing with his army to harass outlying Roman towns, leaving his senators to guard Corioli. Aufidius' hatred and fear of Rome, his respect for Marcius, are suggested. Here again Shakespeare's invention brings in the rivalry between Marcius and his Volscian enemy which will cause the catastrophe.

The next scene likewise is both retrospective and preparative. It advances the narrative of events merely by letting us know that Cominius has marched against Aufidius while Marcius and Titus Lartius 'are set down before their city Corioli' (I.3.102–3); which could have been made clear in I.4; but Shakespeare wished to show Marcius' relations with his family, and in particular with his mother, which will be all-important later, and to develop the First Citizen's hint in Scene 1. In a play with few feminine parts (but those most significant) the sooner they are introduced the better. So in a pleasant domestic scene whose quietness contrasts with what precedes and what comes after, Volumnia (Marcius' mother) and Virgilia (his wife) discuss him and are visited by Valeria (who in Plutarch was much later to suggest the embassy of women). She helps to make the scene one of Roman womanhood at its noblest. On Plutarch's description of Marcius as training for war from his earliest youth, and of his mother (Veturia) as delighting in his exploits [*inf.* 508] the dramatist has built up a portrait of self-disciplined devotion to a rigid code of martial honour. She tells the soft-hearted Virgilia, 'If my son were my husband, I would freelier rejoice in that absence wherein he won honour than in the embracements of his bed wherein he would show most love' (I.3.2–5). The passion for arms which in Plutarch was native to his own mind, is claimed by Volumnia as due to her ('To a cruel war I sent him . . .'). For her a bloody brow 'more becomes a man / Than gilt his trophy' (*ibid.*, 40–1). When Virgilia fears Aufidius, the mother is sure that Marcius would beat him in any fight. Further proof of martial family-traits is supplied when Valeria describes how Marcius' little son tore a gilded butterfly to pieces in childish rage: 'One on's father's moods', comments Volumnia (*ibid.*, 54–69). In Plutarch Valeria did not appear until she suggested the embassy of women and came to Coriolanus' mother's house to request her to lead them out to the Volscian camp. The sister of Publicola, a hero of the resistance against the Tarquins, she shared his noble spirit. Shakespeare diminishes her importance (and does not here mention Publicola, whose name few in the audience would know), but because she will accompany Volumnia on her mission she is brought in now, and a faint reflection of her part in Plutarch appears when she asks the other two women to go out with her. The gentle passive disposition of the wife Virgilia is shown: 'I'll not go over the threshold till my lord return from the wars' (*ibid.*, 75–6). Austere fortitude, mild patience, witty energy, are contrasted in the rapidly sketched characterization of this scene.

From Plutarch's account of the siege of Corioli [*inf.* 511] Shakespeare takes the division of the Roman army (I.4.21); the Volscian sally which drove the Romans back; Marcius' rallying call—which becomes violent abuse (*ibid.*, 30–42); his entry into the city and solitary fight within the gates, and the capture of Corioli by Titus Lartius. I.5 shows Marcius' anger with the looters, and his request to be allowed to go and help the hard-pressed other part of the army under Cominius. In I.6 the ebb and flow of battle is well represented, with tardy news giving a black report of the situation to Cominius, but all set right by the appearance of Marcius, victorious and eager to advance against the Antiates. Shakespeare ignores Plutarch's note about the Roman soldiers making their wills, but Marcius inveighs against 'the common file', who would have lost the battle 'but for our gentlemen' (*ibid.*, 42–5); even in the thick of the fight he contemns the lower orders. Plutarch did not refer to Tullus here, but Shakespeare makes him leader of the Antiates so that (after another glance at the captured city whence Lartius issues to rejoin the fight (I.7)), he may invent a doughty but unfinished hand-to-hand combat between Aufidius and Marcius. By I.9 the victory is complete, and Shakespeare brings forward from the next day (Plutarch, *inf.* 514) the praises showered on Marcius by Cominius. He inserts a terse speech of manly modesty by Marcius (I.9.13–19) who accepts but one horse of the booty and one prisoner (not a friend but a poor man, once his host, whose name he cannot remember. Shakespeare makes a fine stroke of Plutarch's failure to give it). Marcius' modesty is revealed as an austere pride when he savagely rejects the soldiers' applause as 'praises sauc'd with lies'. So at every turn the dramatist displays two sides of the hero's nature, his courage and harshness, his scorn of baseness which suspects even decent feelings, his contempt for common weaknesses and for personal gain, his arrogant distaste for other men's good opinions. Even his mother, he says, 'when she does praise me, grieves me'. But he accepts the title 'Coriolanus' and will try to deserve it. To keep Tullus Aufidius in our minds he is seen raging in defeat and against Marcius who has beaten him five times in combat, 'And wouldst do so, I think, should we encounter / As often as we eat'. He is prepared to use dishonourable means to destroy his enemy (I.10).

Act II begins with an invented scene: Coriolanus' homecoming. The division of opinion about him and the dislike felt by the patricians ('us o' the right-hand file') appear when Menenius berates the tribunes Sicinius and Brutus for calling Marcius proud, for currying favour with the poor, for self-importance, for tangling up legal processes, and for being 'the herdsmen of the beastly plebeians' (II.1.1–97). 'I cannot call you Lycurguses', he says (57), referring no doubt to Plutarch's *Life* of the great law-giver of Sparta.

With Volumnia and Virgilia Menenius expresses his joy at Marcius' victory. Maybe his reference to a letter from the hero: 'It gives me an estate of seven years' health: in which time I will make a lip at the physician' was suggested by Shakespeare's knowledge (from Livy [*inf.* 499]) that the historical Menenius died in 'that same year'. Hence also Coriolanus' greeting: 'And live you yet?' (184). Virgilia shrinks on hearing that her husband has been wounded; Volumnia thanks the Gods for it (II.1.123), ambitiously looking forward to the time when he will display his scars (twenty-seven now) to the people. This introduces the consul-motif, which she hints again at 204–6. The welcome of Coriolanus is a splendid example of Shakespeare's power to create a mood of rejoicing and the reactions of different personages. He kneels to his exultant mother, chides Valeria ('My gracious silence') for weeping, then begs her pardon for doing so, and goes to report to 'the good patricians', leaving the dissident Tribunes to marvel acidly at the popular welcome (described in terms reminiscent of the tribune Marullus' account in *Julius Cæsar*, I.1.40–50 of Pompey's triumph), and to plot his downfall should he seek to be consul.

In Plutarch Marcius did not stand for the consulship until he had won the hatred of the people by the enforced colonization of Vellitræ, and by getting great spoil in an attack on Antium [*inf.* 517]. Shakespeare omits both of these (although there is a reference later to the second); and Coriolanus is invited to be a candidate on the day when he receives formal thanks for Corioli (II.2). Before the ceremony the two minor officers, discussing his attitude to the populace, draw on Plutarch's 'Comparison between Alcibiades and Coriolanus' [*inf.* 544ff]. When the Second Officer speaks of 'many great men that have flattered the people, who ne'er loved them', Shakespeare obviously had Alcibiades in mind, who 'ever studied by all devise he could, to currie favour with the common people', and when the First Officer says: 'Now, to seem to affect the malice and displeasure of the people is as bad as that which he dislikes, to flatter them for their love', he is inverting Plutarch:

> 'For as it is an evill thing to flatter the common people to winne credit: even so is it besides dishonesty, and injustice also, to atteine to credit and authoritie, for one to make himselfe terrible to the people, by offering them wrong and violence' [*inf.* 545].

In spite of his faults, they agree that Marcius 'hath deserved worthily of his country' (24–5). The ceremony continues the conflict of attitudes already seen, with Menenius eager to help Coriolanus but anxious about his behaviour, the tribunes wary (but Sicinius more placatory than Brutus (51–64), Coriolanus shy of hearing himself praised in public, and bluntly modifying Menenius' 'He loves your people' into 'I love them as they weigh' (64, 74). Cominius' speech in his honour (88–122) embroiders on Plutarch's story of Marcius' first battle [*inf.* 507], making him wound Tarquin himself, and retelling his exploits at Corioli and his subsequent refusal of booty with an eloquence that owes much to North's phraseology.

According to Shakespeare the Senate 'are well pleas'd to make [Coriolanus] consul' (II.2.132–3) but to be elected he must stand in the Forum, show his wounds, and ask the plebeian passers-by for their votes. This twofold process is not that described in Plutarch, who declares that to obtain 'any office' the candidate must canvass the citizens in the market place for some days before the election; and that Marcius followed this custom, but that on election day 'Marcius came to the market place with great pompe, accompanied with all the Senate, and the whole Nobilitie of the citie about him' and that the effect was to turn the common people (hitherto well disposed) against Coriolanus, and fearing to increase his power 'they refused Marcius in the ende' [*inf.* 518]. So Plutarch regarded the consuls as elected by the common people. In fact the title of 'consul' was not used until after Coriolanus' time (449 B.C. according to Zonaras); and they were always elected by the Comitia Centuriata, which was dominated by the patricians. Shakespeare combines nomination by the Senate with election by the plebeians (as in Plutarch), and he sets the canvassing between the two, thus making it clear to all that Coriolanus is the patricians' nominee. In Plutarch he follows the custom and shows his wounds without any fuss, but Shakespeare's tribunes have already remarked on his reluctance to appear in the market place in 'The napless vesture of humility' (II.1.239), and they now rejoice to hear him say that the custom 'might well / Be taken from the people' (II.2.145–6).

II.3 begins with several citizens displaying the muddled wits of the multitude, but they are willing enough to give him their votes. Coriolanus' behaviour when he asks for their support is insulting, sarcastic and contemptuous, but the citizens promise him their support, though one of them points out the two sides of his past conduct (II.3.93–5). Coriolanus will not show his wounds in public and barely endures the test, but as Menenius says, 'the tribunes / Endue you with the people's voice' (141–2), and he must finally be confirmed in his office at the Senate house. When he goes off to change his clothes, however, the tribunes make use of some citizens' uncomfortable feeling that Coriolanus has mocked them to arouse their fears of what he might do in such 'A place of potency and sway o' the state' (II.3.158–215), and incite them to revoke their 'ignorant election' while preserving themselves from blame (216–57). Not for the first time Brutus counts on Coriolanus' irascibility to make things worse for himself (258–63). All this is Shakespeare's invention—to accentuate Marcius' overweening pride and unsuitability for political life, and to show, on the other side, the fickleness of the mob and the tribunes' insidious sway.

Always preparing the minds of the audience for what is to follow, Shakespeare begins III.1 with a meeting between Coriolanus and the general Titus Lartius in which the latter tells of renewed peril from the Volscians and Tullus Aufidius' undying hatred for Marcius. There is dramatic irony when the latter wishes he had a cause to seek Aufidius at Antium (III.1.1–20). Cause he will have and all too soon. Brutus tells Coriolanus and his friends that the people have changed their minds:

> The people cry you mock'd them, and of late,
> When corn was given them gratis, you repin'd.
> (III.1.41–2)

This is a reference to an incident which in Plutarch occurred after the refusal of the consulship, when Marcius, smarting under the insult, opposed in Senate the free distribution of corn from Sicily, in order to bring the plebeians to heel and bring about the removal of the tribunes; otherwise 'their disobedience . . . would breake out in the ende, to the utter ruine and overthrowe of the whole state' [*inf.* 520]. Shakespeare uses the allusion to reveal the crass folly of Coriolanus who in his 'passion and choler' insists on repeating the main point of his speech (60–138) warning the 'good but most unwise senators' of the evils they are letting in through the tribunes with their popular 'shall' (actually they had the right of veto). The subsequent divisions in Rome were to prove how right he was in foreseeing a bitter future, 'where gentry, title, wisdom, / Cannot conclude but by the yea and no / Of general ignorance' (141–60). When he demands that the tribunes be overthrown, Brutus accuses him of treason and calls the ædiles to arrest him.

The subsequent order of events departs from Plutarch, in whose work ten stages occur before Coriolanus' banishment. (1) On hearing Coriolanus' speech in the Senate the tribunes rushed off calling for help and the people would have attacked the Senate-house but (2) the tribunes sent their ædiles to arrest him and make him answer for his attacks on plebeians and tribunes. Marcius withstood arrest. (3) The tribunes themselves came to support the ædiles, the patricians helped Coriolanus to keep the officers at bay, and night ended the affray. (4) Next morning the consuls held a Senate-meeting at which it was decided to placate the people by offering them the corn cheaply. (5) This was done, but the tribunes demanded that Coriolanus come and answer several charges (knowing that he would either humble himself or, by refusing, enrage the people more). (6) Coriolanus came and defended himself so rudely that Sicinius declared that he must die and ordered him to be taken by the ædiles and cast from the Tarpeian Rock. (7) The patricians defended Coriolanus by force. (8) The death-sentence was withdrawn until a proper trial before the people could be held some eleven or twelve days later. (9) During the interval the patricians discussed how to save Coriolanus without further riot, and were divided about what they should do. Coriolanus solved their problem by agreeing to be tried by the people if the only charge were that he sought to be King and tyrant. (10) The trial was arranged by the tribunes on a tribal basis and they widened the accusations so as to ensure his condemnation to banishment.

In Shakespeare (1) is represented by Sicinius' exclamation, 'Go, call the people' (III.1.173); (2) and (3) are run together when Sicinius tries to arrest him and Marcius refuses; the ædiles are ordered to take him but the senators withstand them (173–87). (4) and (5) are omitted. (6) follows at once but Marcius is hastily condemned to death without making another speech (188–222). As in (7) he and his friends—including the pacific Menenius—prevent his execution (222–28). Shakespeare now expands greatly on (8), showing Coriolanus with difficulty being sent home while Menenius argues with the tribunes until they reluctantly agree to let him act 'as the people's officer' and bring Coriolanus to be tried 'by process' (253–334). This enables Shakespeare to introduce two parallel scenes of persuasion—that in which the tribunes show their rage and malice but are smoothed down by Menenius' 'old wit', and III.2 in which Coriolanus is brought to agree to a trial by the people, not, as in Plutarch, out of consideration for his peers but through the long persuasions of his mother. Volumnia blames him for courting disaster, for not waiting till he was Consul before showing his dislike of popular policies, for not using his brain as well as his heart. She urges him to dissemble his anger and to speak fairly to the people, to go bonnet in hand, even to kneel, to explain away his blunt speech (III.2.1–92). Finally Coriolanus agrees to try and do what she, Menenius and Cominius ask, but with misgivings:

> You have put me now to such a part which never
> I shall discharge to the life. (105–6)

Shakespeare's Coriolanus has not here questioned the legality of trial by the plebeians; but only his mother's repeated pleas drive him out to flatter and 'mountebank' the people's loves, yet still threatening:

> Let them accuse me by invention, I
> Will answer them in mine honour. (143–4)

That to accuse him 'by invention' is precisely what the tribunes intend to do the beginning of III.3 makes clear, when Brutus adds to the charge of tyranny that of keeping back the booty which in Plutarch Coriolanus divided among his soldiers after a raid on the Antiates for which few volunteers could be found. This raid is not mentioned elsewhere by Shakespeare but that does not matter, since the accusation is never made, and Coriolanus does not agree to be tried by the people on condition that the charge is merely that of seeking to be King [cf. *inf.* 524]. Here the dramatist fails to make full use of Plutarch's material, doubtless because his Marcius is too simple a character to be interested in nice points of procedure. The Elizabethan audience too would not spare much thought for legalistic details about Roman institutions.

Hence Shakespeare does not make full use of Plutarch's notes on the difference between voting by centuries and by tribes by which the tribunes worked against Coriolanus. He merely suggests that Brutus and Sicinius were manipulating the trial and the voting and does not explain the significance of having 'a catalogue' of voters in their favour 'collected by tribes' (III.3.8–11). Maybe he was not sure himself, for Plutarch's abbreviation of Dionysius' account is not entirely clear [*inf.* 523–5]. Nor does Shakespeare make any of the patricians question the legality of trial by the people on a capital charge, or assert its novelty. Sicinius indeed speaks of 'the old prerogative' as though the people had the power of life and death (17–18), which was not so before this time. Shakespeare apparently does not realize the full significance of this trial. His play is about political sentiments, principles and personalities rather than about methods of organization or constitutional history. The wily Brutus knows that if Marcius be 'put to choler' he will destroy himself, and so he does. The formal requirement that Coriolanus 'submit to the people's voices' (43) is moved here to give dramatic intensity [cf. *inf.* 523]. He agrees but at once begins to ask why he has been denied the consulship. Told that he is there to answer questions he subsides, but on being charged with aspiring to be tyrant, and as a traitor, he bursts out in fury, and Sicinius, realizing that 'We need not put new matter to his charge' (75), summarizes the articles against him in Plutarch [*inf.* 522] and condemns him to banishment. It is an odd trial. The people's poll, the votes of the tribes are not even mentioned, for, bringing out the clash of personalities, Shakespeare ignores the procedure in Plutarch where after Coriolanus' defence of his action in dividing the Antiates' spoil among his soldiers had caused 'such a noyse, that he could not be heard', the 'voyces of the Tribes' were counted and he was condemned by the narrow majority of three. Marcius' rage, in which he casts off his country ('I banish you') and looks forward to its ingratitude to future defenders (a reference perhaps to Camillus (in the same chapter of Florus, *inf.* 550)), is in entire accordance with his character in the play and with his future actions. But in Plutarch he 'dyd outwardly shewe no manner of passion . . . because he was so caried awaye with the vehemencie of anger, and desire of revenge, that he had no sence nor feeling of the hard state he was in' [*inf.* 525]. This false calm appears however in the next scene (IV.1) where he takes leave of his family and friends at the gate of the city. In Plutarch he comforted his wife and mother at home, 'and persuaded them to be content with his chaunce' [*inf.* 526]. Shakespeare's Coriolanus chides his mother for losing her 'ancient courage', reminds her that 'My hazards still have been your solace', and promises, 'I'll do well yet' (21). His reference to himself as

> Like to a lonely dragon, that his fen
> Makes fear'd and talk'd of more than seen,

may be a reminiscence of the voice which afflicted the evil Marius, saying

A Lyons very denne is dreadfull to behold
Though he himselfe be gone abroade, and be not therein hold.[1]

She begs him not to drift, little knowing what course he will

[1] Wyndham, III, p. 222.

soon pursue (33–7). He says goodbye to Menenius and Cominius and goes off, probably jeered at by the mob which has been sent by Sicinius to 'see him out' (III.1.135–8) (compare IV.5.82–3 'whoop'd out of Rome').

There follows a scene of railing in which, as the tribunes withdraw from the gate where they have watched the exile's departure, they meet his mother and wife. Volumnia vents her rage on them, and even Virgilia joins in, but the mother chides her for weeping and glories in her own fury ('Anger's my meat', 50–3).

In a not entirely necessary scene (IV.3), intended to bridge the few days during which in Plutarch Marcius was in a turmoil of indecision and choler [*inf.* 526], a dissident Roman and a Volsce discuss the implications of Coriolanus' banishment. In Rome the patricians may go so far as to destroy the tribunes. In Antium Tullus Aufidius, who is ready for a new war, will welcome the news.

The news however is brought by Coriolanus himself, who in IV.4 has reached Aufidius' house in disguise, soliloquizes on the effects of his action—dividing friends and making enemies into allies, and is doubtful of his reception. In IV.5 he enters the house, but whereas in Plutarch his majestic looks and silence awe the servants [*inf.* 527], in Shakespeare he bandies words with them[1] and is 'beaten like a dog' before Aufidius comes and he can reveal himself. His explanatory speech (IV.5.70–106) follows North's prose [*inf.* 527–8] more closely than does any other in the play. It is frank, manly, without subservience, and perhaps the only surprising thing about it is that Marcius includes the 'dastard nobles, who / Have all

[1] The name Cotus given to one of them has caused speculation, since it belongs in the classics only to princes of Thrace. 'Where did Shakespeare find it?' asks the *Camb.* editor. Almost certainly in the *Life of Agesilaus* (Plutarch's parallel to Pompey) who himself acted like Coriolanus when he allied himself with the Egyptians and then went over to their enemies. Agesilaus married his ally Cotys, King of Paphlagonia, to the daughter of another ally, Spithridates, who had changed sides in the war. A sentence or two later Plutarch relates that Spithridates changed sides again, being angered by the petty enquiries made about the plunder with which his soldiers had enriched themselves. So Spithridates too was a minor Coriolanus. Probably when turning over the pages of North in search of a name, Shakespeare's eye fell on this passage and he lifted the name from it. Having based Gloucester in *Lear* on Sidney's blind King of Paphlagonia, Shakespeare was no doubt attracted by the reference.

forsook me' in his indictment. Dionysius of Halicarnassus makes much clearer than Plutarch the divided opinions in the Senate, and the likelihood that Coriolanus would have been surrendered to the plebeians had he not agreed to stand his trial. The positive turn given to the conclusion of the speech

> And cannot live but to thy shame, unless
> It be to do thee service (105–6)

(cf. Plutarch's 'and whose service now can nothing helpe nor pleasure thee') is natural enough, but may have been suggested by some words spoken in the *Life of Agesilaus*, by Lysander, who when the former, offended by his popularity, appointed him his meat-carver to humiliate him, said 'I desire only that you will assign me some office and place in which I may serve you without incurring your displeasure'. Shakespeare's exiled Coriolanus is soon to be envied by Aufidius just as Lysander was by Agesilaus.

Shakespeare greatly expands Tullus' brief reply, increasing his expressions of friendship and delight and making him admit ungrudgingly, 'Thou hast beat me out / Twelve several times', and offering him half his army (106–52). 'So he feasted him for that time', wrote North; Shakespeare ends the scene with servants' talk about the Volscian reception of Coriolanus, the diminution of Aufidius' stature likely to result ('our general is cut i' the middle' etc.), and the resolve to make immediate war. Compare Plutarch, 'within a fewe days after, they fell to consultation together, in what sorte they should beginne their warres'. Speed in action is characteristic of Coriolanus as Shakespeare depicts him.

Both source and play now move back to Rome (IV.6). According to Plutarch, the city was 'in marvellous uprore, and discord' and perturbed by 'sightes and wonders in the ayer'. Moreover Jupiter was angry because his rites had been profaned by the whipping of a slave, thus necessitating a repetition of the ceremonies [*inf.* 528]. This time of national dismay afforded a good opportunity for an attack by Tullus and Coriolanus, who also used as a pretext, and maybe actually instigated, the expulsion of all Volscians from Rome during the games. Plutarch's account is less clear and connected than that in Dionysius and Shakespeare does not use it, but moves straight to Marcius' unexpected invasion [*inf.* 531], preferring to present the Roman people as smugly self-complacent at ridding themselves of their enemy, and Coriolanus as a man of explosive energy, who would not seek insidious pretexts. So Sicinius and Brutus are complimenting themselves, taunting Menenius (who has to agree that 'Alls well'), and receiving the thanks of humble citizens, when news is brought that the Volsces 'with two several powers / Are enter'd in the Roman territories' (1–42). The tribunes' insistence that the slave be whipped and 'fore the people's eyes' (48, 61) comes no doubt from the whipping (for purely private reasons) of the slave in Plutarch. But his news is 'seconded' and the thought that Coriolanus has joined Aufidius makes the patricians round first on the tribunes and then on the fearful citizens, though the gentle Menenius accepts a measure of blame

> We loved him; but like beasts,
> And cowardly nobles, gave way unto your clusters,
> Who did hoot him out o' the city. (122–4)

From the hatred and fear of the Romans we move to the Volscian camp near Rome where Aufidius' attitude has changed. Jealous of Marcius' popularity he accuses him of pride, and hints that he is not playing fair with the Volscian state (IV.7.1–26). What Coriolanus has left undone is not made clear. In Plutarch 'the first occasion of the Volsces' envy to Coriolanus' did not come until he gave the Roman ambassadors a thirty-day truce during which he moved his army out of their territory [*inf.* 534]. In Shakespeare this could not yet have happened. Aufidius notes Coriolanus' pride, his 'defect of judgment', his lack of adaptability, yet admits 'he has a merit / To choke it in the utterance'. And Aufidius touches on one of the roots of the tragedy when he adds 'our virtues / Lie in the interpretation of the time', and one force evokes another one to destroy it, 'Rights by rights falter, strengths by strengths do fail'. Marcius' noble qualities are their own undoing, and Aufidius will avenge himself once Rome is taken (IV.7.28–58). Shakespeare has reminded us that Aufidius' friendliness, sincere enough at the moment, was volatile and shortlived. His inveterate hatred has quickly returned.

V.1 broaches the embassies from Rome. In Plutarch these

were four in number: (1) Coriolanus' friends, to whom he granted thirty days respite (during which he withdrew from Rome but harried the towns of their allies); (2) 'another ambassade' to whom he gave three days' grace; (3) the priests, whom he flatly offered war or his conditions; (4) the women's embassy.

Shakespeare compresses greatly, omitting the third embassy altogether. He begins after the failure of the first mission, led by Cominius, who tells us nothing of the people's request that Marcius return home and have his goods restored to him, but describes his rigorous attitude, the small signs of recognition he made against his will, 'his injury / The gaoler to his pity'. Menenius is with difficulty persuaded by the tribunes to try to move him, but Cominius fears that the only chance is through 'his noble mother and his wife'. There is no mention of the thirty days' respite or the specific terms he offered [*inf.* 534]. Only 'what he would do, / He sent in writing after me' etc. (68–9). Since Cominius goes off to entreat Volumnia to help them, the next two scenes follow in rapid succession.

In V.2 the good old Menenius is being turned back by the Volscian guards, despite his protestations of friendship with Coriolanus, when the latter enters, accompanied by Aufidius, and rejects not only Menenius but his own family: 'Wife, mother, child, I know not' (80). Even so he gives Menenius a paper containing the terms (unspecified) which the Romans have already refused.

Shortly afterwards (V.3) he has just told Aufidius (who admires his constancy) that he will hear no more embassies 'Nor from the state, nor private friends, hereafter' (18) when the embassy of women arrives. This has been prepared for only by Cominius' remarks in V.1.71–5. Though Valeria is there, her part in initiating the mission is ignored and what might have been a fine scene [cf. *inf.* 537] is sacrificed to increase the force of this one.

In Plutarch Marcius leaves his chair of state and goes out to meet them, embracing first his mother, then his wife and little children. 'Nature' makes him weep as he yields 'to the affection of his blood'; yet he calls the Volscian chief to hear their interview. His mother does not kneel but makes her first plea. When she pauses he does not answer, so she starts again, this time appealing to his obligations as a son. Then all the suppliants fall on their knees, and Marcius, raising her up, gives way to her demands.

In Shakespeare the conflict in Marcius breaks as soon as he sees them (22–37), and though he cries 'Let it be virtuous to be obstinate!' he melts and strives in vain to cast off the claims of instinct. He kisses his wife first, and even before doing so says, 'Best of my flesh, / Forgive my tyranny' (43). He kneels dutifully to his mother. She blesses him, then kneels to him, and this shocks him into images of nature overturned. (In Dionysius the Volscians turned their heads away at sight of this monstrous occurrence.) Volumnia points to Valeria (whom he greets warmly) and his son (for whom he invokes martial 'nobleness'). When his mother broaches her mission he already recognizes that he is in the wrong:

> tell me not
> Wherein I seem unnatural: desire not
> To allay my rages and revenges with
> Your colder reasons. (78–86)

He calls the Volscian chief to hear what she has to say. Her long appeals follow North closely, developing the ideas of 'nature' and 'nobility' found there, with special reference to his twofold duty to country and family.[1] Shakespeare's Volumnia pauses twice, first at a natural climax when she declares that to destroy Rome he must first tread on his mother's womb (124). Virgilia and the boy support her, and Coriolanus is so moved that he rises to end the interview. But Volumnia will not let him go. She tells him what she wants: reconciliation and peace. She pauses briefly again (153) at the pause in North, and when he says nothing, speaks more angrily, urging her claims as a mother. When she and the others kneel again it is to shame him (169); then they rise in bleak despair. But she has won. Coriolanus ends the 'unnatural scene' by yielding, though he warns her of its evil consequences for him, and Aufidius calls it a victory of mercy over honour which he himself will use against Coriolanus. When Coriolanus tells the ladies that they 'deserve to have a temple built' to them (206–7) he is referring

[1] Cf. Hermann Heuer's paper, 'From Plutarch to Shakespeare: A Study of Coriolanus', in *Sh. Survey*, 10, 1957, 50–9.

to the fact that the Romans built 'a temple of Fortune of the women' in which miracles happened [*inf.* 541].

V.4 represents the fear in which Rome stood, the city's joy on hearing of the ladies' success, and the welcome given to them. A Senator (67–8) is still looking forward to the recall of Marcius. Meanwhile (V.5) in Antium Tullus Aufidius is preparing to remove the man who has betrayed his hospitality. He lays bare to some of his sympathizers his several grudges and they agree to help him kill Coriolanus. The latter, who was got with such difficulty to explain his actions to the Romans, is now humble and 'Intends to appear before the people, hoping / To purge himself with words' (7–8). In Plutarch he is willing to surrender his generalship if the Volscian lords require it, and 'to geve up an accompt unto the people'. A 'common counsaill' is called and he is accused by orators, but when he rises to answer he is killed by Tullus' conspirators. In Shakespeare he enters claiming to have got peace with honour, and bearing the treaty signed by the Romans. Aufidius at once calls him a traitor, and this excites Marcius (as it did in III.3.65ff). Charged with stealing his name 'Coriolanus', betraying his trust 'for certain drops of salt', and not consulting the Council of War (88–100) he appeals to the lords and then bursts out with a reminder how 'like an eagle in a dove-cote, I / Flutter'd your Volscians in Corioli' (114–17). At this the Volscians are enraged and the conspirators, led by Aufidius, kill him. The exultant Aufidius treads on his body and is rebuked by the lords, who did not desire this end. Aufidius apologizes for what he calls an act of rage, and now that his enemy is dead will mourn and admit Coriolanus' greatness. So the end comes suddenly but inevitably.

In working over Plutarch's story Shakespeare concentrated the material so as to focus our attention mainly on Coriolanus and the personal relations of the other characters with him, frequently keeping close to North's language, especially in the more formal speeches, and at times perpetuating his (or Amyot's) errors (as in the booty offered to Marcius at I.9.31)—yet transmuting prose into poetry by infusing it with dramatic tension. The characters were delineated more firmly and with significant detail. By introducing incidents and conversations not in the source he made Volumnia's character and her part in her son's life more decisive, and he gave personality to Virgilia and significance to young Marcius, a young savage adored by his womenfolk as his father had been.[1] Titus Lartius, Cominius, Menenius and Aufidius are also portrayed more fully than in the original. The interweaving of persons who appear only briefly in Plutarch but recur in the play is one of Shakespeare's unifying devices. The total effect is to make *Coriolanus* the most economical and closely designed of all Shakespeare's plays, the history-play with least 'surplusage', the most intense from start to finish, structurally one of his finest achievements.

It is a harsh play filled with rawness of life, rancour and class-struggle (as early Rome was in the chronicles), but the surges of rhetoric and violent action are balanced so as to keep us detached from the partisans on both sides. Plebeian follies and tribunes' intrigues are shown as such, and we are not expected to give ourselves up to Marcius either.

'The theme of the play [writes Professor Enright] . . . is . . . the dangers that are often implied in the word "political"—the dangers of a situation in which each opposing side understands the other (in the way that Coriolanus is right about the plebeians, and the plebeians are right about Coriolanus) but neither side understands itself.'[2] This is broadly true, but each side has some right which the other fails to appreciate. The tragedy of Coriolanus is that, being a blunt soldier, accustomed to command, reared in a notion of honour as austere as Cato's, he blunders into politics where his inability to temporize, to play the hypocrite, even to accept sincere praise graciously, his lack of Henry V's affability, are made manifest, to the ruin of his career, the exacerbation of his violent traits, until the glorious patriot becomes a traitor.

In the end however Coriolanus enlists more sympathy than Macbeth at *his* end,[3] because there is no perfunctory writing here as in that play, and Marcius, unlike Macbeth (who degenerates into an animal), proves that he shares our common

[1] Cf. the butterfly episode (I.3.58–67). The image of 'boys pursuing summer butterflies' recurs in IV.6.95 when Cominius taunts the tribunes with their helplessness against Coriolanus' cruelty.

[2] D. J. Enright, 'Coriolanus', in *The Apothecary's Shop*, 1957, p. 51.

[3] D. A. Traversi, 'Coriolanus', *Scrutiny*, June 1937.

human kindness. He meets death, not fearful like Hardy's hero, but like the fire-eater he has always been, publicly accused as before in Rome, but now by Rome's enemies (again become his own enemies), led by Aufidius' assassins. As the repeated patterns help us to realize, this is a play of poetic justice. Irascible Marcius has lived and irascible he dies, as the taunt of 'Boy!' sweeps away his effort at moderation, and he dares the Volscians to do their worst.

The final effect in us is a balanced judgement, moral and intellectual rather than passionate, for the paradoxes of the hero's character are seen to cohere in a credible personality which excites admiration and dislike, disapproval and pity without engaging us as totally as do Hamlet, Lear and Othello.

I. Probable Source

THE ROMANE HISTORIE OF T. LIVY

translated by Philemon Holland (1600)

The Romane Historie written by T. Livius of Padua. Also, the Breviaries of L. Florus: with a Chronologie to the whole Historie: and the Topographie of Rome in old time. Translated out of Latine into English, by Philemon Holland, Doctor in Physicke. London Printed by Adam Islip 1600.

From The Second Book

[P. Valerius resigned the Dictatorship in protest against the state's failure to put down bankers and usurers. To avoid spreading discontent by disbanding the army, the Consuls ordered the legions to march against the Aequians.]

This hastened the sedition the sooner & set it forward. At first, as men said, they complotted and laid their heads together about murdering and making awaie the Consuls, to the end they might be acquit of their oth unto them: but afterwards being better schooled and advised, that no mans conscience can be clered of scruple, & discharged of an oth once taken, by committing a sinfull act and working mischiefe, they withdrew themselves out of the way by the persuasion of one *Sicinius*, and without *congé* of the Consuls, departed as farre as mount Sacer, on the farther side of the river Anio, three miles from the citie.[1] This is the rifer report, and goeth more currant, than that whereof *Piso* is the author (namelie, that the commons retired themselves to Aventine.) There, without anie head or captaine, they encamped and fortified themselves within a trench and rampiar, and kept quiet for certaine daies, neither taking nor doing harme; as having caried with them such things onelie as were necessarie for the sustenance of their life. Great feare there was in the

[1] *In margin:* 'The first revolt of the commons of Rome into mount Sacer.'

citie, and in this mutuall and reciprocall feare, all men were perplexed and to seeke what to doe. The commons forlorne of their fellow commoners doubted the violence of the Senatours: the Senatours againe stood in feare and jelousie of the commons that remained stil behind; and were in suspense whither it were better they abode still among them, or followed after their fellowes. For how long trow ye, will a multitude once disbanded, rest in quiet? Againe, in case any forrain warre should arise in the meane time, what might ensue therupon in the end? In conclusion, there was no hope behind to be looked for, but in the concord of citizens: and therfore the commons one way or other, either by reasonable conditions or unreasonable, were to be reconciled again and reduced into the citie, there was no remedie. So it was thought good and agreed upon, that one *Menenius Agrippa* (a faire spoken and eloquent man, gratious withall and welbeloved among the commons, for that he was from them descended) should be sent as an Orator to treat with them. Who being received into the campe, after that old and harsh kind of eloquence in those daies, spake as men saith to this effect, and told this tale and parable[1]: Whilome (quoth he) when as in mans bodie, all the parts therof agreed not, as now they do in one, but ech member had a several intent & meaning, yea and a speech by it selfe: so it befel, that all other parts besides the belly, thought much & repined that by their carefulnes, labor, & ministerie, all was gotten, & yet all little enough to serve it: and the bellie it selfe lying still in the mids of them,[2] did nothing else but enjoy the delightsome pleasures brought unto her. Wherupon they mutined & conspired altogether in this wise, That neither the hands should reach & convey food into the mouth, nor the mouth receive it as it came, ne yet the teeth grind & chew the same. In this mood & fit, whiles they were minded to famish the poore bellie, behold the other lims, yea & the whole bodie besides, pined, wasted, & fel into an extreme consumption. Then was it wel seen, that even the very belly also did no smal service, but fed the other parts, as it received food it selfe: seeing that by working and concocting the meat throughlie, it digesteth and distributeth by the veines into all parts, that fresh and perfect blood whereby we live, we like, and have our full strength.[3] Comparing herewith, and making his application, to wit, how like this intestine and inward sedition of the bodie, was to the full stomacke of the commons, which they had taken and borne against the Senatours, he turned quite the peoples hearts.

[1] *In margin:* 'Agr. Menenius his Oration to the commons.' For other versions see Text IV.

[2] Cf. I.1.99.

[3] Cf. I.1.135–41.

Then began some treatie of unitie and concord: and among other articles it was conditioned and granted, that the Communaltie should have certaine sacred and inviolable magistrates of their owne among themselves, such as might have power to assist the Commons against the Consuls: *Item*, that it might not bee lawfull for any Senatour to beare that office. So there were created two Tribunes of the commons, *C. Licinius* and *L. Albinus*.[1] And these elected three other fellow officers unto them. Of whom *Sicinius*, the author of the sedition or insurrection was one, who were the other twaine is not for certaine knowne. Some say there were but two Tribunes created and no more in the mount Sacer, and that the sacred law was there made concerning their immunitie.

During this insurrection and revolt of the commons, *Sp. Cassius* & *Posthumius Cominius* entered their Consulships. In whose time a league was made with the people of Latium. For the establishing wherof, one of the Consuls staied behinde at Rome: the other was sent unto the Volscian warre, who discomfited and put to flight the Volscians of Antium, chafing and driving them into the towne Longula, which he wonne. And immediatlie he tooke Mucamites a towne of the Volscians, and after that with great force assaulted Corioli.

There was in campe, then among the flowre of gallant youths, one *Caius Martius*, a Noble yoong gentleman, right politicke of advise, active besides, and tall of his hands, who afterwards was surnamed *Coriolanus*. Whiles the Romane armie lay at siege before Corioli, and were amuzed whollie upon the townsmen within, whom they kept fast shut up, and feared no present danger at all from anie forraine warre without: behold, all on a suddaine, the Volscian legions that came from Antium, assailed them: at which verie instant the enemie also sallied out of the towne. Which *Martius* seeing, who by good hap quartered and warded there, with a lustie band of elect men, not onely repressed and stopped the violence of those that issued and brake upon him, but also whiles the gate stood open, fiercely rushed in himselfe: and having made a foule slaughter of people thereby, at his first entrance into the cittie, and caught up fire at a venture, flung it upon the houses that stood upon and about the wals. Whereupon arose a great outcrie of the folke within the towne, together with lamentable weeping and wailing of women and children, as commonly is seene in such a fright. Which at the very first, both hardened the Romanes, and also troubled the Volscians: and no marvell, seeing the citie taken before their face, for which they were come to rescue. Thus were the Volscians

[1] *In margin:* 'Tribunes of the common people first created.'

of Antium defeited, and the town Corioli won.[1] And *Martius* through his praise, so much obscured and stopped the light of the Consull his fame, that had it not been ingraven in brasse for a remembrance and monument, That there was a league with the Latines, and the same made by *Sp. Cassius* alone (for that his companion was absent) there had been no record at all, but forgotten quite it had been, that ever *Sp. Cominius* warred with the Volscians.

The same yeare died *Menenius Agrippa*, a man all his life time before beloved indifferently of the Senatours and the Commons: but after the insurrection, much more deere unto the Commons than before. This truchman, this mediator for civile attonement, this Embassadour and messenger from the Senatours to the commons, this reconciler and reducer of the commons home againe into the cittie, had not at his death sufficient to defray the charges of his funerals[2]: the commons therefore made a purse and a contribution of a Sextant[3] by the poll, and were at the cost to interre and burie him worshipfully.

After this were made Consuls, *T. Geganius*, and *P. Minutius*. In which yeare when all was quiet abroad for any warre, and the dissention at home healed up cleane, and skinned: another calamitie farre more greevous entred the cittie. First a dearth of corne, and all manner of victuals, by reason that the grounds upon the departure of the commons were forelet and untilled. Hereupon insued famine, even such as usually is incident to men besieged. And verily the meinie of bondservants, yea and the commons too, had utterly perished for hunger, if the Consuls had not in time made the better provision: by sending purveiours all abroad to buy up corne, not only into Hetruria, by coasting along the river on the right hand from Hostia, and on the left hand by sea, (passing through the Volscians countrie) even as far as Cumes: but also into Sicilie, there to lay for graine. Such was the hatred of the borderers, that Rome was enforced to have need of succour and releefe from afarre. Now when they had bought certain corne at Cumes, it was no sooner embarked, but the ships were staied and arrested there, by *Aristodemus* the tyrant, for the goods of the *Tarquines*, whose heire in remainder he was. In The Volscian country and Pomptinum, they could buy none for mony. There, the very Purveiors themselves were in danger of violence, by the men of the countrey. Out of Tuscane there came corne up the Tyber, wherewith the commons were sustained and refreshed. And considering the streights they

[1] *In margin:* 'Corioli forced.'

[2] *In margin:* 'The death of Menenius Agrippa, and his povertie.' *Truchmar,* interpreter.

[3] *In margin:* 'The sixt part of As, halfe a farthing or cue with us.'

were in for want of victuals, they had been sore distressed and vexed with warres besides, and that in a very ill time, and unseasonable for them: but that the Volscians, who were now in readinesse, and upon the point to make warre, had a pestilence that raigned hote among them. Which heavie crosse and affliction, the enemies were so discouraged with, that when the plague began to stay, even then they continued still afraid.

The Romanes both at Velitree augmented the number of the inhabitants, and also at Norba, sending a new Colonie into the mountaines, to be a fortresse and strength for all the territorie of Pomptinum. Moreover, when *M. Minutius*, and *A. Sempronius* were Consuls, great store of corne was brought out of Sicilie: and it was debated in the Senate house, at what price the commons should be served therewith. Many thought the time was now come to wring the commons, and keep them under, and to recover againe those roialties, which by their departure were forcibly wrested and dismembred from the nobilitie. But above all others *Martius Coriolanus*, an utter and capitall enemie to the Tribunes power and authoritie,[1] 'If they will (quoth hee) have their corne and victuals at the old price, let them restore unto the Senatours their auncient right and preheminence. Why see I (as one brought under the yoke of servitude, and put as it were unto my ransome, by robbers and theeves) these Magistrates of the Commons? why see I *Sicinius* so mightie? Shall I endure these indignities longer than I needs must? I that could not beare *Tarquinius* to bee King, shall I brooke and suffer *Sicinius*? Let him depart aside now, and take his commons with him: the way is open to mount Sacer and other hils: let them carrie away with them the corne out of our possessions and Lordships, as they did three yeares ago: let them enjoy, take for their use, and spend the store, which they in their foolerie and furie have provided. I dare be bold to say, that when they are by this calamitie once tamed, they will rather till and husband the ground themselves, than with weapon in hand, and by way of insurrection, forbid and hinder the tillage thereof.' I cannot so soone say, whether it had beene as meete, as I suppose it was possible and easie to effect, that the Senators by offering more gentle conditions in the prices of corne and victualles, might have eased themselves of the Tribunes authoritie over them, and also have beene disburdened of those impositions which maugre their heads, were laide upon them. Well, this seemed to the Senate a sharpe censure and severe sentence of *Coriolanus*, and for verie anger also it had like to have caused the Commons to rise up in armes. For they muttered and gave it out

[1] *In margin:* 'Coriolanus enveieth against the Tribunes.'

in these tearmes,[1] 'That now they were laide at and assailed with famine like enemies, defrauded and bereft of their meat and pittance: that the outlandish corne, the onely sustenance and food which fortune had ministred unto them beyond all hope, was snatched and plucked from their mouths, unlesse the Tribunes be delivered & yeelded prisoners hand and foot bound to *C. Martius*, unlesse he might have his penniworths of the backe and shoulders of the commons of Rome, For he was now start up & become their tormentor and hangman, to command them either to death, or to servitude." As he went out of the counsell house, they had run upon him with violence, but that the Tribunes, as good lucke was, served him with processe in time, to appeare at a day, and come to his answer. Herewith, their furious anger was suppressed. For now everie man saw, that he was himselfe to be the judge and lord of his enemies life and death. *Martius* at the first scorned the Tribunes thundering threats, & gave the hearing, as though he made final reckoning therof, saying, That their authoritie had power granted by limitation, only to aid, and not to punish: that the Tribunes were Tribunes to the commons, and not to the Senators. But so spightfully were the Commons bent, and all so set upon mischeef, that there was no other remedie, but one man must pay for it, to save and excuse the rest of the Nobles. Howbeit, the Senatours did what they could to withstand them: by opposing hatred and displeasure againe, and making all meanes, what either privately they were able of themselves, or jointly by their whole Order and degree, to procure. And first, this course they assaied to stop and overthrow the suite commensed; namelie, by setting their followers and retainers in sundrie places to deale with the commons severallie one by one, and what they could to affright them from meetings and assemblies together. Afterwards, they came all forth at once into the *Forum* or common place. A man that had seene them would have said they had beene the parties themselves in trouble and accused, readie to hold up their hand at the barre: such praying, such a beseeching they made of the commons, in the behalfe of this one citizen, this onelie Senatour; that if they would not in their love acquit him for their sakes, as innocent and unguiltie, yet they would give him unto them as an offender and faultie person. In conclusion, when his daie came, he made default and appeared not, yet continued they still in their angrie mood against him. And being condemned in his absence, for contumacie, departed into banishment to the Volscians, menacing his own countrie as he went, and carying even then with him the revenging stomacke of an enemie.

[1] *In margin:* 'The murmuring of the commons against Coriolanus.'

The Volscians at his comming received him courteouslie, and friendlie intreated him everie daie more than other, as they perceived his anger more and more toward his countriemen, by many complaints he made of them, & threats withall that he eftsoones gave out against them in their hearing. He made his abode and sojourned in the house of *Accius Tullus*. Who at that time was a mightie great man among the Volscians, and one that ever bare mortall mallice unto the Romanes. And whiles the one of them was provoked with an old cancred grudge, and the other set on and pricked forward upon a fresh quarrell and occasion of anger, they both laid their heads together and complotted to make warre upon the Romanes. This onelie thing stood in their waie to crosse their designes: They thought verilie their Commons would hardlie or uneth at all be brought, to rise and take armes againe, which they had so often unhappilie attempted: And besides, their courages were well cooled, ad their stomacks abated, by the losse of their youth in manie and sundrie warres often times afore, and now at last, by the late pestilence and mortalitie. They were therfore to go cunninglie to worke; that for as much as the old hatred against the Romanes was growne out and worne away, their hearts upon some new anger might be chaufed and galled againe. . . .

[Accius Tullius and Coriolanus won the people to renew war by having the Volscians driven out from Rome during the Games.]

To mannage this war, were chosen Generall commaunders by one consent of all the citties, *Accius Tullius*, and *Cn. Martius* the banished Romane: in whome of the twaine they reposed greater hope, and this their hope failed them not. So as it soone appeared that the puissance of the state of Rome, consisted more in the dexteritie of good captaines, than in strong armies of souldiours. For first he went to Circeios,[1] from whence he expelled the Romane Coloners, and delivered the cittie cleere and free unto the Volscians. Then by crosse waies he passed into the Latine streete, called *Via Latina*: and regained from the Romanes, these their townes newly gotten afore, Satricum, Longula, Pollustia & Corioli. After this he wan Lanuvium againe, & so forward he forced Corbio,[2] Vitelia, Trebia, Labicos, and Pedum. And last of all from Pedum, he marched on toward the cittie of Rome, and at Cluiliæ Fossæ, five miles off, he encamped and forraied the territorie about, sending with the forreiars certaine guides, to keepe them from spoyling and doing harme in the Noblemens lands: were it that he were more spightfull to the Commons, or that thereby some discord might arise, between the

[1] *In margin:* 'Monte Circello.'

[2] *In margin:* 'Civita indovina vique.'

Comminaltie and the Senatours: which doubtlesse had soone growne, so mightily had the Tribunes alreadie by their complaints and accusations, provoked the Commons forward, (who of themselves were shrewd inough) against the heads and magistrates of the cittie, but that the feare of forraine dangers, the greatest bond of civile concord that can be, held them in and knit their hearts togither, were they never so jealous, suspected, and hatefull afore one to the other.[1] Herein onely was all their difference, that the Senate and Consuls, reposed hope in nothing else save onely in warre: the commons on the other side were desirous of any thing whatsoever, but warre.

Now were *S. Nautius*, and *Sex. Furius* Consuls: who as they were surveying and mustering the legions, and disposing of a good *Corpus de guard* upon the walls, and other places wherein they thought it expedient to keep a standing watch and ward: behold a mightie number called and cried hard for peace, & with their sedicious clamors, put them in exceeding feare: yea & afterwards, forced them to assemble the Senatehouse together, and to propose concerning the sending of certaine embassadors to *Cn. Martius*. The Lords of the Senate seeing evidently the commons hearts to faile them, accepted and granted the motion propounded. Whereupon were Oratours sent unto *Martius* to treate for peace. At whose hands they received this heavie and stout answere[2]: 'If so be the Volscians had their lands restored to them againe, then there might be some parle and treatie of peace: but if they will needs at their pleasure still enjoy that bootie which by war they have gotten, then would he in remembrance of private wrongs done unto him by his countrimen, as also of the friendship and courtesie shewed him by strangers that had given him entertainement, do his best to make it knowne unto the world, that his courage and stomacke is incensed, and not abated and quailed by his banishment.' Then were the same Embassadors sent againe the second time, but they might not be admitted once to set foote within the campe. It is reported moreover that the verie priests in their *Pontificalibus*, in their rich vestiments and goodly ornaments, went with supplication to the tents of the enemies, and turned his heart no more than the embassadors had done before them. Then the dames of the cittie came flocking all about *Veturia* the mother, and *Volumnia* the wife of *Coriolanus*. Whether this proceeded from any publike counsell and was done in pollicie, or came onely of womens feare, I find but little in any records. But howsoever it came about, this one thing is certaine,

[1] *In margin:* 'Coriolanus beseegeth Rome.'
[2] *In margin:* 'The answere of Coriolanus to the Romane Orators.'

they persuaded so effectually with them, that both *Veturia* an aged woman, and also *Volumnia* with her two little sonnes that she had by *Martius*, went toward the enemies campe, to see if women by their praiers and teares, might save the cittie, which men with speare and shield could not defend. When they were come into the camp, & word brought to *Coriolanus*, that there was an exceeding great traine of women thither arrived: at the first, he, as one that had relented, neither for that publike majestie in the Embassadours, nor yet at the religious reverence, which he both conceived in mind, & saw with his eies in the clergie, stood much more stifly bent against the teares of seely women. But afterwards one of his familiar friends, who had seen and knowne *Veturia* there, mourning and bewailing exceedingly above the rest, as she stood betwixt her daughter in law and her little nephewes: 'If mine eies be matches (quoth hee) and deceive me not, here is your mother, your wife, and children.' Whereat, *Coriolanus*, faring like a man well neare beside himselfe, arose from his seate, and ran to meete his mother, and to embrace her. But the woman falling in steede of praiers into a fit of choller: 'Let me know (quoth she)[1] before I suffer thee to embrace me, whether I am come to an enemie or to a sonne, whether I be in thy campe as a captive prisoner, or as a naturall mother. And have I lived indeede so long, and rubbed on still in this miserable old age of mine for this, to see thee first a banished man, and after that to become an enemie? Couldest thou finde in thine heart to waste and spoyle that countrey which bred thee, which fostered thee, and brought thee up? And be it that thou hither marched with a cruell intent and full of threats, would not thine anger and fell mood slake, when thou didst set foote within the borders and marches therof? And being come within the sight of Rome, arose not this in thy mind & thought, Within those wals yonder is my house, there are my house goods, my mother, my wife, my children? Why then, belike if I had never been a mother, and borne a child, Rome had not been assaulted. And if I had no sonne at all, I might have died well ynough in my native countrey, whiles it remained free. But as for me, neither can I suffer ought, more for thy dishonestie and shame; nor more to mine owne calamitie and miserie than this: and most wretched caitife though I be, yet long time so I cannot continue. But for these here, looke thou well to it, I advise thee, and have pittie of them, who if thou goe on as thou beginnest, are like to feele untimely death, or indure long captivitie.' Then his wife and children hung about him, and clipped him: whereat the women fell a weeping on all sides, bewailing their owne

[1] *In margin:* 'The speech of Veturia unto her sonne Martius Coriolanus.'

case and the state of their countrey. So as at length the man was overcome. And after he had taken them in his armes likewise, he let them goe: and himselfe dislodged and removed his campe backeward from the cittie. When he had withdrawne the legions out of the territorie of Rome, he gat himselfe, men said, such hatred and displeasure for this action, that it cost him his life; and murdered he was, some report one way, some another. But I find in *Fabius* a most ancient writer, that he lived untill he was an old man: who reporteth this of him: That oftentimes in his latter daies he used to utter this speech, *A heavie case and most wretched, for an aged man to live banisht.* The men of Rome envied not those women their due deserved praises. So devoid was the world in those daies, of depraving and detracting the glorie of others. For in memoriall hereof to all posteritie, there was a temple built and dedicated to *Fortuna Muliebris.* i.e. Womens fortune.[1]

II. Source

PLUTARCH'S LIVES OF THE NOBLE GRECIANS AND ROMANES

translated by Sir Thomas North (1579)

THE LIFE OF CAIUS MARTIUS CORIOLANUS

The house of the Martians at Rome was of the number of the Patricians, out of the which hath sprong many noble personages: whereof Ancus Martius was one, king Numaes daughters sonne, who was the king of Rome after Tullus Hostilius.[2] Of the same house were Publius, and Quintus, who brought Rome their best water they had by conducts.[3] Censorinus also came of that familie, that was so surnamed, bicause the people had chosen him Censor twise.[4] Through whose persuasion they made a law, that no man from thenceforth might or enjoyerequire, the Censorshippe twise.[5] Caius Martius, whose life we intend now to write, being left an orphan by his father, was brought up under his mother a widowe, who taught us by experience, that orphanage bringeth many discommodities to

[1] *In margin:* 'Fortuna Muliebris.'

[2] *In margin:* 'The familie of the Martians.' II.3.240–8.

[3] *In margin:* 'Publius and Quintus Martius, brought the water by conducts to Rome.' II.3.244–5.

[4] II.3.245–7.

[5] *In margin:* 'Censorinus lawe.'

a childe, but doth not hinder him to become an honest man, and to excell in vertue above the common sorte: as they are meanely borne, wrongfully doe complayne, that it is the occasion of their casting awaye, for that no man in their youth taketh any care of them to see them well brought up, and taught that were meete. This man also is a good proofe to confirme some mens opinions. That a rare and excellent witte untaught, doth bring forth many good and evill things together[1]: like as a fat soile bringeth forth herbes and weedes that lieth unmanured. For this Martius naturall wit and great harte dyd marvelously sturre up his corage, to doe and attempt noble actes. But on the other side for lacke of education,[2] he was so chollericke and impacient, that he would yeld to no living creature: which made him churlishe, uncivill, and altogether unfit for any mans conversation. Yet men marveling much at his constancy, that he was never overcome with pleasure, nor money, and howe he would endure easely all manner of paynes and travailles: thereupon they well liked and commended his stowtnes and temperancie. But for all that, they could not be acquainted with him, as one cittizen useth to be with another in the cittie. His behaviour was so unpleasaunt to them, by reason of a certaine insolent and sterne manner he had, which bicause it was to lordly, was disliked. And to saye truely, the greatest benefit that learning bringeth men unto, is this: that it teacheth men that be rude and rough of nature, by compasse and rule of reason, to be civill and curteous, and to like better the meane state, then the higher.[3] Now in those dayes, valliantnes was honoured in Rome above all other vertues: which they called *Virtus*, by the name of vertue selfe, as including in that generall name, all other speciall vertues besides.[4] So that *Virtus* in the Latin, was asmuche as valliantnes. But Martius being more inclined to the warres, then any other gentleman of his time: beganne from his Childehood to geve him self to handle weapons, and daylie dyd exercise him selfe therein.[5] And outward he esteemed armour to no purpose, unles one were naturally armed within. Moreover he dyd so exercise his bodie to hardnes, and all kynde of activitie, that he was very swift in ronning, strong in wrestling, and mightie in griping, so that no man could ever cast him. In so much as those that would trye masteries with him for strength and nimblenes, would saye when they were overcome: that all was by reason of his naturall strength, and hardnes of warde,

[1] *In margin:* 'Coriolanus wit.' [2] Cf. III.1.318–21.
[3] *In margin:* 'The benefit of learning.'
[4] *In margin:* 'What this worde Virtus signifieth.' Cf. I.1.39.
[5] Hence Volumnia, I.3.5ff.

that never yelded to any payne or toyle he tooke apon him. The first time he went to the warres, being but a strippling,[1] was when Tarquine surnamed the prowde (that had bene king of Rome, and was driven out for his pride, after many attemptes made by sundrie battells to come in againe, wherein he was ever overcome) dyd come to Rome with all the ayde of the Latines, and many other people of Italie: even as it were to set up his whole rest apon a battell by them, who with a great and mightie armie had undertaken to put him into his Kingdome againe, not so much to pleasure him, as to overthrowe the power of the Romaines, whose greatnes they both feared and envied. In this battell, wherein were many hotte and sharpe encounters of either partie, Martius valliantly fought in the sight of the Dictator[2]: and a Romaine souldier being throwen to the ground even hard by him, Martius straight bestrid him, and slue the enemie with his owne handes that had before overthrowen the Romaine.[3] Hereupon, after the battell was wonne, the Dictator dyd not forget so noble an acte, and therefore first of all he crowned Martius with a garland of oken boughs. For whosoever saveth the life a Romaine, it is a manner among them, to honour him with such a garland.[4] This was, either bicause the lawe dyd this honour to the oke, in favour of the Arcadians, who by the oracle of Apollo were in very olde time called eaters of akornes; or els bicause the souldiers might easely in every place come by oken boughes: or lastely, bicause they thought it very necessarie to geve him that had saved a cittizens life, a crowne of this tree to honour him, being properly dedicated unto Jupiter, the patron and protectour of their citties, and thought amongest other wilde trees to bring forth a profitable fruite, and of plantes to be the stongest,[5] Moreover, men at the first beginning dyd use akornes for their bread, and honie for their drincke: and further, the oke dyd feede their beastes, and geve them birdes, by taking glue from the okes, with the which they made birdlime to catche seely birdes. They saye that Castor, and Pollux, appeared in this battell, and how incontinently after the battell, men sawe them in the market place at Rome, all their horses being on a white fome: and they were the first that brought newes of the victorie, even in the same place, where remaineth at this present a temple built in the honour of them neere unto the fountaine. And this is the cause, why the daye of this victorie (which was the fiftenth of Julye) is consecrated yet to this daye unto Castor and Pollux. Moreover, it is daylie seene, that honour and reputation

[1] *In margin:* 'Coriolanus first going to the warres.' II.2.87–88.

[2] II.2.89–90.

[3] II.2.92–5 where he also fights Tarquin.

[4] *In margin:* 'Coriolanus crowned with a garland of oken boughes.' II.2.95–8.

[5] *In margin:* 'The goodnes of the oke.'

lighting on young men before their time, and before they have no great corage by nature: the desire to winne more, dieth straight in them, which easely happeneth, the same having no deepe roote in them before.[1] Where contrariwise, the first honour that valliant mindes doe come unto, doth quicken up their appetite, hasting them forward as with force of winde, to enterprise things of highe deserving praise. For they esteeme, not to receave reward for service done, but rather take it for a remembraunce and encoragement, to make them doe better in time to come: and be ashamed also to cast their honour at their heeles, not seeking to increase it still by like deserte of worthie valliant dedes. This desire being bred in Martius, he strained still to passe him selfe in manlines: and being desirous to shewe a daylie increase of his valliantnes, his noble service dyd still advaunce his fame, bringing in spoyles apon spoyles from the enemie.[2] Whereupon, the captaines that came afterwards (for envie of them that went before) dyd contend who should most honour him, and who should beare most honourable testimonie of his valliantnes. In so much the Romaines having many warres and battells in those dayes, Coriolanus was at them all: and there was not a battell fought, from whence he returned not without some rewarde of honour. And as for other, the only respect that made them valliant, was they hoped to have honour: but touching Martius, the only thing that made him to love honour, was the joye he sawe his mother dyd take of him.[3] For he thought nothing made him so happie and honorable, as that his mother might heare every bodie praise and commend him, that she might allwayes see him returne with a crowne upon his head, and that she might still embrace him with teares ronning downe her cheekes for joye.[4] Which desire they saye Epaminondas dyd avowe, and confesse to have bene in him: as to thinke him selfe a most happie and blessed man, that his father and mother in their life time had seene the victorie he wanne in the plaine of Leuctres.[5] Now as for Epaminondas, he had this good happe, to have his father and mother living, to be partakers of his joye and prosperitie. But Martius thinking all due to his mother, that had bene also due to his father if he had lived: dyd not only content him selfe to rejoyce and honour her, but at her desire tooke a wife also, by whom he had two children, and yet never left his mothers house therefore.[6] Now he being growen to great credit and

[1] *In margin:* 'To[o] soden honor in youth killeth further desier of fame.'

[2] *In margin:* 'Coriolanus noble endevour to continue well deserving.' II.2.98–101.

[3] Cf. I.1.37–8.

[4] I.3.15–17.

[5] *In margin:* 'Coriolanus and Epaminondas did both place their desire of honour alike.'

[6] *In margin:* 'The obedience of Coriolanus to his mother.'

authoritie in Rome for his valliantnes, it fortuned there grewe sedition in the cittie, bicause the Senate dyd favour the riche against the people, who dyd complaine of the sore oppression of userers, of whom they borowed money.[1] For those that had litle, were yet spoyled of that litle they had by their creditours, for lacke of abilitie to paye the userie: who offered their goodes to be solde, to them that would geve most. And suche as had nothing left, their bodies were layed holde of, and they were made their bonde men, notwithstanding all the woundes and cuttes they shewed, which they had receyved in many battells, fighting for defence of their countrie and common wealth[2]: of the which, the last warre they made, was against the Sabynes, wherein they fought apon the promise the riche men had made them, that from thenceforth they would intreate them more gently, and also upon the worde of Marcus Valerius chief of the Senate, who by authoritie of the counsell, and in the behalfe of the riche, sayed they should performe that they had promised.[3] But after that they had faithfully served in this last battell of all, where they overcame their enemies, seeing they were never a whit the better, nor more gently intreated, and that the Senate would geve no eare to them, but make as though they had forgotten their former promise, and suffered them to be made slaves and bonde men to their creditours, and besides, to be turned out of all that ever they had: they fell then even to flat rebellion and mutine, and to sturre up daungerous tumultes within the cittie.[4] The Romaines enemies hearing of this rebellion, dyd straight enter the territories of Rome with a marvelous great power, spoyling and burning all as they came.[5] Whereupon the Senate immediatly made open proclamation by sounde of trumpet, that all those which were of lawfull age to carie weapon, should come and enter their names into the muster masters booke, to goe to the warres: but no man obeyed their commaundement.[6] Whereupon their chief magistrates, and many of the Senate, beganne to be of divers opinions emong them selves. For some thought it was reason, they should somewhat yeld to the poore peoples request, and that they should a litle qualifie the severitie of the lawe. Other held hard against that opinion, and that was Martius for one. For he alleaged, that the creditours losing their money they had lent, was not the worst thing

[1] *In margin:* 'Extremitie of userers complained of at Rome by the people.' Cf. I.1.81–2.

[2] Yet Marcus repeatedly calls them cowards.

[3] *In margin:* 'Counsellers promises make men valliant, in hope of just performance.'

[4] *In margin:* 'Ingratitude, and good service unrewarded, provoketh rebellion.'

[5] I.2.17–25.

[6] Not in *Cor.*

that was thereby: but that the lenitie that was favored, was a beginning of disobedience, and that the prowde attempt of the communaltie, was to abolish lawe, and to bring all to confusion.[1] Therefore he sayed, if the Senate were wise, they should betimes prevent, and quenche this ill favored and worse ment beginning. The Senate met many dayes in consultation about it[2]: but in the end they concluded nothing. The poore common people seeing no redresse, gathered them selves one daye together, and one encoraging another, they all forsooke the cittie, and encamped them selves upon a hill, called at this daye the holy hill,[3] alongest the river of Tyber, offering no creature any hurte or violence, or making any shewe of actuall rebellion: saving that they cried as they went up and down, that the riche men had driven them out of the cittie, and that all Italie through they should fine ayer, water, and ground to burie them in. Moreover, they sayed, to dwell at Rome was nothing els but to be slaine, or hurte with continuall warres, and fighting for defence of the riche mens goodes. The Senate being afeard of their departure, dyd send unto them certaine of the pleasauntest olde men, and the most acceptable to the people among them.[4] Of those, Menenius Agrippa was he, who was sent for chief man of the message from the Senate. He, after many good persuasions and gentle requestes made to the people, on the behalfe of the Senate[5]: knit up his oration in the ende, with a notable tale, in this manner. That on a time all the members of mans bodie,[6] dyd rebell against the bellie, complaining of it, that it only remained in the middest of the bodie,[7] without doing any thing, neither dyd beare any labour to the maintenaunce of the rest: whereas all other partes and members dyd labour paynefully, and was very carefull to satisfie the appetites and desiers of the bodie.[8] And so the bellie, all this notwithstanding, laughed at their follie,[9] and sayed: It is true, I first receyve all meates that norishe mans bodie: but afterwardes I send it againe to the norishement of other partes of the same.[10] Even so (quoth he) O you, my masters, and cittizens of Rome: the reason is a like betweene the Senate, and you. For matters being well digested, and their counsells throughly examined, touching the benefit of the common wealth: the Senatours are cause of the common commodi-

[1] *In margin:* 'Martius Coriolanus against the people.' Cf. I.1.220–2.

[2] Hence I.1.57.

[3] *In margin:* 'The people leave the cittie and doe goe to the holy hill.' Ignored by Shakespeare.

[4] I.1.50–53.

[5] I.1.61–78.

[6] *In margin:* 'An excellent tale tolde by Menenius Agrippa to pacifie the people.' I.1.96–155. See *infra*, Text IV.

[7] I.1.99.

[8] I.1.100–105.

[9] I.1.108.

[10] I.1.131–41.

tie that commeth unto every one of you.[1] These persuasions pacified the people, conditionally, that the Senate would graunte there should be yerely chosen five magistrates, which they now call *Tribuni Plebis*, whose office should be to defend the poore people from violence and oppression.[2] So Junius Brutus, and Sicinius Vellutus, were the first Tribunes of the people that were chosen, who had only bene the causers and procurers of this sedition.[3] Hereupon the cittie being growen againe to good quiet and unitie, the people immediatly went to the warres, shewing that they had a good will to doe better then ever they dyd, and to be very willing to obey the magistrates in that they would commaund, concerning the warres. Martius also, though it liked him nothing to see the greatnes of the people thus increased, considering it was to the prejudice, and imbasing of the nobilitie,[4] and also sawe that other noble Patricians were troubled as well as him selfe: he dyd persuade the Patricians, to shew them selves no lesse forward and willing to fight for their countrie, then the common people were: and to let them knowe by their dedes and actes, that they dyd not so muche passe the people in power and riches, as they dyd exceede them in true nobilitie and valliantnes. In the countrie of the Volsces, against whom the Romaines made warre at that time, there was a principall cittie and of most fame, that was called Corioles, before the which the Consul Cominius dyd lay seige.[5] Wherefore all the other Volsces fearing least that cittie should be taken by assault, they came from all partes of the countrie to save it,[6] entending to geve the Romaines battell before the cittie, and to geve an onset on them in two severall places. The Consul Cominius understanding this, devided his armie also in two partes, and taking the one parte with him selfe, he marched towards them that were drawing to the cittie, out of the countrie[7]: and the other parte of his armie he left in the campe with Titus Lartius (one of the valliantest men the Romaines had at that time) to resist those that would make any salye out of the cittie apon them.[8] So the Coriolans making small accompt of them that laye in campe before the cittie, made a salye out apon them, in the which at the first the Coriolans had the better, and drave the Romaines backe againe into the trenches of their campe.[9] But Martius being

[1] I.1.149–55. [2] *In margin:* 'The first beginning of *Tribuni plebis*.'

[3] *In margin:* 'Junius Brutus, Sicinius Vellutus, the 2 first tribunes.' I.1.216–18. Vellutus should be Bellutus; Amyot's error.

[4] I.1.210–22.

[5] *In margin:* 'The cittie of Corioles besieged by the Consul Cominius.'

[6] I.2.27–9. [7] I.3.101–2.

[8] *In margin:* 'Titus Lartius, a valliant Romaine.' I.3.102–3.

[9] I.4.23,34–6.

there at that time, ronning out of the campe with a fewe men with him, he slue the first enemies he met withall, and made the rest of them staye upon a sodaine, crying out to the Romaines that had turned their backes, and calling them againe to fight with a lowde voyce.[1] For he was even such another, as Cato would have a souldier and a captaine to be: not only terrible, and fierce to laye about him, but to make the enemie afeard with the sounde of his voyce, and grimnes of his countenaunce.[2] Then there flocked about him immediatly, a great number of Romaines: whereat the enemies were so afeard, that they gave backe presently. But Martius not staying so, dyd chase and followe them to their owne gates, that fled for life. And there, perceyving that the Romaines retired backe, for the great number of dartes and arrowes which flewe about their eares from the walles of the cittie, and that there was not one man amongest them that durst venter him selfe to followe the flying enemies into the cittie, for that it was full of men of warre, very well armed, and appointed: he dyd encorage his fellowes with wordes and dedes, crying out to them, that fortune had opened the gates of the cittie, more for the followers, then the flyers.[3] But all this notwithstanding, fewe had the hartes to followe him. Howbeit Martius being in the throng emong the enemies, thrust him selfe into the gates of the cittie, and entred the same emong them that fled, without that any one of them durst at the first turne their face upon him, or els offer to staye him. But he looking about him, and seeing he was entred the cittie with very fewe men to helpe him, and perceyving he was environned by his enemies that gathered round about to set apon him[4]: dyd things then as it is written, wonderfull and incredible, aswell for the force of his hande, as also for the agillitie of his bodie, and with a wonderfull corage and valliantnes, he made a lane through the middest of them, and overthrewe also those he layed at: that some he made ronne to the furthest parte of the cittie, and other for feare he made yeld them selves, and to let fall their weapons before him. By this meanes, Lartius that was gotten out, had some leysure to bring the Romaines with more safety into the cittie.[5] The cittie being taken in this sorte, the most parte of the souldiers beganne incontinently to spoyle, to carie awaye, and to looke up the bootie they had wonne.[6] But Martius was marvelous angry with them, and cried out on them, that it was no time now to looke after spoyle, and to ronne straggling here and

[1] Abusive too in I.4.30–42.

[2] *In margin:* 'The propertie of a souldier.' The reference to Cato in I.4.56–61 is an anachronism since Cato died in 46 B.C.

[3] I.4.43–5. [4] I.4.46–56. [5] Cf. I.4.62–3.

[6] *In margin:* 'The cittie of Corioles taken.' I.5.1–3.

there to enriche them selves, whilest the other Consul and their fellowe cittizens peradventure were fighting with their enemies: and howe that leaving the spoyle they should seeke to winde them selves out of daunger and perill.[1] Howbeit, crie, and saye to them what he could, very fewe of them would hearken to him. Wherefore taking those that willingly offered them selves to followe him, he went out of the cittie, and tooke his waye towardes that parte, where he understoode the rest of the armie was: exhorting and intreating them by the waye that followed him, not to be fainte harted, and ofte holding up his handes to heaven, he besought the goddes to be so gracious and favorable unto him, that he might come in time to the battell, and in good hower to hazarde his life in defence of his country men. Now the Romaines when they were put in battell raye, and ready to take their targettes on their armes, and to guirde them upon their arming coates, had a custome to make their willes at that very instant, without any manner of writing, naming him only whom they would make their heire, in the presence of three or foure witnesses.[2] Martius came just to that reckoning, whilest the souldiers were a doing after that sorte, and that the enemies were approched so neere, as one stoode in viewe of the other. When they sawe him at his first comming, all bloody, and in a swet,[3] and but with a fewe men following him: some thereupon beganne to be afeard. But sone after, when they sawe him ronne with a lively cheere to the Consul and to take him by the hande, declaring howe he had taken the cittie of Corioles, and that they sawe the Consul Cominius also kisse and embrace him: then there was not a man but tooke harte againe to him, and beganne to be of a good corage, some hearing him reporte from poynte to poynte, the happy successe of this exployte, and other also conjecturing it by seeing their gestures a farre of. Then they all beganne to call upon the Consul to marche forward, and to delaye no lenger, but to geve charge upon the enemie.[4] Martius asked him howe the order of their enemies battell was, and on which side they had placed their best fighting men. The Consul made him aunswer, that he thought the bandes which were in the voward of their battell, were those of the Antiates, whom they esteemed to be the warlikest men, and which for valliant corage would geve no place, to any of the hoste of their enemies. Then prayed Martius, to be set directly against them.[5] The Consul graunted him, greatly praysing his corage. Then Martius, when both armies came almost to joyne, advaunced him

[1] I.5.4–14.
[2] *In margin:* 'Souldiers testaments.' Not in *Cor.*
[3] I.6.21–9.
[4] I.6.65–76.
[5] *In margin:* 'By Coriolanus meanes, the Volsci were overcome in battell.' I.6.51–62.

selfe a good space before his companie, and went so fiercely to geve charge on the voward that came right against him, that they could stande no lenger in his handes: he made suche a lane through them, and opened a passage into the battell of the enemies. But the two winges of either side turned one to the other, to compasse him in betweene them: which the Consul Cominius perceyving, he sent thither straight of the best souldiers he had about him.[1] So the battell was marvelous bloudie about Martius, and in a very shorte space many were slaine in the place. But in the ende the Romaines were so strong, that they distressed the enemies, and brake their arraye: and scattering them, made them flye. Then they prayed Martius that he would retire to the campe, bicause they sawe he was able to doe no more, he was already so wearied with the great payne he had taken, and so fainte with the great woundes he had apon him.[2] But Martius aunswered them, that it was not for conquerours to yeld, nor to be fainte harted: and thereupon beganne a freshe to chase those that fled, untill suche time as the armie of the enemies was utterly overthrowen, and numbers of them slaine, and taken prisoners.[3] The next morning betimes, Martius went to the Consul, and the other Romaines with him. There the Consul Cominius going up to his chayer of state, in the presence of the whole armie, gave thankes to the goddes for so great, glorious, and prosperous a victorie: then he spake to Martius, whose valliantnes he commended beyond the moone, both for that he him selfe sawe him doe with his eyes, as also for that Martius had reported unto him.[4] So in the ende he willed Martius, he should choose out of all the horses they had taken of their enemies, and of all the goodes they had wonne (whereof there was great store) tenne of every sorte which he liked best, before any distribution should be made to other.[5] Besides this great honorable offer he had made him, he gave him in testimonie that he had wonne that daye the price of prowes above all other, a goodly horse with a capparison,[6] and all furniture to him: which the whole armie beholding, dyd marvelously praise and commend.[7] But Martius stepping forth, tolde the Consul, he most thanckefully accepted the gifte of his horse, and was a glad man besides, that his service had deserved his generalls commendation: and as for his other offer, which was rather a mercenary reward, then an honorable recompence, he would none of it, but

[1] Marcius chooses them in I.6.65ff.
[2] I.6.62–6.
[3] Shakespeare makes Marcius meet Aufidius, I.8.
[4] I.9.1–11.
[5] *In margin:* 'The tenth parte of the enemies goods offered Martius for rewarde of his service, by Cominius the Consul.' I.9.31–6 follow this note.
[6] This suggested the image in I.9.12.
[7] *In margin:* 'Valiancie rewarded with honour in the fielde.'

was contented to have his equall parte with other souldiers.[1] Only, this grace (sayed he) I crave, and beseeche you to graunt me. Among the Volsces there is an olde friende and hoste of mine, an honest wealthie man, and now a prisoner, who living before in great wealth in his owne countrie, liveth now a poore prisoner in the handes of his enemies: and yet notwithstanding all this his miserie and misfortune, it would doe me great pleasure if I could save him from this one daunger: to keepe him from being solde as a slave.[2] The souldiers hearing Martius wordes, made a marvelous great showte among them: and they were moe that wondred at his great contentation and abstinence, when they sawe so litle covetousnes in him, then they were that highely praised and extolled his valliantnes. For even they them selves, that dyd somewhat malice and envie his glorie, to see him thus honoured, and passingly praysed, dyd thincke him so muche the more worthy of an honorable recompence for his valliant service, as the more carelesly he refused the great offer made him for his profit: and they esteemed more the vertue that was in him, that made him refuse suche rewards, then that which made them to be offred him, as unto a worthie persone. For it is farre more commendable, to use riches well, then to be valliant: and yet it is better not to desire them, then to use them well.[3] After this showte and noyse of the assembly was somewhat appeased, the Consul Cominius beganne to speake in this sorte: We cannot compell Martius to take these giftes we offer him, if he will not receave them: but we will geve him suche a rewarde for the noble service he hath done, as he cannot refuse. Therefore we doe order and decree, that henceforth he be called Coriolanus, onles his valliant acts have wonne him that name before our nomination.[4] And so ever since, he stil bare the third name of Coriolanus. And thereby it appeareth, that the first name the Romaines have, as Caius: was our Christian name now. The second, as Martius: was the name of the house and familie they came of.[5] The third, was some addition geven, either for some acte cr notable service, or for some marke on their face, or of some shape of their bodie, or els for some speciall vertue they had. Even so dyd the Græcians in olde time give additions to Princes, by reason of some notable acte worthie memorie. . . .

Now when this warre was ended, the flatterers of the people beganne to sturre up sedition againe, without any newe occasion, or just matter offered of complainte. For they dyd grounde this

[1] *In margin:* 'Martius noble aunswer, and refusall.' I.9.36–40.

[2] I.9.79–87.

[3] I.9.40*s.d.* But Martius rejects their praise.

[4] *In margin:* 'Martius surnamed Coriolanus by the Consul.' I.9.53–66.

[5] *In margin:* 'How the Romaines came to three names.'

seconde insurrection against the Nobilitie and Patricians, apon the peoples miserie and misfortune, that could not but fall out, by reason of the former discorde and sedition betweene them and the Nobilitie. Bicause the most parte of the errable lande within the territorie of Rome, was become heathie and barren for lacke of plowing, for that they had no time nor meane to cause corne, to be brought them out of other countries to sowe, by reason of their warres which made the extreme dearth they had emong them.[1] Now those busie pratlers that sought the peoples good will, by suche flattering wordes, perceyving great scarsitie of corne to be within the cittie, and though there had bene plenty enough, yet the common people had no money to buye it[2]: they spread abroad false tales and rumours against the Nobilitie, that they in revenge of the people, had practised and procured the extreme dearthe emong them.[3] Furthermore, in the middest of this sturre, there came ambassadours to Rome from the cittie of Velitres, that offered up their cittie to the Romaines, and prayed them they would send newe inhabitants to replenishe the same: bicause the plague had bene so extreme among them, and killed such a number of them, as there was not left alive the tenth persone of the people that had bene there before. So the wise men of Rome beganne to thincke, that the necessitie of the Velitrians fell out in a most happy hower, and howe by this occasion it was very mete in so great a scarsitie of vittailes, to disburden Rome of a great number of cittizens: and by this meanes as well to take awaye this newe sedition, and utterly to ryd it out of the cittie, as also to cleare the same of many mutinous and seditious persones, being the superfluous ill humours that grevously fedde this disease.[4] Hereupon the Consuls prickt out all those by a bill, whom they intended to sende to Velitres, to goe dwell there as in forme of a colonie[5]: and they leavied out of all the rest that remained in the cittie of Rome, a great number to goe against the Volsces, hoping by the meanes of forreine warre, to pacifie their sedition at home.[6] Moreover they imagined, when the poore with the riche, and the meane sorte with the nobilitie, should by this devise be abroad in the warres, and in one campe, and in one service, and in one like daunger: that then they would be more quiet and loving together. But Sicinius and Brutus, two seditious Tribunes,[7] spake against either of these devises, and cried out apon the

[1] *In margin:* 'Sedition at Rome, by reason of famine.' Cf. I.1.5,10,&c.

[2] I.1.190–1. [3] I.1.17–22; 79–86. [4] Cf. I.1.226–7.

[5] *In margin:* 'Velitres made a colonie to Rome.' Not in the play.

[6] *In margin:* 'Two practises to remove the sedition in Rome.'

[7] *In margin:* 'Sicinius and Brutus Tribunes of the people, against both those devises.'

noble men, that under the gentle name of a colonie, they would cloke and culler the most cruell and unnaturall facte as might be: bicause they sent their poore cittizens into a sore infected cittie and pestilent ayer, full of dead bodies unburied, and there also to dwell under the tuytion of a straunge god, that had so cruelly persecuted his people. This were (said they) even as muche, as if the Senate should hedlong cast downe the people into a most bottomles pyt. And are not yet contented to have famished some of the poore cittizens hertofore to death, and to put other of them even to the mercie of the plague: but a freshe, they have procured a voluntarie warre, to the ende they would leave behind no kynde of miserie and ill, wherewith the poore syllie people should not be plagued, and only bicause they are werie to serve the riche. The common people being set on a broyle and braverie with these wordes, would not appeare when the Consuls called their names by a bill, to prest them for the warres, neither would they be sent out to this newe colonie: in so muche as the Senate knewe not well what to saye, or doe in the matter. Martius then, who was now growen to great credit, and a stowte man besides, and of great reputation with the noblest men of Rome, rose up, and openly spake against these flattering Tribunes. And for the replenishing of the cittie of Velitres, he dyd compell those that were chosen, to goe thither, and to departe the cittie, apon great penalties to him that should disobey[1]: but to the warres, the people by no meanes would be brought or constrained.[2] So Martius taking his friendes and followers with him, and such as he could by fayer wordes intreate to goe with him, dyd ronne certen forreyes into the dominion of the Antiates, where he met with great plenty of corne, and had a marvelous great spoyle, aswell of cattell, as of men he had taken prisoners, whom he brought awaye with him, and reserved nothing for him selfe.[3] Afterwardes having brought backe againe all his men that went out with him, safe and sounde to Rome, and every man riche and loden with spoyle: then the hometarriers and housedoves that kept Rome still, beganne to repent them that it was not their happe to goe with him, and so envied both them that had sped so well in this jorney, and also of malice to Martius, they spited to see his credit and estimation increase still more and more, bicause they accompted him to be a great hinderer of the people.[4] Shortely after this, Martius stoode for the Consulshippe: and the common people favored his sute, thinking it would be a shame to them to denie, and refuse, the chiefest

[1] Hence perhaps III.1.262–3.

[2] Cf. III.1.121–3. *In margin:* 'Coriolanus offendeth the people.'

[3] *In margin:* 'Coriolanus invadeth the Antiates, and bringeth rich spoyles home.'

[4] Cf. III.3.3–5; II.3.94–5.

noble man of bloude, and most worthie persone of Rome, and specially him that had done so great service and good to the common wealth.[1] For the custome of Rome was at that time, that suche as dyd sue for any office, should for certen dayes before be in the market place, only with a poore gowne on their backes, and without any coate underneath, to praye the cittizens to remember them at the daye of election[2]: which was thus devised, either to move the people the more, by requesting them in suche meane apparell, or els bicause they might shewe them their woundes they had gotten in the warres in the service of the common wealth, as manifest markes and testimonie of their valliantnes.[3] Now it is not to be thought that the suters went thus lose in a simple gowne in the market place, without any coate under it, for feare, and suspition of the common people: for offices of dignitie in the cittie were not then geven by favour or corruption.[4] It was but of late time, and long after this, that buying and selling fell out in election of officers, and that the voyces of the electours were bought for money. . . . Now Martius following this custome, shewed many woundes and cuttes apon his bodie, which he had receyved in seventeene yeres service at the warres, and in many sundrie battells, being ever the formest man that dyd set out feete to fight.[5] So that there was not a man emong the people, but was ashamed of him selfe, to refuse so valliant a man: and one of them sayed to another, We must needes chuse him Consul, there is no remedie.[6] But when the daye of election was come,[7] and that Martius came to the market place with great pompe, accompanied with all the Senate, and the whole Nobilitie of the cittie about him, who sought to make him Consul, with the greatest instance and intreatie they could, or ever attempted for any man or matter: then the love and good will of the common people, turned straight to an hate and envie toward him,[8] fearing to put this office of soveraine authoritie into his handes, being a man somewhat partiall toward the nobilitie, and of great credit and authoritie amongest the Patricians, and as one they might doubt would take away alltogether the libertie from the people. Whereupon for these considerations, they refused Martius in the ende, and made two others that were suters, Consuls.[9] The Senate being marvelously

[1] II.2.24–34.
[2] *In margin:* 'The manner of suyng for office at Rome.' II.2.135–8
[3] *In margin:* 'Whereupon this manner of suyng was so devised.'
[4] *In margin:* 'Offices geven then by desert, without favour or corruption.'
[5] Contrast his reluctance, II.2.135–50; II.3.40–133, 169.
[6] Cf. II.3.1–13, 87–140.
[7] The same day in II.3.141ff.
[8] *In margin:* 'See the fickle mindes of common people.'
[9] In II.3.177–258 the tribunes cause the refusal.

offended with the people, dyd accompt the shame of this refusall, rather to redownd to them selves, then to Martius[1]: but Martius tooke it in farre worse parte then the Senate, and was out of all pacience. For he was a man to full of passion and choller, and to muche geven to over selfe will and opinion, as one of a highe minde and great corage, that lacked the gravity, and affabilitie that is gotten with judgment of learning and reason, which only is to be looked for in a governour of state: and that remembred not how wilfulnes is the thing of the world, which a governour of a common wealth for pleasing should shonne, being that which Plato called solitarines. As in the ende, all men that are wilfully geven to a selfe opinion and obstinate minde, and who will never yeld to others reason, but to their owne: remaine without companie, and forsaken of all men.[2] For a man that will live in the world, must nedes have patience, which lusty bloudes make but a mocke at. So Martius being a stowte man of nature, that never yelded in any respect, as one thincking that to overcome allwayes, and to have the upper hande in all matters, was a token of magnanimitie, and of no base and fainte corage, which spitteth out anger from the most weake and passioned parte of the harte, much like the matter of an impostume: went home to his house, full fraighted with spite and malice against the people, being accompanied with all the lustiest young gentlemen, whose mindes were nobly bent, as those that came of noble race, and commonly used for to followe and honour him.[3] But then specially they floct about him, and kept him companie, to his muche harme: for they dyd but kyndle and inflame his choller more and more,[4] being sorie with him for the injurie the people offred him, bicause he was their captaine and leader to the warres, that taught them all marshall discipline, and stirred up in them a noble emulation of honour and valliantnes, and yet without envie, praising them that deserved best. In the meane season, there came great plenty of corne to Rome,[5] that had bene bought, parte in Italie, and parte was sent out of Sicile, as geven by Gelon the tyranne of Syracusa: so that many stoode in great hope, that the dearthe of vittells being holpen, the civill dissention would also cease. The Senate sate in counsell upon it immediatly, the common people stoode also about the palice where the counsell was kept, gaping what resolution would fall out: persuading them selves, that the corne they had bought should be solde good cheape, and that which was geven,

[1] Cf. his warning, III.1.67–111.

[2] *In margin:* 'The fruites of selfe will and obstinacie.'

[3] Cf. III.1.229, 233, 239.

[4] Coriolanus needs no incitement, III.2.1–6.

[5] *In margin:* 'Great store of corne brought to Rome.'

should be devided by the polle, without paying any pennie, and the rather, bicause certaine of the Senatours amongest them dyd so wishe and persuade the same. But Martius standing up on his feete, dyd somewhat sharpely take up those, who went about to gratifie the people therein: and called them people pleasers, and traitours to the nobilitie.[1] 'Moreover he sayed they nourrished against them 'selves, the naughty seede and cockle, of insolencie and sedition, 'which had bene sowed and scattered abroade emongest the people, 'whom they should have cut of, if they had bene wise, and have 'prevented their greatnes: and not to their owne destruction to have 'suffered the people, to stablishe a magistrate for them selves, of so 'great power and authoritie, as that man had, to whom they had 'graunted it.[2] Who was also to be feared, bicause he obtained what 'he would, and dyd nothing but what he listed, neither passed for 'any obedience to the Consuls, but lived in all libertie, acknow-'ledging no superiour to commaund him, saving the only heades 'and authours of their faction, whom he called his magistrates. 'Therefore sayed he, they that gave counsell, and persuaded that 'the corne should be geven out to the common people *gratis*, as they 'used to doe in citties of Græce, where the people had more absolute 'power: dyd but only nourishe their disobedience, which would 'breake out in the ende, to the utter ruine and overthrowe of the 'whole state.[3] For they will not thincke it is done in recompense of 'their service past, sithence they know well enough they have so ofte 'refused to goe to the warres, when they were commaunded: neither 'for their mutinies when they went with us, whereby they have 'rebelled and forsaken their countrie: neither for their accusations 'which their flatterers have preferred unto them, and they have 'receyved, and made good against the Senate: but they will rather 'judge we geve and graunt them this, as abasing our selves, and 'standing in feare of them, and glad to flatter them every waye. By 'this meanes, their disobedience will still growe worse and worse: 'and they will never leave to practise newe sedition, and uprores.[4] 'Therefore it were a great follie for us, me thinckes to doe it: yea, 'shall I saye more? we should if we were wise, take from them their 'Tribuneshippe, which most manifestly is the embasing of the 'Consulshippe, and the cause of the division of the cittie.[5] The state 'whereof as it standeth, is not now as it was wont to be, but becom-'meth dismembred in two factions, which mainteines allwayes civill 'dissention and discorde betwene us, and will never suffer us againe

[1] *In margin:* 'Coriolanus oration against the insolencie of the people.' Cf. III.1.41–4; 112–60.

[2] III.1.69–73; 88–111. [3] III.1.112–17. [4] III.1.119–38. [5] III.1.164–70.

'to be united into one bodie.'[1] Martius dilating the matter with many such like reasons, wanne all the young men, and almost all the riche men to his opinion: in so much they range it out, that he was the only man, and alone in the cittie, who stoode out against the people, and never flattered them. There were only a fewe olde men that spake against him, fearing least some mischief might fall out apon it, as in dede there followed no great good afterward. For the Tribunes of the people, being present at this consultation of the Senate, when they sawe that the opinion of Martius was confirmed with the more voyces, they left the Senate, and went downe to the people, crying out for helpe, and that they would assemble to save their Tribunes.[2] Hereupon the people ranne on head in tumult together, before whom the wordes that Martius spake in the Senate were openly reported: which the people so stomaked, that even in that furie they were readie to flye apon the whole Senate. But the Tribunes layed all the faulte and burden wholy upon Martius, and sent their sergeantes forthwith to arrest him, presently to appeare in persone before the people, to aunswer the wordes he had spoken in the Senate. Martius stowtely withstoode these officers that came to arrest him.[3] Then the Tribunes in their owne persones, accompanied with the Ædiles, went to fetche him by force, and so layed violent hands upon him. Howbeit the noble Patricians gathering together about him, made the Tribunes geve backe, and layed it sore apon the Ædiles: so for that time, the night parted them,[4] and the tumult appeased. The next morning betimes,[5] the Consuls seing the people in an uprore, ronning to the market place out of all partes of the cittie, they were affrayed least all the cittie would together by the eares: wherefore assembling the Senate in all hast,[6] they declared how it stoode them upon, to appease the furie of the people, with some gentle wordes, or gratefull decrees in their favour: and moreover, like wise men they should consider, it was now no time to stande at defence and in contention, nor yet to fight for honour against the communaltie: they being fallen to so great an extremitie, and offering such imminent daunger. Wherefore they were to consider temperately of things, and to deliver some present and gentle pacification. The most parte of the Senatours that were present at this counsaill, thought this opinion best, and gave their consents unto it. Whereupon the Consuls rising out of counsaill, went to

[1] III.i.141–60.
[2] In III.i.170–9 they try to arrest him at once.
[3] *In margin:* 'Sedition at Rome for Coriolanus.' III.i.180–228.
[4] Cf. III.i.259, 'I would they were a-bed!'
[5] At III.i.262, the rabble returns that evening.
[6] Not in Shakespeare.

speake unto the people as gently as they could,[1] and they dyd pacifie their furie and anger, purging the Senate of all the unjust accusations layed upon them, and used great modestie in persuading them, and also in reproving the faultes they had committed. And as for the rest, that touched the sale of corne: they promised there should be no disliking offred them in the price. So the most parte of the people being pacified, and appearing so plainely by the great silence and still that was among them, as yelding to the Consuls, and liking well of their wordes: the Tribunes then of the people rose out of their seates, and sayed: Forasmuche as the Senate yelded unto reason, the people also for their parte, as became them, dyd likewise geve place unto them: but notwithstanding, they would that Martius should come in persone to aunswer to the articles they had devised.[2] First, whether he had not solicited and procured the Senate to chaunge the present state of the common weale, and to take the soveraine authoritie out of the peoples handes. Next, when he was sent for by authoritie of their officers, why he dyd contemptuously resist and disobey. Lastely, seeing he had driven and beaten the Ædiles into the market place before all the worlde: if in doing this, he had not done as muche as in him laye, to raise civill warres, and to set one cittizen against another. All this was spoken to one of these two endes, either that Martius against his nature should be constrained to humble him selfe, and to abase his hawty and fierce minde: or els if he continued still in his stowtnes, he should incurre the peoples displeasure and ill will so farre, that he should never possibly winne them againe. Which they hoped would rather fall out so, then otherwise: as in deede they gest, unhappely, considering Martius nature and disposition.[3] So Martius came, and presented him selfe, to aunswer their accusations against him, and the people held their peace, and gave attentive eare, to heare what he would saye. But where they thought to have heard very humble and lowly wordes come from him, he beganne not only to use his wonted boldnes of speaking (which of it selfe was very rough and unpleasaunt, and dyd more aggravate his accusation, then purge his innocencie) but also gave him selfe in his wordes to thunder, and looke therewithall so grimly, as though he made no reckoning of the matter.[4] This stirred coales emong the people, who were in wonderfull furie at it, and their hate and malice grewe so toward him, that they could holde no lenger, beare, nor indure his bravery and careles

[1] Cf. Menenius, III.1.264ff.

[2] *In margin:* 'Articles against Coriolanus.' Cf. III.1.168–70; 173–9; 182–228; III.3.62–5; 77–9.

[3] II.3.258–63; III.1.253–9.

[4] *In margin:* 'Coriolanus stowtnes in defence of him selfe.' Cf. III.3.24–91.

boldnes. Whereupon Sicinius, the cruellest and stowtest of the Tribunes, after he had whispered a litle with his companions, dyd openly pronounce in the face of all the people, Martius as condemned by the Tribunes to dye. Then presently he commaunded the Ædiles to apprehend him, and carie him straight to the rocke Tarpeian, and to cast him hedlong downe the same.[1] When the Ædiles came to laye handes upon Martius to doe that they were commaunded, divers of the people them selves thought it to cruell, and violent a dede. The noble men also being muche troubled to see such force and rigour used, beganne to crie alowde, Helpe Martius: so those that layed handes of him being repulsed, they compassed him in rounde emong them selves, and some of them holding up their handes to the people, besought them not to handle him thus cruelly. But neither their wordes, nor crying out could ought prevaile, the tumulte and hurly burley was so great, untill suche time as the Tribunes owne friendes and kinsemen weying with them selves the impossiblenes to convey Martius to execution, without great slaughter and murder of the nobilitie: dyd persuade and advise not to proceede in so violent and extraordinary a sorte, as to put such a man to death, without lawfull processe in lawe, but that they should referre the sentence of his death, to the free voyce of the people. Then Sicinius bethinking him self a litle, dyd aske the Patricians, for what cause they tooke Martius out of the officers handes that went to doe execution? The Patricians asked him againe, why they would of them selves, so cruelly and wickedly put to death, so noble and valliant a Romaine, as Martius was, and that without lawe or justice? Well, then sayed Sicinius, if that be the matter, let there be no more quarrell or dissention against the people: for they doe graunt your demaunde, that his cause shalbe heard according to the law.[2] Therfore sayed he to Martius, We doe will and charge you to appeare before the people, the third daye of our next sitting and assembly here, to make your purgation for such articles as shalbe objected against you, that by free voyce the people maye geve sentence apon you as shall please them.[3] The noble men were glad then of the adjornment, and were muche pleased they had gotten Martius out of this daunger. In the meane space, before the third day of their next cession came about, the same being kept every nineth daye continually at Rome, whereupon they call it now in Latin, *Nundinæ*: there fell out warre against the Antiates, which gave some hope to the nobilitie, that this adjornment would come

[1] *In margin:* 'Sicinius the Tribune, pronounceth sentence of death upon Martius.' III.1.265–9; 284–8.

[2] Cf. III.1.32ff.

[3] *In margin:* 'Coriolanus hath daye geven him to aunswer the people.'

to litle effect, thinking that this warre would hold them so longe, as that the furie of the people against him would be well swaged or utterly forgotten, by reason of the trouble of the warres. But contrarie to expectation, the peace was concluded presently with the Antiates, and the people returned again to Rome. Then the Patricians assembled oftentimes together, to consult how they might stande to Martius, and keepe the Tribunes from occasion to cause the people to mutine againe, and rise against the nobilitie.[1] And there Appius Clodius (one that was taken ever as an heavie enemie to the people) dyd avowe and protest, that they would utterly abase the authoritie of the Senate, and destroye the common weale, if they would suffer the common people to have authoritie by voyces to geve judgment against the nobilitie. On thother side againe, the most auncient Senatours, and suche as were geven to favour the common people sayed: that when the people should see they had authoritie of life and death in their handes, they would not be so cruell and fierce, but gentle and civill. More also, that it was not for contempt of nobilitie or the Senate, that they sought to have the authoritie of justice in their handes, as a preheminence and prerogative of honour: but bicause they feared, that them selves should be contemned and hated of the nobilitie. So as they were persuaded, that so sone as they gave them authoritie to judge by voyces: so sone would they leave all envie and malice to condemne anye. Martius seeing the Senate in great doubt how to resolve, partely for the love and good will the nobilitie dyd beare him, and partely for the feare they stoode in of the people: asked alowde of the Tribunes, what matter they would burden him with? The Tribunes aunswered him, that they would shewe howe he dyd aspire to be King, and would prove that all his actions tended to usurpe tyrannicall power over Rome.[2] Martius with that, rising up on his feete, sayed: that thereupon he dyd willingly offer him self to the people, to be tried apon that accusation. And that if it were proved by him, he had so muche as once thought of any suche matter, that he would then refuse no kinde of punishment they would offer him: conditionally (quoth he) that you charge me with nothing els besides, and that ye doe not also abuse the Senate.[3] They promised they would not. Under these conditions the judgement was agreed upon, and the people assembled. And first of all the Tribunes would in any case (whatsoever became of it) that the people would proceede to geve their voyces by Tribes, and not by hundreds: for by this meanes the

[1] Shakespeare substitutes III.2, with Volumnia's good counsel.

[2] *In margin:* 'Coriolanus accused that he sought to be King.' Cf. Brutus in Coriolanus' absence, III.3.1–2.

[3] III.3.38–46.

multitude of the poore needy people (and all such rable as had nothing to lose, and had lesse regard of honestie before their eyes) came to be of greater force (bicause their voyces were numbred by the polle) then the noble honest cittizens, whose persones and purse dyd duetifully serve the common wealth in their warres.[1] And then when the Tribunes sawe they could not prove he went about to make him self King: they beganne to broache a freshe the former wordes that Martius had spoken in the Senate, in hindering the distribution of the corne at meane price unto the common people, and persuading also to take the office of Tribuneshippe from them. And for the third, they charged him a newe, that he had not made the common distribution[2] of the spoyle he had gotten in the invading the territories of the Antiates: but had of his owne authoritie devided it among them, who were with him in that jorney. But this matter was most straunge of all to Martius, looking least to have bene burdened with that, as with any matter of offence. Wherupon being burdened on the sodaine, and having no ready excuse to make even at that instant: he beganne to fall a praising of the souldiers that had served with him in that jorney. But those that were not with him, being the greater number, cried out so lowde, and made suche a noyse, that he could not be heard. To conclude, when they came to tell the voyces of the Tribes,[3] there were three voyces odde, which condemned him to be banished for life.[4] After declaration of the sentence, the people made suche joye, as they never rejoyced more for any battell they had wonne upon their enemies, they were so brave and lively, and went home so jocondly from the assembly, for triumphe of this sentence,[5] The Senate againe in contrary manner were as sad and heavie, repenting them selves beyond measure, that they had not rather determined to have done and suffered any thing whatsoever, before the common people should so arrogantly, and outrageously have abused their authoritie. There needed no difference of garments I warrant you, nor outward showes to know a Plebeian from a Patrician, for they were easely decerned by their lookes. For he that was on the peoples side, looked cheerely on the matter: but he that was sad, and honge downe his head, he was sure of the noble mens side. Saving Martius alone, who neither in his countenaunce, nor in his gate, dyd ever showe him selfe abashed, or once let fall his great corage[6]: but he only of all other gentlemen that were angrie at his fortune, dyd outwardly shewe no manner of

[1] Hence III.3.8–11. [2] III.3.4–5.
[3] In III.3.8–12 the votes are already collected.
[4] *In margin:* 'Coriolanus banished for life.' III.3.91–117.
[5] III.3.134–41.
[6] *In margin:* 'Coriolanus constant minde in adversitie.'

passion, nor care at all of him selfe.[1] Not that he dyd paciently beare and temper his good happe, in respect of any reason he had, or by his quiet condition: but bicause he was so caried awaye with the vehemencie of anger, and desire of revenge, that he had no sence nor feeling of the hard state he was in, which the common people judge, not to be sorow, although in dede it be the very same. For when sorow (as you would saye) is set a fyre, then it is converted into spite and malice, and driveth awaye for that time all faintnes of harte and naturall feare. [2] And this is the cause why the chollericke man is so altered, and mad in his actions, as a man set a fyre with a burning agewe: for when a mans harte is troubled within, his pulse will beate marvelous strongely. Now that Martius was even in that taking, it appeared true sone after by his doinges. For when he was come home to his house againe, and had taken his leave of his mother and wife, finding them weeping, and shreeking out for sorrowe, and had also comforted and persuaded them to be content with his chaunce[3]: he went immediatly to the gate of the cittie, accompanied with a great number of Patricians that brought him thither, from whence he went on his waye with three or foure of his friendes only, taking nothing with him, nor requesting any thing of any man. So he remained a fewe dayes in the countrie at his houses, turmoyled with sundry sortes and kynde of thoughtes, suche as the fyer of his choller dyd sturre up. In the ende, seeing he could resolve no waye, to take a profitable or honorable course,[4] but only was pricked forward still to be revenged of the Romaines: he thought to raise up some great warres against them, by their neerest neighbours. Whereupon, he thought it his best waye, first to stirre up the Volsces against them, knowing they were yet able enough in strength and riches to encounter them, notwithstanding their former losses they had receyved not long before, and that their power was not so muche impaired, as their malice and desire was increased, to be revenged of the Romaines. Now in the cittie of Antium, there was one called Tullus Aufidius,[5] who for his riches, as also for his nobilitie and valliantnes, was honoured emong the Volsces as a King. Martius knewe very well, that Tullus dyd more malice and envie him, then he dyd all the Romaines besides: bicause that many times in battells where they met, they were ever at the encounter one against another, like lustie coragious youthes, striving in all emulation of honour, and had encountered many times together.[6] In so muche, as besides the common quarrell betweene them, there

[1] Contrast III.3.118–33. [2] *In margin:* 'The force of anger.'
[3] IV.1. [4] Cf. Volumnia, IV.1.35, 'Determine on some course.'
[5] *In margin:* 'Tullus Aufidius, a greate persone emong the Volsces.'
[6] Cf. I.10.7, 'five times'.

was bred a marvelous private hate one against another. Yet notwithstanding, considering that Tullus Aufidius was a man of a great minde, and that he above all other of the Volsces, most desired revenge of the Romaines, for the injuries they had done unto them: he dyd an acte that confirmed the true wordes of an auncient Poet, who sayed:

It is a thing full harde, mans anger to withstand,
  if it be stiffely bent to take an enterprise in hande.
For then most men will have, the thing that they desire,
  although it cost their lives therefore, suche force hath wicked ire.

And so dyd he. For he disguised him selfe in suche arraye and attire, as he thought no man could ever have knowen him for the persone he was, seeing him in that apparell he had upon his backe: and as Homer sayed of Ulysses,

So dyd he enter into the enemies towne.

It was even twy light when he entred the cittie of Antium, and many people met him in the streetes, but no man knewe him.[1] So he went directly to Tullus Aufidius house, and when he came thither, he got him up straight to the chimney harthe,[2] and sat him downe, and spake not a worde to any man, his face all muffled over. They of the house spying him, wondered what he should be, and yet they durst not byd him rise.[3] For ill favoredly muffled and disguised as he was, yet there appeared a certaine majestie in his countenance,[4] and in his silence: whereupon they went to Tullus who was at supper, to tell him of the straunge disguising of this man. Tullus rose presently from the borde, and comming towards him, asked him what he was, and wherefore he came. Then Martius unmuffled him selfe, and after he had paused a while, making no aunswer, he sayed unto him[5]: 'If thou knowest me not yet, Tullus, and seeing 'me, dost not perhappes beleeve me to be the man I am in dede, I 'must of necessitie bewraye my selfe to be that I am. I am Caius 'Martius, who hath done to thy self particularly, and to all the 'Volsces generally, great hurte and mischief, which I cannot denie 'for my surname of Coriolanus that I beare. For I never had other 'benefit nor recompence, of all the true and paynefull service I have 'done, and the extreme daungers I have bene in, but this only

[1] *In margin:* 'Coriolanus disguised, goeth to Antium, a cittie of the Volsces.' IV.4.

[2] IV.5.26, 84. [3] Contrast IV.5.32–6. [4] IV.5.65–7.

[5] *In margin:* 'Coriolanus oration to Tullus Aufidius.' IV.5.59–62, 70–106.

'surname: a good memorie and witnes, of the malice and displeasure 'thou showldest beare me. In deede the name only remaineth with 'me: for the rest, the envie and crueltie of the people of Rome have 'taken from me, by the sufferance of the dastardly nobilitie and 'magistrates, who have forsaken me, and let me be banished by the 'people. This extremitie hath now driven me to come as a poore 'suter, to take thy chimney harthe, not of any hope I have to save 'my life thereby. For if I had feared death, I would not have come 'hither to have put my life in hazard: but prickt forward with spite 'and desire I have to be revenged of them that thus have banished 'me, whom now I beginne to be avenged on, putting my persone 'betweene thy enemies. Wherefore, if thou hast any harte to be 'wrecked of the injuries thy enemies have done thee, spede thee now, 'and let my miserie serve thy turne, and so use it, as my service 'maye be a benefit to the Volsces: promising thee, that I will fight 'with better good will for all you, then ever I dyd when I was 'against you, knowing that they fight more valliantly, who knowe the force of their enemie, then such as have never proved it. And if it be 'so that thou dare not, and that thou art wearye to prove fortune 'any more: then am I also weary to live any lenger. And it were no 'wisedome in thee, to save the life of him, who hath bene heretofore 'thy mortall enemie, and whose service now can nothing helpe nor 'pleasure thee.' Tullus hearing what he sayed, was a marvelous glad man, and taking him by the hande, he sayed unto him: Stande up, O Martius, and bee of good chere, for in profering thy selfe unto us, thou dost us great honour: and by this meanes thou mayest hope also of greater things, at all the Volsces handes.[1] So he feasted him for that time, and entertained him in the honorablest manner he could, talking with him in no other matters at that present[2]: but within fewe dayes after, they fell to consultation together, in what sorte they should beginne their warres. Now on thother side, the cittie of Rome was in marvelous uprore, and discord, the nobilitie against the communaltie,[1] and chiefly for Martius condemnation and banishment.[3] Moreover the priestes, the Soothesayers, and private men also, came and declared to the Senate certaine sightes and wonders in the ayer, which they had seene, and were to be considered of: amongest the which, such a vision happened. There was a cittizen of Rome called Titus Latinus, a man of meane qualitie and condition, but otherwise an honest sober man, geven to a quiet life, without superstition, and muche lesse to vanitie or lying. This man had a vision in his dreame, in the which he thought

[1] Expanded in IV.5.106–52. [2] IV.5.203–7.

[3] *In margin:* 'Great dissention at Rome about Martius banishment.' Not in IV.6.1–37.

that Jupiter appeared unto him, and commaunded him to signifie to the Senate, that they had caused a very vile lewde daunser to goe before the procession: and sayed, the first time this vision had appeared unto him, he made no reckoning of it: and comming againe another time into his minde, he made not muche more accompt of the matter then before. In the ende, he sawe one of his sonnes dye, who had the best nature and condition of all his brethern: and sodainely he him selfe was so taken in all his limmes, that he became lame and impotent. Hereupon he tolde the whole circumstance of this vision before the Senate, sitting upon his litle couche or bedde, whereon he was caried on mens armes: and he had no sooner reported this vision to the Senate, but he presently felt his bodie and limmes restored again, to their former strength and use. So raising up him self upon his couche, he got up on his feete at that instant, and walked home to his house, without helpe of any man. The Senate being amazed at this matter, made diligent enquierie to understand the trothe: and in the ende they found there was such a thing. There was one that had delivered a bondman of his that had offended him, into the hands of other slaves and bondemen, and had commanded them to whippe him up and down the market place,[1] and afterwards to kill him: and as they had him in execution, whipping him cruelly, they dyd so martyre the poore wretch, that for the cruell smarte and payne he felt, he turned and writhed his bodie, in straunge and pittiefull sorte. The procession by chaunce came by even at the same time, and many that followed it, were hartely moved and offended with the sight, saying: that this was no good sight to behold, nor mete to be met in procession time. But for all this, there was nothing done: saving they blamed and rebuked him, that punished his slave so cruelly. For the Romaines at that time, dyd use their bondemen very gently, bicause they them selves dyd labour with their owne hands, and lived with them, and emong them: and therefore they dyd use them the more gently and familliarly. For the greatest punishment they gave a slave that had offended, was this.[2] They made him carie a limmer on his showlders that is fastened to the axeltree of a coche, and compelled him to goe up and downe in that sorte amongest all their neighbours. He that had once abidden this punishement, and was seene in that manner, was proclaimed and cried in every market towne: so that no man would ever trust him after, and they called him Furcifer, bicause the Latines call the wodd that ronneth into the axeltree of the coche, *Furca*, as muche to saye, as a forke.[3] Now when

[1] Contrast the slave in IV.6.37–63.

[2] *In margin:* 'The Romaines manner of punishing their slaves.'

[3] *In margin:* 'Whereof Furcifer came.'

Latinus had made reporte to the Senate of the vision that had happened to him, they were devising whom this unpleasaunt daunser should be, that went before the procession. Thereupon certain that stoode by, remembred the poore slave that was so cruelly whipped through the market place, whom they afterwardes put to death: and the thing that made them remember it, was the straunge and rare manner of his punishment. The priestes hereupon were repaired unto for advise: they were wholy of opinion, that it was the whipping of the slave. So they caused the slaves master to be punished, and beganne againe a newe procession, and all other showes and sightes in honour of Jupiter. . . . Now Tullus and Martius had secret conference with the greatest personages of the cittie of Antium, declaring unto them, that now they had good time offered them to make warre with the Romaines, while they were in dissention one with another. They aunswered them, they were ashamed to breake the league, considering that they were sworne to keepe peace for two yeres. Howbeit shortely after, the Romaines gave them great occasion to make warre with them.[1] For on a holy daye common playes being kept in Rome, apon some suspition, or false reporte, they made proclamation by sound of trumpet, that all the Volsces should avoyde out of Rome before sunne set. Some thincke this was a crafte and deceipt of Martius, who sent one to Rome to the Consuls, to accuse the Volsces falsely, advertising them howe they had made a conspiracie to set apon them, whilest they were busie in seeing these games, and also to set their cittie a fyre.[2] This open proclamation made all the Volsces more offended with the Romaines, then ever they were before: and Tullus agravating the matter, dyd so inflame the Volsces against them, that in the ende they sent their ambassadours to Rome, to summone them to deliver their landes and townes againe, which they had taken from them in times past, or to looke for present warres. The Romaines hearing this, were marvelously netled: and made no other aunswer but thus: If the Volsces be the first that beginne warre: the Romaines will be the last that will ende it. Incontinently upon returne of the Volsces ambassadours, and deliverie of the Romaines aunswer: Tullus caused an assembly generall to be made of the Volsces, and concluded to make warre apon the Romaines. This done, Tullus dyd counsell them to take Martius into their service, and not to mistrust him for the remembraunce of any thing past, but boldely to trust him in any matter to come: for he would doe them more service in fighting for them, then ever he dyd them displeasure in

[1] *In margin:* 'The Romaines gave the Volsces occasion of warres.'

[2] *In margin:* 'Martius Coriolanus craftie accusation of the Volsces.' Shakespeare omits this.

fighting against them. So Martius was called forth, who spake so excellently in the presence of them all, that he was thought no lesse eloquent in tongue, then warlike in showe: and declared him selfe both expert in warres, and wise with valliantnes. Thus he was joyned in commission with Tullus as generall of the Volsces, having absolute authoritie betwene them to follow and pursue the warres.[1] But Martius fearing least tract of time to bring this armie togither with all the munition and furniture of the Volsces, would robbe him of the meane he had to execute his purpose and intent: left order with the rulers and chief of the cittie, to assemble the rest of their power, and to prepare all necessary provision for the campe. Then he with the lightest souldiers he had, and that were willing to followe him, stale awaye upon the sodaine, and marched with all speede, and entred the territories of Rome, before the Romaines heard any newes of his comming.[2] In so much the Volsces found such spoyle in the fields, as they had more then they could spend in their campe, and were wearie to drive and carie awaye that they had.[3] Howbeit the gayne of the spoyle and the hurte they dyd to the Romaines in this invasion, was the least parte of his intent. For his chiefest purpose was, to increase still the malice and dissention betweene the nobilitie, and the communaltie[4]: and to drawe that on, he was very carefull to keepe the noble mens landes and goods safe from harme and burning, but spoyled all the whole countrie besides, and would suffer no man to take or hurte any thing of the noble mens. This made greater sturre and broyle betweene the nobilitie and people, then was before. For the noble men fell out with the people, bicause they had so unjustly banished a man of so great valure and power.[5] The people on thother side, accused the nobilitie, how they had procured Martius to make these warres, to be revenged of them: bicause it pleased them to see their goodes burnt and spoyled before their eyes, whilest them selves were well at ease, and dyd behold the peoples losses and misfortunes, and knowing their owne goodes safe and out of daunger: and howe the warre was not made against the noble men, that had the enemie abroad, to keepe that they had in safety. Now Martius having done this first exploite (which made the Volsces bolder, and lesse fearefull of the Romaines) brought home all the armie againe, without losse

[1] *In margin:* 'Coriolanus chosen generall of the Volsces, with Tullus Aufidius against the Romaines.'

[2] *In margin:* 'Coriolanus invadeth the territories of the Romaines.' IV.6.39.

[3] IV.6.76–80.

[4] *In margin:* 'A fine devise to make the communaltie suspect the nobilitie.' Ignored in *Cor.*

[5] *In margin:* 'Great harte burning betwext the nobilitie and people.' IV.6.81–162.

of any man. After their whole armie (which was marvelous great, and very forward to service) was assembled in one campe: they agreed to leave parte of it for garrison in the countrie about, and the other parte should goe on, and make the warre apon the Romaines. So Martius bad Tullus choose, and take which of the two charges he liked best. Tullus made him aunswer, he knewe by experience that Martius was no lesse valliant then him selfe, and howe he ever had better fortune and good happe in all battells, then him selfe had. Therefore he thought it best for him to have the leading of those that should make the warres abroade: and him selfe would keepe home, to provide for the safety of the citties and of his countrie, and to furnishe the campe also of all necessary provision abroade. So Martius being stronger then before, went first of all unto the cittie of Circees, inhabited by the Romaines, who willingly yelded them selves, and therefore had no hurte. From thence, he entred the countrie of the Latines, imagining the Romaines would fight with him there, to defend the Latines, who were their confederates, and had many times sent unto the Romaines for their ayde. But on the one side, the people of Rome were very ill willing to goe: and on the other side the Consuls being upon their going out of their office, would not hazard them selves for so small a time: so that the ambassadours of the Latines returned home againe, and dyd no good. Then Martius dyd besiege their citties, and having taken by force the townes of the Tolerinians, Vicanians, Pedanians, and the Bolanians, who made resistaunce: he sacked all their goodes, and tooke them prisoners.[1] Suche as dyd yeld them selves willingly unto him, he was as carefull as possible might be to defend them from hurte: and bicause they should receyve no damage by his will, he removed his campe as farre from their confines as he could. Afterwards, he tooke the cittie of Boles by assault, being about an hundred furlonge from Rome, where he had a marvelous great spoyle, and put every man to the sword that was able to carie weapon. The other Volsces that were appointed to remaine in garrison for defence of their countrie, hearing this good newes, would tary no lenger at home, but armed them selves, and ranne to Martius campe, saying they dyd acknowledge no other captaine but him.[2] Hereupon his fame ranne through all Italie, and every one praised him for a valliant captaine, for that by chaunge of one man for another, suche and so straunge events fell out in the state. In this while, all went still to wracke at Rome. For, to come into the field to fight with the enemie, they could not abyde to heare of it, they were one so muche against another, and full of seditious wordes,

[1] Cf. IV.7.28. [2] Hence IV.7.1.

the nobilitie against the people, and the people against the nobilitie. Untill they had intelligence at the length that the enemies had layed seige to the cittie of Lavinium, in the which were all the temples and images of the goddes their protectours, and from whence came first their auncient originall, for that Æneas at his first arrivall into Italie dyd build that cittie.[1] Then fell there out a marvelous sodain chaunge of minde among the people, and farre more straunge and contrarie in the nobilitie. For the people thought good to repeale the condemnation and exile of Martius. The Senate assembled upon it, would in no case yeld to that. Who either dyd it of a selfe will to be contrarie to the peoples desire: or bicause Martius should not returne through the grace and favour of the people. Or els, bicause they were throughly angrie and offended with him, that he would set apon the whole, being offended but by a fewe, and in his doings would shewe him selfe an open enemie besides unto his countrie: notwithstanding the most parte of them tooke the wrong they had done him, in marvelous ill parte, and as if the injurie had bene done unto them selves. Reporte being made of the Senates resolution, the people founde them selves in a straight: for they could authorise and confirme nothing by their voyces, unles it had bene first propounded and ordeined by the Senate. But Martius hearing this sturre about him, was in a greater rage with them then before: in so muche as he raised his seige incontinently before the cittie of Lavinium, and going towardes Rome, lodged his campe within fortie furlonge of the cittie, at the ditches called Cluiliæ. His incamping so neere Rome, dyd put all the whole cittie in a wonderfull feare: howbeit for the present time it appeased the sedition and dissention betwext the Nobilitie and the people. For there was no Consul, Senatour, nor Magistrate, that durst once contrarie the opinion of the people, for the calling home againe of Martius. When they sawe the women in a marvelous feare, ronning up and downe the cittie: the temples of the goddes full of olde people, weeping bitterly in their prayers to the goddes: and finally, not a man either wise or hardie to provide for their safetie: then they were all of opinion, that the people had reason to call home Martius againe, to reconcile them selves to him, and that the Senate on the contrary parte, were in marvelous great faulte to be angrie and in choller with him, when it stoode them upon rather to have gone out and intreated him. So they all agreed together to send ambassadours unto him, to let him understand howe his countrymen dyd call him home againe, and restored him to all his goodes, and besought him to deliver them from this warre. The ambassadours that were sent,

[1] *In margin:* 'Lavinium built by Æneas.'

were Martius familliar friendes,[1] and acquaintaunce, who looked at the least for a curteous welcome of him, as of their familliar friende and kynseman. Howbeit they founde nothing lesse. For at their comming, they were brought through the campe, to the place where he was set in his chayer of state, with a marvelous and an unspeakable majestie, having the chiefest men of the Volsces about him: so he commaunded them to declare openly the cause of their comming. Which they delivered in the most humble and lowly wordes they possiblie could devise, and with all modest countenaunce and behaviour agreable for the same. When they had done their message: for the injurie they had done him, he aunswered them very hottely, and in great choller. But as generall of the Volsces, he willed them to restore unto the Volsces, all their landes and citties they had taken from them in former warres: and moreover, that they should geve them the like honour and freedome of Rome, as they had before geven to the Latines. For otherwise they had no other meane to ende this warre, if they dyd not graunte these honest and just conditions of peace. Thereupon he gave them thirtie dayes respit to make him aunswer. So the ambassadours returned straight to Rome, and Martius forthwith departed with his armie out of the territories of the Romaines.[2] This was the first matter wherewith the Volsces (that most envied Martius glorie and authoritie) dyd charge Martius with.[3] Among those, Tullus was chief: who though he had receyved no private injurie or displeasure of Martius, yet the common faulte and imperfection of mans nature wrought in him, and it grieved him to see his owne reputation bleamished, through Martius great fame and honour, and so him selfe to be lesse esteemed of the Volsces, then he was before.[4] This fell out the more, bicause every man honoured Martius, and thought he only could doe all, and that all other governours and captaines must be content with suche credit and authoritie, as he would please to countenaunce them with. From hence they derived all their first accusations and secret murmurings against Martius. For private captaines conspiring against him, were very angrie with him: and gave it out, that the removing of the campe was a manifest treason, not of the townes, nor fortes, nor of armes, but of time and occasion, which was a losse of great importaunce, bicause it was that which in treason might both lose and binde all, and preserve the whole. Now Martius having

[1] *In margin:* 'The Romaines send ambassadours to Coriolanus to treate of peace.' Cominius is one; V.1.6–7.

[2] No such respite in *Cor.*

[3] *In margin:* 'The first occasion of the Volsces envy to Coriolanus.' Is this behind IV.7.24–6?

[4] IV.5.208–10; IV.7.1–16.

geven the Romaines thirtie dayes respit for their aunswer, and specially bicause the warres have not accustomed to make any great chaunges, in lesse space of time then that: he thought it good yet, not to lye a sleepe idle all the while, but went and destroyed the landes of the enemies allies, and tooke seven citties of theirs well inhabited, and the Romaines durst not once put them selves into the field, to come to their ayde and helpc: they were so fainte harted, so mistrustfull, and lothe besides to make warres. In so muche as they properly ressembled the bodyes paralyticke, and losed of their limmes and members: as those which through the palsey[1] have lost all their sence and feeling. Wherefore, the time of peace expired, Martius being returned into the dominions of the Romaines againe with all his armie, they sent another ambassade unto him, to praye peace, and the remove of the Volsces out of their countrie[2]: that afterwardes they might with better leysure fall to suche agreementes together, as should be thought most mete and necessarie. For the Romaines were no men that would ever yeld for feare. But if he thought the Volsces had any grounde to demaunde reasonable articles and conditions, all that they would reasonably aske should be graunted unto, by the Romaines, who of them selves would willingly yeld to reason, conditionally, that they dyd laye downe armes. Martius to that aunswered: that as generall of the Volsces he would replie nothing unto it. But yet as a Romaine cittizen, he would counsell them to let fall their pride, and to be conformable to reason, if they were wise: and that they should returne againe within three dayes, delivering up the articles agreed upon, which he had first delivered them.[3] Or otherwise, that he would no more geve them assuraunce or safe conduite to returne againe into his campe, with suche vaine and frivolous messages. When the ambassadours were returned to Rome, and had reported Martius aunswer to the Senate: their cittie being in extreme daunger, and as it were in a terrible storme or tempest, they threw out (as the common proverbe sayeth) their holy ancker. For then they appointed all the bishoppes, priestes, ministers of the goddes, and keepers of holy things, and all the augures or soothesayers, which foreshowe things to come by observation of the flying of birdes (which is an olde auncient kynde of prophecying and divination amongest the Romaines) to goe to Martius[4] apparelled, as when they doe their sacrifices: and first to intreate him to leave of warre, and then that he would speake to his contrymen, and conclude peace with the Volsces. Martius suffered

[1] Cf. Menenius' 'palsied intercession', V.2.43.

[2] *In margin:* 'Another ambassade sent to Coriolanus.' Menenius in V.1 and 2.

[3] Given to Menenius, V.2.88.

[4] *In margin:* 'The priestes and soothesayers sent to Coriolanus.' Not in the play.

them to come into his campe, but yet he graunted them nothing the more, neither dyd he entertaine them or speake more curteously to them, then he dyd the first time that they came unto him, saving only that he willed them to take the one of the two: either to accept peace under the first conditions offered, or els to receyve warre. When all this goodly rable of superstition and priestes were returned, it was determined in counsell that none should goe out of the gates of the cittie, and that they should watche and warde upon the walles, to repulse their enemies if they came to assault them: referring them selves and all their hope to time, and fortunes uncertaine favour, not knowing otherwise howe to remedie the daunger. Now all the cittie was full of tumult, feare, and marvelous doubt what would happen: untill at length there fell out suche a like matter, as Homer oftetimes sayed they would least have thought of. For in great matters, that happen seldome, Homer sayeth, and crieth out in this sorte,

The goddesse Pallas she, with her fayer glistering eyes,
dyd put into his minde suche thoughts, and made him so devise.

And in an other place:

But sure some god hath ta'ne, out of the peoples minde,
both wit and understanding eke, and have therewith assynde
some other simple spirite, in steede thereof to byde,
that so they might their doings all, for lacke of wit misguyde.

And in an other place:

The people of them selves, did either it consider,
or else some god instructed them, and so they joynde together.

Many reckon not of Homer, as referring matters unpossible, and fables of no likelyhoode or trothe, unto mans reason, free will, or judgement: which in deede is not his meaning. But things true and likely, he maketh to depend of our owne free wil and reason. For he oft speaketh these wordes:

I have thought it in my noble harte.

And in an other place:

Achilles angrie was, and sorie for to heare
him so to say, his heavy brest was fraught with pensive feare.

And againe in an other place:

Bellerophon (she) could not move with her fayer tongue,
so honest and so vertuous, he was the rest among.

But in wonderous and extraordinarie thinges, which are done by secret inspirations and motions, he doth not say that God taketh away, from man his choyce and freedom of will, but that he doth move it: neither that he doth worke desire in us, but objecteth to our mindes certaine imaginations whereby we are lead to desire, and thereby doth not make this our action forced, but openeth the way to our will, and addeth thereto courage, and hope of successe. For, either we must say, that the goddes meddle not with the causes and beginninges of our actions: or else what other meanes have they to helpe and further men? It is apparaunt that they handle not our bodies, nor move not our feete and handes, when there is occasion to use them: but that parte of our minde from which these motions proceede, is induced thereto, or caried away by such objectes and reasons, as God offereth unto it. Now the Romaine Ladies and gentlewomen did visite all the temples and goddes of the same, to make their prayers unto them: but the greatest Ladies (and more parte of them) were continuallie about the aulter of Jupiter Capitolin, emonge which troupe by name, was Valeria, Publicolaes owne sister. The selfe same Publicola, who did such notable service to the Romaines, both in peace and warres: and was dead also certaine yeares before, as we have declared in his life. His sister Valeria was greatly honoured and reverenced amonge all the Romaines[1]: and did so modestlie and wiselie behave her selfe, that she did not shame nor dishonour the house she came of. So she sodainely fell into suche a fansie, as we have rehearsed before, and had (by some god as I thinke) taken holde of a noble devise.[2] Whereuppon she rose, and thother Ladies with her, and they all together went straight to the house of Volumnia, Martius mother[3]: and comming into her, founde her, and Martius wife her daughter in lawe set together, and havinge her husbande Martius young children in her lappe. Now all the traine of these Ladies sittinge in a ringe rounde about her: Valeria first beganne to speake in this sorte unto her[4]: 'We Ladies, are come to visite you Ladies (my Ladie Volumnia and Virgilia) by no direction from the Senate, nor 'commaundement of other magistrate: but through the inspiration '(as I take it) of some god above. Who havinge taken compassion 'and pitie of our prayers, hath moved us to come unto you, to 'intreate you in a matter, as well beneficiall for us, as also for the 'whole citizens in generall: but to your selves in especiall (if it please 'you to credit me) and shall redounde to our more fame and glorie,

[1] *In margin:* 'Valeria Publicolaes sister.' V.3.64–7.

[2] Cf. A. Hardy, *Coriolan*, IV.1. Not in Shakespeare.

[3] *In margin:* 'Volumnia, Martius mother.'

[4] *In margin:* 'The wordes of Valeria, unto Volumnia and Virgilia.'

'then the daughters of the Sabynes obteined in former age, when 'they procured lovinge peace, in stead of hatefull warre, betwene 'their fathers and their husbands. Come on good ladies, and let us 'goe all together unto Martius, to intreate him to take pitie uppon 'us, and also to reporte the trothe unto him, howe muche you are 'bounde unto the citizens: who notwithstandinge they have sus- 'teined greate hurte and losses by him, yet they have not hetherto 'sought revenge apon your persons by any discurteous usage, neither 'ever conceyved any suche thought or intent against you, but doe 'deliver ye safe into his handes, though thereby they looke for no 'better grace or clemency from him.' When Valeria had spoken this unto them, all thother ladyes together with one voyce confirmed that she had sayed. Then Volumnia in this sorte did aunswer her[1]: 'My 'good ladies, we are partakers with you of the common miserie and 'calamitie of our countrie, and yet our griefe exceedeth yours the 'more, by reason of our particular misfortune: to feele the losse of 'my sonne Martius former valiancie and glorie, and to see his 'persone environned nowe with our enemies in armes, rather to see 'him foorth comminge and safe kept, then of any love to defende his 'persone. But yet the greatest griefe of our heaped mishappes is, to 'see our poore countrie brought to suche extremite, that all hope 'of the safetie and preservation thereof, is nowe unfortunately cast 'uppon us simple women: bicause we knowe not what accompt he 'will make of us, sence he hath cast from him all care of his naturall 'countrie and common weale, which heretofore he hath holden more 'deere and precious, then either his mother, wife, or children. Not- 'withstandinge, if ye thinke we can doe good, we will willingly doe 'what you will have us: bringe us to him I pray you. For if we can 'not prevaile, we maye yet dye at his feete, as humble suters for the 'safetie of our countrie.'[2] Her aunswere ended, she tooke her daughter in lawe, and Martius children with her, and being accompanied with all the other Romaine ladies, they went in troupe together unto the Volsces campe: whome when they sawe, they of them selves did both pitie and reverence her, and there was not a man amonge them that once durst say a worde unto her. Nowe was Martius set then in his chayer of state, with all the honours of a generall, and when he had spied the women comming a farre of, he marveled what the matter ment: but afterwardes knowing his wife which came formest, he determined at the first to persist in his obstinate and inflexible rancker.[3] But overcomen in the ende with naturall affection, and being altogether altered to see them: his

[1] *In margin:* 'The aunswere of Volumnia to the Romaine ladies.'

[2] Cf. A. Hardy, *Coriolan*, IV.3. Not in Shakespeare.

[3] V.3.22–6; 33–7.

harte would not serve him to tarie their comming to his chayer, but comming downe in hast, he went to meete them, and first he kissed his mother, and imbraced her a pretie while, then his wife and litle children.[1] And nature so wrought with him, that the teares fell from his eyes, and he coulde not keepe him selfe from making much of them, but yeelded to the affection of his bloode, as if he had bene violently caried with the furie of a most swift running streame. After he had thus lovingly received them, and perceivinge that his mother Volumnia would beginne to speake to him, he called the chiefest of the counsell of the Volsces to heare what she would say.[2] Then she spake in this sorte[3]: 'If we helde our peace (my sonne) and determined not to speake, the state of our poore bodies, and present 'sight of our rayment, would easely bewray to thee what life we have 'led at home, since thy exile and abode abroad. But thinke now with 'thy selfe, howe much more unfortunatly, then all the women livinge 'we are come hether, considering that the sight which should be most 'pleasaunt to all other to beholde, spitefull fortune hath made most 'fearefull to us: making my selfe to see my sonne, and my daughter 'here, her husband, besieging the walles of his native countrie.[4] So 'as that which is thonly comforte to all other in their adversitie and 'miserie, to pray unto the goddes, and to call to them for aide: is the 'onely thinge which plongeth us into most deepe perplexitie. For we 'can not (alas) together pray, both for victorie, for our countrie, and 'for safety of thy life also: but a worlde of grievous curses, yea more 'then any mortall enemie can heape uppon us, are forcibly wrapt up 'in our prayers. For the bitter soppe of most harde choyce is offered 'thy wife and children, to forgoe the one of the two: either to lose the 'persone of thy selfe, or the nurse of their native contrie. For my 'selfe (my sonne) I am determined not to tarie, till fortune in my life 'time doe make an ende of this warre. For if I cannot persuade thee, 'rather to doe good unto both parties, then to overthrowe and 'destroye the one, preferring love and nature, before the malice and 'calamitie of warres: thou shalt see, my sonne, and trust unto it, 'thou shalt no soner marche forward to assault thy countrie, but 'thy foote shall treade upon thy mothers wombe, that brought thee 'first into this world.[5] And I maye not deferre to see the daye, either 'that my sonne be led prisoner in triumphe by his naturall country 'men, or that he him selfe doe triumphe of them, and of his naturall 'countrie.[6] For if it were so, that my request tended to save thy 'countrie, in destroying the Volsces: I must confesse, thou wouldest 'hardly and doubtfully resolve on that. For as to destroye thy

[1] Contrast V.3.38–53. [2] V.3.92–3.
[3] *In margin:* 'The oration of Volumnia, unto her sonne Coriolanus.' V.3.94–148.
[4] Cf. V.3.101–3. [5] *Ibid.*, 103–24. [6] *Ibid.*, 111–18.

'naturall countrie, it is altogether unmete and unlawfull: so were it 'not just, and lesse honorable, to betraye those that put their trust 'in thee. But my only demaunde consisteth, to make a gayle deliverie 'of all evills, which delivereth equall benefit and safety, both to the 'one and the other, but most honorable for the Volsces. For it shall 'appeare, that having victorie in their handes, they have of speciall 'favour graunted us singular graces: peace, and amitie, albeit them 'selves have no lesse parte of both, then we. Of which good, if so it 'came to passe, thy selfe is thonly authour, and so hast thou thonly 'honour. But if it faile, and fall out contrarie: thy selfe alone deser'vedly shall carie the shamefull reproche and burden of either partie. 'So, though the ende of warre be uncertaine, yet this notwithstand'ing is most certaine: that if it be thy chaunce to conquer, this 'benefit shalt thou reape of thy goodly conquest, to be chronicled the 'plague and destroyer of thy countrie. And if fortune also overthrowe 'thee, then the world will saye, that through desire to revenge thy 'private injuries, thou hast for ever undone thy good friendes, who 'dyd most lovingly and curteously receyve thee.'[1] Martius gave good eare unto his mothers wordes, without interrupting her speache at all: and after she had sayed what she would, he held his peace a prety while, and aunswered not a worde. Hereupon she beganne againe to speake unto him, and sayed[2]: 'My sonne, why doest thou 'not aunswer me? doest thou thinke it good altogether to geve place 'unto thy choller and desire of revenge, and thinkest thou it not 'honestie for thee to graunt thy mothers request, in so weighty a 'cause? doest thou take it honorable for a noble man, to remember 'the wronges and injuries done him: and doest not in like case thinke 'it an honest noble mans parte, to be thankefull for the goodnes that 'parents doe shewe to their children, acknowledging the duety and 'reverence they ought to beare unto them? No man living is more 'bounde to shewe him selfe thankefull in all partes and respects, 'then thy selfe: who so unnaturally sheweth all ingratitude. More'over (my sonne) thou hast sorely taken of thy countrie, exacting 'grievous payments apon them, in revenge of the injuries offered 'thee: besides, thou hast not hitherto shewed thy poore mother any 'curtesie.[3] And therefore, it is not only honest, but due unto me, that 'without compulsion I should obtaine my so just and reasonable 'request of thee. But since by reason I cannot persuade thee to it, 'to what purpose doe I deferre my last hope?' And with these wordes, her selfe, his wife and children, fell downe upon their knees before him.[4] Martius seeing that, could refraine no lenger, but went

[1] V.3.132–8.
[2] So in V.3.148–82, but more intimately.
[3] V.3.160–1.
[4] V.3.168–82.

straight and lifte her up, crying out: Oh mother, what have you done to me? And holding her hard by the right hande, oh mother, sayed he, you have wonne a happy victorie for your countrie, but mortall and unhappy for your sonne: for I see my self vanquished by you alone.[1] These wordes being spoken openly, he spake a litle a parte with his mother and wife, and then let them returne againe to Rome, for so they dyd request him[2]: and so remaining in campe that night, the next morning he dislodged,[3] and marched homewardes into the Volsces countrie againe, who were not all of one minde, nor all alike contented. For some misliked him, and that he had done. Other being well pleased that peace should be made, sayed: that neither the one, nor the other, deserved blame nor reproche. Other, though they misliked that was done, dyd not thincke him an ill man for that he dyd, but sayed: he was not to be blamed, though he yelded to suche a forcible extremitie. Howbeit no man contraried his departure, but all obeyed his commaundement, more for respect of his worthines and valiancie, then for feare of his authoritie. Now the cittizens of Rome plainely shewed, in what feare and daunger their cittie stoode of this warre, when they were delivered. For so sone as the watche upon the walles of the cittie perceyved the Volsces campe to remove, there was not a temple in the cittie but was presently set open, and full of men, wearing garlands of flowers upon their heads, sacrificing to the goddes, as they were wont to doe upon the newes of some great obteined victorie. And this common joye was yet more manifestly shewed, by the honorable curtesies the whole Senate, and people dyd bestowe on their ladyes.[4] For they were all throughly persuaded, and dyd certenly beleeve, that the ladyes only were cause of the saving of the cittie, and delivering them selves from the instant daunger of the warre. Whereupon the Senate ordeined, that the magistrates to gratifie and honour these ladyes, should graunte them all that they would require. And they only requested that they would build a temple of Fortune of the women, for the building whereof they offered them selves to defraye the whole charge of the sacrifices, and other ceremonies belonging to the service of the goddes. Nevertheles, the Senate commending their good will and forwardnes, ordeined, that the temple and image should be made at the common charge of the cittie.[5] Notwithstanding that, the ladyes gathered

[1] *In margin:* 'Coriolanus compassion of his mother.' V.3.182–9.

[2] V.3.202–6.

[3] *In margin:* 'Coriolanus withdraweth his armie from Rome.' V.4.42.

[4] V.4.53–70.

[5] *In margin:* 'The temple of Fortune built for the women.' Cf. Coriolanus, V.3.206–7.

money emong them, and made with the same a second image of Fortune, which the Romaines saye dyd speake as they offred her up in the temple, and dyd set her in her place: and they affirme, that she spake these wordes: Ladyes, ye have devoutely offered me up.[1] Moreover, that she spake that twise together, making us to beleeve things that never were, and are not to be credited. For to see images that seeme to sweate or weepe, or to put forth any humour red or blowdie, it is not a thing unpossible.[2] For wodde and stone doe commonly receyve certaine moysture, whereof is ingendred an humour, which doe yeld of them selves, or doe take of the ayer, many sortes and kyndes of spottes and cullers: by which signes and tokens it is not amisse we thincke, that the goddes sometimes doe warne men of things to come. And it is possible also, that these images and statues doe somtimes put forth soundes, like unto sighes or mourning, when in the middest or bottome of the same, there is made some violent separation, or breaking a sonder of things, blowen or devised therein: but that a bodie which hath neither life nor soule, should have any direct or exquisite worde formed in it by expresse voyce, that is altogether unpossible. For the soule, nor god him selfe can distinctly speake without a bodie, having necessarie organes and instrumentes mete for the partes of the same, to forme and utter distinct wordes. But where stories many times doe force us to beleeve a thing reported to be true, by many grave testimonies: there we must saye, that it is some passion contrarie to our five naturall sences, which being begotten in the imaginative parte or understanding, draweth an opinion unto it selfe, even as we doe in our sleeping. For many times we thinke we heare, that we doe not heare: and we imagine we see, that we see not. Yet notwithstanding, such as are godly bent, and zealously geven to thinke apon heavenly things, so as they can no waye be drawen from beleeving that which is spoken of them, they have this reason to grounde the foundation of their beleefe upon. That is, the omnipotencie of God which is wonderfull, and hath no manner of resemblaunce or likelines of proportion unto ours, but is altogether contrarie as touching our nature, our moving, our arte, and our force.[3] and therefore if he doe any thing unpossible to us, or doe bring forth and devise things, without mans common reache and understanding, we must not therefore thinke it unpossible at all. For if in other things he is farre contrarie to us, muche more in his workes and secret operations, he farre passeth all the rest: but the most parte of goddes doings, as Heraclitus sayeth, for lacke of faith, are hidden and unknowen unto

[1] *In margin:* 'The image of Fortune spake to the ladyes at Rome.'
[2] *In margin:* 'Of the sweating and voyces of images.'
[3] *In margin:* 'Of the omnipotencie of God.'

us. Now when Martius was returned againe into the cittie of Antium from his voyage, Tullus that hated and could no lenger abide him for the feare he had of his authoritie: sought divers meanes to make him out of the waye, thinking that if he let slippe that present time, he should never recover the like and fit occasion againe.[1] Wherefore Tullus having procured many other of his confederacy, required Martius might be deposed from his estate, to render up accompt to the Volsces of his charge and government.[2] Martius fearing to become a private man againe under Tullus being generall (whose authoritie was greater otherwise, then any other emong all the Volsces) aunswered: he was willing to geve up his charge, and would resigne it into the handes of the lordes of the Volsces, if they dyd all commaund him, as by all their commaundement he receyved it. And moreover, that he would not refuse even at that present to geve up an accompt unto the people, if they would tarie the hearing of it. The people hereupon called a common counsaill, in which assembly there were certen oratours appointed, that stirred up the common people against him[3]: and when they had tolde their tales, Martius rose up to make them aunswer. Now, notwithstanding the mutinous people made a marvelous great noyse, yet when they sawe him, for the reverence they bare unto his valliantnes, they quieted them selves, and gave still audience to alledge with leysure what he could for his purgation. Moreover, the honestest men of the Antiates, and who most rejoyced in peace, shewed by their countenaunce that they would heare him willingly, and judge also according to their conscience. Whereupon Tullus fearing that if he dyd let him speake, he would prove his innocencie to the people, bicause emongest other things he had an eloquent tongue, besides that the first good service he had done to the people of the Volsces, dyd winne him more favour, then these last accusations could purchase him displeasure: and furthermore, the offence they layed to his charge, was a testimonie of the good will they ought him, for they would never have thought he had done them wrong for that they tooke not the cittie of Rome, if they had not bene very neere taking of it, by meanes of his approche and conduction.[4] For these causes Tullus thought he might no lenger delaye his pretence and enterprise, neither to tarie for the mutining and rising of the common people against him: wherefore, those that were of the conspiracie, beganne to crie out that he was not to be heard, nor that they would not suffer a traytour[5] to usurpe tyrannicall power over the tribe of the Volsces, who would not yeld up his estate and authoritie. And in saying these wordes, they all fell

[1] *In margin:* 'Tullus Aufidius seeketh to kill Coriolanus.' V.5.1–49.

[2] No such delay in *Cor.* V.5.

[3] Contrast V.5.50–9.

[4] Cf. Coriolanus V.5.76–84.

[5] V.5.54–6; 84–103.

upon him, and killed him in the market place, none of the people once offering to rescue him.[1] Howbeit it is a clere case, that this murder was not generally consented unto, of the most parte of the Volsces[2]: for men came out of all partes to honour his bodie, and dyd honorably burie him, setting out his tombe with great store of armour and spoyles, as the tombe of a worthie persone and great captaine.[3] The Romaines understanding of his death, shewed no other honour or malice, saving that they graunted the ladyes the request they made: that they might mourne tenne moneths for him,[4] and that was the full time they used to weare blackes for the death of their fathers, brethren, or husbands, according to Numa Pompilius order, who stablished the same, as we have enlarged more amplie in the description of his life. Now Martius being dead, the whole state of the Volsces hartely wished him alive againe. For first of all they fell out with the Æques (who were their friendes and confederates) touching preheminence and place: and this quarrell grew on so farre betwene them, and frayes and murders fell out apon it one with another. After that, the Romaines overcame them in battell, in which Tullus was slaine in the field,[5] and the flower of all their force was put to the sworde: so that they were compelled to accept most shamefull conditions of peace, in yelding them selves subject unto the conquerers, and promising to be obedient at their commandement.

THE COMPARISON OF ALCIBIADES WITH MARTIUS CORIOLANUS

Now that we have written all the dedes of worthie memorie, done by either of them both[6]: we maye presently discerne, that in matters of warre, the one hath not greatly exceeded the other. For both of them in their charge, were a like hardie and valliant for their persones, as also wise and politike in the warres: unles they will saye, that Alcibiades was the better captaine, as he that had foughten more battells with his enemies, both by sea and lande, then ever Coriolanus had done, and had allwayes the victorie of his enemies. For otherwise, in this they were much a like: that where they were both present, and had charge and power to commaund, all things prospered notably, and with good successe on the parte they were

[1] *In margin:* 'Coriolanus murdered in the cittie of Antium.' V.5.112–31.
[2] V.5.133–4; 143–7.
[3] *In margin:* 'Coriolanus funeralles.' V.5.154.
[4] *In margin:* 'The time of mourning appointed by Numa.'
[5] *In margin:* 'Tullus Aufidius slaine in battell.'
[6] *In margin:* 'The acts done by both.' See Vol. VI for Alcibiades in *Timon*.

of: and also when they tooke the contrary side, they made the first have the worse every waye. Now for matters of government, the noble men and honest cittizens dyd hate Alcibiades manner of rule in the common weale, as of a man most dissolute, and geven to flatterie: bicause he ever studied by all devise he could, to currie favour with the common people. So dyd the Romaines malice also Coriolanus government, for that it was to arrogant, prowde, and tyrannicall: whereby neither the one nor the other was to be commended. Notwithstanding, he is lesse to be blamed, that seeketh to please and gratifie his common people: then he that despiseth and disdaineth them, and therefore offereth them wrong and injurie, bicause he would not seeme to flatter them, to winne the more authoritie. For as it is an evill thing to flatter the common people to winne credit: even so is it besides dishonesty, and injustice also, to atteine to credit and authoritie, for one to make him selfe terrible to the people, by offering them wrong and violence. It is true that Martius was ever counted an honest natured man, plaine and simple, without arte or cunning: Howbeit Alcibiades merely contrarie, for he was fine, subtill, and deceiptfull.[1] And the greatest faulte they ever burdened Alcibiades for, was his malice and deceipt, wherewith he abused the ambassadours of the Lacedæmonians, and that he was a let that peace was not concluded, as Thucydides reporteth. Now, though by this acte he sodainly brought the cittie of Athens into warres, yet he brought it thereby to be of greater power, and more fearefull to the enemies, by making alliance with the Mantinians and the Argives, who by Alcibiades practise entred into league with the Athenians. And Martius, as Dionysius the historiographer writeth: dyd by craft and deceipt bring the Romaines into warres against the Volsces, causing the Volsces maliciously, and wrongfully to be suspected, that went to Rome to see the games played. But the cause why he dyd it, made the fact so much more fowle and wicked. For it was not done for any civill dissention, nor for any jelouzy and contention in matters of government, as Alcibiades dyd: but only following his cholerike moode, that would be pleased with no thing, as Dion sayed, he would needes trouble and turmoile the most parte of Italie, and so beinge angrie with his countrie, he destroyed many other townes and cities that could not helpe it, nor doe with all. This is true also, that Alcibiades spite and malice did worke great mischiefe and miserie to his countrie: but when he saw they repented them of the injurie they had done him, he came to him selfe, and did withdrawe his armie. An other time also, when they had banished Alcibiades, he would not yet suffer the captaines of the

[1] *In margin:* 'The manners of Alcibiades and Coriolanus.'

Athenians to runne into great errours, neither would he see them cast away, by followinge ill counsell which they tooke, neither would he forsake them in any daunger they put them selves into. But he did the very same that Aristides had done in olde time unto Themistocles, for which he was then, and is yet so greatly praised. For he went unto the captaines that had charge then of the armie of the Athenians, although they were not his friendes, and tolde them wherein they did amisse, and what they had further to doe. Where Martius to the contrarie, did first great hurte unto the whole citie of Rome, though all in Rome had not generally offended him: yea, and when the best and chiefest parte of the citie were grieved for his sake, and were very sorie and angrie for the injurie done him. Furthermore, the Romaines sought to appease one onely displeasure and despite they had done him, by many ambassades, petitions and requestes they made, whereunto he never yelded, while[1] his mother, wife, and children came, his harte was so hardned. And hereby it appeared he was entred into this cruell warre (when he would harken to no peace) of an intent utterly to destroy and spoyle his countrie, and not as though he ment to recover it, or to returne thither againe. Here was in deede the difference betwene them: that spialls being layed by the Lacedæmonians to kill Alcibiades, for the malice they did beare him, as also for that they were affrayed of him, he was compelled to returne home againe to Athens. Where Martius contrariwise, having bene so honorably received and entertained by the Volsces, he could not with honestie forsake them, consideringe they had done him that honour, as to choose him their generall, and trusted him so farre, as they put all their whole armie and power into his handes: and not as thother, whome the Lacedæmonians rather abused, then used him, suffering him to goe up and downe their citie (and afterwardes in the middest of their campe) without honour or place at all. So that in the ende Alcibiades was compelled to put him selfe into the handes of Tisaphernes: unlesse they will say that he went thither of purpose to him, with intent to save the citie of Athens from utter destruction, for the desire he had to returne home againe. Moreover, we read of Alcibiades, that he was a great taker, and would be corrupted with money[2]: and when he had it, he would most licentiously and dishonestly spend it. Where Martius in contrarie maner would not so much as accept giftes lawefully offered him by his Captaines, to honour him for his valliantnesse. And the cause why the people did beare him such ill will, for the controversie they had with the Nobilitie about clearing of dettes, grew: for that they knewe well

[1] until. [2] *In margin:* 'Alcibiades and Coriolanus manner for money.'

enough it was not for any gayne or benefit he had gotten thereby, so much as it was for spite and displeasure he thought to doe them. Antipater in a letter of his, writing of the death of Aristotle the philosopher, doth not without cause commend the singular giftes that were in Alcibiades, and this inespecially: that he passed all other for winning mens good willes. Wheras all Martius noble actes and vertues, wanting that affabilitie, became hatefull even to those that received benefit by them, who could not abide his severitie and selfe will: which causeth desolation (as Plato sayeth) and men to be ill followed, or altogether forsaken. Contrariwise, seeing Alcibiades had a trimme enterteinment, and a very good grace with him, and could facion him selfe in all companies: it was no marvell if his well doing were gloriously commended, and him selfe much honoured and beloved of the people, considering that some faultes he did, were oftetimes taken for matters of sporte, and toyes of pleasure. And this was the cause, that though many times he did great hurte to the common wealth, yet they did ofte make him their generall, and trusted him with the charge of the whole citie. Where Martius suing for an office of honour that was due to him, for the sundrie good services he had done to the state, was notwithstanding repulsed, and put by. Thus doe we see, that they to whome the one did hurte, had no power to hate him: and thother that honoured his vertue, had no liking to love his persone. Martius also did never any great exployte, beinge generall of his contry men, but when he was generall of their enemies against his naturall contrie: whereas Alcibiades, being both a private persone, and a generall, did notable service unto the Athenians.[1] By reason whereof, Alcibiades wheresoever he was present, had the upper hande ever of his accusers, even as he would him selfe, and their accusations tooke no place against him: onlesse it were in his abscence. Where Martius being present, was condemned by the Romaines: and in his person murdered, and slaine by the Volsces. But here I can not say they have done well, nor justly, albeit him selfe gave them some colour to doe it, when he openly denied the Romaine Ambassadors peace, which after he privatly graunted, at the request of women. So by this dede of his, he tooke not away the enmity that was betwene both people: but leaving warre still betwene them, he made the Volsces (of whome he was generall) to lose the oportunity of noble victory. Where in deede he should (if he had done as he ought) have withdrawen his armie with their counsaill[2] and consent, that had reposed so great affiance in him, in making him their generall: if he had

[1] *In margin:* 'Alcibiades and Coriolanus love unto their contrie.'

[2] Cf. Aufidius, V.5.96–7.

made that accompt of them, as their good will towards him did in duety binde him. Or else, if he did not care for the Volsces in the enterprise of this warre, but had only procured it of intent to be revenged, and afterwards to leave it of, when his anger was blowen over: yet he had no reason for the love of his mother to pardone his contrie, but rather he should in pardoning his contrie, have spared his mother, bicause his mother and wife were members of the bodie of his contrie and city, which he did besiege. For in that he uncurteously rejected all publike petitions, requestes of Ambassadors, intreaties of the bishoppes and priestes, to gratifie only the request of his mother with his departure: that was no acte so much to honour his mother with, as to dishonour his contrie by, the which was preserved for the pitie and intercession of a woman, and not for the love of it selfe, as if it had not bene worthie of it. And so was this departure a grace, to say truly, very odious and cruell, and deserved no thankes of either partie, to him that did it. For he withdrew his army, not at the request of the Romaines, against whom he made warre: nor with their consent, at whose charge the warre was made.[1] And of all his misfortune and ill happe, the austeritie of his nature, and his hawtie obstinate minde, was the onely cause: the which of it selfe being hatefull to the worlde, when it is joyned with ambition, it groweth then much more churlish, fierce, and intollerable. For men that have that fault in nature, are not affable to the people, seeming thereby as though they made no estimacion or regard of the people: and yet on thother side, if the people should not geve them honour and reverence, they would straight take it in scorne, and litle care for the matter. For so did Metellus, Aristides, and Epaminondas, all used this manner: not to seeke the good will of the common people by flatterie and dissimulation: which was in deede, bicause they despised that which the people coulde geve or take awaye. Yet would they not be offended with their citizens, when they were amerced, and set at any fines, or that they banished them, or gave them any other repulse: but they loved them as wel as they did before, so soone as they shewed any token of repentaunce, and that they were sorie for the wrong they had done them, and were easely made frendes againe with them, after they were restored from their banishment. For he that disdaineth to make much of the people, and to have their favour, shoulde much more scorne to seeke to be revenged, when he is repulsed. For, to take a repulse and deniall of honour, so inwardly to the hart: commeth of no other cause, but that he did too earnestly desire it. Therefore Alcibiades did not dissemble at all, that he was not very glad to see him selfe

[1] V.5.65–9.

honored, and sory to be rejected and denied any honour: but also he sought all the meanes he could to make him selfe beloved of those amongest whome he lived. Whereas Martius stowtnes, and hawty stomake, did stay him from making much of those, that might advaunce and honour him: and yet his ambition made him gnawe him selfe for spite and anger, when he sawe he was despised. And this is all that reasonably may be reproved in him: for otherwise he lacked no good commendable vertues and qualities. For his temperaunce, and cleane handes from taking of bribes and money, he may be compared with the most perfect, vertuous, and honest men of all Græce[1]: but not with Alcibiades, who was in that undoutedly alwayes too licentious and losely geven, and had too small regard of his credit and honestie.

THE END OF CAIUS MARTIUS CORIOLANUS LIFE

III. Possible Source

From THE ROMAN HISTORIES OF LUCIUS FLORUS
translated by E. M. B. [?1621]

The Roman Histories of Lucius Julius Florus, from the foundation of Rome, till Cæsar Augustus, for above DCC. yeares, & from thence to Trajan near CC. yeares, divided by Florus into IV ages. Translated into English. London. By Wil. Stansby. [Col.: translated into English by E. M. B.]

From Lib. I. Chap. XI.
[Marcius' victory in perspective]

Over *Veii* and *Bovilli*, a shame to say it, yet wee triumphed. *Tibur* which is now but a suburbe, and *Praeneste*, but our summer-recreation, were then demaunded of the Gods as mightie matters, with vowes for victories made solemnly first in the Capitol. *Fæsulae* were then what *Taphrae* were of late; and the forest of *Aricinum* the same, which in these dayes the huge *Hercinian* woods; *Fregellae* what

[1] *In margin:* 'Coriolanus notable abstinence from bribes.'

Cessoriacum; and *Tibris* what *Euphrates*. Nay it was then held an act of so great glory to have overcome but *Corioli*, that *Caius Marcius* (fie upon it) was thereof called *Coriolanus*, as if hee had conquered *Numantia* in *Spaine*, or the worlds third portion, *Africa*.

Lib. I. Chap. XXII.

Of Seditions

This is the second age of the *Roman* people, and as it were their youth, a time in which they were most fresh, and budding out in certaine fierie shoots, boild over as it were in jollitie of spirit. On the other side, that wildenes which they retaind of their shepheardish originall, breathd foorth some-what still, *which was* untamed *in them*. Thence it came, that the armie, making a mutinie in the campe, stoned *Postuminus*, their Generall, to death, for refusing to give them the shares he promised. . . That under Generall *Volero*, most withdrawing their service, they crusht the Consulls *fasces*. Thence it was, that they punisht the most honourable commanders they had, with banishment, for resisting their pleasure, as *Coriolanus*, whom they condemned to the plough. Which injurie he would as harshly have chastised with his sword, if his mother *Veturia*, when he was now readie to charge, had not disweapond him with weeping. Yea, as *Camillus* himselfe, because in their conceits hee had not made the shares of the *Vaientine* spoiles indifferent, between the Commonaltie, and the souldier. But he, a much better *man*,[1] did rescue the besieged in *Rome* taken, and revenged *their quarel* upon the Galls their enemies, to whom but even now they were humble suitours. In such sort they contended also with the *Senate* itselfe about settling the rules of right, that abandoning their houses, they threatned emptinesse, and utter decay to their native countrey.

Lib. I. Chap. XXIII

The cities first discord

The first *intestine* dissention hapned through the unrulinesse of *Usurers*, who exercising villanous crueltie, the whole people departed in armes to the *Sacred Hill*, and very hardly, nor but untill they were given *Tribunes*, and were perswaded also by the authoritie of *Menenius Agrippa*, a wise, and eloquent man, could be drawne to return. The fable of that old oration, effectuall enough to induce concord, is extant. In which is fained, that the parts of mans bodie were once upon a time at ods together, for that, all the rest doing their severall offices, the bellie only was idle: but in the end, when

[1] than Coriolanus.

they found themselves almost pined to death by the separation, they became good friends againe, for that by the meate, which by the stomakes ministerie was converted into bloud, the veines were filled with nourishment.

IV. Sources

VERSIONS OF MENENIUS' FABLE[1]

(a) From *An Apology for Poetrie.* By Sir Philip Sidney (1595)

Infinite proofes of the strange effects of . . . poeticall invention might be alledged; onely two shall serve, which are so often remembred, as I thinke all men knowe them; The one of *Menenius Agrippa*, who, when the whole people of Rome had resolutely devided themselves from the Senate, with apparent shew of utter ruine, though hee were (for that time) an excellent Oratour, came not among them upon trust of figurative speeches or cunning insinuations, and much lesse with farre fet *Maximes* of Phylosophie, which (especially if they were *Platonick*) they must have learned Geometrie before they could well have conceived; but forsooth he behaves himselfe like a homely and familiar Poet. Hee telleth them a tale, that there was a time[2] when all the parts of the body made a mutinous[3] conspiracie against the belly, which they thought devoured the fruits of each others labour: they concluded they would let so unprofitable a spender starve. In the end, to be short, (for the tale is notorious, and as notorious that it was a tale) with punishing the belly they plagued themselves. This applied by him wrought such effect in the people, as I never read that ever words brought forth but then so suddaine and so good an alteration, for upon reasonable conditions a perfect reconcilement ensued.

(b) From *Remaines of a greater worke concerning Britaine.* By William Camden (1605)

Pope Adrian the Fourth, an Englishman born, of the Family of Breakspeare, in Middlesex, a man commended for converting Nor-

[1] For other versions see Livy [Text I] and Plutarch [Text II] above.

[2] I.1.96. [3] I.1.112, 'mutinous parts'.

way to Christianity before his Papacy, but noted in his Papacy for using the Emperour Frederick the Second as his page in holding his stirrop, demanded of John of Salisbury, his countreyman, what opinion the world had of the Church of Rome and of him; who answered: The Church of Rome which should be a mother is now a Stepmother, wherein sit both Scribes and Pharisees; and as for yourself, whenas you are a father, why do you expect pensions from your children? &c. Adrian smiled, and after some excuses told him this tale which, albeit may seem long, and is not unlike that of Menenius Agrippa in the Roman History, yet give it the reading, and happily you may learne somewhat by it.

All the members of the body conspired against the stomacke, as against the swallowing gulfe[1] of all their labors; for whereas the eyes beheld, the ears heard, the handes labored, the feete traveled, the tongue spake, and all partes performed their functions,[2] onely the stomacke lay idle and consumed all. Here uppon they joyntly agreed al to forbeare their labors, and to pine away their lasie and publike enemy. One day passed over, the second followed very tedious, but the third day was so grievous to them all, that they called a common Counsel; the eyes waxed dimme, the feete could not support the bodie, the armes waxed lasie, the tongue faltered, and could not lay open the matter; therefore they all with one accord desired the advise of the Heart.[3] Then Reason layd open before them that hee against whome they had proclaimed warres, was the cause of all this their misery: For he as their common steward, when his allowances were withdrawne of necessitie withdrew theirs fro them, as not receiving that he might allow. Therefore it were a farre better course to supply him, than that the limbs should faint with hunger. So by the perswasion of Reason, the stomacke was served, the limbes comforted, and peace re-established. Even so it fareth with the bodies of Common-weale; for albeit the Princes gather much, yet not so much for themselves, as for others: So that if they want, they cannot supply the want of others; therefore do not repine at Princes herein, but respect the common good of the whole publike estate.

[1] Cf. I.1.98. [2] I.1.99–105. [3] I.1.117, 'The counsellor heart.'

V. Accounts of Historical Sources

(a) The Oxfordshire rising of 1597[1]

From John Stow's Annales (1631 edn.)[2]

Bartholmewe Stere carpenter and singleman, and placed in verie good service about a fortnight before Michellmas was the first deviser of this insurreccon, his owtward pretence was to overthrowe enclosures, & to helpe the poore cominaltie that were readie to famish for want of corne, But intended to kill the gentleman of that countrie, and to take the spoile of them affirming that the Commons, long sithens in Spaine did rise and kill all the gentlemen in Spaine, and sithens that time have lyved merrily there. That after this he meant to have gonne to London and joyned with the prentices, who as he thought would joyne with him, for that some of them were lately hanged for the like attempt. And said yt was but a monethes work to overrunne England. He continewally persuaded others to joyne with him in this treason, and specially Roger Symondes who was a poore man, and had a great charge of children, and therefore should have some Collour to rise in respect of hunger.

He and Richard Bradshawe (who willingly joyned with him), agreed that the place where they should first assemble should be at Enslowe Hill, on the Monddie next after Saint Hughes daie. For Bradshawe said the sooner the Better. And Barth: Stere said, that there was ons a rising at Enslowe Hill by the Commons and they were perswaded to goe downe, and after were hanged like dogges. But said he wee will never yeeld but goe through with yt.

He at the first entering to this treason served the L. Norreis meant to have spoiled his howse, and to have taken his horse armour and artillarie, and to have victualled themselves with his wine, Beere, & other necessaries, and perswaded his Lordships carter, and coachman to joyne with him meaning to use them for their carriages.

He expected that the Gentlemens servantes of his Countrie would joyne with him in cutting their masters throates, for that he said they kepte like dogges.

He hadd allso drawne two of Sir William Spencers servantes videlt his Cater, and Carter, to be as he termed them sownde

[1] S.P. Dom. James I, Vol. 28, No. 64. Ascribed to 1597 by E. F. Gay, *Trans. of Royal Hist. Soc.*, New Series, XVIII, 1904, App. I.

[2] Annales, or, A Generall Chronicle of England. Begun by John Stow: Continued and Augmented with matters Forraigne and Domestique, Ancient and Moderne, unto the end of this present yeere, 1631. By Edmund Howes, Gent. Londini, Impensis Richardi Meighen, 1631.

fellowes. At the time and place appointed Barth Stere, Edward Bompas Robert Burton mason, and Thomas Horne, mett about ix of the Clock in the night well weoponed, especially Barth: Steere, and continewed there untill xi of the clock, and then departed for that others fayled.

Next to Barth: Steeir these to be principall offendors
Richard Bradshawe miller
Edw: Bompas fuller
Robt: Burton mason
and James Bradshawe miller . . .

Roger Symons did before the tyme appointed discover this treason, and never used speach of consent But to understand and reveale the treason. The clerest way to proceade against these is to procead uppon the statut of 13 of her majesties raigne uppon which lawe the prentices of London were attainted for the like offence.

Upon that lawe they must have 2 witnesses uppon there arraigment or their owne confession, and be proceaded against within five moneths.

(b) The unrest in 1607-8

About the middle of this moneth of May, 1607, a great number of common persons, sodainly assembled themselves in Northamptonshire, and then others of like nature assembled themselves in Warwickshire, and some in Leicestershire, they violently cut and brake downe hedges, filled up ditches, and laid open all such inclosures of Commons, and other grounds as they found inclosed, which of auncient time had beene open,[1] and imployed to tillage, these tumultuous persons in Northamptonshire, Warwicke, and Leicestershire grew very strong, being in some places of men, women, and children, a thousand together, and at Hill Norton in Warwickshire there were three thousand, and at Cottesbich there assembled of men, women, and children to the number of full five thousand: these riotous persons bent all their strength to leavell and lay open inclosures, without exercising any manner of theft, or violence upon any mans person, goods, or cattell, and wheresoever they came, they were generally relieved by the neere inhabitants, who sent them not onely many Carts laden with victuall, but also good store of Spades and Shovells, for speedy performance of their present enterprize, who untill then, some of them were faine to use Bills, Pykes, and such like tooles in stead of Mattocke and Spades.

[1] *In margin:* 'An insurrection for the laying open of enclosures.'

The twenty seaventh of this moneth, there were severall Proclamations made, straightly charging them to surcease their disorder, yet neverthelesse they ceased not, but rather persisted more eagerly, and thereupon the Sheriffs and Justices, had authority given them to suppresse them by force, by vertue whereof they raised an Army and scattered them, using all possible meanes to avoide bloudshed, and after that the king sent *Henry* Earle of Huntington, *Thomas* Earle of Excester, *Edward* Lord *Zowch*, *William* Lord *Compton*, *John* Lord *Harrington*, *Robert* Lord *Spencer*, *George* Lord *Carew*, Sir *Edward Coke* Lord chiefe Justice of the Common pleas, with divers other learned Judges, assisted by the Mayor of Coventry, and the most discreet Justices of peace, and of Dyer and Termyner in their severall Counties, to doe justice upon the leavellers, according to the nature of their offences.

And the 28. of June, the King made Proclamation, signifying his great unwillingnesse to have proceeded against them, either by Marshall law, or civill justice, if lenity or gentle admonition mought any wayes have prevailed with them, to desist from their turbulent, rebellious, and trayterous practise.

At the first those fore-said multitudes assembled themselves, without any particular head or guide, then start up a base Fellow called *John Reynoldes*, whom they surnamed Captaine *Powch*,[1] because of a great leather powch which he wore by his side, in which purse he affirmed to his company, that there was sufficient matter to defend them against all commers, but afterward when hee was apprehended, his Powch was searched, and therein was onely a peece of greene cheese. Hee told them also, that hee had Authority from his Majestie to throw downe enclosures, and that hee was sent of God to satisfie all degrees whatsoever, and that in this present worke hee was directed by the Lord of Heaven, and thereupon they generally inclined to his direction, so as hee kept them in good order, hee commaunded them not to sweare, nor to offer violence to any person: but to ply their businesse, and to make faire worke, entending to continue this worke, so long as God should put them in mind, at the beginning of these disordered assemblies untill their suppression, and due examination of many of the offenders, it was generally bruted throughout the land, that the special cause of their assemblies and discontent was concerning Religion, and the same past currant with many according to their severall opinions in religion, some sayd it was the Puritane factien, because they were the strongest, and thereby sought to enforce their pretended reformation, others said it was the practise of the Papists, thereby to obtaine restauration or tolleration, all which reports proved false as

[1] *In margin:* 'He was either a Pedler or a Tinker.'

appeared plainelie, by the examination of all such as were examined, whose generall pretence of grievances and cause of stirring in this riotous, and trayterous maner was onely for the laying open of inclosures. The prevention of further depopulation, the encrease and continuance of tillage to relieve their wives and children, and chiefely because it had beene credibly reported unto them by many, that of very late yeeres, there were three hundred and forty Townes decayed and depopulated, and that they supposed by this insurrection, and casting downe of inclosures to cause reformation.[1]

Some of them were indicted of high treason, and executed for leavying warre against the King, and opposing themselves against the Kings forces, Captaine *Powch* was made exemplary.[2]

Others for fellonie in continuing together by the space of an houre after proclamation to cease and depart according to the Statute, the rest were indited for Ryots, unlawfull assemblies and throwing downe of hedges and ditches.

(c) The Midland Revolt of 1607

(i) The Earl of Shrewsbury to the Earl of Kent,[3]

Your Lordship hath harde of the tumultuous rable of people that have assembled them selves fyrst in Northamptonshyre on May eve, throwynge downe sondry inclosures in dyvers parts, bothe in that countie, and synce in Warwykeshyre, and lastly in Leycestershyre, wher now they are, continuynge to doe the lyke / before this, your Lordship hathe (I thynke) seene the proclamation, and perhaps have bene informed of more particulars of theyr proceedynges then I know, although there is daly advertisement to the privy counsell from those severall counties, nevertheles I thought good to lett you understande, that his Majestie is nothyinge well pleased with the remiss course that bothe the sheriff and Justices of peace have taken in that matter, and also the deputy Liuetenants, [who ought to have arrested the ringleaders,] wheras on the contrary, they have only used perswations, and no force at all, and now very lately, the sheriffe and Justices of Warwykeshyre havynge hadd conference with a great number of them, perswadynge them to departe and desist from theis unlawfull courses, and shewynge them the danger of the Law, &c: they answered, that if the sayd sheriff and Justices wolde acquaynt his Majestie that the cause of theyr rysing was oute of no undutifull mynde to his Majestie but only for reformation of

[1] *In margin:* 'The pretences of their assemblies.'

[2] *In margin:* 'Their inditements.'

[3] Lansdowne MSS., vol. 90, no. 23. Cited from E. F. Gay, *ibid.*, App. II.

thos late inclosures which made them of the porest sorte reddy to pyne for wante, and that they myght heare answere from his Majestie within vi dayes and that his Highness wolde promis to reforme thos abuses, they wolde then all departe home, and rely uppon his Majesties promis and performance therof &c: which motion of theyrs, to acquaynt his Majestie they promised and sent up Sir Thomas Leygh, who yesterday in the afternoone made the privy counsell acquaynted therwith, which we conceaved to be a course very strange to expostulate with suche insolent, base and rebellious people who they sholde not have voutesafed to have spoken with in any other tearmes then theis (and not untill they hadd suffitient strengeth by them) vidz: to have opened to them theyr extreme folly and lewdeness to enter into so unlawfull and insolent an action and to have layed before them theyr perell and danger, and so to have perswaded them to disperse them selves and reterne home, which if they wolde have instantly done, then to have proceeded no further agaynst them, otherwise to have used force, and to have sett uppon them and used them as rebells and traytors, and to this effect we have (by his Majesties commandement) wrytten severall letters, and lykewise divers other letters (provisionally) into some other shyres adjoining directyng them to take the lyke course, if any suche tumultuous persons rise in theyr counties. And now I the rather troble your Lord[ship] with relation hereof, to thend that if ther shall happen any suche lose or bad people to aryse in bedfordshyre that yow will cause that sounde and sharpe course to be taken with them at the begynninge, and in no sorte otherwise to temporise with them, but to cutt them of at fyrst if perswation will not prevayle, neyther to use any perswation at all till you have some 40 or 50 horss well apoynted, which will run over and cutt in peeces a thousand of suche naked roges as thos are. Your Lordship may doe well to provyde before hande such numbers to be in redynes uppon a dayes warninge, if any suche cause shall happen ther espetially of horss. Which leavynge to your good consideration, I will heare take my leave not forgettynge my wyves most frendly commendacons to your Lordship we bothe ever wyshynge unto yow all honorable happyness. At the cowrte at Whytehall this 2 of June, 1607: In hast,

Your Lordships most affectionate
Lovyng brother and frend.
Gilb: Shrewsbury.

(ii) The Earl of Kent to the Earl of Shrewsbury.[1]

My very honourable good Lord / notwithstandinge all my best

[1] Talbot MSS. (Shrewsbury Letters), No. 89. Cited from E. F. Gay, *op. cit.*, App. II.

direccõns and comaundes by authoritie of his Majesties Commission of my Lieuetenauncye in this his hignes Countie of Bedfordshire (together with all the best care and diligence I possibly could both privately & publikely to prevent and suppresse theis and the like offences and offenders) have bene nowaie wantinge (as your Lordship hath of late partely understoode yet nowe your Lordship shall see, how many discontented obstinate people there be, who (even in this Contrye nowe of late, aswell as in diverse others) without all regard of lawe or reason, feare not tumultuously to disturbe (& what they can to overthrowe) the publike tranquilitie and precious peace, that they they and we all (by the great blessinge of God) do injoye underneath his Majesties happie government. That our Bedfordshire people should offend in this sorte, I am very sorie for it; but I hope that the censure and punishment allready imposed and that hereafter maie be further laid upon some of theis, wilbe such a warninge and example unto them and other the like affected people, that they will presume no more hereafter to committ the like offence: which god graunt. / I have made bold (my good Lord) to send unto your Lordship herewith my letter directed to your honours of the privie Councell concerninge the late troublesome buisines wee have had in this Contrye, as also the Copie of a warrant which I lately sent out for inquiry of unlawfull inclosures & depopulacõns accordinge to your and theire Honours direccõns unto me by your late letters; . . .

(d) Dearth in England, 1608

[William Combe to the Earl of Salisbury] [1]

I am overbold to acquaint your lordship with such grievances as the common people of this country (whereof for this year I have the custody under his Majesty) are troubled with: *videlicet*, with the dearth of corn, the prices rising to some height, caused partly by some that are well stored, by refraining to bring the same to the market out of a covetous conceit that corn will be dearer, and by engrossing of barley by maltsters, of the chief townsmen in every corporation, amongst whom the Justices of the country have no intermeddling. These matters make the people arrogantly and seditiously to speak of the not reforming of conversion of arable land into pasture by enclosing.

[1] S.P. Dom. James I, Vol. 34, No. 4. Text from E. I. Fripp, *Shakespeare Man and Artist*, 1938, II, 706.

VI. Factual Source

(a) From Annales, or A Generall Chronicle of England. Begun by John Stow . . . 1631

(i) [The Frost of 1564/5]

The 21. of December began a Frost, which continued so extreamely, that on New-yeares even people went over and along the Thamis on the Ice from London-bridge to Westminster[1], some played at foote-ball as boldly there, as if it had beene on the dry land, divers of the Court being then at Westminster, shot daily at pricks set upon the Thamis: and the people both men and women went on the Thamis in greater number then in any streete of the City of London.[2] On the third day of January at night it began to thaw: and on the fift day was no Ice to be seene betweene London bridge and Lambeth, which caused great flouds and high waters, that bare downe bridges and houses, and drowned many people in England, especially in Yorkeshire, Owes bridge was borne away with other.[3]

(ii) [The Frost of 1607/8]

The eight of December began a hard frost, which continued seven dayes, and then thawed gently five daies space[4]: and the two and twentieth of the same moneth, the Frost began againe very violently, so as within foure dayes many persons did walke halfe way over the Thamis upon the Ice, and by the thirtieth of December, the multitude at every ebbe, and halfe floud passed over the Thamis in divers places: and although the vyolence of the frost abated now and then, yet it helde from the third of January, unto the fifteenth of the same, so as many set up boothes and standings of sundry things to sell upon the Ice, and some shot at prickes, and playd at bowles with other exercises of pleasure upon the Ice, whereof I have spoken sufficiently in my abridgement. From the foure and twentieth of January unto the thirtieth of the same, the frost was most violent, and the next morning it began to thaw, and the first of February the Ice began to breake by little and little, and the next day in the afternoone all the huge rockes and over-spreading Ice was either quite

[1] *In margin:* 'The Thamis frozen over.'
[2] *In margin:* '1564.'
[3] *In margin:* 'Owes bridge borne downe.'
[4] *In margin:* 'A great frost.'

dissolved or sunke, so as then there remained no manner of signe of frost. And although this great frost continued of and on, by the space of seven weeks yet the Ice was not so delicate smooth and even and pleasant, as was that great frost in the yeere 1564. by reason that frost helde firme, from the beginning unto the ending, but this did not so: this frost brake downe and spoyled many faire bridges and destroyed much wild fowle, especially water foule and smale byrds, and much fish perished, as well in the sea, as in fresh waters, and were found dead upon the shore in divers parts of this Land: this frost destroyed much Herbage in gardens, especially Hartichokes and Rosemary; this Frost was more grievous in Fraunce, then in England. The Russians, Norwayes, and other nations of the North: upon the certaine knowledge of this frost, laughed the French & English to scorne, saying, how foolishly and shamefully, you complaine of one poore sixe weekes cold, which happeneth not in your countries, but once in fiftie yeeres, when wee in fiftie yeeres space, have seldome lesse frost then five moneths, continually every yeere, and with more extremity: this frost was also very violent in Ireland.

(b) From The Great Frost. [By Thomas Dekker?] 1608

The Great Frost. Cold doings in London, except it be at the Lottery. With News out of the Country. A familiar talk between a Countryman and a Citizen touching this terrible Frost, and the great Lottery, and the effects of them, Printed at London for Henry Gosson.

[A Citizen of London and an old Countryman from Ripon in Yorkshire discuss the effects of the Great Frost, 'the harms that this frost hath done to the City,' 'The misery that the country people are driven into by the means of this frost' etc.].

COUN. . . . But I beseech you tell me. Is that goodly river of yours—I call it yours because you are a citizen, and that river is the nurse that gives milk and honey to your city—but is that lady of fresh waters all covered over with ice?

CIT. All over, I assure you, father. The frost hath made a floor upon it, which shows like grey marble roughly hewn out. It is a very pavement of glass, but that it is more strong. The Thames now lies in: or rather is turned, as some think, bankrupt: and dares not show her head; for all the water of it floats up and down like a spring in a cellar.

COUN. God help the poor fishes! It is a hard world with them, when their houses are taken over their heads. They use not to lie under such thick roofs. . . .

. . . And do not the western barges come down upon certain artificial pulleys and engines, sliding on the ice; to serve your city with fuel?

CIT. That were a wonder worth the seeing, and more strange than the rowing over steeples by land in a wherry. I assure you these stories shall never stand in our chronicles. There is no such motion.

COUN. But I hope, Sir, you and I may drink a pint of sack in the tavern that runs by wheels on the river, as well as a thousand have done besides, may we not? The motion of that wine cellar, I am sure is to be seen. Is it not?

CIT. The water cellar is, but the wine cellars have too good doings on the land to leave that, and to set up taverns on the river. You know more in the country I perceive than we do in the city of these matters.

COUN. Nay, Sir, we hear more but know less. We hear the lies, and you know the truth . . .

CIT. . . . You shall understand that the Thames began to put on his freeze-coat, which he yet wears, about the week before Christmas; and hath kept it on till now this latter end of January: how long time soever besides to come none but God knows.

COUN. Did it never thaw in these many weeks?

CIT. Only three days, or four at most; and that but weakly, to dissolve so great a hardness. The cakes of ice, great in quantity and in great numbers, were made and baked cold in the mouth of winter, at the least a fortnight or three weeks befor they were crusted and cemented together; but after they had once joined their strengths into one, their backs held out and could not be broken.

COUN. We may make this good use, even out of this watery and transformed element; that London upholdeth a State: and again, that violent factions and combinations, albeit of the basest persons, in a commonwealth are not easily dissolved; if once they be suffered to grow up to a head. On, Sir, I pray.

[The Citizen describes how first boys then older people dared to walk on the river]

CIT. . . . As the ice increased in hardness, so men's hearts increased in hardiness: so that at the length . . . both men, women, and children walked over and up and down in such companies; that, I verily believe and I dare almost swear it, the one half, if not three parts of the people in the city have been seen going on the Thames. The river showed not now, neither shows it yet, like a river, but like a field, where archers shoot at pricks, while others play at football. It is a place of mastery, where some wrestle and some run; and he that does best is aptest to take a fall. It is an alley to walk upon without dread, albeit under it be most assured danger. The gentlewomen that tremble to pass over a bridge in the field, do here walk boldly. The citizen's wife that looks pale when she sits in a boat for fear of drowning, thinks that here she treads as safe now as in her parlour. Of all ages, of both sexes, of all professions, this is the common path. It is the roadway between London and Westminster, and between Southwark and London. Would you drink a cup of sack, father? here stand some with runlets to fill it out.

COUN. Ah ha! that is the tavern then that is talked on.

CIT. Thirst you for beer, ale, usquebaugh, &c.; or for victuals? There you may buy it, because you may tell another day how you dined upon the Thames. Are you cold with going over? You shall ere you come to the midst of the river, spy some ready with pans of coals to warm your fingers.[1] If you want fruit after you have dined, there stand costermongers to serve you at your call. And thus do people leave their houses and the streets; turning the goodliest river in the whole kingdom into the broadest street to walk in.

. . . .

COUN. . . . This cold ague of the earth must needs have warmth to help it. That warmth must come from fire, and that fire cannot be had without cost: how then, I pray you, in this so general an affliction how did poor people shift for fuel to comfort them?

CIT. Their care for fire was as great as for food. Nay, to want it was a worse torment than to be without meat. The belly was now pinched to have the body warmed: and had not the provident Fathers of this city carefully, charitably and out of a good and godly zeal, dispersed a relief to the poor in several parts and places about the outer bounds of the City, where poverty most inhabiteth; by storing them beforehand with sea coal and other firing at a reasonable rate, I verily persuade myself that the unconscionable and unmerciful raising of the prices of fuel by chandlers, woodmongers, &c.—who now meant to lay the poor on the rack—would have been the death of many a wretched creature through want of succour.

COUN. Not unlikely, Sir. . . .

CIT. . . . As I have discovered unto you what cold doings we have

[1] Cf. I.1.174.

had during this frost in the city; so, I pray, let me understand from you what kind of world you have lived in, in the country.

COUN. The world with us of the country runs upon the old rotten wheels, For all the northern cloth that is woven in our country will scarce make a gown to keep Charity warm; she goes so a-cold. Rich men had never more money, and Covetousness had never less pity. There was never in any age more money stirring nor never more stir to get money. Farmers are now slaves to racking young prodigal landlords. Those landlords are more servile slaves to their own riots and luxury. But these are the common diseases of every kingdom, and therefore are but common news. The tunes of the nightingale are stale in the middle of summer, because we hear them at the coming in of the spring: and so these harsh notes which are sung in every country do by custom grow not to be regarded. But your desire, Sir, is to know how we spend the days of this our frozen age in the country.

CIT. That I would hear indeed, father.

COUN. Believe me, Sir, as wickedly you must think as you can hear in your City. It goes as hard with us as it doth with you. The same cold hand of WINTER is thrust into our bosoms. The same sharp air strikes wounds into our bodies. The same sun shines upon us; but the same sun doth not heat us any more than it doth you. The poor ploughman's children sit crying and blowing their nails, as lamentably as the children and servants of your poor artificers. Hunger pinches their cheeks, as deep into the flesh as it doth into yours here. You cry out here, you are undone for coals: and we complain, we shall die for want of wood. . . .

BIBLIOGRAPHY

I. Historical Works

ALLEN, B.M. *Augustus Cæsar.* 1937.

BOAK, A. E. R. *A History of Rome to 565 A.D.* N.Y., 1943.

COWELL, F. R. *Cicero and the Roman Republic.* 1948.

FERRERO, G. *The Greatness and Decline of Rome* I–III. 1907–8.

FOWLER, W. W. *Julius Cæsar and the Foundation of the Roman Imperial System.* 1904.

HEITLAND, W. E. *The Roman Republic.* 2 vols. Cambridge, 1923.

MOMMSEN, THEODORE. *History of Rome.* 5 vols. 1854–85.

OMAN, SIR CHARLES. *Seven Roman Statesmen.* 1902.

SCULLARD, H. H. *History of the Roman World from 753 to 146 B.C.* 1935.

—— *Roman Politics, 220–150 B.C.* Oxford, 1951.

—— *From the Gracchi to Nero.* 2nd edn. 1963.

TAYLOR, L. R. *Party Politics in the Age of Cæsar.* Berkeley and Los Angeles, 1949.

WALTER, GERARD. *Julius Cæsar.* 2 vols. 1953.

II. Knowledge and Influence of the Classics

BALDWIN, T. W. *Shakspere's Small Latine and Lesse Greeke.* 2 vols. Urbana, 1942.

BOAS, F. S. *University Drama in the Tudor Age.* Oxford, 1914.

CHARLTON, H. B. *The Senecan Tradition in Renaissance Tragedy.* Manchester, 1946. (Also as Introduction to *Works of Sir W. Alexander,* ed. L. Kastner and H. B. Charlton. Manchester, 1920.)

CONLEY, C. H. *The First English Translators of the Classics.* New Haven, 1927.

CREIZENACH, W. *The English Drama in the Age of Shakespeare.* 1916.

CUNLIFFE, P. W. *The Influence of Seneca on Elizabethan Tragedy.* 1893.

ELIOT, T. S. *The Classics and the Man of Letters.* 1943.

FARNHAM, WILLARD. *Shakespeare's Tragic Frontier.* Berkeley, 1950.

FRIPP, E. I. *Shakespeare, Man and Artist.* 2 vols. 1938.

HARVEY, SIR PAUL. *The Oxford Companion to Classical Literature.* Oxford, 1955 edn.

HIGHET, GILBERT. *The Classical Tradition.* 1951 edn.

HONIGMANN, E. A. J. 'Shakespeare's Plutarch'. *ShQ.* x. 1959, 25–33.

KNIGHT, G. WILSON. *The Imperial Theme.* 1951.

LUCAS, F. L. *Seneca and Elizabethan Tragedy*. Cambridge, 1922.
MACCALLUM, M. W. *Shakespeare's Roman Plays and their Background*. 1910.
PALMER, JOHN. *Political Characters in Shakespeare*. 1945.
PHILLIPS, J. E. *The State in Shakespeare's Greek and Roman Plays*. N.Y., 1940.
RIBNER, IRVING. *Patterns in Shakespearian Tragedy*. 1960. Article in JEGP, LVI, 1957, 10–22.
ROOT, R. K. *Classical Mythology in Shakespeare*. N.Y., 1903.
SANDYS, J. E. *A History of Classical Scholarship*. 3 vols. Cambridge, 1903–8; 1958.
SIMPSON, P. 'Shakespeare's Use of Latin Authors', in *Studies in Elizabethan Drama*. Oxford, 1955.
SPENCER, T. J. B. 'Shakespeare and the Elizabethan Romans', *ShSurvey*, 10. Cambridge, 1957.
STAPFER, P. *Shakespeare and Classical Antiquity* (tr. E. J. Carey). 1880.
STIRLING, BRENTS. *The Populace in Shakespeare*. N.Y., 1949.
—— *Unity in Shakespearian Tragedy*. N.Y., 1956.
THOMSON, J. A. K. *The Classical Background of English Literature*. 1948.
—— *Classical Influences on English Poetry*. 1951.
TILLEY, A. A. *The Literature of the French Renaissance*. 2 vols. Cambridge, 1904.
TRAVERSI, D. *Shakespeare. The Roman Plays*. 1964.
WHITAKER, V. K. *Shakespeare's Use of Learning*. 1953.
WILSON, J. D. 'Shakespeare's "Small Latin"—how much?' in *ShSurvey*, 10. Cambridge, 1957.
WOODWARD, A. M. 'Greek History at the Renaissance', *Journal of Hellenic Studies* 63, 1943, 1–14.

III. Editions and Criticism of Individual Plays

Julius Cæsar

1. Editions of (*a*) the Play, (*b*) Sources and Analogues.

(*a*) Fl 1623. Modern edns.: A. D. Innes, *Warwick*, 1893; M. Hunter, 1900; M. MacMillan, *Arden*, 1902; F. H. Sykes, 1909; H. H. Furness, Jr., *New Variorum*, 1913; L. Mason, *Yale*, 1919; G. L. Kittredge, 1939; J. D. Wilson, *Cambridge*, 1949; T. S. Dorsch, *New Arden*, 1955.
(*b*) ALEXANDER, SIR WILLIAM. *Julius Cæsar*, in *The Monarchicke. Tragedies*. 1607. Modern edn.: *Poetical Works of Sir W. Alexander*, ed. L. E. Kastner and H. B. Charlton, 2 vols. Manchester, 1921.
[Anon.] *The Tragedie of Cæsar and Pompey, or Cæsar's Revenge*. 1607. Modern edns.: W. Mühlfeld, *ShJb*, xlvii, 1911, 132–55; *MalSoc*, ed. F. S. Boas, 1911.
APPIAN OF ALEXANDRIA. *Roman History*. Greek: Paris, 1551. Latin: tr. P. Candidus, Venice, 1477. Other Lat. edns.: 1500, 1526, 1529, etc. French trans. by C. de Seyssel,

Lyons, 1544; Italian, A. Braccio, Vinegia, 1538; Spanish, D. de Salazar, 1536. English: *An Auncient Historie and exquisite Chronicle of the Romanes Warres. both Civile and Foren. . . . The second part . . . trans. . . . by W.B.* 1578. Modern trans.: H. White. 6 vols. (Loeb), 1912. Modern selection: E. Schanzer, *Shakespeare's Appian*, 1956.

BLENERHASSET, THOMAS, ed. *The Second Part of the Mirrour for Magistrates.* 1578.

[BOTERO, G.] *Observations upon the Lives of Alexander, Cæsar and Scipio. Newly Englished.* 1602. [From *I Prencipi*. Torino, 1600.]

CÆSAR, GAIUS JULIUS. *Works.* Rome, 1469 etc.; Venice, 1471; Milan, 1477, etc. . . . *C. Julii Cæsaris commentarii. . . .* London. A. Hatfield & N. Newton. 1585; 1601. English trans.: *Julius Cæsars Commentaryes. Newly translatyd in to englyshe as much as concernyth thys realm of England* . . . [by John Tiptoft]. 1530. *The eyght bookes of C. J. Cæsar* . . . trans. Arthur Goldinge. 1565, 1595. *Observations of the five bookes of C's Commentaries, setting fourth the practise of the art military in the Time of the Roman Empire . . . by Clement Edmondes.* 1600, 1604, 1609.

CARION, JOHAN. *Chronica* [ed. P. Melancthon] Wittemberg [1532]. Several later edns. English trans.: *The thre bokes of Cronicles whyche John Carion . . . Gathered wyth great diligence* . . . [trans. Walter Lynne] 1550. French trans.: *Chronique et Histoire Universelle*, [tr. S. Goulart], Geneva, 1595.

CHAUCER, GEOFFREY. *Works.* Pynson's edn. 3 pts. 1526. *The Workes of Geffray Chaucer.* Ed. W. Thynne. 1532; 1542; ed. J. Stow, 1561; ed. T. Speght, 1598; 1602. Modern edns. W. W. Skeat, 6 vols. 1894–7; F. N. Robinson, Boston, 1933. *The Monkes Tale*, ed. W. W. Skeat, Oxford. 1874; 1898.

CICERO, MARCUS TULLIUS. *Brutus.* Rome, 1469; Venice, 1514–5, etc. Modern edns.: G. L. Henderson and H. M. Hubbell (Loeb), 1942; J. Marthe (French) Paris, 1960. *Philippics.* Rome, 1470?, Venice, 1474, etc. London (R. Pynson) 1521; Paris, 1544; Basle, 1551, etc. Modern edn.: W. C. A. Ker (Loeb), 1926. *Familiar Letters.* Rome, 1467; Venice, 1469, 1471 etc.; Paris, 1531; 1579; 1585. Eng. trans.: J. Webbe, 1620. Modern edn.: W. G. Williams (Loeb), 1928.

DION CASSIUS. *Roman Histories.* Greek: Paris, 1548. Latin trans.: (selection) 1481?; Venice, 1526; Lyons, 1559; Frankfurt, 1592; Geneva, 1592. Italian trans.: 1533, 1542 etc. Modern edn.: E. Cary (Loeb), 9 vols. 1914–27.

EEDES, RICHARD. *Cæsar Interfectus.* Epilogue only in F. S. Boas, *University Drama in the Tudor Age.* 1914.

ELYOT, SIR THOMAS. *The Boke named The Governour.* 1531. 8 edns. by 1580.

EUTROPIUS, FLAVIUS. *Breviarium ab Urbe Condita.* Rome, 1471;

1475; 1510; 1516, etc. Eng. trans. Nicolas Haward, *A briefe Chronicle* ... 1564; J. S. Watson (Bohn) 1848. Modern edn.: W. H. S. Jones, 1905.

FLORUS, L. (J.) ANNAEUS. *De Gestis Romanorum libri quatuor.* Paris, 1470–2; Venice, 1472; 1475; 1493; Parma, 1473; Cologne, 1475; 1490, etc. Basle, 1532; Paris, 1539; Cologne, 1540; Antwerp, 1584; English trans.: *The Roman Histories ... Trans. by E.M.B*[olton]. [1619], 1621.

GARNIER, ROBERT. *Cornélie tragédie.* R. Estienne. Paris, 1574. *Les Tragedies* ... Paris, 1580; 1585; 1588; 1592; 1595 etc. Modern edn.: *Œuvres complètes, théâtre et poésies* ... ed. L. Pinvert. 2 tom. Paris, 1923. English trans.: See T. Kyd.

GREVIN, JACQUES. *Le Théâtre de Jacques Grévin* ... Paris, 1562. Modern edn.: ed. Lucien Pinvert. Paris, 1922. *César*, ed. G. A. D. Collischonn, 'Grévins Tragödie *Cæsar* in ihrem Verhältniss zu Muret' (in Stengel, E. M., *Ausgaben und Abhandlungen* ... No. 52, 1882).

HIGGINS, JOHN. *The Mirror for Magistrates.* 3 pts. 1587.

KYD, THOMAS. *Cornelia.* Printed by James Roberts for N.L[ing] and John Busbie. 1594. Modern edns.: R. Dodsley, *Old Plays*, XI, 1744; Hazlitt's Dodsley, IV, 1874; H. Gassner, Munich, 1894; F. S. Boas, 1901 (in *Works*).

LIVIUS, TITUS. *Decades.* Rome, 1469, 1470, etc.; Venice, 1470; Cologne, 1525; Basle, 1535; Lyons, 1542; Frankfurt, 1578; London (E. Bollifant) 1589. French trans.: Paris, 1487, 1514, etc. Italian: 1476; German, 1505; Dutch, 1541. English: *The Romane Historie*, by Philemon Holland, 1600.

LUCANUS, MARCUS ANNÆUS. *Pharsalia.* Rome, 1469; Venice, 1471; 1477; 1486; Vicenza, 1482; Paris, 1506; 1514; Many editions. London, 1589. Italian trans., 1492. English trans.: *Lucans first Booke, translated Line for Line, by Chr. Marlow*, P. Short, 1600. Sir A. Gorges, 1614; T. May, 1627; J. Duff, 1928; R. Graves, 1956. Modern edn. of Marlowe: L. C. Martin, *Poems*, 1931.

MURET, MARC ANTOINE. *Julius Cæsar.* First printed in *M.A. Mureti Opera.* 5 vols. Verona, 1727–30. Modern edn.: in Collischonn, G. A. D., 'Grévins Tragödie *Cæsar* in ihrem Verhältniss zu Muret.' (Stengel, E. M. *Ausgaben und Abhandlungen* ... No. 52. 1882).

OROSIUS, PAULUS. *Historiæ adversus Paganos.* 1471. Vicenza; 1475, etc. Paris, 1524; Cologne, 1526, etc. French trans.: 1509; 1526; Italian: 1525; German: 1539. English: *King Alfred's Anglo-Saxon Version* ... ed. J. Bosworth, 1859; H. Sweet, 1883; *Seven Books* ... trans. I. W. Raymond. N.Y., 1936.

OUTREMEUSE, JEAN DES PREIS. *Ly Myreur des Histors* ... ed. A. Borgnet. 7 vols. Bruxelles. 1864–87.

PESCETTI, ORLANDO. *Il Cesare, tragedia d'Orlando Pescetti* . . . Verona, 1594.

PETRARCA, FRANCESCO. *Il Libro degli Homini Famosi* . . . (tr. from Latin by Donato degli Albanzani), 1476; 1527. Modern edn.: *Historia Julii Cæsaris*, ed. C. E. C. Schneider. Lipsiae, 1827.

PLUTARCH. *Parallel Lives of Greeks and Romans*. Greek: Florence, 1517; Venice, 1519; Basle, 1533 etc. Latin: Rome, 1470?; Strasburg, 1472; Venice, 1478 etc. Basle, 1552 etc. Frankfurt, 1580. Many other edns. French trans.: J. Amyot, 1559; English: *Lives of the Noble Grecians and Romanes*, by Sir Thomas North, 1579; 1595; 1603; 1612; 1631. Modern edns.: George Wyndham, 6 vols. 1895–6; W. W. Skeat, *Shakespeare's Plutarch*, 1875; C. F. T. Brooke, *Shakespeare's Plutarch*, 2 vols., N.Y., 1909; P. Turner, *Select Lives*, 2 vols., 1963.

SALLUSTIUS CRISPUS, CAIUS. *Works*. Venice, 1470; 1474, etc. Paris, 1471, etc. Many edns. French trans.: Paris, 1547; 1577. Spanish trans.: Saragossa, 1493; German: 1515; Italian: 1518; French: 1547; 1577. English (*Jugurthine War*) Sir A. Barclay, 1520?; 1525?; 1557. *The Two Most worthy and Notable Histories, the Conspiracie of Cateline and the Warre which Jugurth maintained* . . . T. Heywood, 1608–9.

SCHIAPOLLARIA, S. A. *La Vita di C. Julio Cesare*. Antwerp, 1578.

SUETONIUS TRANQUILLUS, CAIUS. *Vitae Duodecim Caesarum*. Rome, 1470; Venice, 1471; 1480, etc. Florence, 1515; Basle, 1518; 1533; 1560; Paris, 1535; 1543; Antwerp, 1548; 1591, etc.; Geneva, 1595. Many edns. Italian trans.: 1539; 1554; French: 1541; English: *The Historie of Twelve Cæsars* . . . Philemon Holland, 1606.

TACITUS, PUBLIUS CORNELIUS. *Opera*. Venice, 1470?; 1497; 1534; Rome, 1515; Basle, 1519; 1533; Florence, 1527; Antwerp, 1589. French trans.: 1594; Italian: 1611; Spanish, 1614. English trans.: *Annales* and *Germanie*, R. Grenewey, 1598; 1604, etc. *Fower Bookes of the Histories* . . . [Sir H. Savile] 1591; 1598; 1604, etc. Modern edn.: *Works*, trans. A. Murphy, 4 vols. 1793, etc.; *Histories*, C. H. Moore, and *Annals*, J. Jackson. 4 vols (Loeb) 1931–51.

TUIM, JEAN DE. *Li hystoire de Julius Cæsar* . . . ed. F. Settegest [*Romania*, xii]. Halle, 1881.

VALERIUS MAXIMUS. *Facta et Dicta Memorabilia*. Strasburg, c. 1470; Venice, 1471; 1474; 1502; Antwerp, 1585; Paris, 1475, etc. Many edns. French trans.: 1488; English: *Romæ antiquæ Descriptio* . . . by Samuel Speed. 1678.

VELLEIUS PATERCULUS, CAIUS. *Roman History*. Basle, 1520; Florence, 1525; Padua, 1590; Frankfurt, 1589; Lyons, 1592. English trans.: *V.P. his Romane Historie*, trans. S^r^. R. Le Grys, 1632.

2. Critical Studies of Sources, etc.

ALTKAMP, I. *Die Gestaltung Cæsars bei Plutarch und Shakespeare.* Würzburg, 1933.

AYRES, H. M. 'Shakespeare's *Julius Cæsar* in the Light of some other Versions', *PMLA*, n.s. 18, 1910, 183–227.

BEDE. *Ecclesiastical History.* Strasburg, 1475?; Antwerp, 1550. *Opera*: Paris, 1544; Basle, 1563. Modern edn.: J. E. King (Loeb) 1930.

BOAS, F. S. *The Works of Thomas Kyd.* 1901 (Introduction.)

BOECKER, ALEXANDER. *A Probable Italian Source of Shakespeare's Julius Cæsar.* N.Y., 1913.

BROOKE, C. F. T. *Shakespeare's Plutarch.* 2 vols. N.Y., 1909.

COLLISCHONN, G. A. D. 'Grévins Tragödie *Cæsar* in ihrem Verhältniss zu Muret' in Stengel, E. M., *Ausgaben und Abhandlungen* . . . No. 52. 1882.

CASTELAIN, M. *Jules César.* Paris, 1945.

DELIUS, N. 'Shakespeares *Julius Cæsar* und seine Quellen in Plutarch', *ShJb*, xvii. 1882.

DUNN, F. E. 'Julius Cæsar in the English Chronicles', in *Classical Journal*, xiv, 1918, 280–94.

EDMONDS, SIR C. *Observations upon the Five Books of Cæsar's Commentaries.* 1600.

ELLEHAUGE, MARTIN. 'The Use of his Sources made by Shakespeare in *Julius Cæsar* and *Antony and Cleopatra*', *EngStud.*, 65, 1930/1, 197–210.

FOWLER, W. WARDE. '*Julius Cæsar*', in *Roman Essays and Interpretations.* Oxford, 1920.

GRAF, A. *Roma nella memoria e nelle imaginazioni del medio evo.* Rome, 1882–3.

GUNDOLF, F. *The Mantle of Cæsar.* 1929.

HALL, VERNON. (ed.) *Studies in the English Renaissance Drama.* 1959.

HUNTER, SIR M. 'Politics and Character in Shakespeare's *Julius Cæsar*', in *Essays by Divers Hands. Trans. R. Soc.*, Lib. X, 1931.

MACCALLUM, M. W. *Shakespeare's Roman Plays and their Background.* 1910, pp. 1–299.

MAXWELL, J. C. '*Julius Cæsar* and Elyot's *Governour*', *N & Q* Vol. 201, 1956, p. 147.

PALOGI, B. *Giulio Cesare nella poesia drammatica italiana e straniera.* 1918.

PARODI, E. G. *Le Storie di Cesare nella letteratura italiana dei primi secoli.* (Studi di filologia romanza, Vol. 4.) 1889.

REES, JOAN. '*Julius Cæsar*—an Earlier Play, and an Interpretation.' *MLR*, L, 1955, 135–41.

SARRAZIN, G. 'Shakespeare und Orlando Pescetti.' *EngStud.*, xlvi. 1913.

SCHANZER, ERNEST. *Shakespeare's Problem Plays.* 1963.
'A Neglected Source of *Julius Cæsar*', *N & Q*, 199, 1954, 196–7.
'The Problem of *Julius Cæsar.*' *ShQ*, vi, 1955, 297–308.
'The Tragedy of Shakespeare's Brutus', *ELH*, xxii, 1955.

SHACKFORD, M. H. '*Julius Cæsar* and Ovid', *MLN*, xli, 1926.
SKEAT, W. W. *Shakespeare's Plutarch.* 1875.
SMITH, W. D. 'Duplicate Revelations of Portia's Death', *ShQ*, iv. 1953.
WESEMANN, H. *Cæsar fabeln des Mittelalters.* Löwenberg-i-Schl, 1879.
WILSON, J. D. 'Ben Jonson and *Julius Cæsar*', *ShSurvey*, 2. 1949.

Antony and Cleopatra

I. Editions of (*a*) the Play, (*b*) Sources and Analogues

(*a*) F1 1623. Modern edns.: R. H. Case, *Arden*, 1906, 1930; H. H. Furness, Jr., *Variorum*, 1907; H. S. Canby, *Yale*, 1921; T. Spencer, 1948; J. D. Wilson, *Cambridge*, 1950; M. R. Ridley, *New Arden*, 1954.

(*b*) Anon. *I Fatti di Cesare*, ed. L. Banchi. Bologna. 1863.

APPIAN OF ALEXANDRIA. *An Auncient Historie and exquisite Chronicle of the Romane Warres, both Civile and Foren. Written in Greeke by . . . Appian of Alexandria . . .* [Translated by W.B.] 1578. Modern selection: Ernest Schanzer. *Shakespeare's Appian.* Liverpool, 1956.

DANIEL, SAMUEL. *The Tragedy of Cleopatra.* In *Delia and Rosamond Augmented*, 1594, 1595; *The Poetical Essayes of Samuel Danyell. Newly corrected and augmented.* 1599; *Works.* 3 pts. 1601, 1602; *Certain Small Workes heretofore divulged by S.D.* 1607, revised 1611; *The Whole Workes of S. Daniel . . .* 1623. Modern edns.: *The Complete Works in Verse and Prose*, ed. A. Grosart, 5 vols. 1885–96; *Cleopatra*, ed. M. Lederer (*Materialien*, xxxi) 1911.

FLORUS, LUCIUS ANNÆUS. *The Romane Histories*, trans. E. M. B[olton]. [1619] 1621.

GARNIER, ROBERT. *Marc-Antoine, tragedie.* Paris, 1578. Huits Tragedies, Paris, 1580; 1585; 1588, etc. Modern edns.: *Œuvres complètes, théâtre et poésies* . . . ed. L. Pinvert, 2 tom. Paris, 1923; Paris, 1949. English trans.: Mary Herbert, Countess of Pembroke, *The Tragedy of Antonie* [see below].

GIRALDI CINTHIO, G. B. *Cleopatra, tragedia.* Venice, 1583; also in *Le Tragedie di G. G. Cinthio . . .* Venice, 1583.

HERBERT [SIDNEY], MARY, COUNTESS OF PEMBROKE. *Antonius, A Tragoedie . . . done in English by the Countesse of Pembroke.* 1592. *The Tragedie of Antonie. Doone into English by the Countesse of Pembroke.* 1595. Modern edn.: Alice Luce. Weimar, 1897.

JODELLE, E. *Cléopatre Captive*, in *Oeuvres et meslanges poétiques*, 1574; 1583; 1597–Modern edn.: L. B. Ellis. Philadelphia, 1946.

JOSEPHUS, FLAVIUS. *Works.* Greek: Basle, 1544. Latin: Paris, 1513–14; 1519; Basle, 1534; 1540; 1548; Cologne, 1534; Frankfurt, 1580; 1599; Geneva, 1595. English trans.: *The*

Famous and Memorable Workes of Josephus. Faithfully translated out of the Latin, and French. By Thomas Lodge. 1602; 1609; 1620, etc.; W. Whiston, 4 vols., 1820.

LUCAN, MARCUS ANNÆUS. *Pharsalia.* translated by Thomas May (1627). [See also under *JC*].

PLUTARCH. *Lives of the Noble Grecians and Romanes* . . . trans. Sir T. North. 1579, 1603 [see also under *JC*].

2. Critical Studies of Sources, etc.

ADLER, FRITZ. 'Das Verhältnis von Shakespeares *Antony and Cleopatra* zu Plutarchs Biographie des Antonius', *ShJb*, xxxi. 1895.

BALD, R. C. 'Shakespeare and Daniel', *TLS*, Nov. 20, 1924, p. 776.

BETHELL, S. L. *Shakespeare and the Popular Dramatic Tradition.* 1944.

BRADLEY, A. C. 'Antony and Cleopatra', *Oxford Lectures on Poetry*, 1909, pp. 279–305.

CECIL, LORD DAVID. 'Antony and Cleopatra', in *Poets and Storytellers.* 1949.

DICKEY, FRANKLIN M. *'Not Wisely But Too Well': Shakespeare's Love Tragedies.* San Marino, Cal. 1957.

ELLEHAUGE, MARTIN. 'The Usc of his Sources made by Shakespeare in *Julius Cæsar* and *Antony and Cleopatra.*' *EngStud.*, 65, 1930/1, 197–210.

ELLIS, O. C. DE C. *Cleopatra in the Tide of Time.* 1947.

GARRETT, R. M. 'Cleopatra the Martyr and her Sisters.' *JEGP*, xxii, 1923, p. 64.

GHOSH, P. C. 'Cleopatra's death in Chaucer's Legende of Gode Wommen', *MLR*, xxvi, 1931, p. 332.

GRANVILLE-BARKER, H. *Prefaces to Shakespeare.* Ser. 2. 1930.

GUNDOLF, F. 'Antonius und Cleopatra', *ShJb*, lxii. 1926.

KNIGHTS, L. C. 'On the Tragedy of Antony and Cleopatra', *Scrutiny*, xvi. 1949.

MACCALLUM, M. W. *Shakespeare's Roman Plays and their Background*, 1910, pp. 300–453.

MURRY, J. M. *Countries of the Mind*, 2nd. Series. 1931.

NORGAARD, H. 'Shakespeare and Daniel's "Letter from Octavia"', *N & Q* 200, 1955, 56–7.

NORMAN, A. M. Z. 'Daniel's *The Tragedie of Cleopatra* and *Antony and Cleopatra*', *ShQ*, ix. 1958.

REES, JOAN. 'Daniel's *Cleopatra* and Two French Plays', *MLR*, xlvii. 1952.

SCHÜCKING, L. L. *Character Problems in Shakespeare's Plays.* 1922.

SCHÜTZE, J. 'Daniel's Cleopatra und Shakespeare.' *EngStud.*, lxxi. 1936.

SEATON, ETHEL. 'Antony and Cleopatra and the Book of Revelation', *RES*, xxii, 1946, 219–24.

SELLERS, H. 'A Bibliography of the Works of Samuel Daniel', *Proceedings of Oxford Bibliog. Soc.*, II. 1928–30.

STOLL, E. E. 'Cleopatra' in *Poets and Playwrights*. Minneapolis, 1930.

TATLOCK, J. S. P. 'Cleopatra's Serpent-pit', *MLN*, xxix, 1914, p. 99.

WILSON, E. C. 'Shakespeare's Enobarbus', in *J. Q. Adams Memorial Studies*. Washington, 1948.

WITHERSPOON, A. M. *The Influence of Robert Garnier in Elizabethan Drama*. 1924.

Coriolanus

1. Editions of (*a*) the Play, (*b*) Sources and Analogues

(*a*) Fl 1623. Modern edns.: E. K. Chambers, *Warwick*, 1898; G. S. Gordon, 1912; W. J. Craig and R. H. Case, *Arden*, 1922; C. F. T. Brooke, 1924; H. H. Furness, Jr., *Variorum*, 1928; J. D. Wilson, *Cambridge*, 1960.

(*b*) CAMDEN, WILLIAM. *Remaines of a greater Worke concerning Britaine*. 1605; 1614; 1623, etc. Modern edn.: 1870.

DEKKER, THOMAS? *The Great Frost. Cold doings in London . . . With News out of the Country* . . . 1608.

DION CASSIUS. *Roman Histories*. Modern edn.: E. Cary (Loeb), 9 vols. 1914–27.

DIONYSIUS OF HALICARNASSUS. *Roman Antiquities*. Modern edn.: ed. E. Cary. 7 vols. (Loeb) 1939–50.

FLORUS, LUCIUS ANNÆUS. *The Roman Histories of Lucius Julius Florus*, translated by E.M.B[olton]. [1619, 1621.]

FRIPP, E. I. [Dearth in England, 1608] *Shakespeare, Man and Artist*, II, 1938, 706.

GAY, E. F. [The Risings of 1597 and 1607] in *Trans. of Roy. Hist. Soc.*, n.s. XVIII, 1904, Appendices I, II.

HARDY, ALEXANDRE. *Coriolan. Tragedie*, in Le Théâtre de A. Hardy, 5 vols. Paris, 1625–8. Modern edn.: ed. E. Stengel. 5 vols. Marburg, 1883–4.

LIVIUS, TITUS. *The Romane Historie of T. Livy*, translated by Philemon Holland. 1600.

PLUTARCH. *Lives of the Noble Grecians and Romanes*, trans. by Sir Thomas North. 1579, 1595, 1603.

SIDNEY, SIR PHILIP. *An Apology for Poetrie*. 1595.

STOW, JOHN. *The Annals of England . . . Begun by John Stow . . . Continued unto . . . 1631. By Edmund Howes*. 1631.

2. Critical Studies of Sources, etc.

BRADLEY, A. C. 'Coriolanus' in *Proc. of the British Academy*. V. 1911–12, 457–73; and in *A Miscellany*, 1929.

BÜTTNER, RICHARD. 'Zu Coriolan und seiner Quelle.' *ShJb*, xli, 1905.

DELIUS, NICOLAUS. 'Shakespeares Coriolanus in Seinem Verhältnis zum Coriolanus des Plutarch', *ShJb*, xi. 1876.

DRAPER, J. W. 'Shakespeare's Coriolanus: a Study in Renaissance Psychology', *West Virginia Univ. Bull.*, III. 1939.

GRANVILLE-BARKER, H. 'Coriolanus', *Prefaces to Shakespeare*, Ser. V. 1947.

HEUER, HERMANN. 'From Plutarch to Shakespeare: A Study of *Coriolanus*', *ShSurvey*, 10, Cambridge, 1957, pp. 50–59.

JORGENSEN, P. A. 'Shakespeare's Coriolanus: Elizabethan Soldier', *PMLA*, xliv, 1949, 221–35.

MACCALLUM, M. W. *Shakespeare's Roman Plays and their Background.* 1910. pp. 454–627.

MUIR, K. 'In Defence of the Tribunes', *Essays in Criticism*, IV, 1954.

MURRAY, J. M. 'A Neglected Heroine of Shakespeare' [Virgilia], *Countries of the Mind.* 1922.

PETTET, E. C. '*Coriolanus* and the Midlands Insurrection of 1607', *ShSurvey*, 3. Cambridge, 1950, 34–42.

TOLMAN, A. H. 'The Structure of Shakespeare's Tragedies, with Special Reference to *Coriolanus*', *MLN*, xxxvii. 1922.

WYNDHAM, G. 'North's Plutarch', reprinted in *Essays in Romantic Literature*, 1919. pp. 117ff.

VIEHOFF, H. 'Shakespeares Coriolan', *ShJb*, iv, 1869, 41–61.

[illegible]

INDEX TO THE INTRODUCTIONS